Spyflights and Overflights

US Strategic Aerial Reconnaissance

Volume 1: 1945-1960

Spyflights and Overflights

US Strategic Aerial Reconnaissance
Volume 1: 1945-1960

Robert S Hopkins III

HIKOKI PUBLICATIONS

To William Ochsenwald
and Mel Leffler

First published in 2016 by
Hikoki Publications Ltd
1a Ringway Trading Est
Shadowmoss Rd
Manchester
M22 5LH
England

Email: enquiries@crecy.co.uk
www.crecy.co.uk

Line drawings: © Chris Gibson
Layout by Russell Strong

ISBN 9 781902 109503

Printed in Malta by Melita Press

Front cover Illustrations:

Top: SILVER KING was the ultimate RB-47H ELINT platform. The large pod on the starboard fuselage housed the AN/ALD-4 automatic ELINT collection system, and the AN/APR-17 D- and I-band early warning intercept receivers were next to the wingtips. RB-47H 53-4288 after refueling with its KC-135 tanker. *Author's collection*

Bottom: WB-57F 63-13302 was originally HEART THROB RB-57A 52-1433. It conducted overflights of the USSR 1955-57. Three HEART THROB airplanes were converted into RB-57Fs (and later WB-57Fs) with bigger wings, two more engines, and new serial numbers. Seen at NAS Atsugi on 28 January 1972. *Harry Tyrpak via Stephen Miller*

Back cover illustrations:

Top: The Skunk Works converted seven P2Vs into RB-69As for CIA overflights of Eastern Europe and Red China. All eventually served with the RoCAF. Three were lost to MiGs, including this RB-69A 54-4041 (BuNO 141233), shot down on 19 June 1963 by a MiG-17 *Fresco. Stephen Miller*

Center left: The U-2 became an icon of Cold War strategic aerial reconnaissance after the Soviets shot down CIA pilot Frank Powers on 1 May 1960. There were only 24 U-2 overflights of the USSR, but hundreds of US Air Force and Navy overflights by RB-45s, RB-47s, RB-57s, RF-86s, RF-100s, P4M-1Qs, and P2Vs. *Courtesy Chris Pocock*

Center middle: Soviet, Chinese, and North Korean interceptors routinely attacked reconnaissance aircraft in international airspace. A few managed to limp to safety. P2V-5 131515 was shot at by MiG-15s over the Bering Sea on 22 June 1955, but crash landed on St Lawrence Island. *Author's Collection*

Center right: Maintenance crews suffered in the cold (-40°) to prepare RB-47 flights from Eielson AFB, Alaska. Despite the weather, Alaska's location was ideal for sorties along the Soviet coast to Japan or 'over the top' to England, missions later duplicated by COTTON CANDY and BURNING WIND RC-135s. *Author's Collection*

Bottom: The 'grandfather' of all BIG SAFARI aircraft was the PIE FACE C-97A. The airplane carried the 'Big Bertha' camera, originally tested in a B-36. Flown by the 'Berlin for Lunch Bunch,' 49-2592 is seen here on short final to Berlin Tempelhof AP. *Ralf Manteufel*

Half-title page: RF-80s and RF-86s under the operational control of Far Eastern Air Forces commanders conducted multiple overflights of the USSR and PRC. Presidents Truman and Eisenhower approved military overflights. HAYMAKER RF-86F 52-4864 *Pretty Billie* prepares for its next flight. *Tom Hagler photo courtesy Doug Gordon*

Title page, top: A number of reconnaissance airplanes carried spurious serial numbers to obscure their true mission and confuse foreign observers. LULU BELLE C-54D 42-72684 is seen here as '17206'. *Ralf Manteufel*

Title page, bottom: RB-45Cs were among the first SAC overflight jets flown from Yokota AB, as well as the RAF JU JITSU missions from RAF Sculthorpe. 48-027 leads this lineup at Lockbourne AFB. *NMUSAF via Geoff Hayes*

Contents

President Truman approved a September 1951 B-47 overflight of the Soviet Union from Alaska, but the airplane, B-47B 49-2645, caught fire during ground servicing and was destroyed before the flight. 49-2645 is seen at Eielson AFB on 20 September 1951 hours before the fire. *Boeing Photo*

Acknowledgements

As with any book this has been a labour of many. I have benefitted greatly from the informed contributions, critical assessments, and moral support offered by friends and colleagues, old and new. These include Matthew Aid, Lennart Andersson, Bob Archer, Joe Bruch, Bill Burrows, John Calvert, Peter Cary, Jim Cloninger, Mark Conversino, Paul Crickmore, George Cully, Dwayne Day, Nicholas Dujmovic, Charles Dunlap, Betsy Elliot-Meisel, Ken Ellis, Scherry, Darrell, and Emeleigh Englebrecht, John Ferris, John Frederickson, Kris Fulkerson, John Lewis Gaddis, Mike Ginn, Peter Grose, Dan Hagedorn, Gerald Haines, Chuck Hansen, Bill Harrington, Ann Heiss, Walter Hixson, Bryan LeBeau, Steve Link, Gene Matthews, Ernest May, Walt Moody, Maria Morrison, Michael O'Brien, Dave Osborne, Chester Pach, John Prados, Brian 'Buck' Rogers, Mike Rip, Martin Smisek, Ilicia Sprey, William Taubman, John Taylor, Wesley Wark, Wayne Weiss, Jan Wouters, and Vlad Zubok. Among the many photo contributors Alan Scholefield, Kurt Finger, Doug Gordon, Mike Habermehl, Geoff Hays, Dennis Jenkins, Ralf Manteufel, Stephen Miller, and Yefim Gordon deserve great credit for their willingness to provide images. Dave Brown championed clearer prose and argumentation. I am grateful to David Snead, Jeff Richelson, and Bill Burr for their incisive comments and 'golden' sources. Dave Lavery – in between putting rovers on Mars – provided a place to sleep, terrifying rush hour drives to the Library of Congress and the National Archives, and ambrosia. Dave's link to this book is equally personal. His father, John D Lavery, was a courier for U-2 overflight films returning to the United States.

Although they differ markedly in their conclusions about strategic aerial reconnaissance during the early years of the Cold War, I have been the happy beneficiary of support, discussions, critiques, and source materials from Cargill Hall and Paul Lashmar. Despite their profound disagreements over the motives of US peripheral and overflight reconnaissance between 1945 and 1960, they each deserve great credit for their pioneering efforts to illuminate this previously unheralded story. Neither gentleman will be completely satisfied with what I have written. Perhaps that is a good thing.

I have had the privilege of interviewing or corresponding with many of the participants in these events, among them Hal Austin, Bruce Bailey, Richard Bissell (who told me that he never quite got around to flying in 'his' U-2), John Farquhar, Don Hillman, Robb Hoover, Bruce Holloway, Rex Knaak, John Kovacs, John McCone, Vance Mitchell, Bruce Olmstead, John Roche, 'Doc' Savage, Maury Seitz, and Reggie Urschler. After 50 years many of those I interviewed were still sensitive about the secrecy surrounding the programs and asked simply to be remembered as 'Anonymous.' No one better exemplifies the 'corporate memory' on the U-2 and its operational history than fellow author and friend Chris Pocock. Colleague Dino Brugioni has long championed the need to tell the story of US intelligence analysis. Gary Powers, Jr, provided invaluable input.

The University of Virginia and Creighton University both approved travel grants that enabled me to present these ideas in Protean form. The Harry S Truman Library supported my efforts with a generous grant. I also received financial support from the Air Force Historical Research Agency (AFHRA). Maranda Gilmore at the AFHRA worked magic in locating documents.

I owe an immeasurable debt to Mel Leffler. His ongoing patience, good cheer, and insistence on unparalleled excellence all informed my research and thinking. I am equally grateful to Brian Balogh, Norman Graebner, Nelson Lichtenstein, Allen Lynch, Woodford McClellan, Peter Onuf, and Kenneth Thompson. William Ochsenwald inspired a passion for history in not one, but two generations of my family, and taught me how to write good history despite my better efforts.

Considerable thanks go to the people who did so much to convert this manuscript into an actual book. Chris Gibson focused the relevance of the content and provided the maps. Russell Strong deserves great credit for his superb layout work. I am especially grateful to Jeremy Pratt and Gill Richardson at Crécy for their confidence and support.

As he has for 30 years, Jay Miller provided moral support and deep insight into the relation between airplanes and how they are used. Neil Lewis showed great patience in bringing this project to fruition. Without his transoceanic commitment this book would not be in your hands.

The life of a recon pilot and a historian share few attributes. Among these, however, is time away from home and family, either flying around the world or ensconced in an archive somewhere. To those who have felt this absence most of all – Robert and Eula Mae Hopkins, Robin, Sarah, Mike and Sam, Robert, Emily, and Christopher – you have my deepest thanks. And to Amy, who spent a birthday sitting patiently in the National Archives, I promise all the rest will be so much better.

Robert S Hopkins, III
Dallas, Texas, March 2016

Glossary

AAA	Anti-aircraft artillery
AAC	Alaskan Air Command
AB	Air Base
ACRP	Airborne COMINT Reconnaissance Program
ADC	Air Defense Command
ADIZ	Air Defense Intercept Zone
AFB	Air Force Base
AFCRL	Air Force Cambridge Research Laboratory
AFHRA	Air Force Historical Research Agency
AFSHO	Air Force History Support Office
AMARC	Aerospace Maintenance and Regeneration Center
ANG	Air National Guard
ARDC	Air Research and Development Command
ASRP	Airborne SIGINT Reconnaissance Program
ASW	Anti-submarine warfare
ATRAN	Automatic Terrain Recognition and Navigation
AWACS	Airborne Warning and Control System
BBC	British Broadcasting Corporation
BDA	Battle damage assessment
BuNO	Bureau of Naval Operations (number)
CAT	Civil Air Transport
CIA	Central Intelligence Agency
CIG	Central Intelligence Group
CINCSAC	Commander-in-Chief, Strategic Air Command
CMF	Combat mission folder
COMINT	Communications intelligence
CPA	Closest point of approach
DA	*Dal'naya Aviatsiya* (Soviet Long Range Aviation)
DDEL	Dwight D Eisenhower Library
DDRS	Declassified Document Reference System
DefPat	Defensive Patrol
DEFSMAC	Defense Special Missile and Astronautics Center
DGZ	Designated Ground Zero
DMZ	Demilitarized Zone
DoD	Department of Defense
ECCM	Electronic counter-countermeasures
ECM	Electronic countermeasures
ELINT	Electronic intelligence
FBI	Federal Bureau of Investigation
FEAF	Far Eastern Air Forces
FICON	Fighter conveyer
FOIA	Freedom of Information Act
FRG	Federal Republic of Germany
FRUS	*Foreign Relations of the United States*
FY	Fiscal year
GCI	Ground-controlled intercept
HF	High frequency
HSTL	Harry S Truman Library
HUMINT	Human intelligence
IAC	Intelligence Advisory Committee
IADS	Integrated Air Defense System
IAP	International Airport
ICAO	International Civil Aviation Organization
ICBM	Intercontinental ballistic missile
IFR	Inflight Refueling
IRAN	Inspect and Repair as Necessary
IRBM	Intermediate range ballistic missile
JCS	Joint Chiefs of Staff
JIC	Joint Intelligence Committee
JIIC	Joint Intelligence Indications Committee
JSTARS	Joint Surveillance Target Attack Radar System
JSTPS	Joint Strategic Target Planning Staff
JRC	Joint Reconnaissance Center
kW	Kilowatt
LimDis	Limited Distribution
LoC	Library of Congress
LORAN	Long Range Navigation
LRDP	Long Range Detection Program
MASDC	Military Aircraft Storage and Disposal Center
MASINT	Measurement and Signature Intelligence
MDS	Mission-Design-Series
MID	Military Intelligence Division
MiG	Mikoyan/Gurevich – Soviet aircraft manufacturer
NARA	National Archives and Records Agency
NATO	North Atlantic Treaty Organization
NiAct	Night Action
NIC	National Indications Center
NIE	National Intelligence Estimate
NKVD	*Narodnyy Komissariat Vnutrennikh Del* (Soviet security)
nm	Nautical mile
NMUSAF	National Museum of the US Air Force
NNTRP	National Nuclear Test Readiness Program
NSA	National Security Agency
NSArch	National Security Archives
NSAM	National Security Action Memorandum
NSC	National Security Council
NSCID	National Security Council Intelligence Directive
NSTL	National Strategic Target List
OB	Order of battle
OCAMA	Oklahoma City Air Materièl Area
ONI	Office of Naval Intelligence
OSS	Office of Strategic Services
PACAF	Pacific Air Forces
PHOTINT	Photographic intelligence
PLAAF	People's Liberation Army – Air Force
PNIO	Priority National Intelligence Objectives
PRC	People's Republic of China
PRG	Photographic Reconnaissance Group
PRS	Photographic Reconnaissance Squadron
PSF	President's Secretary's Files
PVO	*Protivo Vozdushnaya Oborona Strany* (Soviet Air Defense)
R&D	Research and development
RAF	Royal Air Force
RAMP	RAdiation Monitoring Program
RG	Record group
RoCAF	Republic of China Air Force
RS	Reconnaissance Squadron
RTAFB	Royal Thai Air Force Base

SAC	Strategic Air Command
SAF	Swedish Air Force
SAM	Surface-to-air missile
SDI	Strategic Defense Initiative
SEATO	Southeast Asia Treaty Organization
SENSINT	Sensitive Intelligence
SESP	Special Electronic Airborne Search Project
SHORAN	Short Range Navigation
SIGINT	Signal intelligence
SIOP	Single Integrated Operations Plan
SLAR	Side looking airborne radar
SLBM	Sea-launched ballistic missile
SMG	Special Mission Group
SNIE	Special National Intelligence Estimate
SOI	Signal of interest
SRS	Strategic Reconnaissance Squadron
SRW	Strategic Reconnaissance Wing
SW	Strategic Wing
TCP	Technical Capabilities Panel
TDY	Temporary duty
TELINT	Telemetry intelligence
TEMCO	Texas Engineering and Manufacturing Company
TRG	Tactical Reconnaissance Group
TRG	Technical Research Group
TRS	Tactical Reconnaissance Squadron
UFO	Unidentified flying object
USAAF	United States Army Air Force
USAF	United States Air Force
USAFE	United States Air Forces, Europe
USN	United States Navy
USSR	Union of Soviet Socialist Republics
VHF	Very high frequency
WF	Ann Whitman Files
wfu	Withdrawn from use
WHO	White House Office Files
WS	Weather Squadron
WSEG	Weapon System Evaluation Group
w/o	Written off

Terminology

For Soviet aircraft, missiles, and weapons this books uses Western designations, typically those assigned by NATO (for instance, the R-7 *Semyorka* ICBM is referred to as the SS-6 *Sapwood*). Similarly, references to Chinese equipment purchased or copied from the Soviet Union use the designation of the original Soviet design (for instance, J-5 is cited as MiG-17). NATO codenames for Soviet and Chinese aircraft are assigned based on airplane and engine type, and are printed in italics. Bombers are given names beginning with 'B', fighters with 'F', cargo planes with 'C'. Piston-powered planes are given names with one syllable and jet-powered planes have two-syllable names. Hence the piston-powered Tu-4 and Tu-95 bombers are named *Bull* and *Bear*, respectively, while the jet-powered Tu-16 and Mya-4 and named *Badger* and *Bison*, respectively.

Some sources use the names Russians and Soviets interchangeably, and this is repeated here. The People's Republic of China is sometimes listed as Red China, and the Republic of China is also referred to as Taiwan or Formosa. In all cases traditional Western transliteration is used for Russian and Chinese names and places.

This work relies heavily on abbreviations, acronyms, special program names, and code words. Many of these acronyms are commonplace (CIA, USSR, SAC) and printed in capital letters without periods. Program names (COBRA BALL, CONGO MAIDEN, HOME RUN) are presented in small caps. Code words (Chalice, Byeman, Idealist) are treated as proper nouns.

Military personnel are referred to by rank and name instead of the incorrect usage of title and name. For example, Chairman of the Joint Chiefs of Staff (CJCS) General Nathan F Twining is correctly identified as 'General Twining' rather than the erroneous 'CJCS Twining'. The title of the commander, Strategic Air Command (SAC), changed twice in the early years of the command, all of them during the tenure of Curtis LeMay. From 1948-1953 the title was 'Commanding General, Strategic Air Command.' From 1953-1955 the title was 'Commander, Strategic Air Command.' This changed in 1955 to the more familiar 'Commander-in-Chief, Strategic Air Command' (CINCSAC) as part of the Department of Defense realignment of certain commanders such as CINCPAC and CINCLANT. For the sake of continuity the term CINCSAC is used throughout this book. LeMay was assigned to SAC in October 1948 as a Lieutenant General. He was promoted to General in October 1951, and is consistently referred to as such irrespective of date.

US airplane designations describe the mission and function of the airplane. USAF bombers are assigned the prefix 'B' as in B-29 and B-47. Bombers converted into reconnaissance platforms add the letter 'R' as in RB-29 and RB-47. Cargo planes are assigned the prefix 'C' as in C-54 and C-130, and reconnaissance versions are similarly modified into RC-54 and RC-130. Fighter aircraft are designated with 'F' such as the F-86 and F-100 and their reconnaissance variants are shown as RF-86 and RF-100. USN reconnaissance aircraft are largely derived from patrol airplanes and are designated, *inter alia*, P2V-3W or PB4Y-2. The U-2 was given a 'Utility' designation as part of the effort to maintain secrecy.

US Air Force bases within the Continental United States are designated as 'Air Force Base' – that is, Offutt AFB. USAF bases located elsewhere are designated as 'Air Base' – that is, Yokota AB. Bases in Alaska, notably Eielson and Shemya, changed designation, especially once Alaska achieved statehood in 1959. For the sake of consistency, both are listed as 'AFB' regardless of date.

Preface
A Personal Journey

I arrived at Eielson AFB, Alaska, in September 1987 just in time for the first snow. As a pilot I was excited about my new assignment, flying the RC-135S COBRA BALL. The mission was particularly satisfying because it furthered my commitment to use reconnaissance capabilities to prevent conflict. In this case, the airplane was part of the 'national technical means' to verify foreign (read Soviet) compliance with international arms limitation and reduction treaties.[1] There was an air of adrenalin and drama about it as well: no-notice launches from a tiny island in the Bering Sea, orbiting off the coast of the Soviet Union, and monitoring the re-entry of Soviet nuclear warheads. There was also a real sense of danger. Shemya AFB is an island two miles wide by four miles long located at the tip of the Aleutians at the confluence of the Northern Pacific Ocean and the Bering Sea. Shemya is among the worst places in the world for flying. One RC-135S slid off the icy runway and broke in half. Another RC-135S landed short, killing six crewmembers. After departing Shemya, the sole RC-135E RIVET AMBER (partner to the RC-135S) disappeared somewhere over the Bering Sea, likely the result of structural failure, taking all 19 souls on board to a watery grave.[2]

Most COBRA BALL missions followed a common pattern. The Defense Special Missile and Astronautics Center (DEFSMAC), a component of the National Security Agency (NSA), would determine that a Soviet missile launch was imminent and alert the COBRA BALL crew to take off immediately.[3] Within 15 minutes the RC-135S would be airborne, often in winds of up to 50mph and blinding snow. It would then proceed to an orbit area in international airspace east of the Kamchatka Peninsula to await the re-entry of the ICBM end-stage booster, bus, and warheads. During a successful 'collection,' sensors recorded telemetry data and measured optical and spectrographic images of re-entry objects. The view of these missile components and warheads at the Kura Test Range near Klyuchi, especially at night, was extraordinary – the opening seconds of World War Three would be beautiful if not horrific.

The locals say the warhead flights are spectacular. At first, there's a bright star in the night sky, rapidly approaching the ground. Then a flash so powerful the street's lit like daytime, but doomsday lasts not more than a second. In an instant, the big star separates into several smaller ones. Up to 10 warheads separate from the platform and fly at their own targets. Cooler than any fireworks.[4]

Sometimes the launches never happened due to unreliable pre-launch intelligence, technical delays, or just the Soviets changing their minds because they knew that the COBRA BALL, among other assets, was on station and ready to observe the re-entry. Initially the Soviet launches took place with no warning. As evolving arms agreements stipulated verification

The loss of COBRA BALL RC-135S 61-2664 on 15 March 1981 at Shemya AFB (claiming six lives) attests to the personal risks that are part of flying strategic reconnaissance missions. The RIVET AMBER RC-135E LISA ANN disappeared on 5 June 1969 during a flight from Shemya AFB to Eielson AFB, with the loss of all 19 on board. For years this monument, which includes the actual nose number from the RC-135S, was on display at Shemya AFB (later Eareckson AS) and finally moved to Offutt AFB, where it remains. *Stephen Miller*

Above: Following in the rich tradition of the Incirlik-based TELL TWO EB-47Es that collected TELINT from Soviet ICBM launches, the RC-135S COBRA BALL sat alert on the tiny and windswept Shemya Island. A 3:00 AM 'gronk' with a radio-silent launch inside of 15 minutes in blowing snow followed by a 'take' made the Cold War mission important and exciting. *Toshiyuki Toda via Stephen Miller*

Below: Watching the watcher. WANDA BELLE RC-135S 59-1491 catches a Soviet 'trawler' fishing for intelligence near Shemya. Because a warning from the trawler could lead to a cancelled missile test, RC-135S and RC-135E launches from 'the Rock' were radio silent. It was all part of the game, and both sides played it well. *via 55th Wing Association website.*

Opposite, top: The MiG-31 *Foxhound* may turn out to be the last design by OKB-MiG to intercept Western reconnaissance aircraft, as the company struggles to compete with rival Sukhoi. Armed with eight missiles and a cannon, the MiG-31's radar and speed makes it a highly capable platform. Not well suited for dogfighting with an F-15 or JAS-39, it is a real – but not absolute – threat for any RC-135. *via Yefim Gordon*

Opposite, bottom: An Su-15TM *Flagon-F* pulls up abruptly in front of a ferret on a peripheral sortie in an effort to discourage it from continuing its mission. During the height of the Cold War antics such as this were commonplace. Intercepts some 20 years after the end of the Cold War, however, have been fraught with danger due to occasional collisions resulting from interceptor pilot arrogance and inexperience in flying in close proximity to large aircraft whose aerodynamics destabilize the fighter. *via Geoff Hays*

procedures, the Soviets were obligated to provide a minimum pre-launch notification, sometimes as little as 30 minutes. Coupled with an average 25-minute ballistic flight time, this left COBRA BALL crews with little less than an hour to get to the airplane, take off, climb to altitude, and fly nearly 400 miles to the collection orbit. The Soviets occasionally had a 'fishing trawler' in the vicinity of Shemya. Known colloquially as the 'Cobra Boatski,' the ship would listen for radio transmissions indicating a COBRA BALL launch. This information could then easily be used to delay or postpone the missile launch to avoid collection. Consequently, COBRA BALL missions were typically radio silent.

Spending hours flying in circles waiting for a missile launch gave me plenty of time to appreciate the rugged beauty of Kamchatka, home to the largest number of active volcanoes in the world. Missions where nothing happened were called 'tuna patrols,' as the imaginary fish was all we brought home. On some missions we would leave the 'sensitive area' and join up with a tanker to refuel in flight, extending the duration of our sortie. Missions usually lasted 6-8 hours, but with in-flight refueling we could stay on station for 10-18 hours to ensure collection of an event or cover multiple launch windows. My longest flight was 21 hours. Most of the time, however, our sorties reflected the old reconnaissance adage: 'Alone, unarmed, and unafraid.'

That changed on 16 November 1988. As my crew orbited late on a bright afternoon, we received a visitor. For the first time in many years a Soviet fighter came out to escort the COBRA BALL.[5] The MiG-31 was a beast, carrying four AA-8 *Aphid* heat-seeking missiles, four AA-9 *Amos* radar-homing missiles, and a GSh-6-23 23mm cannon. The MiG, NATO codenamed *Foxhound*, followed international protocols

and stayed between us and Soviet airspace, flying just 70 feet from where I sat. We followed a time-honored tradition in the recon community: we waved at them and they waved at us. After an hour or so the MiG ran low on fuel, lit the afterburner, and headed home as we remained on station until our collection window expired.

Fighter escorts (for other than the COBRA BALL) have long been commonplace for US strategic reconnaissance flights beginning in the 1940s and continuing to the present day. Ironically, until the end of the Cold War most American fighter pilots who trained daily to engage and shoot down Soviet fighters never saw one throughout their entire career. For the crews of P2Vs, RB-47s, EP-3s, and RC-135s, however, seeing Russian fighters 'up close and personal' was a daily occurrence. Indeed, US recon crews knew some Soviet interceptor pilots by name. As American reconnaissance requirements increased and the geographic coverage expanded accordingly, so too did the interceptions by Soviet and Chinese MiGs, Mirages and MiGs from the Arab world, even US-built F-16s flown by the Norwegians and the Israelis.

Not all intercepts have been friendly. Pilots of all nations understand the meaning of an extended middle finger. Sometimes fighter pilots would fly perilously close to the big reconnaissance aircraft, trying to intimidate the crew into leaving.[6] In 1987 a Soviet Sukhoi Su-27 *Flanker* struck a Norwegian P-3 Orion after several harassing passes. In April 2001 a People's

Republic of China (PRC) Jian-8D *Finback* collided with a US Navy Lockheed EP-3E after the J-8 pilot had made passes as close as 10 feet. The EP-3E made an emergency landing on Hainan Island but the J-8 pilot perished after he lost control and crashed into the sea.[7] By 2014, increasing US-Russian tensions led to aggressive intercepts of RC-135s by Su-27 *Flankers* in the Baltic Sea and the Sea of Japan.[8] At the extreme, both Soviet and Chinese fighters have attacked US and allied reconnaissance planes. Between 1945 and 1960, 43 airplanes were fired upon, and additional 28 were shot down and destroyed.

***

I arrived in Charlottesville, Virginia, in August 1992 as the leaves along the Blue Ridge Parkway were beginning to change from green to orange to red. A civilian now with a newly minted MA in History in hand, I was about to embark on the final academic journey to earn a PhD in 'diplomatic history' with a particular interest in the relationship between technical capabilities and national policy. Talk about being thrown into the deep end of the pool. I knew who Kennan was and could tell one Dulles from the other but beyond that was woefully ignorant. For someone with historical training in the Middle East and the History of Science, the process of mastering American history was as challenging as landing at Shemya at night and in horrible weather.

I immersed myself in the literature of the Cold War both at home and abroad. I was quick to champion scholars who held historical viewpoints similar to my own, and eager to refute those who did not. To my surprise, I could do neither.

I discovered that however they might be labeled – traditionalists, revisionists, New Left, post-revisionists – historians view the same events through far different lenses. The Korean War, for example, was an ongoing part of a monolithic Communist plan to establish a global classless, atheist utopia one domino at a time. It might have been a legitimate reaction by the sovereign government of the Democratic People's Republic of Korea to external threats of territorial aggrandizement. Perhaps it was the need to have a unified Korea as a market for Japanese goods to ensure domestic prosperity and hence a friendly liberal capitalist nation to complete the encirclement of Communist Asia. Or maybe it was just Dean Acheson forgetting to point to Korea on a map as he gave a speech about America's vital interests in Asia. Despite my initial uncertainty, I found it necessary to inform my thinking on the role of strategic aerial reconnaissance with these many different perspectives in mind. What was once black and white was now shades of grey. Clarity and certainty had given way to subtlety and nuance.

The research environment was equally ambiguous. Some military colleagues argued that I had sold out to a left-wing academy that pandered to the politically correct, and considered me a pariah. Some academic colleagues worried that I was an untrustworthy vestige of right-wing militarists, and saw my research as apologetic. Equally I was exposed to the divide between military and diplomatic history. Some viewed the former as 'counting rivets on battleships' or rehashing the combat effectiveness of different belt buckles on Union troops at Little Round Top. Others viewed the latter as stolid diplomatic cables or the abdication of Von Rankian narrative history to Derrida-infused English Departments. Just as I had learned that there were varying conceptual frameworks and methodologies to assess the role and impact of strategic aerial reconnaissance on US and Soviet national security policy, so too were there varying opinions about the messenger. No matter what his argument or evidence, Cargill Hall would never have credibility among readers of *The New Statesman* nor would Paul Lashmar be the keynote speaker at the annual banquet of the 55th Wing Association.

As with countless scholars before me, I had the privilege of discussing my research with the late John Taylor at the National Archives. He said simply, 'What a good idea.' He then listed all the reasons why it was an impossible task: endless classified material, compartmented classifications, official denial that some organizations even existed, multiple alphabet-soup agencies with a long track record of refusing to declassify documents, aging participants who had signed life-long non-disclosure agreements, immensely long delays in getting Freedom of Information Act (FOIA) requests processed, or trying to interpret documents so heavily redacted that they were a black square on a white page.[9] When he finished, Mr Taylor smiled and told me, 'You'll do just fine.'

***

To steal a phrase from the title of a controversial Cold War history book, we now know that strategic reconnaissance flights – both civilian and military – were far more numerous than previously believed. We know that they were influential in military matters such as targeting

Understanding the history of Cold War aerial reconnaissance requires bridging the gap between aviation history and diplomatic and intelligence history. Few scholars care about MDS and serial numbers while few enthusiasts are interested in the policy requirements for the missions. It is essential to link these disparate fields to appreciate why RB-47H 53-4280 was at Eielson AFB – a capability – and the missions assigned to it – a purpose. *Author's Collection*

and early warning. So, too, did they provide essential information about the Soviet nuclear weapons program. The intelligence gathered from these flights informed decision makers at the highest levels in US policy, and reaffirmed presidential authority over the military and intelligence communities. We have learned more about foreign responses to the missions and their potential as a *casus belli*.

Most importantly, the study of these flights and their impact on national security policy demonstrates a useful and informative analytic and descriptive framework. Since my first meeting with John Taylor, there have been numerous conferences and television documentaries on Cold War aerial reconnaissance, including those sponsored by the CIA, reconnaissance associations, and the BBC. Many participants are now willing (indeed eager) to tell the story of their role in strategic reconnaissance flights. New books have appeared in the popular press describing the personal price of these missions. Increasingly, researchers are incorporating components from other fields into their work. For example, far from simple 'nuts and bolts' descriptions of the airplane, Chris Pocock's multiple books on the U-2 demonstrate a deep understanding of the domestic and international political environment surrounding U-2 operations. Indeed, the CIA's official history of the U-2 program calls Pocock's work 'by far the most accurate unclassified account of the U-2.'[10] Fortunately – and to the benefit of scholars and enthusiasts alike – this list of multi-field study is growing.

Twenty years have passed since this project began life. It has been updated and rewritten many times as I pursued an unrelated career in the improvement of health care quality and safety. With the end of the Cold War, strategic aerial reconnaissance dropped from the public eye, almost an anachronism. As this book is published, however, crises in the Ukraine, the Baltic, Crimea, and the Spratly Islands have reinvigorated tensions between East and West, and once again aerial reconnaissance missions have been at the forefront of these events. Past has become present, and the lessons of strategic reconnaissance flights and their effect on international policy are just as relevant today as they were under Truman and Eisenhower a half century earlier. By combining my first-hand piloting and command experience in the elite reconnaissance community with an objective, critical scholarly framework, I believe I offer a unique perspective on an important component of early Cold War – and contemporary – history.

A changing post Cold War world has seen old enemies become friends. This Cuban Revolutionary Air Force MiG-21 *Fishbed-L* backs *away* from the wingtip of a 55th SRW RC-135 during the 1980s. Cuba and the United States normalized relations in 2015, ending 50+ years of hostility. *USAF via Geoff Hays*

1 A Better Understanding

Hervey Stockman cut a dashing figure with a personality to match. He attended Princeton University until 1942 when he entered military service. During the Second World War he flew P-51 Mustangs including missions on D-Day over Normandy. By war's end he was credited with two destroyed German warplanes. After the war he returned to civilian life, earned a degree in industrial engineering and went to work for General Motors designing Cadillacs. As with many post-war pilots, he was recalled to military duty in the wake of the Korean War and flew the latest jet fighters. Tempted by an intriguing offer, he accepted a job flying a highly classified airplane for the Central Intelligence Agency (CIA) known simply as 'the Article.' Difficult to fly and unforgiving of a pilot's inattention, the airplane – known to the rest of the world as the Lockheed U-2 – was designed to fly at extremely high altitudes and take photographs of cities, roads, and military installations beneath it.

On 4 July 1956, America's Independence Day, Stockman climbed into the tiny cockpit of Article 347 and departed Wiesbaden Air Base (AB) in West Germany. Wearing an uncomfortable pressure suit and sitting on a metal ejection seat, he began his climb to 70,000 feet. Then, alone some 13 miles above the earth and in complete radio silence, Stockman crossed the border into the Belorussian Soviet Socialist Republic. Turning the aircraft's cutting-edge cameras on and off at locations carefully marked on his map, he photographed bomber bases in Belorussia and turned north. Now over Russia proper he flew to Leningrad, the birthplace of the Bolshevik Revolution. Again Stockman photographed bomber bases and shipyards before heading west to the Baltic states and back to Wiesbaden. Mission #2013 lasted 8 hours and 45 minutes, and the intelligence it gathered was stunning. Much to the surprise of CIA planners and Lockheed designers, however, the U-2 was tracked by Russian radar the entire time it was over Soviet territory. Stockman watched in his view scope as Soviet MiG interceptors tried – but failed – to climb high enough to shoot him down. Although he described the flight as 'very exciting,' Stockman held no illusions about his safety. The MiGs were trying to destroy his airplane, and although he had an ejection seat and a parachute, American officials were certain that in the event his aircraft was shot down he would not survive. In fact, they were counting on it.[1]

Hervey Stockman had the Right Stuff. Opportunity and success followed throughout his career as a pilot flying P-51 Mustangs over Normandy on D-Day to the excitement of the inaugural U-2 overflight of the USSR. After a mid-air collision over North Vietnam, he endured six years in a prison camp. In this photo, taken in 1953, he was the SAC F-84F contestant in the annual Bendix Trophy Dash won by noted ace William Whisner. *Author's Collection*

Francis Gary Powers could hardly have been more different from Hervey Stockman. Square jawed and too young to see military service in World War Two, Powers graduated in 1950 from Milligan College in Tennessee. A year later he was finally an Air Force pilot headed for Korea but a case of appendicitis kept him stateside. He had missed yet another opportunity. Powers – known as Frank to his friends and colleagues – was an excellent pilot with strong flight skills, and attracted the attention of the CIA as it looked for pilots for its secret U-2 program. After four years of flying the U-2, including overflights of the USSR and Red China as well as the Middle East during the Suez Crisis, Powers was considered the most experienced operational U-2 pilot in the unit. He was an appropriate choice to make the first attempt 'to fly all the way across the Soviet Union.'[2]

On 1 May 1960, International Worker's Day, he departed Peshawar AB in Pakistan in Article 360 for the longest, most dangerous U-2 flight yet. Operation GRAND SLAM was planned to take

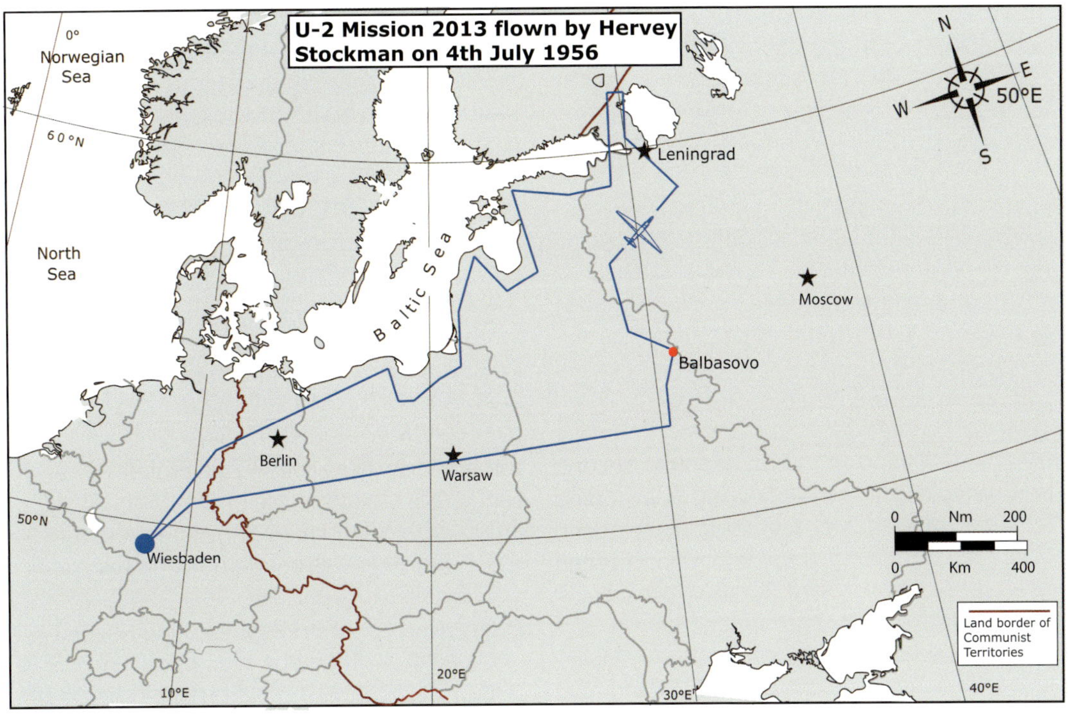

The first U-2 overflight of the Soviet Union included Balbasovo AB in the Belorussian SSR, a key Soviet bomber base and nuclear weapons facility. PHOTINT gleaned from this mission would indicate the extent of Soviet bomber production and preparedness, critical factors in assessing the Soviet bomber threat to Western Europe and the United States. Despite CIA beliefs, the Soviets tracked Stockman throughout his flight.

Powers from the southern border of the Soviet Union over its main ballistic missile facility at Tyuratam, key industrial and atomic weapons development facilities at Chelyabinsk, then northward to the missile test site at Plesetsk, the naval base at Murmansk, and finally recovering into Bodø, Norway. Scheduled for nine hours, Mission #4154 was at the absolute maximum range of the newer U-2C. Immediately upon entering Soviet airspace Russian radar began tracking the U-2. As with Stockman, Powers watched as multiple Soviet fighters scrambled to shoot him down, including one Sukhoi Su-9 *Fishpot* pilot – Igor Mentukov – who was told to go airborne without any weapons and simply ram the U-2. As the airplane neared Sverdlovsk, formerly known as Yekaterinberg, where Tsar Nicholas II and his family were murdered in 1918 and birthplace of Boris Yeltsin, a Soviet SA-2 *Guideline* surface-to-air missile (SAM) detonated close to the U-2, rendering it uncontrollable and sending it spiraling to the ground. To the glee of Soviet Premier Nikita S Khrushchev and the eventual embarrassment and dismay of US leaders,

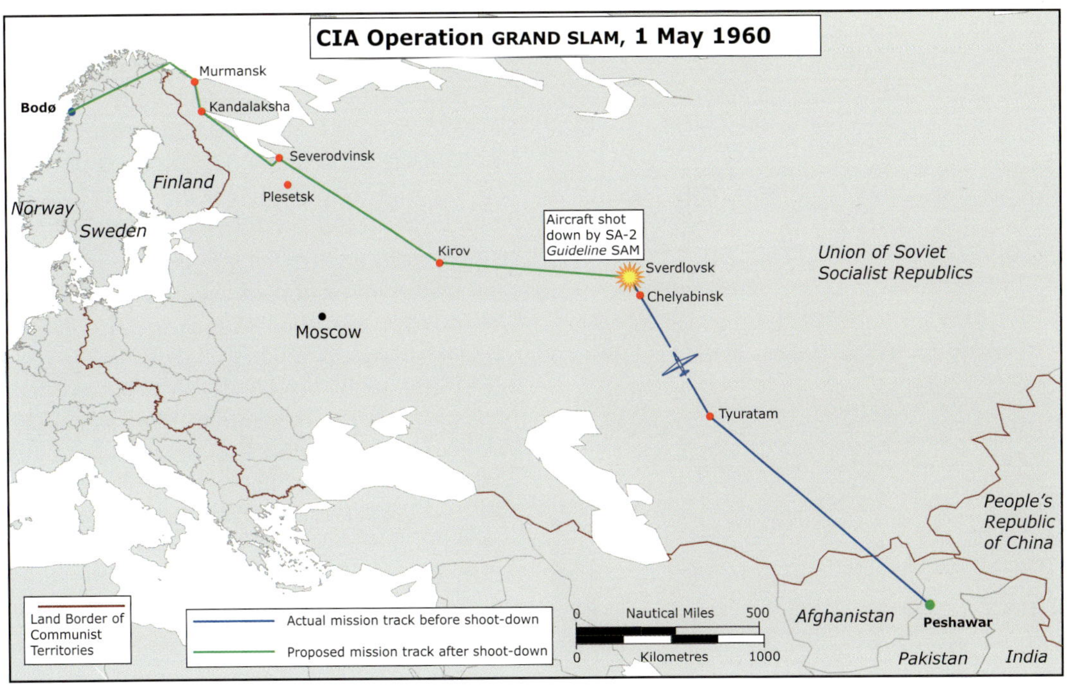

The final U-2 overflight of the Soviet Union was the most ambitious and arguably the most dangerous, but was defined by chance. For the US, luck was bound to run out and a U-2 mission be compromised. For the USSR, luck brought down Frank Powers on the 24th overflight. For both countries, luck was an irresponsible factor in Cold War confrontation.

Powers survived the attack. The 'U-2 Incident' had become part of the Cold War lexicon.[3]

During the 46 months between Hervey Stockman's first mission and the final mission by Frank Powers, the CIA conducted 22 additional U-2 overflights of the Soviet Union. US intelligence officials, military planners, and President Dwight D Eisenhower considered the photographs collected by the U-2 to be of such value to US national security policy that they were worth the risk and adverse impact of any potential compromise.

Others were not so sure. Journalists David Wise and Thomas Ross condemned the flight, especially its timing just ahead of the Four Powers Summit in Paris. Writing during 1962 in *The U-2 Affair*, the authors argued that US intelligence officials had run amok and were 'worried not so much that the U-2 might endanger the summit as that the summit might endanger the U-2' and that 'instead of serving as a basis for policy-making, intelligence-gathering had become an end in itself.' Senior intelligence officials and imagery analysts feared that the summit might sufficiently ease US-Soviet tensions to end U-2 overflights permanently. They therefore pressured Eisenhower to approve the flight, which took place without the President or his advisors aware 'at the time that Powers was in the air over the Soviet Union.'[4] Criticism of Powers came from within the intelligence community as well. CIA Director John McCone ordered a classified inquiry into Powers' operational conduct. The Prettyman Board 'unequivocally cleared' Powers of any misdeed or improper behavior. Convinced of Powers' complicity in the loss of the U-2, or at best his incompetence, McCone rejected the board's conclusions. The National Security Agency (NSA) also rejected the results, arguing that it had evidence that discredited Powers' story about the loss. According to an NSA voice intercept, Soviet radar operators reportedly claimed the U-2 descended from its cruise altitude, enabling defense forces to shoot it down. President John F Kennedy, however, accepted the board's report that Powers did not attempt to defect to the Soviet Union and directed McCone to drop the matter.[5]

When Frank Powers took off on Operation GRAND SLAM, Allen Dulles (right) was CIA Director. Dulles had no doubt that a compromised U-2 mission would prove fatal to the pilot and protect America's public image. When Frank Powers came home from the Lubyanka Prison in Moscow, John McCone (left) had replaced Dulles. Despite an investigation that exonerated Powers, McCone never wavered in his vituperative belief that Powers was complicit in the shoot down. *Author's Collection*

Following impressive congressional testimony about the affair, Frank Powers was publicly exonerated and quietly welcomed home, but some within the intelligence and aviation communities persisted in their uncharitable consideration of him as an outcast who 'screwed the pooch.' Powers did not receive the CIA's 'Intelligence Star' award in 1963 along with his cohorts due to political reasons (it was awarded in 1965). In 2000 he was posthumously awarded several Air Force decorations and the CIA's 'Director's Medal.' His family received his Silver Star medal in 2012 for conspicuous bravery in captivity. (Powers was not the only modern American aviator shunned as a failed hero. Astronaut Virgil I 'Gus' Grissom was equally ostracized for 'losing' the *Liberty Bell 7* capsule after splashdown in 1961, dramatically portrayed in Tom Wolfe's *The Right Stuff*).

After his stint in the U-2, Stockman returned to the Air Force and eventually flew McDonnell Douglas F-4s. While on a 1967 combat mission over North Vietnam Stockman's F-4 collided with another US airplane. After ejecting, he was held as a prisoner of war until 1973. Throughout his captivity the North Vietnamese (and the Russians who took a keen interest in their prisoners) never learned that Stockman was a former CIA U-2 pilot, particularly the one who flew first over the Soviet Union. It is ironic that the two CIA pilots who flew the first and last overflights of the USSR both ended up as prisoners. The U-2 that Stockman flew on the first overflight is on display in the Smithsonian Air & Space Museum, Steven F Udvar-Hazy Center in Chantilly, Virginia. Pieces of the one Powers flew are on display in three locations; at the Central Museum of the Air Forces at Monino, near Moscow, at the Central Museum of the Armed Forces in Moscow, and the Museum of Military Technology in Yekaterinberg.

The acrimony over the U-2 incident persisted, particularly among researchers and journalists interested in the issue of overflights. With the advent of revisionist scholarship on Eisenhower, the positive influence of the U-2 and overflights gained increasing acceptance. Seminal studies such as *Ike's Spies* by Stephen Ambrose and

Mayday by Michael Beschloss established Eisenhower's wisdom in authorizing the U-2 flights in general, but were still circumspect in their judgment about the timing of the May 1960 mission so close to the Paris summit. Additional studies acknowledged the essential role of U-2 overflights in the detection and peaceful resolution of the October 1962 crisis over Soviet nuclear missiles in Cuba. Still, there was dissent about the value of the flights. Distinguished US diplomat George F Kennan argued that the flights were needlessly antagonistic and 'virtually indistinguishable from…a state of war' and were a likely cause of war between the United States and the Soviet Union.[6] Other critics, writing after the 1983 Soviet destruction of a Korean airliner, warned that reconnaissance flights were a constant source of danger, not only for the major countries involved but for peace-loving peoples everywhere.

The May 1960 incident created a popular myopia. U-2 missions acquired a certain primacy in the study of intelligence, which was already significantly circumscribed by the highly technical nature of modern intelligence gathering and the deep shroud of secrecy surrounding the collection and analysis of intelligence in general. These barriers often placed such study beyond the realm of interest or understanding of many researchers who 'do not feel comfortable with technological questions and seldom deal with the impact of technological development on strategic affairs [including] electronic intelligence.'[7] Given the increasing accessibility of material, relevant studies by aviation writers also focused on the U-2, but these works were typically overlooked by academics. Historian Garry Clifford, for example, identified the need to

Frank Powers seemed to be surrounded by bad timing or bad luck. A true patriot, he was too young to see service in World War Two and missed duty in Korea due to appendicitis. His misfortune at being the pilot of the U-2 Incident added to this unearned notoriety. Powers was an outstanding flier, and was chosen for Operation GRAND SLAM because he was the most experienced U-2 pilot in Det B at Incirlik AB. Like his contemporary, astronaut 'Gus' Grissom, Powers never overcame this infamy and died without the full recognition he justly deserved. *Author's Collection*

Part of the remains of Article 360 which Frank Powers flew on 1 May 1960 rest beneath an inert SA-2, credited with finally shooting down a U-2 overflight after 23 prior missions. Despite Khrushchev's bluster, the inability to destroy a U-2 was largely the result of his own short-sighted emphasis on ICBMs instead of conventional air defenses and ongoing internal secrecy. *Yefim Gordon*

'rescue intelligence history from the espionage buffs,' a lament equally applicable to airpower history and aviation enthusiasts.[8] Such limits further constrained the ability of researchers to incorporate these technical sources into more traditional histories. Indeed, one observer tartly noted, 'academic historians have been less than enterprising in their investigations and tend towards a culture of archival dependency.'[9] Consequently, a number of researchers focused on important treatises of the organizational history of American intelligence agencies, especially during the transition from the wartime Office of Strategic Services (OSS) to the postwar Central Intelligence Group (CIG) to the CIA. Nonetheless, a lack of evidence, either archival or anecdotal, was problematic in the field of aerial intelligence gathering. As one scholar lamented, historians have been content – or at least obliged – to presume that US intelligence policy during the 1950s 'consisted essentially of coups and U-2s.'[10]

By the late 1980s and early 1990s researchers devoted substantial attention to the description and assessment of more esoteric, high-priority national programs such as billion-dollar satellites orbiting above the Soviet Union. Concurrently they identified an essential component of aerial intelligence gathering that had always been in the public shadow of the civilian CIA U-2 program: military reconnaissance flights. Books such as *Deep Black* by William Burrows and *American Espionage and the Soviet Target* by Jeffrey Richelson clearly linked Cold War peripheral reconnaissance flights of the 1970s and 1980s with many previously unknown US agencies and national security policies, while *The History of Big Safari* by Bill Grimes provides a full accounting of this essential military reconnaissance program. Researchers were quick to encourage similar studies of the early Cold War period.[11]

Initial efforts identified diplomatic exchanges and brief accounts in back issues of the *New York Times* of a few US Air Force (USAF) and US Navy (USN) 'ferret' flights that were attacked or shot down. Between August 1946 and July 1960, defense forces from the Soviet Union, People's Republic of China (PRC), and the Democratic People's Republic of Korea (DPRK – North Korea) attacked at least 44 US Air Force and Navy reconnaissance planes. Nearly all were fired upon in international airspace or over non-Communist territory. Twenty-nine planes were destroyed and over 100 crewmembers killed, considered missing, or taken prisoner. During the next decade Communist forces downed nine more reconnaissance planes with the loss of nearly 40 crewmembers. Additional Cold War aerial losses included reconnaissance planes from Britain, Sweden, and the Republic of China, gathering intelligence which they shared with the United States.[12] (See Appendix I)

Ironically, access to new material on these peripheral military reconnaissance missions derived in no small measure from Russian *glasnost*. Not only did the putative end of the Cold War mean an increased American willingness to talk about intelligence gathering activities, it meant an equal willingness of the former Soviet

Although MiGs accounted for the majority of Cold War air-to-air reconnaissance aircraft losses, none were shot down by radar-guided missiles such these AA-1 *Alkalis* and AA-3 *Anabs* being loaded onto MiG-17PFUs and MiG-19PMs. The nascent state of Soviet beam-riding and semi-active radar homing made these weapons unreliable, and pilots preferred using guns even at night and in bad weather. *via Yefim Gordon*

Union to talk about the many 'visits' it received. In 1992, for example, Russian President Boris Yeltsin told US President George H W Bush that the former Soviet Union would co-operate with American officials to determine if any missing crewmembers from lost peripheral flights had been taken prisoner and if they were still alive. Much of the impact of this announcement was lost amidst Yeltsin's later disproven claim that US prisoners of war in Vietnam were taken to the Soviet Union and might still be alive. More recent efforts confirmed that Cold War reconnaissance crews were indeed held or buried in the USSR.[13] Subsequently, detailed accounts of a number of the destroyed flights were made public, along with the declassification of relevant American and Russian documents. These accounts included only *military* reconnaissance aircraft attacked or lost, and pointedly excluded *civilian* losses other than the U-2 Incident, such as those associated with CIA Projects CHERRY and OSTIARY. Richard Bissell talks freely in his memoirs about the U-2 program, but does not mention other possible CIA overflight or peripheral collection efforts. This may be due to the compartmentalized nature of intelligence collection, and Bissell may have been unaware of the other programs. As CIA Director Allen W Dulles's trusted advisor, however, this explanation is less plausible than Bissell's general unwillingness to talk about still-classified programs. Given the CIA's reluctance to admit participation in or declassify materials on known CIA operations, evidence that can corroborate additional civilian flights may be long in coming.

During a June 1992 visit to the United States, Russian Federation President Boris N Yeltsin provided US President George H W Bush with documents relating to Soviet attacks on US military peripheral reconnaissance missions. This openness did not clarify the status of any US crewmembers believed captured and held as prisoners in the Soviet gulag. *Author's Collection*

Of equal importance was the increasing availability of personal recollections by many of the participants in military peripheral and overflight missions as well as the efforts of journalists and scholars to declassify key documents, most of which were simply unknown a decade prior. Using stories told by crewmembers, unit operational histories, award citations, airplane photographs, and disparate documents acquired under the Freedom of Information Act (FOIA), *US News and World Report* published multiple articles on ferret flights and Cold War aerial losses. The following year the British Broadcasting Corporation (BBC) aired an important documentary by British television producer Paul Lashmar chronicling Western military reconnaissance flights around and over the Soviet Union.

These efforts demonstrated that military peripheral and overflight missions far exceeded those by CIA U-2s. In 1995 CIA Director John M

Experience begets experience. A number of early overflight pilots went on to subsequent overflight programs. Capt Cecil Rigsby, seen here in front of RF-86F *Ruby Pearl*, would later fly SLICK CHICK RF-100As. Fellow HAYMAKER pilot Mele Vojvodich would fly the CIA A-12. Their stories are finally being told. *Cecil Rigsby via Doug Gordon*

Deutch revealed that during the entire U-2 Soviet overflight program between 4 July 1956 and 1 May 1960, there were only 24 U-2 overflights of the USSR, a figure far below the 200 overflights assumed by some historians. Deutch acknowledged that the first successful CORONA reconnaissance satellite covered 1,650,000 square miles of Soviet territory, providing 'more overhead photographic coverage of the Soviet Union than the U-2 obtained in all of its 24 flights over Soviet territory.'[14] Military flights – both peripheral and overflights – were by far more numerous. During peak periods of interest, for example, peripheral reconnaissance sorties around the Soviet Union numbered as many as a half dozen *per day,* with one or two flights along the Kurile Islands or the Kamchatka and Chukotskii Peninsulas in the Pacific, one over the Baltic Sea, one over the Black Sea, one along the East German border, one around the Kola peninsula and Novaya Zemlya Island, and often one along the Siberian north flown between Alaska and England. During July 1948 crews of the 72nd Reconnaissance Squadron (RS) flew eleven electronic 'ferret' missions in the vicinity of Russia's Anadyr Bay and around the Chukotskii Peninsula. Concurrently, the 375th Weather Squadron (WS) flew daily weather missions along the Kamchatka Peninsula and the Siberian coastline. There were seven USAF RB-50G electronic ferret sorties 'through the Black Sea area' between 1 January and 1 October 1953, with two sorties during September alone. The 91st Strategic Reconnaissance Squadron (SRS) based at Yokota AB, Japan, completed 27 'special reconnaissance' missions (a euphemism for overflight or border incursion) and nine peripheral 'photo mapping' missions throughout East Asia, including Vladivostok, during the month of August 1954. 'Repeat' or 'continuous' missions – where a reconnaissance airplane flew the same route monthly, weekly, or even daily – dramatically increased the total number of military reconnaissance sorties. Repeat photographs taken a week or month apart could reveal recent construction or the stockpiling of weapons, suggesting a facility's increasing importance and potential threat. Conversely, a lack of new activity over time could suggest that a facility was of little or no importance to an enemy, and hence less of a threat to the United States.[15] Military overflights of the Soviet Union began in 1946 and continued over the next decade.[16] During just six weeks in 1954 Operation HOME RUN completed 156 overflights of Siberia. Although this was the largest number of military missions over the USSR in any one period, there were

RB-50F 47-144 *Mac's Effort* carried SHORAN for mapping and precision PHOTINT. By making regular flights near an area of interest, photos taken days or weeks apart would show any changes – new installations, deployment or withdrawal of forces – that might suggest an increased danger of war or a new threat to US or allied forces. *Andy Meyer photo from the Dave Menard Collection at NMUSAF*

dozens more, often over a several week or month period (See Appendix II).

Despite the initial assertions by Wise and Ross that the U-2 incident in May 1960 represented Eisenhower's loss of control over the intelligence community, most researchers considered otherwise. Eisenhower approved each civilian U-2 overflight of the Soviet Union, and was not afraid to reject those he deemed poor risks. Once he approved a specific flight he delegated operational authority – the actual execution of the mission – to appropriate authorities in the CIA. The discovery of the sheer number of military overflights of the USSR, however, created a significant dilemma. In the absence of a 'paper trail' similar to the well-chronicled civilian U-2 authorizations, it appeared that the military overflights were conducted without the knowledge or consent of the president. Many of these flights were under the operational control of Strategic Air Command (SAC) and its commander, General Curtis E LeMay. Known for his gruff attitude, his harsh wartime success as a bomber commander and architect of the devastating Tokyo fire raids, and his strident anticommunism, LeMay quickly became the culprit amid claims that he not only ordered these flights illegally and without Eisenhower's knowledge but that he intended the flights to provoke general nuclear war with the Soviet Union. Researchers and writers on both sides of the ideological barricade were quick to engage the debate which focused more on LeMay than on aerial reconnaissance operations. Lashmar and Pulitzer Prize-author Richard Rhodes, for example, argued in television documentaries, books, and the pages of *The New Yorker* that LeMay was a 'killer on the edge.'[17] A number of writers and researchers responded that these claims were agenda driven and were based on highly selective misuse of dubious facts or 'proof by assertion.'[18]

In the ensuing decade multiple conferences on military overflights, the ongoing declassification of key documents, and new research expanded the understanding of civilian and military reconnaissance flights in informing US national security policy and the essential role of the president in authorizing these flights. William Burrows' *By Any Means Necessary* as well as Larry Tart and Robert Keefe's *The Price of Vigilance* and Tart's magisterial multivolume *Freedom Through Vigilance: History of the US Air Force Security Service*, showed the personal investment of those who flew the missions, including those who did not return. Dino Brugioni's *Eyes in the Sky* offered the perspective of

Liberal animus toward General Curtis E LeMay led to specious claims that he ordered SAC overflights of the USSR without presidential authorization and, despite the absence of any evidence, that these flights were intended to provoke World War Three to satisfy LeMay's roll-back agenda. *USAF photo*

a distinguished CIA photo analyst involved from the very beginning of the U-2 program as well as the follow-on SR-71 and satellites. He demonstrated the link between aerial reconnaissance and policy making, as well as the tension between the CIA and SAC over operational authority of the U-2. Most importantly, Brugioni argued that Eisenhower enabled a 'revolution' in intelligence collection capability thanks to strategic aerial reconnaissance, which has since served the nation well.

Researchers have certainly appreciated that strategic aerial intelligence flights affected the evolution of early Cold War national security policy. They have given the U-2 primacy of place in disproving the Bomber Gap and the Missile Gap, as well as the peaceful resolution of the Cuban Missile Crisis. Beyond these high-visibility events, however, we are left to wonder exactly *how* these flights contributed to US military planning and to the formulation of American policy. As historian Robin Winks asked, 'does intelligence truly matter? …[is the world] a safer place today because of' intelligence?'[19] Or, as Winks wondered, for all the money spent, the planes and lives lost, and the political and diplomatic damage done, were aerial intelligence flights worth the cost and effort to US security?

To date researchers have reached a general consensus about early Cold War aerial intelligence gathering. Strategic reconnaissance flights, particularly military peripheral and overflights of the Soviet Union and its allies, were more numerous than previously believed. Intelligence gleaned from these civilian and military missions directly informed US policy-making and

Above: Arguably the ultimate Cold War strategic aerial reconnaissance aircraft, the Lockheed SR-71 was the culmination of airframe, engine, and sensor technology. Flying at Mach 3 and 82,000 feet, it traced its operational lineage to the RB-50s and other early ferrets that flew at 200 KIAS and 24,000 feet. Expensive to operate, its career ended in 1998 – every agency wanted its capability but no one wanted to pay for it, and it was replaced by satellites and drones. SR-71A 61-7964 finishes air refueling on the Viking North track over the North Sea during an operational mission on 6 October 1981. *Paul Crickmore*

Opposite: For all the interest in the different types of airplanes that flew adjacent to or over the USSR, or the historical legacy of the political impact of the missions, or the ideological debate over their provocative nature, strategic aerial reconnaissance was about people. Thousands of fliers risked (and many gave) their lives to preserve peace in a Cold War overshadowed by the spectre of nuclear warfare. Their names might not be remembered, but their efforts will never – must never – be forgotten. RF-86F HAYMAKER pilots. *Photo courtesy Doug Gordon*

military planning, particularly in the areas of war plans, assessing the Soviet nuclear capability, and early warning of any impending attack on the United States. These flights also provided timely information about ongoing international crises, such as Suez or the Taiwan Straits. Aerial reconnaissance flights, especially military overflights, were undertaken with the knowledge and approval of the Joints Chiefs of Staff, the Secretaries of State and Defense, and, most importantly, the President. Early Cold War aerial reconnaissance flights contributed directly to stability in US-Soviet relations not because they reassured American leaders that Soviet military capabilities or intentions were less threatening than generally believed, but because the flights provided sufficient strategic early warning that the Soviet Union was not preparing a 'nuclear Pearl Harbor' attack on the United States or its key allies. In addition, intelligence from the flights reassured American military planners that the United States was increasingly prepared for armed conflict with Russia. War between the superpowers may still have been possible, perhaps even inevitable, but it would neither be a surprise nor would it be an impossible task. As such, US policies were less belligerent toward the USSR, but this moderation did not prevent or eliminate a spiraling Cold War arms race or international hostility. Indeed, the U-2 Incident, along with the 1983 Soviet downing of a Korean airliner, are still considered defining events that needlessly escalated US-Soviet tensions.

These assessments have, over the course of some 50 years, become well entrenched in the Cold War canon. They remain essentially descriptive, however, and do not satisfactorily explain the consequences of aerial intelligence on American and Soviet policy and planning. Moreover, this inadequacy reflects the widespread, uncritical acceptance of the fundamental assumptions about the importance and effect of strategic aerial reconnaissance on the early Cold War. For example, the improvement in Cold War aerial reconnaissance capability did not necessarily influence US policy and military plans in positive ways. Contrary to widely held belief, aerial intelligence created pressure for more sophisticated and more numerous weapons systems as well as more nuclear weapons. Despite the President's desire to balance the budget by limiting needless or excessive defense spending, he did not or was unable to use aerial intelligence to constrain spending on strategic forces. Peripheral and overflight missions provided essential intelligence prior to and during the 1956 Suez Crisis and the 1958

Taiwan Straits Crisis. In both cases Eisenhower used this information to mitigate the conflicts, but did not or could not use such information to prevent them or resolve them more quickly, challenging critical assumptions about the efficacy of aerial reconnaissance in strategic early warning. The issue of military overflights as illegal and the trigger for preventive war has wrongly focused on the person of Curtis LeMay and ignored the extant White House and Pentagon procedures to authorize the flights under both Truman and Eisenhower. It equally presumes that reconnaissance flights were as important then to Soviet leaders as they are now to modern scholars and journalists, and that the Russians reacted only with violence against peripheral missions and overflights alike. No matter the public rhetoric, the Soviet Union never considered overflights – civilian or military – as justifiable reasons to initiate war, nor did these flights poison Soviet-American relations and make for a 'longer, colder' Cold War. Eisenhower's approach to overflights was inconsistent, demanding that U-2 overflight pilots be civilians to avoid warlike provocation in the event of a compromised mission, yet he allowed hundreds of military crewmembers to undertake separate military overflights. He dissembled in his approval for overflights by falsely arguing that similar missions carried different risks. He openly claimed that he would start World War Three in response to a single, hypothetical Soviet overflight of the United States but simultaneously authorized hundreds of American overflights – military and civilian – of the USSR. By behaving unpredictably, however, Eisenhower shrewdly strengthened his control over demands for overflights and shut down the potential for preventive war.

For Hervey Stockman, Frank Powers, and the thousands of other pilots, navigators, engineers, gunners, and intelligence specialists who strapped on an airplane and flew into harm's way in pursuit of photographs, electronic recordings, or transcripts of radio conversations, strategic aerial reconnaissance was a deeply personal commitment to fulfill an urgent and compelling national security objective. They all knew the danger, and they all knew someone who didn't come back. For Truman, Eisenhower, Twining, LeMay, Dulles, Bissell, and the other leaders who sent them alone into the darkness, strategic aerial reconnaissance was both a professional and international risk justified by the unfamiliar territory of a 'cold' war. Their legacy, however, has been defined by the journalists, scholars, champions, and critics who have exaggerated the importance and adverse effect of these flights while overlooking their limitations. After nearly 70 years, new evidence and new interpretations provide a new and more sophisticated understanding of the importance of strategic aerial reconnaissance under Truman and Eisenhower.

2 From Post War to Cold War

The Cold War did not suddenly begin one day in 1945. Nearly 30 years earlier US President Woodrow Wilson and his successors saw communism as a direct threat to the liberal capitalist world order they viewed as essential to American and Western personal and national prosperity. American liberals and conservatives alike found communism to be gratuitously violent and destructive to human nature. They viewed it as the basis for a totalitarian state that reduced the spirit of individual achievement and vision to that of an automaton in a society that sought to make everyone equally miserable in a God-less world. The 1917 Bolshevik Revolution took place in the midst of the Great War to contain Germany, and Lenin's separate peace to preserve the revolution at home was seen as Bolshevik complicity in German expansion. In the 1920s Red Scares erupted in the United States as fears of anarchism and radical politics threatened traditional American values. With the global economic collapse of the 1930s, people around the world turned to extreme ideologies such as Nazism and communism as the panacea for social and economic failures. The United States finally recognized the Soviet Union in 1933 when Franklin D Roosevelt saw Russian markets as a potential relief valve for the economic strife at home, not because he chose to welcome the USSR into the fold of global nationhood.

With the onset of the Second World War, the United States joined with Britain, France, China, and other nations in their commitment to prevent Nazi Germany and its allies from dominating Europe and Asia, both critical to Western economic recovery and to preserve liberal democracy around the world. The 1939 Molotov-Ribbentrop Pact echoed Lenin's earlier unwillingness to contain a now-revanchist Germany. It also allowed the USSR to occupy half of Poland after failing to conquer that country during the 1919-1921 Polish-Soviet War, reaffirming Russian expansionist behavior. The Nazi invasion of Russia in 1941 changed the global dynamic. Under the Grand Alliance Roosevelt and British Prime Minister Winston Churchill chose to support 'the devil' in Soviet General

The Cold War didn't necessarily start at Potsdam in 1945, but it certainly got colder, where the distance between Harry Truman (left) and Joseph Stalin (center) was more than literal. Neither side trusted the other. America feared Communist ideology and the huge Soviet army of occupation throughout Eastern Europe. Russia feared the US atomic monopoly and encirclement. Both sides turned to espionage – US spy flights and Soviet moles – to learn about their wartime ally turned adversary. *US Army Signal Corps, Courtesy of Harry S Truman Library*

Secretary Joseph Stalin against Adolf Hitler. By May 1945 Russian armies had captured Berlin, occupied Eastern Europe, and were preparing to assault Japanese forces in Manchuria. For Harry S Truman (who had become president in April upon FDR's death) the wartime expedient of Soviet-American friendship was at an end. Truman was not about to trade one totalitarian government in control of Europe and Asia for another. Two weeks after assuming the presidency he told Soviet Foreign Minister Vyacheslav Molotov in no uncertain terms that the United States would not tolerate Soviet duplicity in honoring their wartime agreements. 'Uncle Joe' (FDR's name for Stalin which Stalin found vulgar and offensive), had ceased to be the partner in the war against fascism. In the absence of a common foe, the Soviet Union resumed its place as the primary threat to American (and world) economic prosperity and democracy.

Although few US officials, military or civilian, imagined a direct Soviet attack on the United States, the Soviets and the West clashed on a variety of issues, some of which could easily have led to war between the former allies. The continued presence of Soviet troops in Iran and claims of a planned Soviet invasion of Turkey in 1946, civil strife in Greece and Turkey during 1947 and 1948, the establishment in 1947 of a Polish Communist government, the 1948 *coup d'état* in Czechoslovakia and the Berlin Crisis, the 1949 Communist victory in the Chinese civil war and the Soviet detonation of an atomic device, and the 1950 Communist invasion of South Korea were all sources of friction, if not potential conflict, between the two leading powers of the post-war world.

War, if it came, might well begin in Europe with a scenario that saw post-war Communist parties in Italy, France, and Greece subverting democratic governments prior to Soviet military occupation. The key to preventing such fifth column threats and Soviet territorial aggrandizement was post-war economic recovery, exemplified by the Marshall Plan, and military support to friendly governments, exemplified by the Truman Doctrine. Should these and other efforts fail, America needed to be ready for general war with the Soviet Union. After the Great Patriotic War the Soviet Union had a huge superiority over the United States in terms of sheer numbers of ground troops and conventional military equipment. From the US point of view this Soviet quantitative edge effectively negated the American qualitative advantage made possible by technologically sophisticated weapons and an atomic monopoly, but this perspective overlooked the widespread demobilization of Soviet ground forces.[1] Nonetheless, by 1950 the Soviet Union had gone from a potent ally of the United States and Great Britain to a potent adversary.

To counter this perceived threat, American policy makers and planners sought the means to prevent a Soviet attack on the United States or its allies and, if need be, attack and defeat the Soviet Union. Any potential conflict with the USSR would necessitate considerable challenges for American forces. The Soviet Union was for all purposes landlocked. American naval and amphibious forces so successful in the Pacific theater would be of little value in attacking just the ice-free ports of Murmansk and Vladivostok. Similarly the Soviet Union had just successfully repelled the largest land invasion in history by using millions of Red Army soldiers to defeat millions of Nazi troops. US ground forces were grossly fewer in number, lacked a suitable starting point, had no supply chain or support infrastructure, and had little chance to overcome the popular Soviet commitment to defend the Motherland. Fresh from the experience of World War Two where strategic bombing of Germany and Japan was held to be a decisive determinant of Axis surrender, American officials opted to use strategic airpower as the cornerstone of US national security policy, and with it strategic aerial reconnaissance was born.

During World War Two the collection and use of intelligence became an essential component of warfare, and post-war officials appreciated its value. Historian John Keegan writes that in 'no war before that of 1939-45...had intelligence been accorded a greater importance,' an influence that would increase dramatically in the years after the war. In September 1945 General Carl Spaatz chaired a committee 'to determine at the earliest date the effect of the atomic bomb on the size, organization, composition, and employment of the Air Force.' Among the 'Spaatz Report's' conclusions was a call for the establishment of an 'essential' strategic intelligence collection and analysis organization within the Air Force 'that will know at all times the strategic vulnerability, capabilities, and probable intentions of any potential adversary.' The September 1945 *United States Strategic Bombing Survey* emphasized that to be successful in any future war US military forces required 'more accurate information, especially before and during the early phases' of conflict. In November 1945

Believed to be Lieutenant Colonel Henry 'Hap' Arnold, this image taken during the 1934 YB-10 Alaska mission represents the deep personal connections within the reconnaissance community. Arnold's team included Captain George Goddard, who oversaw the technical photographic aspects of the operation. Goddard would eventually serve as mentor to Richard Leghorn, arguably the most influential thinker in Cold War aerial reconnaissance. *Museum of Flight P91-3-26/1 [3 of 4] courtesy Dan Hagedorn*

General Henry H 'Hap' Arnold echoed this sentiment by telling Secretary of War Robert Patterson that American leaders and policy makers required 'continuous knowledge of potential enemies.'[2] As the leading American thinker on aerial reconnaissance Lieutenant Colonel Richard S Leghorn warned: *it obviously becomes essential that we have prior knowledge of the possibility of an attack, for defensive action against it must be taken before it is launched. Military intelligence is the agency for providing this information, and our national security rests upon its effectiveness, next to a sound international political structure.*[3]

These recommendations first came to fruition with the establishment of the Strategic Air Command (SAC) in March 1946. In addition to its strategic bombardment duties, SAC would 'conduct maximum range reconnaissance over land or sea either independently or in co-operation with land and naval forces.'[4] The intelligence SAC was ordered to collect would benefit not only military and civilian policy makers, but would satisfy SAC's global targeting requirements as well. Most importantly, aerial intelligence would provide the margin needed for America to learn of an impending attack, no doubt with atomic weapons.

Military planners were long familiar with the value of aerial intelligence to meet 'tactical' and 'operational' requirements. Tactical intelligence revealed, for example, where an artillery piece was located while operational intelligence indicated the amount of ammunition for that gun, a possible warning of an impending attack. Both tactical and operational intelligence remained vital during the Cold War, especially in targeting and war planning, but were of little direct value to senior civilian and military policy makers. Of greater interest to American policy makers was 'strategic' intelligence. Sherman Kent, who headed the CIA's Board of National Estimates from 1952 through 1967, called strategic intelligence 'the knowledge *vital for national survival.*' It involved 'long-range speculation on the strength and intentions of other states,' as well as 'estimates of their probable responses to acts which we ourselves plan to initiate.' Considered the father of strategic intelligence and author of the defining work on the subject, Kent argued that strategic intelligence was 'indispensible to our welfare and security' and the cornerstone 'upon which our nation's foreign relations, in war and peace, must rest.'[5]

Beginning with the Truman administration, US policy makers used strategic intelligence to achieve three major objectives crucial to the formulation of US national security policy. Most importantly the United States should 'develop and maintain an intelligence system' for early warning of Soviet aggression against the continental United States (and secondarily against Western Europe and Japan). Strategic intelligence would also provide US military planners, especially in SAC, with the defense capabilities of 'foreign countries, friendly and neutral as well as enemy' in the event of general war. Finally, strategic intelligence would forecast potential developments that would affect US national security and contribute to day-to-day planning and policy formulation concerning the USSR and its allies.[6]

Clark Clifford, one of President Truman's advisors, highlighted the necessity of strategic intelligence in the formulation of American national security policy during the post-war years. Clifford and George Elsey argued in September 1946 that only through an 'accurate understanding of the characteristics of the one nation which can endanger the United States will our government be able to make and carry out policies which will reestablish order in Europe and Asia and protect this nation at all times.' According to Clifford, this report (actually written by Elsey) reflected widespread consensus throughout the Pentagon and Department of State, indicating the breadth of support for the collection and analysis of intelligence information about the USSR.[7]

The Clifford-Elsey report clearly linked the collection of adequate intelligence to America's post-war goals of reconstruction in Europe and Asia, as well as America's own national security. Given that very few people in the Truman administration ever saw the Clifford-Elsey report because of its provocative tone – perhaps only the president himself read the final report – it is difficult to assess its role in the creation of policy. Nonetheless, if the report *was* as representative of administration attitudes as Clifford later contended, it illuminated the importance Truman administration officials assigned to intelligence gathering. Indeed, some researchers argue that the report's influence was substantial, saying that it 'helped coalesce an uncertain attitude toward the Soviets' and was a 'blueprint for Truman's postwar strategic policy.'[8] Truman agreed with the Clifford-Elsey report's call for improved US intelligence capabilities and took a variety of steps to establish new or reorganize old intelligence agencies. In addition to highly visible efforts, such as the founding of the Central Intelligence Agency, Truman supported less visible military intelligence gathering programs, especially those of the Air Force and Navy.

After much acrimonious debate that focused upon US military 'roles and missions,' the B-36 controversy, the 'Revolt of the Admirals,' the Finletter Commission, and other budgetary and operational battles, American officials endorsed the 'strategic air offensive' model. The United States would deter aggression by promising to defeat an enemy through a sustained and overwhelming atomic attack delivered by American strategic bombers against key industrial and population centers. As early as 1947 and 1948, an atomic air offensive was an integral part of US war plans such as FROLIC and HALFMOON. By fiscal year (FY) 1953, the Truman administration had begun laying the foundation for a policy attributed to his successor: 'Massive Retaliation.'

Assigning priority to strategic bombing facilitated the use of strategic aerial reconnaissance to satisfy American intelligence requirements, largely because long-range American bombers converted into reconnaissance planes were the only means by which the necessary intelligence

Considered the 'father' of strategic intelligence, Sherman Kent argued that strategic intelligence was 'the knowledge vital for national survival' and the cornerstone 'upon which our nation's foreign relations, in war and peace, must rest.' Strategic aerial reconnaissance flights became the primary means to gather this intelligence during the early years of the Cold War. *CIA photo*

Left and far left: Among the most influential Cold War documents the 1946 Clifford-Elsey Report articulated the Soviet threat to America. American and European security and post-war economic recovery were hostage to adequate intelligence about Soviet intentions and capabilities. Perhaps only Truman saw the report, which provided the intellectual basis for strategic aerial reconnaissance to meet Cold War policy needs. Although George Elsey (left) wrote the report, Washington insider Clark Clifford is typically credited as primary author (right). *Copyright Unknown, Courtesy of Harry S Truman Library*

could be collected. The use of converted bombers, however, created additional problems. American RB-29s equipped with cameras en route to reconnoiter the Soviet border were indistinguishable from B-29s equipped with an atomic bomb en route to their targets. Soviet defense forces could easily misidentify a reconnaissance RB-29 flying near the USSR and, fearing an American attack, unleash a retaliatory strike.

There was little debate among Truman and his senior advisors over the wisdom of such flights, their implications for US-Soviet relations, or the institutional management of these flights on a day-to-day basis. US reconnaissance flights were simply accepted as a necessary part of American security requirements. For example, Truman reacted to the 1950 Soviet aerial attack and destruction of a US reconnaissance airplane not by wondering if such missions were prudent given US-Soviet tensions, but by ordering better defensive measures to protect the airplanes from future Soviet attack. John Farquhar, a historian and participant in later strategic reconnaissance flights, notes that 'Truman's [1950] approval of the formal guidelines for aerial reconnaissance not only established the framework of operations to be conducted, but set the stage for a decade of aerial confrontation' with the Soviet Union.[9]

Truman also deferred operational policy decisions on aerial reconnaissance flights to the Joint Chiefs of Staff (JCS). The Air Force, however, gained practical control over the missions during the Truman years even though other agencies such as the CIA and the Navy had legitimate requirements for and undertook efforts to fulfill their own aerial reconnaissance needs. Truman sided with the Air Force on the issue of primary responsibility, approving National Security Council Intelligence Directive (NSCID) 2 and NSCID 3 'with the provision that the dominant interest in air intelligence is assigned to the Department of the Air Force.'[10] Truman also directed the JCS to strengthen the military aerial reconnaissance program, and on 5 May 1950 the JCS approved the Special Electronic Airborne Search Project (SESP) to acquire 'the maximum amount of intelligence concerning foreign electronic developments as a safeguard to national defense.'[11]

Consequently the Air Force had a vested institutional interest in the success of the flights, as much for their intelligence value as for their effect on increasing Air Force influence and advantage over other services and government agencies. Although the Navy conducted only a small percentage of strategic reconnaissance flights, it did not abandon its prerogative to conduct clandestine reconnaissance operations. Submarines conducted a variety of intelligence-gathering missions, including those well within Soviet territorial waters. The Army and Marine Corps had no strategic aerial reconnaissance capacity at all. The Air Force could therefore argue that it deserved the lion's share of funding to support the continued operation of these flights. It could also use the intelligence these flights produced to advance its own interests, especially in times of limited military budgets. Consequently, the Air Force made a firm organizational commitment to satisfy Truman's approval of increased military aerial intelligence-gathering: six groups – nearly ten per cent – of the planned 70-group air force would be dedicated to and equipped for long-range reconnaissance.

With Truman's mandate American leaders embraced strategic aerial reconnaissance to resolve serious weaknesses in US intelligence collection capabilities in and around the Soviet Union. The demand for accurate intelligence was particularly critical after the Soviet Union acquired atomic weapons, which many US pundits and policy makers perceived as capable of delivering a knock-out blow to Western democracies, especially in a surprise attack. The United States had been badly surprised by the Japanese attack at Pearl Harbor and by the North Korean invasion of South Korea. There was no guarantee that another such intelligence failure would not happen again, this time involving the Soviet Union armed with atomic weapons. As Sherman Kent warned in his seminal assessment of the relationship between strategic intelligence and America's survival, 'never before in our peacetime history have the stakes of foreign policy been higher.'[12] The *Saturday Evening Post* made the relationship between early warning intelligence and the Soviet threat even clearer: *If our intelligence services fail us and we are struck with a surprise atomic attack that catches our big planes on the ground – as the Korean War caught us with our land forces unready – then, the tough and realistic men who boss the Strategic Air Command believe, we will have lost the war.*[13]

Unfortunately the means to gather this intelligence was generally unavailable during the early years of the Cold War. What little intelligence the United States had about the Soviet Union in 1945 came from open-source materials gathered through the Library of Congress, Russian émigrés, Tsarist-era maps and travelogues, debriefings of German prisoners of war recently released from Russian prison camps, or captured German air force aerial photographs. By 1953 these sources had expanded greatly, but were still considered insufficient for the precision needed by US military planners and civilian policy makers.[14] This vacuum prompted an accelerated search for more reliable sources, particularly as the need grew for increasingly technical intelligence associated with atomic weapons, electronic warfare, and radar bombing. The technological change in weapons and targets, from massed conventionally armed ground forces along a border to atomic research facilities hidden within the vast expanse of the Soviet Union, proved especially troublesome. Major General Earle E Partridge, then the Air Force Director of Training and Requisition, bemoaned in 1948, 'The scope of the [aerial] reconnaissance needed to carry out atomic bomb attacks in Russia staggers my imagination.'[15]

The promise of long-range airplanes did not necessarily translate promptly into flying reconnaissance missions. Early US strategic aerial operations were hampered by mundane problems such as limited operational budgets, poor aircrew retention, and inadequate airplane numbers, issues which adversely affected SAC bomber operations as well. Between 1948 and 1949 SAC global strategic reconnaissance was severely constrained because of a shortage of airplanes and higher priorities. Beginning in November 1949, for example, the entire RB-29 fleet, SAC's primary reconnaissance platform, was grounded for several months pending essential structural modifications. Reconnaissance units were compelled to borrow unmodified B-29 bombers from other units just to meet minimum training standards, let alone conduct worldwide operational requirements. A lack of proven aerial photography procedures further reduced the effectiveness of SAC's reconnaissance fleet. Finally, a major reorganization in SAC temporarily affected aerial reconnaissance operations and training during late 1949 and early 1950. Shortly after taking command of SAC, LeMay lamented this shortcoming in intelligence gathering capability, saying 'the bottleneck in expanding our present two-squadron reconnaissance capability appears to lie in the availability of reconnaissance type aircraft.'[16] By June 1950 SAC had 30 RB-29s in two reconnaissance wings and planned for nearly 80 RB-50s, RB-36s, and jet-powered RB-45s by late 1951. Given the shortages of aircraft and spares this was not a realistic scenario.[17]

SAC's reconnaissance capacity was also hindered by the lack of trained personnel to fly and maintain the airplanes, and by a severe shortage of specialists trained in the emerging science of electronic intelligence (ELINT), one subcategory of signals intelligence (SIGINT). During the early 1950s ELINT was still in the gestational phase; aerial equipment operators and ground analysts were almost non-existent. New squadrons had to be assembled, equipment delivered, training undertaken, and results calibrated, all efforts that took considerable time. Even more troublesome for the emerging ELINT cadres was the lack of budgetary support for many of these programs by some of SAC's bomber-oriented commanders, who saw ELINT as a form of 'voodoo warfare.'[18]

These shortages affected SAC's ability to gather the intelligence needed to provide early warning of an impending Soviet attack or to help policy makers determine Soviet intentions. Such shortages also seriously hindered SAC's ability to fulfill its combat mission of striking Soviet targets. In February 1950, for example, the Weapon System Evaluation Group (WSEG) reported that SAC's ability to hit Soviet targets was adversely affected by SAC's lack of accurate target information, in particular information regarding the Soviet attack force of Tupolev Tu-4 bombers, atomic weapons development sites, and Soviet air defense bases and equipment.[19]

The Air Force sought to address these deficiencies in target intelligence by establishing or expanding civilian scientific committees. During May 1951, as a spin-off of Project LINCOLN at the Massachusetts Institute of Technology (MIT), the Air Force sponsored Project JEFFERSON, later renamed WINCHESTER. Popularly referred to as the Beacon Hill Study Group because it met in Boston's prestigious Beacon Hill neighborhood, Kodak physicist Carl F P Overhage chaired the group which included Polaroid Corporation founder and president Edwin 'Din' Land (later influential in the Killian Panel and the U-2 program), Harvard University's Edward M Purcell and James G Baker, and Allen F Donovan from Cornell Aeronautical Laboratory. Leghorn served as the Air Force liaison.

The Air Force charged the Beacon Hill group with suggesting 'areas for increased research and development in the fields of reconnaissance and intelligence, with principal concern directed toward technical methods of collecting and utilizing intelligence data.' Of particular interest to the Air Force were issues such as 'pre-D-Day penetration vehicles for air acquisi-

ECM antennas protrude from an RB-36. When this image was taken on 16 May 1955, electronic warfare was still an inexact science and had as many champions as opponents. Eventually Ravens achieved great professional credibility for their work in both ELINT reconnaissance and combat EW. *Lockheed Martin via Dennis Jenkins*

tion of data (GOPHER, a reconnaissance Snark, the proposed earth–satellite, etc).' GOPHER was a balloon overflight program, also known as GRANDSON, GRAYBACK, and GENETRIX. The Northrop SM-62 Snark was a predecessor to ground-launched cruise missiles.[20] That same year the Air Force established its Scientific Advisory Board's Panel on Physical Sciences (renamed more appropriately in 1953 as the Intelligence Systems Panel, and renamed again in 1955 as the Reconnaissance Panel). Clearly, the military in general and SAC in particular needed better support for intelligence collection, support which materialized in the form of strong civilian endorsement of aerial reconnaissance.

No one entered the presidency more appreciative of or more inclined to use intelligence gathering, particularly by aerial means, in the promotion of US national security than did Dwight D Eisenhower. He acknowledged the importance of strategic aerial intelligence to US national security, saying that the United States 'had been the leader for peace in the world. In order to remain the leader, we must remain strong and in order to be strong we must obtain intelligence information.'[21]

Eisenhower commissioned multiple blue-ribbon panels of scientists, industrialists, and military leaders to address the need for better intelligence gathering and analysis. Shortly after taking office Eisenhower chartered Project SOLARIUM, an in-depth analysis of US national policy. A key assumption in the SOLARIUM study was the availability of accurate intelligence about Soviet capabilities and intentions. Two years later, in its 14 February 1955 report to President Eisenhower, the Technological Capabilities Panel of the Science Advisory Committee (also known as the 'Killian Panel' or the 'TCP') made a clear call for improved and better use of intelligence. *We must find ways to increase the number of hard facts upon which our intelligence estimates are based, to provide better strategic warning, to minimize surprise in th[is] kind of attack, and to reduce the danger of gross overestimation or gross underestimation of the threat. To this end, we recommend adoption of a vigorous program for the extensive use, in many intelligence procedures, of the most advanced knowledge in science and technology.*[22]

The Killian Report specified seven courses of action to accomplish these intelligence objectives. These included: the discovery of intelligence hoaxes; increased accessibility during wartime of classified information about enemy capabilities; the gathering and exploitation of electronic intelligence or 'ELINT' (implemented under NSCID-17); support for the small earth satellite to establish the precedent of 'freedom of space' (implemented under NSC 5520); application of data management and retrieval systems to intelligence information; and substantial long-term investment in preparing covert agents.[23] The Killian Report also viewed intelligence not just in terms of gathering data about potential enemies, but in terms of how that material would inform American policy making: *If intelligence can uncover a new military threat, we may take steps to meet it. If intelligence can reveal an opponent's specific weakness, we may prepare to exploit it. With good intelligence we can avoid wasting our resources by arming for the wrong danger at the wrong time. Beyond this, in the broadest sense, intelligence underlies our estimate of the enemy and thus helps to guide our political strategy.*[24]

The report devoted a separate section to 'Intelligence' as well as an appendix entitled 'Intelligence: Our First Defense Against Surprise,' both of which remain classified. A glimpse of what the Intelligence Panel Report contains, however, appears in Richard Bissell's memoirs. As Bissell recalls, the TCP intelligence group received 'extensive briefings on state-of-the-art optical and camera designs, as well as on potential aircraft and power plants.' Clearly thinking about aerial reconnaissance and its relation to early warning, military planning, and American security, the Intelligence Panel 'strongly recommended' that the United States 'initiate with maximum security and urgency a project to develop an advanced-technology system of overhead reconnaissance.'[25] Eisenhower no doubt welcomed this recommendation, which independently reaffirmed his decision in late 1954 to approve development of the U-2.

Echoing the findings and recommendations of the Killian Panel, the November 1957 report 'Deterrence and Survival in the Nuclear Age,' commonly known as the Gaither Report, articulated weaknesses in US intelligence. 'We have too few solid facts on which to base essential knowledge of USSR capabilities and too few solid facts to learn how they are changing with time. From such observations, intentions may often be deduced.' The Gaither Report recommended that: *because of their utmost importance to our actual survival, we urge exploitation of all means presently at our disposal to obtain both strategic warning and hard intelligence, even if some risks have to be taken, together with the vigorous development of new techniques.*[26]

One might wonder if the 'risks to be taken' represented the Gaither Committee's support for existing or proposed military overflights, and in particular revealed its knowledge of the U-2 program. It is widely held that the Gaither Committee was unaware of the U-2 overflights and was not given access to U-2 photos.[27] However, at least three members knew of the U-2 photos and what they revealed. Lieutenant General James H 'Jimmy' Doolittle had been briefed regularly on the U-2 program and had seen U-2 photos prior to his participation on the Gaither Committee. Doolittle was also a member of the TCP Intelligence Panel, which was subsequently briefed on the development and operations of the U-2. As a Shell Oil executive Doolittle helped U-2 designer Clarence 'Kelly' Johnson produce the low–vapor kerosene fuel necessary for the high-flying U-2. Of course Killian was aware of the U-2, as was fellow TCP member James B Fisk. U-2 data probably contributed directly to Eisenhower's positive response to those portions of the Gaither report which endorsed strategic aerial reconnaissance.

Policy makers, both military and civilian, clearly recognized the need for strategic intelligence and its essential relation to American national security. They also recognized the value of aerial reconnaissance in fulfilling this intelligence objective. They did not always agree, however, on what constituted appropriate intelligence or how to interpret the information, reflecting the analyst's dilemma: 'The more you know the less you understand.' For example, accurate forecasts of foreign behavior based upon strategic intelligence rely heavily upon understanding that nation's *intent*, something not easily determined by examining photographs of airplane factories or counting submarines in a naval yard. Just because the Soviets *had* the production capability to build a large fleet of strategic bombers did not necessarily mean that they *would*. US intelligence analysts often mapped their own assumptions about Soviet behavior (presumed to be aggressive and expansionist) onto Soviet capabilities and thereby derived a fallacious Soviet intent to build a massive bomber fleet or outpace American ballistic missile production.

Some policy makers were equally worried about America's increasing 'gadget bias,' its increasing use of sophisticated equipment that gathered quantitative but not qualitative intelligence. Former Ambassador and State Department official U Alexis Johnson, for example, 'was impressed by [technical means of collection] and the intelligence data they could pro-

An intercept provided the ultimate intelligence collection. COMINT would record the radio conversation between ground controllers and pilots, revealing operational frequencies and procedures. ELINT would collect radar and ECM data used by the airplane and ground defense forces. PHOTINT would show new modifications, nose numbers, aircraft technical details, and even the metal used in construction based on skin color. A Yak-25M *Flashlight-A* shows this to good effect while intercepting an RC-135. *USAF via Geoff Hays*

duce,' but felt that the United States was 'becoming unduly enamored' with them 'to the detriment of our abilities in the hard, dangerous drudgery of old-time espionage.' Technical reconnaissance was 'excellent for revealing what an enemy's capabilities [were, but seldom disclosed] how, or if, he intends to use them.'[28] There were also organizational and bureaucratic differences that arose in the interpretation of raw intelligence. The Air Force and CIA, for example, clashed on issues of operational control of reconnaissance assets, collection priorities, and analytic implications. This variation extended to international intelligence operations, as US and British analyses from the same intelligence sources often yielded different conclusions. These analytic and interpretive shortcomings were more institutional than operational, however, and did not reflect adversely on aerial reconnaissance as a means of intelligence collection. Once policy makers and military planners decided on the primacy of technical intelligence gathered by these flights, the mindset they brought to the analysis of the information predisposed the conclusions they would draw, contributing to major strategic intelligence failures such as the 'Bomber Gap' and the 'Missile Gap,' a problem that remained largely unresolved throughout the Cold War.

Discerning Soviet capabilities and intentions proved increasingly difficult as the Cold War evolved. Russia's closed society, the severe restrictions on Soviet citizens, and an extensive Soviet counterespionage effort all limited the efficiency of US agents in place or those sent to the USSR. Analysts needed new collection methods that could provide the highly technical information associated with modern Soviet weapons. Moreover, merely counting missiles or bombers did not necessarily indicate how effective they were. Consequently, the traditional reliance upon subjective human intelligence (HUMINT) gave way to other objective sources such as technical analysis based upon electronic transmissions, although not all policy makers were enthusiastic about this shift toward highly technical intelligence. Analysts considered these newer forms of intelligence more reliable than human sources, and encouraged the development of sophisticated technical means to collect photographic intelligence (PHOTINT), SIGINT and its subfield of ELINT, communications intelligence (COMINT), telemetry intelligence (TELINT), and other, more esoteric forms of intelligence. Although these methods were in Spartan use before 1945, they were not accorded the importance they achieved during the Cold War. SIGINT, especially ELINT, became increasingly essential to American Cold War military planning as the tools of warfare became increasingly electronic in nature. By 1980 ELINT collection accounted for 80 per cent of US intelligence.[29]

The stereotypic notion of collecting intelligence is based upon a Kim Philby who infiltrates a secret agency or a Mata Hari who seduces enemy officers. To be sure, there were numerous cases of Cold War HUMINT intelligence coups such as Klaus Fuchs and US atomic secrets, Oleg Penkovsky and Soviet missile secrets, and Aldrich Ames and CIA operatives abroad. Compared with overhead and aerial photography, as well as all sources of SIGINT, however, these known HUMINT examples represent only a small portion of US intelligence sources. US moles in the Soviet Union were usually caught and executed, or once dropped behind Soviet borders, as in Operation REDSOX, were never heard from again.[30] One consequence of this shortage of reliable agents was an overestimation of Soviet capabilities. A 1950 Department of Defense (DoD) memorandum

MIND THE GAP

The Cold War epitomized the definition of 'arms race.' It began with US and British technology commanding a decisive lead over Soviet strength of numbers. The atomic bomb and B-29s negated millions of Russian troops and tanks. This Western lead did not last long, as the Soviets introduced their copy of the B-29 – the Tu-4 *Bull* – into operational service with the *Dal'naya Aviatsiya*. To almost everyone's shock and surprise, the Soviets detonated their first atomic bomb on 29 August 1949, by some accounts five years earlier than expected. It was not Soviet parity with the West, however, that exacerbated Western fears, but the *speed* at which the Soviets were able to achieve technological and strategic equality with the West. American military analysts believed this demonstrated that the Soviets had the capability to out produce the United States. Within another five years, they feared, Russian industrial might would exceed that of America and Europe combined. Two key events appeared to reaffirm this belief, despite the fact that both were the result of errors in intelligence and judgment.

THE BOMBER GAP

During the early 1950s America emphasized jet engines for its B-47s and B-52s. Although the Soviets had modest success with the jet-powered Tu-16 *Badger*, they were far more successful with the turboprop-powered Tu-95 *Bear*. For SAC analysts this was a throwback to the B-36, and at the time was seen as only an interim long-range bomber pending improvements in Soviet jet engine technology. The 1954 appearance of the Myasishchev Mya-4 *Bison* led Western officials to believe that time had come. The Mya-4 was both large and jet-powered, so USAF planners equated it with the B-52 in operational capability. They also believed that because the Soviets had the *potential* to build several hundred of these bombers a year that they necessarily *would* build that many.

The 1955 Aviation Day air show near Moscow fanned these alarmist predictions. Ten Mya-4s flew past the reviewing stand and then out of sight. They returned from the opposite direction, along with eight more *Bisons*. The ruse worked. Western air attachés and the foreign press dutifully reported a total of 28 Mya-4s were already flying, and projected some 800 in service by 1960. This substantially exceeded ongoing B-47 and B-52 production, and the 'Bomber Gap' was born. Congressional hawks, especially those whose constituents stood to gain from increased acquisition of US bombers, demanded that more B-47s and B-52s be purchased.

US RB-47 and U-2 overflights of the USSR through 1956 revealed the small number of *Bisons* in service, effectively demonstrating the 'Bomber Gap' to be a myth. The public environment remained suspect, however, and LeMay used that tension to push through modest additional acquisitions of new SAC bombers. Most ominously, the 'Bomber Gap' predisposed a US mindset that made what happened next inevitable

THE MISSILE GAP

On 4 October 1957 people around the world could tune their radios to listen to the 'beep beep beep' of the first artificial satellite in orbit around the Earth. This was *Sputnik* – Russian for (ironically enough) 'Fellow Traveler'. It wasn't so much the satellite that created the greatest fear among Western officials, however, as it was the means to get *Sputnik* into space. Today the Soviet R-7 *Semyorka* rocket lofted the tiny satellite into orbit. Tomorrow the same rocket could loft Soviet atom bombs at targets in Europe and America. To be sure, the United States had a fledgling rocket and space program led by former Nazi scientist Werner von Braun, but it had been fraught with failures and lack of meaningful Congressional support. According to Nikita Khrushchev, the Soviets were pumping out R-7s 'like sausages', indicative of both a robust development program and a mature production capability.

The 'Missile Gap' preyed on the same fears and mentality that had yet to abate from the earlier 'Bomber Gap'. Young Russians studied science to become engineers and, ahem, 'rocket scientists.' Young Americans studied the hula hoop and Elvis Presley, undermining the academic edge which had previously served US technological superiority so well. Prospective US Democratic presidential candidate Senator John Kennedy coined the phrase 'Missile Gap', and used it throughout his campaign to emphasize how the Republican Eisenhower administration and its presumptive presidential candidate, Vice President Richard Nixon, were 'soft on defense.'

As with the 'Bomber Gap', US strategic aerial reconnaissance missions ranging from EB-47E(TT) TELL TWO sorties out of Turkey to U-2 overflights of Tyuratam and ground-based listening posts undermined Kennedy's claims. Ultimately CORONA satellite imagery drove the final nail in the coffin, but not until Kennedy had already been elected and inaugurated as president.

THE MINE SHAFT GAP

By 1964 the 'Bomber Gap' and the 'Missile Gap' had become so deeply ingrained into Western culture that they appeared in Stanley Kubrick's farce *Dr Strangelove: Or How I Learned to Stop Worrying and Love the Bomb*. Faced with the inevitability of a Soviet 'Doomsday Machine' that will destroy all life on the planet, Dr Strangelove (one of three parts played by Peter Sellers) opines that some people could survive the irradiated holocaust if they moved quickly into deep mine shafts. General 'Buck' Turgidson (George C Scott) warns that it would be necessary to ensure that more Americans survive than Russians in order to 'win' the war. This would require more American than Soviet mine shafts, and Turgidson expressed deep reservations about a 'Mine Shaft Gap'. Strategic aerial reconnaissance would likely have been useful in debunking such a gap, as the images collected could reveal not only possible entryways but the mine shaft depth needed to survive the radiation based on the amount of dirt excavated from the mine and deposited nearby. Still, there wouldn't have been anyone alive to fly the missions anyway. Certainly not Major Kong....

commenting upon a CIA report that minimized Soviet atomic capacity warned that: *there are areas in Russia that are* not *covered by our agents so that the CIA report is based on intelligence from* incomplete coverage *of the Soviet Union. The CIA figure is more likely to represent a minimum capability of the Soviet Union. We ought at least to look at the other end of the bracket...*[31]

The DoD report did just that, emphasizing a significantly greater Soviet atomic capability than was justified by the evidence at hand.

Even when it was available the intelligence gleaned from HUMINT was suspect. Refugees or defectors, as well as Western travellers visiting the USSR (as in Operation REDSKIN), might report seeing something that looked like a radar installation. What an illiterate peasant or

Below: Preserved under the wing of B-36J 52-2220 at the NMUSAF, the 'Boston Camera' gives a clear indication of its actual size. Initially tested in an RB-36D, it saw operational use in the PIE FACE C-97A 49-2592 as part of the 'Berlin for Lunch Bunch' missions during the 1950s. Its value there was limited, however, as Soviet restrictions to corridor flights limited the PIE FACE to an altitude of 10,000 feet. Each image was 18 x 36 inches, offering remarkable detail for the benefit of eager photo interpreters. *Stephen Miller*

Opposite: The Berlin corridors proved fruitful venues for US strategic reconnaissance flights. The proximity of Soviet and East German bases and command centers allowed for robust PHOTINT and COMINT collection. Moreover, Soviet ground-based and aerial radars and electronic gear made for an ELINT-rich environment for the C-97s, T-29s, C-54s, and C-118s of the 'Berlin for Lunch Bunch' which plied these routes on a daily basis. However routine, these flights were not without risk as MiG-15 harassment was common and MiGs shot down several military and civilian airplanes.

a casual visitor described as a radar unit may well have turned out to be merely a chicken-wire fence. Further, the sighting of a radar dish did not reveal its range or accuracy. HUMINT was also vulnerable to disinformation, where double agents planted bogus information intended to confuse US intelligence analysts. Should war erupt, refugees and defectors would be even less accessible and reliable, especially given the time constraints of a global war involving atomic weapons. Air Force Intelligence highlighted this vulnerability in a 1951 appeal for greater aerial reconnaissance assets: 'Defectors and refugees…supply us with some information but the flow is not steady. [Aerial] Reconnaissance will solve much of our problem and quickly, once hostilities start…'[32] In view of the inherent weaknesses to HUMINT, as well as its interpretive vulnerabilities, US analysts sought more reliable sources of information.

Even before the use of spy cameras, agents drew maps of enemy locations. Once cameras were introduced, the reliability of visual intelligence increased substantially. Still, it took an agent in place to take the needed pictures, often an impossible undertaking in the USSR. Moreover, US analysts required photographs in greater quantity and detail than available from agents. A single spy photo hastily taken outside the fence at a Soviet bomber base might show one or two distant airplanes. The photo could not disclose the total number of bombers at the base, how they were dispersed, the level of maintenance they received, how much fuel was available to them, or if they were on alert for a pre-emptive strike against the United States.

The answer was PHOTINT. A single aerial photo could show all these things and more, such as on-going construction, quantity of fuel available in nearby storage tanks, or the presence of a weapons bunker and what kind of bombs it might contain. The length of a runway, for example, reveals the takeoff distance required by a bomber, which tells the maximum takeoff weight, which in turn suggests the amount of fuel on board (and hence the range of the bomber and targets it might reach) as well as the bomber's potential to carry heavy atomic weapons. To a trained eye, even the number of wooden crates at a site and how they were arranged might reveal the imminent deployment of a new weapon.

Secretary of State Henry L Stimson declared his distaste for espionage during the administration of Herbert Hoover by saying 'Gentlemen do not read each other's mail.' He would no doubt be aghast to learn that gentlemen not only read one another's mail, but they listen in on one another's telephone calls as well. This is one form of communications intelligence – COMINT – perhaps the most valuable source of information about an enemy's intentions.

COMINT is the interception of communications passed by radio, wire, or other electromagnetic means. By intercepting a message between a field commander and his headquarters, analysts could determine if an attack was forthcoming, could deduce enemy operational procedures and their effectiveness, could identify specific command and control links between higher headquarters and their reporting units, and could suggest ways to jam or exploit enemy communications links.[33] COMINT could also reveal sensitive diplomatic information, such as messages from Moscow telling Beijing and Pyongyang that the USSR wished to remain out of the Korean War, and that aid to North Korea would have to come from the People's Republic of China (PRC). COMINT was vulnerable to disinformation, as an adversary might create spurious conversations designed to give the appearance of one action while undertaking another. Moreover, COMINT was typically in a language other than English and was often encrypted, requiring multiple levels of translation and decoding which slowed the analytic process considerably. Thus informed of Soviet intentions, American policy makers could – but did not necessarily – plan wisely.

As with PHOTINT, airplanes provided an excellent platform to collect COMINT. The listening range of a surface-based station adjacent to the USSR is limited by the transmitting

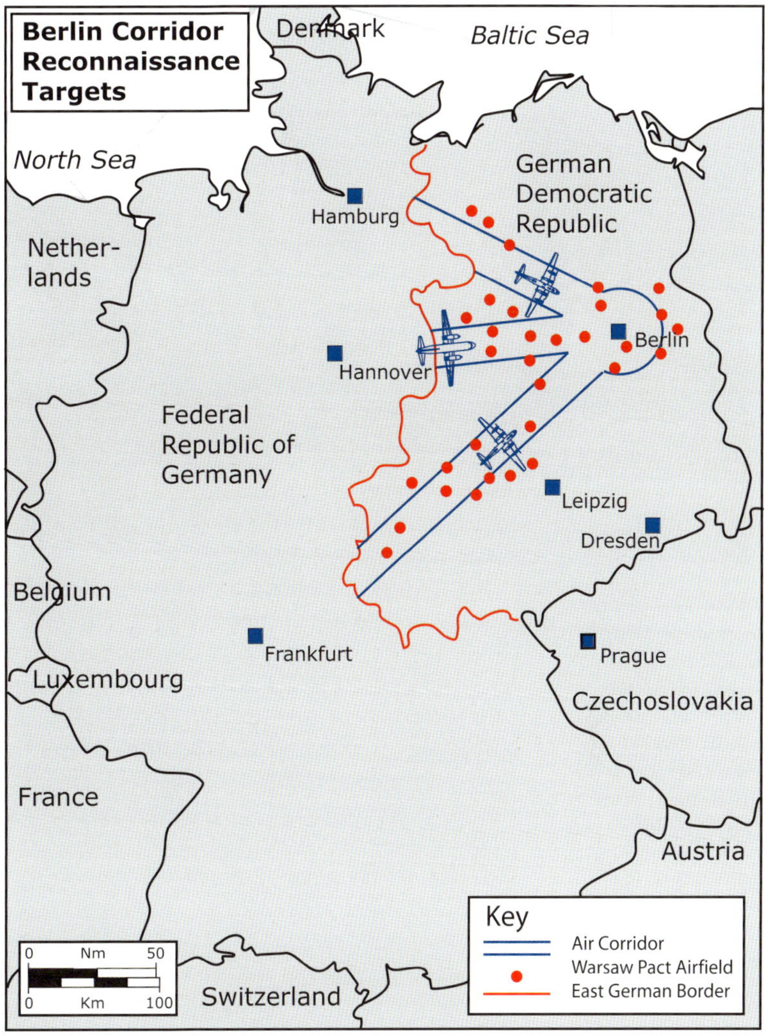

radio's line-of-sight capability, a function of the curvature of the earth and the local terrain. At sea level, this range for a very high frequency (VHF) radio can be as small as tens of miles. Although high frequency (HF) transmissions have global range depending on atmospheric conditions, their unpredictability was unsuitable for continuous monitoring. By raising the listening post to 35,000 feet, the height at which an electronic 'ferret' might fly, this intercept range for VHF increases to 230 miles, a distance especially relevant to potential hostile forces poised a few miles behind a border or defensive anti-aircraft sites and command nodes within the Soviet Union. It was neither economically feasible nor politically practicable to build listening posts every 100 miles or so around the Soviet Union for maximum coverage, especially where some areas were of little interest or adjacent governments were unwilling to allow such sites on their territory. Good examples of these geopolitical limitations include initial Pakistani reluctance to accept US listening posts and U-2 bases, the British unwillingness to permit U-2 flights after an unsavory incident involving British espionage and a visiting Soviet naval vessel, or Sweden's second thoughts about hosting a US ballistic missile radar.[34] Airplanes, however, could routinely cover these areas with considerable flexibility in their routes, frequency, and timing, thereby increasing their value as collection assets. A 1958 study confirmed this, saying the 'intercept productivity [of airplanes] was far higher than at fixed sites.'[35]

ELINT is among the newest forms of intelligence gathering, making its debut during the Second World War. It is the collection of 'information derived from foreign noncommunications electromagnetic radiations emanating from other than atomic detonations or radioactive sources.' ELINT includes 'frequencies, signal strengths, pulse lengths, pulse rates, and other specifications' of radars and electronic warfare equipment.[36] Although there were efforts by British and Americans during World War Two to gather details about German and Japanese electronic gear, it was not until the Cold War that electronic equipment became a substantial threat to US military operations and elicited concern over its scope and effectiveness.

SAC's RB-50 and RB-47 ELINT airplanes were 'designed to accomplish electronic reconnaissance, involving the locating and analyzing of electronic radiations' of enemy radars.[37] During 1958, for example, the CIA used ELINT gleaned from USAF RB-47s to assess the capability of the Soviet BAR LOCK radar used to detect and track U-2 overflights and how it might be jammed.[38] Electronic 'data [were] the primary source for establishing an enemy perimeter and interior radar order of battle and [were] an absolute necessity for successfully implementing offensive action by the United States and its allies.'[39] Knowledge of enemy radar sites allowed US military planners to devise bomber penetration routes that skirted dangerous areas, minimizing bomber losses en route to their targets and improving the probability that the target would be struck. ELINT also enabled US scientists and engineers to develop electronic countermeasures (ECM) capable of jamming enemy radars. Installed in American bombers, ECM further enhanced an airplane's ability to penetrate enemy defenses.[40] As with COMINT, ELINT signals are limited by the earth's curvature or can be masked by mountainous terrain. Airborne collection platforms overcame these obstacles and could carry the necessary heavyweight detection and recording equipment. In addition, the airplanes could loiter as needed, allow-

Above: ELINT collection could be broad spectrum, where an airplane such as RB-47H 53-4280 would gather any signals that happened to be 'up' as the aircraft passed by. In other cases, ELINT could be a dedicated search for specific signals such as those emitted by the *Bar Lock* radar that tracked CIA U-2 overflights. By 13 May 1967, when this photo was taken at RAF Upper Heyford, the RB-47H fleet was just months from final retirement. *Stephen Miller Collection*

ing crewmembers to make on-the-spot analyses of signals of interest (SOIs).

If COMINT offers a glimpse of an enemy's intentions and ELINT peers into an enemy's capabilities, TELINT is a kind of divination into an enemy's future. TELINT is: *associated with the testing and operational deployment of aerospace, surface, and subsurface systems that may have military or civilian applications...includ[ing] but...not limited to signals from telemetry, beaconing, electronic interrogators, tracking/fusing/aiming/command systems, and video data links.*[41]

For example, as the Soviets tested their prototype ballistic missiles, Russian scientists would analyze the telemetry data sent from the missile during each flight. This telemetry would tell the scientists how well the rocket was performing or where its weaknesses were hampering its range, acceleration, or payload capacity. Despite routine encryption and ambiguity, telemetry could be and was intercepted to tell US scientists the same information relayed to Soviet scientists.

Most accounts accord PHOTINT from CIA U-2 overflights of the USSR with near-absolute responsibility for identifying the weaknesses in Soviet ballistic missile capability, thereby ending the missile gap. This view ignores, however, the role of airborne assets such as the USAF EB-47E TELL TWO peripheral TELINT reconnaissance program associated with the CIA IRON WORKS program. Beginning in 1958, and in conjunction with a ground-based radar in Turkey, three TELL TWO airplanes collected substantial TELINT demonstrating the foibles of Soviet missiles. Whereas U-2 photos showed how *few* missiles the Soviets had, TELL TWO TELINT revealed just how *ineffective* those few missiles were, disarming critics who charged that the Soviets

Right: Large flat antennas on the nose and in the wingtips of the Boeing-configured TELL TWO EB-47E collected TELINT from Soviet missiles and rockets. Early jet engines were 'gas guzzlers,' so reconnaissance B-47s needed air refueling for long-duration missions or to get to bases in England, Greenland, Turkey, Japan, or Alaska. *John Kovacs*

needed only the limited number of missiles shown in U-2 photographs because they were so accurate and powerful (to be sure, U-2s did collect TELINT). Richard M Bissell, the director of CIA U-2 operations, acknowledged that 'the TELL TWO data corroborated the U-2 photography in downgrading the notion of a missile gap.'[42] Despite the importance of the TELL TWO missions and other sources of information on Soviet missile tests such as informer Oleg Penkovsky, ground listening posts in Turkey and Alaska, and ultimately the CORONA satellite program the bias toward the U-2's omnipotence in defusing the missile gap proved difficult to overcome.[43]

Accurate TELINT did not necessarily translate in accurate assessments. Following the display at the 1967 Paris Air Show of the Soviet SS-6 *Sapwood* intercontinental ballistic missile (ICBM), CIA analysts were afforded the opportunity to compare their conclusions drawn over the preceding decade with the actual hardware in question. The results showed 'many weaknesses' in the evaluation process. Although the telemetry data were accurate and some analysts did indeed correctly assess the SS-6's true capabilities, 'unfortunately their [analytic] adversaries, guided by the 'divine righteousness' of [US rocket] design concepts overruled their superior technical judgments.'[44]

Although the importance of ground- or ship-based TELINT collection sites should not be minimized, airplanes were an ideal source for gathering TELINT. In addition to overcoming the common limits of range and terrain, airplanes offered a quick-response capability to collect 'one-shot' intelligence data. US analysts might learn of an impending Soviet missile test only hours ahead of the scheduled launch. Forewarned, the TELINT airplane could take off, climb to altitude, wait for the launch, record the desired telemetry, and return the data for prompt analysis.[45]

The new post-war demand for accurate intelligence about Soviet intentions and capabilities dictated collection methods capable of overcoming major obstacles such as long distances, remote locations, excessive secrecy, and ambiguous observations. Moreover, the changing environment of warfare from traditional land- and sea-based conventional forces to highly technical exoatmospheric weapons such as ICBMs and the growth of electronic warfare necessitated substantial changes in the tools used to acquire these data. Strategic aerial reconnaissance satisfied both of these requirements, and did so in conjunction with the increasing US commitment to strategic airpower as the core of American national security strategy. American military and civilian leaders, especially the president, endorsed ongoing collection efforts around the periphery of Communist bloc nations, as well as overflights of the Soviet Union, the PRC, and their client states. Truman, Eisenhower, and their advisors like Allen Dulles and General Nathan Twining were willing to risk direct confrontation with the Soviet Union to gather strategic intelligence they deemed essential to the long-term safety of the United States. As General Partridge warned in 1948, the effort to achieve this over the next 15 years was staggering.

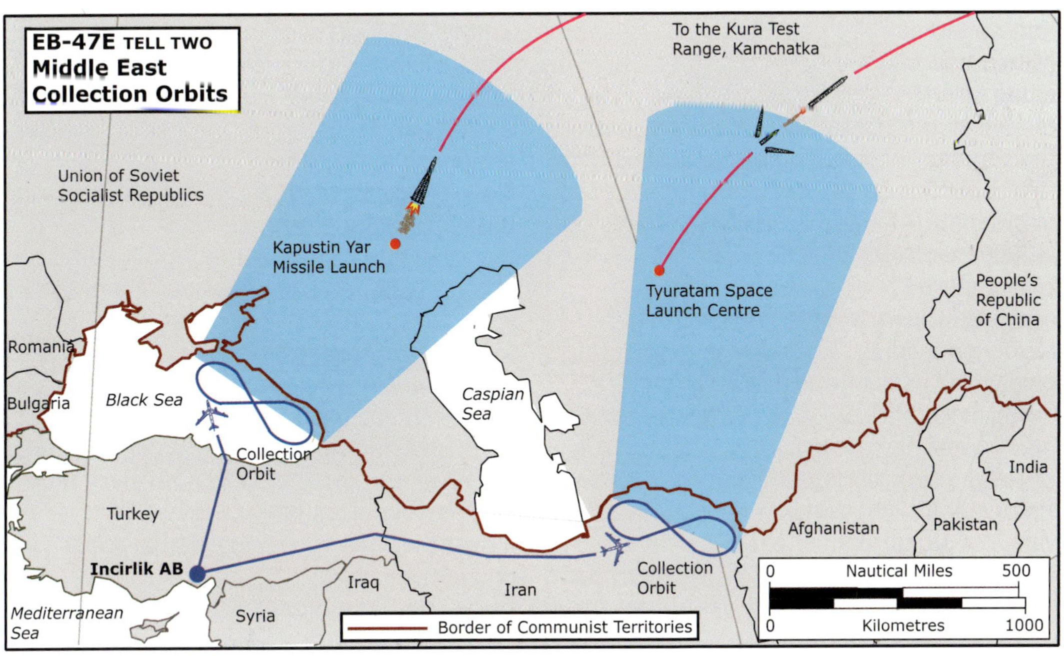

A TELL TWO EB-47E on alert at Incirlik AB could be airborne within 15 minutes and en route to an orbit where it would gather launch-phase TELINT from Soviet missiles. This revealed how well (or not) the ICBM was performing. Interestingly, the TELL TWO would remain it its orbit for some two hours after the Soviets launched a satellite from Tyuratam. The TELL TWO was then able to collect the initial telemetry downlink from the satellite, a considerable intelligence coup.

3 Aerial Containment

They lived in places like Topeka Kansas, Lockbourne Ohio, and Brunswick Maine. Gas for their Packards and DeSotos cost 29 cents a gallon. Before taxes the officers earned $350 per month and the enlisted men brought home $288. On Thursday nights they might watch Jack Webb as Sergeant Joe Friday in the new television version of the popular radio show *Dragnet*. Many of them no doubt smoked Chesterfields, the show's sponsor. Dean Martin's 'That's Amore!' was popular among the older men, who didn't care much for new music like Bill Haley and His Comets singing 'Shake, Rattle, and Roll.' They all worked nearby at 'the base,' essentially a runway or two, a place to park and work on airplanes, and flimsy buildings that housed administrative and operational offices, remnants of facilities hastily built throughout America during the Second World War. Once or twice a week they would fly local training sorties for pilot and navigator proficiency. There was also a lot of 'practice bleeding,' the derogatory euphemism for simulated wartime operations.

Every six weeks or so they deployed overseas on temporary duty (TDY). They told their wives and girlfriends, children and parents, and friends and neighbors only that they would be home in 30-45 days. Wives could usually figure out where their husbands were going based on the contents of their suitcases: extra long johns meant Alaska or Greenland and extra sports shirts meant Turkey or Morocco. Departures were particularly tough. Sweethearts were left behind. Fathers were gone for Christmas, school plays, or the birth of a child. Wives were forced to cope with traditional 'man-of-the-house' duties like income tax preparation, mowing the lawn, or fixing the clutch in the car all while fulfilling their ubiquitous role as homemaker. For the fliers TDY meant getting away from the routine of life, enjoying some 'male bonding,' and shopping and sightseeing. The global deployments and long flights were infinitely more enjoyable than sitting 'SAC alert' every third week.

For all the importance and excitement accorded the aerial intelligence mission, reconnaissance crews – especially those in the US Navy – frequently operated in substandard conditions. These P4M-1Q Mercator crews no doubt longed for the open-bay barracks at home. USAF crews considered Navy billeting contemptible and avoided diverting to a Navy base at all cost. *Author's Collection*

Reconnaissance airplanes were a harsh place to work. The airplane was sweltering in the heat and freezing in the cold (especially at night while cruising at high altitude). In the RB-47, for example, the pilot, co-pilot, and navigator suffered from the same discomforts as standard B-47 crewmembers: long missions (perhaps 10-12 hours), wearing a helmet, oxygen mask, and parachute, strapped into an uncomfortable ejection seat in a noisy environment. In-flight box lunches were appalling. Transit time to and from the area of interest was excruciatingly boring. For the two or three Ravens (or more familiarly, the 'Crows') it was worse. They worked in a tomb-like capsule installed in the bomb bay. There were no windows, so a few floodlights and the lights of their equipment were the only source of illumination. Non-smokers agonized in the tiny compartment that quickly filled with cigar or cigarette smoke, making the sortie a miserable physical experience, especially for a flier hung over from last night's antics at the officer's club or the pub 'just outside the gate.'

Such unpleasantries did not dampen the fliers' enthusiasm. New signals were puzzles waiting to be collected and analyzed. Changing weather made the flight path anything but routine. Fuel management and aircraft performance were critical as there was no place to land in an emergency. Any deployment carried the risk of the aircraft crashing due to mechanical problems, bad weather, or crew error, but for these crews the hazard was even greater. The 'other guy' had a track record of attacking and destroying their airplanes. Far from the hyperbole and rhetoric of the Cold War, these fliers were the main attraction in a hidden shooting war. Even 60 years later, 'crew dogs' gather annually to swap lies and remembrances in an elite fraternity whose unofficial motto is 'Recon is my life, danger is my business.'

For many years military reconnaissance flights along the periphery of (and occasionally over) Communist bloc nations were unknown to Americans outside of a small group of fliers, their families, and key officials with a 'need to know.' Flights were often over remote stretches of Arctic oceans where rescue was impossible in the event of a malfunction or attack. Survival time in the frigid waters was less than four minutes as fliers might lose consciousness and freeze to death before they could even reach a life raft. Radio communication was severely limited due to the long distances involved and the vagaries of HF transmission in the polar region. Calls for help in an emergency were useless as they would likely go unanswered. Most importantly, any rescue or defensive forces were simply too far away to provide timely assistance. Should an aircraft go down near hostile rescue forces or even local fishing boats the crew's future was still in grave doubt. Beginning with the first shoot-down in 1950 and over the following decade, a number of unverified claims arose of dozens of crewmembers rescued, imprisoned, interrogated, and forgotten. A Russian fishing trawler rescued Captains John McKone and Bruce Olmstead after the Soviets shot down their RB-47H on 1 July 1960. Ravens Major Eugene Posa and Captains Oscar Goforth and Dean Phillips perished, likely unable to eject from the out-of-control airplane. Major Willard Palm's body was recovered and returned to the United States. McKone and Olmstead were held in Moscow's notorious Lubyanka prison alongside Frank Powers. They came home on 24 January 1961, the only surviving military reconnaissance crewmembers to be imprisoned and then repatriated.

For the families of these missing fliers there was little hope of understanding what happened and what became of their loved one. In an effort to preserve the intelligence value of the flights the US government refused to acknowledge their existence. Wives and parents were told their husbands and sons were lost due to a 'navigation error' or a 'technical malfunction,' suggesting that their misfortune was of their own making. Other times relatives were told they were conducting a routine study of magnetic wave propagation or other scientific analysis and disappeared without a trace due to the remoteness of their flight. Unless the episode reached the *New York Times* or other public forums, US officials were loath to press the Soviets or Chinese for information about the crash or the whereabouts of the crew. As journalist William Burrows writes, American officials saw the downed fliers as 'problems without a solution.'[1] In some cases the Soviets knew what happened but either refused to provide assistance or intentionally misled American rescue and recovery efforts. On 17 April 1955, for example, Soviet MiG-17s shot down RB-47B-I 51-2054 near Petropavlovsk on the Kamchatka Peninsula. Soviet officials reported only that the airplane crashed and gave a spurious location to keep US forces away from the actual impact site in an effort to cover up details of the Soviet attack. What became of the crew of three remains unknown.

Despite a general unwillingness to acknowledge peripheral reconnaissance flights, the US military and government attempted to honor the fliers in discreet but meaningful ways. Medals for valor and distinguished airmanship were awarded for specific missions, but the citations were vague about what happened. The flight time accrual record for reconnaissance crewmembers was given a special designation, ranking it just below combat flying time in importance to acknowledge the risk inherent in the missions. According to a declassified NSA history, in 1963 the JCS implemented a highly secret 'White Wolf Advisory Warning Program to protect American aircraft flying reconnaissance missions essentially worldwide.' Using ground-based listening stations as well as onboard linguists, flight crews could be warned of impending hostile action, allowing time for the aircraft to avoid attack (even with this safety net the North Koreans still shot down a USAF EC-121 on 15 April 1969).[2] Eventually the word spread throughout the military that a handful of units flew these hazardous missions, and they acquired a respect and mystique accorded a small, elite group of fliers. Equally, there was no shortage of volunteers seeking to transfer into these squadrons.

In their studies of Cold War aerial reconnaissance researchers have traditionally focused on the two dozen U-2 overflights of the Soviet Union or the occasional public announcement of Soviet or Chinese attacks on a US ferret. The extensive nature of the American aerial reconnaissance program, particularly military overflights and peripheral sorties, went beyond these events and reveals a well established com-

A US Navy publicity photo of the crew of P2V-5 BuNO 131515 which was attacked on 22 June 1955 by MiG-15s and managed to crash land on St Lawrence Island in the Bering Sea. Most Soviet and Red Chinese attacks on western reconnaissance aircraft ended with injuries, fatalities, or even the total loss of the airplane and crew. Sadly, the US government failed to support the families of lost or missing crewmen. *US Navy*

Opposite, top: YB-10 153 at Ladd Field in late summer 1934 as part of the effort to photograph Alaska. Whether or not the airplanes overflew Siberia is a contentious issue. If so, it was likely the first US military reconnaissance overflight of the USSR. *Museum of Flight P91-3-26/1 [2 of 4] courtesy Dan Hagedorn*

mitment at the highest levels of government to utilize these flights as a primary means of acquiring intelligence about the Soviet Union. The intensive frequency of military flights, the development and procurement of increasingly capable airplanes, the amount of budgetary outlay to support the missions, and the establishment of global bases and infrastructure all reaffirmed the strong organizational commitment to putting intelligence assets in the air at the right place and the right time.

Existing accounts of American aerial reconnaissance of the Soviet Union emphasize post-1945 operations, but there is some reason to believe that US intelligence-gathering flights around or over the Soviet Union may predate post-war missions by some 12-15 years. Anecdotal evidence suggests that as early as 1934 the United States prepared to undertake aerial reconnaissance of territory that included the Soviet Union. An attempt that year, purportedly at the behest of the US Army, 'to fly out [from Alaska] toward the Russian coast and take pictures' was canceled as the airplanes and crews prepared to leave for Alaska. In addition to cameras, the mission gear included unidentified electronic equipment, suggesting the first planned aerial collection of SIGINT from the USSR. Such a mission was entirely in keeping with FDR's preference for using 'amateurs' in collecting intelligence, and resembles the alleged intelligence-gathering role of Amelia Earhart's ill-fated trans-Pacific flight. This also comports with official Army reluctance to use Air Corps G2 (intelligence) resources to satisfy Army war planning needs, instead relying upon other 'unidentified' sources.[3]

Another possible aerial photography mission of the Soviet Union took place later that year in July or early August. To focus attention on the Army Air Corps' growing capabilities, Secretary of War George H Dern announced that ten new Martin YB-10 bombers would participate in a 'training and photographic' flight from Washington, DC, via Canada, to Fairbanks, Alaska, and back. The mission was under the command of Lieutenant Colonel Henry H 'Hap' Arnold, later the only General of the Air Force. Ten planes made the flight to and from Alaska, but one aircraft was damaged in Alaska and did not participate in the photographic missions. Shortly after their 24 July arrival in Alaska, the nine YB-10s surveyed '12,000 square miles of territory' 'to the westward' of Fairbanks. The flight was also intended to establish 'military aviation stations throughout Alaska.' Captain George W Goddard, the Army's dean of aerial photography, was in charge of the 'mass photographic effort' which took place over a three-day period. (One of Goddard's protégés was Richard Leghorn).[4]

Tensions between the Soviet Union and Japan over the Chinese Eastern Railway in Manchukuo and fishing rights off the Kamchatka Peninsula sparked rumors of war between the two nations in 1934. Soviet Commissar for War and Marine Klementi Voroshilov warned the Japanese in February that the USSR had increased its defenses in the 'Far East' with substantial 'fortified areas.' The *New York Times* reported that by early April the USSR had strengthened its military position in Eastern Siberia with a 'powerful concentration of Russian forces.' This buildup was both rapid and robust: 'Russia, which two years ago was too weak to oppose Japan when the latter began her Manchurian adventure, has now outstripped the island empire in military preparation.'[5] In addition to these developments, Roosevelt worried that Japan would demand increased naval capacity by renouncing the 1922 Washington Naval Conference agreement, which it did in December 1934. Roosevelt sought to use the Soviet Union as a counter to Japanese power in the region, and may well have discouraged any overflights of Soviet territory for fear of weakening Soviet willingness to support this goal.[6]

Historian John Murphy asserts that a major purpose of the Army photographic mission, which covered not only Alaska and the Arctic Ocean but 'most of the home islands of Japan, Korea, all of [Manchukuo] and much of Siberia,' was to collect intelligence on Soviet capabilities in eastern Siberia related to the Sino-Japanese situation.[7] American interest in the region was understandable, but Murphy's evidence hardly supports his argument that the Arnold flights were undertaken to provide photographic evidence of Russian and Japanese military forces throughout Siberia, or that the flights were intended to identify potential threats from the Soviet Union or Japan with an eye to a possible invasion of Alaska (geographically distant from the 'Lower Forty-eight,' Alaska was a tempting 'quick prize'). Arnold's photographs revealed sites for bases within Alaska as well as other geographic and cartographic information that could prove vital in any defense of the territory. In addition, the flight itself sent 'a signal to both the Japanese and the Russians that Alaska was not so vulnerable to considerations of expansion.'[8] Murphy's conclusions place too much emphasis on what was only an incidental benefit rather than a primary motive for the photographic flights. Moreover, his claim that the flights covered 'much of Siberia' (unlikely at over 5 million square miles) gives too much credit to the technical and operational limits of the airplanes and their cameras. This claim also overestimates US pre-war aerial reconnaissance capabilities. As late as November 1941 an American plan to use two Consolidated B-24s for long-range aerial reconnaissance of Japanese military positions throughout the South Pacific failed miserably due to lack of co-ordination and logistics support. This also suggests that by 1941, on the eve of war, the United States had yet to demonstrate a resolve and commitment to using aerial reconnaissance that it would eventually display during the Cold War years.[9]

During the early years of the Cold War, reconnaissance aircraft continued with the tradition established during World War Two: small, fast, maneuverable, and filled with cameras. Existing airplanes like the Supermarine Spitfire, the North American P-51 Mustang, and the de Havilland Mosquito reflected this postwar 'need for speed', as did the newer jet-powered Lockheed RF-80 Shooting Star, the Republic RF-84 Thunderflash, and later the McDonnell RF-101 Voodoo. Low altitude sorties provided highly detailed images of combatant forces and battle damage assessment (BDA). High altitude sorties gathered photographs of entire battlefields, towns or cities, or industrial complexes. When combined, these photos provided a clear understanding of targets and their defenses. Although originally fighters, reconnaissance airplanes typically had their guns and armour

removed to lessen their weight. This not only compensated for the added weight of the photography gear but increased the speed and altitude they could achieve. Speed was the essential ingredient in reconnaissance operations. This allowed surprise of enemy forces and prevented efforts to hide or camouflage the mission's objectives. It meant that enemy forces would be unprepared to intercept the airplane, either by defensive fighters or ground-based antiaircraft fire. It also allowed the possibility that the flight would be undetected, an added advantage. As such, reconnaissance pilots knew that they had just one opportunity to take their photographs and head home – 'one pass then haul ass.' Anything else could easily compromise the mission or result in a destroyed airplane.

The geography and evolving technology of the Cold War substantially altered this equation. High-speed photoreconnaissance remained important, to be sure, but it was substantially constrained by the increasing distances involved and the growing demand for SIGINT, ELINT, and COMINT. Converted fight-

Below: Early post-war aerial reconnaissance emphasized speed and maneuverability to get the photos, exemplified by Swedish P-51 Mustang 26051 from J26. Addition of heavy, bulky, highly technical reconnaissance gear to meet evolving ELINT and COMINT demands meant that converted bombers and transports quickly replaced fighters as the primary platform. *G Larsson via Lennart Andersson*

ers simply did not have the range to fly long distances to reach remote regions along the borders of the Soviet Union, for example, or to undertake deep overflights. Air refueling would surely help, but might well require hitting a tanker just before crossing the border, a complicated operation sure to attract unwanted, if not lethal, attention to both tanker and the reconnaissance airplane. With the growing emphasis on radar and electronic warfare, converted fighters lacked the capacity to carry the bulky, heavy receivers needed to collect ELINT. External configuration changes to accommodate the gear or antennas would compromise their speed and altitude advantages. Moreover, this equipment was not automated so it required human intervention to operate. In a single-seat reconnaissance airplane the pilot was busy enough flying the airplane, navigating a precise route, avoiding hostile forces, and starting or stopping cameras according to the mission-timing chart. To require the pilot to stare into a hooded oscilloscope while tweaking frequency dials and recording the signal onto a wire was a sure recipe for flying the airplane into the ground. Including a dedicated reconnaissance crewmember – even if there was room to do so – would resolve this issue but add more weight, further degrading the airplane's operational capability and increasing the risk of a failed mission.

Every strategic reconnaissance airplane had a crucial vulnerability. FEATHERWEIGHT RB-36s could reach nearly 60,000 feet and fly for two days carrying cameras and crew. Unfortunately, it was slow. As MiG-15s equaled the RB-36's cruise altitude, it became a very large target. Still, it took considerable skill as a MiG-15 pilot to zoom climb and reach the RB-36 at the right moment. This is 5th SRW RB-36E 44-92020. *Frederick A Johnsen Collection via Dennis Jenkins*

Whereas PHOTINT emphasized the need for surprise and speed, the growing demand for newer forms of intelligence dictated patience. An airplane gathering TELINT, for example, might need to loiter for hours at a remote location waiting for a missile launch. A COMINT platform might need to monitor lengthy communication exchanges between a headquarters and field unit. In any case, these evolving requirements meant that endurance now trumped speed as the primary flight capability. Coupled with the requirement for heavy equipment and additional operators, strategic reconnaissance aircraft shifted toward large converted bomber, patrol, and cargo aircraft, although the U-2 and its successors (the Lockheed A-12 and SR-71) proved the exception.

The postwar surplus of medium and heavy bombers, as well as large cargo transports, solved the problems of range, endurance, and capacity. Boeing B-29s and B-50s equipped with cameras or electronic listening gear had the range to fly missions from Japan to Alaska, or could orbit for hours waiting to observe and record the emissions from an upgraded radar site. Similarly, they could carry additional Ravens to study ELINT or linguists to monitor COMINT. The behemoth Convair RB-36D-III was potentially the ultimate reconnaissance platform. Capable of 50-hour missions from the United States covering 8,000nm (eliminating the diplomatic need for bases in foreign countries) at altitudes above 58,000 feet, an RB-36 could carry 15-20 optical cameras, a crew of 22 (including on-board analysts), or even the RF-84K parasite reconnaissance jet, and was virtually immune to interception by Soviet piston-powered fighters or existing AAA. Indeed, American planners incorrectly assumed that the RB-36 would operate above the height limits of Soviet radar. The RB-36's weakness, however,

was its speed. To achieve its great range the airplane cruised at only 200 KIAS. Even with the addition of its four J47 jet engines the airspeed would nearly double to 350 KIAS but with a significant range penalty. In any case, this was not enough to deal with existing interceptors, let alone the threat of jet-powered MiG-15s.

Soviet fighter production during World War Two focused on ground attack and low-altitude air-to-air combat. The service ceiling of Soviet interceptors such as the Yakovlev Yak-9 *Frank* and the Lavochkin La-9 *Fritz* ranged from 30,000-34,000 feet, well below the cruising altitude of an RB-36. Moreover, these piston-powered airplanes had comparatively poor climb performance – typically 2,500 feet per minute, which degraded substantially as the airplane reached higher altitudes. This meant that it would take some 15-20 minutes to reach maximum altitude, by which time a passing ferret would be long gone. With the delivery in 1949 of the MiG-15 *Fagot*, the RB-36 was now at genuine risk. The MiG-15's airspeed was 550 KIAS, it could reach 50,000 feet, it had an impressive 10,000 feet per minute initial rate of climb, and it needed only 6 or 7 minutes to intercept the plodding RB-36. Given the MiG-15's superior speed, the RB-36 (along with RB-50s and Consolidated PB4Y-2s) could no longer rely on outpacing any interceptors, especially with overflights. This led to the use of jet-powered reconnaissance platforms such as the RB-47 and RB-57, although improvements in speed and rate-of-climb performance in interceptors such as the MiG-17 *Fresco* and Su-9 *Fishpot* significantly reduced these advantages.

Post-war USAAF (USAF after 18 September 1947) and USN peripheral reconnaissance missions around the USSR began in 1945 as a continuation of wartime photoreconnaissance and maritime patrol missions. The Air Force utilized long-range bomber variants such as RB-29s and RB-50s plus RB-36s, and the Navy pressed its PB4Y-2 Privateers, Lockheed P2V, Neptunes, and P4M-1Q Mercators into service on medium- to high-altitude photographic runs near and over Communist targets and their defenses.[10] By August 1948 US aerial reconnaissance assets were well established around the world. One Top Secret report listed SAC B-29s deployed: *in Japan, Alaska, and Germany for Electronic Counter Measures and weather reconnaissance. ...There are also other planes of this type in other parts of the world, operating on detached service for reconnaissance, weather observation, and Electronic Counter Measures.*[11]

During these initial years peripheral aerial reconnaissance flights were most numerous in East Asia where they quickly evolved from wartime maritime patrol missions. The flights operated over the Sea of Japan, the Northern Pacific Ocean, and the Bering Sea. Pacific Ocean peripheral programs included Operation LEOPARD, flown by the 46th Reconnaissance Squadron (RS) – later redesignated the 72nd RS – from Ladd Field, Alaska, which gathered 'oblique photography of fair scale and quality along the Soviet Chukotskii Peninsula.' Operation STONEWORK, again conducted by the 46th/72nd RS, covered most of the Kurile Islands, now in the hands of the Soviet Union.

Navy patrol planes from World War Two such as the Martin PBM-5 Mariner were among the initial US Cold War aerial reconnaissance assets. They were no match for even piston-powered Soviet interceptors including the Yak-9 *Frank* and La-9 *Fritz*. Communist forces attacked at least nine PBM-5s and Red China shot down one on 7 November 1953. *Robert Stachowiak via Stephen Miller*

US Military Reconnaissance Bases and Operating Locations, 1945-1961

Base and Location	Operating Areas
RAF Brize Norton, UK	Barents Sea, Baltic Sea, East European border
Yokota AB, Japan	Yellow Sea, South China Sea, East China Sea, Sea of Japan, Sea of Okhotsk, Kurile Islands, Kamchatka Peninsula
Athens, Greece	Mediterranean Sea, Adriatic Sea
Incirlik, Turkey	Black Sea
Dhahran, Saudi Arabia	Southwest Asia
Thule AB, Greenland	Kara Sea, Laptev Sea
Ladd Field/Eielson AFB/ Shemya AFB, Alaska	East Siberian Sea, Bering Sea, Kamchatka Peninsula
Wiesbaden AB, FRG/ Rhein-Main AB, FRG	Baltic Sea, East European border, Adriatic Sea
Clark AB, Philippines	South China Sea, Indonesia, Southeast Asia

A peripheral program known as Project 5 (later FLOODLIGHT) took place from August 1946 through September 1948, photographing areas close to Siberia between 160-180°E and 73-77°N, around the west and north coasts of Alaska to search for previously undetected land masses. Project 20 was a 1947 peripheral operation involving two RB-29 flights a month to take photographs of eastern Siberia. Additional operations such as RICKRACK and OVERCALLS took photos of the Kamchatka Peninsula as well as the Chukotskii Peninsula. In general these flights looked for evidence that would detect new Soviet bomber bases or show the operational status of existing bases in Siberia, those closest to the United States from which an attack could take place. In addition to PHOTINT missions, reconnaissance airplanes often carried rudimentary ELINT or COMINT equipment. By July 1948 two RB-29s were dedicated exclusively to ELINT collection.[12] The purpose of these missions was to monitor radio communications and radar emissions that would reveal the level of readiness of Soviet bomber units and bases.

Although US foreign policy emphasized European post-war recovery, Soviet bomber bases in Siberia, the proximity of Soviet forces to Japan, the 'loss' of China to communism, the outbreak of war in Korea, and the development of Soviet ICBMs made the Pacific Theater the top US intelligence priority from 1945-1960. Indeed, most of the incidents and losses of US reconnaissance aircraft took place in the Far East.

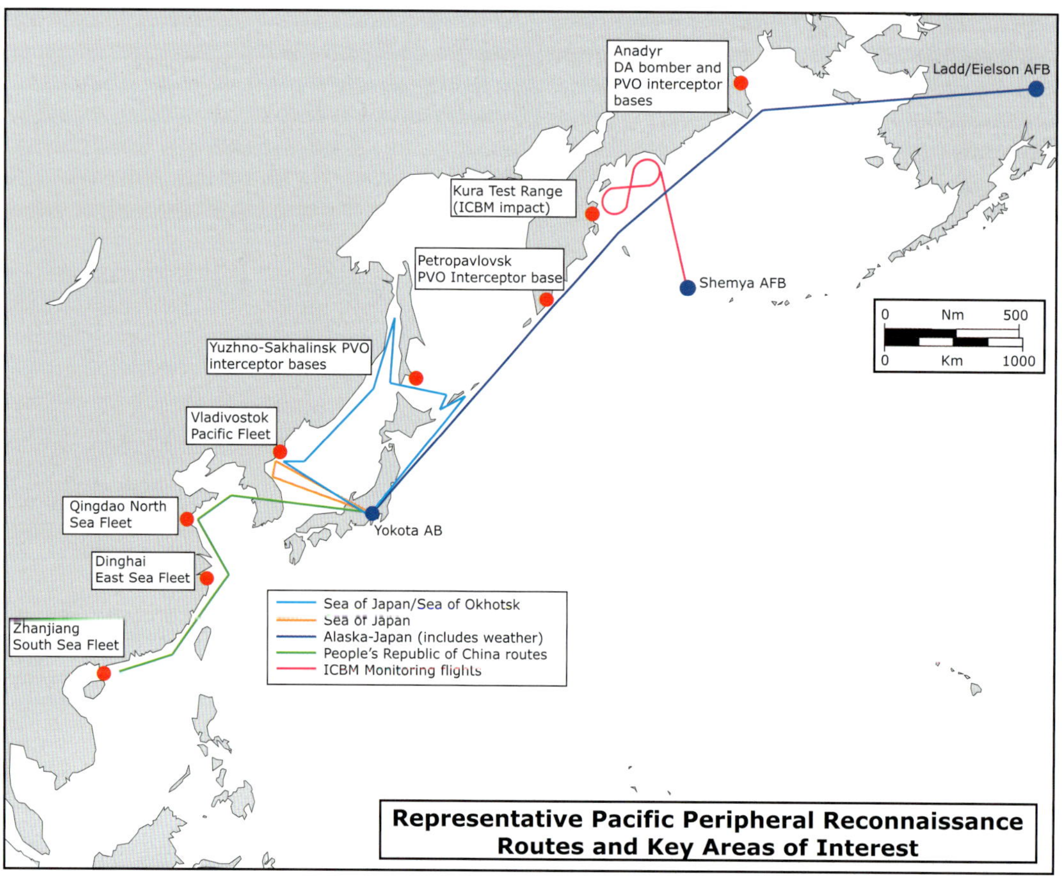

Representative Pacific Peripheral Reconnaissance Routes and Key Areas of Interest

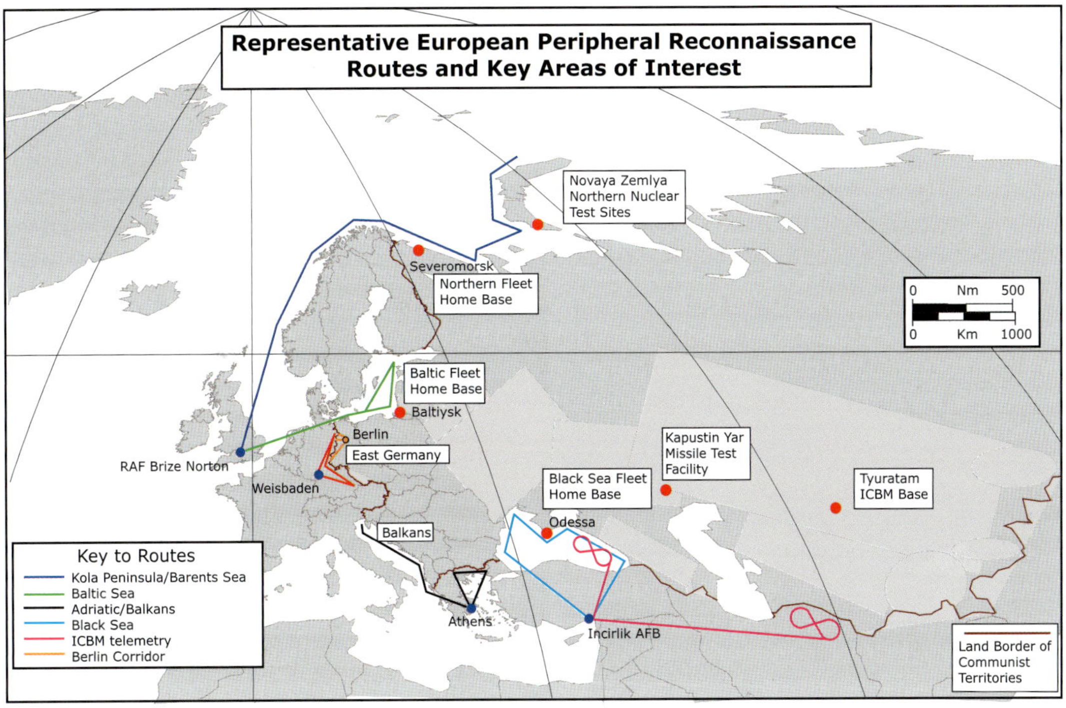

Peripheral reconnaissance flights in Europe evolved from occasional USAF sorties 'along the fence' between East and West Germany to routine USAF, US Navy, RAF, and Swedish AF patrols covering roughly one third of the circumference of the Soviet Union and Warsaw Pact. These missions regularly monitored some of the most important military and test facilities in the USSR.

Peripheral sorties in Europe began in late 1945 and early 1946 with USAAF RB-26s assigned to the 45th Reconnaissance Squadron at Fürth, West Germany. These quickly expanded in number with the addition of PHOTINT- and ELINT-configured RB-17s and RC-47s, although these were limited by their slow cruise speed and lack of pressurized crew compartments, forcing them to operate at lower altitudes, ultimately decreasing their reconnaissance value while increasing their vulnerability.

SAC RB-17Gs were primarily used for photomapping, most notably with Operation EARDRUM, the trimetrogon aerial mapping of Greenland and North American polar regions to identify potential locations for SAC bomber bases and routes from the United States (especially Alaska) to Greenland and onward to the Soviet Union. USAAF/USAFE RB-17 flights such as the CASEY JONES missions – typically conducted ELINT missions in the Baltic and Adriatic Seas, along the border separating Eastern from Western Europe, as well as photographing portions of Europe and North Africa to update existing maps. During July 1947, for example, the US State Department approved a USAF request for three ferret missions in the 'Norther[n] area' of Europe between the Swedish island of Gotland in the Baltic Sea and the Latvian Soviet Socialist Republic, with the promise that 'more flights will be made in the near future.'[13] Other sorties were COMINT flights intended to intercept diplomatic and military communications that might reveal Soviet intentions toward the West.

Additional US peripheral sorties included atomic detection flights, known by the nicknames CENTERING and COTTONSEED. By 1948 WB-29s assigned to the LRDP flew daily missions over the Arctic Ocean and the northern areas of the Pacific Ocean collecting air samples which could reveal the presence of radioactive material produced by an atomic detonation. One such mission bore fruit on 3 September 1949, when a WB-29 on a routine mission from Misawa AB, Japan, to Ladd Field collected the first unmistakable indications of the 29 August detonation of the first Soviet atomic device at Semipalatinsk, known as 'First Lightning'.[14] USAF RB-29s flew the majority of their missions in the Pacific theater, typically from Yokota AB, Japan, and Ladd Field. Once the Korean War erupted in 1950, RB-29s from the 91st SRW shared mission tasking for both tactical reconnaissance over Korea as well as strategic reconnaissance along the Chinese and Soviet coasts. The RAF also operated three RB-29As (*not* Washington B.1s) in the ELINT role.

Officially, peripheral missions were obligated to remain 'well clear' of Soviet airspace, an ill-defined limit prompted by a Soviet claim that a US reconnaissance flight intruded into Soviet airspace in December 1947. Through 1948 this directive to avoid Soviet airspace tended to exist more in theory than in practice as the Joint Chiefs of Staff, the Air Force, and the State Department vacillated in their definition of 'well

RB-17G 44-8889 assigned to the 7499th SS for peripheral PHOTINT and some ELINT mission, including CASEY JONES. SAC and USAFE RB-17Gs were largely a stop-gap measure pending delivery of RB-50s with better aircraft performance and improved cameras or ELINT gear. *Author's Collection*

clear.' At times the closest point of approach (CPA) to the Soviet landmass or airspace varied from 3 to 12 to 20 to 40 miles. This distance often depended upon the international situation and specific US reconnaissance needs. In May 1948, for example, the Air Force established a 40-mile limit, but this changed three months later to 20 miles. Even at this closer distance long-range photography failed to yield suitable images, and the Air Force sought to reduce this range to 12 or even three miles.[15] Field units did not always comply with these parameters, however. Mismanaged communications and broad interpretations of the regulations often allowed flying units like the 72nd RS to fly closer to the USSR than desired by senior military and civilian policy makers. An inquiry into a 23 December 1947 violation of Soviet airspace revealed that a 72nd RS RB-29 on a 'Project 23 [electronic reconnaissance] mission' flew closer to the Soviet shoreline than the State Department-mandated 12 mile minimum, although it was 'impossible to determine that the Soviet frontier [had] been violated as alleged.' Air Force investigators found 'that the pilot may not have complied' with existing regulations.[16] Project 23 was indeed a planned border incursion, if not outright overflight, and was an early example of a 'co-ordinated' mission involving two or more airplanes operating together but at different locations. Project 23 missions took place from August through December 1947 and covered the 'North and South coasts of Siberia adjacent to Alaska.' According to the mission summary, one airplane operating at 'very high altitude flies directly over the coastline while the second aircraft, at a lesser altitude, flies parallel to the first plane [but is] several miles out to sea,' recording the Soviet reaction to the high-flying intruder.[17]

Despite their absence from traditional accounts of the Cold War, planned US military overflights of the Soviet Union were certainly a regular part of American intelligence-gathering efforts and were well known to senior officials. President Eisenhower told an NSC meeting after the U-2 incident that 'reconnaissance activity' such as the ill-fated overflight 'had been going on for years.' At a 24 May 1960 NSC meeting Air Force Chief of Staff General Nathan F Twining expressed fear that 'if the investigators probed CIA [U-2 overflights], they would want to investigate JCS operations' as well, and 'wondered whether there was anything [the NSC] could do to stop the investigation.' In executive session testimony before the Senate Foreign Relations Committee on 2 June 1960, Secretary of Defense Thomas S Gates, Jr, acknowledged that the United States 'had overflown Soviet territory without their permission in 1954, 1955, and even perhaps before that.' When pressed, Gates elaborated, asking that his answers be held in confidence. As early as 1950, Gates said, the United States 'did engage in overflights of the Soviet Union from the Department of Defense point of view, but none since 1956. When in 1950, precisely I don't know.' Twining boasted in a 1967 interview that once in 1950, 'I had 47 airplanes flying all over Russia.' (This remark reflected his 'sour grapes' braggadocio related to the Air Force not getting control of the U-2 program in 1956 rather than an accurate assessment of US overflights. There is as yet no corroborative evidence of Twining's claim).[18]

Post-war American reconnaissance flights over the Soviet Union may have started as early as 1946, but certainly by 1947. Claims by participants in supposed overflights remain unsubstantiated by official military or civilian records, but not all reconnaissance operations were adequately documented (most units did not have an assigned historian, nor did any of the few historians in place have sufficient security clearance even to know about the flights). Some flights may have taken place with the tacit approval of senior Air Force officials, notably General George C Kenney, SAC's first Commanding General, under the assumption that brief shallow incursions were acceptable as long as they offered 'plausible deniability' should they create an incident.

Major Maynard E White was the squadron commander of SAC's first operational reconnaissance unit, the 46th Reconnaissance Squadron (Very Long Range), Photographic, assigned to Ladd Field, Alaska. White recalls that his squadron's RB-29s conducted 'reconnaissance flights over the Soviet Union as early as 1946.' Some members of White's squadron dispute this claim, while others allow that overflights may have happened but, given the 'compartmentalized' nature of squadron operations, not everyone may have been aware of these highly sensitive flights. During a 15 October 1946 visit to Ladd Field, LeMay – then USAF Deputy Chief of Staff for Research and Development – spoke with White 'at length about the feasibility of flying reconnaissance missions across the Soviet Union, landing in Europe, and returning a few days later on parallel routes.'[19] It is tempting to assert that LeMay's interest in such an overflight represented an early commitment to peacetime aerial violations of the Soviet Union in an effort to look for Soviet bomber bases or other future targets for SAC. LeMay would not be assigned as SAC's commander for another two years, and his inquiry actually reflected the potential for these flights to fulfill the need for pre- and post-strike aerial reconnaissance once hostilities began. Nonetheless, one reason for LeMay's discretion in discussing this matter with White was his squadron's purported experience in undertaking such reconnaissance missions, but no documentary evidence has been uncovered to support White's overflight claims.

Military overflights of the USSR reportedly continued in 1947 when an RB-29 on a PHOTINT mission overflew a Soviet airfield, confirming the existence of the Soviet copy of the B-29 bomber, the Tu-4. Richard Meyer, a retired SAC crew member who claims to have participated in early overflights, recalled one sortie 'in the summer of 1948' that penetrated 'deep into Soviet territory on a ferret mission.' This 5 August overflight mission, nearly 20 hours long, departed Ladd Field and arrived at Yokota AB after flying over Siberia. The airplane and crew returned to Ladd Field on 8 August, reversing the original course across the Soviet Union. Another round-robin overflight took place on 1 and 6 September.[20] All of these flights, if they indeed took place, occurred during the height of the 1948 Berlin crisis. Arguably, the missions may have been in search of evidence of any impending Soviet military action against the United States. Conversely, these missions could have easily provoked open confrontation or even general war between the United States and the Soviet Union, so presidential approval for them would have been improbable. A likely explanation for these flights is that in the absence of a well-defined authorization process, senior area commanders (at this time Lieutenant General Nathan Twining) could approve flights on a case-by-case basis. It is worth noting that at the height of the Cuban Missile Crisis in 1962 a SAC U-2 on a routine sampling mission flown by Captain Charles Maultsby from Eielson AFB got lost and inadvertently overflew the Soviet Union. President John F Kennedy said of the incursion, 'There's always some son-of-a-bitch that doesn't get the word,' so it should not be surprising that similar events might have taken place nearly 15 years earlier.[21] Moreover, these undocumented overflights may have served as examples that influenced Truman and his advisors to create a greater centralized control mechanism for military aerial reconnaissance.

Clearly Alaska served as an essential site for collection of intelligence related to Soviet bomber bases in eastern Siberia. SAC capitalized on this proximity to acquire what it defined as 'radar scope photography,' 'target verification photography,' '"Pioneer" or target development photography,' and the 'procurement, by ferret methods, of intelligence concerning enemy electronic emissions (radar, etc).' During the summer of 1949 SAC reconnaissance aircraft completed overflight mapping and SIGINT missions out of Alaska 'to determine hostile ELINT in the area.'[22]

Tactical overflights of the USSR from bases in Japan reportedly took place as early as 1949 and continued through 1955. Lockheed RF-80As from the 8th Tactical Reconnaissance Squadron (TRS) flew missions along the Kurile

Pilot Tom Hagler and crew chief finish their pre-flight inspection of RF-86F 52-4864 *Pretty Billie*. The HAYMAKER RF-86Fs operated in conjunction with HONEYBUCKET and ASHTRAY RF-86As and RF-86Fs for tactical reconnaissance during the Korean War as well as post-war overflights of the Soviet Union and Red China. *Tom Hagler photo courtesy of Doug Gordon*

Islands as early as 10 May 1949, with overflights of Vladivostok and other Soviet bases from 10 March through 18 August 1950, as well as Dairen and Shanghai in the People's Republic of China. One pilot flew 19 such missions. RF-86A ASHTRAY and HAYMARKET overflights continued through 1953.[23] Tactical missions in Europe in 1951-1952 included Navy Project PEGASUS, utilizing Grumman F2H-2P jets that overflew Eastern bloc countries. A follow-on proposal called for overflights of the Crimea, Ukraine, and western Russia, but apparently was not enacted.[24]

Peripheral aerial reconnaissance continued through the 1950s. Beginning in early 1950 RB-29s flew COMINT missions along the Pacific coast of the USSR and PRC. These were supplemented by RC-47 BLUE SKY (later ROSE BOWL) flights in Korea. The eruption of war in June 1950, however, altered the strategic aerial reconnaissance dynamic. The combat debut over Korea of the MiG-15 was an unwelcome surprise to American aviators. Impressive in performance, especially in comparison to most US combat planes then in service, the MiG-15 posed an even greater threat to America's strategic aerial reconnaissance force. The MiG-15's high speed, maneuverability, rate of climb, and high-altitude performance made easy targets of the lumbering piston-powered converted bombers for use as reconnaissance platforms. During the Korean War MiG-15s destroyed a number of B-29 bombers flying in large, self-protective groups. US aerial recon-

Crews push a 5th SRW RB-36D into a mammoth hangar at Thule AB for maintenance during operation BLUE NOSE II in 1954. ELINT antennas are aft of the bomb bay door and under the chin. ECM antennas and a large camera window are forward of the bomb bay. Interestingly, the BLUE NOSE II missions were flown at 15,000 feet. *AFHRA photo, 5th SRW History, 1954, courtesy Maranda Gilmore*

naissance planners feared that a lone RB-29 would be even more vulnerable.[25] Solo reconnaissance airplanes actually fared much better than this dour forecast suggested. B-29s shot down by MiG-15s were attacked in daylight and with good visibility. Ferret flights routinely operated at night and in bad weather, times when the MiG-15s were ineffective due to their lack of airborne radar. Further, the older RB-29s, which had been stripped of their defensive armament to make room for reconnaissance equipment, were being replaced by newer RB-50s that carried both reconnaissance gear and a full complement of defensive armament.[26] Nonetheless, USAF RB-29s and RB-50s, as well as USN Privateers, Neptunes, and Mercators largely – but not totally – discontinued their overflights and remained along the periphery of 'denied airspace,' ostensibly safe from attack. Even so, MiG-15s attacked a 91st SRS RB-29 on 9 November 1950 during a peripheral sortie. The RB-29's tail gunner destroyed at least one MiG-15 and the damaged airplane limped back to Johnson AB, Japan, but crashed upon landing. Over the next five years, all US losses to Communist fighters were claimed by MiG-15s. These attacks prompted repeated efforts to initiate jet reconnaissance B-47 operations.[27]

Pending the arrival of a dedicated jet-powered long-range reconnaissance platform, SAC RB-36s, capable of reaching heights of 58,000 feet, undertook peripheral sorties around and overflights of Communist countries until the early to mid 1950s. Operations began in 1951, and the flights were all consistently detected by Soviet radar (which should have been a clear warning to U-2 designers and mission planners in 1954, let alone in 1956, that it was foolish to believe the U-2 could fly undetected only 12,000 feet above RB-36s). Peripheral RB-36 missions were commonplace. In August 1954, for example, RB-36Ds from the 5th SRW at Fairfield-Suisin AFB, California, flew 11 reconnaissance sorties, as well as Operation BLUE NOSE II, designed to 'determine if clandestine Soviet communications activities exist in an area of interest along the [uncharted] northeastern coast of Greenland' as well as remote regions of Canada.[28]

Reported RB-36 overflights took place near Murmansk, Siberia, Armenia and the Caucasus, and the PRC. During late 1952, for example, six RB-36s deployed to Yokota AB and conducted overflights of Manchuria. Former RB-36 electronics countermeasures officer Ken McCoy recalls 'recon runs over [the People's Republic of] China' at 'such great heights' that the MiGs could see but not engage the 'prowling Peacemakers.' Retired RB-36 crewmembers hint that they also overflew the USSR at these extreme altitudes, including the 'Murmansk Run,' which searched for evidence of Soviet atomic weapons development at Novaya Zemlya, and the enigmatic 'Operation 21', but these remain unverified.[29] From 1955 through April 1956, RB-36Ds carrying GRF-84Ks reportedly undertook 'Fighter Conveyor' (FICON) missions that made short incursions into Soviet and Red Chinese airspace (See Appendix III).[30]

Despite their age and operational limits in the jet age, piston-powered RB-50, Douglas

The FICON parasite program solved the dual dilemma of RB-36 vulnerability to MiGs and the limited range of RF-84s. The short-lived program flew peripheral missions and (by some accounts) shallow incursions. The promise of the U-2 spelled the end of the FICON program. RF-84K 52-7266 approaches GRB-36D 49-2692. *USAF photo via Dennis Jenkins*

C-54D 42-72684 (spuriously marked here as '17206') was the sole LULU BELLE airplane. Originally part of the ATRAN program, it was later modified to a covert infrared collection system with a KC-1 camera just forward of the APS-27 radar fairing and a KA-1 camera at the center of the wing box. By 1958 it had the ability to downlink photos for rapid interpretation. *Ralf Manteufel*

C-54, Douglas C-118, and Boeing C-97 variants expanded during the early to mid 1950s. Units such as the 7499th Support Squadron (SS), the 7405th SS, the 7406th SS, and the 7407th SS at Rhein-Main AB, West Germany, all undertook a variety of intelligence gathering missions. Many of these aircraft were converted under the secretive BIG SAFARI program with operational names like PRETTY GIRL, LULU BELLE, and SARA JANE. In 1955-56, the 7405th, for example, undertook Operation SQUINT using HOT PEPPER RC-54Ds converted for PHOTINT. These regular missions photographed Soviet naval vessels in the Baltic Sea. Other USAFE aircraft gathered ELINT or COMINT emitted by these ships. In addition to reconnaissance flights the 7405th SS operated three C-118 transports on behalf of 'another agency' – presumably the CIA – for routine cargo and passenger operations.

Opposite, top: Early Cold War strategic aerial reconnaissance relied substantially on three different RB-50 variants that undertook mapping, PHOTINT, ELINT, and COMINT missions. The RB-50 was a definite improvement over the RB-29, but lacked the range and speed of the RB-47 or the altitude of the RB-57. RB-50F 47-138 was used in mapping and PHOTINT roles while assigned to the 338th SRS, 55th SRW at Ramey AB. *Andy Meyer via the Dave Menard Collection at NMUSAF*

RB-50s saw widespread operational use in Europe and in the Pacific as part of the Airborne COMINT Reconnaissance Program (ACRP). The 7406th SS flew two HALF TRACK RB-50Ds on aerial mapping sorties and five DREAM BOAT RB-50Gs on ACRP missions. During the first six months of 1957, for example, two RB-50Gs flew 97 missions resulting in '1,535 hours of actual intercept, much of it unique, and accounting for several 'first heards,' including Soviet line-of-sight VHF communications beyond the intercept range of fixed field sites.' By 1955 the USAFE RB-50Gs had been replaced by Lockheed C-130A-IIs under the SUN VALLEY-I and C-130B-IIs under the SUN VALLEY-II program.[31] The RB-50s were transferred to PACAF where they flew ACRP missions in the Pacific theater as part of the BIG FIVE program.

RB-50 overflights were rare, but included one joint-service 'co-ordinated mission' between 2 April and 29 June 1952. Operating from Shemya AFB at the tip of the Aleutian Islands, a Navy P2V-3W and an Air Force ELINT RB-50E flew nine or ten missions covering three tracks over the Bering Sea. The P2V-3W would detect radar and electronic signals from Soviet bases in Siberia. After homing in on them the P2V-3W would overfly them and, in conjunction with the RB-50E, take precision measurements and photographs used to plot the exact location of the radar.[32]

During 1954 and 1955 Lockheed modified seven Navy P2V-7 Neptunes, painted them in USAF markings, redesignated them as RB-69s, and delivered them to the CIA. They were used for operations known as Projects CHERRY and WILD CHERRY, which may have been European components of the OSTIARY program. The RB-69s flew from Wiesbaden AB with crews made up of expatriate Poles or Czechs for COMINT purposes. The RB-69s flew 'a mix of penetration and border surveillance flights.' Operations over Red China began in early 1957 when the airplanes received Taiwanese markings and flew with mixed US-Taiwanese crews. From 1958 through 1964 there were 81 penetrations of PRC airspace, some as deep as Beijing and Kwangchow.[33]

Western strategic aerial reconnaissance officially entered the jet age during the early 1950s with the arrival of the North American RB-45C Tornado and the English Electric Canberra (manufactured under license in the United

C-130A-IIs replaced ACRP RB-50s in the COMINT role under the SUN VALLEY-I program. These were replaced with C-130B-IIs as part of SUN VALLEY-II. The ACRP C-130s had room for more operators and better equipment. Note the fiberglass 'wing tank' hiding COMINT antennas but designed to dupe observers about the airplane's true mission. C-130B-II 59-1533 prepares to depart Da Nang AB in early 1968. *Roger Pollack via Stephen Miller*

RB-69A 54-4041 (BuNO 141233) displays the APQ-56 SLAR antenna on the aft fuselage (located on both sides). This was also installed on the 14 PETER PAN RB-47Es. All seven RB-69As were transferred to the RoCAF. A PLAAF MiG-17 *Fresco* shot down this RB-69A on 19 June 1963. *Stephen Miller*

States by Martin as the RB-57). Although jet powered, the RB-45 did not necessarily provide an adequate solution to the MiG problem. A 1951 report detailed extensive flight tests involving US fighters simulating attacks on an RB-45C under a variety of conditions. The results were disappointing, and the report recommended that 'RB-45 aircraft fly into areas well defended by high speed jet aircraft *only under suitable jet fighter escort* and/or in bad weather and at night.'[34] Despite these criticisms RB-45Cs conducted PHOTINT overflights of the USSR and PRC from 1951 through 1954. In Europe, three of these airplanes operated from the Royal Air Force (RAF) Base at Sculthorpe in England, and flew 'deep penetration' sorties of the USSR and Eastern Europe under the mission name of JU JITSU. The American-made RB-45Cs were marked with British roundels and fin markings and flew with all-British crews.[35] The British commander and lead pilot, Squadron Leader John Crampton, said the highly classified program 'rivaled [in fact outranked] the Manhattan Project for secrecy.'[36] The first operational mission overflew Berlin on 21 March 1952, and the first overflight of the USSR took place on the night of 17-18 April 1952 when three RB-45Cs simultaneously entered Soviet airspace on separate tracks at altitudes in excess of 35,000 feet and lasted twelve hours or more, including aerial refueling over Western Europe.

In addition to the JU JITSU RB-45C overflight missions, the British flew English Electric Canberras and Americans flew HEART THROB RB-57As on intelligence sorties at altitudes above 60,000 feet. RB-57As conducted peripheral missions along the borders and overflights of Eastern Europe and the USSR.[37] One supposed Canberra flight has become the stuff of overflight legend. In August 1953, as part of Operation ROBIN (an RAF high-altitude peripheral PHOTINT program along the 'fence' between East and West Germany), an RAF Canberra was allegedly attacked and badly damaged during a mission which overflew Kiev, Kharkov, Stalingrad, and the vicinity of the Soviet missile research facility at Kapustin Yar, although it managed to land safely in Iran. These ROBIN photographs were reportedly of such poor quality that they were unusable in assessing the status of the ICBM facility.[38] Aviation writer and U-2 historian Chris Pocock has shown convincingly that this flight did not happen, but the flight and its blurry photographs remain an entrenched part of aerial reconnaissance history.[39]After a two-year hiatus, RB-45C flights resumed on 28 April 1954, with three airplanes flying deep penetrations over the 'West Central Soviet Union.' The last RB-45C overflight of the Soviet Union from RAF Sculthorpe took place on 1 March 1955, again with three aircraft involved.[40]

RB-45Cs also conducted peripheral and overflight reconnaissance missions in the Pacific, typically by the 91st SRS based at Yokota AB and in collaboration with other 91st SRS reconnaissance assets. Many of these missions were dedicated to intelligence gathering as part of the Korean War effort, but some

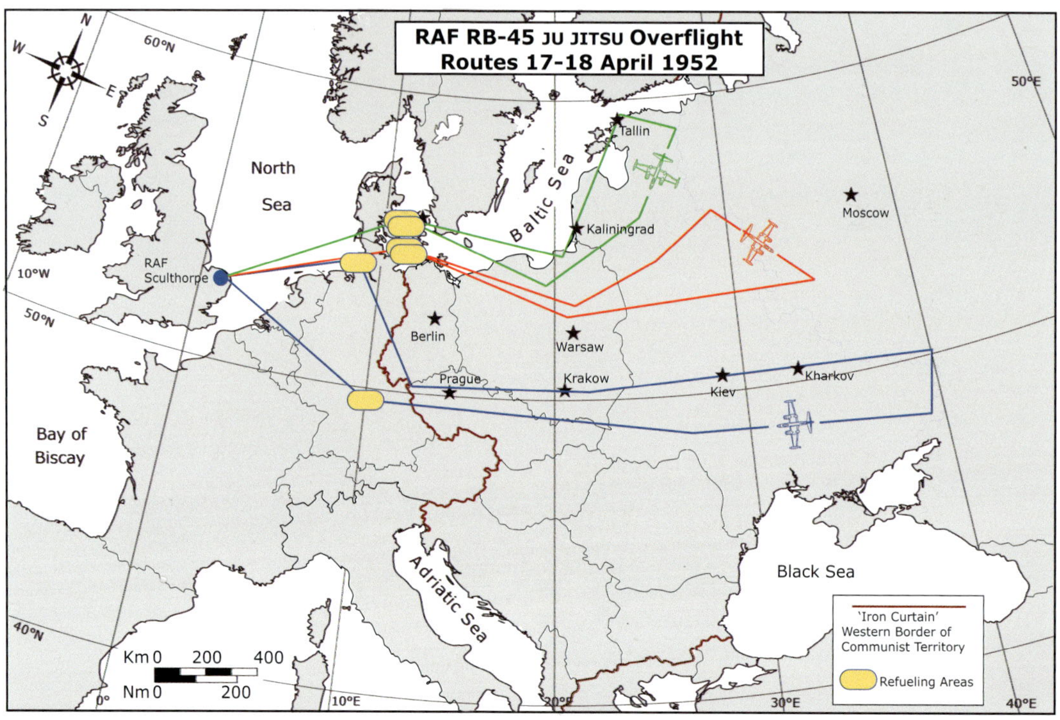

The three RAF RB-45 JU JITSU overflights reflect US willingness to rely on its partners to conduct dangerous missions of mutual interest. The Republic of China flew multiple sorties over Red China as well. Truman embraced the JU JITSU flights, asking General Twining, 'Why don't you do more of it?'

RB-45C (and RB-29) missions, including overflights, were assigned targets in the Soviet Union's maritime provinces and the People's Republic of China. Between 1951 and 1952 the unit flew 'night radar deep-penetration missions into China as far as Mukden [Shenyang] and at least three over Beijing.' On 25 August 1951, for example, the sole 91st SRS RB-29A directly overflew Shanghai on a 'special photographic mission'. Another mission took place on 9 October 1951 when a 91st SRS RB-45C overflew Sakhalin Island at 18,000 feet. On 17 December 1952 an RB-45C flying from Yokota AB conducted a 'deep penetration' mission over the Soviet Union and China. Other RB-45C overflight missions near Vladivostok occurred in March and May 1952 and continued through April 1953.[41] Throughout this period the 91st SRS routinely conducted electronic reconnaissance missions 'performed by specially equipped aircraft which fly adjacent to or over Communist controlled territory seeking to detect, analyze, and determine the source of non-friendly radar signals.'[42] By July 1954 aircraft of the 91st SRS operating from Yokota AB had conducted a total of 27 overflight missions in the vicinity of Vladivostok, Harbin, and Mukden.

Overflights were not restricted to Communist-controlled countries. On 31 March 1954 an RB-50 on mission #R421 overflew Laos, Vietnam, and the Vietnamese-Chinese border. That same month mission R414 overflew 'certain areas of French Indochina,' as did the same RB-29 on mission R425 in April 1954. These flights gathered intelligence related to the French defense of Dien Bien Phu and activities of Viet Minh or other forces hostile to French interests, and may have contributed to high-level military and policy planning related to possible American intervention, especially Operation VULTURE.[43] Similar sorties included Boeing C-97 transports modified for SIGINT and COMINT that overflew Indonesia in 1958 and 1959 as part of the ULCER GULCH program. Interestingly, European-based RB-50s and RB-36s routinely photographed all of Western Europe as part of Operation ROUNDOUT. This provided continually up-to-date maps and target photos in the event of a successful Communist invasion, facilitating targeting for retaliatory strikes. ROUNDOUT Phase II covered 31 targets in France, Italy, and Holland. Phase III missions covered these nations again, as well as Belgium and Portugal. Although flights adjacent to Communist territory carried the danger of being shot down, 'milk run' sorties had their

Long overlooked by historians and enthusiasts, the RB-45C flew clandestine missions over Eastern Europe, the Soviet Union, and the People's Republic of China. It lacked the maneuverability and speed to tangle with MiG-15s, which claimed one during a mission over North Korea. Still, it survived the RAF JU JITSU flights and myriad missions by the 91st SRS from bases in the Pacific. RB-45C 48-025 of the 91st SRW prepares to depart from Kimpo (K-14) AB. *NMUSAF via Geoff Hays*

A single RB-47H mission from England to Alaska could easily monitor multiple Soviet facilities, ranging from potential strategic bomber bases to early warning radars to nuclear weapons test sites to the home port of the Soviet Atlantic fleet. Aerial refueling by KC-97s or KC-135s at the entry and exit points of the 'sensitive area' (near the northern tip of Norway and north of Alaska) made the missions practical. Crews held no illusion about the safety of the route, however, as mechanical failure would have proven lethal in the remote and brutal Arctic environment.

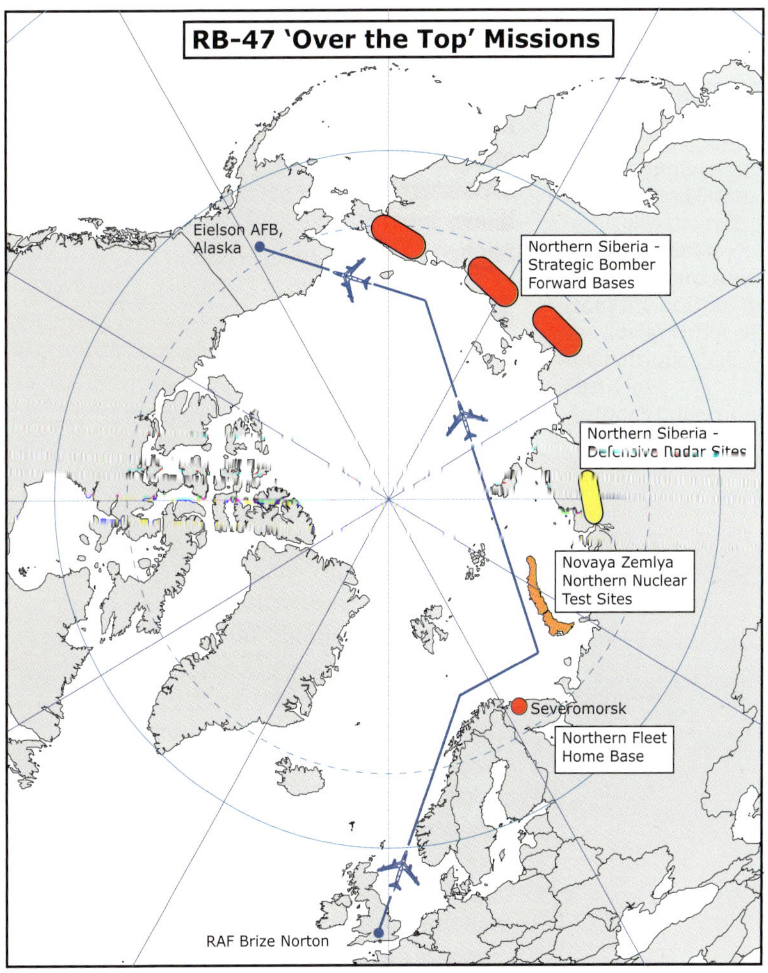

By 1961 the SILVER KING RB-47H (53-4294 seen here) represented the ultimate in early Cold War reconnaissance capability. Three Ravens operated manual and automatic ELINT gear. In addition, the automated BOX TOP system collected COMINT. Converted bombers had reached their useful limit, however, as unarmed cargo jets like the C-135 proved more capable and less threatening. *USAF via Mike Habermehl*

own risks. On 5 August 1953, an engine fire on RB-36H 52-1369 forced the pilot to ditch in the Atlantic Ocean while en route to England on a ROUNDOUT deployment, claiming 19 lives of the 23 on board.[44]

Throughout the 1950s SAC expanded its aerial reconnaissance efforts and undertook several organizational changes to improve collection and dissemination of aerial intelligence material. Most importantly, SAC began to replace its older, slower RB-50s with newer, faster jet-powered RB-47s. These airplanes offered substantial improvements in peripheral coverage due to their ability to fly longer distances in less time. SAC leaders also believed that RB-47s would be less vulnerable to attack given their speed advantages over MiG-15 interceptors.

RB-47 missions began from RAF Brize Norton and quickly expanded to Eielson AFB and Thule AB, affording ready access to existing reconnaissance routes along the periphery of the Soviet Union. These missions now required mid-air refueling from KC-97 tankers that were often co-located at these bases. Peripheral sorties included Project SEASHORE in March 1955 that photographed air defense sites on the northern and eastern shores of Siberia.[45] In addition to the PHOTINT missions associated with the YRB-47B and RB-47E, and the ELINT missions flown by RB-47Hs, SAC undertook proof-of-concept flights to gather COMINT in high performance aircraft in a program known as BONUS BABY. A linguist flew in place of the one of the Ravens in a small number of RB-47Hs equipped with radio receivers, providing not only a COMINT collection ability but a modest degree of self-protection. Missions were flown from RAF Brize Norton and Eielson AFB, and proved successful. Given the limited space for crew in the RB-47H, an automated COMINT collection system was installed as part of an overall reconnaissance system upgrade known as BOX TOP.

Reconnaissance B-47s were also used for overflight missions. The first of these – specifically approved by President Truman – failed in September 1951 when the airplane (B-47B 49-2645) caught fire during routine maintenance and was destroyed on the ground at Eielson AFB. The second B-47 mission approved by Truman, this time successful, took place on 15 October 1952. The airplane overflew northeastern Siberia and the Chukotskii Peninsula to determine the operational status of Soviet bomber bases in the area. A back-up airplane orbited near the USSR in case the primary mission airplane experienced mechanical problems and had to abort the mission.[46] Concerns about the deployment of the jet-powered Myasishchev Mya-4 *Bison* bomber prompted the next overflight on 8 May 1954 with a single-plane mission over Murmansk and the Kola Peninsula.[47] There is some evidence to suggest that at least one other mission took place over Murmansk in 1954 as well as four over Siberia.[48] In addition to ongoing peripheral sorties, during 1955-1956 14 RB-47Es configured with the APQ-56 side-looking airborne radar (SLAR) conducted shallow overflights under the MONTICELLO and PETER PAN programs along the southern border of the USSR in order to gather intelligence about the Soviet ICBM facility at Kapustin Yar.[49]

The US Marine Corps conducted a brief series of overflights of the People's Republic of China from 11 May – 12 June 1954 using McDonnell F2H-2P Banshees. Assigned to VMJ-1 at NAS Atsugi, they searched for (but did not find) evidence of a PRC buildup of an imminent invasion of Quemoy or Matsu.[50]

Concerns about the production and operational capability of the Mya-4 *Bison* heavy jet bomber prompted the 8 May 1954 RB-47E overflight of Murmansk. Western analysts equated the *Bison* with the B-52, although it looked more like an overgrown B-47 with embedded engines. The Mya-4 never achieved a similar potential as a bomber, although a number were used as air refueling tankers, stoking SAC's fears of a maturing Soviet long-range bomber force. *via Yefim Gordon*

Overflights of the USSR and Eastern Europe continued through February 1955 as North American RF-86s made high-altitude incursions over Khabarovsk from April 1954 through 19 February 1955. During the same period, North American SLICK CHICK RF-100As – six early F-100As modified to fly at supersonic speed at altitudes above 50,000 feet – made 'shallow penetrations' over Eastern bloc countries while assigned to Detachment 1, 7407th SS at Bitburg AB, West Germany.[51] As with the fictitious ROBIN Kapustin Yar flight, at least one researcher argues that from May 1955 through June 1956 SLICK CHICK RF-100As operated from Turkey and supposedly conducted 16 overflights of Kapustin Yar. There is no evidence that any Turkish flights took place. Brugioni discounts these overflights altogether, and a SLICK CHICK pilot makes no reference to any flights from Turkey. Three SLICK CHICK RF-100s were assigned to the 6008th Composite Group at Yokota AB where they undertook similar missions.[52]

From September 1955 through August 1956 specially modified RB-57As participated in numerous peripheral reconnaissance sorties in the Pacific and European theaters. The airplanes had improved engines and armament removed under a program known as LIGHTWEIGHT, which was later changed to HEART THROB. Flown from bases in Japan, the HEART THROB missions included fewer than a half dozen overflights of the eastern Soviet Union and Sakhalin Island. The 7407th SS at Rhein-Main AB conducted some 15-19 HEART THROB overflight missions of Eastern Europe. Clearly, SAC did not have a monopoly on Air Force peripheral or overflight reconnaissance.[53]

The largest single military reconnaissance overflight operation of the Cold War took place between 21 March and 10 May 1956. Known as Project HOME RUN, these missions involved 16 RB-47E PHOTINT aircraft from Lockbourne AFB and four RB-47H SIGINT aircraft from Forbes AFB plus 28 Boeing KC-97 aerial tankers from the same bases. Deployed to Thule AB, the RB-47s undertook as many as four or five overflights a day with a total of 156 missions flown. Flights covered the Kara Sea and Laptev Sea area, as well as portions of Siberia near the Bering Sea. On a typical sortie an RB-47E would take photographs while an RB-47H would collect SIGINT from Soviet ground defenses, par-

SLICK CHICK RF-100A 53-1551 at the North American facility following modification. Under fuselage fairings are clearly visible, although the side fairing beneath the cockpit does not show well. The airplanes operated with four drop tanks, a configuration which pilots disliked due to center of gravity and yaw issues. *North American Aviation photo via Cecil Rigsby via Doug Gordon*

ticularly those which reacted to the RB-47E. Crews photographed Novaya Zemlya Island, the northern Soviet nuclear weapons test site, and also determined that the USSR had few defenses east of the Ural Mountains. In one final mission during May 1956, six RB-47Es from Thule AB overflew the USSR from Ambarchik, along the northern Siberian coastline, to the Chukotskii Peninsula, recovered at Eielson AFB, and then returned to Thule AB.[54]

Despite the improvements in speed and performance, RB-47s were not immune from attack. SAC officials told Captain Harold 'Hal' Austin and his crew that there would be 'only MiG-15s' that might threaten his 8 May 1954 mission over Murmansk, and that the weather would be favorable to preclude the formation of condensation trails (contrails) behind the airplane that would reveal its position hundreds of miles away. Instead of the predicted MiG-15s the interceptors were more advanced MiG-17 *Frescos*, easily capable of the speed and altitude needed to reach the RB-47, and the bomber produced long, white contrails against the blue sky.[55] Austin's aircraft was hit by cannon fire from the MiG-17s but managed to return safely to RAF Fairford.

Reconnaissance B-47 losses include an RB-47B-I (one of two which carried a 100-inch camera for peripheral PHOTINT) shot down on 17 April 1955 and the ELINT RB-47H on 1 July 1960, although there are doubtful claims for others. For example, aviation writer Al Lloyd asserts that the 3 April 1965 loss of 55th SRW EB-47E(TT) 53-2320 was because it 'fought a running gun battle with MiGs and crashed on landing' resulting in four fatalities. In fact the airplane crashed because of loss of control in strong crosswinds during landing, killing two.[56] Similarly, author Jan Tegler reports a possible RB-47H shot down over the Caspian Sea in the 'early 1960s.' However, every RB-47H is accounted for, the RB-47 reconnaissance community has no knowledge of such an incident or losing any members to hostile fire after 1 July 1960, and the NSA has no SIGINT record for any such loss.[57]

At first glance 63-13302 appears as a standard WB-57F when photographed at NAS Atsugi on 28 January 1972. In fact, the airplane was originally HEART THROB RB-57A 52-1433, albeit with smaller wings and two fewer engines. Three of the HEART THROB airplanes were converted into RB-57Fs with new serial numbers, and then further modified into WB-57Fs, attesting to the type's value in high-altitude operations. *Harry Tyrpak via Stephen Miller*

There are persistent reports of two (perhaps three) B-47s converted by Lockheed-Marietta during the late 1950s for CIA overflights. Known as 'Black Beauties' for their all-black paint scheme, the airplanes were ostensibly part of a 1950s and 1960s program. These unverified RB-47s had their wings lengthened considerably and their six General Electric J47 engines replaced with four Pratt & Whitney J57s or TF33s similar to the proposed YB-47C or B-56. Range of the airplane was said to be on a par with the U-2, and the CIA RB-47s could reach altitudes well above 60,000 feet. One reportedly crashed while on a training mission over Tennessee, and another was supposedly shot down over the USSR. Few aviation researchers believe in the existence of Black Beauty RB-47s, especially seconded to the CIA. However, some enthusiasts continue to argue that an 'ERB-47H' supposedly lost over the Caspian Sea in 1967 was in fact a CIA Black Beauty RB-47 operating from Iran. No loss of any of the three actual ERB-47Hs is known to have occurred; all three were retired and scrapped. Others argue that the Tennessee accident was actually a cover story using the crash of an unspecified cargo aircraft. At least three KC-135 boom operators each swear they refueled such an airplane. One claimed that his tanker was ordered to orbit at a point just outside the USSR and refuel 'whatever showed up,' which happened to be an all-black B-47. Another asserted that he refueled an all-black B-47 near Alaska. A third said the B-47 was used for missions against Cuba in 1958, but this makes little operational sense. (In 1958 Cuba was still an 'American playground' under the absolute control of President Fulgencio Batista. There was no need for such a sophisticated aerial asset to collect what could easily have been gathered by wandering unimpeded around the island with cameras.)

The name 'Black Beauty' was indeed associated with the B-47, but only as part of a $37 million subcontract to Douglas-Tulsa Aircraft Division to perform routine Inspect and Repair as Necessary (IRAN) maintenance on 204 standard B-47 bombers, and certainly not as part of some ultra-clandestine overflight program. As with the ROBIN Canberra and the SLICK CHICK

RF-100A Kapustin Yar missions, claims of CIA RB-47s are almost certainly apocryphal.

After much bureaucratic wrangling and a turf battle between the CIA's Richard Bissell and the Air Force's Curtis LeMay, SAC finally acquired its own U-2s beginning in 1956, although the two programs remained separate despite LeMay's ongoing efforts for SAC to become the sole operational authority for the U-2. This tension is well described by researchers and CIA participants. Brugioni recalls this long-standing, almost adversarial relationship between CIA and SAC over control of the U-2 program, but clearly from the point of view of the CIA. Although the official CIA history of the U-2 refers to SAC and the CIA as 'partners in advancing the state of the art in overhead reconnaissance' and concludes that the 'co-operation between the Agency and Air Force that began with the U-2...remains a major feature in US reconnaissance programs,' it nonetheless notes that the 'struggle between the CIA and the US Air Force to control U-2' was part of a long-standing turf battle that persisted through subsequent intelligence-gathering systems.[58] As with many issues associated with SAC and other agencies, the focus of this animus was not on SAC or the Air Force but was almost certainly on LeMay. On 11 June 1957 the 4080th SRW at Laughlin AFB, Texas, (SAC's RB-57Ds were also part of the 4080th SRW) was declared operational and became the first SAC unit to fly the U-2. At the time, LeMay's victory seemed Pyrrhic. As part of Eisenhower's commitment toward use of civilian pilots in the U-2 program, the president insisted that only the CIA – and not SAC – would conduct U-2 overflights of the Soviet Union and its allies. In the end, however, LeMay triumphed when SAC U-2s conducted overflights of Cuba and Southeast Asia, and when CIA Lockheed A-12s were retired and their mission (including overflights) assumed by SAC SR-71s.

Much to the chagrin of General Curtis LeMay, SAC's foray into the U-2 business was limited to global CROWFLIGHT and peripheral TOY SOLDIER sampling missions and the CONGO MAIDEN peripheral PHOTINT mission. SAC U-2s, such as 56-6953 displaying the 4080th SW badge on the vertical stabilizer, would not have an overflight mission until the Cuban Missile Crisis in 1962. *Courtesy of Chris Pocock*

Perhaps most valuable among SAC's peripheral missions was the High Altitude Sampling Program (HASP), known as Operation CROWFLIGHT. Like the LRDP atmospheric detection program, HASP was intended to identify particles produced by an atmospheric nuclear explosion.[59] To LeMay's displeasure, HASP was intended to assess only US (and arguably British) weapons tests. Beginning in October 1957 SAC U-2s deployed to Ramey AB, Puerto Rico, Plattsburgh AFB, New York, and Ezeiza IAP, Buenos Aires, Argentina, and flew sampling routes over the western Atlantic Ocean and Canada, respectively. Although these were hardly as dramatic as the CIA overflights of the Soviet Union, they provided an essential function with critical implications for future SAC sampling flights. Using data acquired from American nuclear tests, scientists validated the accuracy of the sampling equipment on board the HASP U-2s. Confident that future sampling missions would be more accurate and reliable, US analysts began operations aimed at Soviet weapons tests. CIA U-2s assigned to Detachment C at Yokota AB conducted the first five sampling missions. As part of Operation TOY SOLDIER SAC U-2s deployed to Eielson AFB from

Select Early SAC U-2 Operations

Name	Start	End	Operating Location	Mission
TOY SOLDIER	03 Feb 58	16 Mar 58	Eielson AFB, AK	Sampling
TOY SOLDIER II	10 Sep 58	14 Nov 58	Eielson AFB, AK	Sampling
TOY SOLDIER III	03 Apr 59	19 May 59	Eielson AFB, AK	Sampling
FORTUNE FINDER	20 Mar 59	15 May 59	Eielson AFB, AK	Sampling
FORTUNE FINDER II (cancelled)	Jun 59	Jun 59	RAF Upper Heyford	Sampling
CONGO MAIDEN	23 Mar 59	28 Mar 59	Eielson AFB, AK	PHOTINT
CROWFLIGHT	1957	post-1970s	Ramey AB, Puerto Rico	Sampling
			Plattsburgh AFB	Sampling
			Ezeiza IAP, Buenos Aires	Sampling

Following a wing crack RB-57D-0 53-3973 was repaired and reassigned to ARDC as an NRB-57D, retaining the camera windows on the lower forward fuselage. Except for the orange conspicuity paint, this is how all BLACK KNIGHT RB-57Ds appeared with a white top and black underside. This airplane was configured for air refueling – note red outline on fuselage spine for IFR receptacle. *Jim Morrow via Stephen Miller*

3 February through 16 March 1958 for additional sampling missions as the Soviets detonated two nuclear weapons in January, three in February, and ten weapons in March.[60] SAC U-2s flew TOY SOLDIER-II missions from 10 September to 14 November 1958, TOY SOLDIER-III missions from 3 April to 19 May 1959, along with FORTUNE FINDER sampling missions from 20 March to 15 May 1959.[61] SAC B-52Bs (and later B-52Fs) flew SEA FISH sampling missions as well. B-52s from the 92nd BW at Spokane AFB carried special filters on 'missions involved with the world-wide monitoring of air masses to detect atomic explosions if and when they occurred.' On 1 May 1959 the 93rd BW at Castle AFB, California, took over the SEA FISH flights.[62]

In addition to its high-flying U-2s, SAC's 4080th SRW operated a modest fleet of BLACK KNIGHT RB-57D Canberras. Noted for their increased wingspan, they were capable of reaching altitudes of 60,000 feet. They collected PHOTINT and ELINT on both peripheral and overflight missions of the USSR. The initial BLACK KNIGHT deployment began on 3 September 1956 when six RB-57Ds departed Turner AFB for Yokota AB as part of Operation SEA LION. Some of the aircraft returned to Laughlin on 23 September 1956.[63] The remaining RB-57Ds conducted operational missions as part of Flight A, Detachment 1, 3rd Air Division. By the end of October 1956 the unit had flown 39 missions totaling 168 hours.

The next SEA LION deployment was slated to begin on 27 November 1956. Two RB-57Ds flew from Turner AFB to Yokota AB, and presumably were among the three which overflew Vladivostok (or the three spares) on 11 December 1956. Four days later the Soviets protested the incursion, and Eisenhower directed the suspension of all overflights of 'Iron Curtain' countries. In a 1988 interview LeMay refers to the 11 December mission in his oft-quoted remark about flying 'all the reconnaissance aircraft that SAC possessed over Vladivostok at high noon,' involving 'a whole wing of [RB-57] Canberras.'[64]

Although SAC overflights ended in 1956, the BLACK KNIGHT RB-57Ds continued peripheral missions. Three 4080th SRW RB-57D-2s deployed to RAF Brize Norton on 24 January 1959 as part of Operation BORDER TOWN for 14 ELINT sorties. Operation SAND SHARK involved two RB-57D-2s flying 14 sorties from Eielson AFB. On 20 July 1959, RB-57D-2 53-3965 on Mission FX-020 detected a suspected 'long-range, high-priority Soviet early warning radar' along the Kamchatka Peninsula, which was confirmed by two additional sorties.[65] In April 1958 six BLACK KNIGHT RB-57Ds participated in the HARD TACK series of US nuclear tests at Eniwetok.

SAC transferred the BLACK KNIGHT RB-57Ds to USAFE, where they were used for peripheral PHOTINT and SIGINT missions.[66] Some BLACK KNIGHT RB-57Ds may have overflown Finland, but this is not confirmed. One former B-57 pilot not involved in the BLACK KNIGHT project identifies RB-57D-1 52-3963 as the first of these airplanes to overfly the Soviet Union from Germany, but this claim is unsupported by any official documentation.[67] Still the early HEART THROB and BLACK KNIGHT overflights created a deeply entrenched belief that the only the 'Canberra' could undertake extremely high-altitude missions. Indeed, when civilian U-2 began overflights of the USSR in July 1956 Soviet military officials misidentified it as a twin-engine bomber. Two of the BLACK KNIGHT RB-57Ds were transferred to the Republic of China Air Force (RoCAF) where they undertook some 24 overflight missions of Red China.

SAC continued its U-2 operations in late March 1959 with the CONGO MAIDEN PHOTINT program, operating from Eielson AFB. The U-2s conducted peripheral missions 12-15 miles off the coast of the Chukotskii and Kamchatka Peninsulas to determine the status of known Soviet bomber bases and identify any improvement to them or construction of new facilities. Additional CONGO MAIDEN missions took place a year later. They were hardly without excitement, as at least one SAM was fired at a U-2 mission passing the base at Anadyr but to no effect.[68]

Following the 12 May 1960, cabinet meeting in the wake of the U-2 incident, Eisenhower told Secretary of State Christian Herter that there should be a 'recess or restriction on all intelligence operations of a 'provocative nature'.' Herter had previously issued such a similar directive and 'had already told the Air Force to cut down on 'ferret' operations.' On 1 June, Eisenhower formalized this moratorium by ordering the cessation of 'all activities that might be taken by the Soviets as provocative,' specifically overflights.[69] USAF penetration flights of Eastern Europe allegedly continued. North American RB-66Cs assigned to the 7544th Strategic Group (SG) flew WET STONE missions along the border of Eastern Bloc countries, occasionally making shallow border incursions and recording the results. RB-57D missions included PAPER DOLL and DINAH LEE, as well as continued peripheral sorties, weather reconnaissance, and aerial sampling missions through the mid 1960s.[70]

Not all overflights were violations of foreign airspace. USAF flights through the three so-called 'Berlin corridors,' international airspace over East Germany linking West Berlin's Templehof Airport to the rest of the Federal Republic of Germany and the world, conducted extensive reconnaissance operations. C-97s photographed Communist forces adjacent to the corridors using a huge camera developed as part of PIE FACE program. These were popularly known as the 'Berlin-for-Lunch-Bunch' because of their daily morning flights to Berlin followed by an afternoon return to West Germany. This humorous moniker should not mask the risks these crews undertook, as they often flew right at the edge of the allocated corridor air space or altitude, and even made brief incursions into East German airspace (known as the 'Corridor Dance'). Convair CT-29s collected PHOTINT as part of the CAROL ANN program.[71] A Fairchild C-119 cargo aircraft was equipped with sophisticated power measuring gear for flights through the corridor to assess the operational characteristics of the Soviet *Bar Lock* radars along the route. The *Bar Lock* was tracking CIA U-2 missions, and Lockheed and CIA officials were seeking ways to jam or reduce its effectiveness.[72]

For Western leaders, especially Truman and Eisenhower, there was an essential need for information about Soviet political intentions and military capabilities. Given the long distances involved and the increasingly technical nature of the intelligence required, airplanes carrying powerful cameras, sophisticated electronic equipment, and skilled systems operators and linguists served as the primary means of collecting this information. Far from compiling a mere laundry list of program names, dates of missions, and areas observed, we now understand that peripheral aerial reconnaissance missions – both military and civilian – were widespread and reflected a deep organizational and budgetary commitment by the president and his senior civilian and military advisors. The number of military overflights of the Soviet Union and Communist bloc nations far exceeded civilian U-2 incursions, held to be the cornerstone of US intelligence collection during the Eisenhower administration.

The PIE FACE C-97A 49-2592 on short final to Berlin Tempelhof AP. Even to the trained eye there is very little to indicate the reconnaissance-related modifications to the airplane. Aside from the observation blister on the aft fuselage and the APS-64 radar fairing under the nose, this could be easily mistaken for a stock C-97 transport. *Ralf Manteufel*

4 Targets and Tactics

During the reception following the 1 August 1974 change of command ceremony at which General Russell E Dougherty became SAC's eighth commander, the second and most famous of SAC's leaders – Curtis LeMay – asked Dougherty about his new responsibilities. For LeMay, SAC's first combat mission could well be its last and demanded the highest degree of leadership and command. The new CINCSAC assured LeMay that he appreciated the serious responsibility of commanding SAC and America's nuclear forces. LeMay next asked Dougherty who he remembered from Pearl Harbor. Dougherty replied that he recalled only Army Lieutenant General Walter C Short and Navy Admiral Husband E Kimmel. Both were relieved of their commands for dereliction, and bore the brunt of recrimination for the debacle at Pearl Harbor. LeMay replied quickly, saying, 'You're exactly right. The responsible military commanders are the ones remembered in disasters and defeats. Don't you be remembered in history for a single mistake.'[1]

For each of SAC's commanders and for senior US officials during the Cold War, that single mistake would be to allow an atomic Pearl Harbor, an attack where SAC's nuclear retaliatory power was crippled or destroyed on the ground before it could be used. Blue-ribbon panels and military commissions during the early Cold War years agreed that defense of the United States – and SAC bases in particular – against an atomic attack was nearly impossible. If SAC's bombers were left burning on the runways after a 'bolt from the blue,' as any sudden and unexpected attack came to be known, the United States had little else remaining with which to attack its enemies. America would be defeated.

America's worst nightmare – a nuclear Pearl Harbor – began with a Soviet atom bomb released from a Tu-4A *Bull*. Intelligence failures at Pearl Harbor and Korea were proof to US officials that strategic aerial reconnaissance was essential to determine the status of the Soviet nuclear weapons program and bomber deployment to prevent a 'knock-out blow' surprise attack on SAC bases and American cities. Seen here is a video still shot of a live Soviet atomic bomb test moments after release from a Tu-4. *via Yefim Gordon*

Moreover, as American security relied increasingly upon the might of SAC's atomic bombers as a deterrent force, American security become increasingly linked to SAC's vulnerability. Should a potential enemy realize that a surprise attack with atomic weapons might eliminate America's nuclear strike force, then SAC's deterrent and retaliatory value decreased dramatically, if not disappeared altogether. Consequently, the temptation for an enemy to go to war against the United States increased significantly. Bernard Brodie warned in 1946 that this made such an attack more likely because of its 'low-risk, high-gain' appeal to Soviet leaders.[2] Former naval aviator and future Secretary of Defense Robert A Lovett directly linked future Soviet behavior with the fortunes of American air power. The USSR, he wrote to General Spaatz, 'is keenly aware of the power of an adequate air force, and recognizes that [America's] position and influence in the world will...be in some direct relation with our supremacy, or lack of it, in the air.'[3] The potential for a successful surprise attack against the United States significantly and adversely affected US strategic deterrent and retaliatory war-fighting capabilities.

Even if war between the United States and the Soviet Union erupted under circumstances favorable to America there was no guarantee that SAC's forces could reach, locate, and destroy their assigned targets. There was considerable concern among military planners and civilian defense analysts that SAC simply did not know all the targets it needed to attack. There was open debate in the Pentagon, in Congress, in newspaper editorials, and in the halls of academia about the ability of SAC's bombers to penetrate Soviet defenses and find their assigned targets. The shortage of information about Soviet targets and a profoundly inadequate knowledge of Soviet air defenses meant that SAC's strike capability was severely constrained by sheer ignorance.[4] In addition, US defense planners knew little or nothing about a nascent Soviet strike force and how to defend America against it.

For US officials, ignorance was just as great an enemy as Soviet bombs. Without advanced knowledge of an impending attack, the United States could be quickly and easily destroyed or crippled and compelled to surrender. Without improved knowledge of enemy offensive forces, American defensive forces would be ill prepared to detect and repel any invading force. Without detailed knowledge of enemy targets and defenses, US strikes against an enemy might be marginally effective at best or meaningless at worst. Without broad knowledge of an enemy's capabilities, the prudent allocation of American defense dollars would not be possible, as there was not enough money available to support plans and policies that would address every military contingency.

None of these concerns addressed the broader issue of what exactly would be a desirable outcome of any general war with the Soviet Union. For many strategists the definition of 'winning' was simply 'not losing.' At one extreme CINCSAC General Thomas S Power reputedly said, 'The whole idea is to kill the bastards. At the end of the war if there are two Americans and one Russian left alive, we win!' LeMay held a more realistic if not ambiguous view of an American victory than his successor: 'By *Winning* is meant achieving a condition wherein the enemy cannot impose his will on us, but we can impose our will upon him.'[5] Assuming that both of these definitions are valid, it is difficult to imagine that after a nuclear war there would be any major states intact or even interested in imposing their will on a state on the other side of the world.

During the early years of the Cold War, US military planners needed military information and they needed it quickly. New agencies were established and others reorganized to analyze this vital information. Despite these efforts, the means to collect the information used in such analyses remained woefully inadequate. Strategic aerial reconnaissance provided one expedient and reliable way to resolve this inadequacy.

Military applications of strategic aerial reconnaissance were based on three 'critical intelligence requirements.' In order of priority these were: '1. Indications of the imminence of hostilities [strategic and tactical warning]. 2. Enemy atomic air-strengths which threaten US and Allied strengths at home and abroad. [and] 3. Enemy air and other strengths to resist US penetrations of his air space.'[6] Advanced warning and indications could provide early detection – perhaps months in advance – of an impending Soviet attack on the United States. Long-range intelligence-gathering flights regularly monitored a number of indicators in the Soviet Union which could tip off US analysts to a forthcoming attack. These reconnaissance missions also collected information on the development and operational status of Soviet bombers (and eventually ballistic missiles) and atomic weapons. Learning about enemy defensive capabilities meant locating and mapping targets to be attacked by US forces, as well as the anti-aircraft artillery (AAA), fighters, radar, and other measures in place to defend these targets and Soviet borders. Reconnaissance overflights of the USSR identified, located, and photographed future targets. In addition, peripheral and overflight reconnaissance missions gathered technical information about enemy defenses. ELINT, for example, helped determined the location, range, and frequency of Soviet early-warning radars. This information enabled American military planners to identify safe penetration routes for US strike forces, increasing their likelihood of reaching and destroying their targets. For the US military in the post-war world, strategic aerial reconnaissance was vital to the success of America's offensive and defensive capability.

During the early Cold War years US officials did not believe that the Soviet Union would intentionally attack the United States in the near future. In 1946 Harry Truman told former Vice President John Nance Garner, for example, that there was 'too much loose talk about the Russian situation. We are not going to have any shooting trouble with them....'[7] Instead, American civilian and military officials postulated that war between the two nations and their allies might erupt within five to ten years. President Truman's Air Policy Commission, also known as the Finletter Commission, concluded in 1947 that there was little short-term possibility of a Soviet attack on the United States. The commission noted that any credible Soviet threat hinged upon Soviet efforts to develop atomic weapons and long-range bombers. Neither of these events was, in the opinion of the commission, probable until sometime in the early- to mid-1950s. Lieutenant General Jimmy Doolittle told Secretary of the Air Force Stuart Symington in 1950 that Russia was unlikely to

In 1950 LGEN Jimmy Doolittle dismissed a Soviet first strike because the USSR lacked heavy bombers or air refuelable medium bombers. By the mid-1950s the Soviets could indeed refuel their medium bombers. Ground crew extract the refueling hose from a Tu-16Z tanker capable of wingtip-to-wingtip refueling. The process was inefficient (good luck at night) and dangerous (static discharge and mid-air collisions) but it represented a limited capability. *via Yefim Gordon*

start an 'offensive war against the United States...until she has heavy bombers or more medium bombers which could be used with [aerial] refueling.'[8] A 1952 national security report to President Truman concluded that it was 'unlikely that the Kremlin will deliberately initiate general war' against the United States through the end of 1954. Military planners typically shared this view but were inclined to hedge their bets. SAC's Director of Intelligence Major General James A Walsh argued, 'It is not certain, of course, that the Soviets deliberately will launch an attack on the US. But at the same time we cannot be sure they will not.'[9] This presumes, of course, that the Soviet Union actually *intended* to attack the United States. Stalin held as a matter of faith the Marxist-Leninist inevitability of war first among the capitalist states and then between the surviving capitalist West and socialist East. He believed that such a war would and should begin on Soviet terms, that is, when the USSR was sufficiently strong to defeat the United States. Whether or not this was a real or hyperbolic threat, US officials could ill afford to discount this as purely ideological rhetoric.

Although American leaders believed that a premeditated Soviet attack against the United States was unlikely, they were nonetheless concerned that war between the two countries could erupt by miscalculation or by a crisis escalating rapidly and unexpectedly. The 1946 Clifford-Elsey report warned that 'sudden moves, or unexpected or misunderstood moves, by the Soviet Union might...lead us into a showdown of force for which we would probably be unprepared, or might lead us into blind or hasty diplomatic retreat.' In 1950 Paul Nitze of the State Department's Policy Planning Staff warned that Soviet actions 'might lead to an accidental outbreak of general military conflict. Thus the chance of war through miscalculation is increased.' Two years later Truman administration officials concluded 'there will be continuing grave danger that general war may arise from a series of actions and counteractions in a situation which neither side desired to develop into a general war.'[10]

Irrespective of whether war with the USSR came as a premeditated act on the part of the USSR or by miscalculation, US officials were most concerned that war would come as a surprise, just as it did with Japan in 1941. One might reasonably argue that the Soviet entry into World War Two also started with a surprise Nazi invasion in 1941, so both superpowers had justifiable reasons to be apprehensive about an unexpected attack. The surprise attack on Pearl Harbor transformed American military and national security planning. As historian Gordon Prange argues: *Pearl Harbor drove the idea of surprise attack so deeply into the national psyche that 'Pearl Harbor' became almost a generic term for any sneak attack.... After World War II, it was generally agreed that any future attack almost certainly would be [a] surprise.*[11]

So profound was the post-war US commitment to avoiding surprise attack that every major US operational plan regarding the prosecution of warfare in the Cold War years was based on the assumption that there would be 'no strategic surprise in the initiation of such a war.'[12] This was particularly ironic as US planners concurrently lamented the lack of suitable intelligence and warning capability.

Airpower advocates like General Carl Spaatz warned that American defense policies 'must be properly organized so that there cannot possibly be an air surprise such as occurred at Pearl Harbor.' Should such an attack involve atomic weapons then the devastation to American forces and cities would be overwhelming, as America might be compelled to surrender without *any* military resistance.[13] In 1947 the Joint Chiefs warned President Truman about the consequences of a surprise atomic attack: *Even a nation capable of retaining the will and ability to fight a victorious war after losses far greater than those of the Pearl Harbor surprise attack can be seriously crippled, perhaps defeated, by a well planned and executed atomic bomb attack. This may hold true no matter how great the damage inflicted by belated counter-attack.*[14]

A report by the National Security Council (NSC) Net Evaluation Subcommittee warned that if US strike forces were destroyed by a surprise attack, 'the USSR by [means of] a nuclear attack on the continental United States will emerge as the dominant world power in 24 hours.'[15]

Rapid technological improvements to weapons and aircraft meant that the United States could no longer hide behind its oceans as a primary means of defense. After Stalin's death in 1953 Soviet doctrine shifted away from the traditional defense-in-depth strategy and openly espoused the elements of surprise, long-range air attacks, and the use of nuclear weapons. Soviet rhetoric added to the apprehension of US planners. Air Marshall Konstantin A Vershinin, the Commander-in-Chief of the Soviet Air Force, boasted in 1957 that it was possible to deliver atomic weapons 'instantly to the remotest areas of any continent of the world by intercontinental ballistic missiles,' and that '[m]any of the major cities of the United States and some Western countries, may, in the event of war, be attacked by rockets and bombers as well as submarines.'[16]

At the heart of this new direct threat to America was the degree of SAC's vulnerability to surprise attack. General LeMay had little faith in the US intelligence community's ability to provide SAC with *tactical* warning of an imminent attack on the United States: *Our intelligence system is pretty sorry.... We hope it will get better as time goes on, and I believe it will. I think however – and this is my personal opinion – that it will never be good enough to tell us that so many airplanes are coming off this field at such and such a time to attack the United States.*[17]

As weapon technology improved and tactical warning time decreased to a matter of minutes, the effectiveness of SAC's response dropped significantly. According to one history, 'SAC strike plans were predicated on the amount of warning time the command could expect to receive of impending attack. This time was constantly diminishing.'[18]

The issue of SAC's vulnerability was hardly the parochial, bureaucratic squabbling many considered it to be. As late as 1955 and 1956, Air Force analysts warned Air Force Chief of Staff General Nathan F Twining that SAC remained vulnerable to a Soviet surprise attack. They added that America's 'present warning and fighter control systems are inadequate and obsolete. An enemy aircraft can fly over the United States without detection above 50,000 feet or below 500 feet.' By December 1957 the USAF Air Defense Command (ADC) warned Power that 'under many conditions no [tactical] warning could be guaranteed to any SAC base.'[19] SAC bombers routinely conducted high-altitude, no-notice simulated attacks on American cities as US air defense forces sat idly on the ground, either unaware of the bombers or else grounded by bad weather. If SAC bombers could circumvent American aerial defenses, so too could those of an enemy, especially a nuclear-armed Soviet Union.

The fear of surprise attack against the United States even had humorous implications. During the late 1940s the United States began to experience increased reports of unidentified flying objects (UFOs). In 1948 President Truman discussed these events with his Air Force aide, Brigadier General Robert B Landry. Truman 'hadn't given much serious thought' to these reports but wondered 'if there was any evidence of a strategic threat to the national security' posed by UFOs. Truman ordered Landry to consult with the CIA and to report to the president on a quarterly basis as to whether any of the UFO incidents 'could be considered as having any strategic threatening implications at all.' It did not matter if the UFOs were Soviet bombers or Martian saucers, they were still alien and a potential threat to American security and represented a gap in America's defenses. Landry made his oral reports over the remaining four and half years of Truman's presidency. Unsurprisingly, 'nothing of substance considered credible or threatening to the coun-

Prior to becoming Air Force Chief of Staff, General Hoyt S Vandenberg (left) was Director of Central Intelligence. As such, he had a strong commitment to strategic aerial reconnaissance and encouraged President Truman (center left) to expand the SESP and SENSINT programs. Brigadier General Robert Landry (center right), Truman's military aide, briefed the president on UFOs. The CIA feared a fake UFO invasion might be used to mask a Soviet bomber attack on the United States. *Copyright Unknown, Courtesy of Harry S Truman Library*

try was ever received from intelligence.'[20] Conversely, the CIA worried that the Soviets could exploit the UFO issue by flooding North American air defenses with bogus reports of flying saucers, tying up scarce radar and interceptor resources. A surprise Soviet bomber or missile attack against the United States would then go undetected and unchallenged.[21] This anxiety over UFOs should not be dismissed as a mere social fad. Following the 1938 radio broadcast of 'War of the Worlds,' many Americans (and foreigners) firmly believed in the nationwide hysteria that supposedly erupted. In fact, very little social disruption took place. Still, the CIA was concerned that *Soviet* leaders believed this hype and would attempt to use it to their advantage.[22] In the context of the Cold War, invading aliens from outer space were little different from invading Communists from Russia, and the adverse affect on the American social order could be dramatic.

All of these issues – war by miscalculation, surprise attack with atomic weapons, and SAC's vulnerability – combined to give increasing importance to the collection of strategic aerial intelligence within the Air Force, particularly in SAC. US officials believed that the information gathered by these flights would significantly reduce the possibility of war between the United States and the Soviet Union.

The US intelligence community divided early warning into two broad categories. 'Strategic' early warning provided long-term indications of war based on 'deductive conclusions about Soviet preparations.' 'Operational' early warning alerted officials of an impending attack given 'information on Soviet operations...obtained largely through mechanical means.' These categories were based on an intellectual framework about the Soviet Union that assessed, among other factors, what essential precursors the Russians needed to prepare for war, whether or not Soviet actions were precautionary or preparatory, and what evidence would justify those conclusions. Acquiring this evidence dictated 'new techniques and methods for collection.'[23]

In the years immediately after the Second World War, American agents within the USSR failed to identify any long-term early warnings of general war against the United States. Some US analysts interpreted this absence of warnings by concluding that the agents had *yet to discover* the evidence of preparation for an attack. In reality this 'failure' to detect indicators of an impending invasion was because there *were no* warning signs because there *was no* forthcoming attack. Nonetheless for many American officials, this 'undiscovered' evidence highlighted existing inadequacies in US intelligence gathering and fueled the requirement for more methods to gather and analyze the evidence that could reveal Soviet intentions for war. The 1945 Spaatz Report, for example, urged improvements in intelligence collection regarding Soviet capabilities and intentions, which would prove especially useful in early warning of a surprise attack. By 1946 the intelligence community had made 'early warning' a 'panicky requirement' of nearly obsessive levels.[24]

Efforts to develop an early warning system of an impending Soviet attack accelerated in 1948 when the unexpected Soviet blockade of Berlin exacerbated existing fears of a surprise attack by the USSR. President Truman created a special group within the CIA known as the Watch Committee to monitor the many warning signs of an impending Soviet attack. The Watch Committee made four basic assumptions about any Soviet attack:

- *The Soviets, together with other Communist states, are seeking an opportune time to initiate hostilities to achieve their ends.*
- *The attack will attempt maximum surprise, possibly during periods of international calm.*
- *The decision to initiate hostilities may be made without the requisite military capability which we [the United States] would consider requisite.*
- *Any estimates which argue from other assumptions may be quite wrong.*[25]

Analysts built an 'indicator list' of activities that the Soviet Union would take to meet these assumptions. Such indicators would provide several months' warning, while Soviet logistical and operational preparations were still under way. The Watch Committee was especially busy during the Korean War, looking for evidence that the war portended a spread of conflict to Europe, an attack on Japan, or even a direct Soviet assault on the United States. By 1954 this group gained such importance that President Eisenhower reorganized it into the National Indications Center, which monitored 'direct military threats to the United States and its allies.'[26] The heart of the NIC remained the Watch Committee, and its first chairman after the reorganization was Major General Charles P Cabell, the CIA's Deputy Director. Cabell's influence on the Watch Committee was substantial, particularly in his appreciation of the potential of strategic aerial reconnaissance in an early warning role.[27] In addition to the NIC, Eisenhower sought other ways to detect and prevent surprise attack. On 27 March 1954 he ordered the Office of Defense Mobilization's Science Advisory Committee (the Killian Panel) to examine the 'current vulnerability of the United States to surprise attack' and 'how science and technology could be used to reduce that vulnerability.' The Killian Panel looked for new technologies that might 'prevent or forestall' a surprise attack on the United States.[28] One of the key arguments in approving the development and operation of the U-2 was that overflight 'photo-intelligence...would greatly help protect the United States from surprise attack.' A 1955 symposium on strategic aerial reconnaissance warned 'there is no problem more serious, *or* more challenging, *or* more deserving of our greatest effort toward solution than the problem of "strategic warning".'[29] In 1958 NSC 5802/1 encouraged 'vigorous efforts...to collect and accurately evaluate indications of hostile intentions that would give maximum prior strategic warning of hostile action against the United States.' Late that same year US and Soviet officials met in Geneva to discuss 'technical' ways to prevent surprise attack.[30]

Reducing or eliminating American vulnerability to surprise attack depended upon solid intelligence gathering and analysis. The Killian Panel clearly articulated this crucial relationship. Its members defined 'strategic warning' as the ability to warn 'of an attack while it is in the preparative stage,' *before* Soviet bombers or missiles were launched. Strategic warning would detect 'the buildup of the striking force, its vehicles, weapons, crews, and bases.' JCS Chairman Admiral Arthur Radford told Secretary of Defense Charles Wilson that 'safeguards against surprise long-range attack include the surveillance of [long-range striking forces] and their support, and measures to detect preparation for such an attack.' Indicators 'most likely to provide against the possibility of surprise attack' included weapons and delivery systems suitable for surprise attack (bombers, missiles, and submarines), transportation systems and telecommunications, and the status and positioning of armed forces. SAC, too, watched specific indicators, specifying those of 'particular value' as 'aircraft activity, stockpiling of fuel, supplies, etc.'[31]

The warning time gleaned from this information was estimated to be 'months, weeks, days, or hours,' but was deemed adequate 'to deny to the enemy the enormous advantages of surprise attack in modern war.' US officials felt confident that they could detect Soviet preparations for war 'six to twelve months or longer in advance' of any attack, but still worried that Soviet tactical surprise would be 'successful to some extent.'[32] The CIA's 1954 Special National Intelligence Estimate 'Probable Warning of Soviet Attack on the US Through Mid-1957 (SNIE 11-8-54)' said that 'indicators would probably...give warning 15-30 days prior to attack,' or as much as 'four or possibly even six months prior to D-Day.' The lengthy warning of an impending attack could be used not only to prepare for a preemptive or retaliatory attack, but also afforded policy makers an opportunity to resolve diplomatically the issues that led to the Soviets' plans for war. Should all options to prevent war fail, this early warning could then translate into American military action with the launching of SAC's bomber force.[33]

Severe limits on traditional forms of espionage – such as agents, moles, and defectors – meant that early warning had to come from other sources. Moreover, indicators had to be monitored regularly, often, and undetected in order to observe routine behavior. Finally, the evidence gathered had to be as objective as possible (a photograph of enemy bombers rather than a hearsay report) and easily subject to quantification (exactly how many submarines were in port).

Strategic 'aerial reconnaissance appeared to have great promise for meeting [these] requirements,' and provided 'a series of routine monitoring-type missions against selected targets.'[34] These flights offered direct, timely, and objective access to key indicators. In a classic example of the aerial intelligence requirements cycle, a defector reported in early 1951 'that a Tu-4 base, capable of supporting 125 Tu-4s, had been established on Franz Josef Land.' From there bombers could easily strike the United States, an ominous threat if true. Photographs taken by SAC's long-range reconnaissance planes would provide objective evidence to support or refute the defector's claim. If true, the photographs could offer clues about the base's operational readiness and capability. Beginning in January 1952 a request for a reconnaissance overflight of the archipelago started through the Departments of Defense and State, concurrent with another request to overfly Siberia and the Chukotskii Peninsula. Truman approved both missions on 2 August 1952. After several weather and mechanical delays, a SAC RB-50E departed Thule AB in the early morning hours on 17 September. High, thick clouds obscured the islands, so pilot Major Roy Kaden descended from the planned altitude of 20,000 feet to 2,500 feet. The crew saw and photographed nothing 'that would indicate a Soviet presence, let alone military activity. There was no evidence of airfields, of construction of any sort, or of ships, wharves, or docks.'[35] Aerial reconnaissance disproved the defector's initial report, eliminating the need to add the fictitious base to current and future war planning.

The possibility of air bases on Franz Josef Land underscored the belief of American analysts that the most important early warning indicator of impending general war was the status of Soviet bombers. Most US officials in the early 1950s proclaimed publicly that the Soviet air force had too few bombers with too little range to reach targets in the United States. Although true, such comments tended to reflect the inadequacy of *both* the Soviet and American strategic bomber forces, as SAC was beset with similar problems. At the same time, however, these same officials warned that the Soviet Union already had the basis for a substantial strike force, and America had to plan for the future possibility of a surprise Soviet attack.

Prior to the Second World War Soviet long-range aviation was generally limited to exploratory flights to the Arctic and trans-polar record-setting flights to Oregon and California. After the outbreak of war with Germany in 1941 the Soviet Air Force primarily acquired airplanes designed to attack enemy ground forces while operating from air bases immediately behind the front lines. The Tupolev TB-3 four-engine bomber, first delivered in 1930, was already obsolete but pressed into use in a support role. The Petlyakov Pe-8 heavy bomber also saw service including a few 'morale' bombing raids on Berlin, but there were fewer than 20 on hand at any one time and more than 60 percent of its losses were due to faulty engines rather than combat. The focus on Soviet airpower remained tactical ground attack. Russia produced some 120,000 combat airplanes during four years of war, including more than 36,000 'Flying Tank' Ilyushin IL-2 *Sturmoviks*, the most numerous combat airplane in history. Coupled with Lend-Lease airplanes from the United States like the B-25 Mitchell and Douglas A-20 medium-range bombers and the Bell P-39 and P-63 fighters, the Soviets amassed nearly 150,000 airplanes designed to repel German invaders.

The United States twice rebuffed Soviet requests for Lend-Lease B-29s, but during 1944 four US B-29s landed in the Soviet Union after bombing raids on Japan. Three of these were used for reverse engineering, flight testing, and production of a B-29 copy made by the Tupolev design bureau known as the Tu-4, NATO codename *Bull*. Following its successful first flight in 1947 and operational debut in 1949, nearly 850 had entered service when serial production ended in 1952. They remained in use through the 1960s.

Although there were only two Soviet bases in 1948 – one near Moscow and one near Vladivostok – capable of supporting the heavyweight Tu-4, US officials noted that there were at least five bases east of Vladivostok in the Chukotskii and Kamchatka regions close to Alaska that could be surreptitiously upgraded in a matter of weeks using forced labor from the Kolyma camps to support Tu-4 operations.[36] US military planners were equally concerned that the Soviet Union would gain strategic bomber bases outside of Russia, particularly in Iceland. From such insular bases Soviet bombers could easily strike the United States, especially the eastern seaboard.[37]

USAF intelligence analysts feared in 1948 that by building Tu-4s at an accelerated pace the Soviets could by 1954 deploy a sizeable strategic bomber fleet, and it was this future fleet that would participate in a potential Soviet surprise attack. Such concern was hardly an exaggeration. By the end of 1949 the Soviets had some 300 Tu-4s in operational service with the *Dal'naya Aviatsiya*, the long-range aviation force.[38] By comparison, in 1949 SAC had 390 B-29s (identical to the Tu-4), 36 B-36s, and 99 B-50s. Skeptics might argue that the fledgling Soviet

Left and below: Soviet weapons development emphasized defensive fighters and ground attack aircraft, and early Soviet attempts to build a four-engine bomber were less than successful. Both the Tupolev TB-3 (top) and Petlyakov Pe-8 (bottom) saw limited and disappointing service during the Great Patriotic War and were hardly suited for strategic bombardment. This changed when four USAAF B-29s landed in the USSR following raids on Japan. By acquiring copies of the B-29, the Soviet *Dal'naya Aviatsiya* – Long Range Aviation – abruptly achieved the same capability as Strategic Air Command between 1945 and 1950. *via Yefim Gordon*

bomber force lacked the experience of American crews. When LeMay took over SAC in 1948, however, he found that SAC's bombing and maintenance reliability was nonexistent.[39] In early 1950 the Soviet long-range bomber force was briefly comparable to SAC both in terms of numbers and equally low operational readiness. During 1954 no less an authority than LeMay summarized this situation: *One thing really worries me. In questioning the defectors that have shown up on our side of the line, we find the Russians have apparently understood the value of air power and are doing their best to attract good people into it. ...[they are] bound to produce at some future time a really good air force.*[40]

None of this should suggest that in 1950 the Soviet Union possessed a strike force comparable to a 1956 level Strategic Air Command, or it was this Soviet force-in-being that led US planners to fear a surprise bomber attack. In 1950 SAC was in very poor shape, so the comparison with a similar Soviet force demonstrates the general inadequacy of both forces. Moreover, no US official ever claimed in 1949 or 1950 that the extant Soviet bomber fleet would participate in an imminent surprise attack against the United States. Instead they consistently argued that this strike force would form the basis of a future bomber fleet that would train just as dutifully as would SAC to achieve the potential to strike the United States. LeMay (and ultimately Presidents Truman and Eisenhower) believed that SAC would overcome its own operational deficiencies and become the cornerstone of US defense policy. He also believed that the Soviet bomber force could do the same, and he acted accordingly.

Aside from the availability of Tu-4s in sufficient number to attack the United States, the range of those airplanes was of equal concern. In a travelogue written in 1944 while accompanying US Vice President Henry Wallace to Siberia and China, Sinologist Owen Lattimore described the ease of prospective airline flights from the Soviet Union to America. Airliners could fly non-stop and unrefueled from Siberia 'straight to the heart of America...down to such points as Minneapolis, Omaha, and Chicago.' If so uninformed an observer as Lattimore could discern the potential for interna-

tional airline travel from the Soviet Union to the United States, then US defense planners could easily see the same potential for Soviet bombers to reach American targets.[41] Identifying the location and operational status of potential and existing bomber bases in Siberia was of paramount importance. By 1950 these included 'bounce airdrome' facilities at Anadyr', Mys Shmidta, and Tiksi under the control of the Soviet Air Force Arctic Control Group based in Tiksi. Bombers would fly from their home bases to these locations to refuel, load bombs and ammunition, and then depart for their attacks on the United States. For American early warning observers the presence of dozens of bombers each at multiple Siberian bases which were previously empty would be a strong indicator of a potential attack (reaffirming the value of frequent repeat aerial reconnaissance missions to maintain constant surveillance of these bases). Within five years the number of facilities increased as construction began on bases at Chekurovka, Ostrov Bolshevik, Tiksi North, and Dresba, as well as Vorkuta, Norilsk, Sredniy Island, Olen'ya, and bases along the Alaska-Siberia Lend-Lease routes. These many airstrips allowed the Tu-4 to reach key US cities such as Chicago, Seattle, and New York, especially during the winter months when the high-altitude west-to-east jet stream winds were at their strongest, adding five- to ten-percent to the bomber's range.[42]

In addition to these land-based facilities, the Soviets had a well-established ability to conduct operations from ice floes as a result of their experience in Arctic aviation during the 1930s. 'North Pole-6' (NP-6), for example, served as a staging base for Tu-4s as it slowly drifted among pack ice in Arctic waters.[43] Hardly the stuff of Hollywood action movies, the Soviets built entire bases on 'ice islands.' A SAC RB-36 crewmember recalls overflying one such facility: *As we approached the airfield we again descended to 1,500 feet. We could see the airfield. It had large, permanent looking buildings, even hangars and a tower. Our cameras were turned on as we flew directly down the runway. The only thing we saw moving was a jeep-like vehicle racing down the runway.*[44]

One CIA assessment warned that Soviet Tu-4s could be painted with bogus US markings and fly unmolested through North American airspace. Tu-4s carrying atomic bombs might even have the audacity to land in Alaska or Canada, refuel using spurious orders, and then take off to strike targets farther to the south,

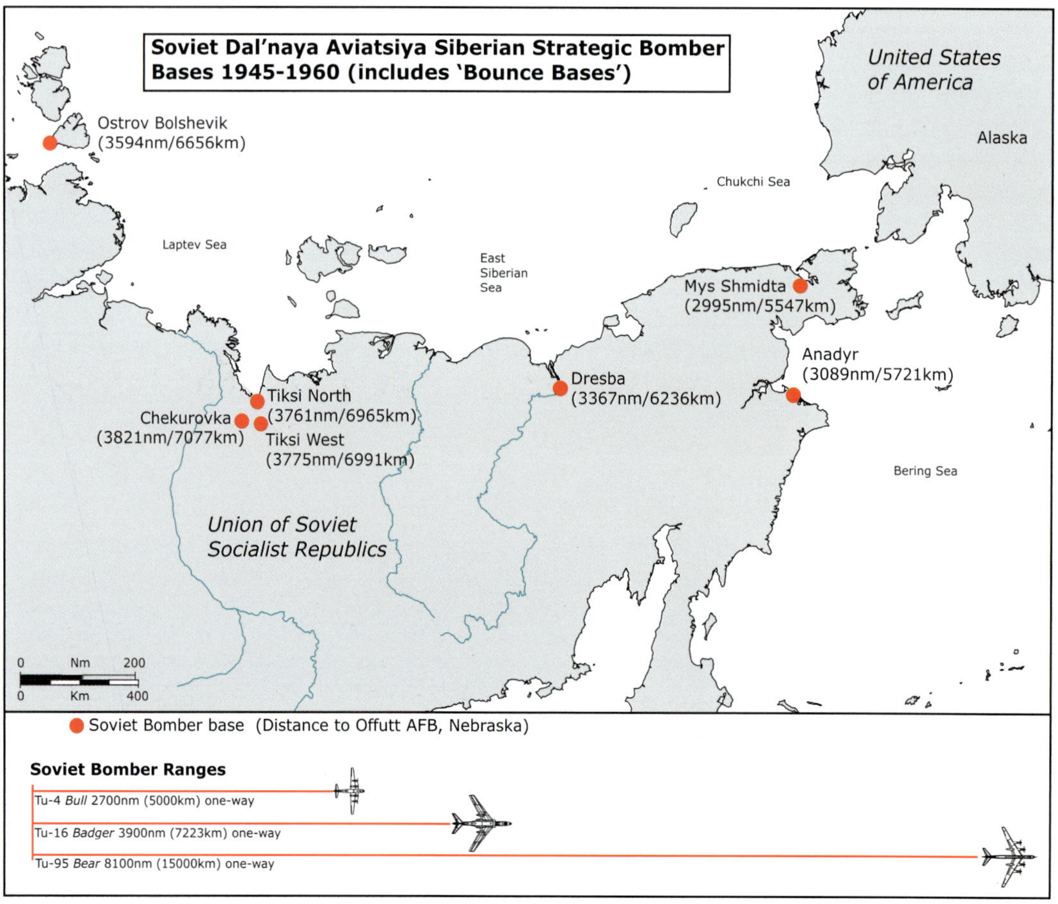

Erroneous claims that the US was behind the USSR in bomber production – the Bomber Gap – should not mask legitimate US concerns about Soviet bomber capability. By 1950 Tu-4 *Bulls* could reach SAC bases such as Rapid City AFB and Larson AFB. At the 1956 height of the Bomber Gap controversy Tu-16 *Badgers* and Tu-95 *Bears* could reach all SAC bases and major US cities.

The post-war maturity of aerial refueling meant that range limitations to the Tu-4 *Bull* were effectively eliminated. Soviet air refueling development stagnated, however, but American assessments of Soviet capability did not. Indeed, US planners incorrectly considered the USSR would have a fully robust air refueling capability by 1954, exaggerating the realities of the Soviet bomber threat. *via Yefim Gordon*

although such a scenario was highly improbable. It was *possible*, though, and for some analysts that was enough to treat it seriously. One need only remember even the limited effectiveness of Nazi troops masquerading as Americans during the 1944 Battle of the Bulge to appreciate how disastrous this might be.[45]

Just as the Americans were developing an active air-to-air refueling capability, so too were the Soviets. Secretary of the Air Force Stuart Symington warned that with in-flight refueling Soviet bombers had 'the capacity to deliver the [atomic] bomb against [the United States] without resorting to suicide missions. Soviet use of aerial refueling 'would increase the combat radius of the Tu-4 by 40 percent if one refueling was employed, and by 75 percent if two refueling operations were conducted.' Even without aerial refueling Soviet bombers could still reach targets in the United States – and certainly those in Western Europe and Japan – making the bombers a genuine threat. Ultimately only a few Tu-4s were configured for wingtip-to-wingtip refueling, and there was little evidence of an operational Russian aerial refueling capability during the late 1940s, although this began to change with other Russian airplanes in the 1950s. Unaware of this limited Soviet implementation, US planners nonetheless assumed that air refueling would become a key ingredient in Soviet offensive plans not in 1950 but in 1954 or 1956.[46] Again, it was not the Soviet bomber force of 1950 that posed the threat but the one Americans feared would be ready in the mid-1950s.

Through the mid- to late-1940s not all USAF B-29s had the SILVERPLATE modification that enabled them to carry atomic weapons. The B-29s Truman sent to England in 1948 as a show of force during the Berlin crisis were non-SILVERPLATE airplanes incapable of carrying atomic bombs. Not that Truman intended to use them, but his message about their potential was unequivocal. Early US war plans called for a single atomic-bomb-armed B-29 to fly to its target escorted by three to six conventionally armed B-29s. SAC may have had the airplanes, but they didn't necessarily have the bombs to fill them. The Soviet Air Force was little different.

The Soviet equivalent to the USAF SILVERPLATE B-29 was the Tu-4A. It entered operational service in 1951 at Balbasovo AB in the Belorussian SSR, which was among the targets overflown by Hervey Stockman in July 1956 and would have been targeted against European cities such as London, Paris, and Berlin. Known as the fictitious 'Training Unit Number 8', it began with seven airplanes, and this number eventually grew to 22. By 1953 the unit had participated in the test drops of atomic bombs at the Semipalatinsk facility in Kazakhstan, as well as performed air-sampling flights following Soviet atmospheric tests akin to the US LRDP missions. Two additional front-line Tu-4A units were established in 1954. On 14 September 1954, as part of Operation SNOWBALL, one of these Tu-4As dropped a 40kt atomic bomb near Totskoye in Russia. Minutes after the detonation Soviet MiG-17s and IL-28s conducted simulated attacks on the same target, and three hours later some 45,000 unprotected troops and vehicles 'seized' the target, exposing them to atomic radiation (an exercise similar to US Operation DESERT ROCK).[47] Although there were only fewer than two dozen atomic-capable Tu-4As in service, if they were mixed among the hundreds of Tu-4s carrying conventional weapons

A Tu-4A during take off roll for Operation SNOWBALL, a 1954 live drop of an atomic bomb followed by ground and air forces entering the blast zone to conduct conventional exercises. To American analysts, this was clear evidence that Soviet planners intended to *fight* a nuclear war begun with strategic bombers, rather than *deter* an attack on the USSR. *via Yefim Gordon*

then US air defense forces would be compelled to destroy all the *Bulls* to ensure that no nuclear-equipped bombers reached their targets. Both the United States and the Soviet Union could play the same effective shell game.

The 1956 introduction of the Tu-95 *Bear* made the range issue even more critical. Whereas Tu-4s were limited to some 3,000nm, Tu-95s could fly 8,000nm without refueling and all were configured to carry atomic bombs. As such, the *Bear* could reach any target in the United States without the need to resort to one-way 'suicide missions' required for the Tu-4. In order to reach America from bases in Siberia, Tu-4s would have to fly their maximum range, drop their weapons, and either crash land in the United States or attempt to fly to Mexico and land there. Military planners considered this not only a realistic possibility but correctly deduced that it was indeed the Soviet intention, although not necessarily with the safe haven 'south of the border.' As Soviet General Secretary Nikita Khrushchev admonished one bomber designer, 'What do you think Mexico is – our mother-in-law? You think we can simply go calling any time we want?' Civilian analysts as well as many pundits and researchers discounted this suicidal view. They argued that it was irrational for Soviet planners to lose their bombers and crews. They also asserted that American bomber crews were not asked to attack the USSR without the expectation of safe recovery after striking their targets, so neither would the Soviets ask this of their own bomber crews in a general war plan based on Kamikaze attacks.[48] Therefore, they concluded, the military's perceived threat of Soviet bombers was highly exaggerated. In this case, the civilians were wrong.

Americans grossly underestimated the psychology of the huge Russian loss of life during the Great Patriotic War. Nearly 8.7 million Soviet combatants were killed or missing and some 15 million civilians perished. Ruthless commanders like Georgii Zhukov and Vasilii Chuikov sent hundreds of thousands of troops to their death in stop-gap measures with little hope of success. Stalin's 28 July 1942 General Order No.227 'Not a step back!' resulted in tens of thousands of troops shot by Soviet NKVD 'blocking detachments' or executed for cowardice. *Shtraf* penal battalions were comprised of Stavka-specified quotas of 'undesirables' or troublemakers and sent into battle unarmed or made to walk through mine fields in advance of regular Soviet troops.[49] Given these extraordinary and callous losses it is not unreasonable to assume that the Soviets would send a few thousand aviators on one-way bombing missions, a view privately shared among American planners about their own forces.

Whereas the Tu-4 could just reach targets in the US, the Tu-95 *Bear* could do so without trusting to a tail wind and luck. The Tu-95 had the unsurpassed range and weapon capacity of the B-36 and the technology of the newer B-52, making it a potent threat as a strategic bomber. Dismissed as anachronistic for its turboprop engines, one need only recall that both the Tu-95 and B-52 remain in front-line service over 50 years after their introduction. *via Yefim Gordon*

Even with the increasing American use of aerial refueling it was not until the late 1950s and early 1960s that SAC bombers had the capacity to strike their targets and then proceed to recovery destinations outside of the USSR. Prior to this, SAC crews were trained to crash land in or bail out over the Soviet Union, evade detection or capture by a hostile population whom they had just bombed, and make their way on foot hundreds of miles through irradiated territory in sweltering heat or freezing blizzards to predetermined recovery points. Once there, crews were expected to survive with no resources and sit out the duration of global nuclear war and await further orders or rescue as part of the JACK POT Recovery Plan.[50] The confidence of SAC bomber crews in 'reaching their target areas [was] more than offset by pessimism over the chances of returning from such missions, even in the B-36.' The one-way loss rate of SAC bombers was expected to be so great that SAC planners considered it 'unlikely that enough [bombers] would return so that [the United States] could count on continuing raids on the three-month schedule thought necessary and feasible.'[51] One pilot who flew B-47s and B-52s assigned to targets in the Soviet Union related that the consensus among crewmembers was that there would be nothing to come home to after a Soviet first strike on the United States, there would be no chance of surviving within the 'smoking radiating ruin' of the Soviet Union, and little purpose in creating a new life in remote regions of Afghanistan or Iran where they were expected to land on dirt airstrips and await fuel, new weapons, and orders from SAC for additional strikes. Instead many crewmembers indicated they would opt for the 'Valhalla option' where they would intentionally crash into their final target and be incinerated by the atomic blast. Knowing that US bomber crews would have been sent on one-way missions, it is not unreasonable to assume that Soviet bomber crews would have been expected to fly similar missions, lending greater credibility to the early threat of Soviet long-range bombers.

Clearly, the long-term requirement to monitor Soviet bomber bases was both a legitimate security concern and a viable early warning indicator. According to SNIE 11-8-54, last-minute strategic early warning of a Soviet surprise attack without routine Soviet preparations, the worst-case Pearl Harbor scenario, would come primarily from one source. The 'critical indicators would be those relating to increased levels of activity at staging bases in the Chukotskii, Kamchatka, and Kola areas.' Indeed, the report continued, 'warning of air attack would depend almost entirely on indicators received during the staging of aircraft through [forward] bases,' in eastern Siberia. In a 1952 address to the Air War College, LeMay said: *The fact that the Soviets do possess a fleet of atomic bombers (some twenty wings of Tu-4s) creates a demand for Intelligence information of a magnitude and quantity which we have not possessed heretofore. … this air fleet is only a few hours away from this country and it is far more important that we have accurate and timely information about its equipment. We have no alternative but to develop the means to get day-to-day information regarding this long-range force.*[52]

By 1950 US estimates of the Soviet Tu-4 fleet reached 20 wings – some 300 airplanes. This was a reasonable number and raised genuine concern among SAC planners. Although there were insufficient nuclear weapons in the Soviet arsenal for all of these airplanes to carry an atom bomb, US and Canadian defenses would have to shoot down every airplane to make sure that one armed with a nuclear weapon did not get through to its target. As such, accurate and regular intelligence about the Tu-4 fleet became a top SAC priority. *via Yefim Gordon*

Strategic aerial reconnaissance efforts to detect and monitor Soviet bomber bases in Siberia and the Kola Peninsula began during late 1946. RB-29 peripheral PHOTINT missions included Project POLARIS, which searched for undiscovered islands in the Arctic Ocean that could be used as forward bomber bases. Project 5 was a general search for any clandestine Soviet activity of any type in the Arctic region. Project 23 utilized PHOTINT and ELINT gathered during overflight missions to locate Soviet bomber bases. By 1947 the 46th RS undertook ELINT collection in the Arctic and Bering Sea regions searching for electronic indications of bomber bases and their defenses. Other flights from Yokota AB, Ladd Field, and Shemya AFB monitored bomber operations along the Soviet coastline from Wrangel Island to the southern tip of Kamchatka as part of Project RICKRACK.[53]

The US Air Force's Alaskan Command recognized the value of strategic aerial reconnaissance in determining the number and status of Soviet bomber bases in Siberia: *[B]uilding up supplies, enlarging bases and improving facilities must precede the realization of a state of readiness for attack. This command believes that continuous surveillance of Northeast Siberia...will yield sufficient indication of Soviet buildup to...make necessary plans and dispositions and to achieve a maximum state of combat readiness prior to a Soviet attack.*[54]

A 23 November 1951 ADC request identified the need for reconnaissance of 'Soviet territory north of 64° Latitude, all Soviet territory east of 150° E longitude and for the Soviet Polar Islands.' A 26 August 1952 message articulated an 'urgent need' for 'aerial reconnaissance photography to confirm reports of airfield construction activity...in the Kuril island Group.' The region had been photographed previously by the 91st SRS on 6 April 1952, but that photo revealed little of interest to the intelligence analysts seeking a more current assessment. Approval for this follow-up overflight photography came on 13 November 1952.[55]

Throughout the late 1950s efforts to monitor Soviet bomber bases continued. Peripheral flights included those conducted by SAC's CONGO MAIDEN U-2s from Eielson AFB flying along the Kamchatka Peninsula beginning in 1959 and recurring in 1960. Early warning indicators began to change during this time as well. In addition to Soviet bombers, American analysts were increasingly worried about Soviet ICBMs. Efforts to detect preparations for launch against American or allied targets were perhaps even more critical than those used to determine bomber readiness. Once an ICBM was launched there were some 30 minutes before it reached its target. During that time the president and his advisors had to determine if the United States should launch a retaliatory attack against the Soviet Union. This created the need for an early warning mechanism capable of providing real-time information. U-2 designer Clarence 'Kelly' Johnson proposed a fleet of modified U-2s capable of detecting ICBM launches given their launch and boost-phase heat signatures. These U-2s would orbit outside the periphery of the Soviet Union to provide tactical early warning. The proposal, known as LOW CARD, was deemed too expensive and required more infrastructure that the US government was willing to support.[56] The Air Force did, however, undertake additional efforts beyond Johnson's suggestion. During 1957 the Air Force Cambridge Research Laboratory (AFCRL) started Project SKYSCRAPER, a pair of Boeing JKC-135A airborne platforms designed to collect multi-spectrum optical signatures of ballistic missiles during the re-entry phase. By 1959 this had expanded to include the RAdiation Monitoring Program (RAMP), which focused on the launch phase. Like Johnson's LOW CARD proposal, these airplanes would fly outside the USSR and detect ICBM launches. Predating President Ronald Reagan's Strategic Defense Initiative (SDI) effort by some 30 years, these airplanes would then use an unspecified on-board laser-type weapon to shoot down the ICBM during the boost phase.[57]

Long-range reconnaissance flights also determined the extent to which Soviet weather stations might be used in strikes against the United States. These remote stations on ice islands could provide wind and other meteorological data essential to strategic bombers en route to the United States. Aerial photography would show how many stations there were, their locations, and, in conjunction with COMINT, identify specific sites. Not only could this information be used to warn of an impending Soviet attack (by virtue of an increase the frequency of weather reports), it could be exploited for use by American bombers headed in the opposite direction.[58]

The use of strategic aerial reconnaissance in long-range strategic early warning was so important that efforts to use aerial reconnaissance in others areas was often circumscribed or prohibited altogether. Air Force Intelligence rejected a 1952 Army request for aerial reconnaissance around or over Romania and Bulgaria. Major General John A Sanford, the USAF Director of Intelligence, argued that: *A require-*

ment exists now for reconnaissance operations in certain selected areas of the USSR for the purpose of determining Soviet readiness to take direct military action. This requirement is of the highest priority. Any prior action [that is, the Army's request]...would seriously tend to compromise or render unlikely the success of operations designed to fulfill these much more critical needs.[59]

The results of these early peripheral flights were not surprising. RB-29s gathered 'oblique photography of fair scale and quality...of the Delena Lavrentiya, Mys Chaplin, and Provideniya areas,' providing 'fairly conclusive evidence that there was very little activity...and no visible bases at these particular sites, from which long-range bombing attacks [against the United States] could be launched.'[60] Despite this reassuring evidence, fears of a Soviet surprise attack from long-range bomber bases in Siberia did not abate. US analysts concluded that the photographs which revealed so little activity could 'in no way discount the possibilities of an air attack from the general area of the Chukotskii Peninsula, since there might well be elaborate inland bases on which no information is available or of which no photographic coverage exists.'[61]

This fear meant that peripheral reconnaissance alone was inadequate to satisfy the need for monitoring strategic early warning indicators. To be absolutely certain that all potential Soviet bomber bases were detected and monitored, it was necessary to photograph regions in the USSR beyond the 40-50nm range of cameras carried by peripheral PHOTINT flights. This requirement dictated the use of overflight missions to reveal Soviet preparations for an attack, which would include 'improving airfields, maintenance and fuel storage facilities in the Chukotskii, Kamchatka, and Kola areas, [and] bringing personnel and equipment to full strength in long-range air units.' A 1950 Air Force memorandum noted that: *Critical areas, in so far as Soviet capability for delivering atomic bombs on targets within the United States is concerned, are the Chukotskii Peninsula area and the Murmansk area...but positive intelligence on both areas is lacking. Both of these areas could probably be penetrated by aerial reconnaissance without detection.*[62]

The first well-documented intentional overflight of Siberia took place in 1952, looking for bomber bases. The overflight was not only detected but pursued by Soviet MiG-15s in an effort to shoot it down. That same year joint USN and USAF overflights of Siberia took place.[63] Austin's 1954 mission, the 1956 HOME RUN sorties, and most of the CIA U-2 overflights looked for and monitored Soviet bomber bases. These overflights were highly dangerous, but US officials believed that the low risk of an international incident or even armed conflict with the USSR was acceptable in view of the alternative – a nuclear Pearl Harbor.

Aerial reconnaissance, both peripheral and overflight, also monitored strategic early warning indicators other than bomber and ICBM bases. SAC RB-29s and RB-50s operated from England and flew around Norway to the Kola Peninsula and Murmansk. They were also based at Dhahran, Saudi Arabia, where they flew missions into the Black Sea area and near Soviet Armenia. During 1948 RB-29s undertook

Concerns about Soviet bomber bases in the Chukotskii region of Siberia prompted SAC's first overflights of the USSR. Beyond the sheer number of Tu-4s, what did the images reveal about their operational readiness? How much fuel was available (affecting range)? Were there weapons storage facilities (especially for atomic bombs)? Were the airplanes in disrepair (or undergoing routine maintenance)? Was the runway in regular use and cleared of snow (or was this a 'dummy' base)? *via Yefim Gordon*

reconnaissance missions from England over the Baltic Sea and along the border separating East and West Germany as part of Project BIOGRAPH.[64] Navy P4M-1Qs and PB4Y-2s flew in the same regions while flying from Port Lyautey, Morocco, and deployment bases in Turkey and Germany.

These flights adjacent to or over the Soviet Union and its allies provided PHOTINT that would show, for example, increased civil defense activities, 'large-scale troop movements in East Germany,' and 'the movement of large numbers of locomotives and rolling stock from East Germany to the Soviet border in order to prepare for resupply and reinforcement operations to support and expand the offensive.' COMINT derived from these flights would indicate the 'evacuation of key personnel or even considerable segments of population from potential target areas, [and other] measures to increase Soviet ability to recuperate from nuclear blows.' Peripheral PHOTINT missions would indicate the replenishment in port and dispersal of Soviet submarine fleets, information that 'would support up to two weeks warning of Soviet preparation for attack against the US and key overseas installations.' From peripheral COMINT missions, analysts could identify Soviet 'diplomatic approaches to some states designed to influence them toward abandonment of their alliances with the US,' and 'instructions to Communist parties to ready themselves for their sabotage and subversion missions in the event of war.'[65]

One should not overlook the value of these flights in reassuring American officials. By detecting nothing, reconnaissance flights could assuage officials that even if there was a long-term possibility of confrontation with the Soviet Union, there were no indications that the conflict was imminent. As long as strategic early warning could successfully detect preparations for war as far as a year in advance, American leaders could be comfortable knowing that the absence of any indications offered a sense of breathing room, and the need to build American defenses was not so urgent. It afforded time to pursue peaceful strategies designed to prevent any future conflict. It also enabled the United States to take diplomatic, political, or military risks which it might otherwise be reluctant to undertake. Strategic reconnaissance flights often came home with nothing of interest, which may have been enough evidence to convince some analysts and policy makers that the 'threat' was neither as severe nor as imminent, nor perhaps even as 'real' as some believed. This could have led to a more tempered intelligence analysis, which could have – but did not necessarily – prevented the unnecessary escalation of the Cold War.[66] American perceptions and *a priori* assumptions of Soviet intentions often colored these conclusions. This was particularly true in assessing the potential use of Soviet atomic weapons.

A 1949 CIA report to the National Security Council warned that 'Russian intent and plans to engage in aggressive warfare will be influenced by the progress she can make in her atomic energy program.'[67] Air Force Secretary Symington told Secretary of Defense Louis Johnson after the first Soviet atomic test in 1949 that he feared 'an immediate atomic attack upon the United States,' and that 'the survival of the United States may be involved.' Truman disagreed with Symington's histrionics. In remarks prepared for a press conference on the Soviet atomic test, Truman exuded calm. Should he be asked if he viewed the Soviet atomic blast with alarm, Truman's written answer said 'No, not with alarm.... We do not think that Soviet possession of this weapon necessarily makes war more probable.'[68] Nonetheless, accurate estimates of Soviet atomic weapon production were 'key elements in estimating Soviet capabilities for delivering a decisive attack against the West.'[69] On 22 May 1950 the JIC approved the 'Critical Intelligence Objectives of the Department of Defense with Respect to the USSR.' The number one priority was determining 'Soviet capabilities for delivering atomic bombs to targets within the United States.' Fourth on the list of priorities was the determination of 'Soviet production and stockpiling capabilities, including location of facilities and installations [of] Atomic and related weapons.'[70]

Strategic aerial reconnaissance was already the primary means of monitoring Soviet delivery capability, and offered the same utility for detection of Soviet atomic weapons. Indeed, the Soviets themselves considered these US flights to be the 'best collecting sources..., allowing for successful tracking of many aspects of Soviet nuclear programs.'[71] Aerial reconnaissance could do this in two ways. Direct detection involved photographing Soviet atomic production and test facilities, observing atomic tests at Novaya Zemlya, and gathering SIGINT and COMINT related to atomic tests. Indirect detection gathered atmospheric evidence of Soviet atomic blasts or confirmed evidence collected by other sources.

Direct detection was primarily PHOTINT. For example, intelligence analysts predicted that one indicator of Soviet weapons production was a substantial increase in electrical production plants. A 1947 estimate showed that the six hydroelectric plants in the Lake Baikal area produced approximately 9 million kilowatts (kW) of electricity, compared with America's Tennessee Valley Authority which produced only 3 million kW. Three hydro-electric facilities in the Uzbek-Kazakh region produced some 6 million kW, compared with the Grand Coulee Dam's 2.7 million kW. The report concluded that these 'abnormal' power requirements in such low-population areas were 'startling evidence' of Soviet atomic weapons programs. Although these power supplies could support heavy industry or rural electrification as well as atomic production, the Uzbek-Kazakh facilities had no industry or rural regions to support and the report deemed them exclusively for the 'production of fissionable material.' Reconnaissance planes photographed these dams and hydroelectric plants, as well as the production facilities themselves, verifying their role in developing and manufacturing atomic weapons.[72] Over the next 15 years, reconnaissance planes overflew known and suspected Soviet atomic weapons plants and test areas, as well as flew downwind collection missions. So sensitive was this US atomic detection effort that the 31 December 1950 *New York Times* newspaper column 'How Red A-Blast Was Detected' written by Joseph and Stewart Alsop prompted an FBI investigation.[73]

The addition in the early 1950s of air-refuelable, jet-powered RB-47s meant that SAC reconnaissance coverage extended to previously inaccessible regions of the Soviet coastline such as the Soviet atomic test area at Novaya Zemlya. Beginning in 1956 CIA U-2 deep-penetration flights photographed other sites such as the nuclear production facility at Alma Ata.[74] On 22 August 1957, for example, a CIA U-2 flown by James Cherbonneaux overflew the Soviet nuclear test facility at Semipalatinsk in Soviet Kazakhstan. In recalling the experience Cherbonneaux's story has become part of U-2 lore: *I looked through my drift sight and saw a startling sight ...*Could it really be? *We had no idea that this test site even existed. I...focused on a large tower...[that] held a large object at the top, and there were signs of activity around a huge blockhouse about two miles away. And then a paralyzing thought slammed me: what if those bastards were getting set to let that nuclear weapon blow just as I was directly overhead?*[75]

Cherbonneaux photographed the site and continued on safely, both embarrassed by his transient fear and certain he would be 'received as a hero for having uncovered a Soviet nuclear test site with a bomb in the tower.' Instead, CIA officials in Pakistan sternly criticized Cherbonneaux for questionable credibility and judgment. 'There is no atomic test facility in that part of central Russia,' he was told. The next day his observations were vindicated with an official apology. A local CIA official told Cherbonneaux that collateral 'intelligence sources just reported that a nuclear bomb was detonated from that tower less than two hours after you overflew it.' In fact, the 520 kiloton detonation was not placed on the tower that Cherbonneaux observed but was dropped later that day from a Russian bomber visible in the film collected by Cherbonneaux. There was a weapon on the tower nonetheless, which was finally detonated in a test on 13 September 1957. The local CIA briefers who castigated Cherbonneaux were not 'in the know' about Semipalatinsk and its role in nuclear testing.[76]

Although direct detection and monitoring of the Soviet atomic weapons programs was perhaps the most desirable evidence of Soviet progress, the most accessible information came

Footage taken by Jim Cherbonneaux as he overflew the Soviet nuclear test facility at Semipalatinsk on 22 August 1957 during U-2 Mission #4050. The shot tower holding an atomic device which Cherbonneaux feared would detonate casts a long shadow. Study of the test facility contributed to a better overall analysis of each blast. By combining atmospheric residue, seismic and other physical data, US scientists could calculate more precisely the yield of a blast and its components, key indicators of the maturity of the Soviet nuclear effort. *CIA via Chris Pocock*

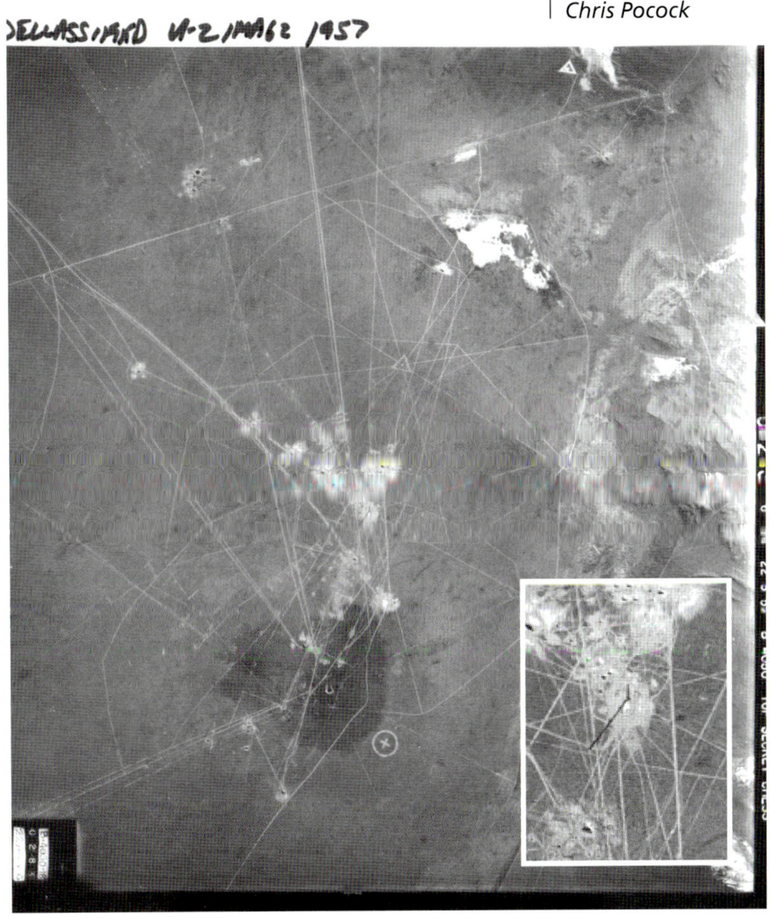

Indirect detection of nuclear blasts was the most common method of assessing foreign nuclear maturity. Sampling aircraft such as 58th WRS WB-50D 48-115, seen here at Ladd Field in 1957, flew regular Pacific routes to collect any post-detonation particulate matter using the E-1 sampler atop the fuselage and with the wingtip pods. Parachute on display board is for a dropsonde, which served the 'Weather' mission. *Dave Menard via Geoff Hayes*

from indirect detection and monitoring by long-range aerial weather reconnaissance. This proved extremely effective and demonstrated '[o]utstanding success in collecting good early [atomic] debris samples.' Aerial collection has since become an essential ingredient in nuclear test ban agreements.[77] These efforts date at least to September 1947, when Secretary of War Kenneth C Royal announced that overall responsibility for the Long Range Detection Program (LRDP) would be assigned to the Army Air Force. Secretary of the Navy James V Forrestal concurred in this recommendation, and on 16 September 1947 the US Army chief of staff officially charged the newly constituted 'US Air Force with responsibility for detecting atomic bomb explosions.' The CONSTANT PHOENIX aerial detection program was born. By July 1948 USAF Air Weather Service (AWS) airplanes were in operation with special filters to collect radioactive materials from the atmosphere.[78] The first Soviet atomic test – Operation 'First Lightning' – on 29 August 1949 was detected five days later by a WB-29 from the 375th Weather Squadron (WS) flying over the Northern Pacific Ocean. Aerial reconnaissance worked in close co-ordination with ground-based detection and monitoring facilities to identify and monitor other Soviet tests. For example, on 24 September 1951 an Air Force ground station detected an 'acoustic signal of unusual intensity' near the Soviet test facility at Semipalatinsk. To corroborate the conclusion that the Soviets detonated an atomic device, long-range weather reconnaissance flights were increased over the next few days. On 28 September these flights collected 'large amounts of radioactivity.' Analysis of the collected particles revealed that they 'could only have come from a high order atomic explosion.' From this US analysts concluded that there 'was indeed a bona fide atomic explosion' within the USSR. In fact this was the second Soviet nuclear test, 'Joe 2'. Specially configured SEA FISH B-36s flying from bases in Guam and Washington state collected evidence of the 22 November 1955 Soviet detonation.[79] Eventually B-52s would replace the SEA FISH B-36 samplers, and WB-50s, WB-47s, and later WC-135s would replace the WB-29s in these near-daily flights, along with SAC's HASP U-2 missions.

Should deterrence fail and America be forced into a nuclear war with the Soviet Union, there was still the crucial problem of where SAC bombers should attack and how they could penetrate Soviet defenses along the way. US officials and military planners knew of few industrial and military facilities other than those in major cities. Given the limited (but steadily increasing) number of atomic bombs in the American arsenal, planners had to decide which targets should be struck with nuclear weapons and which could be destroyed with conventional high explosive or incendiary bombs. From the very onset of the Cold War, the demand for detailed knowledge about Soviet targets served as a powerful impetus for the collection of intelligence, particularly by airplane, about the USSR. The need for target intelligence was among LeMay's highest priorities: *Obtaining information on all types of targets represents a major item of concern in the field of intelligence, and I believe the Air Force should press for a large-scale intelligence project which would insure we obtain the current information necessary to destroy the enemy's long-range atomic forces. I believe that you will agree that this is important enough to warrant the formation of a project equal in nature and scope to the Manhattan Project.*[80]

Military leaders throughout recorded history have relied upon intelligence gathering to identify and plan attacks on enemy targets. With a relatively small effort commanders could plan assaults that paid huge dividends. In 1948 Major General Earle Partridge recalled a story 'that a small boy with a $1.00 Brownie camera could produce in peacetime photographs which could cost millions of dollars or hundreds of lives during combat.'[81] Airpower in particular depended increasingly upon accurate intelligence as aircraft had to fly great distances, often in bad weather or at night, to reach their targets.

At the end of the Second World War US military planners were unable to compile a list of targets in the Soviet Union. American data on potential Soviet targets came from an exhaustive search of the holdings of the Library of Congress as part of the TREASURE ISLAND program and from debriefings of displaced persons and former prisoners of war held in the Soviet Union. One in four of these debriefings provided information vital to SAC target planning and operations, as well as identified additional strategic early warning indicators.[82] Project WRINGER interrogated German, Austrian, and Japanese prisoners of war repatriated from the Soviet Union, and correlated these reports for target planning and other purposes. Throughout post-war Europe former Nazi general Reinhard Gehlen's intelligence apparatus also provided information on Soviet defenses and capabilities. Another source was the US Army's Intelligence Interrogation Team in Athens, Greece. Considered 'one of the most valuable sources' of HUMINT, the USAF sought to assign two full-time intelligence specialists to this two-year project 'for the purpose of interrogating deserters from Russia and from Russian dominated areas.' Another source for SAC target data was 'pre-World War II and even Tsarist-era maps, or at best German aerial photos from 1942-43.'[83] Coverage from these sources ranged from adequate to nonexistent. By 1948, for example, the 'industrial areas of Dnepr and Don Basins' had '1941-43 cover[age]… available' while the top priority targets of the 'industrial area of the Urals' had 'no cover[age] at present.'[84]

This absence of accurate target data severely hampered the development of US plans for general war with the Soviet Union. Conversely, Soviet strike aircraft were less vulnerable to a shortage of intelligence about specific US targets because of the open nature of US society.

GIANT FISH sampler pod seen on a B-52H in 1986. Earlier versions were similar. Top view, looking aft, shows two of the five intakes through which particulate matter would flow to reach filters for collection. These were closed until reaching the sampling area to avoid contamination. Bottom view, looking forward, shows the proximity of the sampler openings to an aircraft exhaust vent. B-52Bs proved unsuitable as samplers because of efflux from this vent, which was mitigated in the B-52Fs and B-52Hs that later flew the missions. *Both photos Brian C Rogers*

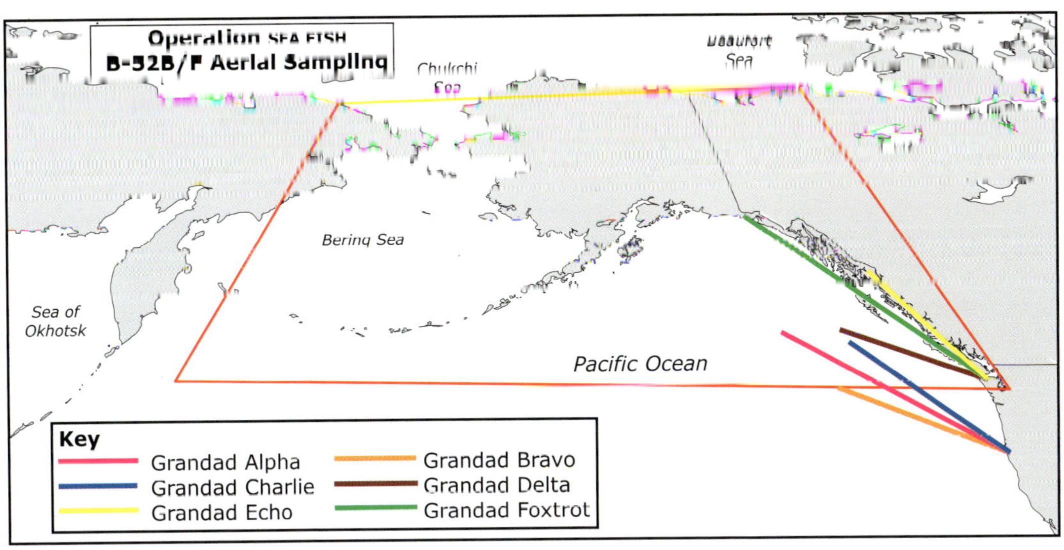

By the late 1950s aerial sampling for atmospheric evidence of Soviet nuclear detonations had become quite complex. SEA FISH B-52s from Castle AFB, for example, flew specific 'Grandad' tracks to different points and altitudes most likely to yield traces of an explosion. The B-52s would then fly westward into the prevailing winds or orbit to maximize collection.

A Phillips 66 road map of Fort Worth, Texas, for example, available from any 'filling station' in the area, would have given Soviet navigators and bombardiers a decided advantage in looking for nearby Carswell AFB over their American counterparts looking for a Tu-4 base 'somewhere in Kazakhstan.' Such maps could be easily acquired by Soviet espionage sources and forwarded to the *Dal'naya Aviatsiya* for mission planning.

Early US war plans were based upon assumptions and guesses using target data sometimes 50 years old. The JCS were aware of these limits in their assessment of the 1946 PINCHER war plan: *The scarcity of reliable and detailed intelligence on the USSR precludes the determination at this time of specific target systems for air attack. Any strategic bombing program established at this time would be provisional even for purposes of current planning; it is certain to be altered radically when additional information becomes available. The current lack of intelligence on the USSR is due not only to the rigid security maintained by that country, but also the fact that such information as is available has not yet been properly assembled.*[85]

A committee chaired by Lieutenant General Hubert R Harmon found in May 1949 that although the planned American atomic offensive against the USSR would reduce Soviet industrial capacity by up to 40 per cent and kill some 2.7 million Soviet citizens, it would not cripple the Soviet economy, and might even harden the Soviet population's will to resist.[86] The Harmon Report identified the lack of adequate target intelligence as a crucial weakness in the US war plan. At the same time, the Weapon System Evaluation Group (WSEG) reached similar conclusions. The WSEG cited shortcomings in intelligence gathering and targeting as significant impediments to the success of the SAC war plan. Of the priority targets assigned in the SHAKEDOWN war plan SAC had no intelligence on 29 per cent.[87]

SAC was keenly aware of its target intelligence problem. General LeMay told the House Foreign Affairs Committee on 23 June 1950 that SAC 'did not have sufficient reconnaissance [aircraft] to find,' let alone attack, 'the [Soviet] atomic bases.' In August 1950 the JCS assigned 'first priority'' to 'the destruction of known targets affecting the Soviet capability to deliver atomic bombs,' the BRAVO (or blunting) mission. LeMay called the BRAVO mission SAC's 'most difficult task,' primarily because of the inadequacy of target data. Other nuclear missions assigned to SAC included the ROMEO (or retardation) mission to slow a potential Soviet advance across Europe, and the DELTA (or disruption/destruction) mission designed to affect Soviet war-making capability. The BRAVO mission was SAC's highest priority, but despite the shortage of target intelligence LeMay claimed that SAC was 'prepared and capable [of] carry[ing] out operations against all three categories of targets simultaneously.' Moreover, SAC's limited knowledge of enemy defenses and the growing danger of jet-powered MiG interceptors meant that bomber crews could only hope to reach their targets under cover of darkness or bad weather. This necessitated aiming at the target by radar, which required detailed radar target maps for pre-strike study. Unfortunately, LeMay said, SAC had 'no radar scope photos of Russian targets.'[88]

LeMay also worried that there were too many targets that required pre-strike photo or radar reconnaissance in order to be targeted effectively, something beyond SAC's existing limited reconnaissance capability. LeMay said that his command had: *enough information in our target folders to put down the first few missions. The reconnaissance [aircraft would then] go out to get additional information that we require to put down attacks on targets where we do not have the information. Then, of course, they will bring back information of new targets we know nothing of now. We knew much more about Japan [during World War Two] than we know about Russia [today]; yet when we got to flying over Japan and taking some pictures, we covered twice as many targets as we knew about. We think the same thing will happen in Russia. And of course, we have machinery for grinding that stuff out into target material to get it to the units so the attack can be brought about.*[89]

This was hardly an efficient, timely means to facilitate follow-on nuclear strikes in a war predicted to be a one-shot affair, which physicist and nuclear pundit Herman Kahn eventually called 'wargasm.'

In a recommendation that predates the 'counter force versus counter value' argument, LeMay recommended that the target set shift to strictly industrial targets which could be struck with less accurate planning. A Soviet bomber base had to be hit precisely with conventional weapons in order to render it inoperative and eliminate it as a future threat. To do so effectively required disabling the runway, a target a mile or more long but only 150 feet wide. A city that encompassed several industrial sites, however, could be set ablaze with incendiary bombs destroying its factories, much like those in Japan during World War Two. Moreover, the scarcity of American atomic weapons in the early years of the Cold War meant that A-bombs had to be targeted judiciously. Wasting one on a target of low priority or on a spurious target was ineffective planning and warfighting. Indeed, the Spaatz Report stressed that most Soviet targets would still be struck with conventional high explosive or incendiary weapons.[90]

The limits of target intelligence affected the early evolution of US strategic doctrine. War plans like PINCHER, which called for attacks on specific Soviet military and industrial targets, were hamstrung by their lack of accurate target intelligence. US planners did not know the precise location of planned targets. This meant that bomber crews would have to waste valuable time in hostile territory searching for their target, time that could easily allow Soviet interceptors to shoot them down. Even more ominously, without the specific latitude and longitude or radar signature of their target, US bomber crews might be compelled to drop their bombs only in the general vicinity – perhaps within tens of miles – of where they thought their target might be. This was hardly an appropriate way to destroy a factory or an air base. To be effective the US bombing campaign required precision, but without accurate target data this was highly unlikely.[91]

This lack of target data compelled the United States to shift its war plan priority from precision to area bombing. Later plans such as BROILER overcame limits in target intelligence by relying upon the broad-area destructive force of atomic weapons rather than the doctrine of precision bombing advocated by airpower theorists before and during World War Two. OFFTACKLE relied on a relatively indiscriminate massive atomic attack against Soviet cities rather than against key targets.[92] Large industrial centers became primary targets less for the 'terror appeal of mass destruction' than for the ease in identifying and striking them with limited advance intelligence. Other targets, in order of descending priority, included command and control centers, population centers, transportation centers, and petroleum production facilities.[93]

LeMay also acknowledged in 1954 that 'the predominance of [SAC] target systems lies in the area where the cloud coverage is over 60 percent of the time,' severely hampering the collection of target intelligence.[94] Weather hindered not only intelligence collection but air strikes themselves. Unpredictable winds could affect the trajectory of a free-fall weapon dropped from high altitude, causing it to miss its target completely. Excessive headwinds could significantly reduce the range of a bomber. Crosswinds could blow it off course to the degree that it might not be able to find and strike its target. Forecasted good weather at a target might change during the 10+ hour flight from SAC bases to the target. Weather intelligence was therefore nearly as important as data on the targets themselves. Major General Partridge warned that either for peacetime recon-

Weather has always affected the outcome of battles, none more so than those involving air power. WB-50Ds such as 49-313 seen here at RAAF East Sale, Australia, flew daily weather missions to improve en route and target forecasts in the event of general war. The E-1 filter pod on the dorsal fuselage also facilitated air sampling, a crucial tool in detecting and analyzing nuclear detonations. *Kurt Finger*

Months before *Sputnik* made Soviet ICBMs a household word, US analysts were studying the facility at Tyuratam. Beyond the actual launch pad, the location of preparation facilities and fuel storage depots gave clear indications about the time required to launch an ICBM, a key early warning factor. This U-2 image, taken by Eugene 'Buster' Edens on 5 August 1957 during Mission #4035, shows Scientific-Research Test Range Number 5, Area 1, Pad 1, from which both *Sputnik* and Yuri Gagarin were launched into space. *CIA/USAF via Geoff Hays*

naissance flights near or over the Soviet Union or during any future war with the USSR, the United States would: *be required to forecast the weather in a locality several thousand miles distant from the nearest [US] observation post and provide consistently accurate results. In the face of the weather bureau's inability to forecast the local weather at Washington, I believe there is a great deal of work to be done in this field alone.*[95]

Clearly US war plans and all-weather attack capabilities were hampered by the lack of accurate target intelligence.

Finding, identifying, and classifying these targets became a serious issue. Long-range reconnaissance flights provided an expedient and reliable source for this crucial intelligence. During February 1948 the Air Force Director of Intelligence, Major General George C McDonald, initiated a program for the 'strategic photographic reconnaissance of the USSR and satellite states.' The program guidelines dictated that the effort accommodate targeting requirements as well as other issues: *It is imperative that suitable aerial photographic cover of all important industrial, power, and transport (including air) facilities which be used by the USSR, be available to the US for use in*

a. The selection and evaluation of strategic target systems and individual targets, and
b. The preparation of strategic target materials for operational units.[96]

This proposal was soon translated into action with Harry Truman's December 1950 approval of RB-47 overflights of Siberia (which actually began in 1952) in search of Soviet bomber bases, targets of the highest priority. This delay in fulfilling a high-priority mission was due to operational exigencies. Truman approved the mission on 2 September 1950, but B-47B 49-2645 caught fire on the ramp at Eielson AFB on 20 September 1951 and burned to destruction. The mission was cancelled. A new request was submitted to Truman who approved it on 12 August 1952 and another B-47B was configured for the mission. That flight took place on 15 October 1952.[97] Other overflights gathered aerial radar scope photography of potential targets. These photographs showed, for example, the layout of the Kremlin or a major naval base. SAC crews studied these photographs to improve their ability to locate the target using radar under any weather conditions and to drop their weapons precisely. CIA U-2 pilot Marty Knutson recalled his July 1956 U-2 over flight of the USSR: *Leningrad was my target as a SAC pilot and I spent two years training with maps and films, and here I was, coming in from the same direction as in the SAC battle plan, looking down on it through my [U-2] sights. Only this time I was lining up for photos, not a bomb drop.*[98]

The photos Knutson studied as a SAC pilot were most likely taken by RB-45 overflights in 1952.

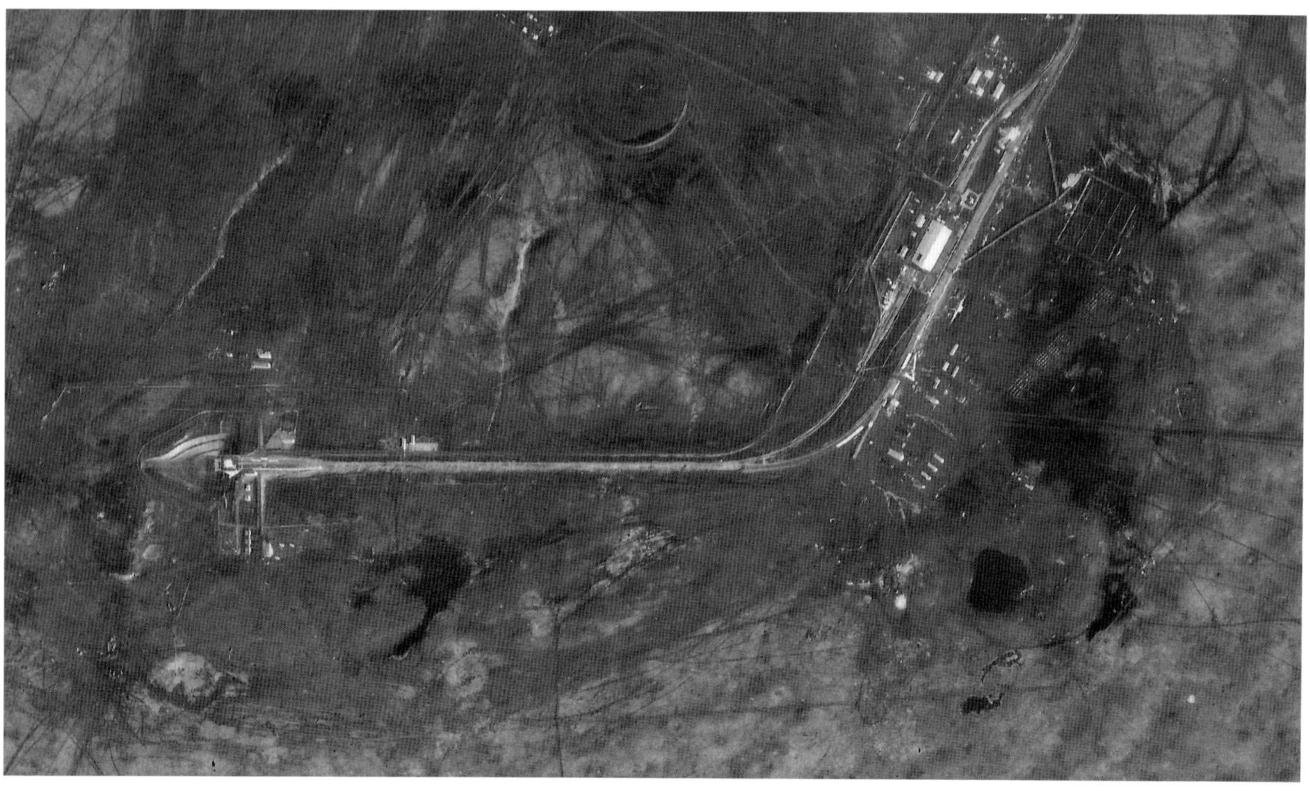

A CIA *ad hoc* committee identified key targets essential to defeating the USSR in war and prepared a list of prioritized targets to be reconnoitered by the U-2 and 'other [aerial] means of collection.' These included Soviet long-range bomber bases, ballistic or guided missile research or test facilities, and nuclear energy or atomic weapons sites.[99] These targets emphasized Soviet military capacity and overlooked industrial, agricultural, and commercial facets that could be used to gauge Soviet intentions to attack as well as the vulnerability of the Soviet economy to atomic attack.

There were limits to aerial reconnaissance in satisfying targeting requirements, however. Potential targets deep within the USSR could only be photographed by overflights, which were highly dangerous, politically sensitive, and extremely difficult to authorize. There simply were not enough overflights during the late 1940s and very early 1950s to satisfy these target intelligence demands. President Truman would not approve the large numbers of flights needed. He did approve some overflights which gathered useful target intelligence, but by and large US planners were denied the high number of aerial reconnaissance missions they desired.

Another limit was the continually changing nature of potential Soviet targets. Efforts to map Soviet bomber bases during the late 1950s decreased. This was in part because most had already been identified and targeted. More importantly, Khrushchev's shift in strategy from bombers to missiles had a significant effect on American target requirements. Despite a decade of aerial intelligence gathering the Eisenhower administration lacked adequate knowledge of the newest Soviet threat, intercontinental ballistic missiles (ICBMs). On 12 February 1959, for example, Secretary of Defense Neil McElroy asked President Eisenhower for additional U-2 overflights of the Soviet Union, stating that the United States knew 'the location of no [ICBM] launching platforms within the USSR.' More U-2 flights would alleviate this shortcoming.'[100] So important was this information that in March 1959 the Air Force Directorate of Targets initiated the Missile Launch Site Target Acquisition Program (MILSAP) to combine U-2 PHOTINT and material gleaned from the National Security Agency (NSA), the Joint Intelligence Bureau in London, and the Air Research Division of the Library of Congress in order to 'identify, locate and evaluate missile...installations which Soviet security and counterintelligence does its best to conceal.' MILSAP would identify key indicators of Soviet ICBM activity such as 'airfields, certain transportation facilities, special weapons facilities and special propellant plants.' Revealing 'clusters of these indicators' would allow 'high priority collection activities [specifically PHOTINT overflights] to be focused on these localities in an effort to confirm or disprove the presence of missile installations.'[101] Given the vast expanses of the Soviet Union, reconnaissance overflights remained the only means by which specific target data – precise location, defenses, and support – for Soviet ICBM sites could be acquired. Merely locating these facilities did not necessarily mean that they would be properly recognized. CIA Deputy Director Charles Cabell took photo analysts to the US rocket launch base at Cape Canaveral, Florida, so they could see first hand what to look for in covert photographs.[102]

The potential threat of Soviet military conquest and domination of Western European industrial sources also received the scrutiny of strategic aerial reconnaissance. Should the USSR control these vital resources, US bombers required accurate target information to attack and destroy them, preventing their use in supporting any future attack against the United States. Operation ROUNDOUT, flown by SAC RB-50s and RB-36s, provided 'photo reconnaissance on all significant targets in the whole of Western Europe this side of the Soviet zone and the production of target materials therefrom.'[103]

Accurate target information also contributed to the ability of military planners to avoid unintended targets. During the Korean War strategic aerial reconnaissance identified hospitals and other sensitive sites in North Korea, enabling planners to devise bombing missions that avoided these, minimizing collateral damage and the resulting propaganda criticisms that could adversely affect the United States in world opinion.[104]

Locating targets with the aid of strategic aerial reconnaissance addressed one of SAC's major problems in executing its wartime mission, but did little to show how to reach those targets safely. If US strike aircraft were to fulfill their mission against the USSR, evading Soviet defensive forces would mean the difference between the success or failure of the American war plan.

The first obstacle for US strike planners was to avoid the growing ring of electronic detection and tracking sites around the USSR. Bombers detected by radar sites were easy prey for defensive fighters controlled by those ground-based radars. Events in Korea reaffirmed this. Jet-powered MiG-15s proved surprisingly effective in disrupting SAC bomber operations, especially during daylight and good weather. US military planners believed, and were correct in assuming, that Communist aerial combat tactics in Korea – the use of early warning radars and ground controlled intercept (GCI) vectoring of jet fighters against USAF heavy bombers – represented the tactics US bombers would encounter en route to targets within the USSR. Moreover, a number of Soviet pilots flew those MiG-15s on behalf of North Korea, and were sure to share their experiences with their PVO colleagues. After a fact-finding visit to Korea, Air Force Chief of Staff General Hoyt S Vandenberg opined that current Communist air defenses meant that 'the US might not be able to fulfill its atom bomb retaliation mission, if and when Russia strikes.'[105]

Finding and avoiding Soviet radar sites and their associated interceptor bases was the first step in building a successful strike mission. As early as 1948 the Air Force advocated 'a suitable electronic reconnaissance program' intended to:

a. *Determine the exact location, density and effectiveness of early warning defensive nets of radar...*
b. *Investigate any other types of radio emissions which might be used as control or motivation of guided missiles or pilotless aircraft.*[106]

This 'electronic reconnaissance should be provided around the perimeter of the USSR and satellite states to a depth of several hundred miles and in the vicinity of strategic industrial and population centers within the critical areas.' These critical areas included 'all of the Russo-European landmass and in the maritime areas of the Far East between Korea and the Bering Strait.'[107] In addition, knowledge of Soviet interceptor and defensive fighter bases was 'nonexistent.' Where these bases were located, their operational status, the number and capabilities of interceptors located there, and the specific radar control sites which coordinated their missions were all completely unknown to SAC planners.[108]

Whether a B-47 on its EWO strike mission or an RB-47 on a peripheral SIGINT sortie, Soviet early warning radars – such as this P-14 *Tall King* – were the initial threat. As such, ELINT reconnaissance missions recorded the radar's operating characteristics, enabling the development of ECM to jam the radar. *Author's Collection*

Strategic aerial reconnaissance offered an ideal solution to these problems. NSCID 10, entitled 'Collection of Foreign Scientific and Technological Data,' specifically identified the need for and the use of long-range strategic reconnaissance flights, among other sources, to satisfy early US ELINT requirements. A 1950 proposal for reconnaissance overflights of the Soviet Union made this link clear: 'To determine Soviet capabilities to interfere with the US strategic air attack, aerial reconnaissance in the Leningrad-Moscow areas would probably provide us with useful information.'[109] Six years later U-2 overflights and peripheral missions were justified by the requirement to detect enemy electronic defenses. U-2s joined SAC RB-50s and RB-47s and USN P2Vs in collecting ELINT that would help identify, locate, and target 'Soviet radar, tracking, and communications along the entire [Russian-European] border.'[110]

PHOTINT-configured airplanes took pictures of enemy interceptor bases, counted the number of fighters present, located enemy anti-aircraft guns or missiles, and mapped geographic features such as mountains or valleys that might create 'blind spots' in enemy radar coverage. ELINT flights often confirmed what PHOTINT flights or other sources suggested, specifically the location of radar sites that could be used to defend the USSR by detecting American bombers. By flying close to Soviet airspace (or even undertaking brief incursions), ELINT flights could provoke a full Soviet defensive response involving interceptors and anti-aircraft defenses. This enabled the ferret to record Soviet defensive operations in a war-like situation, perfect for training and exploitation by SAC bomber crews.[111] COMINT-configured airplanes could record the communications between ground controllers and interceptor pilots, revealing specific defensive tactics that US bombers could later avoid or overcome for safe passage. In addition, the radio frequency used by controllers could be identified for future jamming.

Although these flights eventually provided a fairly accurate map of Soviet defenses and radar coverage, not all analysts were satisfied with the results. Some planners argued that the holes in Soviet defenses were in reality 'gaps in our intelligence – gaps in our electronic reconnaissance coverage – rather than gaps in Soviet electronic defenses.'[112] Even though this was a spurious conclusion, more pragmatic analysts were aware that Soviet radar coverage would eventually encompass the USSR completely. US bombers entering the Soviet Union would by necessity have to penetrate Soviet electronic defenses. This meant that US bombers would have to jam or deceive these radars in order to pass safely.

Aerial operations in Korea showed that the use of radar and electronic countermeasures were essential. Indeed, the Korean War proved to be kind of a combat laboratory for electronic weapons and countermeasures. Initial efforts to acquire and exploit ELINT for ECM purposes were heavily circumscribed. US military planners were deeply concerned that the use of ECM in Korea might tip off the Soviets about US general war plans and tactics and hence were unwilling to use equipment and tactics to their fullest, actually increasing US combat losses in Korea to electronic weapons.[113] LeMay had such a strong commitment to ECM and its security that he considered SAC electronic warfare 'tactics to have a higher classification than the Atomic Energy Commission and the Congress have placed on atomic secrets.'[114]

ELINT allowed US engineers the opportunity to evaluate enemy electronic defenses and devise equipment and tactics that would negate their effectiveness. The 1956 HOME RUN series of overflights contributed directly to expanding the database of the Soviet electronic order of battle. Knowing the operating frequencies of enemy long-range early warning radars meant that the United States could manufacture ECM devices specifically designed to jam or blind these radars. By 1954 ELINT flights showed that Soviet interceptors were carrying air-to-air radar, increasing their ability to detect, track, attack, and destroy penetrating American bombers without their previous absolute dependence on GCI. SAC bombers were consequently equipped with specific ECM gear designed to jam not only ground radars but the radar carried in Soviet interceptors.[115] ELINT also allowed the development of simulators that could mimic Soviet radars and weapons. SAC bomber crews could thus train in realistic situations and react to specific threats just as they would in time of war. All of these efforts were intended to improve bomber penetration capability, and hence strike effectiveness.

ELINT acquired by aerial reconnaissance became even more essential to the US war plan as SAC tactics relied increasingly upon ECM. Not only would ECM derived from strategic aerial reconnaissance allow bombers to penetrate the Soviet ground-based radar defenses, it improved the ability of the bombers to evade detection and attack by Soviet interceptors. SAC bombers in the first Emergency War Plan, for example, would travel to their targets in cells of eleven planes. Six airplanes would carry only electric jamming equipment (such as the Phase V ECM EB-47E) and would lead a single atomic bomber through Soviet defenses. These seven planes would then be followed by three more ECM aircraft and a second atomic bomber. Similar tactics were eventually incorporated into the HALFMOON, FLEETWOOD, and TROJAN war plans.[116] SAC planners considered ECM sorties expendable. They would either jam Soviet defenses or induce the fighters and SAMs to

The three ERB-47Hs, including 53-6245, had a specialized ELINT suite that served as a precursor to the RC-135U COMBAT SENT. In a 6 February 1960 mission two ERB-47Hs flew from Turkey along the Black Sea coast of the USSR at 200 feet until reaching Yalta, then popped up to 22,000 feet. Soviet radars and fighters lit up the ELINT spectrum. The ERB-47Hs collected unique data that SAC bomber crews would see should they go to war. *USAF photo, Author's Collection*

attack them, allowing the bomb-carrying airplane to get through to its target. One electronic warfare officer recalled that his mission was to 'orbit between Moscow and Leningrad [to jam defenses] for as long as they had fuel' or until they were shot down, neither of which was expected to take very long.[117]

Acquisition of this intelligence by aerial platforms was not without its unintended consequences. The inability of Soviet fighters and AAA to intercept and destroy Western reconnaissance aircraft that were believed to have violated the Soviet border prompted Soviet generals to convince Soviet officials 'that the best way to stop the American flights would be to create special ground-to-air anti-aircraft missiles [SAMs].'[118] Ironically, these early flights which sought but found no evidence of powerful Soviet defenses against aerial penetration ultimately compelled the Soviets to develop the very weapon – the SA-2 *Guideline* surface-to-air missile – that would not only destroy Frank Powers's U-2 in 1960 but kill the future development of America's high-altitude bomber – the North American B-70 – in the early 1960s.[119]

American perceptions of the Soviet threat were clearly linked to Russia's prospective ability to deliver atomic bombs *en masse* against US cities and military bases, most likely in a surprise attack. Believing that traditional defense against such an attack was impossible if not absurdly expensive, the United States relied upon intelligence collection to detect the early warning signs that would allow the United States time to prevent a Soviet surprise atomic attack, either by means of diplomacy or by a US pre-emptive attack on Soviet strategic offensive forces. Although US intelligence agencies used a variety of sources and methods to gather this information, strategic aerial reconnaissance became the main source for objective and regular assessments of Soviet bomber and later ICBM preparedness during the first two decades of the Cold War.

The issue of Soviet *preparedness* should not be confused with *production*. Strategic aerial reconnaissance was not conducive to estimates of potential Soviet bomber production, as the so-called 'Bomber Gap' showed. Reconnaissance flights could and did, however, reliably show the level of operational preparedness of Soviet bombers once they were delivered to front-line units where they were monitored as one indicator of future war. In general, strate-

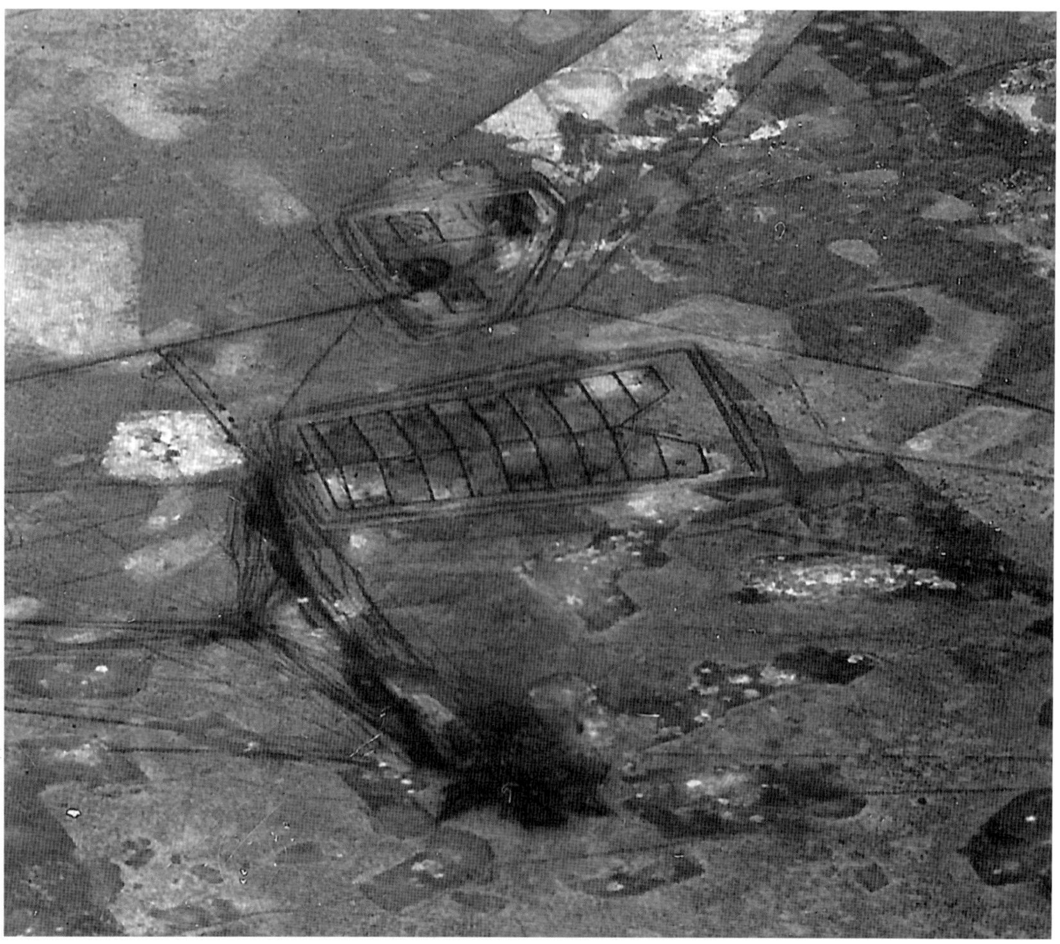

An RAF image of Kapustin Yar – not from the unverified 1953 Canberra ROBIN mission but instead the 6 December 1959 U-2 overflight Mission # 8005 by Robbie Robinson. This is R&D Test Range Number 8, used to evaluate the S-25 *Berkut* (SA-1 *Guild*) SAM, first used in 1954. Deployed exclusively around Moscow, the distinctive pattern of the SA-1 launch site represented a real threat to B-47s targeted against the Soviet leadership in the Kremlin. *CIA/USAF via Geoff Hays*

gic aerial reconnaissance consistently showed that an attack by Soviet bombers was possible but not probable. PHOTINT showed that reports of widespread 'potential' Soviet bomber bases were often highly exaggerated. Some US planners insisted that the bases were there but they simply had not been discovered, a belief fueled by their fear of another Pearl Harbor, this time with atomic weapons. Despite this extreme view, aerial reconnaissance reliably monitored the status of Soviet offensive forces, reducing, if not alleviating, fears of an imminent future attack against the United States. However accurate or prudent the conclusions derived from aerial intelligence, the method of gathering it proved highly effective.

Aerial reconnaissance efforts to monitor the Soviet atomic weapons program paid both short- and long-term dividends. Immediate benefits included the detection of the first and subsequent Soviet atomic blasts. Using aerial samples collected by airplanes like WB-29s and HASP U-2s, scientists could accurately scrutinize the sophistication and operational status of Soviet nuclear weapons. Long-term benefits included the establishment of a reliable means to monitor Soviet atomic weapons tests. By virtue of a decade of experience, aerial detection platforms played an important role during the 1960s in convincing many US officials that Soviet compliance with an atmospheric test ban was verifiable.

In the event of war, US war plans required accurate knowledge of Soviet bases and industrial sites to be attacked and destroyed. In addition, SAC strike planners needed to know about enemy defenses which could preclude SAC bombers from reaching their targets. Strategic aerial reconnaissance attempted to resolve many of these problems by photographing targets, gathering ELINT, and recording enemy defensive reactions to peripheral and penetration reconnaissance flights. Early Cold War offensive plans against the Soviet Union called for precise strategic aerial bombardment of specific Soviet targets such as factories, military facilities, and hydroelectric plants. The most reliable means to redress the acute lack of intelligence about Soviet targets was US military overflights of the USSR to locate and then take optical and radar photographs of potential targets.

Presidents Truman and Eisenhower did not approve deep overflights in any meaningful number prior to 1956 to alleviate this intelligence shortcoming. This lack of target data in turn forced a major reconsideration of US offensive strategic doctrine. Lacking precise means to destroy a specific target, US strike plans shifted to imprecise area bombing with atomic weapons, planning to destroy a target of uncertain location by sheer force of a nuclear explosion that encompassed an entire city. Consequently, US target planners allocated multiple atomic weapons on general areas in an effort to ensure the destruction of a specific target within that area. Moreover, bigger bombs were needed to destroy larger areas, an evolution that contributed to the approval of the hydrogen bomb. By the time of Project HOME RUN and the U-2 overflights, both important sources of precise target data, the decision to build and use larger, more destructive bombs in an indiscriminate rain of nuclear bombing had already been made. The evolution of US Cold War strategic doctrine from precision bombing raids to relatively imprecise area bombing was therefore directly related to the American inability to gather sufficient, exhaustive, and accurate target intelligence, which was itself a function of the reluctance of American leaders to use and exploit strategic aerial reconnaissance to its fullest.[120]

***

Strategic aerial reconnaissance was clearly essential to the identification of areas of interest that would eventually become targets for potential US strikes against the Soviet Union. This new information should have reassured US military planners that they were indeed aware of key threats and could accurately target them for destruction, reducing anxieties that might feed a tolerance for preventive war. But the same 1950s mindset that led some Americans to believe there was a Communist spy in every pumpkin patch led SAC planners to believe that every new discovery in the USSR that derived from aerial reconnaissance was a potential target. For example, CIA U-2 photos and SAC RB-47 pictures might pinpoint a Soviet nuclear weapons storage facility, an appropriate target in the event of war. Those same images would also show railroad tracks leading from the storage facility to train yards in nearby towns, from which the weapons could be transshipped to multiple bomber bases. To ensure that the Soviet nuclear weapons did not reach these sites in wartime, SAC planners assigned weapons to destroy not only the storage facility but also the railroads leading from it, any key bridges the tracks might cross, and the marshaling yard in each town. This meant that SAC targeting demands created an almost exponential growth in weapons requirements. SAC now needed one or two bombs to interdict each rail line, another one for each key bridge, and perhaps two for the rail yard in each town. Where once a single bomb (or perhaps two or three given the arcane math behind target damage calculations) would likely meet SAC's target requirements, SAC planners now asked for as many as five or more bombs. Because each B-47 could carry only one Mark 6 atomic bomb, the increased number of weapons meant a corresponding increase in the number of bombers, tankers, and EW jamming planes – not to mention the peacetime infrastructure required such as bases, training, and fuel – to deliver American bombs on Russian targets. The weapon-to-bomber ratio was an evolving number. Early strategic nuclear weapons were large and heavy, and bombers like the B-29 and B-50 carried only a single atomic bomb. Beginning in 1951 the primary US atomic bomb was the Mark 6, which weighed some 8,000 pounds and was the size of a small car. Its dimensions and weight meant that medium bombers such as the B-50 and B-47 could carry only one weapon. Until the operational debut of the B-52, the B-36 was the only airplane that could carry the massive Mark 17 15-megaton bomb. Significant size and weight reductions in weapon design, greater efficiency in weapon yield, and improved delivery precision led to more bombs per bomber. For the early years of the Cold War, however, it is not unreasonable to think of 'one bomb, one bomber' as a useful approximation of US delivery capability.[121] As such, strategic aerial reconnaissance missions contributed materially not only to assessing the Soviet threat and how to defeat it in the event of war, they had the *unintended* effect of escalating strategic defense budgets and 'overkill'. One might even wonder if these flights were among the seminal causes of a spiraling Cold War arms race – each mission discovered new targets which required more weapons and bombers or ICBMs to deliver them, thereby increasing the size and sophistication of the Western nuclear strike force, compelling a commensurate Soviet buildup.

The extreme secrecy associated with US target strategy has made a clear understanding of the targeting process and its evolution a difficult proposition. Pioneering work by Rosenberg and others nonetheless offers a glimpse into what is arguably the very core of American nuclear war plans and Cold War national security policy: what to attack and with what assets in order to protect and preserve the United States, its key allies, and a favorable global political economy.[122]

Until the first operational deployment of the Navy's Polaris SLBM submarine in November 1960, SAC was the primary delivery means for America's strategic nuclear arsenal. By default this meant that SAC was the primary planning agency for nuclear war targeting and operations. Although SAC was required to submit its war plan to the Joint Chiefs of Staff for review and inter-service integration, in practice this did not always happen. The JCS lacked the analytic capability to assess and validate the SAC plan, and there is evidence that LeMay intentionally withheld the plan out of security concerns.[123] Although the Navy created its own nuclear war plan and was prepared to execute it, SAC officials had little doubt that *their* plan was the *American* plan in case of general war.

In developing its blueprint, SAC utilized intelligence it received from other agencies such as the CIA and the British as well as its own aerial reconnaissance assets, including RB-47 and RB-57 overflights. SAC did not routinely, however, share the results from these flights with others, and, according to former CINCSAC General Bruce K Holloway, SAC's internally acquired aerial intelligence gained a disproportionate level of influence in war planning and operations.[124] The SAC Warning Center operated independently of the NIC to warn the CINCSAC of an impending threat, providing the opportunity to disperse or launch the bomber and tanker force under positive control but *not* execute their SIOP mission. SAC's Intelligence Directorate included five operational divisions: 1) Air Estimates; 2) Targets; 3) Target Materials; 4) Collections; and 5) Trajectory Center. The Air Estimates Division was the primary intelligence source for the SAC Warning Center and provided assessments of enemy capabilities, ELINT analysis, and penetration guidance for SIOP sorties. The Targets Division produced 'target and weapon requirements for command EWO and SIOP documents.' Target Materials provided combat mission folder (CMF) materials for SAC crews, including standardized scale navigation charts and training materials. Collections Division was responsible for acquiring and disseminating SAC's intelligence. ELINT gathered by SAC aircraft underwent automated computer-based analysis with equipment such as the aptly named FINDER (Ferret Intelligence Data Evaluator). The Trajectory Center 'computed target trajectories for the command's missiles and those belonging to our allies.'[125]

Armed with this proprietary intelligence, SAC planning went 'well beyond' JCS 'assigned' targets, resulting in a 1954 war plan, for example, that listed '1,700 DGZs [Designated Ground Zeros – targets] ...includ[ing] 409 airfields.'[126] By 1954 there were perhaps three or four dozen Soviet airfields capable of supporting Tu-4 *Bull* and Tu-16 *Badger* strategic bomber operations, which constituted the primary threat against the United States. Even assuming another 100 airfields equipped with interceptors that might interdict SAC bombers en route to their targets within the USSR (totaling some 150 bases), the targeting of '409 airfields' reveals the unchecked results of SAC's 'target creep'. This in turn compelled the acquisition of additional nuclear weapons. Between 1958 and 1960, thanks to increased target data acquired by U-2s, the US nuclear inventory rose by more than 11,000 weapons.[127] In a 1958 assessment, the war plan was expected to 'destroy Soviet military targets numbering in the thousands.' In the first 15 hours of a nuclear exchange across four continents, some '7 million kilotons (over half of it in the first three hours) would be detonated.' Within 'a half-day,' US nuclear detonations would be '350,000 times as great in magnitude as the nuclear explosion at Hiroshima.' These staggering numbers reveal not only the appalling nature of nuclear war but also the preposterous number of SAC targets and the absurdity of overkill built into target calculations.[128]

The total US target base was further inflated as the US Navy, the US Far East Air Forces, British strike forces, and others enumerated their own targets, many of them duplications of other listings. Through 1960, of the 2,400 DGZs in the war plan some 300 were unknowingly targeted by more than one strike force. Not only was this a wasteful allocation of limited strategic resources, it raised the real and undesired potential for fratricide (such as when an undetonated Navy Regulus missile warhead approaching its target would be destroyed by the blast generated by a free-fall bomb concurrently dropped from a SAC B-47). In the 1960 study there were over '200 time-over-target conflicts' where the US would not only destroy enemy targets, but its own strategic forces as well.[129]

The targeting issue was a central component of fierce JCS strategy debates during 1958 and 1959. The Army and Navy argued that the existing target lists and the 'counterforce versus countervalue' mix were sufficient and appropriate. The Air Force contested this viewpoint, ultimately proposing a new unified US Strategic Command that included not only SAC's bombers and fledgling ICBM force, but the Navy's forthcoming Polaris SLBM submarine force. This bureaucratic infighting led JCS Chairman General Twining to poll the service chiefs to go on record regarding a 'national strategic target system,' the types of targets it might include, which organization would maintain such a list, and the merits of a single integrated nuclear war plan.[130] The parochial issues remained. It fell to Secretary of Defense Gates to recommend to the president that instead of creating a new Strategic Command, all matters related to America's nuclear war plan should be assigned to the only existing organization that had the computing capacity and operational experience necessary to produce a single integrated war plan – Strategic Air Command. Eisenhower, tired of the Navy's insular thinking, agreed with Gates. On 11 August 1960 the president authorized the creation of the Joint Strategic Target Planning Staff (JSTPS) responsible for the development and maintenance of the National Strategic Target List (NSTL) and the production of a Single Integrated Operations Plan (SIOP), America's nuclear war plan.[131] Located at SAC's Offutt AFB, Nebraska, headquarters, the JSTPS produced the first NSTL and SIOP in only three months.

If the JSTPS goal was to resolve issues related to target planning, the organizational inbreeding at Offutt in fact made matters worse. 'SAC's control over targeting doctrine, especially target selection and damage criteria, led to an increase in the number of targets and to multiple strikes on those targets to meet very stringent damage requirements.' The original SIOP had a target database of 4,100 sites, of which JSTPS selected 2,600 to be attacked, leading to 1,050 DGZs. A year later there were 80,000 potential targets and 3,729 were to be attacked. U-2 overflights alone added more than 20,000 potential targets. This growth in DGZs 'artificially boosted weapons requirements.'[132] Although each DGZ was a single target, typically more than one atomic bomb was assigned to each DGZ in order to assure the desired level of target damage or destruction. Rosenberg says that some 3,000 atomic bombs were slated for the 1,050 DGZs in the first SIOP.[133] Delivering those 3,000 bombs required an equal combination of bombers and ICBMs, plus tankers and collateral strike forces. Consequently, the targeting process – identification (driven substantially by strategic aerial reconnaissance), analysis, and assignment of weapons – dictated American defense procurement and strategic policy. Nuclear-warfare scholar and former Minuteman ICBM launch control officer Bruce Blair argues that the targeting process at the heart of SIOP 'defines our procurement needs. It defines our policy toward deterrence and the way we frame the problem of deterrence generally.' This determines how many weapons are needed and therefore drives weapons production and policy.[134] As SAC and CIA reconnaissance flights discovered more targets in the USSR and its allies, more dollars for additional weapons were needed to guarantee their destruction in the event of war. The results of aerial intelligence flights were therefore directly linked to the procurement of new weapons.

Researchers have traditionally focused on the Missile Gap controversy as a case study that examines the direct relationship between intelligence collection and defense budgets.[135] Their consensus is that claims leveled by Senate Democrats such as John Kennedy, Stuart Symington, and Lyndon Johnson that the Eisenhower administration was 'weak' on defense by allowing the Soviets to achieve superiority in ICBMs were more rhetoric than reason. U-2 photographs and TELINT from ground stations and aerial reconnaissance flights reassured the president that his defense policies were prudent and that greater military spending to 'catch up' with the USSR was needless and wasteful. As such, the president could focus on his primary goal of economic prosperity through a balanced budget and no tax increases. Richard Bissell captured the essence of this argument, saying that Eisenhower relied upon U-2 intelligence as he 'repeatedly frustrated the attempts of America's military-industrial complex to gain financing for larger and more expensive weapon systems. An economically strong America, unhobbled by huge budget deficits, was one of Eisenhower's greatest legacies.' James Killian praised the U-2 program for moderating the Air Force's budget, saving 'billions of dollars.' Historian Michael Beschloss echoes this sentiment. 'For years, Eisenhower resisted unnecessary defense spending almost single handedly against immense pressure. This was perhaps the principal achievement of the U-2 program and of his Presidency.' Scholar John Sloan notes that the 'constraint [Eisenhower] exercised over the military budget following *Sputnik* may have been the most remarkable budget achievement in recent US history. No other politician could have done it.'[136] These laudatory assessments credit Dwight Eisenhower with keeping the lid on annual defense spending in general but fail to acknowledge that the president had little effective control over how those dollars were allocated. As political scientist Peter Roman first recognized, although 'the budget *level* remained relatively constant' under Eisenhower, 'the *content* of the defense budget changed dramatically.'[137]

Following his re-election, Eisenhower grew increasingly worried about the adverse effect of defense spending on the economy. For the president the issue was not merely concern that the United States was buying too many bombers or frigates, but that a growing proportion of the defense budget was allocated to a number of blue-sky programs, many of which were redundant and others offered little hope for success. The relatively new field of research and development (R&D) had acquired a budgetary life of its own, feeding the 'military-industrial complex.' Eisenhower's use of this term did not refer exclusively to some insidious sales link between the Pentagon and manufacturers such as Boeing or North American. Rather, he correctly perceived that manufacturers had come to view the Pentagon as a cash cow, funding corporate growth and profits through increased spending on intangibles such as R&D. Buying bombers was one thing, pouring huge amounts of cash into pure research with little demonstrated potential was another.

The greatest single budget buster was the burgeoning ballistic missile R&D program. Fraught with technical complexity, this represented the inherent risks that inflated the budget – multiple redundant programs (each service had one or more ballistic missiles in development), high costs (already at ten per cent of the current defense budget, with projected increases to 20 per cent over the next five years), and low immediate returns (a handful of initial deliveries over a period of months two or three years down the road had little practical military or political value). In 1955 Eisenhower approved NSC Action 1433 which established the ICBM project as 'a research and development program of the highest priority above all others'. For ICBM proponents, this offered (but ultimately fell short of) 'a streamlined decision-making process, their own separate budget... [and the actual] ability to override everything else.' Two years later the president reined in this carte blanche, worried that the existing R&D process promoted the acquisition of unproven equipment and weapons. Eisenhower noted 'that we should not approve components of production models unless we were sure the missiles would work.' Echoing similar sentiments from Secretary of Defense Charles Wilson, Eisenhower concurred 'that if Atlas did not work, neither would Titan.'[138] Concerned that R&D would become insatiable, Eisenhower told Wilson in the spring of 1957 that beginning with the FY59 budget then under development, the Department of Defense should plan for an annual budget cap of $39 billion over the next five years. This limit would necessitate hard choices, but Wilson agreed that it could be done.[139] That assessment changed on 4 October 1957.

The launch of *Sputnik* (and its successor a month later, carrying Laika the dog) had a profound effect on all aspects of American politics, security, and culture. Most significantly, the R-7 *Semyorka* rocket which carried the *Sputniks* into orbit was the same SS-6 *Sapwood* ICBM that could rain Soviet nuclear warheads on American and Western cities. Russia clearly seemed ahead in ICBM development and operations. America seemed behind primarily because it had not invested the necessary funds in rocket and ballistic missile R&D. To further complicate the defense budget equation, four days after the second *Sputnik* launch Eisenhower received the Gaither Report. The Gaither Committee concluded that in order for America to have a sufficient deterrent force capable of defeating the Soviet Union, suitable military defenses to protect against a Soviet attack on the United States, and a meaningful civil defense capability in the event a Russian attack evaded American bomber and missile defenses, the United States needed to spend some $44 billion a year on defense, $5 billion more than the maximum the president had mandated. This report was an irritant to the president, who was reluctant to adopt its recommendations given the costs involved as well as some of its naïve assumptions, like the futility of a widespread civilian bomb shelter program – more Band-aid than cure for the cancer of nuclear war. Faced with widespread criticism from the public, Congress, and the Pentagon over *Sputnik* as well as the fanciful recommendations contained in the Gaither Report, Eisenhower softened his $39 billion budget cap by adding another $500 million.

How this modest 1.28 per cent increase affected the budget *components* is particularly telling. Officials slashed $1.6 billion from the original budget by cutting conventional weapons procurement, capital investments such as new construction, and by reductions in personnel. They then added an additional $2.14 billion to reach the $39.5 billion cap by increasing funding for strategic weapons, expanded bomber alert, and other strategic programs.[140] After 16 months of U-2 overflights which reassured Eisenhower and his closest advisors that the Soviet ballistic missile threat was overstated and that additional strategic weapons such as more bombers and greater ICBM funding were neither essential nor expedient, the president yielded to pressure to raise his budget cap and approve additional expenditures on the very strategic forces he believed were unnecessary and wasteful. The pressure continued as the JCS requested supplemental FY59 funding in excess of $10 billion, although Secretary of Defense McElroy pared this to $1.648 billion which Eisenhower and the Congress accepted. The president made it clear that additional exorbitant requests such as the $10 billion from the JCS would not be considered, but added that future annual defense budgets would 'hopefully' not exceed $40 billion.[141]

The FY60 defense budget was even more contentious. The JCS asked for $43.1 billion, of which nearly $20 billion was for new weapons procurement and R&D. This included 'significant increases' in strategic forces: the number of Polaris SLBM submarines rose from 6 to 12, projected ICBM deployment accelerated from 130 to 200, and B-52 production would continue at five aircraft per month rather than the planned reduction to three aircraft. McElroy was able to trim the budget to $40.95 billion, a figure the president grudgingly approved. Expressing his displeasure with even this amount, Eisenhower told his Secretary of Defense that he 'had been 'dragooned' into approving the Defense programs as presented'

Despite solid evidence acquired by U-2s, EB-47E(TT)s, and other sources that the US was not behind in a Missile Gap with the USSR, Eisenhower was unable to limit wasteful spending on unneeded strategic weapons. CINCSAC General Thomas S Power (left) and ARDC Commander Lieutenant General Bernard A Schriever (right) were among those who successfully urged Congress to buy more bombers and ICBMs. *Author's Collection*

and that his approval was 'reluctant but it was given only because he felt he had no choice.'[142]

Dragooned? Reluctant? No choice? These are hardly words that describe a president showing decisive leadership in constraining unnecessary budget increases. Even if the internal budget shuffling moved funds from conventional forces to strategic forces, the sheer cost of new and unproven weapons systems demanded a disproportionately deep cut in the conventional budget. This produced the doubly undesirable result of cutting traditional forces which limited war advocates such as the Army argued were necessary, and failed to produce newer strategic weapons such as ICBMs and SLBMs in greater quantities and with earlier deliveries as hardliners in the Air Force and Navy urged. Eisenhower thus allowed the budget to increase while simultaneously undermining optimal conventional and strategic force requirements.

Critics such as Stuart Symington attacked the president on both counts. Congressional hearings gave equal billing to anyone – general, admiral, politician, or academic – who would argue that the Eisenhower administration was endangering American security through excessive fiscal conservatism and obliviousness to the Soviet threat. Conflicting testimonies and leaks added to the confusion, suggesting that the president was out of touch with his intelligence community and was unaware of the true danger facing the United States.[143] In spite of this public hysteria, Eisenhower chose not to share the U-2 photos and other intelligence derived from aerial reconnaissance with Symington, the first Secretary of the Air Force and now a Democratic senator from Missouri. Had he done so the president may well have disarmed much of the furor over the growing missile gap controversy and limited its subsequent impact on defense spending. Eisenhower thought Symington a demagogue and prone to leak classified information for political purposes, not least of which was the Senator's prospective presidential run in 1960. To suggest that the president chose not to show the U-2 images to Symington out of fears of leaks that might compromise the U-2 effort, however, is disingenuous. Eisenhower had already shared U-2 images with the British in 1956 in an effort to dissuade them from invading Egypt, and they had equal access to them given that RAF pilots flew U-2s over the USSR. Charles de Gaulle had also seen the photos. Several Gaither Committee members were aware of the U-2 missions. Key JCS officials knew both of the U-2 overflights as well as those by SAC. It may be flippant to say but it seems that of all those in Washington who ought to have known about the U-2 overflights and the images they returned, Symington was the only one who did not seem to know anything about them at all. Even if the photos themselves would not convince Symington that there was no gap, they certainly would have buttressed his waning confidence in Eisenhower's awareness of the state of the Soviet threat and attenuated the Senator's public calls for more defense spending.

As Secretary of the Air Force, Stuart Symington warned that the first Soviet atomic detonation in 1949 meant 'an immediate atomic attack upon the United States.' As Democratic Senator from Missouri, Symington led Senate hawks like Lyndon Johnson and John Kennedy in lambasting Eisenhower's modest defense budget which they argued caused the Missile Gap. It is unknown if Symington saw U-2 photos or intelligence which minimized this threat, but Eisenhower was unable to use aerial intelligence to constrain Congressionally mandated expenditures on strategic weapons. *US Air Force, Courtesy of Harry S Truman Library*

Defense spending for the FY61 and FY62 budgets was equally problematic. Both years saw an annual budget just below $43 billion, but the focus remained primarily on strategic weapons. Indeed, in the FY61 budget the Air Force asked for $19.3 billion, almost half of the total defense budget. Eisenhower seemed surprised at the difficulty in limiting spending increases: '[I] had not realized the budgetary situation is this severe.' He told McElroy 'the defense budget could exceed the ceiling, even if such an increase meant cutting nondefense spending.' Bomber programs remained a source of considerable controversy, and the president eventually approved an additional $1 billion in spending for B-58 procurement.[144]

Beginning with the original FY59 budget cap of $39 billion through the FY62 budget of $42.5 billion, defense spending rose by 8.97 per cent, some $3.5 billion overall. Whether or not this constitutes proof that Eisenhower 'resisted unnecessary defense spending' is certainly debatable. What this rise – however large – does not show is the unplanned shift in defense spending away from a budget that balanced conventional weapons and force retention with spending on strategic weapons and a seemingly bottomless pit of research and development. Bissell's assertion that because of U-2 data Eisenhower 'frustrated attempts' to fund 'larger and more expensive weapon systems' is simply not true. Expenditures for Polaris missile submarines doubled. More strategic B-52 and B-58 bombers were procured than originally planned, along with a similar increase in KC-135 tankers to support them.[145] ICBM research and procurement increased well beyond the pre-*Sputnik* allocations. To be sure, Eisenhower eliminated the absurd nuclear-powered bomber and eventually reduced other strategic programs to insignificance, such as the B-70, Skybolt, and Nike-Zeus, all of which eventually died during the Kennedy administration.[146] Despite claims by Bissell and others to the contrary, these changes suggest that the president either did not – or could not – use intelligence derived from aerial reconnaissance effectively to limit demands for more strategic defense dollars and keep the defense budget under control.

The Joint Chiefs, especially Air Force Chief of Staff General White and Chief of Naval Operations Admiral Arleigh Burke, were the primary sources of pressure for budget increases after *Sputnik*. White and JCS Chairman General Twining were aware of overflights of the USSR by SAC and CIA reconnaissance planes, although it is not certain if the other chiefs (especially Burke) were briefed on the U-2 missions. The images and intelligence these flights gathered did not moderate JCS calls for increased strategic spending. Eisenhower did not – or could not – use aerial intelligence to make a compelling case to his senior defense advisors that their calls for increases in strategic weapons were unnecessary and that they should refrain from asking for more dollars, especially in public forums.

The chiefs were equally disingenuous in their post-*Sputnik* budget shuffling, and the president did not – or could not – challenge this duplicity. For example, in the FY59 budget the chiefs cut $1.6 billion from conventional forces in order to allocate those dollars (plus an additional $2.14 billion) to strategic weapons. If the $1.6 billion was not sufficiently critical that the chiefs could afford to cut it from the original budget, and the net increase of $3.74 billion for *strategic* weapons was unnecessary given the U-2 imagery, then Eisenhower should have held his ground and saved the country nearly $4 billion in unwarranted defense spending. In short, Eisenhower could have done far more than simply 'resisted unnecessary defense spending' as Beschloss claims, but could have actually *decreased* net defense spending overall.

Based in hawkish Senator Lyndon B Johnson's (D-Tex) backyard, Convair benefitted from LBJ's arm-twisting to procure far more B-58 bombers than sought by President Eisenhower. Convair also enjoyed deep federal pockets to cover extensive R&D for ballistic missiles, in this case the Atlas ICBM. *Lockheed, Author's Collection*

Moreover, the president did not – or could not – exert his executive leadership in stipulating an absolute limit on the budget from one of his cabinet secretaries. Other executive branch budgets complied with Eisenhower's spending cap but the Defense Department did not. If Secretary of Defense McElroy could not deliver a budget that met with his boss' limitations (a central feature of the corporate worldview that infused much of the Eisenhower administration) then he should have either resigned or the president should have fired him.

Why Eisenhower displayed this ambivalence is certainly paradoxical. He wanted to limit all spending in general, and defense spending in particular. After *Sputnik*, however, he was unable to constrain spending on strategic weapons such as Polaris submarines. He worried that increased R&D-type expenditures would hemorrhage the budget and achieve few meaningful improvements in national security. Nonetheless, programs such as the Atlas ICBM and early to mid-cycle development of the B-70 and Skybolt all saw substantial budgetary infusions. He knew from U-2 photos and other intelligence sources that the Soviet threat was not as great as hardliners lamented. Despite this intelligence he was unable to make a convincing argument that additional expenditures on strategic weapons were unnecessary and wasteful.

Given this elementary exercise in budget analysis and this laundry list of 'did nots' and 'could nots,' it is tempting to conclude that

Eisenhower failed to use intelligence derived from strategic aerial reconnaissance – in particular U-2 images – to constrain unreasonable budget increases. Indeed, the overall defense budget rose by nearly 10 per cent and allocations for strategic weapons systems and new R&D increased disproportionately to the president's perception of their need. To yield to temptation and accept this conclusion, however, requires that Eisenhower actually *intended* to use this intelligence to limit defense spending.

To begin with there is some ambiguity about the firmness with which Eisenhower stipulated the DoD budget caps. Referring to a 'rigid ceiling' on the budget, the president said 'he had never wished it to be called that.' He added that he did not seek 'to establish a [maximum] figure at all, but had done so on the repeated request of Secretary Wilson.'[147] Conversely, Eisenhower's later remarks that he 'had no choice but to accept' and was 'dragooned' into accepting these increases arguably undermine this implication of flexibility.

But is it necessary to conclude that the president must have meant or believed only *one* of these diametric perspectives? Just as he did in other areas related to aerial reconnaissance – military versus civilian overflight pilots, high- versus low-risk overflights of the USSR, his willingness to declare nuclear war with the USSR based on a single hypothetical Soviet military overflight of the United States – the president spoke with two equal voices about the defense budget. His 'rigid ceiling' was more akin to the 'manufacturer's suggested retail price' for a new car – a dollar amount that starts the haggling but which no one realistically believes will be the final price. As a politician Eisenhower could ill afford to be seen as acquiescent to unbridled defense spending. It was to his political advantage and image to be viewed as the voice of reason and moderation in constraining fiscally irresponsible demands. Eisenhower was the wise and avuncular president who refused to get bogged down in tactical budget battles and focused instead on 'the long haul.' As such it was expedient to be firm in announcing a firm budget cap but wise in negotiating changes.

Finally, there is as yet no documentary evidence that Dwight Eisenhower ever said or thought that CIA or SAC overflight intelligence could be or was instrumental in his desire to maintain a balanced budget and American economic health. That he *could* have done so does not mean that he *meant* to do so. Instead, the notion that Eisenhower used U-2 data to limit unbridled defense spending is little more than a historical cliché, a shibboleth, a legend. With the clarity of hindsight, Bissell wrote in his memoirs that the U-2 program – which attracted so much opprobrium in the aftermath of the 1 May 1960 loss – had in fact contributed in positive ways to issues far beyond simple intelligence collection. One of these, Bissell asserted without evidence, was to limit defense spending. Subsequent researchers such as Beschloss and Sloan have uncritically echoed Bissell's self-serving theme as part of the scholarly rehabilitation of the Eisenhower presidency. Along with the entrenched belief in the phantom ROBIN overflight of Kapustin Yar, the myth of Eisenhower using U-2 images to constrain defense spending has become one of the enduring legends of strategic aerial reconnaissance.

However ingrained the 'legend' has become, it should not obscure the effects, intended or otherwise, of strategic aerial reconnaissance on the evolution of strategic military planning and policy under Harry Truman and Dwight Eisenhower. Indeed, these effects were two sides of the same coin. Aerial reconnaissance provided the information needed to alert America of a potential Russian attack, and plan – if necessary – to defeat the Soviet Union. Aerial reconnaissance equally provided the justification for more American weapons and spending in the name of strategic security. Used initially to understand the extent and sophistication of the Soviet military threat to the political and economic security of the West, intelligence derived from reconnaissance flights ultimately became the key factor in exaggerating that threat.

Despite unsubstantiated claims by Bissell and echoed by historians, Eisenhower was unable to use U-2 intelligence to constrain defense spending on strategic weapons. The president felt 'dragooned' into approving budgets that funded unneeded bombers, was 'reluctant' but felt he had 'no choice' but to double the number of Polaris missile submarines, and struggled to limit R&D funding for multiple ICBM programs. Secretary of Defense Neil McElroy (right) administers the oath to his replacement Thomas Gates (left) as Ike looks on. *Author's Collection*

5 Who's in Control?

Expressing his reluctance to give interviews during his retirement, Curtis LeMay said in 1976, 'Well, I take a dim view of these less swank professors and so forth going down and digging in my file and then writing an adverse article about the Air Force quoting me or misquoting me and so forth....'[1] LeMay's concern proved to be more than mere paranoia or animus toward writers and researchers. Nearly 20 years later journalists and scholars were using LeMay's own words as evidence of an American military aerial reconnaissance fleet run amok, the tool of hard-line, rollback generals seeking to provoke World War Three on terms favorable to the United States, all without presidential knowledge or approval.[2]

Evidence to support such bold claims has been largely fragmentary. At the time a handful of documents were declassified, often only in part. These were coupled with personal recollections quoted as verbatim some 40 years after the fact, and were then linked by an explanation driven more by an author's thesis than in terms of what likely happened. Intelligence historian Sheila Kerr admonished that ongoing 'spasmodic' declassification of portions of interviews and operational documents would contribute to 'sensational scoops and counter scoops, scurrilous allegations and immortal conspiracy theories.' She added that 'competitive and politically motivated declassification [would] distort history, and create the worst conditions in which to declassify the most sensitive government documents, those concerning intelligence and security.'[3] As Kerr warned, making sense of then-newly declassified evidence proved a formidable task for researchers seeking to understand strategic aerial reconnaissance in the early Cold War years. It also made it relatively easy to use that same incomplete evidence to portray the flights as provocative and driven by an ulterior, sinister motive.

One of the most hotly contested issues in understanding the early years of strategic aerial reconnaissance has been the question of authority for the missions, especially military overflights of Communist countries. For some researchers the absence of a clearly defined 'paper trail' from the president to the flight crew raised the specter that someone other than the president authorized the flights. This in turn suggested that some senior military commander acted not only without presidential knowledge but with purposes that contradicted US policy. Other than the president, who had the wherewithal to plan, order, and carry out military overflights of the Soviet Union and its allies?

The answer was obvious.

Curtis Emerson LeMay's legacy evolved in parallel with America's Cold War fortunes. During the Second World War he was hailed as a brilliant commander for his relentless but ruthless bombing campaigns, first against Germany and then against Japan. With the end of the war LeMay led research and development efforts for advanced airplanes and weapons on behalf of the newly constituted Air Force. Although justifiably associated with the brutality of aerial bombardment in war, it was LeMay in 1948 who launched Operation VITTLES – the Berlin Airlift – the humanitarian resupply of the former German capital. As the newly formed Strategic Air Command failed to mature into the force intended by American military and civilian planners, it was natural for LeMay to replace its middling commander, General George Kenney. American fears of the Soviet Union and the choice of strategic airpower to deter or defeat Soviet aggression gave LeMay unprecedented clout in building SAC and defining the American atomic agenda.

But LeMay was no longer fighting fascists. By the 1950s whatever broad political cachet he and other early Cold War commanders once held began to wane. Liberals who previously supported a strong military led by fervent generals to defeat the Nazis now questioned the equal hostility directed toward the Soviet Union. With SAC as the centerpiece of American military preparedness for war with Russia, LeMay quickly became an icon for conservatives

Frank Lovejoy (left) played an articulate SAC Commander in *Strategic Air Command*, opposite disgruntled SAC wife June Allyson (center). Popular opinion of General Curtis LeMay (right) remained high throughout his career, despite being vilified by liberals and intellectuals for his hard-line attitude toward the USSR. *Ernest Bihler, Author's Collection*

who embraced a tough line in American foreign policy and a lightning rod for those who argued for a more conciliatory approach to US-Soviet relations. There was little, if any, middle ground when talking about Curtis LeMay; polemic substituted for critical thinking.

He was lionized on the cover of *Time*, went on hunting safaris with influential public figures like Arthur Godfrey, and was reverently portrayed by gravelly voiced actor Frank Lovejoy as a tough-talking commander opposite real-life Air Force Reserve Colonel Jimmy Stewart seeking to safeguard the United States in the 1954 film *Strategic Air Command*. Conversely, intellectuals such as I F Stone vilified LeMay, and called him a 'tough old troglodyte.' They were appalled by the 'jingoist, militant philosophy he represented.'[4] As Air Force Chief of Staff, LeMay never fit in with Kennedy's 'Best and Brightest,' and chroniclers of the Cuban Missile Crisis are quick to recall his gratuitously offensive 'appeasement' remark.[5] He was contemptuously treated in Stanley Kubrick's 1964 farce *Dr Strangelove*, where he was cartoonishly portrayed as an admixture of a war-mongering buffoon and a cigar-chomping psychotic. Actor George C Scott was General 'Buck' Turgidson, a bombastic lothario (hence his name) who couldn't decide if he should talk with his mistress or wrestle with the Russian ambassador. Sterling Hayden was Brigadier General 'Jack' Ripper, a sexually repressed lunatic who wanted 'peace on earth' but thought preventive nuclear war with the Soviet Union was the best way to achieve it. For many viewers Ripper was in fact then-CINCSAC General Thomas Sarfield Power, but it is hard to ignore Ripper's cigar, which does not appear with Turgidson. (Scott later earned but refused the 1971 Best Actor Oscar for his portrayal of another hard-line general in *Patton*.)

LeMay was equally paradoxical as a person. Critics said he roared 'like a just-neutered bull' and 'characteristically bellowed' when he spoke, but he had a soft voice and seldom used it in his own defense.[6] Even when disciplining his troops he was quietly intimidating. In one story, likely apocryphal, a Wing Commander stood before LeMay expecting to be fired following the loss of an airplane by his unit. The colonel stood sweating at attention for several minutes, ignored by the cigar-chewing CINCSAC shuffling papers at his desk. Finally LeMay mumbled, 'The next time a plane crashes at your base you had better be in it. Dismissed.' LeMay was tough, but he was never cruel, an assessment LeMay reserved for his successor at SAC General Power. When he did speak extemporaneously it was often in ill-considered phrases.[7] He was called a 'racist blowhard' who wanted to 'nuke the Chinks' but astutely told Robert McNamara that had Japan won the war then he and other Americans would have been tried as war criminals.[8] If indeed some rogue officer ordered illegal overflights of the Soviet Union to provoke World War Three, LeMay had both the means and the motive, and he quickly became the *bête noire* in the historical debate over the role of aerial reconnaissance in the Cold War.

Two of the earliest and most vocal proponents of this argument were British television producer and researcher Paul Lashmar and Pulitzer Prize-winning author Richard Rhodes. Citing declassified documents and interviews with overflight participants, Lashmar wondered if the 'lax control of LeMay and his colleagues by successive presidents led to a much colder Cold War?' Lashmar asserted that 'Eisenhower did not have tight control on the military,' and this enabled LeMay to use strategic reconnaissance as a 'global political tool' to 'pressure' the Soviet Union into complying with hard-line American objectives. Finally, Lashmar claimed, 'LeMay and the JCS did not tell Ike of the extent of their aggressive reconnaissance missions.'[9] Rhodes went even farther, claiming that LeMay sought to usurp presidential authority in authorizing the use of nuclear weapons. 'LeMay had decided,' charges Rhodes, 'at the beginning of the Korean War, if not before, that there were circumstances under which he would override the Commander-in-Chief's prerogative' to use nuclear weapons. Rhodes added that LeMay 'readied his nuclear armada while he prodded the Soviet bear with reconnaissance flights.'[10] Unlike Lashmar's documents and interviews, Rhodes offered no evidence for his claim that LeMay sought to circumvent presidential authority in the release and use of nuclear weapons and that the trigger would be military overflights. Perhaps Rhodes was thinking about the story related by Gaither Committee member Robert C Sprague following a visit to SAC Headquarters. After boasting that SAC had reconnaissance planes over the USSR that would warn of an impending Soviet bomber attack LeMay added, 'I'm going to knock the shit out them before they take off the ground.' Sprague replied, 'But General…that's not national policy.' 'I don't care' answered the CINCSAC, '[i]t's my policy. That's what I'm going to do.' This verbatim conversation is highly suspect, however. Sprague visited SAC twice in September 1957, nine months *after* Eisenhower suspended all military overflights of the USSR. Moreover, LeMay left SAC on 30 June 1957 to become Air Force Vice Chief of Staff at the Pentagon, and was replaced as CINCSAC by General Power. At the time of the purported conversation, LeMay was no longer in a position to control, let alone launch, SAC forces.[11]

LeMay's defenders fared little better in their rebuttals, relying on character defenses to reject the claims summarily or argue that LeMay would not have acted inappropriately, all without evidence of any sort. Aviation historian Al Lloyd said dismissively 'These allegations are blatantly untrue.' Biographer Warren Kozak argued that LeMay 'had a rock solid belief in the Constitution…and was under the absolute and complete control of the commander in chief,' adding 'LeMay never stepped outside the chain of command or even tried to advance his personal views.' Indeed, LeMay and SAC are so synonymous that it is impossible to believe that LeMay's personal opinions did not influence SAC plans or even national policies. Pentagon Papers journalist Neil Sheehan (like Rhodes, a Pulitzer Prize recipient) wrote that LeMay was no 'outlaw militant' and 'had always remained subordinate to civilian authority.' Sheehan added that Rhodes' and Lashmar's accusations 'were untrue;' he was never 'an advocate of preventive war.' CIA analyst Dino Brugioni, certainly no LeMay admirer, said that the 'flights were ordered at the highest level, and General LeMay was carrying out those orders.'[12] None of these rejoinders, however, served as proof that LeMay acted legally and with the knowledge and approval of the president.

The heart of these arguments is that the military – particularly SAC under LeMay – conducted strategic aerial reconnaissance flights, especially overflights of the Soviet Union, without presidential authorization or even knowledge under both Truman and Eisenhower. The proximal purpose of these illegal overflights was to intimidate the Soviet Union into 'good behavior,' an idea advanced in an Air Force study known as Project CONTROL. Even more disturbing is the claim that these missions were inseparably linked to the central thesis of preventive war. The flights were intended to provoke a Soviet military response that LeMay – not the president – would use as a *casus belli* to initiate World War Three on terms favorable to SAC, with or without presidential approval or even awareness.

Regardless of the veracity of these claims, strategic reconnaissance flights, particularly those which overflew 'denied territory,' were a critical juncture in the evolution of civilian control of the military in the United States. If, as Rhodes and Lashmar claimed, LeMay used these flights to advance a dangerous political agenda, then the missions represent a successful effort to subvert presidential control of US military forces and brought America and the West perilously close to general nuclear war with the Soviet Union. Conversely, if Presidents Truman and Eisenhower wielded their authority as commander-in-chief to constrain military and civilian leaders seeking to increase the number and scope of strategic reconnaissance flights and their international political implications, then the missions reaffirm civilian control over the military and reduced the potential for hostilities between the United States and its Communist adversaries. Either way, these flights were as much about civilian military relations in the United States as they were about Soviet-American relations in the Cold War.

* * *

By the late 1940s, different regional commands such as the Pacific Far East Air Forces, US Air Forces Europe (USAFE), or Alaskan Air Command had established their own operational procedures and policies for peripheral reconnaissance missions, and these guidelines served as the basis for future overflights. In July 1949 Air Force Chief of Staff General Hoyt S Vandenberg sought to consolidate and co-ordinate all intelligence flights by establishing the operational 'policies, plans, and requirements' of the USAF Electronic Reconnaissance Program.'[13] Four months later the Departments of State and Defense agreed that the Air Force would 'maintain close co-ordination with the Department of State on the pattern and frequency of operations by ferret aircraft.[14] Beyond this bureaucratic liaison, there appears to have been no formal executive branch policy on US aerial reconnaissance flights from 1945 through at least May 1950. Moreover, there is no direct link showing that President Truman was involved with any decision-making associated with these early US flights.

The first evidence to illuminate the relationship of the president to the 'chain of command' in the formative years of the US aerial reconnaissance program comes from the 8 April 1950 loss of a US Navy PB4Y-2 on a peripheral ferret mission over the Baltic Sea. In his report on the incident to the president and Secretary of Defense, Chairman of the Joint Chiefs of Staff General Omar N Bradley told Truman and Secretary of Defense Louis Johnson that the Air Force and Navy 'have been codirecting' ferret flights to obtain the 'maximum amount of intelligence concerning foreign electronic developments as a safeguard to national defense.' Bradley noted that the 'operations have been carried on without a formal statement of policy but on a basis of an informal working agreement between the Navy and Air Force.'[15] A month later Truman approved clearly defined operating procedures for future missions. Responding to a JCS recommendation that all reconnaissance flights be 'armed and instructed to shoot in self-defense,' Truman penciled the note 'Good sense, it seems to me' directly on the paper, implicitly approving the flights and explicitly approving actions needed to protect them in the face of direct military confrontation with the Soviet Union.[16] Indeed, Truman appears to have been more concerned with learning what actions reconnaissance planners would take in the future to prevent further losses instead of asking if such flights were appropriate or should continue. Truman took it for granted that they should. In the immediate aftermath of the 8 April loss, the relevant correspondence between the White House and the Department of State focused only on clarifying the details of the incident and how to handle the Soviet protests rather than exploring the value and risks inherent in such flights.[17] Truman responded favorably to the JCS argument that 'there would be more serious disadvantages occurring to the United States if the cessation of [reconnaissance] operations were to be extended over an excessively longer period' than the brief moratorium established after the Privateer loss. He approved the JCS recommendation to form the Special Electronic Airborne Search Project (SESP) to co-ordinate all US ferret operations.[18] Hardly circumspect, Truman 'approved the resumption of [ferret] ECM activities around the world at the same tempo' as before the Baltic incident 'except that all the aircraft would be armed and ordered to shoot in self defense.' This resumption was to take effect 'immediately.'[19] Truman's decision made the Joint Chiefs of Staff the agency responsible for the scheduling and conduct of these missions. From this point onward, as historian John Farquhar notes, 'no longer would ferret operations be conducted informally by the military services.'[20]

Truman's endorsement of defensive measures to protect the airplanes against hostile attack shows his awareness of peripheral flights, their potential for overt conflict between the United States and the Soviet Union, and his strong commitment to allow them to continue. He was aware that peripheral reconnaissance flights were planned, approved, and conducted by the military on the basis of informal agreements between the military and the Department of State. There is no evidence that the president was involved in any step in this process, nor is there any indication that Truman felt that he should have been involved. After 1950, with the establishment of the SESP, Truman endorsed these earlier efforts and codified them by delegating reconnaissance policy and operations to the Joint Chiefs. There is also no evidence that he explicitly maintained any discretionary power to himself, such as reserving for the president the sole approval authority for these flights. More significantly, he applied this laissez-faire approach to at least some overflights. For example, in 1950 Truman and the NSC ordered that the Departments of State and Defense 'will jointly work out an arrangement to accomplish the required [military] reconnaissance' overflights of the coast of the People's Republic of China. By overflying the coastal borders of Communist China the missions had the potential to provoke a Chinese (or even Soviet) military reaction against the United States. Despite this possibility, Truman delegated all of the details of these operations – their objectives, when and where they would take place, and how often they might be repeated – to the JCS, the Department of Defense, and the State Department. The precedent of delegated authority was clearly established.[21]

This was consistent with Truman's relatively hands-off management style in handling other substantial national security issues. For example, Truman did not receive his first full briefing on SAC's mission and the US air atomic offensive until September 1948, some 30 months after its establishment as the centerpiece of American strategic airpower and three years after he assumed the presidency.[22] That same month Truman approved NSC 30, which served as the 'sole specific statement on American policy for atomic [warfare] approved by the NSC until 1960.' This seminal document did not address important national issues such as justification for use of atomic weapons, atomic weapons objectives, or even targets, much as the SESP did not address similar issues on reconnaissance matters. Truman left details on atomic planning to others, beginning with the JCS who translated 'high policy guidance into strategic plans and concepts.' The final level included the operational commands that would execute these strategic plans, and in practice this meant LeMay and the Strategic Air Command.[23] At the 6 December 1948 DUALISM conference at Maxwell AFB, Alabama, senior Air Force civilian and military leaders reaffirmed the primary mission of the Air Force as accomplishing the strategic air offensive. However, there was no joint war plan. As SAC's commander, it officially fell to LeMay to prepare such a plan, which he did. The plan received the complete support of senior Air Force leaders, and was put into effect. SAC was also unique among the military services in that it reported not only to the Air Force Chief of Staff (as the other branches did to their respective chiefs) but also reported directly to the JCS. This direct channel from the JCS to SAC meant less interference and oversight from Air Force Headquarters, allowing SAC considerable discretion in planning and conducting not only the atomic war plan but highly sensitive aerial reconnaissance missions as well.[24]

Although this illustration specifically addresses US nuclear policy under Truman, it could easily apply to his outlook on reconnaissance policy. Once Truman approved in principal the idea of strategic aerial reconnaissance, as he did with strategic atomic policy, he delegated its development and implementation to the Joint Chiefs, who then passed it on to SAC and LeMay: 'The responsibility for the operational phases of the USAF electronic reconnaissance program will rest with the Commanding General, Strategic Air Command.'[25] By 1949 the operational jurisdiction of US strategic aerial reconnaissance flights became the domain of General LeMay as SAC's commander. If Truman felt the need to codify presidential authority in using atomic weapons as he did in NSC 30, he would have had little reservation in asserting a similar prerogative regarding overflights.[26] He chose not to, and delegated that decision to the State and Defense Departments. This did not mean that Truman remained ignorant of or disinterested in the issue of strategic aerial reconnaissance, particularly overflights. During April 1951 General Matthew B Ridgway, commander of United Nations forces in Korea, asked the JCS for 'higher authority approval' to conduct additional 'aerial reconnaissance over Manchuria' in support of US military efforts in Korea. The Departments of State and Defense discussed and co-ordinated Ridgway's request. On the evening of 27 April, the Joint Chiefs and Secretary of State Dean Acheson met with Truman, who approved Ridgway's overflight request. It is not clear if the chiefs and Acheson were obligated to seek Truman's approval or if they informed him as a courtesy prior to the flights with an expectation that he would disapprove any missions he deemed unacceptable rather than approve only missions he thought appropriate, a significant difference. In short, overflight missions planned by SAC, the Navy, or the JCS and under State Department guidelines were going to happen unless the president specifically stopped them.

LeMay's 1949 SESP charter specified only peripheral ferret operations, not overflight missions, and included clear constraints. The State Department issued a directive 'that national claims of sovereignty over coastal water and airspace out to twelve miles from shore should be respected,' but left to SAC's discretion any other limits 'based on perceptions of what the target nation would or would not tolerate.'[27] By 1950, peripheral flights would operate 'no closer than twenty miles to the USSR [or Soviet]-satellite controlled territory,' and would not deviate from or alter planned flight courses for reasons other than safety.' These guidelines were 'applicable to all aerial reconnaissance which may be conducted in sensitive areas adjacent to the USSR' or its satellites.[28] Some researchers have argued that Truman endorsed these limits because of his fear that border violations might provoke general war. Rosenberg noted in 1986 that by '1950, SAC RB-36 and RB-50 aircraft were flying [peripheral] electronic and photo reconnaissance missions, although few if any of the spy flights actually crossed the border.' Farquhar added in 1991 'since penetration flights [ran] counter to President Truman's fears of war caused by unintentional provocation of the Soviets, it is hard to believe that he would approve such missions.'[29]

This early research did not benefit from subsequent declassification of evidence that Truman not only endorsed armed peripheral missions in close proximity to Soviet and Red Chinese borders, he approved multiple overflights of the Soviet Union and the People's Republic. Truman had 'mixed feelings' over the issue of covert operations. He condemned the CIA under Eisenhower for what he considered its excesses in covert operations, but, as one historian argues, similar activities 'began on a more modest scale during [Truman's] presidency and almost certainly with his knowledge.'[30] After the U-2 Incident Truman expressed public concern not about the use of overflights as an intelligence-gathering tool but about the level of Eisenhower's awareness of the flights.[31] Given the modest number of Air Force and Navy overflights of the Soviet Union and China between 1946 and 1952 approved by the president, it is clear that Truman had no opposition to covert military operations – specifically overflights or planned border incursions of the Soviet Union and PRC – and he actively participated in their oversight and approval.

In an oral history conducted in 1967, General Twining recalled that after Truman authorized a plan in 1950 to undertake military reconnaissance overflights of the USSR, the president asked him, 'Why in the devil hasn't [the Air Force] been doing this before?'[32] Researchers have either dismissed Twining's story as self-serving or embraced it as proof that this was the presidential 'green light' to the Air Force and SAC to begin military overflights without further presidential approval. Neither conclusion is true.

By 1950 the US Air Force had identified the need for overflight reconnaissance of the Soviet Union but had not yet made a concerted effort to convince the president that such flights were desirable and worth the risk, especially in light of the war in Korea. A 1950 report on SAC reconnaissance says that LeMay, 'with an awareness of the peculiar position of reconnaissance in peace and war, has given special consideration to the reconnaissance force. Its position, as a support group to atomic bombardment, has been more clearly defined than, perhaps, ever before.'[33] That same year LeMay asked Vandenberg to institute a program to rescue crews downed 'within the USSR.' Although this was ultimately intended for bomber crews stranded during an atomic strike, LeMay was well aware that such a program would benefit peacetime reconnaissance crews operating over the Soviet Union.[34] In 1954 LeMay told an audience at the National War College that one reason SAC bombers would succeed in penetrating Soviet airspace despite claims to the contrary is that 'we have good reason to believe our [bomber] forces can penetrate any defense system in existence today....'[35] LeMay based this assertion on the empirical success of previous reconnaissance incursions into the Soviet Union such as Hal Austin's 8 May 1954 overflight of Murmansk.

LeMay was not the only one who advocated these overflights. A January 1948 proposal from the Air Force director of intelligence called for '[e]lectronic reconnaissance...on a search and investigation basis covering any locations [inside the USSR] which are determined to be experimental or testing areas.'[36] A 1949 Air Force policy paper entitled 'Penetration Problems of Strategic Reconnaissance' identified the opposition that ELINT and reconnaissance 'RB-29s would encounter photographing Russian industrial areas within the next year or so.' The report enumerated key problems such as weather, Soviet early warning and defenses, and reconnaissance crew training, and offered suggestions on how to 'traverse an area defended by enemy forces.' The author further asserted, based on meteorological data, that overflight missions could best be conducted during the winter by 'low altitude night' sorties and during the summer by 'high altitude day' sorties.[37] A Top Secret October 1952 memorandum discussed the optimum bureaucratic handling procedures of aerial photography obtained over the previous two years by 'Air Force overflights of Soviet territory' and 'Soviet dominated territory.'[38]

The Air Force, however, was ambivalent over the issue of overflights. In response to a 5 April 1948 request by then-Senator Symington to General Spaatz as to why there was no detailed photographic coverage of possible Soviet bomber bases along the Chukotskiii Peninsula, the Air Intelligence Requirements Division replied that 'photographs of sovereign territory cannot be made without risking the loss of aircraft and crew and without risking a grave international crisis.' The report went on to recommended 'that no attempt be made by the United States Air Force to photograph airfields on Chukotskii Peninsula' by overflights.[39] Interestingly, the first verified overflights of the region took place four months later. During 1950 Colonel William A Adams, SAC's director of intelligence, prepared a study on 'possible reconnaissance routes over the USSR.' Despite the need for such routes, senior Air Force intelligence officials responded to the proposal by saying, 'It cannot be done, however, without detection and without risk of loss of aircraft.'[40] General Cabell at CIA agreed and disagreed, clearly articulating the breadth of authorities involved in approving overflights: *My own view, although recognizing the desirability, is that its essentiality is questionable in light of present conditions. My forecast is that it [the request for overflights] would not get by either the* A.F. front office, the JCS, Defense or State.... *If SAC wants to formally request it anyhow, I would recommend against it, and unless SAC specifically requested otherwise, I would not forward it.*[41]

In a back-handed way of encouraging future overflight proposals, Cabell added, 'All this is entirely aside from the desirability for SAC Recon to perfect the capability, looking forward to a day when it becomes either more essential or less objectionable.' Indeed, during the Korean War Cabell wanted USAF RB-45Cs to overfly not only North Korea but the Soviet Union as well.[42] Other Air Force officials also discouraged overflights and recommended different sources to satisfy US intelligence needs: *No one is satisfied with the intelligence yield on the USSR.... Everyone agrees on a major collection effort. The only problem is how to accomplish it. Overt efforts are completely thwarted by the extraordinary security measures in effect. [Overflight] photo reconnaissance cannot be employed without creating serious incidents. Our only hopeful resources are defectors, refugees, and covert agencies.*[43]

This institutional schizophrenia over the wisdom or desirability of overflights reflects the robust gestational debate about the missions during the Truman administration, and demonstrates the extent to which multiple senior defense officials were part of or aware of the evolving overflight program.

Ultimately the Air Force opted to pursue overflight missions – which were known throughout the Defense Department as 'sensitive intelligence' missions (SENSINT) – and did not hesitate to seek Truman's approval for them. Perhaps the most well-documented example is the first B-47 overflight in October 1952. On 5 July 1952 the Air Force Chief of Staff forwarded a proposed overflight to LeMay at SAC. The mission would cover the Chukotskii Peninsula looking for Soviet bomber bases. Hardly a *carte-blanche*, the directive stipulated that SAC would undertake 'such operations if and when JCS approval and authority is received.'[44] Pending authorization SAC would plan the specific route, assign appropriate airplanes, crews, and support, and be ready to execute the mission when told to do so. On 12 August Secretary of Defense Johnson briefed Truman on the proposed mission, and the president 'approved the recommendation of the Joint Chiefs of Staff with respect to the Northern run.' Truman did not approve a second 'Southern' route over concerns about vulnerability of the airplane and crew. Truman also 'emphasized that his approval of the Northern route was subject to full discussion with appropriate officials of the State Department and their concurrence.'[45] Such approval appears to have been immediate. The following day Major General Roger Ramey, the Air Force Deputy Chief of Staff for Operations, informed LeMay that the 'President has approved the implementation of Project Number 52 AFR-18' and added Truman's restrictions. Ramey gave LeMay a large measure of discretion in carrying out the mission, saying that SAC should 'take necessary action to undertake this operation during the month of September at a date most likely to insure its successful completion.'[46] The actual flight, commanded by Lieutenant Colonel Don Hillman, took place on 15 October 1952. This example demonstrates that the conduct of overflights followed a clear procedural pattern and with the knowledge and consent of multiple senior military and civilian officials, including the president. The mission was first articulated by personnel in the office of the Air Force Chief of Staff and briefed to the Secretary of Defense who presented it to the president for his approval. Truman approved a modified plan subject to objections by the State Department, and gave execution authority to LeMay and SAC to carry out the mission. These flights were hardly undertaken surreptitiously by order of a rogue commander, nor were they result of a cabal of Pentagon militarists operating in contravention of any presidential prohibition. The president and his Secretaries of Defense and State knew about these flights, approved these flights, and held military officials accountable for these flights. Moreover, Truman and his senior advisors were not the only heads of government in the early Cold War years who were aware of or

The first B-47 overflight of the Soviet Union provides clear and compelling evidence of Presidential authorization for these missions. After extensive planning by the Air Staff, the Secretary of Defense briefed Truman on the mission, who approved it on the condition that it met with State Department approval. It did. The Air Staff then ordered LeMay to conduct the overflight.

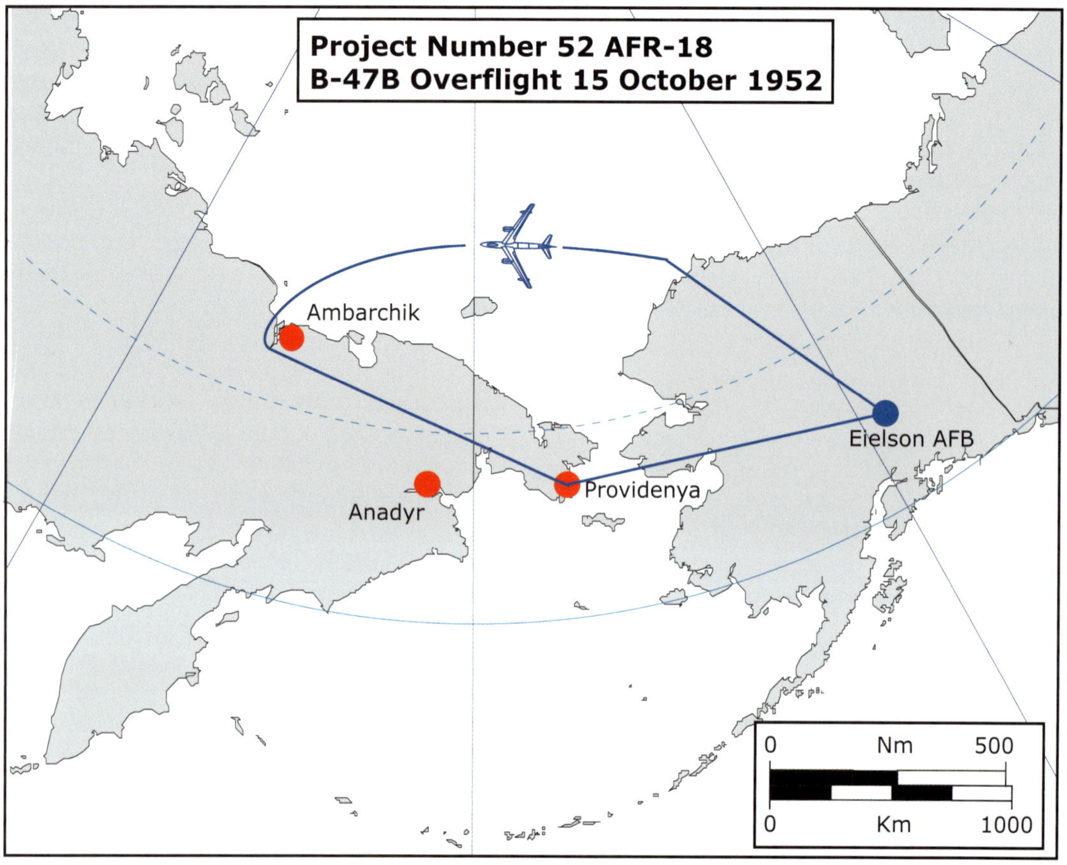

authorized US military overflights of the Soviet Union.

During the middle of 1951, the United States arranged to give three RB-45s to the Royal Air Force for use in reconnaissance overflights of the Soviet Union.[47] The 'High Altitude Reconnaissance Flight' would 'undertake certain joint research work, required by the USAF and [the RAF].' Although the 'political agreement' had yet to be obtained, the RAF arranged the training of flight crews within the United States. Once trained in the RB-45 they would return to RAF Sculthorpe to await political approval from the United States to fly the penetration missions. The airplanes would have their US markings 'painted out and would be replaced by Royal Air Force roundels.'[48] This project, known as JU JITSU, was so secret that the only American military personnel aware of it were Generals Vandenberg, Twining, LeMay, and Thomas D White. Even General Ramey, responsible for training the crews, was kept in the dark. The British liaison to the USAF dealt directly 'with Twining on such points as concerned the true purpose of the Mission, and with Ramey on such points as concerned the ostensible purpose of the Mission.'[49]

The first RAF RB-45C overflight of Eastern Europe took place on 21 March 1952, and the first overflight of the Soviet Union followed on 17 April. During late summer 1952, when Twining briefed Truman on the need for the 15 October US RB-47 overflight of Siberia (which Truman approved), Twining also updated the president on the RAF RB-45 JU JITSU overflights. It is as this point in 1952, rather than two years earlier, that Truman apparently uttered his encouraging remark to Twining. In a 3 September 1952 letter to RAF Air Marshal John C Slessor, Twining said that Truman responded to the overflight issue by saying 'Why don't you do more of it?' Subject to the vagaries of oral history, Twining's 1967 recollection of '1950' should not be taken literally. Slessor was happy to oblige the president's entreaty to 'do more of it' and told Vandenberg on 12 September that the RAF wanted another JU JITSU mission in November. This proposed mission would include three RAF and, for the first time, three USAF crews to enable '6 sorties simultaneously.' Slessor worried about flying the missions at close intervals, suggesting an overflight in the Spring after the proposed November mission. He indicated that he could more readily obtain 'the Old Man's [Prime Minister Winston Churchill] approval to [undertake] another JU JITSU' flight if he could claim 'that this time US as well as British crews would take part.'[50] The

November 1952 mission never took place. RAF RB-45 flights resumed in April and May 1954, and none operated with joint British-American crews.

Critics rightly observe that Truman's awareness of a handful of American and British military overflights of the Soviet Union prior to 1953 did not necessarily mean that his successor, Dwight Eisenhower, was aware of the hundreds of US military overflights of the Soviet Union and its allies between 1953 and 1957. Indeed, Lashmar and Rhodes suggest that LeMay became so emboldened by his ability to undertake these flights under Truman, however legal, that he took it upon himself to authorize 'aggressive reconnaissance missions' without bothering to inform Eisenhower or LeMay's own superiors at the Pentagon. Even if LeMay wrongly believed that he had blanket presidential permission, Lashmar points out, LeMay still acted illegally and provocatively, risking the possibility of general war with the USSR.[51]

If the Air Force was ambivalent about the need and suitability of overflights during the Truman administration, this indecisiveness virtually disappeared during the Eisenhower years. The Air Force's senior reconnaissance theorist, Colonel Richard Leghorn, had long championed the need for overflights despite their associated opprobrium. As early as 1946 he articulated the key critique of overflights: 'whereas peacetime spying is considered a normal function between nation states, military aerial reconnaissance – which is simply another method of spying – is given more weight as an act of military aggression.' Without a substantial change in international legal thinking, Leghorn warned, 'reconnaissance flights will not be able to be performed in peace without permission of the nation state over which the flight is to be made.'[52] Given that the Soviet Union or the PRC would hardly be inclined to allow such flights, Leghorn recommended by the 1950s that they be undertaken anyway. 'I think this photography, whether authorized or unauthorized [by the overflown country], is the greatest key to international peace that we've got.'[53] Commenting on Eisenhower's Open Skies program, Leghorn said in August 1955 that if the Soviets rejected the Open Skies overflights, the United States 'would carry out the inspection covertly, even in the face of Soviet military opposition.' He added that '[a]erial spying on the Soviet Union – done covertly and without Soviet permission – can be carried out with a very, very small probability of loss and with great gains for the West.' Leghorn firmly believed 'that we *can* conduct such reconnaissance missions over Soviet territory without their being able to do anything about it – with very rare exceptions.' These overflights would take advantage of new equipment that predated modern stealth technology. Leghorn revealed in 1955 that future reconnaissance aircraft would be covered with a 'paint developed early in World War Two which hides from the human eye an aircraft flying at high altitude.' He hinted at work under way that would help make the U-2 and its successors nearly invisible to hostile radar: 'we can develop better material and shapes for aircraft surfaces that will absorb or scatter radar beams so as to make radar detection of reconnaissance aircraft quite difficult.' Kelly Johnson and the Skunk Works tried all of these to render the U-2 undetectable to Soviet radar, but none worked.[54]

Civilian policy makers under Eisenhower were not so overt in their endorsement of overflights, but supported them nonetheless. According to Richard Bissell, the Killian panel made at least one recommendation to Eisenhower 'so sensitive that it was omitted entirely from the committee's final [written] report.' In a private meeting with Eisenhower in late 1954, well before the balance of the Killian Report was presented in early 1955, Killian urged the president to approve construction of 'a reconnaissance aircraft capable of flying at very high altitudes and that the plane *should engage in overflights of the USSR*.'[55] Clearly, the need for US overflights had become, to use General Cabell's earlier remark, 'more essential and less objectionable.'

In addition to the unquestioned need for overflights as a solution to America's demands for passive intelligence relating to war planning and early warning, there was an active benefit of these flights. If American intelligence-gathering airplanes could overfly the USSR at will, then Soviet leaders would surely recognize that the airplanes which one day carried cameras could the next day carry atomic bombs. Reminded of this vulnerability every time a US reconnaissance aircraft overflew the USSR, Soviet leaders would be compelled to 'behave' or risk atomic bombardment.

Project CONTROL first appeared in US policy making circles in 1954 when Air Force Colonel Raymond S Sleeper headed a study at the Air War College at Maxwell AFB, Alabama. Sleeper learned that from 1919 through the 1930s the RAF successfully used 'air control' to intimidate and police hostile people in British territories. Why not, Sleeper wondered, apply this to US policy toward the "hostile' Soviet people? By controlling Soviet airspace, the United States could issue ultimatums to Soviet leaders to alter their political behavior. Here at last was a direct means for applying US strategic air power to achieve Cold War political ends.[56]

Project CONTROL was a 'persuasive reconnaissance offensive' designed to establish a constant, threatening presence over the Soviet Union which would simultaneously gather precise target intelligence. If the Soviets failed to comply with US demands or took aggressive action to defend themselves from these overflights, the United States would initiate an 'armed reconnaissance offensive' against the USSR, including the use of atomic weapons. Sleeper naively believed that the Russian people would then overthrow the Soviet government, leading to democratic elections.[57] Such conclusions roundly contradicted the lessons from the strategic bombardment of Germany. As early as 1943 Carl Spaatz argued that attempts to undermine the Nazi regime by bombing the populace were fruitless: 'Morale in a totalitarian society is irrelevant so long as the control patterns function effectively.' Indeed, according to historian Richard Overy, bombing only increased 'the dependence of the population on both the state apparatus and the Party organizations responsible for welfare, reducing even further the space for more serious dissent. Survival depended on not challenging the system.'[58] Oblivious to nearly a decade of post-war doctrinal analyses, Sleeper proposed the ultimate in roll-back fantasies.

On 24 May 1954, a little more than two weeks after Austin's overflight of Murmansk, Sleeper presented his briefing at the Air Force World Wide Commander's Conference, attended by every senior officer in the Air Force, including LeMay. They were 'very favorably impressed,' and Secretary of the Air Force Harold E Talbott 'discussed methods of getting [the briefing] into [t]he White House for the President immediately.'[59] Among others, Sleeper later briefed Secretary of Defense Charles Wilson, CIA Director Allen Dulles, and the Joint Chiefs of Staff. Military officials were generally sympathetic but non-committal. State Department officials and think-tank pundits who heard the presentation were appalled and openly hostile to the plan as tantamount to preventive war. Despite Talbott's enthusiasm for the project, there is no evidence that Eisenhower was ever briefed on Project CONTROL. By the end of 1954 the Eisenhower administration categorically rejected preventive war as an option for US policy, and Project CONTROL quietly disappeared.

Or did it? According to a 1993 interview with Sleeper, LeMay was a 'big supporter' of Project CONTROL and was one of the few senior officials aware of CONTROL prior to the May 1954 mass briefing. Sleeper claimed that he spoke to LeMay 'several times a month' about the program, and that the SAC commander told him 'that he [LeMay] carried around a summary of the plan wherever he went.'[60] This unsubstantiated claim almost certainly exaggerates Sleeper's own importance and LeMay's interest in Project CONTROL. Nonetheless, in his memoirs LeMay described his conceptual support of the philosophy behind Project CONTROL: *...from the time when the Russians achieved The Bomb, until after they had The Bomb but didn't yet own a stockpile of weapons...it would have been possible, I believe, for America to say to the Soviets, 'here's a blueprint for your immediate future. We'll give you a deadline of five or six months' – something like that – 'to pull out of the satellite countries, and effect a complete change of conduct. You will behave your damn selves from this moment forth.'*[61]

LeMay wasn't the only person closely linked with US overflights of the Soviet Union to realize the importance of 'compellence.' Richard Bissell recalled: *As soon as we had a few successful [U-2] overflights, however, it did occur to me that, if you could demonstrate to an enemy country that you could overfly it with impunity and it couldn't do a goddamn thing to prevent you, that in itself would be a good deterrent. I believe this strongly, and it's a point that has never been made about the history of the U-2. The U-2 was a deterrent because it showed that the United States possessed a significant technological capability that the Soviets could not match. That was a great accomplishment.*[62]

John Foster Dulles was equally aware of the impact of the U-2 flights as pressure to compel the Soviet Union to contemplate reform.[63]

Lashmar hedged few bets that Project CONTROL influenced LeMay's thinking on the political value of reconnaissance overflights of the Soviet Union. 'It would seem likely that Project Control was in his mind when he ordered the missions and it cannot be discounted that he was trying to force the Russians into a major hostile response.' Lashmar continued: *With the further discovery of the Project Control archives I began to see where LeMay's agenda of aggressive airpower had come from. I have concluded that under LeMay and then Power reconnaissance missions transcended their usual use as an intelligence tool; they had became [sic] a global political tool. Apparently using a covert air power doctrine derived from Project Control, LeMay put a great deal of pressure on the Soviet Union. These missions were a systematic provocation in a game of hard nosed poker.*[64]

Lashmar also interviewed an impeccable witness who stated that LeMay hoped that these flights would provoke open hostilities between the United States and the Soviet Union, perhaps even general war. In 1954 LeMay told Colonel Hal Austin, the aircraft commander of the May 1954 RB-47E overflight of the Murmansk region, 'Well, maybe if we do this overflight right, we can get World War Three started.' In another meeting some 30 years later, LeMay again told Austin 'Well, we'd have been a hell of a lot better off if we'd got World War Three started in those days.'[65]

Was LeMay a loose cannon ready and willing to start a global nuclear war by initiating unauthorized overflights of the Soviet Union as Rhodes claims? Did he attempt to circumvent presidential authority by covertly implementing the ideas behind Project CONTROL, as Lashmar argues? The evidence shows that he did not.

LeMay freely acknowledged the presence and clandestine nature of SAC's overflights of the Soviet Union. In a frequently cited interview, he said that during the 1950s he 'flew all the reconnaissance aircraft that SAC possessed over Vladivostok at high noon' involving 'a whole wing of Canberras.'[66] In another widely credited source, LeMay is reported to have told Gaither Committee member Robert Sprague in September 1957 that America 'had airplanes flying secret missions over Soviet territory twenty-four hours a day, picking up all sorts of intelligence information, mostly [COMINT] from Soviet military radio transmissions.' LeMay added 'those statements the Soviets periodically made about American spy planes penetrating Russian airspace were true. We always said the incidents were accidental, but they were not; they were very deliberate.' The COMINT flights were almost certainly only peripheral sorties, not overflights which gathered PHOTINT and SIGINT. LeMay would not necessarily have felt compelled in his remark to Sprague to discriminate between peripheral and overflight missions.[67]

Critics have been quick to emphasize that in the absence of a direct documentary link between these overflights and the president – the only person who could have legally authorized them – LeMay's boasts demonstrate his willingness to undertake the flights without higher authority. For example, LeMay admitted that he did not report Austin's May 1954 overflight to Washington because he would 'have to explain this mission to too many damn people who don't need to know.'[68] Critics argue, therefore, that this and other overflights took place without proper presidential authorization. This conveniently overlooks the rest of LeMay's remarks and actions, as well as other evidence.

Although LeMay was conceptually sympathetic to Project CONTROL and its value in directing the Russians to 'behave your damn selves from this moment forth,' he said more in his memoirs than just this provocative bluster. In the sentence following this oft-cited quote LeMay added 'whether we *should* have presented such a blueprint was not for me to decide. That was a question of national policy.'

RB-47Es (53-4253 seen here) had an elongated nose and clean lines, making it an ideal high-speed, high-altitude reconnaissance platform capable of evading MiG-15s. On 8 May 1954, however, MiG-17s attacked Major Harold 'Hal' Austin's RB-47E during his overflight of Murmansk and Archangelsk. *via Mike Habermehl*

He continued '[t]hat is not something for the military to say. It is for our Administration to say.... Our job in SAC was not to promulgate a national policy or an international one.'[69]

On the issue of overflights, LeMay identified his role in the organizational chain of command originating with the president. Referring to the December 1956 overflight, which was expressly approved by President Eisenhower, he said it was not 'my idea...I was ordered to do it. They [the Eisenhower administration's intelligence chiefs] were worried about something going on at Vladivostok. So I laid out a mission.'[70] LeMay's assertion that he was 'just following orders' was hardly the self-serving 'cop out' offered by former SS prison camp guards. As the example of the 1952 overflight of Siberia showed, Air Force headquarters ordered LeMay at SAC to plan and carry out Project Number 52 AFR-18; he was indeed complying with a legal directive from his superiors, including the president. LeMay told historians in 1972 that overflights were a: *primarily political consideration and not a military consideration in peacetime and I don't think the military commander should be the final judge on this. He may be the final judge as to the necessity but...as to whether it is to be done or not has to come from the highest level of the land.*[71]

LeMay also recognized the essential balance between the military's need for intelligence and the constraints on the military's ability to gather intelligence. He noted SAC's atomic offensive: *requires the highest possible order of intelligence. And, equally important, it requires a freedom of initiative not likely to be provided a military commander in a democracy. Within these limits, and they are severe, we are prepared to perform this task.*[72]

Regarding the 1954 overflight and LeMay's refusal to report it in detail to Washington, Austin recounted that LeMay told him the secrecy was due to LeMay's fears of spies or 'pinkos' in the State Department, who would then compromise the safety and secrecy of future missions. LeMay's concerns were hardly just conservative paranoia. Soviet mole Kim Philby may have tipped off the Soviets about future RB-45C overflights in 1952, accounting for why they were canceled. He is also credited for 'betraying' the fictional 1953 RAF Canberra ROBIN flight. Philby, who finally defected to the Soviet Union in 1963, has also been linked to advance Soviet knowledge of Frank Powers' U-2 overflight in 1960.[73] LeMay's refusal to communicate with Washington was equally related to recommending Austin and his crew for decorations. LeMay thought Austin deserved the Silver Star for his bravery under combat conditions, but this award required Pentagon-level approval justified by a detailed narrative of the event. Unwilling to reveal this highly sensitive information to 'shoe clerks' – administrative personnel in the 'awards and decorations' division – LeMay chose instead to use his prerogative as CINCSAC to award Austin and his crew *two* Distinguished Flying Crosses apiece, an award which did not require Pentagon approval. Eventually LeMay and Twining discussed the award of medals and ribbons to aircrews and units for their participation in these missions, and several subsequent overflight pilots received the Silver Star.[74] Moreover, LeMay did communicate details of this and earlier missions to his military superiors at the Pentagon. Norwegian historian Fredrik Fagertun shows that although it was LeMay who ordered his crews to undertake the flights, he was 'supported by the Joint Chiefs of Staff' and other military officials.[75] For example, in 1953 Air Force Vice Chief of Staff General Thomas White sought LeMay's guidance on the establishment of a 'pre-hostilities reconnaissance' unit that would overfly the USSR immediately before the outbreak of war to gather last-minute target data. White asked for LeMay's opinions because 'of the extent of [SAC's previous] operations in this area.' Although White's project was 'dropped from further consideration,' he stressed to LeMay that: *From time to time there do arise requirements for sensitive reconnaissance missions [overflights] to be performed. A large number of these will be delegated to the Strategic Air Command for accomplishment. When special operations dictate unusual equipments [sic] or modifications, every assistance necessary will be afforded the Strategic Air Command to fulfill the mission.*[76]

Claims that the 1954 flight was intended to provoke the Soviets into shooting down the RB-47 as a *casus belli* ignore the fact that LeMay did not know for certain the Soviets could attack the RB-47 on this mission. According to Austin, SAC planners believed that the Soviets had only older, less capable MiG-15s in the region, not the more advanced MiG-17s which could successfully attack the RB-47. Other sources suggest that one purpose of the mission was to determine if indeed there were even operational MiG-17s in the area. Either way, if LeMay wanted the Soviets to attack the RB-47 as a provocation for a US military response, he would have chosen a route that guaranteed MiG-17s were in place and operationally ready

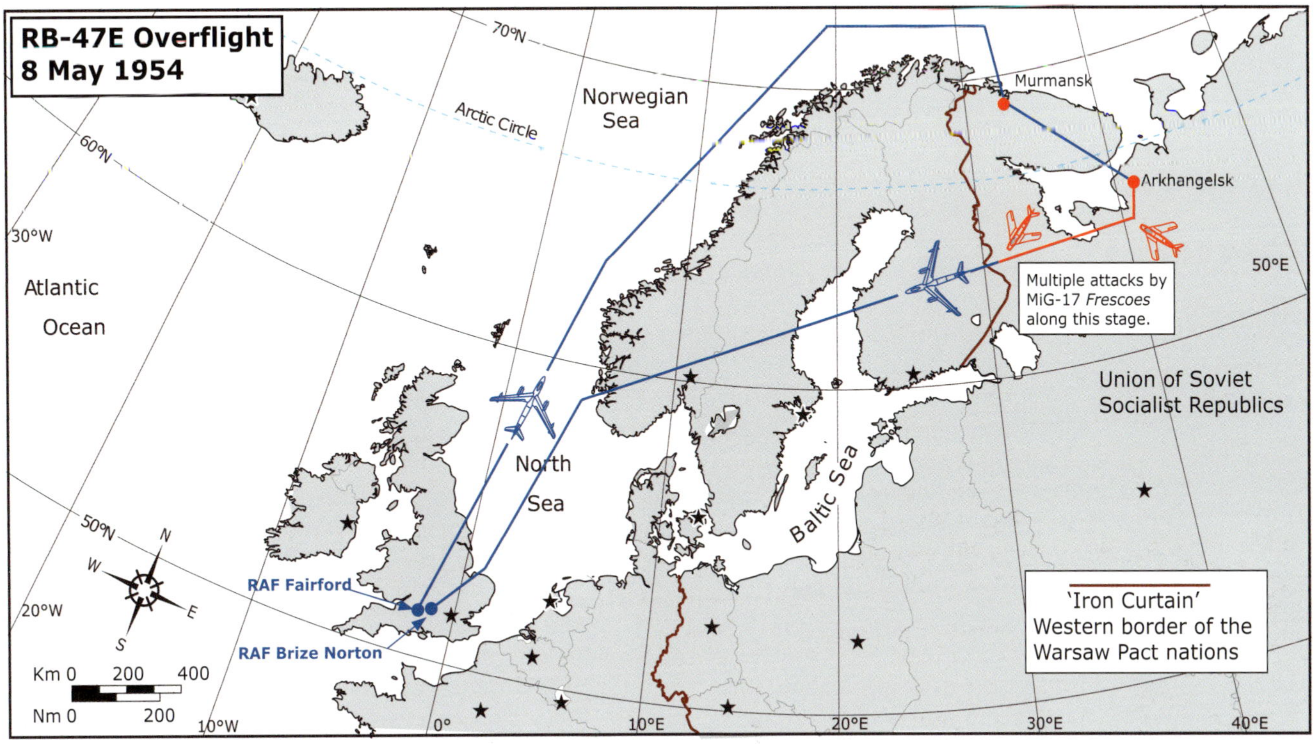

to intercept and attack the RB-47. LeMay did not expect this airplane to be attacked, so would therefore not trust that this flight would provoke a US military response.[77] Arguably one could make a case that LeMay knew that the Soviets would intercept Austin's RB-47 with the more capable MiG-17 and that SAC planners told Austin there would only be MiG-15s, deluding Austin into a clash that LeMay could use as a *casus belli*. There is no evidence to support such a wild claim, nor can it be disproven sufficiently, making it the perfect conspiracy theory.

But what of LeMay's remarks, reported 30 years later, that he thought it advantageous to use overflights to provoke a third world war? Throughout the 1950s many US officials, both civilian and military, considered a war between the United States and the Soviet Union to be inevitable. Whether based upon their own anxieties, incomplete or inaccurate intelligence, or worst-case scenarios derived from Soviet rhetoric associated with the inevitability of a cataclysmic clash between capitalism and communism, many US officials held that World War Three was just a matter of time. If this war was unavoidable, LeMay and others may have thought, then better to have it on terms and at a time when it was most favorable to the United States, at a time when the US nuclear stockpile and strike force were still superior to those of the Soviet Union. The issue of preventive war was hardly the private domain of the 'lunatic fringe' during the early Cold War, and included such diverse thinkers as John von Neumann, Bertrand Russell, and even George Kennan and Charles 'Chip' Bolen. Moreover, preventive war – launching an attack against an enemy when there is no indication that an attack by that enemy is imminent or even planned – should be distinguished from a preemptive war, which begins when an enemy's attack is imminent.[78]

Preparing for such a war did not necessarily mean that LeMay wanted it to happen at his discretion, or that he took steps to make it happen. LeMay believed that US forces could strike the USSR with only minimal losses to SAC forces – comparable to then-existing daily training attrition.[79] He was equally aware that even with a favorable American first strike the Soviets would still be able to attack bases and cities in the United States in an atomic exchange, and that meant huge American casualties. Critics might charge that even these losses were acceptable to LeMay when compared with the hundreds of millions of dead Americans in an eventual nuclear war with a fully prepared Soviet Union. Austin discounts this assertion. LeMay, Austin said, was the 'soldier's soldier,' meaning he absolutely followed orders just as he expected his own troops to do the same. Starting World War Three on his own was simply not something that LeMay would have considered, according to Austin, let alone undertaken. Claims that LeMay actually intended to start World War Three by using

Critics refer to the 8 May 1954 overflight as ultimate proof that LeMay ordered missions to start global thermonuclear war. LeMay supposedly told Hal Austin, the RB-47 pilot, 'Well, maybe if we do this overflight right, we can get World War Three started.' Truman, Eisenhower, and even Stalin made similar wistful remarks, but no one has argued they intended to provoke global war.

aerial reconnaissance are, recalled Austin, 'just plain fancy.'[80]

It might be tempting to lump Austin's dismissal along with other supporters who defend LeMay by appealing to intangible and unprovable references to LeMay's professional integrity. In Austin's case, however, he was part of the conversation incorporating these statements and considered them wistful – rather than wishful – thinking. To assert that LeMay's provocative remarks were anything other than his well-known off–the-cuff bluster, that they were proof of LeMay's insidious intent to start a global conflagration, would be a grievous misinterpretation akin to believing that a homeowner who openly laments that he would need to rob a bank to pay his bills was actually plotting to do so. Indeed, Truman 'fantasized' along similar lines: 'Get plenty of Atomic Bombs on hand – drop one on Stalin, put the United Nations to work and eventually set up a free world.' Eisenhower asked rhetorically if 'our duty to future generations did not require us to *initiate* war at the most propitious moment that we could designate.' During the 1956 Suez Crisis Ike told his physician that 'if he were a dictator, he would tell Russia if they moved a finger, he would drop our entire stock of atomic weapons on them.' Not surprisingly Stalin held a nearly identical view, wondering in 1950 if war with the United States wouldn't be preferable before Japan was rearmed.[81] No one has cited these quotes or others in suggesting that Truman or Eisenhower or Stalin seriously sought to start a preventive war with the Soviet Union. Selectively using LeMay's similar remark as proof of his active intent to provoke World War Three is disingenuous.

It is clear from guidance provided to SAC by the State Department and the Pentagon on the conduct of aerial reconnaissance missions that LeMay was aware of his limits to initiate overflights and his responsibility to senior civilian authorities. Does this suggest then, as Lashmar and Rhodes claim, that the flights were undertaken with the knowledge of senior Air Force personnel but without the knowledge of President Eisenhower or his civilian advisors? Again, the evidence suggests otherwise.

Lieutenant Colonel Roger Rhodarmer was the Air Force project officer in the Pentagon for overflight operations. (During 1946, then-Major Rhodarmer flew RB-26C BIRDSEYE PHOTINT missions over West Germany and along the Iron Curtain.) In 1954 the Air Force Deputy Chief of Staff for Operations, Lieutenant General Frank Everest, directed him to co-ordinate all military overflight plans and missions, as well as liaise with William Armstrong, the Special Assistant for Intelligence to Secretary of State Dulles. According to Rhodarmer there was a very specific mechanism by which each overflight request was considered and then either approved or disapproved. Theater commanders or intelligence agencies would submit a request to Everest at Air Force Headquarters, who would then forward it to the JCS. If they felt it had merit they would send the request to a variety of key individuals including the President's Special Assistant for National Security Affairs, the Secretaries of State and Defense, the Director of Central Intelligence, and the Chairman of the Joint Chiefs of Staff. If all concurred that the mission should be undertaken then typically the Secretary of Defense would brief President Eisenhower. If he approved, then the mission was referred to SAC for execution. This process clearly demonstrates that not only senior military officials but multiple civilian leaders were aware of ongoing military overflights. Rhodarmer is equally emphatic in terms of Eisenhower's awareness. He recalls sitting outside the Oval Office as AF Vice Chief of Staff General White briefed the president on the state of the overflight program. As White left the Oval Office he told him 'the President's reviewed the program and it's Okay.' Rhodarmer added, 'Apparently the President already knew about the program, but I do not know whether he knew it had been that successful.'[82]

This approval process also included a review and critique of each mission as well as the intelligence collected. During one HOME RUN flight the pilot deviated from the planned flight route by turning around to photograph his target a second time. This violated a cardinal rule in aerial photography to rely on surprise during a mission and never give the enemy a second chance to shoot at the airplane. According to Rhodarmer, White sent LeMay a terse warning, if not outright reprimand. The letter admonished LeMay that SAC was not authorized to deviate from the approved plan and that such variation could jeopardize future missions. LeMay should instruct his crews accordingly. The letter also mentioned potential disciplinary action. Rhodarmer delivered the letter in person to LeMay and awaited his reply. True to form, LeMay was the consummate commander who recognized that in spite of operating outside the specified guidelines that the pilot in question achieved the objective thereby eliminating the need for a second mission, a valuable lesson LeMay

As part of the 1956 HOME RUN overflights, RB-47Hs operating from Thule AB gathered ELINT as RB-47Es photographed large portions of Siberia. Flight crews demonstrated great courage in making these flights, as well as considerable skill in flying in harsh conditions – not to overlook the maintenance crews who 'kept 'em flying.' *Author's Collection*

learned as a bomber commander. He wrote, 'I have looked into this matter and I support my aircrews.' To Rhodarmer's surprise, LeMay was cordial and quiet, and bore him no animosity in subsequent encounters.[83] (John Lappo was the pilot of the RB-47, and later earned equal measures of admiration and notoriety for flying an RB-47 under the Mackinac Bridge in Michigan on 29 April 1959). If White was this careful to warn LeMay over a procedural violation of an approved overflight mission routing, then it strains credibility that White and other senior officials – military or civilian – would have looked the other way if LeMay was conducting 156 unauthorized overflights.

Ironically, there were *civilian* efforts to go behind Eisenhower's back for overflights of the Soviet Union. Richard Bissell recalls in his memoirs that he 'saw a limiting factor in [CIA U-2] operations – namely, the ability to obtain the president's permission to conduct the flights.' Bissell says that he 'conceived the scheme' of involving the Royal Air Force in U-2 overflights, in which the British government could approve a U-2 overflight of the Soviet Union if President Eisenhower had already rejected it. Bissell adds, 'the last thing I wanted was to make it more difficult for political authorities to approve flights. Indeed I wanted to make it easier, of course.' Bissell's efforts to secure additional approving authorities did not stop in London. 'Late' in the overflight program, probably during 1959 or 1960, Bissell decided on his own to 'add another partner.' Without the approval or even the knowledge of the CIA or State Department and presumably President Eisenhower, Bissell invited French President Charles de Gaulle to join the U-2 effort. To Bissell's surprise, de Gaulle refused. For Bissell this proved fortuitous, as de Gaulle's approval would have provoked 'a fight back at the agency' or a 'potential diplomatic problem if the agreement had been reached and later had to be broken because it was undertaken without formal approval.'[84]

Eisenhower was equally uninformed of another CIA program related to overflight intelligence deep within the Soviet Union. During 1959 CIA Director Allen Dulles proposed that the president's personal airplane – Air Force One – be secretly configured to take photographs during Eisenhower's planned 1960 trip to Moscow. Flying at half the altitude of a CIA U-2, cameras secreted away in the presidential Boeing VC-137B could provide stunning detail of aerial defenses, railyards, roads, and military installations surrounding Moscow, Leningrad, and several other locations which Eisenhower would likely visit. A similar program known as SARA JANE had begun in 1955 using Douglas C-54s. These VIP-configured aircraft flew throughout Europe on seemingly benign 'embassy runs' to shuttle personnel and diplomatic pouches, all the while conducting aerial

CIA's Richard Bissell successfully fought with Curtis LeMay to keep U-2 overflights out of SAC's control. Bissell also sought to circumvent President Dwight Eisenhower's limits to U-2 overflights, and unsuccessfully tried to give the British and French authority to approve U-2 overflights of the Soviet Union. *CIA photo*

Using VIP transports as intelligence-gathering aircraft was commonplace. The SARA JANE C-54s, likely including C-54E 44-9075, shuttled diplomats unfettered throughout East and West (note flags below cockpit window). The LIDA ROSE VC-137B for President Eisenhower fulfilled a similar role. Hardly a Western monopoly, the Tupolev Tu-114 *Cleat* which Nikita Khrushchev flew to New York in 1959 was comparably configured. Did the officials know? Did it matter? *Ralf Manteufel*

photography using cameras in secret compartments that would close while on the ground. Efforts to detect these cameras proved fruitless, and the program was quite successful.[85]

Dulles did not tell the president of the Air Force One project – undertaken by Lockheed Aircraft Services at their Jamaica, New York, facility and named LIDA ROSE – in an effort to allow Eisenhower the political option of 'plausible deniability' should the airplane's intelligence-gathering capabilities be compromised. Much like the CIA U-2 pilots who simply turned

President Eisenhower waves to Parisians as he departs the failed 1960 Summit aboard VC-137A 58-6970. In 1959 Allen Dulles directed the CIA LIDA ROSE hidden-camera modification in one VC-137A, undertaken at the Lockheed Air Services' Jamaica, NY, facility, without Eisenhower's knowledge to ensure deniability as Air Force One overflew the USSR during Ike's planned visit. *Author's Collection*

their cameras on and off at specified locations on their flight charts, Air Force One's copilot was the camera operator. Test flights demonstrated the success of the project, estimated to cost $1,000,000, and the airplane was readied for the president's trip to Moscow. The U-2 Incident, however, scuttled the trip. The camera gear remained in Air Force One until January 1961, when John Kennedy took office. With the imminent transition to satellite photography of the USSR and the likely cessation of U-2 overflights due to their extreme risk, it is ironic that Eisenhower himself would have been aboard the last US reconnaissance overflight of the Soviet Union.[86]

One might argue that the military planning and execution mechanism worked effectively when applied to those missions that LeMay or other senior military officials chose to reveal to Eisenhower. It is possible that there were other overflights kept secret from him. Was the president ill-informed by his Air Force advisors about these overflights, weakening civilian control over the military, leading, as Lashmar suggested, to a 'much colder Cold War?'[87]

During Eisenhower's presidency the United States started four major aerial reconnaissance systems: the GENETRIX balloon program and its successors (a flop), the Aquatone U-2 program, the CIA's OXCART A-12 and the Air Force's SR-71 programs, and the CORONA satellite program, all successful. Eisenhower's commitment to overflights has been well documented. This has been due in large measure to the extraordinary written records produced by General Andrew J Goodpaster, Eisenhower's military liaison officer.[88] His meticulous memoranda serve as the basis for most scholarly analyses of the formulation of national security policy during the last half of the Eisenhower presidency. General Goodpaster not only took minutes of so many crucial policy meetings, he was – along with Gordon Gray – one of Eisenhower's key national security advisors. Consequently, Goodpaster's initial public repudiation of military overflights contributed to doubts over presidential awareness and control of the missions. In a 1997 television interview with Paul Lashmar, Goodpaster discounted the existence of the military overflights: *I would be astonished a) that it happened, and b) that I don't remember it if it did happen. And I do think I would have known, because that was my job.... And I doubt if the Air Force would have ventured into anything like that on their own. That's why I say it's astounding to me to hear reports that such flights did in fact occur.*[89]

Although he admitted the possibility that Goodpaster's memory was faulty, Lashmar still relied on this and other quotes as evidence that Eisenhower was unaware of the military overflights and that they were part of a 'hidden agenda' by LeMay to compel Soviet good behavior or even start World War Three.[90] Although General Goodpaster may not have remembered details about the flights in 1997, his records from 40 years earlier show that he – and Eisenhower – had a clear understanding of the extent of military overflights.

On 28 May 1956 President Eisenhower met with a small group of his advisors to discuss the 'matter of special reconnaissance flights,' a euphemism for overflights or shallow peripheral penetration missions. Present at the meeting were Under Secretary of State Herbert C Hoover, Jr, Allen Dulles, Chairman of the Joint Chiefs of Staff Admiral Arthur M Radford, Air Force Chief of Staff General Nathan F Twining, and then-Colonel Goodpaster. This meeting is particularly important because it establishes that Eisenhower was aware that a planned US military incursion into Soviet airspace had taken place and that Goodpaster took notes to that effect.[91] In printed remarks to a 2003 symposium on military overflights, General Goodpaster distanced himself from his 1997 comments to Lashmar and acceded to the documentary record. 'My own memory is not clear or detailed, but it is my belief that authorizations were handled by direct, very brief comment between Eisenhower and the chairman of the Joint Chiefs of Staff, either US Navy Admiral Arthur W Radford or US Air Force General Nathan F Twining.'[92] Goodpaster added that orders relating to the missions were often given verbally and written records kept to a minimum

Undersecretary of State Herbert C Hoover, Jr (right), son of America's 31st president, served as the State Department liaison to President Eisenhower (left) in approving US military overflights of the Soviet Union. He was present at the key meeting on 28 May 1956 when the HOME RUN overflights were discussed. Hoover frequently sat in for the ailing Foster Dulles as Secretary of State, and was aware of US military overflight programs undertaken with State Department approval. *Author's Collection*

HOME RUN was the largest single overflight operation of the Cold War. SAC RB-47s flew 156 missions from Thule AB to collect PHOTINT and ELINT of Soviet bomber bases, radar facilities, and frozen tundra in Siberia. Some viewed the initial absence of a 'paper trail' from President Eisenhower to General LeMay authorizing the flights as proof that LeMay ordered the flights illegally and with nefarious intent. Recent evidence shows, however, that Eisenhower knew and LeMay carried out legal orders.

President Eisenhower promoted LeMay (center) to Vice Chief of Staff and appointed Thomas Power (right) as his successor at SAC, hardly the action of a leader unaware that his top airpower commander was secretly trying to provoke global thermonuclear war. When John Kennedy (left) became president he chose LeMay as Air Force Chief of Staff. LeMay had enough political enemies who would have gladly used the illegal overflight issue to force his retirement *if* it had any merit, which it did not. *Author's Collection*

to preserve secrecy or deniability. Indeed, in a cover note for the 15 November 1956 memorandum regarding increased oversight of missions in the Far East, Goodpaster instructed his aide to 'take this around to Adm Radford *by hand*. You shd [*sic*] not leave a copy.'[93]

Eisenhower was aware of the exact nature of the overflight discussed in the May 1956 meeting. According to Goodpaster, 'General Twining said the operation protested [by the Soviets] has been stopped. All actions were completed. It was set up last February and conducted in recent weeks.'[94] This was Operation HOME RUN, the sweeping series of overflights from Thule AB, encompassing 156 penetrations of Soviet airspace by SAC RB-47s during a several week period. As it was General Twining, a military leader, and not Allen Dulles, the head of the civilian CIA, who explained the operation to Eisenhower, as well as the fact that HOME RUN was a SAC operation, the president must have understood that the overflights were a military, rather than a civilian, undertaking. Moreover, as of 28 May there had yet been no civilian U-2 overflights of Eastern Europe or the USSR (the first flight over the Communist bloc occurred nearly a month later on 20 June), further confirming in Eisenhower's mind the military nature of the overflight.

Significantly, Eisenhower said nothing in response to Twining's remarks about this operation, which served to conclude the meeting. This suggests that Eisenhower did not find Twining's statement or its content sufficiently provocative to merit further inquiry. If, as Lashmar suggests, Operation HOME RUN was undertaken without presidential authorization or knowledge, then it is surely reasonable to assume that Eisenhower, ever the five-star general, would have immediately held Twining to account for these 'unauthorized' or 'illegal' overflights. By saying and doing nothing Eisenhower accepted the military overflights, hardly the action of a president caught unawares by a subordinate revealing a clandestine operation with implications that included nuclear war with the Soviet Union.[95] Had Eisenhower not known of the military overflights prior to Twining's remarks, there is little doubt that the president would have sought prompt disciplinary action against those responsible. For Operation HOME RUN, that included Twining as the Air Force Chief of Staff and LeMay as SAC's commander. Instead Eisenhower presently promoted both Twining and LeMay. When Admiral Radford retired in August 1957 as the chairman of the Joint Chiefs of Staff, Eisenhower named Twining as his replacement. In July 1957 Eisenhower selected LeMay as the new Air Force Vice Chief of Staff, and accepted LeMay's recommendation of Power to replace him as CINCSAC.[96] These actions hardly reveal a president dissatisfied with his military subordinates. If Twining had known about these surreptitious overflights but not told the president then Eisenhower could not trust Twining to counsel him as chairman of the Joint Chiefs. Even if Twining did not know about the flights, Eisenhower would not want a senior military advisor so grossly ignorant of his own service's actions. At a 1958 meeting to discuss additional U-2 overflights, Twining told Eisenhower that overflights of the Soviet Union had been 'a rather regular practice for the last ten years.'[97] Given that civilian U-2 overflights had begun only two years earlier, Eisenhower must have appreciated that the preceding eight years of overflights were therefore by military airplanes, including missions approved by his presidential predecessor. If Twining had kept Eisenhower in the dark about any of these military incursions over the Soviet Union – as some researchers suggest – then this episode again provided an opportunity for the president to fire his Chairman of the Joint Chiefs for these past transgressions and his duplicity.

Nor is it likely that Eisenhower brought LeMay to Washington so he could 'keep a close eye on him.' It would be far easier to ask for his retirement and be done with his treachery than to recommend him for a position of greater trust and responsibility. Neither would Eisenhower have accepted LeMay's recommendation to select Power as his replacement as commander of the Strategic Air Command. Power was a ruthless LeMay protégé who would have had little compunction about undertaking operations outside the chain of command. Indeed, Eisenhower was not afraid to censure senior or popular US commanders or discipline their subordinates for actions or decisions that brought discredit upon the United States. He seconded President Truman's 1951 decision to fire General of the Army Douglas MacArthur (Eisenhower's former boss) for insubordination. After learning in 1958 that US reconnaissance balloons landed in the interior of the Soviet Union rather than in Denmark as intended because of an error by the Air Force officer who programmed them, Eisenhower told Secretary of State Dulles in a 30 July telephone conversation that he would 'take the man who ordered that and fire him. There will be a great thing before the Supreme Court but in the meantime the man will suffer.'[98] It is not difficult to imagine what Eisenhower would have done to LeMay or Twining for secretly taking actions that could have led to global thermonuclear war.

Moreover, there were simply too many generals and admirals who were involved in military overflights to keep the process secret from the president. During the six weeks prior to Austin's overflight, for example, American RF-86Fs based in Japan conducted three overflights of the USSR involving six airplanes. These overflew the naval base at Vladivostok and regional airfields, locating Tu-4 bases. These HAYMAKER RF-86Fs were under the operational control of

Charges that LeMay sought to provoke World War Three by secretly ordering SAC RB-47s to overfly the USSR conveniently ignore other military overflights that were beyond LeMay's control. Tactical aircraft, such as this HAYMAKER RF-86F, flew missions under the authority of FEAF/PACAF commanders including General Earle Partridge. *Tom Hagler photo courtesy of Doug Gordon*

During the Korean War F-86s were modified for reconnaissance under the ASHTRAY, HONEYBUCKET, and HAYMAKER programs. These conducted overflights of the PRC and Soviet Union during and long after the end of the war under the authority of FEAF commanders, including General Earle Partridge, *not* Curtis LeMay.

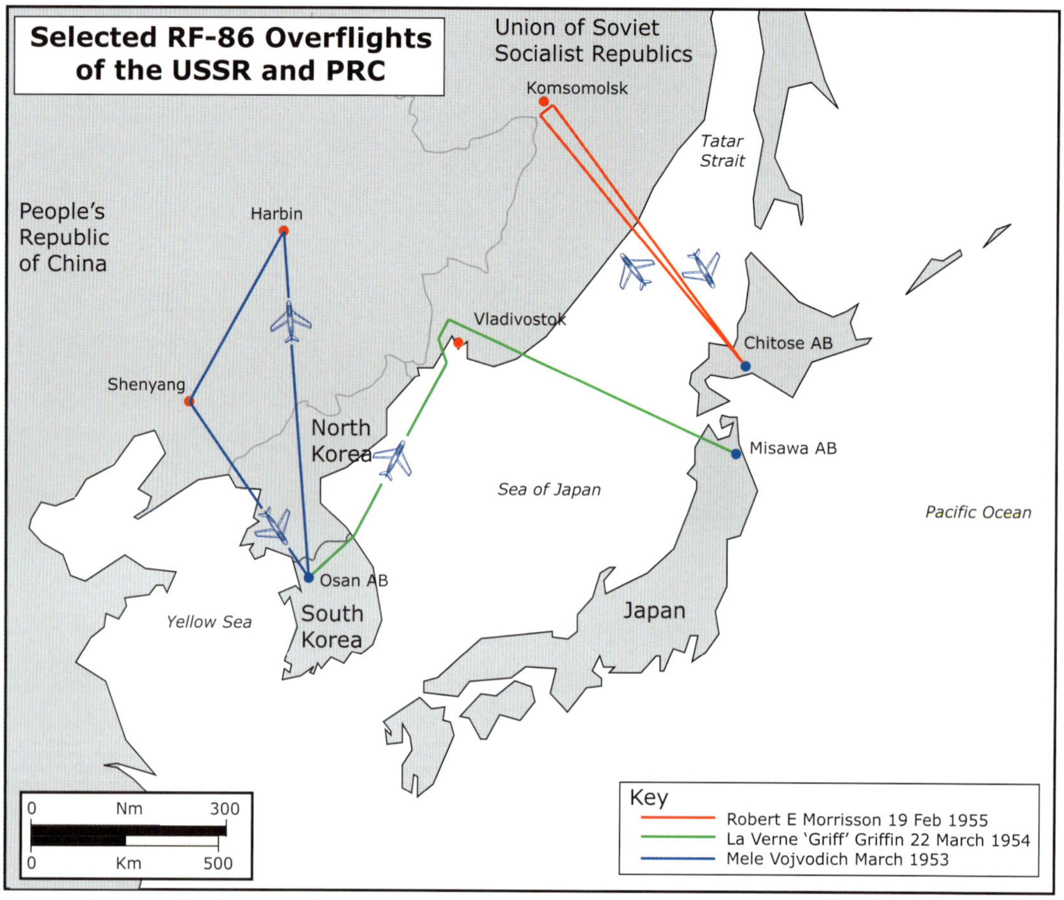

the Pacific Air Forces, commanded by General Earle Partridge, not Curtis LeMay. Partridge authorized all subsequent RB-57A HEART THROB and RF-100A SLICK CHICK overflight missions in the Pacific theater, while General Lauris Norstad was the authorizing authority for those missions in Europe.[99] Partridge, famous for having been one of the stunt pilots in the Oscar-winning movie *Wings*, reported to the Commander, Pacific Forces Army General Lyman

Lemnitzer, who was also briefed on each mission. Eisenhower promoted Lemnitzer to Army Chief of Staff in 1957 and then replaced Twining with him as Chairman of the Joint Chiefs in 1960; again, hardly the sign of a president dissatisfied with rogue officers. Navy commanders were sufficiently aware of SAC overflights (and their own) that they requested copies of USAF photographs taken during specific missions. Had they not received this material it would have been a simple matter to take their grievance to the JCS chairman US Navy Admiral Radford, the Secretary of Defense, or even the president. The Navy could then blame LeMay or Twining for conducting illegal overflights and be rid of them permanently.

Similarly, during World War Two Eisenhower commanded dozens of general officers from multiple nations, including those with extraordinary egos and personal agendas such as British Field Marshal Bernard Law Montgomery and his nemesis General George S Patton. Eisenhower was the inaugural NATO Supreme Allied Commander in Europe, again with oversight of dozens of multinational senior officers. In both cases Eisenhower's success as a leader derived in no small measure from knowing what his subordinates were doing and what they were attempting to achieve, a skill he continued to exercise once he became president. It difficult to believe that upon his election Eisenhower would have lost this attribute and abruptly become unaware of what his two most important 'New Look' commanders – Twining and LeMay – were planning and carrying out. Eisenhower clearly knew about the military overflights and that LeMay was responsible for their execution. Once again, LeMay, Twining, Partridge, Norstad, and others acted as they had under Truman, only this time with Eisenhower's approval in authorizing the overflights. They were carrying out, rather than making, American national security policy articulated by President Dwight D Eisenhower. If the purpose of the flights was to provoke World War Three, as Lashmar and Rhodes claim, then it was Eisenhower's purpose, not LeMay's, and no one has been willing to make such a bald assertion.

Two months after the May 1956 meeting Gordon Gray asked Foster Dulles to approve the transfer of two HEART THROB RB-57A-1s to Taiwan for the express purpose of deep penetration overflights. The RoCAF previously operated a variety of US-built reconnaissance airplanes on missions near and over Red China 'under the specific supervision of J–2, Commander-in-Chief, Pacific (CINCPAC) and the Intelligence Officer, Taiwan Defense Command.' Gray emphasized that the 'information gained from these *overflights* has been shared equally by the GRC [Government of the Republic of China] and American intelligence agencies' and 'have been and continue to be a principal source of vital early warning intelligence to the US Forces charged with defending Taiwan.' He added that 'the presently programmed squadron of RF–84F aircraft must therefore be supplemented with aircraft having a higher operating ceiling capability if deep penetration reconnaissance missions are to be undertaken' by the RoCAF. The solution was 'two RB–57 aircraft of the 'Heart Throb' configuration which do have deep penetration characteristics.' Gray concluded that 'the Department of Defense, therefore, requests the concurrence of the Department of State in the assignment of these aircraft in order that the Commander-in-Chief, Pacific, may fulfill the deep penetration portion of his intelligence mission.'[100]

There is no ambiguity in Gray's request, nor is it couched in euphemism or implication. Gray specifically requested two *military* RB-57A HEART THROB aircraft because of their 'deep penetration' capability, proven in 1955 with USAF RB-57 HEART THROB overflights of the USSR and Eastern Europe. Gray knew clearly that US military aircraft had overflown the USSR as part of this established program. Secretary of State Foster Dulles understood the operational history of the HEART THROB program, and approved the transfer to Taiwan after a phone conversation with his brother at CIA, knowing full well why the airplanes were suited for deep penetration overflights. As with Goodpaster, if Gray knew about official military overflights of the USSR with the 1955 HEART THROB program, then Eisenhower knew about US military overflights of the Soviet Union.

In the aftermath of the Russian protests of the December 1956 SAC RB-57D BLACK KNIGHT mission over Vladivostok, the president ordered the cessation of all 'flights by US reconnaissance aircraft over 'Iron Curtain' countries.'[101] He ended this moratorium for CIA U-2 flights over the Soviet Union, which resumed on 18 March 1957. He did not authorize the resumption of any military overflights of Iron Curtain countries. During the 1958 Taiwan Straits crisis, however, the RoCAF undertook 'high-altitude reconnaissance flights to the mainland [of China] with the understanding that permission had been granted by the President.' Eisenhower angrily told Secretary of State Foster Dulles and General Twining after learning of these RoCAF overflights using the former HEART THROB RB-57A-1s that he was not briefed in advance.[102] On 24 April 1958 the president directed Goodpaster to tell Twining and Allen Dulles that there were to be 'no reconnaissance flights, by *military* or other aircraft, over the territory of the USSR or other Communist countries.'[103] The president authorized at least one exception in late 1958 when Twining and Secretary of Defense McElroy asked Eisenhower for permission to fly a RoCAF RB-57 'over the mainland of China' (believed to be the 6 December 1958 STAGE SHOW mission), a request which the president approved.[104] As late as 1 June 1960, when a SAC RB-47H was shot down along the periphery of the USSR, Eisenhower suspended not only all future civilian U-2 overflights, but any similar military operations. The president ordered Secretary of Defense Thomas Gates, Jr, 'to take action to assure such things were called off.' The following day Goodpaster specifically repeated the directive to Twining.[105] This language reflects the president's desire to be clear that there would be no overflights of any kind, military or civilian. It equally indicates that Eisenhower sought to end all overflights of *any* country, not just those in the Communist Bloc.

Opposite, bottom: The Joint Chiefs of Staff had a clear understanding of military overflights. USAF General Nathan Twining (left) oversaw HOME RUN and other SAC missions, and likely authorized very early RB-29 overflights from Ladd Field. Army General Lyman Lemnitzer (l ctr) was briefed on RF-86 and RB-57 HEART THROB missions in the Pacific theater. JCS Chairman and naval aviator Admiral Arthur Radford (r ctr) and Chief of Naval Operations Admiral Robert Carney (right) were aware of joint USAF-USN overflights of the Chukotskii Peninsula as well as SAC missions. *Author's Collection*

Indeed, during 1958 and 1959 there were MILL TOWN and SOUTH GATE U-2 overflights of Indonesia, Tibet, Laos, and North Vietnam, and possibly military flights over additional countries as well. Other CIA overflights included those associated with the OSTIARY program in Tibet and Indonesia, but these were primarily agent and supply drops with intelligence gathering as a secondary objective.[106] There were also military overflights of non-Communist nations, but none over the USSR. One former B-57 pilot writes that beginning in January 1959, RB-57Ds assigned to the 4080th SW conducted overflights of the Soviet Union. This is incorrect as the BLACK KNIGHT RB-57s purportedly overflew only Finland.[107] Air Force COMINT missions may have overflown Indonesia in 1958 during the ULCER GULCH operations.

Ultimately, Eisenhower acted decisively in ending overflights. His 1960 ban on any aerial incursions into Soviet or Eastern Bloc nations remains unchanged to the present day. He did this not only to reduce the risk of conflict, but because the value of the U-2 missions had been supplanted by nascent satellite technology which provided greater coverage and included all aspects of intelligence collection from PHOTINT to SIGINT to COMINT. Eisenhower did not, however, end overflights of Communist China in 1960, but restricted those operations to missions flown by Republic of China pilots under the aegis of the CIA.[108] Overflights of Red China continued until 1974 when Eisenhower's former vice president, Richard Nixon, ended them as part of his ongoing presidential efforts to establish and improve relations with the PRC.

In the last year of his presidency Eisenhower went beyond eliminating overflights of the Soviet Bloc. He tackled the increasingly thorny problem of vastly expanding numbers of peripheral reconnaissance flights and their organizational control. Truman's decision to defer operational matters on aerial reconnaissance missions to the JCS created a significant degree of parochial turf issues. LeMay was frustrated that SAC aircraft and crews 'doing ECM work in the Baltic' were under the day-to–day authority of the United States Air Forces Europe (USAFE) commander, not himself as SAC's commanding general. He was particularly upset that the JCS assigned Black Sea missions to Navy aircraft and crews, a task which SAC leaders felt was not being accorded the urgency they believed it deserved.[109] Few agencies knew of another's operations, and few of the results were willingly shared outside of the gathering agency. Indeed, the Air Force (especially SAC) and the CIA had a particularly antagonistic relationship as they evaluated the same threats to US national security but often reached profoundly different conclusions. The intelligence community spoke with too many voices, each clamoring for presidential attention and a greater share of the budgetary pie.

As NATO commander Eisenhower certainly knew about Air Force and Navy peripheral missions, and was likely briefed on the March 1952 RAF JU JITSU RB-45C overflights of Eastern Europe and the Soviet Union. Upon becoming president in 1953, he inherited both this relatively inchoate intelligence system and a maturing strategic aerial reconnaissance program. Sometimes Eisenhower accepted existing JCS authority for its conduct and operations established under Truman. At other times Eisenhower reined in the program to ensure the strictest presidential control. As a matter of policy for aerial intelligence gathering, Eisenhower relied on a 'universally accepted military premise' that allowed military commanders to 'exercise no more prerogatives than are necessary to the performance of [their] mission,' effectively delegating the planning of 'clandestine intelligence collection' to the field commander as he saw fit, but not without strict accountability.[110] Eisenhower's disposition to delegate responsibility (but not authority) derived from his own military experience. He was certainly willing to allow others to make decisions having critical foreign policy implications.[111] Eisenhower believed that his actions improved the effectiveness of the program while limiting its potential liabilities. But this delegation of decisions addressed only *how* strategic aerial reconnaissance would be undertaken, not *if* they would be undertaken. For example, by the mid-1950s the JCS became increasingly concerned about the 'commonplace' nature of peripheral and overflight missions. In August 1956 the chiefs warned the responsible field commanders (like LeMay) that the 'real danger [of confrontation with the Soviet Union] lies in routine operations of this type becoming so routine as to lead to careless operational practices.'[112] Eisenhower shared this concern. After the 1958 downing of a USAFE C-130A-II SUN VALLEY I COMINT aircraft that had inadvertently strayed over Armenia, the president 'stressed the necessity of command emphasis and supervision' as suitable action to prevent future recurrences. Air Force Chief of Staff General White told Goodpaster 'that he had taken steps to tighten up further the conduct and supervision of such reconnaissance flights....' For many years it was held that

MiG-17s and J-5s shot down 10 ferrets, including C-130A-II 56-0528, on peripheral missions. Critics charge that the RB-47E overflight of Murmansk and its crew were sacrificial bait intended to draw Soviet MiG-17 fire, justifying LeMay's nefarious plan to start World War Three. This conspiracy theory requires that LeMay knew there would be MiG-17s and not MIG-15s along the RB-47E's route, but told the crew they would encounter only MiG-15s. Great Hollywood movie fodder, but there is no evidence whatsoever that it is true. *via Yefim Gordon*

the C-130A-II was lured into Soviet airspace and then shot down. Current research shows that the airplane inadvertently crossed the Turkish-Armenian border and was attacked by multiple MiG-17s and crashed with no survivors.[113] After learning of the unapproved 6 January 1959 RoCAF STAGE SHOW RB-57D overflight of the PRC, the president told Secretary Dulles and General Twining that permission for future overflights of the PRC or anywhere else 'must be secured on a mission-by-mission basis from the President.' Eisenhower also stipulated that the flights not include 'the northern sector' – likely meaning the Chinese region adjacent to the Soviet Union – and must not operate from bases in Korea.[114]

These correctives initially satisfied the president, but failed to put an end to the problem. Exactly two months after the U-2 was shot down over the Soviet Union, a SAC RB-47H on a peripheral SIGINT mission was attacked and destroyed over the Barents Sea.[115] Although the airplane was over international waters when attacked – despite Soviet claims to the contrary – the incident underscored Eisenhower's perception that the US reconnaissance flights were becoming 'sloppy' (interestingly, there was some doubt among the president and his advisors that the Soviets actually shot down the RB-47H, believing it may have crashed due to mechanical failure or similar causes).[116] In keeping with his increasing centralization efforts over the intelligence community as a whole, the president felt the time had come to transfer day-to-day operational authority for aerial reconnaissance from SAC and the Air Force where it had been for the past 15 years to the Joint Chiefs of Staff.[117] According to one of the military officials involved in this transformation, Eisenhower told JCS Chairman General Twining after the RB-47H loss that Twining 'personally' should 'keep a handle' on all aerial reconnaissance flights, adding 'you are responsible.' After several months, Secretary of Defense Thomas Gates approved the establishment of the Joint Reconnaissance Center (JRC) on 24 October 1960.[118] The JRC reported directly to the JCS and subsequently to the Secretary of Defense, and would 'monitor all reconnaissance operations conducted by' the military. The president also ordered Twining to determine the suitability of a strategic reconnaissance variant of the Convair B-58 to facilitate peripheral missions at speeds which would offer a modicum of defense against interception.[119] Just months before leaving office, Eisenhower centralized the daily conduct of peripheral reconnaissance flights. Planning and conducting missions would no longer be the purview of multiple theater commanders or the Navy and Air Force. There would be one entity overseeing all peripheral reconnaissance and that was the JCS. As chairman, Twining and his successors were solely responsible and fully accountable to the president for their efficient and effective conduct.[120] Eisenhower's centralization of supervision over the US aerial reconnaissance effort, however, did not mean a radical change in the way the program did business. As one declassified Air Force history notes, 'the Joint Reconnaissance Center duplicated the reconnaissance control mechanism already established within the Air Force.'[121] Several years earlier Eisenhower appointed a blue ribbon panel (known as the Hull Committee) to oversee organizational improvements to the US intelligence community. Among its many recommendations, on 4 October 1960 the committee endorsed 'the peripheral ELINT ferret operations of SAC and we recommend their renewal and continuation under the careful safeguards which have characterized the conduct of this program over the years.' The president concurred, authorizing the full-scale resumption of peripheral flights using SAC's existing procedures, but now 'under the safeguards which have been directed by the JCS.'[122] As such, the JRC was largely an organizational, rather than an operational, change to US strategic aerial reconnaissance policy. The JRC became the single source of oversight for the continuation of procedures developed and adopted by the Air Force and Navy over the preceding 15 years, rather than an agency committed to the critical analysis and alteration of the motives, means, and methods of long-range aerial reconnaissance missions, peripheral or overflight. This created a paradoxical situation where Eisenhower strengthened control over a key part of the military intelligence community while simultaneously allowing it to operate on its own under the aegis of the Joint Chiefs of Staff.

***

Access during the mid-1990s to newly declassified material and many of the participants contributed substantially to an improved understanding of the role of strategic aerial reconnaissance during the first 25 years of the Cold War. Not surprisingly, two disparate conclusions emerged from these analyses: 1) that the flights were an acceptable part of US military operations, approved and condoned by the president as part of the American effort to determine the precise nature of the Soviet threat to the United States; or 2) that the flights were illegally undertaken by SAC Commander Curtis LeMay – either singly or in concert with other senior military officials and without the knowledge of the president – to advance LeMay's personal conservative political agenda which included initiation of preventive nuclear war with the Soviet Union.

Fragmentary release of documents easily supported both of these diverse arguments that opponents held were either an apologetic justification for rogue officers seeking World War Three or a liberal attack on a distinguished American officer while ignoring the positive value of legal overflights in constraining the Cold War. Both sides of the barricade based their arguments primarily on LeMay's comments and his reputation viewed through the patina of time and ideology. Although the evidence was often ambiguous, the conclusions derived from the documents and interviews were not, and were often fallacious. Lashmar, for example, wrote 'it cannot be discounted that [LeMay] was trying to force the Russians into a major hostile response.'[123] Any number of conclusions is possible from LeMay's remarks and actions, but Lashmar chose the most threatening because it fit his overall theory of a 'killer on the edge.'

Lashmar's argument, however compelling or convincing, was hardly original. Nearly 40 years earlier Nikita Khrushchev told an auditorium packed with delegates of the Supreme Soviet on 5 May 1960 that the U-2 flight could well have been an 'aggressive act committed by Pentagon militarists without the President's knowledge.' Indeed, Khrushchev went on, if 'American military men can take actions on their own, the world should be greatly concerned.' Two days later, as he sprung the news that Powers was still alive, Khrushchev again opined that Eisenhower knew nothing about the U-2 flight and it was instead 'the American military giving its own orders,' which was dangerously ominous. 'When the military starts bossing the show, the results can be disastrous. Such a pirate, prone to dizziness, may in fact drop a hydrogen bomb on foreign soil.' Khrushchev feared that 'insubordinate Western officers' could start World War Three, and may even have believed that the May Day flight, along with the U-2 mission on 9 April, was the doing of some US general.[124] Arguably Khrushchev was giving Eisenhower an out – a way to save face and the impending Paris summit. But the consequences, had the president chosen to accept the offer, were profoundly troubling.

One contemporary appraisal of Eisenhower was that he was 'too tired or lazy or dumb to take command of his job' and that he played golf while the 'government was run by faceless White House aides.'[125] To admit that some subordinate authorized the overflight without presidential awareness would have been an admission that Eisenhower was indeed out of touch with his responsibilities as the leader of the free world and that it was renegade generals who held their fingers to button, not the president. American actions after the U-2 loss did little to dispel this implication that Eisenhower had lost control of the intelligence-gathering community in general and reconnaissance flights in particular. A press announcement on 7 May noted that '[a]s a result of the inquiry ordered by the President, it has been established that insofar as the authorities in Washington are concerned, there was no authorization' for the U-2 flight. Two days later a State Department press release said '[s]pecific missions…have not been subject to Presidential authorization'.[126]

Given the piecemeal availability of evidence surrounding overflights in general it is understandable that Lashmar and others found ready arguments in Khrushchev's 'party line' and critique of Eisenhower, particularly when coupled with the highly politicized vituperation surrounding LeMay as the suspected culprit. Subsequent declassification of new materials and fuller declassification of older documents demonstrate, however, that Presidents Truman and Eisenhower were clearly aware of the extent of and endorsed the strategic aerial reconnaissance program. They understood the distinction between peripheral missions and overflights. Both presidents approved military overflights and were not afraid to disapprove any they felt were unnecessary risks. Although the bulk of military overflight missions were delegated primarily to SAC for execution, they were reviewed and approved not only by the Joint Chiefs of Staff but by civilian leaders such as the Secretaries of Defense and State and their civilian subordinates. Military overflights were duly authorized by commanders who were held accountable for their success or failure. Policies and procedures for all aerial reconnaissance missions evolved under Truman and Eisenhower, leading to a greater degree of centralized control and in the eventual elimination of all overflights, military or civilian, of the Soviet Union and Eastern Bloc countries.

Truman and Eisenhower were both strongly committed to the need for more intelligence about the Soviet Union and were appreciative of the value of aerial reconnaissance, peripheral or overflights, in acquiring this information. Until the debut of CIA U-2 operations in 1956, it fell to the Navy and the Air Force – predominantly SAC – to conduct these missions. Both presidents were aware of the risks entailed with the missions, and sought to mitigate their impact on US-Soviet relations. Irrespective of ideological views about Curtis LeMay, there is no evidence that he was ever a rogue officer driven by a rollback agenda that included preventive nuclear war instigated by military overflights. Indeed, the evidence shows just the opposite. LeMay followed procedures established by senior military and civilian leaders, and he executed overflights approved by the President of the United States. Civilian oversight of the military, in this case SAC and its overflight program, worked as advertised.

To argue that President Eisenhower was unaware of US military overflights of the Soviet Union requires that the President's National Security Advisor and his senior military advisor (both close friends of Ike), the Secretaries of Defense and State and their undersecretaries, the Chairman of the Joint Chiefs of Staff, the Air Force Chief of Staff, and a dozen or more other four-star generals and admirals (each well known to the president), the head of the CIA, and a host of senior departmental functionaries throughout the government all knew about these military overflights but somehow managed to keep them secret from the president for years despite Soviet protests. To blame Curtis LeMay and his 'killer on the edge' rollback agenda for these flights as an unconstitutional mechanism for provoking war with the USSR on terms favorable to LeMay and SAC equally requires that the same individuals colluded with one another for years to enable LeMay to authorize these flights, whether as a co-conspirator or as a dupe, while keeping them secret from the president. In either case, it requires that one of the most astute military and political leaders in American history suddenly lost the operational knowledge and acumen which had served him so well as supreme commander of allied forces in Europe during the Second World War and had abruptly become the naïve and ignorant puppet of a cabal which sought publicly to preserve global peace during the Cold War while surreptitiously trying to start World War Three. At best these suppositions make for ridiculous Hollywood fodder, at worst they are a conspiracy theorist's dream.

Eisenhower knew, and LeMay did as the president ordered.

In 1957, well after the 1956 SAC HOME RUN RB-47 and BLACK KNIGHT RB-57 overflights of the USSR, President Eisenhower promoted LeMay to Air Force Vice Chief of Staff. Ike understood that LeMay carried out orders approved by the Departments of Defense and State. Ironically, the red ribbon on LeMay's left side, third row from the bottom is the Soviet Order of the Patriotic War, First Class. *Author's Collection*

6 Planes and Policies

Intelligence collected by SAC RB-47s, Navy PB4Y-2s, and CIA U-2s was an essential tool in developing military plans and strategic national security policies. Analysts studied photographs to locate potential enemy defenses or cross check suspected targets with other sources, an often time-consuming and tedious process. Target planners would then sit down with maps and painstakingly draw bomber penetration routes to avoid SAMs or enemy airfields. Such variations in flight paths increased fuel burn rates, so each airplane's load of jet fuel had to be recalculated precisely with each change, a laborious task in a world without computers. For a thousand bomber missions, this effort was Herculean.

Communications intercepts had to be translated, transcribed, and then culled by subject-matter experts to determine what nuggets they might contain. Did they reveal a previously unidentified command center with improved survivability? Did they indicate a new tactic by interceptor pilots who would then catch SAC's bomber force unaware and vulnerable? Did they eavesdrop on the private conversation of senior officials complaining about the shift in strategy from bombers to ICBMs? Or did they simply record the drunken ramblings of a radio operator at some remote outpost, ranting about being away from his sweetheart?

Recordings of a new radar signal were shared with scientists and engineers who attempted to divine its purpose, whether as a new tracking radar, a ballistic missile detection facility, or simply a better way to forecast the weather. Repeated collections of the signal over months would determine if the device was entering operational service or was merely an experiment. If it was the former then American military and civilian technical experts would take months, perhaps years, to design, test, and produce electronic jamming equipment to be installed in a B-47 or B-52.

Even policies made at the highest levels of government were the product of a lengthy intelligence process. Analysts would study the information, subject their initial conclusions to repeated critique sessions across multiple agencies, write draft after draft of their interpretation and assessment of the data, and ultimately produce an NIE or other document that the president or the Secretary of State might actually read during deliberations over a new NSC statement of policy.

Strategic aerial reconnaissance was designed as a solution for the long-term, continually evolving security environment. It offered the benefit of careful study, reflection, consensus, and dissent in understanding the motives and capabilities of an adversary, real or potential. Policies could then be implemented judiciously and with the option to modify them or change them altogether. The flights also offered another – unplanned – tool in the policy making process that allowed for short-term analyses and decisions. In times of tension or crisis, aerial intelligence could expeditiously tell senior officials what was happening, what was about to happen, and suggest what they might do about it. Strategic reconnaissance that informed policy over months or years acquired a tactical role in a dynamic situation. In some cases such missions showed that further American involvement in a region would be imprudent. During 1958 and 1959, for example, the United States limited – or avoided altogether – potential or escalated military intervention in places such as Indonesia, Laos, and Tibet. In other cases the flights provided PHOTINT and COMINT that enabled the president and his advisors to assess the extent of an ongoing conflict and develop a measured American response, most notably during the Suez Crisis in 1956 and the Taiwan Straits crisis of 1958.

Researchers have not been shy in their efforts to relate intelligence to policy. Their focus, however, has largely been on long-term or strategic issues such as the formulation of national intelligence estimates (NIEs), the relationship of intelligence to strategic force planning, or the use of intelligence to verify strategic arms agreements. In a more recent illustration of this relationship, intelligence collected off Kamchatka by the RC-135E RIVET AMBER in May 1969 appeared to validate the belief among hard-line US policy makers that the Soviet SS-9 *Scarp's* three nuclear warheads were multiple independently targetable reentry vehicles (MIRVs). If true, this represented a significant first-strike capability and would be a critical issue in ongoing strategic arms limitation negotiations. In fact, the RIVET AMBER intelligence was at first incorrectly analyzed. Subsequent study correctly showed that it was not MIRV capable and the three warheads were not configured for independent targeting. Consequently, the SS-9 was not an extreme threat to US Minuteman silos and hence less of a bargaining chip in the negotiations, much to the dismay of US National Security Advisor Henry Kissinger.[1]

The 1962 Cuban missile crisis remains the definitive example of US flights contributing to the day-to-day deliberations of the president and his senior advisors in a crisis situation. From the initial detection by U-2s of the Soviet medium-range ballistic missiles, to the daily updates of missile site construction and operational status, to verifying the withdrawal of Soviet weapons and forces from Cuba, US strategic aerial reconnaissance missions provided President Kennedy, the Executive Committee, and the Department of Defense with the information necessary to attack and destroy the missiles, as well as to make informed, measured decisions to achieve a peaceful resolution to the crisis. Of the Cuban missile crisis Ray Cline, the head of the CIA's Directorate of Intelligence at the time, wrote, 'I cannot imagine a more intimate linking of [aerial] intelligence in all functional categories with the highest level of decisionmaking.'[2] Despite this clear and compelling connection, one wonders if the use of aerial reconnaissance during the Cuban missile crisis was an exceptional or representative case. The historical record suggests that it was indeed typical, although how US officials under Truman and Eisenhower used the intelligence collected by aerial methods during a crisis has varied in its overall effectiveness.

There are as yet few examples of Harry Truman's use of strategic aerial reconnaissance in times of duress. This is most likely due to the adolescent nature of the aerial reconnaissance program and its primary purpose to collect military intelligence rather than any reluctance on Truman's part to utilize peripheral missions and overflights to gather political intelligence. No doubt reconnaissance flights assessed the deployment and operational status of Soviet forces during the 1948 Berlin Blockade, particularly in determining Soviet response to Operation VITTLES. From the onset of the war in Korea in June 1950, the Air Force and the Navy used reconnaissance and patrol flights to gather PHOTINT and SIGINT over and around the battlefield, but this information was used more by the military in its reaction to the invasion than by civilian officials in the formulation of US policy in response to the surprise invasion. Still, there is at least one case which shows that Truman took advantage of strategic reconnaissance flights outside of the Korean theater – but clearly linked to the conflict there – to develop a restrained US response to potential Soviet aggression.

One common fear among US policy makers was that the North Korean invasion of South Korea was a feint intended to divert American attention away from Europe, where a Soviet invasion was secretly imminent. Less than a week after DPRK forces crossed into South Korea, the Soviets staged extensive naval maneuvers in the Black Sea, a possible indicator of an impending invasion of Turkey. These operations might have been a warning sign of a mass Soviet naval breakout through the Bosphorus into the Mediterranean, threatening Greece, Italy, France, or Spain, particularly if undertaken in conjunction with land-based attacks in Germany. US strategic reconnaissance missions constantly monitored these exercises. Indeed, surveillance flights 'of Soviet Fleet movements in this and other areas' were 'intensified and further reports [to the president were] made on a priority basis.'[3] From this continuous observation as well as other intelligence indicators, US analysts were able to determine early in the Korean crisis that there was no evidence these naval maneuvers were a harbinger of a Soviet invasion of Western Europe, the Eastern Mediterranean, or the Middle East. Soviet military maneuvers were typically well orchestrated to ensure the desired outcome, so having complex naval operations less than a week after the invasion with little planning time strongly suggests that the two events were coincidental but unrelated. Truman and his advisors were thus reassured that the war in Korea was not part of a larger Soviet war plan. The United States then tailored its military response to the Korean invasion to suit a regional, rather than a global, conflict, precluding inadvertent escalation with the Soviet Union.

President Eisenhower was equally able to use strategic reconnaissance flights to preclude poor policy choices, to customize a US response that was less threatening to the USSR or its allies, to avoid unnecessarily engaging US military and economic resources in fruitless situations, and – unusually in many foreign policy decisions – to know when to withdraw. By using aerial photos and SIGINT, Eisenhower was able to avoid altogether or disengage from foreign entanglements that would otherwise unintentionally obligate America to a no-win military commitment.

For many members of the Eisenhower administration, a nation's neutrality during the Cold War was nearly as sinful as its embrace of communism. The non-aligned movement, epitomized by figures such as Jawaharlal Nehru of India and Gamal Nasser of Egypt, stressed a course of action that cut strongly against the Washington mentality that if a nation was not with America in its containment of communism, then that country was against the United States. Moreover, a neutral country was more likely to fall under Soviet sway, further aggregating an already bipolar world. One of the most important non-aligned leaders was Ahmed Sukarno, the mercurial president of Indonesia, who hosted the 1955 Bandung Conference. Eisenhower and Foster Dulles saw Sukarno not only as a driving force in the non-aligned movement but vulnerable to anti-American (read Communist) influence. Combined with Sukarno's revolutionary nationalism – another red flag in the Eisenhower administration – the conditions appeared ripe for a major Soviet presence in Southeast Asia.

To US policy makers, Indonesia was of considerable importance. The island nation was essential to Australian security and Japanese economic prosperity, was a vital source of natural resources such as rubber, tin, copper, and petroleum, and was a large and influential 'domino.' Viewing Indonesia in strictly Cold War terms, American officials feared that the ascension of pro-Communist forces to power in Indonesia during the late 1950s would lead to the denial of its rich resources to the United States and their subsequent availability instead to the Soviet bloc, would threaten vital sea lanes throughout Southeast Asia, would jeopardize US defense commitments to Southeast Asia, especially the Philippines, and would 'weaken the resolve of some Southeast Asian states to remain oriented primarily to the west.'[4] These fears appeared more credible when, during 1957, Indonesia acquired Soviet-designed fighters and bombers imported from Czechoslovakia. Most ominously, this included IL-28 *Beagle* bombers capable of carrying low-yield atomic weapons. Although Indonesia did not possess atomic bombs, nor was the Soviet Union about to give any to the island nation, American officials were concerned over the possibility that the Soviets themselves would use the IL-28 base in Indonesia to deliver Soviet atom bombs on US facilities in the Philippines or to close shipping lanes.[5] The Joint Chiefs considered the Indonesian Air Force as the most 'pro-Communist' of the Indonesian military services, and the Czech sale reinforced these US anxieties. By turning to the Soviet bloc to arm its military, American military planners feared that Indonesia would receive not just Soviet equipment but Soviet advisors and their attendant influence.[6] Understanding the resources and capabilities of the Indonesian Air Force became paramount in US policy calculations.

CIA efforts to influence Indonesian elections in favor of anti-Communist groups failed, and the United States began to consider more drastic measures. One opportunity arose when the CIA recommended support of a rebellion by dis-

Czech-built IL-28s represented a threat by the pro-Communist Indonesian Air Force. Vital shipping lanes essential to the economic recovery of East Asia were at risk, raising the possibility of a US-backed coup. U-2s and other aerial sources indicated that few of the *Beagles* had been delivered and that chances for a successful coup were poor. Eisenhower demurred. *via Yefim Gordon*

CIA U-2 Detachments and Mission Numbers

Detachment	Numbers	Mission Type
Det A, Wiesbaden AB, Germany	2XXX	Eastern Europe/USSR Overflights
Det B, Incirlik AB, Turkey	14XX	Middle East/Suez Sorties, US Pilots
	4XXX	USSR/Tibet Overflights
	8XXX	USSR Overflights, RAF Pilots
	86XX	Middle East Sorties, RAF Pilots
Det C, NAS Atsugi, Japan	6XXX	USSR/PRC Overflights

gruntled Indonesian Army officers known by the Indonesian acronym PEMESTA. In what turned out to be a dress rehearsal for the Bay of Pigs, the CIA provided $7 million worth of weapons, training, and aerial support for the rebels as part of the CIA's Operation HAIK.[7] The United States utilized COMINT derived from aerial reconnaissance missions, such as the USAF ULCER GULCH C-97s, to determine Indonesian (both loyalist and rebel) military plans and operations. During 1958 Richard Bissell dispatched U-2s from NAS Atsugi to NAS Cubi Point in the Philippines as part of Operation ROBIN HOOD to photograph the many Indonesian islands to determine the disposition of troops and rebel forces. CIA U-2s flew some 30 missions from the end of March to the middle of June.[8] Aerial reconnaissance revealed the construction of a substantial airstrip on the island of Natuna Besar, north of Sumatra. The long runway meant that the base was clearly intended for use by bombers. US naval leaders feared that Sukarno might allow Soviet-manned bombers to operate from this base, threatening shipping routes throughout the Indonesian archipelago. For Americans, the potential of a Soviet atomic bomber base was frightening enough, but it did not necessarily teach the Americans what the Soviets must have felt like surrounded by US bomber bases in England, Morocco, Okinawa, and elsewhere. During the 1960s the Indonesians acquired at least 20 Tupolev Tu-16KS-1 bombers from the Soviet Union, each capable of carrying two air launched AS-1 anti-ship missiles. These airplanes had a longer range than the IL 28s, so could carry atomic weapons or sink ships over an even greater area.[9] Aerial detection of this new bomber base exacerbated American fears of a potential Soviet presence – direct or indirect – in the region. US reconnaissance flights also sparked direct conflict between the United States and Indonesia, when Indonesian Air Force fighters attacked and damaged a US Navy patrol aircraft, ostensibly conducting aerial reconnaissance.[10]

Most importantly, aerial reconnaissance revealed the pro-American, anti-Sukarno coup's limited potential for success. COMINT showed that the rebels were poorly organized – perhaps too much so to benefit from American assistance – and that the Indonesian military was far better prepared to mount counterattacks and search-and-destroy missions designed to cripple the rebellion. PHOTINT showed that rebel forces were widely scattered through inhospitable terrain and appeared incapable of launching effective co-ordinated attacks against crucial targets. In the face of this disconcerting evidence, the Joint Chiefs 'seriously worried' that increasing Russian influence and the defeat of the rebels 'would almost certainly lead to Communist domination of Indonesia.' This, in turn, would cause a 'serious reaction' in Malaya and Thailand, 'probable trouble' in Laos, and 'possible trouble' in Cambodia. The JCS predicted that a Communist Indonesia 'could result in the disappearance of [the Southeast Asia Treaty Organization (SEATO)] as a viable pact' and contribute to the extension of communism in the Muslim Middle East given its religious affinity with Islamic Indonesia.[11]

Eventually the coup – modeled after the successful CIA overthrow of Guatemala's Jacobo Arbenz – failed. Allen Dulles told the NSC that the rebels had 'moved rather too fast and ...without carefully counting their military assets.'[12] Despite the dire predictions issued by the JCS regarding the future of a pro-Communist Indonesia should the coup fail, little substantive US effort was made to reinforce the rebels. The unwillingness of the White House and Langley to support the rebels derived in no small measure from aerial reconnaissance. Intelligence flights showed that there was no evidence of Soviet military forces, particularly bombers, which could compromise American interests in the region. Moreover, reconnaissance flights showed that few of the Czech-built MiG-15 and MiG-17 fighters and IL-28 bombers had even arrived in Indonesia, let alone become operational. Coupled with intelligence reports that the Indonesian crews were still training in Egypt and Czechoslovakia, there was no evidence of an immediate threat – either Indonesian or Soviet – requiring any direct US military intervention, further reducing the Eisenhower administration's willingness to commit substantial resources to support the rebels.[13] US reconnaissance flights also monitored the highly fluid battlefield between the rebels and government forces as well as their deployment and operational readiness. When U-2 photos and COMINT showed that rebel forces were badly organized and ill-suited to fight government forces across the expanse of the archipelago, Eisenhower understood that increased support for the rebels would prove useless and further publicly embroil the United States in a no-win situation. Indeed, American complicity in the coup became undeniable when an American CIA pilot flying tactical combat missions in support of the rebels was shot down and captured, along with incriminating documents. On 18 May 1958 CIA pilot Allen Pope was shot down in a Douglas B-26B Invader during an attack on an Indonesian convoy. One wonders why this incident did not serve as a warning to Eisenhower about the potential of U-2 overflight compromise. CIA officials believed that pilots were unlikely to survive any crash, but Pope did, just as would Powers two years later. Any further American action on behalf of rebel forces would be ineffective and politically damaging abroad, and US efforts to prolong the coup would necessitate a far greater degree of overt assistance than the United States was willing to offer.

Eisenhower was equally prudent elsewhere, thanks in part to intelligence gleaned from aerial reconnaissance. Throughout 1959 and 1960, the stability of Laos (given Communist influence from the Soviet Union, PRC, and North Vietnam) raised concerns over American policy in Southeast Asia. The CIA flew U-2 missions out of Takhli RTAFB in Thailand, looking for evidence of foreign troops, supplies, and equipment, the status of roads and supply lines, and the disposition of Lao forces. U-2 photos showed no evidence of any foreign intervention in Laos. To be sure, the value of these photos was limited. Despite the clarity of the photos, interpreters could not see through the dense jungle canopy. It was impossible to know what forces might be in place but otherwise obscured by the foliage. Myriad caves in the region could hold supplies and command centers. Roads marked on maps might in actuality be little more than footpaths or otherwise unusable by motor vehicles. Such limits to intelligence interpretation certainly constrained options in the policy process. Coupled with Eisenhower's military experience and awareness of the challenges in guerilla warfare, he opted not to escalate the American presence in Laos by deploying substantive military forces to support Lao forces and defend key areas. Eisenhower's reluctance to commit troops to Southeast Asia in geography and conditions that would have severely constrained their ability to achieve American goals is a lesson that was lost on subsequent presidents and their advisors.[14]

Similarly, following the departure of the Dalai Lama from Tibet in 1959, Eisenhower sought to exploit the tensions between the Tibetans and their Communist Chinese occupiers. The president considered giving increased American support to Tibetan rebels, but US knowledge of the region was severely limited. Given that Tibet was not easily accessible, aerial reconnaissance provided a ready solution to acquire the intelligence needed to make appropriate policy decisions. CIA U-2 missions from Thailand and the Philippines acquired excellent and often dramatic images of the imposing terrain, and showed an extensive road network built by the Chinese following their invasion in 1950.[15] It was clear from the images that supplies to the Tibetan rebels could not be trucked in en masse and would have to be airdropped in small but frequent quantities. Moreover, given the extent of the PRC's military infrastructure and deployment of forces – the product of nearly a decade of occupation – Eisenhower was extremely pessimistic about the chances for the rebels' success.[16] Just as he had in Indonesia, the president elected not to support the Tibetan forces beyond modest supply drops under the CIA OSTIARY program (averaging seven per month) as well as missions undertaken by the Republic of China as part of Project CIRCUS.[17] Ongoing aerial intelligence showed that rebel forces were badly outmatched by Red Chinese troops, many of whom had prior combat experience from the Korean War. As much as Eisenhower would have liked to see Tibet free of the Communist Chinese yoke, he was not willing to commit American resources or troops at the levels necessary and in an almost inaccessible region to enable a successful Tibetan rebellion.

If the 1962 Cuban Missile Crisis represented the extraordinary value of aerial reconnaissance during the Kennedy years, the Suez Crisis of 1956 and the second Taiwan Straits Crisis in 1958 are touted as great successes in using intelligence flights during the Eisenhower administration. Both events hold primacy of place in existing histories of the Eisenhower presidency, intelligence studies, and profiles of the U-2. As both crises carried a great risk of direct US confrontation with the Soviet Union or its allies, the legacy of the U-2 in resolving these conflicts has become almost canon, and for good reason. In 1956, at the very time when a show of Western unity could have fully exploited, if not constrained, harsh Soviet repression in Hungary, the United States was compelled to rein in its greatest allies who were engaged in naked aggression. More importantly, should the USSR decide to pursue a military solution to the Anglo-French-Israeli attack on its Egyptian and Syrian allies, the United States would have had little choice but to react militarily. The Suez Crisis could have easily led to direct US-Soviet military confrontation. One might even consider the Suez Crisis as Eisenhower's 'eyeball to eyeball' moment.[18] Similarly, during the summer of 1958 the People's Republic of China seemed bent on capturing the disputed islands of Quemoy and Matsu, an action that some believed presaged a Communist invasion of Taiwan. Pledged to its defense, the United States might have resorted to the use of 'small yield atomic weapons' to protect or rescue the Nationalist Chinese. US officials believed that this surely would have led to a Soviet nuclear retaliatory strike on behalf of the People's Republic, which would have escalated quickly into general war between East and West.[19]

In both of these cases, US reaction to the developing situation would influence the Soviet or Chinese Communist response. Too belligerent a policy by the Americans could provoke an otherwise unintended Soviet military reaction, leading to war between the two atomic powers. Too weak a response by the Americans could lead to the loss of territory, resources, or political collapse of friendly governments and increased Soviet influence in what some saw as a zero-sum, bipolar world. What Eisenhower needed was a way to determine quickly and accurately what was happening on the battlefield or deep beyond adjacent borders, and he fully appreciated the benefits of intelligence, especially aerial reconnaissance, to meet these key demands.[20] By exploiting American strategic aerial reconnaissance assets along with other sources, Eisenhower could choose an 'appropriate response' that was well suited to the situation, a response neither too antagonistic nor too timid.

The Middle East epitomized many of the key foreign policy issues facing the Eisenhower administration, particularly during its first term. The rise of revolutionary nationalism, the vacuum created by the withdrawal of former colonial powers, charismatic leaders with strong non-aligned rhetoric, the Arab-Israeli dispute, increasing Arab radicalism, unfettered access to oil, and traditional regional conflicts all combined to exacerbate Eisenhower's primary fear of growing Soviet influence in the Middle East. NSC 5428, approved on 23 July 1954, warned that the 'security of the United States would be critically endangered if the [Middle East] should fall under Soviet influence or control.' Of the six major policy objectives outlined in NSC 5428, half were devoted to containing Soviet advances in the region. The United States sought to deny 'resources and strategic positions to the Soviet bloc,' to seek 'friendly governments in the area, capable of withstanding Communist-inspired subversion from within, and willing to resist Communist aggression,' and to prevent 'the extension of Soviet influence in the area.' Throughout the Cold War, the United States had only three objectives in the Middle East: 'access to oil, containing Soviet advances, and protecting Israeli security.' All three were directly linked to fears of a Soviet presence in the Middle East.[21] The benefits of stable Arab states, access to oil, and improved US trade opportunities were essential but secondary to the objective of limiting Soviet inroads in the region. Eisenhower's Middle East policy was never free from the shadow of the Soviet threat. Prior to 1955 the Soviet Union had no meaningful presence in the Middle East. They had no influence over the many monarchs or conservative leaders in the region, and played no part in efforts to resolve the Arab-Israeli dispute. This changed in 1955 when the Soviet Union negotiated a substantial arms deal with Egypt through Czechoslovakia (as they did two years later with Indonesia), marking the first real opportunity for Soviet military and political advisors to appear in the region. The 1956 US objective of containing the Soviet presence in the Middle East, therefore, was intended more to keep the door closed rather than limiting further expansion.

Arab nationalism was equally unsettling to Eisenhower and US Secretary of State Foster Dulles. They believed that the willingness of Arab leaders to turn to the USSR for economic and military assistance reflected gross Arab naiveté about Soviet intentions and a tacit acquiescence to Soviet expansionism. Eisen-

An Egyptian pilot preflights his MiG-17F *Fresco* during the 1956 Suez Crisis. With Soviet aircraft came Soviet influence, and Eisenhower was deeply concerned that Nasser's anti-Western rhetoric meant a growing Russian presence in the Middle East. Ike used U-2 overflights from Det B at Incirlik AB, including several flown by Frank Powers, to monitor the battlefield situation once war began.
via Yefim Gordon

hower was particularly concerned that Egypt's President Gamal Nasser's effort to distance his country from its former economic, political, and military reliance upon the West would destabilize the region sufficiently to allow the Soviet Union to increase its own influence throughout the area. This fear profoundly affected American policy toward Middle Eastern countries. As one scholar concluded, 'containment of Soviet influence ...became the overriding US goal in the region and shaped the Eisenhower administration's reaction to Arab nationalism.'[22]

Events seemed to justify this fear. Presaging similar events in Indonesia, the 1955 Egyptian arms agreement with Czechoslovakia and Nasser's May 1956 recognition of the People's Republic of China portended a further 'tilt to one side' in Egyptian relations with Communist countries. Two months later the United States abruptly withdrew its support and funding of Egypt's Aswan Dam project because of Nasser's virulently anti-American denunciations and increasing US doubts about the stability of the Egyptian economy.[23] Six days later Nasser nationalized the Suez Canal and closed the Straits of Tiran and the Gulf of Aqaba to Israeli vessels. Closing the canal effectively doubled the shipping distance of oil from the Persian (or Arabian) Gulf terminals to British ports, for example, doubling the transit time and raising the cost by 140 per cent. Great Britain and France quickly undertook efforts to regain the canal and their influence in the region. By the end of October their diplomatic overtures had failed. War erupted on 29 October when Israel, after prior co-ordination with France and Britain, dropped paratroopers into the Sinai Peninsula. French and British forces attacked Egypt two days later. All of this occurred as the Soviet Union sent its forces into Hungary to quash a popular anti-Communist uprising. For Eisenhower these concurrent crises could not have come at a worse time, less than a week before the 1956 presidential and congressional elections.

Strategic aerial reconnaissance played a central role in the evolution of American actions during the 1956 Suez Crisis.[24] Although SAC, USAFE, and the Navy continued their peripheral aerial COMINT and SIGINT missions in the eastern Mediterranean Sea, CIA U-2s were the main source of aerial intelligence throughout the crisis. Beginning on 29 August, CIA U-2s based in Turkey flew missions over Israel, Egypt, Syria, and Jordan, as well as areas throughout the Mediterranean. Ultimately there were four U-2 Suez missions in August, seven in September, ten in October, and fourteen in November.[25] According to Richard Bissell the CIA was 'encouraged to obtain any [U-2] coverage that might be useful.'[26] The PARAMOUNT Committee, established by the Intelligence Advisory Committee (IAC) on 5 September, evaluated the U-2 photos. These revealed nearly three times as many French-built Mystère fighter-bombers transferred to Israel than the French and Israelis had reported to the United States. On 26 October the PARAMOUNT Committee reported '40 British jet light bombers had arrived on Cyprus on 23 October. On the following day the committee reported to the IAC the arrival of 18 French aircraft.'[27]

This infuriated Eisenhower. In an appendix to a 15 October memorandum he wrote, 'Incidentally, our high-flying reconnaissance planes [U-2s] have shown that Israel has obtained some 60 of the French Mystère pursuit planes, when they had reported the transfer of only 24. This violated an agreement between the United States, Britain, and France to apprise each other of the assistance they gave to Israel.[28] Eisenhower also felt betrayed by French and British deception when, despite claims to the contrary, CIA U-2 overflights of Malta, Cyprus, and even Toulon, France, showed extensive French and British preparations for Operation MUSKETEER, their joint invasion of Egypt. Foster Dulles was equally outraged at being intentionally misled by the French and British for 'plotting behind his back.' He was especially upset because the invasion drew attention away from Soviet action in Hungary. 'It is nothing less than tragic,' he said, 'that at this very time, when we are on the point of winning an immense and long-hoped-for victory over Soviet colonialism in Eastern Europe, we should be forced to choose between following in the footsteps of Anglo-French colonialism in Asia and Africa, or splitting our course away from theirs.' Dulles's angst over being kept in the dark was primarily theatrical. CIA Director Allen Dulles wrote that the US intelligence community was fully aware of the Anglo-French-Israeli military preparations, and he no doubt passed this knowledge on to his brother. The Secretary of State's ire likely was over 'official' American ignorance because of French and British duplicity through diplomatic channels.[29] Moreover, every senior Eisenhower administration official knew that British and French protestations of innocence were little more than smokescreens for their planned attacks, but could do little to cut through them.

Early U-2 flights also indicated the beginnings of mobilization for Operation KADESH, the Israeli attack the Sinai Peninsula.[30] Despite the precision and detail of these photographs, US analysts were not entirely certain of their implications. The CIA had found no evidence that Israel was allied with France and Britain as part of their invasion of Egypt. Although the photos revealed an Israeli military build-up, American analysts misinterpreted the Israeli target. The 'background noise' of Jordanian instability, active Israeli deception suggesting that Jordan was the intended target, and Allen Dulles's own distraction by the reports of an impending coup in Syria all prevented US analysts from correctly interpreting the U-2 data in terms of the target of Operation KADESH.[31] There was no doubt the Israelis were preparing for war. The problem was figuring out where. The CIA's confusion about Israel's intentions contrasted sharply with a concurrent assessment by the National Indications Center (NIC). On 27 October Major General Cabell, Deputy Director of Intelligence and head of the NIC, urged a reconsideration of Israeli intentions. Two days later the JCS issued a last-minute message to key US military commands warning that 'a major attack' by Israel 'will be launched against Egypt in the very near future.'[32] Once the 29 October Israeli invasion of the Sinai began, followed by the French and British assault on Egypt two days later, U-2s provided continuous and timely intelligence information. Some of this included BDA, which kept Eisenhower informed of the details on a fluid battlefield. A popular anecdote describes the president's satisfaction with some serendipitous pre- and post-strike photos. On 1 November U-2 pilot Bill Hall overflew Cairo in one direction as his cameras recorded the city at peace. He saw RAF Canberra bombers approaching the city and turned his U-2 around. Now heading in the opposite direction, his cameras filmed the just-destroyed Egyptian airfield at Cairo Almaza. Eisenhower was impressed, saying 'Ten-minute reconnaissance. Now that's something to shoot for.'[33]

However valuable these battlefield images were, the real advantage of these flights was in assessing what Eisenhower considered to be the gravest problem associated with these hostilities: direct Soviet military intervention. In retrospect some participants wrote with clarity of hindsight and minimized the Soviet military threat. Charles E 'Chip' Bohlen, then US Ambassador to the Soviet Union, noted in 1973 that the 'Soviets would not take overt action that might put them directly or indirectly into

Gamal Abdel Nasser was among the charismatic leaders in the mid-1950s who rode to power on the tide of revolutionary nationalism. Despite the claim of non-alignment with either East or West, Nasser clearly 'tilted to one side' by purchasing Czech-built airplanes and weapons, nationalizing the Suez Canal, and closing the Straits of Tiran to Israeli traffic. CIA U-2s were an integral part of monitoring the 1956 conflict, just as SAC U-2s were a key peacekeeping component after the 1973 October War, initiated by Anwar el-Sadat, Nasser's successor as President.
Author's Collection

Allen Dulles was the Director of the CIA and his brother John Foster Dulles was the Secretary of State under Eisenhower, an extraordinary coupling of knowledge and power. In some cases it worked well – as in Indonesia. In other cases inaccurate intelligence hampered good decision making – as in Suez. Allen Dulles accomplished much as Director, including the U-2 program and its successor the A-12. He and Richard Bissell left the Agency after the Bay of Pigs fiasco, for which they were responsible.
CIA photo

Allen Dulles badly misread Israeli intentions, anticipating an invasion of Jordan rather than Egypt. Nonetheless U-2 photos provided stunning images of both Israeli forces in the Sinai and French and British forces along the Suez and in Egypt. Although this intelligence kept Eisenhower well informed about battlefield events, it had little effect on his ability to stop the fighting. In this case, as well as the 1958 Taiwan Crisis, knowledge did not equal power.

the fighting in the Middle East.'[34] US Under Secretary of State for Political Affairs Robert D Murphy said in 1964 that Soviet threats 'did not impress him' as credible.[35] During early November 1956, however, senior US officials were far more suspect about the possibility that the Soviet Union would send its forces into the region, an act with ominous consequences.

Eisenhower was especially concerned that Syria would yield to Soviet pressure and offer a base for Soviet military operations in the region. He worried that Syria was the 'immediate objective of Communist domination. By controlling Syria, the Russians could flank Turkey on a wide front and drive a wedge into the Middle East.'[36] Repeated rumors of an impending coup in Syria by pro-Communist forces raised the fear of Syrian bases being offered to Soviet forces. Egypt's transfer of Soviet-built tanks and MiGs to Syria lent further credibility to claims of an expanding Soviet military presence in the region. Another rumor circulating in Washington in late 1956 – later proven to be entirely without merit – warned that the Soviets intended to infiltrate the Syrian military and expropriate Syrian bases without the approval of Syrian authorities.

The Joint Chiefs articulated these concerns on 30 October. They considered the possibility of a direct Soviet reaction to be 'serious' enough to prepare for the 'possible movement' of US military forces to the Eastern Mediterranean, an action which Eisenhower supported.[37] Amidst this fear of Soviet intervention there were claims of 'volunteer' armies forming in the USSR to fight in Egypt. Remembering the Communist Chinese 'volunteer' forces that fought in the Korean War, US policy makers did not dismiss these reports as mere propaganda.[38] Moreover, Syrian President Shukri al-Quwatli was in Moscow at the time of the crisis seeking 'material assistance,' a visit that the JCS interpreted as evidence of Syrian-Soviet complicity. Unbeknown to American planners, Khrushchev scoffed at al-Kuwatli's request and promised only, 'We'll see what we can do,' while Soviet Defense Minister Georgii Zhukov called any intervention 'impossible'.[39] Four days later, Under Secretary of State Herbert Hoover, Jr, described 'great concern' among senior civilian officials over the possible deployment of Soviet forces, volunteer or otherwise, to Syria.

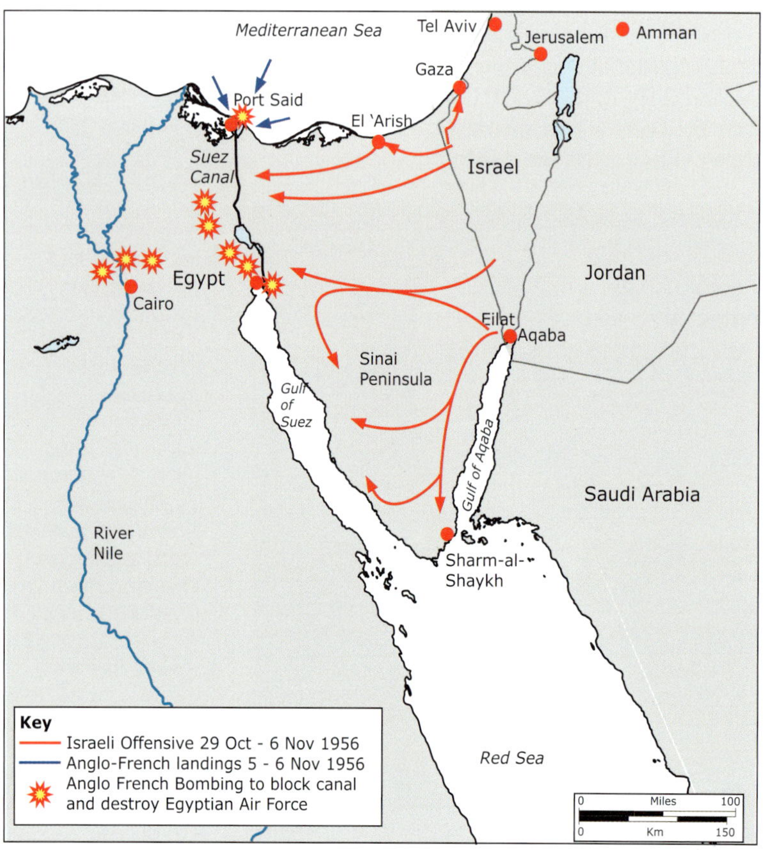

By the morning of 5 November Eisenhower was deeply worried over Russian actions and the potential for direct confrontation with Soviet forces. What moves they might take were uncertain given the logistical constraints of aiding Syria, Egypt, or Jordan (with whom they had just signed an defense pact) as well as the demands of the Soviet operations in Hungary. The president knew (probably from U-2 photos) that Syrian airfields were of poor quality, thus limiting Soviet deployment and operational potential. Nonetheless, Eisenhower considered it 'very important' for the United States to 'keep a close watch' on the Syrian airfields. He asked that 'Allen Dulles give special attention to this matter,' no doubt with the U-2 in mind, to warn 'at the earliest possible moment [of] such possible Soviet action.'[40]

Events later in the day, however, added urgency and legitimacy to this precautionary effort. Soviet Foreign Minister Dimitrii Shepilov asked Ambassador Bohlen to pass to Eisenhower a note signed by Soviet Prime Minister Nikolai Bulganin calling for joint US-Soviet military action against France and Britain. Bulganin suggested that the '[u]nited and urgent use' of America's 'strong naval fleet' in the Mediterranean and that of the USSR 'would be [a] reliable guarantee of [the] termination of aggression against Egyptian people.' Left unchecked, Bulganin warned, the Franco-British-Israeli invasion 'is fraught with danger and [could] grow into [a] third world war.'[41] He also made this proposed joint operation the

Syrian Air Force MiG-17Fs supplied by Egypt worried Eisenhower. Certainly capable of engaging French, British, and Israeli aircraft in combat, Ike's greatest fear was that Soviet pilots would fly the MiG-17s. Indeed, Russians flew MiG-15s in Korea, and would later fly MiG-21s and MiG-25s in combat for Egypt. This *Fresco* was among nine that defected from Syria to Israel in August 1968. *via Yefim Gordon*

basis of a threat to British Prime Minister Anthony Eden, warning that joint US and Soviet 'naval and air forces' would, along with those of other UN countries, 'crush the aggressor and reestablish peace in the East by using force.'[42] Even if the United States did not participate in this joint effort, the Soviet Union would 'reserve its liberty of action,' clearly implying the possibility of unilateral Soviet military action.[43]

Eisenhower appreciated the implications and gravity of these messages. He told Secretary Hoover 'the Soviets, seeing their position and policy failing so badly in the satellites, are ready to take any wild adventure.' Eisenhower repeatedly stressed his concern 'over the possibility of Soviet armed intervention,' calling the Soviets 'scared and furious.' Invoking the memory of Adolf Hitler, Eisenhower added, 'There is nothing more dangerous than a dictatorship in this state of mind.'[44] Robert Murphy told French Ambassador to the United States Hervé Alphand that Soviet reactions and policy were 'developing in a spirit of recklessness.' He added that Shepilov's request for UN approval of joint US-Soviet military intervention on behalf of Egypt might indicate 'a real intention on the part of the Soviet Union to intervene in the Middle East.' The American impression was that this was not the case, but the United States could ill 'afford to exclude the possibility' that it portended imminent unilateral Soviet military action.[45] On the surface Murphy's admonition to Alphand seems to be at odds with Murphy's later assertion that Soviet threats were not credible. Although he did not believe that the Soviet Union would, or perhaps even could, intervene in the Middle East, Murphy clearly articulated the greater American fear that reckless Soviet actions short of direct intervention could complicate the peace process or lead to inadvertent US military action and superpower confrontation.

Not surprisingly, Eisenhower considered joint US-Soviet military operations 'unthinkable.'[46] In a press release that afternoon he warned that the introduction of any new forces into the region – clearly referring to any Soviet action, unilateral or otherwise – would result in American opposition, an unstated but implicit willingness to use military force.[47] Seeking any means to calm the volatile situation, Eisenhower asked the State Department to draft a message to Indian Prime Minister Nehru, asking him to add his 'powerful voice to those counseling restraint with regard to this [Soviet] proposal for expanded [joint US and Soviet] military action,' otherwise the entire situation could 'radically deteriorate.'[48]

The following day brought disturbing news that this deterioration may have already begun. Allen Dulles briefed the president that the Soviet Union alerted the Egyptians that they would 'do something.' The JCS feared a 'very disturbed situation in Moscow [that] may indicate serious intent on the part of the Soviets' to take unilateral military action in the region.[49] Again, American anxieties centered on the potential movement of Soviet air forces to Syria. Eisenhower asked Allen Dulles 'to conduct high reconnaissance in this area, avoiding, however, any flights into Russia. Flights over Syria and Israel should be conducted.' In addition to his earlier worries about the possibility of a US-Soviet confrontation, Eisenhower feared the ominous implication that 'if reconnaissance discloses Soviet Air Forces on Syrian bases ...there would be reason for the British and French to destroy them.'[50] The British told US Ambassador to Great Britain Winthrop W Aldrich that the Soviet deployment of 'air units into Syria' was likely, 'if they have not already begun.'[51] A 6 November CIA Special National Intelligence Estimate (SNIE) discounted the possibility of Soviet military intervention because their ability to do so was constrained by events in Hungary as well as the distances involved.[52] If Aldrich's assertion was true, however, the United States could be drawn quickly and involuntarily into a direct confrontation with the Soviet Union. Eisenhower noted that if the Soviets attacked 'the French and British directly, we would be in a war.'[53]

Of equal concern to Eisenhower and his advisors was the possibility that Soviet forces in Syria would attack Israeli forces or bases. Soviet Communist Party Secretary Nikita Khrushchev told a group of Scandinavian diplomats that the 'Soviet Union could handle the Israelis with regular rockets, without airplanes or atomic rockets.'[54] The CIA learned from sources in Moscow that the USSR intended to 'flatten' Israel the next day. Naturally the Israelis were quite worried about the American reaction to any such attack. Isser Harel, head of Israel's Mossad, pessimistically told Israeli Prime Minister David Ben Gurion 'that the United States would not come to Israel's defense should the Soviet Union take military action against Israel.'[55] Although Eisenhower was willing to risk direct military confrontation with the USSR – perhaps even general war – on behalf of long-time *primum inter pares* allies Britain and France, Harel's doubts appear justified that the United States would risk nuclear war over a conventional Russian attack on Israel.

How the United States would react to these problems – a possible Soviet military presence in Middle East, open conflict between France or Britain and the USSR, or a Soviet attack upon Israel – depended to a considerable degree upon what the constant U-2 missions discovered. A direct Soviet military presence in the Middle East would force Eisenhower to order a major mobilization of American military forces, including SAC's nuclear forces. Ambassador Bohlen warned that 'the dispatch of Strategic Air Command bombers, with all the overtones of nuclear weapons, might ...be regarded by the Soviets as a clear indication of the imminence of an [American] attack, and might, therefore, provoke a convulsive [Soviet] reaction.'[56] The United States might also be compelled to defend other nations in the region. Turkey called for a preventive US strike against Syrian bases to preclude their use by Soviet aircraft that might attack Turkey should the war escalate. Iran would require a sizeable contingent of US troops to shore up the Mohammed Reza Pahlevi regime in the face of potential domestic discord, already hostile to the United States after the 1953 CIA coup there. Eisenhower rejected both the Turkish call for a strike against Syria and the option of sending troops to Teheran. Clearly, the president had to act wisely. To escalate prematurely would lead to an unintended war. Not to escalate in time would lead to humiliation of the three great protectors of Western democracy at the hands a pro-Communist Third World dictator and his benefactors in the Soviet Union.

On Election Day Colonel Goodpaster met Eisenhower as he returned from Gettysburg, Pennsylvania, where he had gone to vote. The news was good: U-2 photos revealed no Soviet deployments. Although Eisenhower did upgrade the readiness of US forces within the eastern Mediterranean, he refused to recall military personnel on leave, an act which could have frightened the American people and alarmed the Soviets. Without the accuracy and rapid availability of the U-2 photos, Eisenhower might well have been forced to mobilize prematurely or excessively, actions that could well have provoked the Soviets into sending forces to Syria and increasing the possibility of inadvertent war between the superpowers.[57] With this tempered assessment of actual Soviet capabilities in the Middle East, Eisenhower did not ask the JCS to order SAC to a higher alert status. Instead the JCS directed SAC only to review existing war plans, to make sure that its airplanes and crews were at the highest peacetime levels of readiness, and to deploy tankers to their forward alert bases but retain bomber forces on alert within the United States, all prudent but not necessarily provocative actions.[58]

Outwardly Eisenhower was gravely concerned with Soviet threats of raining atomic rockets on London and Paris, but he appreciated that they were empty rhetoric. He knew from the handful of U-2 overflights of the USSR in July that the Soviets lacked missiles with the necessary range to reach the two European capitals, especially with nuclear warheads. If they were indeed attacked by Soviet missiles, US forces would retaliate against the USSR, which, Eisenhower believed, lacked the resources to win a general war with the United States. He correctly reasoned that Khrushchev would not risk war with America over the Middle East. Despite the potential for a dangerous Soviet military move in the region, the president knew that substantial Soviet involvement was a practical impossibility.[59] Soviet forces were already strained to their limits by the repression in Hungary. Any meaningful quantities of Soviet troops would have to travel by ship from the Black Sea through the Bosphorus, Dardenelles,

Khrushchev rejected pleas from Syrian President al-Quwatli for 'material assistance' during the Suez Crisis. Russia was already overstretched with the concurrent invasion of Hungary, and any Soviet aid – or troops – would likely need a fleet of transports such as this An-12 *Cub*. These would be vulnerable to interception by carrier-based planes from the US Sixth Fleet. *via Yefim Gordon*

and the Aegean Sea which were controlled by NATO countries Greece and Turkey and could therefore be easily denied passage. Aerial deployment of sufficient troops and equipment to attack British, French, or Israeli forces would necessitate a huge armada that would have to overfly Turkey or Iran, was subject to early detection, and would have been highly vulnerable to their air forces or fighters from the US Sixth Fleet. Soviet submarines might attack French or British ships in the Mediterranean, but the overwhelming presence of the Sixth Fleet meant that while sub attacks represented a potential flashpoint they would have little military effectiveness. Claims of Soviet volunteers clamoring to fight were for public consumption by the Egyptians in an effort to bolster the Arabs' sagging opinion of Soviet reliability. In fact, some 380 Czech and Soviet advisors in Egypt were ordered to leave Cairo for the relative safety of Khartoum, Sudan, until the fighting was over. Still, Eisenhower was genuinely worried that the Soviet Union might react to some unforeseen incident and feel compelled to *try* to intervene.

One can make a good case that the president relied more heavily upon strategic aerial reconnaissance than on other intelligence during the handling and resolution of the events surrounding Suez. Available documents and official histories disclose nothing about other sources of information in resolving this crisis. One Top Secret CIA history, for example, reveals no other CIA efforts that might have been used, and stresses the U-2's importance in gathering intelligence for policy making; another CIA history noted the new role of the U-2 in gathering tactical – rather than strategic – intelligence.[60] Although this assessment reflects a certain degree of parochial self interest, it nonetheless portrays the reality of the U-2 as the significant source of intelligence collection throughout the Suez crisis and reflects the crucial advantages of the intelligence gathered by these flights over information gleaned from other sources. Traditional HUMINT sources within the region had already shown their unreliability by passing on evidence that convinced US analysts that war would come in Jordan, rather than Egypt, along with a coup in Syria. COMINT sources, such as ground–based listening posts in Turkey and naval vessels in the Mediterranean, were equally duped by Israeli disinformation. Diplomatic sources of intelligence from allied countries with strong contacts in the region, allies like the British and French, were obviously constrained because of their own complicity in the invasion. Aerial reconnaissance, which Eisenhower appeared to value more than other forms of intelligence gathering because of its technical sophistication and objectivity, overcame these limits. US planes were able to gather timely photographs that were not vulnerable to the successful deceptive tactics that undermined COMINT and HUMINT.

Intelligence gathered by U-2s during the Suez Crisis contributed directly to critical US short-term options and long-term benefits. U-2 photos demonstrated clearly that there was no evidence of any direct Soviet military presence in the Middle East, particularly in Syria. This meant there was little likelihood of military confrontation between France, Britain, and Israel with the Soviet Union, which would almost certainly force the United States into a conflict which it neither sought nor believed would end without potentially horrible escalation. It also meant that the United States could limit its own military options to avoid provoking the Soviets into taking military action. For the 'long haul,'

American pressure on France, Great Britain, and Israel to protect Egyptian sovereignty signaled other nations, particularly non-aligned countries, that the United States was not inherently hostile to their post-colonial interests. If America was willing to constrain its closest allies in conflict with one of the most vocal critics of US policy, then perhaps the United States wasn't as evil as portrayed by Khrushchev or Mao.

At the height of the crisis, Eisenhower visited Foster Dulles in his room at Walter Reed Hospital and told him of 'his [the president's] satisfaction at having a certain highly classified observation operation available to him at this time. [Eisenhower] felt that others had conducted operations with a similar objective, but these had been detected whereas our own had not been.'[61] No doubt the president felt a certain degree of satisfaction that the U-2, designed to gather strategic 'high-quality results considered more important than speed,' had in fact proven invaluable as a 'tactical reconnaissance unit, [delivering] film immediately after landing for instant interpretation.'[62] Given the peaceful resolution of the perilous events in the Middle East, the money and political capital spent on the U-2 program proved to be a wise investment indeed.

Just as it did during the Suez Crisis, strategic aerial intelligence gathered by peripheral and overflight missions also proved crucial to US policy making in the Far East. During August 1958 aerial and naval clashes between Chinese Communists and Nationalist Chinese intensified amid recurrent fears of an impending Communist takeover of the islands of Quemoy (Jinmen) and Matsu (Mazu). These two tiny Nationalist islands, adjacent to Mao Zedong's People's Republic of China, served as a focal point for Communist-Nationalist Chinese relations throughout the 1950s. Held by Chiang Kai-Shek's (Jiang Jieshi) Nationalists since they departed the mainland after the 1949 Communist victory in the civil war, the islands held symbolic importance disproportionate to their true strategic value. Quemoy was nearly 50 square miles, and Matsu was barely four square miles; together the cluster of largely uninhabitable islets were equal in size to the city of Norfolk, Virginia. The islands were some 1.5 and 10 miles, respectively, from the coast of Red China but 130 and 170 miles from Taiwan. On 23 August 1958 Chinese Communist artillery units began shelling the islands with a barrage of 30,000-50,000 shells per day – an average of one explosion every two seconds. Fearful that these artillery assaults meant that a Communist attack on the islands was imminent and a full-scale invasion of the Nationalist's home island of Formosa would follow, Chiang asked for US assistance under the 1954 US-Taiwan defense treaty.[63]

American officials were not entirely convinced that the events preceding this barrage were precursors to invasion. Based on unidentified intelligence sources, the Joint Chiefs concluded as early as 2 August that there was 'no evidence' of a 'build-up or other military moves suggesting' a Communist Chinese offensive against either the islands or Taiwan itself.[64] Five days later Allen Dulles told the NSC that People's Liberation Army – Air Force (PLAAF) MiG-17 'fighter planes-not bombers' were deployed to forward bases near the Fujian coast on the mainland. Although they could be used to cover an invasion of the islands, the *Frescos* were thought to be primarily defensive interceptors, and their operational range limited their ability to support offensive operations, even over the nearby islands. Dulles added that no strong indicators of an impending attack such as 'ground build-up or movement of naval forces from the Shanghai base had been detected.' In his opinion, there would be no

Opposite page: The geography of Quemoy and Matsu Islands raised crucial doubts about the US willingness to honor its defense treaty with Taiwan. Eisenhower likely would have used nuclear weapons against the PRC following an invasion of Taiwan itself, but not after occupation of the two tiny archipelagos just off the coast of Red China but 150 miles from Taiwan. Mao understood this, so acted without fear of US retribution. Chiang demanded American military intervention, which included use of low-yield atomic weapons. In the end, the US problem was restraining Chiang rather than deterring Mao.

Above: Before the 1958 Taiwan Straits Crisis, U-2 overflights of Red China showed PLAAF MiG-17s such as these at bases along the coast. By August, US intelligence analysts were convinced these were for defensive purposes only in response to aggressive RoCAF overflights. Initial US policy, consequently, was restrained – moving the Seventh Fleet to signal US resolve. That failed to end the shelling. *via Yefim Gordon*

invasion 'without a prior ground forces build-up on the mainland opposite' the two islands, which had not been observed.[65] Two weeks later Dulles again told the NSC that although a Communist amphibious 'attack on the offshore islands could occur with virtually no advance warning,' he did not believe that this likely, saying only that the PRC was 'in a position to do so at any time.' He added that more Communist MiGs had been deployed to 'five or six airfields' in the area, reinforcing his impression that they were defensive in nature.[66] By late September US intelligence analysts believed that these deployments were in response to an increase in Nationalist flights along the coast and over the Chinese mainland as well as lopsided victories in large-scale aerial battles over the region – on 24 September, for example, RoCAF F-86 Sabres shot down at least 10 PLAAF MiG-15s and MiG-17s with no losses.

Among other intelligence sources such as HUMINT and ground-based COMINT interception, the Joint Chiefs and the CIA relied heavily upon strategic aerial reconnaissance to make these confident pronouncements. US and Nationalist Chinese peripheral flights using oblique photography reconnoitered coastal facilities and airfields and took pictures showing the buildup of interceptors but not amphibious assault forces.[67] *Photographic reconnaissance …revealed the presence of 26 aircraft at Chenghai airfield (near Swatow) and at least 29 aircraft at Lungchi airfield (near Amoy), only 40 miles from Quemoy.… No evidence has been received of any corresponding moves to build up Chinese Communist ground and naval strength in the coastal area facing Taiwan.*[68] American CIA U-2 and at least one Nationalist RB-57A overflights photographed Communist military and logistics operations deep within Red China.[69] These flights took 'good photographs' but again found little evidence of preparations for substantial offensive operations.[70]

Not surprisingly, the Chinese Communists reacted strongly to these missions, particularly reconnaissance 'patrols and overflights,' and made 'aggressive attempts to deny [their] airspace to [Chinese Nationalist and US] overflights.' US officials rationalized the build-up of PLAAF fighters along the coast as more in response to these aerial incursions than as a harbinger of offensive operations. President Eisenhower was certainly sensitive to the provocative nature of these reconnaissance flights.[71] After an American CIA U-2 'over-flying the Chinese mainland pursuant to the President's approval' provoked a strong Communist protest, Eisenhower briefly suspended U-2 (and presumably Nationalists) overflights of the PRC.[72]

RoCAF overflights of the PRC were more common than US incursions because of the lack of US restraint on such flights and the Nationalist Chinese willingness to risk direct military confrontation with the PRC in aerial battles. On 8 September 1958, for example, a dozen Nationalist fighters escorted two reconnaissance planes on a mission over Chenghai airfield near Swatow. Five intercepting MiGs were downed with the loss of one Nationalist airplane. The head of the US Taiwan Defense Command, Vice Admiral Roland N Smoot, was not informed in advance about the penetration mission, and subsequently lodged a 'vigorous verbal protest' with his Taiwanese counterpart.[73]

Despite Nationalist Chinese fervor to undertake these dangerous and provocative missions, the United States paradoxically endorsed such flights. Rather than risk direct US-Communist Chinese confrontation should an overflight be intercepted and downed, the USAF provided the Nationalist Chinese with airplanes and technical support to conduct overflight and peripheral missions as part of US intelligence collection efforts. CIA support of Nationalist Chinese overflights of the PRC reportedly began in the 'early 1950s.' Most of these flights were for purposes other than reconnaissance such as dropping leaflets and counterfeit currency printed in Taiwan, or deploying Nationalist guerillas on the mainland. These CIA-sponsored flights were conducted by various 'front' agencies such as 'Western Enterprises,' 'Western International Company,' and Civil Air Transport, as well as the RoCAF Special Operations Unit.[74] During 1956 the Nationalist government asked for additional tactical reconnaissance planes such as the RF-84, North American RF-86, and the RF-101 to replace those lost to overflights of the PRC. The Pentagon recommended approving such requests, saying, 'by making available additional reconnaissance fighter aircraft for such purposes, [the United States] would be significantly improving its own intelligence operations.'[75] A year later the CIA provided Taiwan with RB-69s for reconnaissance overflights using American equipment with Chinese crews.[76] By 1958 Nationalist reconnaissance planes had 'been overflying [the] mainland for years ... with the encouragement of the US to obviate [the] necessity for use [of] US forces to procure vital intelligence.'[77] Unlike the earlier incident that provoked Smoot's ire, these almost daily proxy flights were co-ordinated in detail with US and Taiwanese planners and crews.

As the 1958 crisis developed, US officials were concerned that an invasion of the two tiny islands would cause the Nationalist government to collapse. Foster Dulles said that the crisis 'was not a question just of the loss of some small islands but rather of the possible loss of a whole nation' and 'would almost certainly lead to further Chinese Communist aggressive moves and gains.'[78] Eisenhower did not believe that the PRC sought war with the United States so he ordered only an American naval show of force in the straits by the US Seventh Fleet to demonstrate American commitment to the Nationalist Chinese. This resolve, Eisenhower believed, would dissuade the Communists from taking aggressive action toward Taiwan.[79] By early September, however, these maneuvers and continued diplomatic overtures failed to ease tensions. War remained a real possibility.

Aerial reconnaissance played an important part in preparing for any potential hostilities, particularly in targeting. The US Pacific Air Forces (PACAF) revised their existing war plans by requesting the Air Force Directorate of Targets to update 'materials on three Chinese coastal cities opposite Formosa.' These three primary target updates were later supplemented by the update of 'target materials on an all-source basis on China within a 600 nautical mile radius from Formosa.'[80] On 22 September for example, now-Lieutenant General Cabell and Richard Bissell asked Foster Dulles for permission to resume U-2 overflights of China. These would take advantage of good weather to detect possible Communist transshipments to the coast 'from the interior' and allow US military planners to update their target materials. Foster Dulles discouraged this resumption of overflights, so Cabell deferred his request 'pending what might be another propitious day,' acquiring the needed photography from other sources, most likely oblique peripheral sorties or RoCAF missions.[81]

Irrespective of what Red Chinese preparations for war aerial reconnaissance might detect, any American military response would be ominous. As early as 15 August the JCS warned 'effective US [military] intervention would necessitate nuclear bombing of mainland bases.' At a 2 September meeting, JCS Chairman General Twining indicated that should the United States be compelled 'to intervene militarily' in the crisis, US forces 'would strike at Communist airfields and shore batteries with small atomic weapons' as 'this was the only way to do the job.' Twining added that the United States would use '7-10 kiloton airburst bombs' rather than the more effective but 'dirtier' ground burst weapons. Five bombs would be used in the initial attack, one on each of five coastal airfields.[82] The following day, the JCS indicated that they were also prepared to strike additional Communist Chinese targets within a 500-mile radius of the islands, including military targets near the cities of Shanghai, Nanking, and Canton. Secretary Dulles went so far as to warn British Prime Minister Harold Macmillan of the imminent use of 'small air bursts without fallout.'[83]

In the event of an American nuclear attack, the JCS warned that 'Peiping [Beijing] and its Soviet ally would probably feel compelled to react with nuclear attacks at least on Taiwan and on the Seventh Fleet,' although where Mao would get any atomic weapons was never clarified. A Red Chinese atomic response using Soviet bombs would, they argued, certainly escalate to the use of SAC bombers in 'large-scale nuclear attacks against Communist China,' which would 'very probably lead to general war with the USSR.'[84] Soviet Premier Nikita Khrushchev reinforced this JCS belief in a 7 September letter to President Eisenhower. Any US 'atomic blackmail' over the straits would not succeed, Khrushchev warned, because an American 'attack on the Chinese People's Republic, which is a great friend, ally and neighbor of our country, is an attack on the Soviet Union.' Although there were increasing tensions between the PRC and the USSR, there was no question that Khrushchev viewed any US nuclear attack on the People's Republic as a *casus belli* for general war between the United States and the Soviet Union.[85]

In keeping with the contemporary worldview of 'monolithic communism,' Eisenhower and his advisors assumed that in attacking Quemoy and Matsu Beijing acted in accord with Moscow. This certainly seemed the case when the Russians expressed public support for their Communist ally during the crisis. US strategic aerial reconnaissance flights around the Soviet Union, not surprisingly, found no evidence of military preparations within the USSR to buttress Red Chinese defenses. Mao's shelling of Quemoy and Matsu – an effort to undermine Khrushchev's efforts to improve relations with the West – took place without any warning to Khrushchev.[86] Based on aerial intelligence, as well as other sources, Eisenhower promptly understood that the Red Chinese artillery attack on the islands appeared to be an extemporaneous affair, with little evidence of extensive preparations for either an all-out invasion of the islands, Taiwan, or a provocation for general war with the United States. As such, the president had greater flexibility in his actions ranging from subtle diplomatic efforts to the outright threat of using nuclear weapons.[87]

Researchers are divided over the degree to which President Eisenhower might have been willing to use atomic bombs to resolve the crisis. To some, Eisenhower's atomic saber rattling was a 'game of deception,' and the president 'never intended to permit the use of nuclear weapons.'[88] To others, including the president himself, Eisenhower was clearly prepared, in his words, to 'face the necessity of using small-yield atomic weapons against hostile airfields.'[89] This focus obscures the real dilemma facing Eisenhower and his advisors, the issue of where to draw the line that would trigger an American military response, nuclear or otherwise. Most critically, how would the president know when that line had been crossed? Again, the answer was aerial reconnaissance.

The 1954 defense agreement between Taiwan and the United States guaranteed that America would respond to defend Taiwan should it be attacked by the People's Republic, but the accord did not specify if the US defense perimeter around Taiwan included Quemoy and Matsu.[90] Some scholars have presumed that it did not, and that even if it did President Eisenhower would not have used nuclear weapons to defend them.[91] Historian Gordon Chang, however, has shown that prior to the 1958 crisis, Eisenhower and Dulles were very much willing to use atomic weapons against Red China should it launch an amphibious attack against the offshore islands, and even deployed SAC B-36 bombers to Andersen AB in Guam – where US atomic weapons were stored and ready for use – in preparation for such a retaliatory attack should it become necessary.[92]

By 1958 Eisenhower appears to have reconsidered and changed his commitment to protect Quemoy and Matsu with a US nuclear response. The president indicated his willingness 'to see the [Nationalist] abandonment' of Quemoy and Matsu rather than risk a general war.[93] America might well consider atomic war with the PRC and even the Soviet Union to protect Formosa, but only Formosa. No responsible civilian policy maker was willing to go to war – in all likelihood nuclear war – with the Chinese (and implicitly the USSR) over two tiny clusters of islands both well within the territorial waters of the People's Republic of China. Mao suspected this and cleverly used the bombardment of the islands to embarrass the United States as incapable of fulfilling its pledge to its client state, as well as show 'fraternal solidarity' with the anti-monarchists in the ongoing Lebanon Crisis.[94]

Chiang, however, remained intransigent. Claiming an imminent Communist invasion of the islands, he urgently advocated the use of American atomic bombs to protect them, and hence Formosa, should war erupt.[95] Despite Chiang's claims, US and RoCAF aerial reconnaissance and other intelligence sources found no evidence of Communist preparations for such an invasion.[96] Secretary of Defense Neil

Even with two months of U-2 missions that gathered indisputable evidence of an impending invasion of Suez, the US was unable to find a diplomatic solution to *prevent* war – the underlying premise of strategic aerial reconnaissance in early warning. British Ambassador Sir Roger Makins (left) and French Ambassador Maurice Couve de Murville (center) greet US Secretary of State John Foster Dulles (right) in August 1956 to discuss the impending Suez Crisis. *Author's Collection*

Unfettered access to the Suez Canal was far more an issue than waning British or French colonialism in India or Southeast Asia. Middle East oil that warmed and powered Europe came via the Canal, cutting transit time in half and costs by 70%. Nasser's 26 July 1956 nationalization of the Canal represented a direct challenge to traditional European influence. By September Operation MUSKETEER – the Franco-British invasion of Suez – had become both a necessity and an inevitability.

McElroy told Eisenhower that Jiang was using the pretext of an invasion 'to provoke a big fight [over the islands], with the idea of getting back into China during the aftermath.'[97] What was once a military standoff between the Communist Chinese and the United States had become a political standoff between the Nationalist Chinese and the United States.

Jiang was at first unresponsive to American verbal reassurances of support and seemed indifferent to the political implications of the crisis. Amid this Nationalist bunker mentality Eisenhower suggested to Foster Dulles that 'the tactical approach' to Jiang be changed and instead 'stress be placed on the military aspect of the problem.' US Ambassador to the Republic of China Everett F Drumright concurred, saying it 'would be wise to discuss [holding the islands] purely as military problems and not as political bargaining concessions.'[98] Reconnaissance photographs taken by CIA U-2s and RoCAF RB-57s – Chiang's own air force – provided the undeniable military evidence Eisenhower needed to allay Chiang's fears of an invasion. The president therefore directed 'that the benefits of these flights should be given to the Chinese Nationalists.'[99] Confronted with such compelling evidence, Chiang was subsequently more compliant with US efforts for a mediated response. Moreover, as a further *quid pro quo* for his reduced truculence, Taiwan acquired its own fleet of U-2s, thanks in large measure to the personal intervention of CIA Station Chief Ray Cline. Beginning in 1959 RoCAF pilots received U-2 training, and U-2s with Taiwanese markings and pilots conducted overflights of the PRC until 1974 when ended at the direction of President Nixon.[100] The Taiwanese had previously received several former USAF HEART THROB RB-57As for 'high-altitude reconnaissance operations over the Chinese Mainland,' and were in the process of deploying two FAIR TREAT RB-57Ds during the September crisis. These arrangements benefitted the Republic of China as well as the United States.

Strategic aerial reconnaissance was one of the most important tools in resolving the 1958 crisis. US officials were able to monitor the status of Communist forces arrayed along the coast adjacent to Quemoy and Matsu. Photographs taken by peripheral and overflight missions showed exact numbers, types, and locations of Red Chinese aircraft, as well as the distinct absence of a ready invasion force. Eisenhower used this evidence that showed a less-belligerent PRC to convince Chiang that there was no forthcoming attack on the islands, and most importantly, on Taiwan itself. Armed with the knowledge acquired via aerial reconnaissance, Eisenhower was, through 'a combination of threats, firmness, and resolve, combined with a willingness to negotiate and be reasonable,' able to achieve a satisfactory outcome.[101] Indeed, Secretary Dulles wrote to Chiang shortly after returning from their meeting in Taipei, 'I sense a general feeling of relief, and of recognition of your statesmanship in having been willing to put the mission of your government on a higher plane than mere reliance on force alone.' One wonders if Dulles's allusion to a 'higher plane' was a subtle recognition of the role of high-altitude reconnaissance in resolving the crisis.[102] In addition to avoiding war between the United States and the PRC, Eisenhower held a 'long haul' hope for improved relations with Red China. Perhaps not during his administration, or even that of his successor, but Eisenhower knew that if there would ever be good will between East and West, it would be forever compromised in 1958 if he acted imprudently.[103]

***

Eisenhower's use of CIA U-2s in the evolution of American involvement in Indonesia, Southeast Asia, and Tibet has become an essential case study in the successful applicability of aerial reconnaissance to the formulation of security policy and actions. In each case, there is a clear link between the information acquired and the outcomes. Poorly organized and dispersed rebels, unknowable troop and supply levels, remote locations guarded by experienced combat troops – all detected by U-2 PHOTINT as well as aerial SIGINT and COMINT – influenced Eisenhower and his advisors to avoid deepening commitments to exploit or salvage situations that offered little chance of success and great political risk. Indeed, the intelligence reinforced the president's existing opinions and provided the margin necessary to reach the decisions to stop or prevent intervention altogether.

Similarly, the Suez Crisis of 1956 and the Taiwan Strait Crisis of 1958 form the staple of scholarly assessments of Eisenhower's presidency. Given the peaceful outcome of both crises, it is not unreasonable to consider them as political successes by the Eisenhower administration in general, and the beneficiaries of strategic aerial intelligence in particular. Researchers have traditionally hailed the president for his handling of these tense situations and freely acknowledged the importance of U-2 flights in the resolution of these affairs.[104] In the face of this veritable *festschrift* of academic attention, a careful reassessment of these two seminal events and the role of aerial reconnaissance in their resolution suggest doubts about the effectiveness of Eisenhower's actions and the applicability of strategic intelligence flights in crisis situations.

Despite the apparently resounding importance of U-2 intelligence in *resolving* the Suez Crisis, U-2 photos did nothing to *prevent* the Suez Crisis. The president and his advisors were keenly aware throughout the summer of 1956 of the potential for conflict in the region given the vitriol from Nasser, the animus resulting from the suspension of US aid for the Aswan Dam, the Franco-British reaction to Egypt's nationalization of the Suez Canal, and Israel's critical national interest in freedom of navigation of the now-closed Straits of Tiran. Left unchecked, these events could easily spiral out of control and lead to a regional war. If the Soviet Union joined the conflict the implications were staggering. Only by the end of the summer was Eisenhower sufficiently concerned that war might erupt that he ordered U-2 flights over the Middle East, starting on 29 August, two months before hostilities began. There were 21 U-2 overflights of the region before Israel, France, and Great Britain attacked Egypt and the war started. The U-2 photos revealed undeniable warning signs of war preparations. Within a week of the first U-2 flight the PARAMOUNT Committee began exploitation of the photos to assess French and British preparations for war. Other missions followed. On 11 September a U-2 overflew Toulon, France, revealing the likely embarkation of troops and supplies. Overflights of Cyprus showed the preparation of tents sufficient to house up to 60,000 British troops. Missions covering Malta detected a large number of British naval vessels, including troop transports.[105] Although there was ambiguity about Israeli intentions, the photographs nonetheless showed extensive Israeli mobilization efforts. Israel was clearly preparing to fight someone in the immediate future. By the end of the summer there was little doubt in the president's mind that war was imminent. Armed with 60 days' worth of incontrovertible U-2 evidence of French, British, and Israeli offensive military preparations, Eisenhower was still unable to prevent America's key allies from starting a war with potential global implications.

Why not? The answer lies with the intentions of the British, French, and Israelis as well as the options Eisenhower might wield to prevent conflict. Seeing the nationalization of the Suez Canal as an affront to their waning colonial

influence – not to mention its critical importance in expediting the shipping of goods and oil – both European nations resolved that unless Nasser returned control of the canal there would be war. At the end of August British Foreign Secretary Selwyn Lloyd warned that 'a button [would be] pushed in early September and after that everything would happen automatically and be irrevocable.'[106] Unless Eisenhower could convince Nasser to accede to terms that

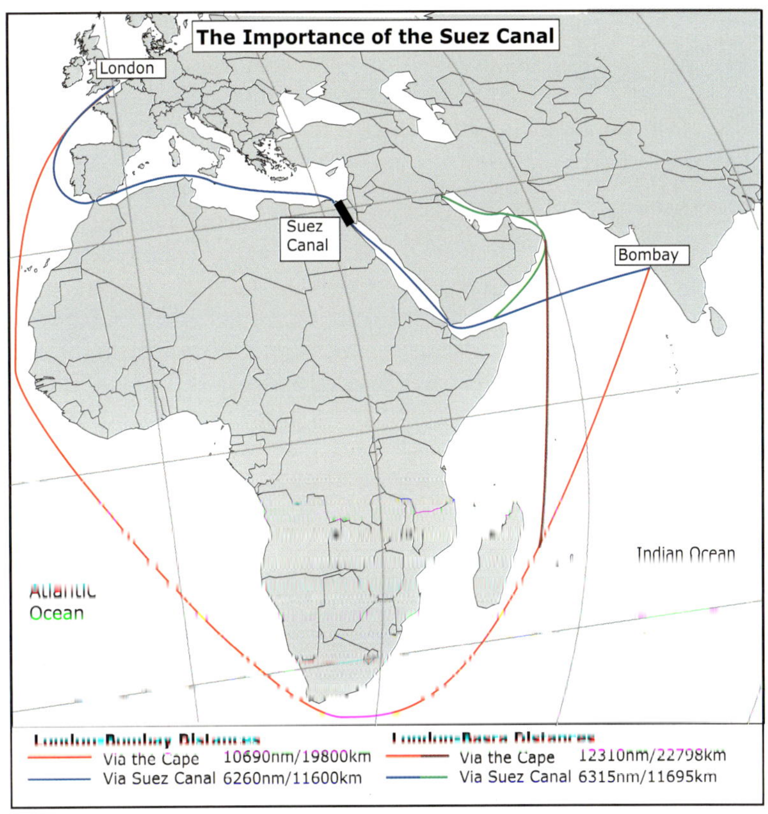

British Prime Minister Anthony Eden (left) meets with President Eisenhower (center) and US Secretary of State Foster Dulles (right). Ike had an extraordinary working relationship as well as deep friendships with British leaders thanks to his wartime role as Supreme Allied Commander, as did his staff, including Walter Bedell Smith (back row, right). Despite this, Eisenhower could not dissuade his friends from going to war – what hope would he have in discouraging his enemies from doing the same? *Author's Collection*

provoked the crisis in the first place – an unlikely possibility – French and British forces would invade Egypt to protect their colonial interests in the canal. Throughout the summer, Eisenhower and his advisors were unable to offer fruitful solutions that would mollify both sides (such as the stillborn Suez Canal Users Association), had little leverage over Nasser (particularly after Eisenhower's roughshod handling of the cessation of aid for the Aswan Dam), and could not cajole his allies (not to mention close personal friends among the British, no less) into acting with restraint. In one misguided attempt to dissuade the British from acting rashly, the president directed that the CIA brief senior RAF and Whitehall officials on the current status of Egyptian, Syrian, and Jordanian forces. At the 11 September meeting, the British viewed the same U-2 pictures seen by the president, but were unresponsive to the tacit 'warning that the Middle East was under careful surveillance.'[107] Eisenhower unwisely approved giving the photos and briefing materials to the British. Unwilling to take the hint that the Americans were fully aware of the situation and that British diplomatic protestations of innocence were a charade, the British instead used the photos to tweak their plans to invade Egypt. Instead of convincing the British not to start a war, U-2 photos actually contributed to honing British military operations.

The best the president could do with Israel was warn its ambassador to the United States Abba Eban that America would honor its pledges to the United Nations to prevent aggression.[108] In addition, the 1950 Tripartite Declaration among the United States, France, and Britain called for protection of 'victims of aggression' in the Middle East, with options including the use of military force to return to a status quo ante. Eisenhower could hardly use American soldiers, sailors, and airmen against its ally Israel in defense of its erstwhile enemy Egypt. The hypocrisy was even greater considering that two of the Declaration's signatories were on the verge of becoming the aggressors. Nor could Eisenhower follow through with threats of sanctions against Israel if he was unwilling to apply those same sanctions equitably to Britain and France.

Even with Israeli military action under way and in the face of overwhelming U-2 photo evidence, Eisenhower still could not dissuade France and Britain from launching Operation MUSKETEER. He was helpless beyond sending pleading letters to British Prime Minister Anthony Eden or asking Foster Dulles to submit cease-fire proposals to the United Nations Security Council. Even the potential use of the American Sixth Fleet as an interim UN peacekeeping force – an idea bruited by Nasser – was fraught with irony and tragic consequences: what would happen if French or British forces fired upon American peacekeepers?

At home the president kept surprisingly mum on the evolving crisis. Throughout the summer the events in the Middle East were of great interest to the American people – any disruption of oil supplies which normally transited the Suez Canal would mean higher gas prices for consumers. Eisenhower chose not to discuss the events in detail to avoid unnecessarily alarming the public, as well as to maintain his flexibility in dealing with allies and opponents alike. His public silence, particularly in the context of the run-up to the 1956 presidential election, gave Democratic opponent Adlai Stevenson the ammunition to charge that Eisenhower was inept and indecisive in his foreign policy and that his health weakened his ability to act in time of crisis. Similar charges would resurface in the years ahead as other Democrats like Senators Lyndon Johnson and John Kennedy argued that Eisenhower was weak on defense despite knowing from U-2 photos that such claims were in fact empty. Indeed, at the height of the crisis – which coincided with Election Day – Democratic members of the Senate Foreign Relations Committee called the Suez crisis the 'worst diplomatic disaster in memory' and castigated the president for his 'indecision, tactlessness, timidity, and bluster.'[109]

Although Eisenhower was re-elected by a wide margin, U-2 photos were of no help in addressing public concerns about the crisis.

Revealing their existence would compromise the U-2 program which was critical in assessing Soviet strategic nuclear capabilities, a mission far more important than any public relations advantage related to a regional war involving American allies. In fact, the U-2 photos could actually have harmed the president politically, verifying Stevenson's claims of Eisenhower's inaction. The photos would show the American people that the president had in fact been aware of but unable to prevent the extensive, months-long military build up and actual onset of hostilities. If he couldn't do so with America's closest allies, how could he stand up to the Russians or the Chinese and prevent them from attacking the United States? To his credit, Eisenhower did use the photos to verify that the Soviets were not planning to join the conflict, which precluded unnecessary and highly risky escalation. The president's critics, however, could easily counter this success by arguing that Eisenhower was merely responding to Soviet behavior, rather than asserting his international leadership of the Free World in setting policy and compelling the Soviet Union to behave itself in the Middle East and its Eastern European satellites. Had he been more presidential and less time playing golf or hosting stag bridge games with his cronies he should have prevented the Suez Crisis months before it began, allowing him to take the moral high ground in focusing global attention on the brutal Soviet reaction to a fledgling pro-democracy movement in Hungary. Indeed, it was not until January 1957 that Eisenhower actually articulated a coherent American policy toward the Middle East – the Eisenhower Doctrine – which the Senate finally approved on 5 March 1957.

Moreover, revealing the U-2 photos would open the door to an embarrassing examination of the American intelligence community's disarray and misjudgment in predicting Israeli intentions and identifying the Franco-British-Israeli alliance. If the CIA – America's premier intelligence agency – could not detect these critical events, then how could it be expected to detect a Soviet surprise attack on the United States? Again, Stevenson might have argued, a passive president whose questionable health kept him away from the helm of government at critical times, coupled with an equally ill Secretary of State – whose brother ran the CIA – offered ineffective oversight of the American intelligence and diplomatic communities. Ultimately this failure could be replicated in their inability to provide early warning of a military threat to America and to democratic peace worldwide.

This argument applies equally to the 1958 Taiwan Straits crisis. If Mao's shelling of Quemoy and Matsu caught Khrushchev by surprise, it equally caught Chiang and Eisenhower off guard. There is no evidence that the United States or Taiwan detected any substantive Communist Chinese gradual or abrupt build up or force mobilization prior to the 23 August onset of the artillery barrages against the tiny islands. The absence of these indicators has been used to support the argument that there was no Red Chinese intent to invade the islands or Formosa. Had there been any such preparations, they surely would have been observed – the crisis, while real and fraught with catastrophic long-term consequences, was essentially a hollow event, more theater than substance.

In fact, aerial reconnaissance missed a genuine threat months earlier. Throughout the summer, Mao assembled an amphibious assault

Intelligence shortcomings revealed by the 1956 Suez Crisis and the 1958 Taiwan Straits Crisis raised critical questions about the ability of the United States to detect and respond to early indications of a Soviet attack. A couple of Tu-16 *Badgers* at a 'bounce' base in Siberia or on an ice floe in the Arctic Ocean would be enough to execute a surprise attack on key facilities, perhaps sufficient to undermine American willingness to retaliate. Only geostationary satellites could provide the continuous, real-time warning needed. *via Yefim Gordon*

force poised to invade the islands, ready to use them when the situation was propitious. On 27 July, a month before the shelling began, Mao changed his mind for some reason. The forces once on the verge of attack were reconfigured into a defensive posture, and it was this later, less hostile deployment which CIA U-2s first observed.[110] Similarly, without continuous, expansive coverage, RoCAF overflights were insufficient in number and frequency to detect the substantial build up of Communist forces. This unnoticed military build up evokes memories of a similar oversight eight years earlier. Aerial reconnaissance did not provide any early warning of the North Korean invasion of South Korea. This was largely because the situation on the peninsula was deemed insufficiently threatening and was therefore not subject to routine monitoring, rather than as an organic failure of aerial early warning in itself. Nonetheless the 1958 crisis raises questions about the American ability to understand and predict Asian intentions, and whether sufficient resources were employed there to detect potential threats.[111]

This failure to observe Red Chinese preparations for an amphibious invasion of Quemoy and Matsu had key security implications for the United States far greater than the control of two tiny islands. What if the extensive US aerial reconnaissance effort devoted to monitoring the Soviet Union for warning signs of an attack failed to detect imminent preparations for war? Just as with Korea in 1950 and Taiwan in 1958, the United States would be surprised by yet another Pearl Harbor scenario, this time involving nuclear weapons. SAC bombers would be caught on the ground, and any American retaliatory actions would thus be heavily circumscribed. Indeed, hard-liners worried, US political will might be undermined sufficiently to accept capitulation rather than risk further attacks – 'better Red than dead.' Aware of this reduced reliability in early warning, American military planners could well demand needless increases in defense spending that would significantly undermine economic prosperity. At the extreme, this weakness in early warning would provide advocates of preventive war with stronger evidence for their reckless intentions.

Did Mao Zedong really plan to invade Quemoy and Matsu, preparations which CIA U-2 overflights did not detect because of mission timing? Evidence suggests that he did but changed his mind. Strategic aerial reconnaissance missed this build up for war, and the implications ranged far beyond the 1958 Taiwan Crisis. If reconnaissance flights could not reliably and consistently fulfill the early warning role on which western security was based, then the United States and its allies were at profound risk of surprise attack. *Author's Collection*

Even with timely and accurate early warning of the summer Red Chinese military buildup, what would Eisenhower have done with this knowledge? Faced with clear indications of an invasion – just as he was in the Middle East two years earlier – the president would have to convince Mao not to attack the islands, and arguably, Formosa. As with the British and French at Suez, Mao's intentions were sufficiently rigid that any American political pressure would have had little restraining effect, and might just as easily have forced Mao's hand. Given the intense domestic pressure from the China Lobby, Eisenhower may have felt that in the absence of his ability to compel Mao to stand down and achieve a diplomatic solution that the president's only options were either to pre-empt the invasion or allow it to happen and respond by escalating to nuclear war with the PRC and Soviet Union. As it happened, it was fortuitous that the Red Chinese build up went unobserved, allowing Eisenhower and his advisors to focus their efforts on restraining Chiang rather than deterring Mao, a far greater, if not impossible, task.

Eisenhower's reliance on strategic aerial reconnaissance in the resolution of both the Suez and Taiwan confrontations reflects the value of this information in crisis management rather than in developing strategy or policy formulation.[112] In each case the intelligence gave the president and his advisors details of what was happening and preparations under way for imminent military actions. Knowing this, however, did not translate into an effective mechanism to prevent the crises from beginning or in expediting their conclusion. Indeed, pre-war intelligence photos should have enabled Eisenhower to ask far-reaching policy questions long before August 1956 or August 1958. For example, what should the United States do politically in the Middle East that would render a hypothetical invasion of Egypt unnecessary, rather than how could America respond to it? As Stevenson claimed, Eisenhower reacted to Suez

A June 1958 CIA U-2 mission flew along the northern coast of the PRC and missed southern preparations for an assault on Quemoy. By the end of July Mao changed his mind and dispersed the invasion force. An August U-2 mission detected this now defensive deployment, leading to a moderate US response to the crisis. This begs the issue, however, of how Eisenhower would have responded if a hypothetical U-2 flight in early July detected the Red Chinese invasion force. For many, Ike's options were a choice of Scylla or Charybdis: pre-empt the invasion and trigger nuclear war with the PRC and its USSR allies, or let the invasion happen and respond with nuclear weapons, escalating into global thermonuclear war.

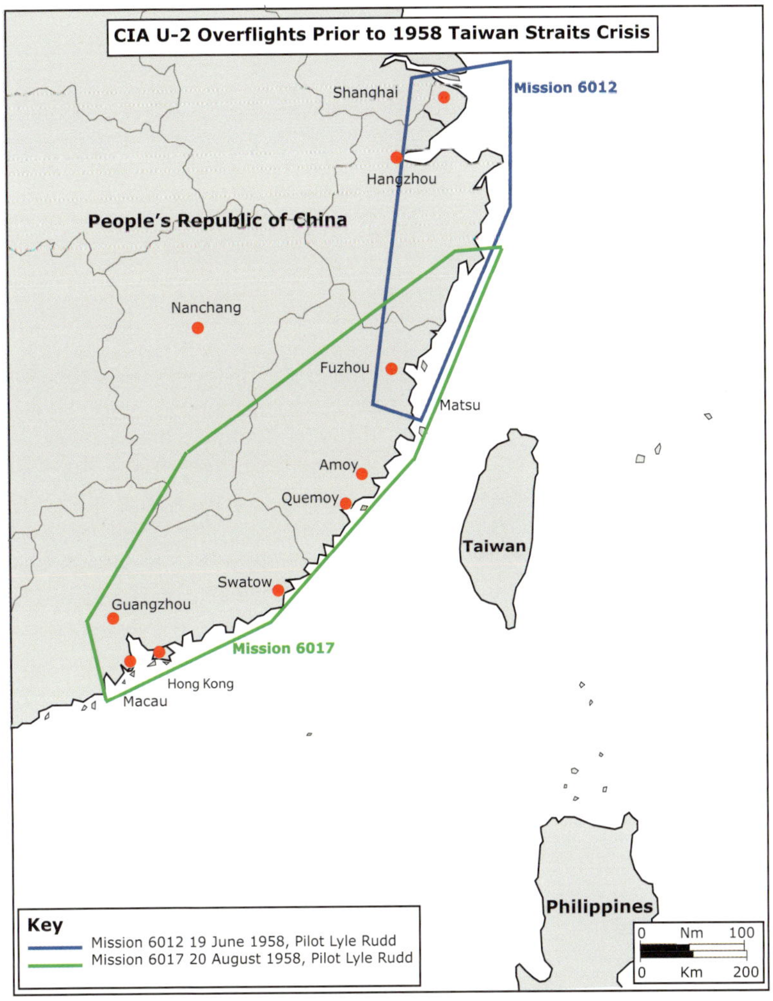

U-2 and RoCAF imagery acquired during the 1958 crisis failed to show an actual offensive build up in preparation for an amphibious invasion of Quemoy and Matsu. Radar-equipped PLAAF MiG-17PFs such as these would have provided aerial cover for night-time operations. US analysts, however, considered these useful only in point defense and missed this as a warning indicator. *via Yefim Gordon*

and Taiwan, using US aerial intelligence assets to understand what the belligerents were doing but did not use those assets to articulate in advance American policies that would ensure an ongoing peace. In Suez, especially, U-2 photos offered Eisenhower an impressive window into battlefield dynamics, but left him on the outside looking in in terms of his ability to influence the overall course of events. In Taiwan U-2 photos enabled the president to restrain Chiang, but failed to alert him earlier to a far greater danger. Ultimately, Suez and Taiwan raise critical challenges about existing assessments of Eisenhower's handling of these crises. They also question the effectiveness of aerial reconnaissance in strategic early warning, and reveal, at best, mixed success in using these flights in 'tactical' situations.[113]

7 Rhetoric and Stability

The crew had been flying in darkness for four hours. Summer sunlight began to illuminate the airplane as it flew northeast over the Sea of Japan. To the left was the narrow border between North Korea and the Soviet Union. Ahead was the naval base at Vladivostok. As the airplane approached the Russian coastline the pilot turned eastward, away from the Soviet border. They were close enough to monitor Soviet defense communications and signals, but far enough to avoid the 12-mile limit of Soviet airspace. For the electronic warfare officers and the Russian-speaking linguists on board the RB-50, the workload increased dramatically as they recorded radar tracking signals and listened to ground controllers who reported the airplane's location and altitude. For the pilots and navigators there was a sense of satisfaction that they were on course and would soon enjoy a beer and some sleep back at Yokota.

Abruptly the airplane lurched at it was struck by cannon fire. Two Soviet MiG-17s were shooting at the RB-50. One of the gunners, Airman Second Class James E Woods, began to shoot at the two MiGs as they continued their attack. His return fire was ineffective as the MiG-17s, highly maneuverable jet fighters, adroitly turned away from the large piston-powered ferret. The damage was done; the wounds were lethal. Engines disintegrated or caught fire. Chunks of the wings fell off. Within a minute the RB-50 spun uncontrollably toward the water below. Most of the crewmembers managed to bail out. Others were not so fortunate.

The loss of this RB-50G, serial number 47-0145 and nicknamed *Little Red Ass*, has been well chronicled.[1] Despite the catastrophic damage to the airplane and its location in such close proximity to the Soviet Union, there was a single survivor, Captain John E Roche, the co-pilot. Forty-five years after the incident Roche recalled that they were on course over international waters 40 miles off shore from the Soviet Union. He noted that the MiG-17 attack was unprovoked and that no one had seen the MiGs until they opened fire, and emphasized that Woods shot at the MiGs only after the RB-50 came under attack. This attack may well have been planned in retaliation for the loss of a Soviet Ilyushin IL-12 *Coach* transport to a US F-86 a few days earlier. Roche's recollection of Soviet rescue vessels in the immediate vicinity (as well as other corroborating evidence) supports this assertion. Several contemporary claims were made that survivors from the *Little Red Ass* were incarcerated in Soviet labor camps. Investigations at the time found these to be without merit, but subsequent research suggests that in fact they were imprisoned but perished.[2]

On the morning of 29 July 1953, however, there were two other pilots in the fatal drama surrounding the *Little Red Ass* whose stories have only recently been told. The very same radars that were of interest to the crew of the RB-50 were actively tracking the airplane's flight path along the periphery of the USSR. According to an internal Russian defense report from Soviet Navy Minister Admiral of the Fleet Nikolai G Kuznetsov to Minister of Defence Marshal Zhukov, the RB-50 entered the airspace over Soviet territorial waters near Cape Gamova at 7:01 AM. It headed toward the heavily fortified Askold Island, held by the USSR and located 25 miles south of Nakhodka. At 7:06 AM local commanders ordered two MiG-17s which were in an airborne defensive patrol (DefPat) south of Vladivostok to intercept the RB-50 with orders to force the airplane to land in the Soviet Union. This was a widely accepted practice for dealing with incursions. By 7:11 AM the MiGs' pilots visually spotted the 'intruder' six miles south of Askold. They approached the airplane to identify it but were fired upon, causing damage to the lead interceptor. The MiG pilots had no choice but to defend themselves and their homeland. They shot at and damaged the RB-50, then watched it lose control and start its spiral toward the sea at a point 70 miles from Vladivostok and 26 miles from Cape Povorotny. For their bravery under fire Senior Lieutenants

Alexansdr Rybakov and Yuri Yablonski were awarded the Order of the Red Banner of Combat and the Order of the Red Star, respectively.[3]

It is not surprising that the American and Russian accounts of the RB-50's destruction should differ. Both sides viewed the attack from two distinct geographic and ideological perspectives. In this case the United States asserted that the airplane had a right to be where it was, well outside even the most liberal definition of Soviet territorial waters. The Russian attack was illegal under international law and reflected the violent nature of a pariah Soviet Union. If the MiG pilots had truly attempted to instruct the RB-50 to land as they claim then it was legally incumbent upon them to ensure that the pilots of the RB-50 had seen and understood these instructions. Instead, the MiG pilots opened fire on an innocent and unsuspecting airplane and were responsible for the murder of some of its crew. Conversely, the Russians argued that the airplane violated Soviet airspace as had many other previous American reconnaissance flights, infringing the sovereignty of the USSR. Despite the peaceful attempt to direct the RB-50 to land in the USSR as allowed by international aviation agreements, the intruding spyplane fired first, provoking the MiG-17s to return fire and shoot it down. Once again, hostile American actions undermined Soviet efforts to preserve a peaceful world.

Highly visible and violent incidents such as this one led many contemporary Western diplomats and observers – not to mention subsequent researchers – to conclude that the Russian reaction to reconnaissance flights was to attack them and shoot them down whenever possible. The Soviets did so, critics argued, because their leaders justifiably viewed the flights as illegal, threatening, or harbingers of war. Aerial reconnaissance missions destabilized East-West relations. Their continued presence compelled the Soviets to defend their country by force. Improved Soviet-American relations and long-term peace could only come by eliminating these gratuitous provocations which needlessly prolonged the Cold War, and even ran the risk of precipitating general war between the two major nuclear powers.[4] The benefit of global peace far outweighed any incremental intelligence benefit derived from these flights.

Understanding the Soviet response to Western aerial reconnaissance has been largely constrained by the inaccessibility of archival material and the barrier of language, longstanding impediments to much Cold War scholarship. With the dissolution of the Soviet Union, however, retired PVO officers have come forward to share their experiences. Russian-speaking scholars have begun to mine the former Soviet archives. Russian aviation researchers such as Yefim Gordon have started to chronicle much of the unwritten history of Soviet-era aerospace. There is now an opportunity to assess – or at least appreciate – the Soviet response to these flights and their overall impact on Soviet-American relations, as well as establish a baseline for future inquiry.

In an early effort to understand the cause and effect of Western aerial reconnaissance on Soviet policy, historian John Farquhar adapted the spiral model of action and reaction from international relations theory to develop an interpretive framework called the 'Circle of Fear.' The United States undertook reconnais-

The *Little Red Ass* was similar to RB-50G 47-161 assigned to the 343rd SRS, 55th SRW, seen here in the Western Pacific during 1953. Although equipped with defensive armament, it strains credibility to imagine that a lumbering aircraft like this would initiate an attack against highly maneuverable MiGs. *NMUSAF via Geoff Hays*

sance flights out of 'mistrust and fear' of the Soviet Union. Once under way, the flights preyed upon Soviet fears of 'capitalist encirclement' and accentuated weaknesses in Soviet defenses. Improvements to these defenses led to attacks and the destruction of American reconnaissance planes. These incidents, especially those with the loss of American lives, seized the public's attention, stirred public outrage, and reinforced an American vision of 'implacable Soviet hostility' toward the United States and of a Soviet Union bent on global military domination. Reports in the *New York Times* and elsewhere stressed the barbarity of the Soviet reaction, especially as all the destroyed aircraft were in international airspace where they had a legal right to fly. These perceptions fueled the US demand for more reconnaissance flights to learn more fully the intentions and capabilities of an increasingly powerful and threatening Soviet Union. The 'Circle of Fear' was now complete and ready to escalate another notch.[5]

This generally accepted view, epitomized by Farquhar's model, is based on three implicit assumptions: (1) that Soviet leaders clearly recognized these as intelligence-gathering flights and reacted to them precisely because they were reconnaissance aircraft; (2) that overflights and peripheral flights contributed equally to Soviet fears; and (3) that the Soviet reaction to Western aircraft that skirted or overflew the Soviet Union was consistently violent from 1945 to 1961. In fact, none of these is true.

Although Soviet leaders justifiably viewed overflights as an irritant in East-West relations, and held arguably far more tolerant views on peripheral flights, the number of Soviet attacks on Western aircraft was extremely low compared to the total number of intelligence-gathering flights undertaken. The number of attacks is even smaller when compared with the total number of Soviet incidents involving all Western aircraft, military or civilian, which varied considerably between 1945 and 1961,

WHERE WAS THE *LITTLE RED ASS*?

Efforts to understand exactly where the *Little Red Ass* was the morning of 29 July 1953 are clouded by the foibles of memory and the requirement to maintain an official story on the part of both American and Soviet participants. Based on interviews and recently declassified American intercepts of Soviet radio transmissions, it is now possible to reconstruct what likely happened and why.

In addition to the crew's five Ravens, two USAF Security Service Russian linguists and an unidentified native-speaking Russian (called a 'displaced person', likely a defector) were also on board the RB-50G. The linguists were to collect COMINT as well as provide an internal self-defense capability. Listening to Soviet ground controllers and interceptor pilots, they would warn aircraft commander Captain Stan O'Kelley if the airplane was in danger, prompting the flight to leave the area.

According to a declassified NSA study, the RB-50G was on a VHF intercept mission and the 'official' route of flight was well south of the 42° parallel. Beginning around 6:45 AM local Vladivostok time (L), US ground-based listening posts monitored Soviet tracking communications that indicated they were following an unidentified airplane, which in fact was the RB-50G (subsequent public statements by Soviet officials described the airplane as a 'B-50'). Soviet position reports indicated that the RB-50G was on a track parallel to but some 50nm *north* of its 'official' route. These reports placed it close to the Soviet 12nm territorial limit, and certainly far closer to the Soviet coastline than the 40nm claimed by survivor John Roche and US officials. At 6:56L the Soviets launched two MiG-17s into a DefPat near Vladivostok. As the RB-50G passed Cape Gamova at 7:01L, Soviet tracking placed it 12nm southeast of Russian territory, violating Soviet airspace. At this point, the RB-50G made a leisurely turn eastward toward Japan, away from the heading that would have taken it to Askold Island. Five minutes later, Soviet controllers ordered the two MiG-17s to intercept the intruder. The RB-50G continued east until 7:17:30L, when it abruptly turned south. By 7:18L the MiG-17s had opened fire on the RB-50G at 42°18' N, 132°36' E, where the *Little Red Ass* began its uncontrolled descent into the Peter the Great Bay, crashing at 7:21L.

[Some reports indicate that the MiGs were MiG-15s from the 9th Army Air Force at Korolsk AB, while others claim they were MiG-17s from Nikolaevka AB, some 35nm closer to Vladivostok. Given the length of time the MiGs were airborne and the distances covered, it is most likely – but not unequivocal – that they were MiG-17s.]

Despite substantial delays, two USAF search-and-rescue SB-29s began looking for the missing RB-50G out of concern that it had crashed due to a mechanical problem, unaware that it had been shot down. Soviet radar tracked one of these as it flew along a path that approximated the RB-50's *actual* – rather than 'official' – flight path. The SB-29 crew flew where they expected to find the RB-50G if it had crashed along its actual flight planned course. In addition, the SB-29 crew had to be given this actual course prior to their departure to look for the *Little Red Ass*. That means that the RB-50G was *on course* as it flew some 20nm – the US limit for ferret flights – off the coast of the Soviet Union as it was tracked by Soviet radar.

The SB-29 crew saw Roche and O'Kelley in the water and dropped an aluminum lifeboat to them. Sadly, O'Kelley did not reach the lifeboat before succumbing to injury and exhaustion. The SB-29 crew also claimed they saw other survivors and debris, as did a second SB-29, and reported multiple Soviet vessels in what appeared to be a well co-ordinated rescue effort, suggesting advance preparation. As darkness and fog set in, the SB-29s returned to Japan. US and Australian naval vessels headed for the crash site to continue the search effort. Some 22 hours after being shot down, John Roche was aboard a US Navy destroyer receiving medical care.

In the days that followed, Roche repeated the official American version of the story that the RB-50G was on course 40nm from shore. But, as one US Navy flier involved in the rescue effort told Roche years later, 'You guys just about parked it [the *Little Red Ass*] in [Vladivostok] harbor; you were close enough so they could see you from the shore.' Although an exaggeration, this nonetheless suggests that the RB-50G had indeed flown where the Soviets claimed it had in order for it to crash at the location where the rescue operations took place.

reaching a peak in 1952 and 1953. Soviet officials frequently used non-violent means to express their displeasure with peripheral flights. Diplomatic protests and propaganda campaigns accounted for many of the Soviet reactions. In other cases the Soviets did nothing, either unaware of the flights or unwilling to admit that they could not take action against them. How and why the Soviets reacted to Western reconnaissance flights was more a constantly evolving function of Soviet Cold War national security capabilities and goals than a specific reaction to foreign aerial espionage. This assessment of the Soviet reaction to Western reconnaissance flights does not take into consideration the reactions of the People's Republic of China which attacked and destroyed several such flights. However, the same general conditions that apply to the Soviet case – reaction to any aerial intruder, real or perceived, and the limited number of violent attacks compared to the total number of flights – are still valid.[6]

Prior to the First World War, champions of the burgeoning field of aviation argued that airspace around and above all states was equivalent to the high seas. This meant that airplanes could fly unrestricted anywhere in the world over land or ocean. Once the military value of aircraft became apparent in the Great War, the view of overflights became more restrictive and more closely linked to traditional interpretations of land and sea sovereignty. This was codified in 1919 with the Paris Convention on the Regulation of Air Navigation, and later in the 1944 Chicago Convention on International Civil Aviation. These accords defined airspace above a state's territory as part of that state's 'full and exclusive sovereignty.'[7] Moreover, these agreements specifically excluded the notion of 'innocent passage' which allowed ships at sea to travel through a state's territorial waters as a matter of expediency while en route to their final destination. The Chicago Convention concluded that an aircraft may not overfly foreign airspace without the authorization of

It may never be possible to ascertain who fired first, but the evidence suggests that it was the MiGs. After the RB-50G turned east at Cape Gamova, it continued at the same slow cruise speed of approximately 215 KIAS. The on-board Russian linguists either did not hear the Soviet controller's order for the two MiG-17s to intercept the RB-50G or, if they did hear it, they did not consider it sufficiently threatening to merit an increase in speed to leave the area in haste (an order to intercept is obviously far less menacing than an order to attack). Indeed, the airplane soon turned northeast back toward Askold Island, and then resumed its eastward journey, hardly indicative of a crew aware that they were in peril.

At 7:17:30L the RB-50G turned abruptly away from the Soviet coastline and headed south, an indication that it was fleeing for safety. Roche did not say that the on-board linguists had warned of an impending attack by hearing orders to the MiG-17 pilots to shoot at the RB-50G, prompting this hasty retrograde. Given that this was (and remained for decades) a highly classified COMINT capability, Roche may have intentionally omitted this detail from his story. The 90-degree turn suggests a high degree of urgency, not what might be expected from simply having the MiGs appear, although Roche's account does not specify that the crew made a turn. If under attack, the crew would have instinctively turned away, and Roche may not have recalled this turn (likely made by O'Kelley) while under fire. This

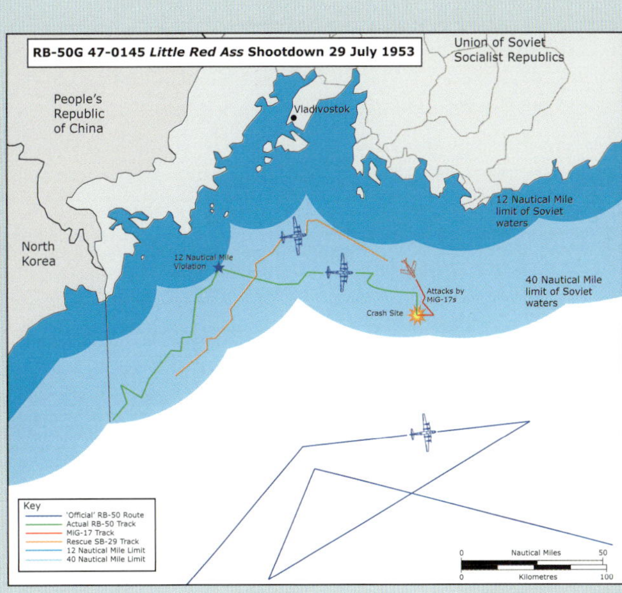

Neither the US nor the Soviet Union was completely honest in their public announcements about the loss of RB-50G *Little Red Ass* on 29 July 1953. The RB-50 was far closer than the 40nm claimed by the Americans, and the Soviets almost certainly shot it down not for violating Soviet airspace but in retaliation for a US attack on a Russian airplane.

suggests that the RB-50G turned under duress.

Given that the entire interception of the *Little Red Ass* appears to have been a planned retaliation for the prior American downing of a Soviet IL-12, it makes sense that the MiG-17s simply opened fire on the RB-50G without warning, having no intention of forcing it to land. That one of the SB-29s also appears to have crossed the 12nm boundary and was not attacked further suggests that the RB-50G was not shot down due to an airspace violation. Damage to one of the MiG-17s might easily have come from return fire, or simply debris from the disintegrating RB-50G.

In short, the official American story was that the *Little Red Ass* was at least 40nm from the USSR, preserving the cover story that US ferrets operated with the greatest of caution and without provocation. The official Soviet story is that the RB-50G violated Soviet territory and attacked the intercepting MiGs, obscuring the Russian intent to shoot it down all along in retaliation for an event unrelated to strategic aerial reconnaissance.

[Sources: Roche, Interview with Author; Peterson, *Cryptologic Quarterly*; Burrows, *By Any Means Necessary*, 310; Tart and Keefe, *Price of Vigilance*, 40-51; and Gordon and Kommissarov, *Soviet Air Defence Aviation*, 37-39.]

the state being overflown. The Convention also clearly reaffirmed the unabridged right of any airplane to fly uncontested in international airspace surrounding any nation. This guarantee applied equally to commercial as well as military aircraft, including Western aerial reconnaissance assets operating in the vicinity of the Soviet Union or People's Republic of China. Indeed, by 1950 the global consensus – including that of Communist bloc nations – was that an airplane of any type and from any country could fly without restriction in international airspace *however close* to Soviet airspace, *even if* that airplane was engaged in reconnaissance activities. Although the Soviet Union was not a signatory to the 1944 accord and its leaders asserted that they were not bound by it, they nonetheless agreed with the right of airplanes to operate freely in international airspace adjacent to the USSR irrespective of the purpose of the flight.[8] Despite this agreement in principle, Soviet and Red Chinese responses to Western peripheral aerial reconnaissance missions ranged from silence to diplomatic protests to propaganda campaigns to outright attacks. For the Soviets, these reactions varied according to the strength – not vulnerability – of Russian military preparedness. As Soviet aerial defense forces increased in quantity and improved in quality, so too did the belligerence of the response, reaching a zenith in 1953, after which the Soviet response to peripheral flights became notably less aggressive.

For the first five years of the Cold War the most common Soviet reaction to peripheral reconnaissance missions was silence given the comparatively small number of flights and their secrecy, the remote areas of the Soviet Union where they took place, and the nascent Soviet policy toward the flights. Sometimes this was a matter of choice, other times a matter of hard reality and not for want of trying. In many instances the Soviets did nothing about the flights because they were of little significance. A single unidentified airplane – reconnaissance platform or airliner – flying adjacent to the Kamchatka Peninsula was hardly of interest. In some cases the Soviets said nothing because they were simply unaware of the flights. Operational secrecy surrounding the flights and huge gaps in Russian radar coverage meant that reconnaissance flights could operate freely and undiscovered near the coast or border. In other situations the Soviets were silent because they could not intercept the flights they did detect. Poor early warning equipment meant insufficient reaction time for PVO fighters to reach the passing airplane.

Between 1945 and 1947 peripheral intelligence flights were hardly commonplace. Most were US Navy maritime patrol flights tracking commercial shipping and naval movements in vital regions such as the Baltic and the Sea of Japan. As evolving US intelligence requirements demanded more information about Soviet war capabilities and defenses, the number of reconnaissance flights – especially those by the newly formed Strategic Air Command – increased commensurately. Still, by early 1949 there were hardly the hundreds of monthly peripheral flights that eventually characterized early Cold War aerial reconnaissance.

Gathering intelligence is inherently a clandestine activity, and Western military officials and civilian leaders clearly understood the need for secrecy in conducting peripheral reconnaissance missions around the Soviet Union and the People's Republic of China. Even with the small number of initial peripheral missions, operational commanders went to great lengths to ensure the flights operated in maximum secrecy to avoid letting an enemy know that they were being monitored. With the exception of the crews themselves and those military or civilian personnel responsible for the on-scene operational conduct of each flight, perhaps only a few dozen officials knew that a flight was planned or under way.

Given the vast expanse of Siberia and the Russian Pacific coastline, these limited flights operated with relative impunity. The northern reaches of Siberia, for example, had few, if any, sites to detect these airplanes, a capability severely constrained by qualitative and quantitative limits to Soviet long-range early warning radars. Even when Soviet defenses did identify Western reconnaissance flights – or any other airplane perceived to be too close to the Soviet border – they were ill suited to take decisive mil-

Soviet attacks on Western aircraft during the early years of the Cold War utilized piston-powered fighters such as this La-7 *Fin*. These airplanes should not be dismissed as 'aging' or 'war surplus' given that most were just a few years old, as were their US and British counterparts. Most importantly, they were effectively dangerous, if not lethal. *via Yefim Gordon*

itary action. Soviet piston-powered fighters typically had insufficient warning time to launch and intercept high-flying RB-29s, as they lacked the climb capability, speed, and operational range to catch up to the faster aircraft. There were occasional engagements and a few shots fired, but these were due more to chance than to any co-ordinated effort by Soviet air defense forces. The first such hostile Soviet reaction to the US postwar aerial reconnaissance effort was the 15 October 1945 attack by Soviet fighters on a US Navy PBM-5 Mariner conducting a routine shipping identification mission. The incident occurred 25 miles from Dairen after the PBM-5 supposedly flew within a mile of Port Arthur, then under Soviet control.[9] Taking place some six weeks after the Japanese surrender, the incident might well have been a case of post-war nerves – hardly any consolation to the Mariner's crew – rather than a matter of Soviet policy. US officials were unable to determine if the attack was just a warning to the airplane to stay clear of Soviet-controlled airspace or was actually intended to destroy the Mariner. Other shots were fired during an intercept on 20 February 1946, and Soviet fighters 'aggressively' escorted a reconnaissance flight on 5 October 1949 but did not fire warning shots. Two weeks later Soviet La-7 *Fin* fighters attacked and damaged an RB-29.[10]

Aside from the operational limits that constrained the Soviet response to Western reconnaissance flights, the apparent unwillingness of the Soviets to take action against them was directly linked to their own evolving view of Cold War security issues. Although Soviet leaders endorsed violence when it suited their policy needs and were capable of employing it when the risks were low, they found it inexpedient to use force routinely against the earliest flights.[11] Part of this moderation was rooted in Stalinist doctrine that held another world war was 'fatalistically inevitable,' first among the capitalist nations and then between the weakened survivors and the great socialist states. However inescapable such a war might be, Stalin and his advisors were genuinely concerned about a premature war between the United States and the Soviet Union. They did not necessarily expect an American surprise attack, but believed that should war erupt the Soviet Union was ill prepared to fight and win (a mirror-image sentiment to one in the White House). Stalin knew that despite a significant residual Soviet land army the American nuclear airpower monopoly was a critical force that as yet could not be overcome. Khrushchev reaffirmed this trepidation, swearing that 'Stalin trembled with fear' of war with the United States. 'How he quivered! He was afraid of war.'[12] The Russian inability to detect or intercept Western reconnaissance flights highlighted this strategic limit. If the Soviets could not stop a reconnaissance aircraft from operating near the USSR, they held little hope that they could stop an attacking bomber from entering the Soviet Union. With this constraint in mind, Soviet leaders reasoned that delaying any potential war was to the advantage of the Soviet Union, allowing it more time to prepare suitable defenses, produce more offensive weapons – including atomic bombs, and cultivate increased revolutionary consciousness abroad.[13]

The example of the Great Patriotic War was still fresh in Stalin's mind. During the spring and summer of 1941, German aerial reconnaissance missions along the border with and over Russian territory preceded the start of Operation BARBAROSSA. Stalin ordered that no action be taken against them to avoid provoking war with Germany. Cold war peripheral missions might similarly portend a US attack on the Soviet Union. Fearful that a violent response to these flights might precipitate harsh American retaliation that could escalate into a premature war between the United States and Russia, Stalin chose a comparable policy of silence. This approach was in keeping with Stalin's personality. He would often say nothing to a potential victim for months, allowing his strategy to percolate until the time was right to act. Nikolai Buglanin supposedly told Khrushchev, 'Sometimes when you go to Stalin's he invites you as a friend. But while you're sitting with him, you don't know where they'll take you afterward: home or to prison.'[14] In this case, one can easily imagine Stalin tolerating Western peripheral flights until the moment was propitious to act decisively to stop them, ready for war if need be. As such, Stalin's restraint was a pragmatic policy intended to avoid precipitating war with the West at a time of relative Soviet weakness while biding his time until the Soviet Union was strong enough to act without fear of defeat. Stalin's concern that an aggressive Soviet reaction to Western flights might trigger premature war with the United States is particularly ironic. American critics feared the flights were a sufficient irritant that could induce Russia to attack them, leading unintentionally to war. He, similarly, worried that any Soviet attack on the airplanes would compel the United States to respond with actions that would equally lead to war.

Initially Stalin could do little about Western reconnaissance flights out of lack of military capability and fear of provoking greater conflict. As Soviet forces improved Stalin became more aggressive toward *all* flights, military or civilian. Most importantly, the lack of substantive US response to Soviet attacks on ferrets and airliners alike emboldened Stalin. From January through December 1952 (he died three months later), incidents involving Western aircraft peaked at 48, only 16 of which comprised reconnaissance aircraft. *Author's Collection*

Opposite: A PVO flight commander briefs his colleagues prior to a mission in their MiG-17PFUs. Fliers would literally walk through the planned mission to ensure absolute compliance with the pre-flight briefing. Without belittling the individual skill and courage of Soviet pilots, the IADS system required pilots to follow the instructions of ground-based radar controllers without delay or deviation. Ultimately, these *Fresco* E pilots were trained to identify a target and pull the trigger if need be, and little more. *via Yefim Gordon*

Although early Soviet response to Western peripheral intelligence flights was driven largely by unawareness or reluctance to act, this changed by 1950. Russian reactions became increasingly strident, intolerant, and hostile. This change resulted from several related factors. The war in Korea heightened tensions between East and West, escalating the hyperbole and vitriol accompanying international diplomacy. In addition, Western peripheral flights had become routine. Their regular routes and times – such as the daily weather reconnaissance flights in each direction between Japan and Alaska – made them sufficiently predictable and hence vulnerable to interception and attack. Some SIGINT and COMINT flights orbited for hours near key coastal installations. Spies near US bases in England, Japan, and Alaska monitored airplane departures and reported that a reconnaissance mission was likely under way. There have been multiple claims that Soviet and Chinese moles or Communist sympathizers within the intelligence or diplomatic communities warned Soviet defense forces of an impending flight. Roche, for example, claims that 'peace at any price' Soviet sympathizers in the US State Department 'tipped off' the Soviets to the location of the flight as Roche claims. None of these assertions has been corroborated.[15] Commercial airliner traffic had increased, particularly along the Great Circle routes from the United States to Japan, which skirted the Soviet Far East, leading to a dramatic increase in the total number of airplanes of any type operating adjacent to the Soviet Union. Moreover, between 1950 and 1955 the number of overflights of the USSR grew, leading to increased Soviet public remonstrance and aggression toward *all flights* – military, civilian, and commercial – in international airspace around the Soviet Union.

Between 1945 and 1947 the Soviet Union issued a modest 15 diplomatic protests concerning aerial violations (or perceived violations) of Russian territory. During these early years Soviet leaders typically issued a protest only when they were unable to take direct military action against a ferret, or when a foreign government or media source revealed the incident. On 25 February 1947, for example, the Soviets complained about claimed US overflights of remote Big Diomede Island that took place on 23 and 25 December 1946. Additional alleged violations by US aircraft of Soviet airspace occurred along the Soviet-Iranian border and in the Sea of Japan, prompting occasional Soviet diplomatic notes asking that the incidents be investigated and measures be taken to prevent their recurrence. Over the next three years, Soviet reticence to complain about aerial incidents abated. From 1947 to 1950, the number of Soviet objections increased dramatically with some 203 protests over Western aircraft allegedly violating Soviet airspace.[16] In addition, Russian grievances were increasingly specific about individual missions involving military aircraft – especially perceived border violations – instead of general grousing about random incidents involving any aircraft type, such as commercial airliners that had strayed off course near or over the Soviet Union.

Most significantly, ongoing technological and organizational improvements in Soviet defense forces meant that more reconnaissance flights could be detected and intercepted. By 1949 the nimble, jet-powered MiG-15 *Fagot* had entered service with frontline PVO units. This new fighter could take off with little notice, climb rapidly to an unidentified airplane's cruising altitude, and loiter with it long enough to escort it, chase it away, or even fire upon it. RB-29s or RB-50s, for example, could no longer rely upon their altitude and speed to avoid contact with Soviet fighters. Similarly, refinements in the quality of Russian early warning and tracking radars, coupled with attendant advancements in communication between radar sites and airborne interceptors, facilitated the deployment of what would become an integrated air defense system (IADS). Rather than a hodgepodge of individual units operating separately and without common information, IADS meant that more precise information could be relayed from radar units to the interceptors, enabling them to locate and attack their targets more often, especially at night or in bad weather. Even older, piston-powered fighters such as the La-7 *Fin*, La-11 *Fang*, and Yak-9 *Frank* were once again effective against Western reconnaissance planes.

IADS was a simple arrangement. Russian long-range early warning radars detected an airplane as it passed or approached the Soviet Union. Radar operators would then alert other crews manning short-range tracking radar of a potential interception. Concurrently, MiG pilots would scramble and fly toward the unidentified airplane. The tracking controllers would tell the MiG pilot when to climb, which way to turn, and when to fire upon the target. The MiG pilot was effectively an automaton, following instructions from commanders on the ground and with little prerogative or room for improvisation. IADS was like much of the Soviet defense community throughout the Cold War – rigid, inflexible, and unimaginative.[17] Nonetheless, it was a vast improvement in Russian capability, and it worked. Unfortunately, it worked too well.

Soviet radars might know precisely where a ferret like an RB-29 was, and would be able to guide the two MiG-15s precisely to the RB-29 and shoot it down. Precision, however, did not mean accuracy. Most Soviet long-range and tracking radars were located well behind the Russian coastline or borders to protect them from invading ground forces. They were also notoriously inaccurate at their extreme limits. Operating under these conditions, spurious radar returns could show a distant airplane to be anywhere from 30 to 50 miles or more from its actual position. If this technical artifact placed the airplane closer than it actually was, Soviet defense forces would falsely conclude that it had crossed into Russian airspace or was even over the mainland. An RB-29, therefore, flying over water in international airspace some 20 miles *outside* the Soviet coastline, might appear to a remote Soviet radar operator to be 10 miles *inside* the Russian coastline. This erroneous position would arguably justify a Soviet attack on an unidentified airplane, even though in fact it had not violated Russian airspace or borders. In short, both the American and Russian versions of the same event were simultaneously plausible. Based on flight crew navigation, the ferret was on course outside Soviet airspace. Based on Soviet radar returns, the ferret was inside Russian airspace.[18]

Just as Soviet radar could not always accurately tell where an airplane was, it could not identify the type of airplane it was tracking. For a 'scope dope' – slang for a radar operator – the blip on his radar screen was just that: a blip. It was impossible to distinguish an RB-50 on an intelligence-gathering mission near the coast from a C-54 medical evacuation flight from Japan that was blown off course by stiff crosswinds. Even Soviet leaders knew that it was a 'practical impossibility' to use radar to identify a reconnaissance aircraft from among the thousands of military and civilian aircraft that flew close to the USSR.[19] Consequently, the Soviets reacted in exactly the same fashion to *any* aircraft even remotely perceived to have violated Soviet

airspace, irrespective of whether it was a military reconnaissance flight, a military cargo or passenger flight, or a civilian airliner. Between 1945 and 1960 there were at least 199 aerial incidents, but only 93 (47 per cent) of these involved US reconnaissance airplanes. Out of the 51 Western airplanes shot down during this period, only 28 were US reconnaissance missions.[20]

Russian pilots faced a similar impediment. An interceptor pilot might have only a few moments to confirm visually the identity of an airplane being tracked by ground radar. The target airplane might be flying in and out of clouds, in poor light conditions, or even darkness, making this task all the more difficult. The interceptor might be at the limit of its range and therefore could only make a single identifying pass, preserving just enough fuel for an attack run if so ordered. The actual appearance of the target airplane could be equally ambiguous. A four-engine airliner flying near or over Communist territory might easily be mistaken at first glance for an RB-50 on a reconnaissance mission. Indeed, on 29 April 1952 Russian MiG-15s based in East Germany attacked an Air France DC-4 on a routine passenger flight from Frankfurt to Berlin; on 22 July 1954 Red Chinese La-9 *Fritz* fighters shot down a Cathay Pacific Airways Douglas DC-4 airliner near Hainan Island while on a flight from Bangkok, Thailand, to Hong Kong; on 27 July 1955 Bulgarian MiG-15s shot down an El Al Airlines Lockheed Constellation near Petrich, Bulgaria. More ominously, RB-29s and RB-50s carrying cameras and electronic recording gear could not be easily differentiated from B-29s and B-50s carrying conventional or atomic bombs. To a MiG pilot all airliners and 'all B-29s looked alike, all carried menacing .50 caliber tail guns and were the enemy – period.'[21]

Improvements in Soviet defenses, however effective, were not specifically linked to Western peripheral reconnaissance flights. One of the earliest and most important reorganizations of the Soviet anti-aircraft forces – the first line of defense against aerial reconnaissance missions – took place in late 1948 in response to Truman's deployment of B-29s to England during the Berlin Crisis.[22] Even when Soviet defenses did undergo changes that could be linked to reconnaissance flights, these improved assets were not necessarily deployed judiciously or in a timely manner. For example, SA-2 *Guideline* SAMs were first stationed in the Russian heartland for use against overflights – primarily by U-2s – and took considerable time to be assigned to forces charged with defending the USSR from perceived border violations by low-altitude peripheral reconnaissance missions.[23] One former air defense commander recalled that his forces along Soviet borders and coastlines were severely circumscribed because Moscow did not 'provide enough resources and budget for the [air defense forces,] and the dif-

This page: The fighter pilot's dilemma: night, bad weather, approaching minimum fuel while over frigid ocean waters 40 miles from the nearest land. The radar controller is screaming over the radio and your eyes are blurry and head is pounding from too much vodka and cigarettes before you went to bed. Is that a reconnaissance B-50 full of cameras or a bomber B-50 full of bombs? Is that blob on top of the fuselage a gun turret or a sampling pod? Do you shoot or go home? The top photo shows WB-50D 49-0261 on 29 April 1956, and the bottom image is B-50D 47-0101 taken on 25 May 1953. *Both photos Alan Scholefield*

Opposite page, top: MiG-15s flown by Soviet pilots shot down or destroyed six RB-29s and an RB-45 during the course of the Korean War. The MiG-15 *Fagot* changed the dynamic of strategic aerial reconnaissance, forcing the flights to operate at night and in bad weather, conditions not favorable to the nimble MiG-15. This meant that PHOTINT would require a faster, higher flying platform, leading to the RF-100A, YRB-47B and RB-47E, RB-57 variants, and ultimately the U-2 at altitudes beyond the MiG-15's ceiling. *via Yefim Gordon*

ficulties and hardships of service in the air defense force…[were] really great.'[24]

Soviet defense spending in general reflected this lack of funding for frontline air defense forces. Beginning in the mid 1950s Soviet military expenditures actually decreased. The 1956 defense budget was approximately 18.5 billion rubles, which dropped to 17.5 billion in 1957 and 15.5 billion in 1958. Although defense spending increased substantially to 19.0 billion rubles in 1959, this level remained constant until 1962. Overall, Soviet defense spending between 1955 and 1962, as a percentage of gross national product, dropped from 11.5 per cent in 1955, hovered between 8.5 and 9.5 per cent through 1961, and then remained nearly constant at 10 per cent for the next five years.[25] Much to the chagrin of senior Soviet defense officials (and mirroring similar sentiments among US military men about their own budget), most of this later increase was dedicated to research and development for the fledgling Soviet strategic rocket force and atomic weapons, not for conventional defense forces such as airplanes, radars, SAMs, and the crews to operate and maintain them. By January 1960, Khrushchev had slashed another 1.2 million troops and made 'deepest cuts in Soviet armed forces since 1924.'[26]

Decreased air defense budgets did not necessarily translate into continued Soviet inaction toward peripheral reconnaissance missions. As the quality – rather than sheer quantity of numbers – of PVO forces improved, so too did the willingness of Soviet leaders to respond more aggressively to border flights. Between 1945 and 1950 Soviet leaders generally could only complain about foreign aerial missions. Although they reserved the right to attack and

destroy them, they lacked the overall capacity to do so. With better radars and higher performance fighters, the Soviet Union could at last prosecute these claims, beginning with the April 1950 Soviet attack and destruction of the US Navy PB4Y-2 Privateer over the Baltic Sea 35 miles west-southwest of Latvia. In 'late 1950' the Soviets attacked a Navy P2V Neptune near Vladivostok, but it managed to escape while destroying one of the MiG-15 interceptors.

During November 1950 a North Korean MiG-15 – flown by a Russian pilot – shot down an RB-29. A month later another Soviet pilot flying a DPRK MiG-15 destroyed an RB-45. The day after Christmas, Soviet pilots led by Stepan Bakhayev claim to have destroyed an RB-29, but the airplane landed and was repaired. Bakhayev, a distinguished World War Two pilot and ace, was among the Russians seconded to fly MiG-15s for the DPRK during the Korean War, based near Antung, China.

Attacks and losses continued. On 6 November 1951 the Soviets shot down another Nep-

Of all US reconnaissance aircraft shot down between 1945 and 1960, the P4M-1Q may well have suffered the highest proportion of losses. Of the 18 total in service, two were shot down and two may have been lost in hostile circumstances – a 22 per cent loss rate. This P4M-1Q visited RAF Blackbushe on 6 September 1956. *Alan Scholefield*

Always the clever orator, Soviet Ambassador to the UN Andreii Vyshinskii (right) earned Stalin's approval as the prosecutor in the infamous 1937-38 Show Trials of Old Bolsheviks. Just as he did then, he used selective evidence, verbal gymnastics, outright denial, and blamed the victim to avoid culpability in the 4 September 1954 shoot down of a US Navy P2V-5 by Soviet MiG-15s. *Author's Collection*

tune over the Sea of Japan. On 7 February 1952 a US Navy P4M-1Q Mercator ran out of fuel while evading Soviet interceptors and was forced to ditch in the Mediterranean Sea with the loss of all 13 crewmen. In 1952 the number of attacks by Soviet and Red Chinese forces reached 14, including the loss of two RB-29s and a Swedish SIGINT DC-3. In January 1953 Russian MiG-15s shot down a B-29 and PRC antiaircraft fire claimed a P2V-5. In March Soviet MiG-15s shot down an RAF Lincoln in Europe and attacked an RB-50 near Kamchatka. The Lincoln was from the RAF Central Gunnery School based at RAF Leconfield in Yorkshire, England. The flight was a routine mission along one of the Berlin Corridors to train gunners in identifying and tracking aerial targets. Hours earlier MiG-15s had entered the corridor and intercepted another Lincoln which they likely believed was an ELINT-configured Lincoln B2/4A. Although Gunnery School Lincolns were not configured as reconnaissance platforms, they operated in the corridor boundaries with the training benefit of acquiring an escort of MiGs, a behavior similar to some SIGINT missions. Later the same day Soviet MiGs harassed a British European Airways Viking on a regular passenger flight through the corridor. Given the quick Soviet apology for the Lincoln downing, it is not unreasonable to conclude that the MiGs either mistook the Lincoln for a reconnaissance flight or were predisposed from the earlier interception to behave more aggressively toward the later flight.[27] Through the middle of 1960 when the last airplane was lost under the Eisenhower administration, there were 51 Soviet and Chinese attacks on Western reconnaissance flights. Of these, 42 were shot down (See Appendix II).[28]

This aggressive change in Soviet behavior stressed twin themes of 'self defense'. The first of these was sovereign defense of the *Rodina* – the Soviet homeland – the internationally recognized legal right of a state to protect its borders from foreign incursions. The second form of self defense was the right to protect the fighters which had intercepted an airplane in international airspace. For peripheral missions this created a complex situation.

Throughout the early years of the Cold War legal scholars and observers from around the world focused their attention on the international legality and liability of the Soviet Union in the downing of American reconnaissance planes operating along the periphery of the USSR. These politically diverse legal opinions – including those from Communist bloc nations – were in near-unanimous accord that because the flights were in international airspace they were legal under existing agreements, were protected from attack, and that the USSR should be held legally and financially accountable for their loss.[29] These arguments applied equally to non-reconnaissance military flights and to civilian airliners that flew in close proximity to Communist airspace along extant air routes. Indeed, the Soviets themselves concurred with these assertions. For example, following the September 1954 destruction of a US Navy P2V-5 by Russian MiG-15s over the Sea of Japan, Soviet Ambassador to the United Nations Andreii Vishinskii told the UN Security Council that it was 'absurd to suggest that I could be defending the right of any State to shoot aircraft down over the high seas.... We are opposed to it...' In this case, however, as with so many of the other incidents, he argued that the issue at hand was not the attack upon an airplane in international airspace but that the P2V-5 had violated Soviet airspace. Vyshinskii added, 'the incident involving the Soviet and United States aircraft occurred over Soviet territory and not over the high seas.'[30]

Soviet radar that tracked an airplane flying in international airspace could easily and erroneously place it inside Soviet territory, justifying an attack on the grounds that they were simply defending their sovereign territory. Perhaps that was the case with the P2V, perhaps not. The Russians, however, did not always insist upon actual violations (however accurate) as the basis for attacking airplanes flying adjacent to their airspace. The Soviets applied what they called a form of 'technical violation.' This meant that although a foreign aircraft – again, whether a ferret or an airliner – *had not yet actually* violated Soviet airspace, Soviet defense officials anticipated that it *might* do so, there-

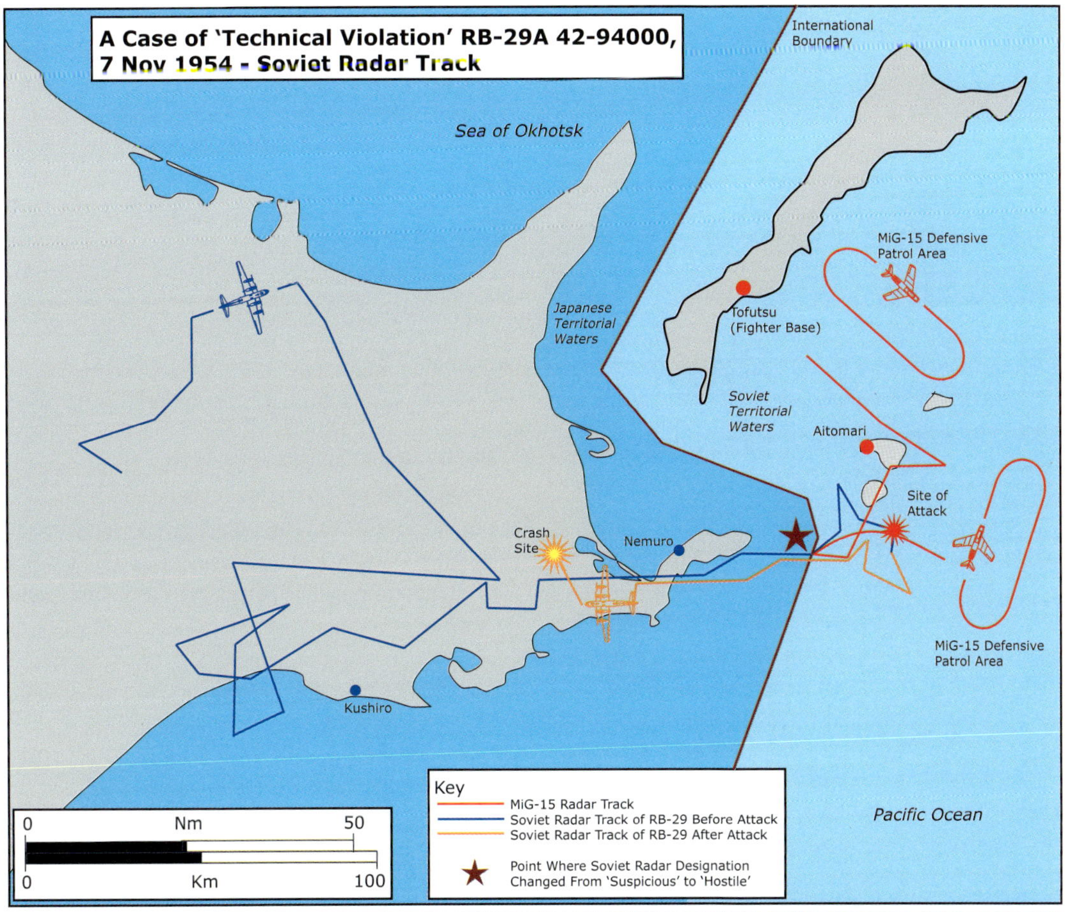

Operational limits of Soviet radar led to significant imprecision in plotting the track of aircraft – military or civilian – along the periphery of the USSR. In the case of RB-29A *Diamond Lil*, the Soviets identified the airplane as 'hostile' just outside Russian airspace and ordered MiG-15s to attack the RB-29A as it clearly *intended* to violate Soviet airspace, justifying the attack. The erratic track after crossing into Soviet airspace and prior to the attack proved its guilt.

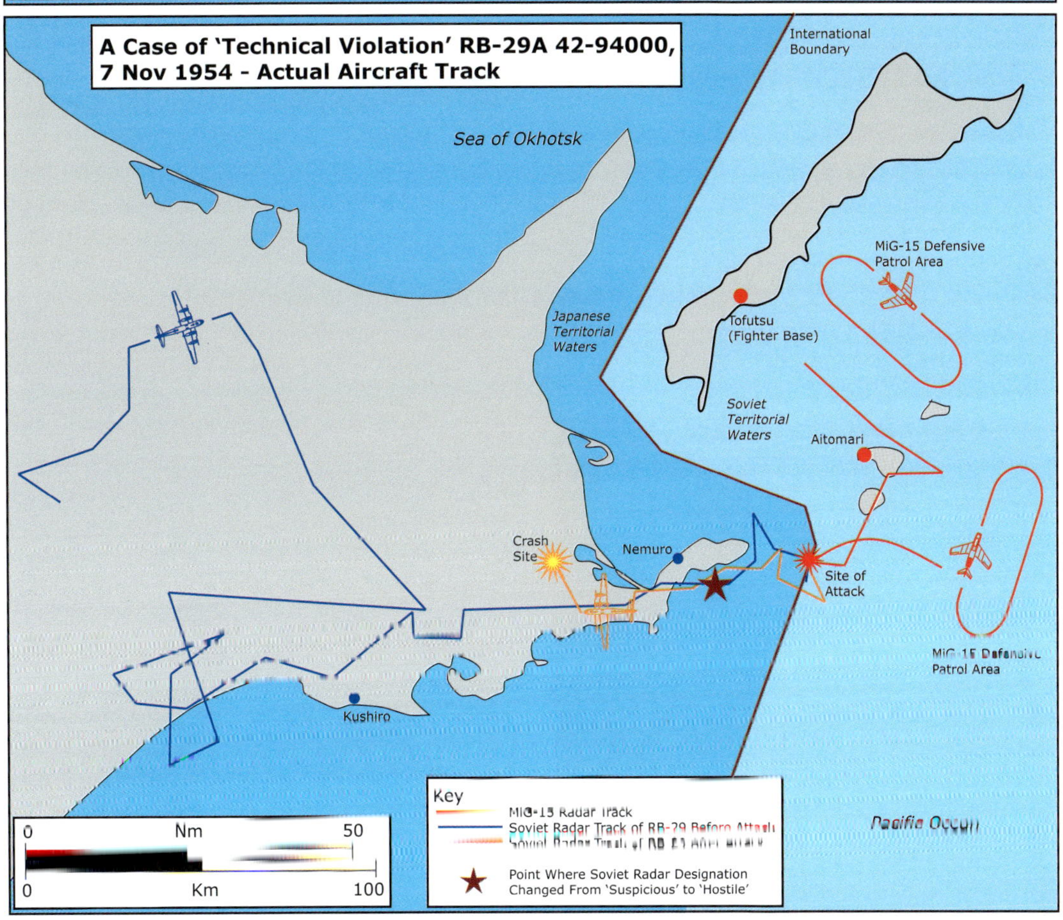

In fact, the Soviet plotted track of the RB-29A was displaced nearly 20 miles due *east* of the actual ground track. Even accounting for the gross inaccuracy of the radar plot, Soviet controllers declared the RB-29A a legitimate target for attack even though it was in Japanese airspace. Moreover, the 'erratic' course is revealed here as a routine ferret maneuver intended to gather ELINT and COMINT. Sadly, it proved mortally effective given the combination of technical limits to Soviet radar and the absurd Soviet policy of 'technical violation.'

fore subjecting it to interception and attack.[31] A potential violation might be imminent or as much as 30 minutes in the future. The airplane's course might be headed straight for Soviet Union, parallel to its borders, or even away from the USSR. No matter. If Soviet officials determined that the airplane might *conceivably* violate Soviet airspace at some point in the future, even if it did not appear that it would, then it was fair game to attack and destroy.

The loss of RB-29A 42-94000 *Diamond Lil* on 7 November 1954 is a good example of both this 'technical violation' and the limits of Soviet radar accuracy. The RB-29 was established on a course over Hokkaido, Japan, some 70-80 miles away from Soviet airspace over the Soviet-claimed Lesser Kuriles. MiG-15 defensive patrols had been airborne for almost two hours, a routine and internationally accepted procedure. According to transcripts from the NSA listening post at Nemuro, as the RB-29 proceeded east toward the southernmost of these disputed small islands, and while still in Japanese airspace, Soviet controllers changed their tracking classification for the RB-29 from 'suspicious' to 'hostile,' and vectored two MiG-15s from the 10th Air Army Regiment T5350D at Tofutsu on Kunashir Island toward the RB-29. A minute or so later Soviet radar plotted the RB-29 over Soviet territorial water and the 'ground controller gave the command to attack, repeating the command three times over the next two minutes.' The MiG-15s began their attack well within Soviet airspace and the RB-29 started evasive maneuvers, turned west, and crash landed on Hokkaido 11 minutes later. In fact, the actual track of *Diamond Lil* was nearly 20nm due west of the plotted track, and the MiG-15 attack was just to the west of the international border in Japanese airspace.[32]

Soviet MiG-17s shot down SUN VALLEY-I C-130A-II 56-0528 on 2 September 1958 after it inadvertently strayed into Armenia during a COMINT mission. The Soviets frequently claimed that the ferrets fired first, forcing MiGs to shoot only in self defense. This C-130A-II, as with so many other victims, was unarmed and could not have fired on the intercepting MiGs. *Stephen Miller*

Whether a Western airplane made an actual or a 'technical' violation of Soviet airspace mattered little once Soviet interceptors had taken off from their bases. Soviet air defense policy was much like the *Code Napoléon*: guilty until proven innocent. Soviet interceptor pilots assumed that they were airborne because their target had indeed violated Soviet airspace and was therefore subject to 'appropriate measures,' which usually meant that Soviet interceptors first tried to force the airplane to land inside the USSR. Naturally the 'intruding' airplane wanted to avoid this unscheduled landing, particularly when the flight was within its legal rights to be in that airspace. A 'force down' meant landing at a remote location where food, accommodations, and access to diplomatic assistance would be unavailable. It meant that the passengers and crew might be held indefinitely and tried as spies, or at best have to wait weeks or months to be repatriated. It meant that the airplane and its cargo or equipment might never be returned. In light of this gloomy outlook, not surprisingly the crew would turn away from Russian territory to avoid further contact. Soviet pilots saw this evasion as implicit proof of guilt, and fired on the fleeing aircraft.[33]

'Self defense' of Soviet interceptors as justification for attacking airplanes in international airspace was equally disingenuous. Most ferrets were built originally as bombers armed with guns designed to defend themselves from attacking fighters while conducting bombing operations as part of declared war. In peacetime their bomb bays were converted to carry cameras, electronic recording gear, or even additional crewmembers to operate the reconnaissance equipment or monitor radio conversations. PVO officials routinely justified MiG attacks on peripheral aircraft because an RB-50 or P2V used their residual guns to fire on Soviet interceptors. After the April loss of the Privateer, Truman approved arming all US reconnaissance flights for protection, and authorized those already equipped with guns to use them if attacked. On several occasions American reconnaissance planes fired upon and even destroyed hostile interceptors. US crews claimed they acted only to protect themselves, but it is impossible to know with absolute certainty. Many American gunners during the early years of the Cold War were very young men looking at an aggressive MiG for the first time. It is not unreasonable to posit that one may have panicked and fired first at the MiG. At one point RB-29 COMINT crews oper-

The 7405th SS operated several C-118As, including 51-3822, shot down on 27 June 1958. Several of these bore spurious markings, such as this C-118A noted at Tempelhof AB on 19 September 1965. Although marked as '0-13842' (actually a C-121), the airplane is in reality 51-3823. Rationale for these changes has yet to be verified. Behind the C-118 is FLINT STONE C-97G 52-2687, part of the 'Berlin for Lunch Bunch' stable. *Ralf Manteufel*

ating in Europe were prohibited from using the tail gun, but did so anyway rather than be shot down.[34] Still, it strains credibility to believe that the crew of a large, relatively unmaneuverable airplane filled with cameras would intentionally fire first at an agile interceptor equipped with machine guns, cannons, or air-to-air missiles. In other cases, however, Soviet claims that their interceptors were fired upon and hence were justified in attacking were ludicrous. The Soviets shot down a British Lincoln, a Swedish DC-3, a USAF C-118A, and a USAF C-130A-II – not to mention multiple civilian airliners – which were all unarmed and clearly could not have fired first. Interestingly, the C-118A (51-3822) was purportedly CIA Director Allen Dulles's personal USAF transport, although he was not on the airplane at the time it was forced down.[35] In fact, this airplane was assigned to the 7405th SS, and was used to support mission tasking from 'other agencies,' which may well have included – but was not limited to – the CIA. No matter what the circumstances, Russian and Chinese forces routinely justified every attack on foreign airplanes of any kind – military or civilian – along their peripheries by asserting they acted in self defense.

Regardless of this legal sleight-of-hand, thousands of Western peripheral reconnaissance flights took place under the full protection and legitimacy of international law and aviation agreements. Claims of self defense were not always compelling, however, and the Soviets were neither afraid of nor incapable of shifting the focus of these events to their own political advantage. In a number of cases, the Soviets sought to manipulate public opinion in an effort to convince the international community that they were forced to attack the airplane. The Soviets again tried to manipulate world opinion to legitimize their destruction of Korean Air Lines flight 007 in 1983. This effort backfired as Soviet officials publicly contradicted themselves, their apologist writers around the world wrote grossly inaccurate accounts of the events which were often at odds with each other, and eventual revelations by the Soviets themselves showed that they had erred in identifying and attacking the aircraft.[36]

Between 1945 and 1960, the degree of Soviet manipulation and exploitation varied, with the harshest campaigns coming during Stalin's regime. Public condemnation of aerial incursions was not always automatic, but was often used when the time seemed most opportune. For example, on 13 June 1952 the Soviets shot down an unarmed Swedish Air Force Douglas DC-3 flying on a SIGINT mission in international airspace over the Baltic, killing all eight on board. Three days later they shot down an unarmed Swedish Air Force PBY Catalina search-and-rescue flying boat looking for the missing DC-3, but a passing cargo ship rescued the Catalina's crew of five. The Soviets promptly denied any involvement in either loss. Rather than respond to Western charges of culpability in the attacks, Soviet officials instead announced that Swedish overflights of Soviet

Soviet MiG-15s shot down this Swedish SIGINT DC-3 79001 (42-5694) on 13 June 1952, as well as search and rescue PBY Catalina 47002 three days later. Not only did the Soviets deny attacking these airplanes, they effectively shifted public opinion, blaming the Swedes for undertaking the flights in the first place.
Author's Collection

territory had taken place nearly a year earlier on 17 and 26 July 1951. Soviet propagandists reversed Western criticism by showing that they were continual victims of these incursions and were therefore justified in taking such Draconian action. Public opinion was no longer critical of the Soviets for attacking the rescue aircraft trying to locate the missing reconnaissance crews but was instead critical of Sweden for flying provocative 'spy' missions in the first place. In 1991 the Russians admitted that they had intentionally attacked the two airplanes. The last known Swedish overflight of the USSR took place on 29 September 1949 over Murmansk.[37]

Soviet publicity campaigns were not always belligerent. After the 12 March 1953 Soviet destruction of the British Lincoln aircraft flying in the Berlin corridor over East Germany, Soviet announcements were surprisingly conciliatory. Senior military officials even apologized for the incident. General Vasilii I Chuikov, chief of the Soviet Control Commission in the GDR, said that Soviet fighters had no choice but to attack the aircraft after repeated and unsuccessful peaceful attempts to force it to land, as provided by international law. Soviet leaders deeply regretted the incident, Chuikov said, but had to behave as severely as they did because of the actions of the British crew. By appearing apologetic, Soviet rhetoric blamed the victim and absolved the Soviet Union of responsibility for destroying an airplane with a legal right to be where it was.[38]

The increasing Soviet capability and willingness to enforce its sovereign rights to attack aerial violators made the years from 1950 through 1953, as one RAND study characterized the period, a time of 'maximum belligerency.' During this period there were no fewer than 31 attacks on aircraft along the Soviet borders, plus four incidents involving commercial airliners.[39] Fourteen reconnaissance planes were shot down. How did this increased hostility square with Stalin's earlier restraint to avoid provoking a war with the United States? One possible explanation derives from America's response to Soviet attacks on US reconnaissance flights.

After the Soviets shot down the first American reconnaissance aircraft in 1950, Alan G Kirk, the US ambassador to the Soviet Union, reflected: *It must, I suppose be accepted privately that the fliers in our plane were on an operational mission, and their lives lost in doing their duty to their best ability. For them the 'Cold War' turned 'hot', and the long forgotten cry of 'no quarter' was revived by these tartar [sic] fighter pilots, now apparently decorated for their job.*[40]

Despite the rhetoric in America and abroad, official US response to Soviet attacks against reconnaissance flights was remarkably low key, hardly the kind of action required for the 'Circle of Fear' model. The United States took no steps that might have escalated each incident into a potential *casus belli*. Moreover, the limited US response to reconnaissance flights lost in the Pacific around the USSR and PRC as part of the conflict in Korea reinforced the appearance that the United States was unwilling to risk war with the People's Republic of China or the Soviet Union over the issue of reconnaissance flights.[41] When the Soviets attacked and destroyed the US Navy Privateer in 1950, the United States showed no signs of a military reaction, nor did US leaders pursue a military response to any subsequent incidents. Stalin could therefore order his forces to attack the flights without fear of a military reaction by the United States that could lead to war.[42] As with many of Stalin's policies toward the West, he did what he could get away with, and in attacking and destroying American reconnaissance flights he got away with a lot.

But this kind of behavior is hardly the basis for policy making. In addition to asserting legitimate sovereign rights, Stalin's willingness to order a harsh military response to modest aerial incursions served a major function in Soviet national security policy: it revealed to the world in general, and the United States in particular, that Soviet air defenses were now more than adequate to defend against an aerial attack, the heart of any potential US strike against the Soviet Union. Whether it was reconnaissance planes carrying cameras or intercontinental bombers carrying nuclear weapons, Soviet fighters could shoot them down. If the United

States was contemplating a preventive or pre-emptive attack against the Soviet Union on the grounds that the USSR was incapable of defending itself, then these successful attacks on American reconnaissance planes – or any other planes, for that matter – would show how wrong such an assumption was. By attacking these planes, Stalin may, in the long term, have believed that he was preventing an American attack fueled by American presumptions of Soviet defenselessness.[43]

Ultimately, increased Soviet hostility toward Western reconnaissance flights from 1950 through 1953 demonstrated Soviet military capability and resolve to the world and to the Soviet people at a time when the America was increasing its own conventional military forces, an effort articulated in US policy NSC-68. Most importantly, the harsh Soviet reaction showed the United States that although Soviet leaders did not expect an imminent US aerial attack on the Soviet Union, Russian officials did not want American planners to get the idea that the Soviet Union was militarily incapable of or politically unwilling to defend itself against potential aerial aggression in the long term, staving off any potential attack in the next three to five years.

The largest number of American peripheral reconnaissance losses to Soviet air defenses took place in 1952, with four confirmed losses. For many observers and subsequent researchers, this reflected an escalating trend toward widespread attacks on peripheral flights described in the 'Circle of Fear.' In retrospect, however, these incidents marked the end of blanket Russian hostility and aggression toward peripheral reconnaissance flights. During the year or so following the 5 March 1953 death of the *Vozhd'* – the 'Boss', Stalin's successors began to formulate a greater tolerance toward the West that would eventually become known as 'peaceful coexistence' or the 'Khrushchev Thaw.'[44] Given that US reconnaissance flights were one source of tension between the Soviet Union and Western forces, the Soviets' increasingly tolerant reaction to these flights reflected their decreased belligerence in general.

Prior to March 1953, Soviet announcements about destroyed aircraft stressed the guilt of the victim – the airplane had violated Soviet airspace or had fired upon Soviet fighters carrying out their legitimate mission to intercept the intruding aircraft and force it land. After Stalin's death this harsh rhetoric halted abruptly. Soviet officials apologized to Great Britain for the 12 March 1953 destruction of the RAF Lincoln and sought co-operation to prevent further episodes. In addition, Soviet fighters no longer attacked those aircraft which *might* violate Soviet airspace, but restricted their attention to those planes which had clearly entered Soviet territory. With Khrushchev's new policy of peaceful coexistence, coupled with the de-Stalinization efforts beginning in 1956, there was less overt Soviet hostility toward the United States in general, and this was reflected in the decreased Soviet rhetoric toward reconnaissance flights. In 1956 Marshal of Aviation Sergei G Rudenko replied to a newsman's query about the Soviet policy of downing foreign planes that violated Soviet territory. Rudenko said that the USSR 'did not want to heighten international tensions, so Soviet planes had orders not to shoot at planes that accidentally strayed over the border.'[45]

Even more illuminating is the generally calm tenor within the Soviet air defense forces during the late 1950s. Soviet pilots who flew these intercepts do not recall any blanket orders to attack and destroy American aircraft that did not clearly violate Soviet borders. Indeed, Soviet pilots held American reconnaissance crews in high regard for their efforts, and bore them no personal ill will for their part in the flights. Vasilii A Polyakov, the pilot who shot down the RB-47H in July 1960, recalled: 'I feel sympathy to the boys who found themselves in such a situation. They were not guilty they were just...fulfilling their duty. Each of us was doing

Under ICAO procedures, an interceptor is required to fly between its airspace and the intercepted airplane, in this case a MiG-19PM *Farmer-D* and an RB-47H. Standardized hand signals allow for rudimentary communication. Most encounters were professional, although a few extended middle fingers or monthly fold-outs appeared occasionally. *USAF via Geoff Hays*

his duty...it is impossible that all could have come out as winners.'[46]

To be sure, Soviet attacks on peripheral flights did not end with Stalin's death. Three American reconnaissance planes were shot down each year in 1954 and 1955, one in 1956 and 1958, and no losses in 1957 or 1959. Most importantly, however, the overall number of attacks on US planes decreased significantly. Following 1953 there were fewer than a handful of incidents where shots were fired. From 1950 to 1960, American and Nationalist Chinese losses to the People's Republic of China were sporadic, with one airplane destroyed in each of four separate years. This changed abruptly in 1958, when four airplanes were shot down, and 1959, with two losses, all related to the Taiwan Straits Crisis. The reduction in confrontations is even more unusual considering that between 1954 and 1956 the United States undertook a number of RB-47 overflights of the Soviet Union, including the hundreds associated with Operation HOME RUN during the Spring of 1956.

Despite the small number of highly visible and sadly fatal encounters – and the families of crew members killed in US aircraft shot down by Soviet forces in international airspace might well disagree – the Soviet response to Western reconnaissance flights following Stalin's death became remarkably subdued. The predictability of many reconnaissance flights, especially weather and atmospheric sampling missions, reassured the Soviets because they were routine and were increasingly interpreted as non-threatening. As such, they did not warrant an interception that might result in a violent confrontation. The total number of peripheral reconnaissance flights increased from dozens or even a few hundred per year in the late 1940s to perhaps as many as 2,000 flights a year a decade later. This meant that the ratio of airplanes shot down to the total number of flights dropped by nearly 85 per cent. Although each incident from 1950 through 1960 represented a potential flashpoint between the US and the USSR, the loss of 21 airplanes over the span of 120 months was, to paraphrase Curtis LeMay, roughly equivalent to SAC's peacetime training attrition rate for just 8 months. For the United States, this marginal loss rate was an acceptable price for the intelligence gained. For the Russians, the flights were at worst an annoyance and generally not worth the international opprobrium should one be attacked and shot down. In short, both the United States and the Soviets had become desensitized to peripheral missions.[47]

Overflights, however, were another matter entirely.

Just as the 1919 Paris and 1944 Chicago Conventions and subsequent worldwide jurisprudence affirmed the right for airplanes to operate freely in international airspace adjacent to any country, including the Soviet Union, so too did they affirm the principle of national sovereignty of airspace above any nation. This meant that a state could take whatever action it deemed appropriate to protect its sovereignty, including attacking and destroying an overflying airplane of any type, military or civilian. Naturally the signatories to these agreements and subsequent legal observers hoped that a state would not resort to such extreme violence when reacting to an overflight, but tacitly acknowledged that to do so was well within its rights. Despite this unanimity over the sanctity of airspace above a nation, there was disagreement over the definition of that airspace. Did it extend indefinitely from the ground out into space? Up to the atmospheric boundary? Or did it share the same conceptual limits as territorial waters – say, three miles or 12 miles? These were hardly esoteric debates. If the limit was three miles (a mere 16,000 feet), then SAC RB-50s flying at 32,000 feet (nearly six miles) over the USSR were not in violation of Soviet airspace. If the limit was 12 miles (about 63,000 feet), then SAC reconnaissance planes were in violation of Russian sovereign airspace but CIA U-2s flying above 70,000 feet were not. The October 1957 launch and orbit of the *Sputnik* satellite further complicated these deliberations. By the time of the U-2 Incident in May 1960, there was at least a *de facto* consensus that if it was an airplane then it operated in sovereign airspace. Conversely, the Soviets established the precedent with *Sputnik* that satellites operated outside the atmosphere in the absolute freedom of space and therefore did not violate national sovereignty.[48] Practically, however, these definitions were of little importance in terms of Western reconnaissance flights over the Soviet Union and the People's Republic of China. Communist policy toward overflights was straightforward. To appropriate a phrase used by fighter pilots patrolling prohibited airspace – 'If it flies, it dies.'

Outwardly the Soviet response to Western overflights was similar to their reaction to peripheral missions. In some cases they said nothing, epitomized by Khrushchev's silence on the U-2 missions during his September 1959 talks with Eisenhower at Camp David.[49] In other situations they issued protests in stultified and surprisingly restrained diplomatic language, such as with the 1956 HOME RUN incursions: *In calling the attention of the Department of State to the inadmissibility of such violations by American planes of the air space of the USSR, the [Soviet] Embassy states that all responsibility for possible consequences of such violations rests upon the Government of the United States. The Embassy expects that the Government of the United States will take the necessary steps to prevent such violations in the future.*[50]

This was hardly the sort of language that portended imminent nuclear hostilities if such infractions did not stop, and which differed little in content or tone from the very first Soviet protest of a peripheral flight in 1947. The Soviets were not hesitant to manipulate opinion regarding US overflights, as the U-2 loss in May 1960 achieved the level of ultimate international theater. Certainly the Soviets (and the Red Chinese) were not hesitant to attack reconnaissance overflights, much to the consternation of fliers like Hal Austin and others. Underlying these similarities with peripheral missions, however, were significant differences in the Soviet response to overflights.

Soviet silence about peripheral reconnaissance flights was largely driven by an early lack of awareness that they were taking place, followed by an uncertainty about what to do with them, eventually giving way to a general sense of indifference. This was not the case with overflights. Beginning with the 1947 Siberia overflight as part of Project 23, the Soviets detected, tracked, and attempted to intercept intruding airplanes with the intent of forcing them to land or destroying them outright. Western pilots who undertook overflights regularly watched Soviet interceptors try in vain to catch them or climb to their altitude, as did SAC pilots like Hal Austin and Don Hillman and U-2 pilots from Hervey Stockman to Frank Powers. The Soviets tracked all 24 U-2 overflight missions and attempted fruitlessly to force down 23 of them, either intact or in pieces if need be. SAC overflights through 1956 provoked a similar Soviet response, although none were shot down.

Despite the fact the Soviets were keenly aware of Western overflights and responded aggressively to them, Russian leaders were loath to discuss them either in public forums or in private diplomatic conversations. The apparent ability of SAC, RAF, US Navy, RoCAF, and CIA reconnaissance planes to fly at will over the USSR and PRC betrayed an absolute vulnerability in Soviet and Red Chinese national defenses. Khrushchev recalled that US overflights 'some-

The second U-2 mission over the Soviet Union was the first over Moscow. The flights were not only irritating for their role in gathering intelligence, they highlighted the military weakness of the USSR. The inability to shoot down a lone spyplane meant that Soviet defense forces – shortchanged by Khrushchev as he focused instead on ICBMs – would have little success in stopping SAC's aerial armada should war erupt.

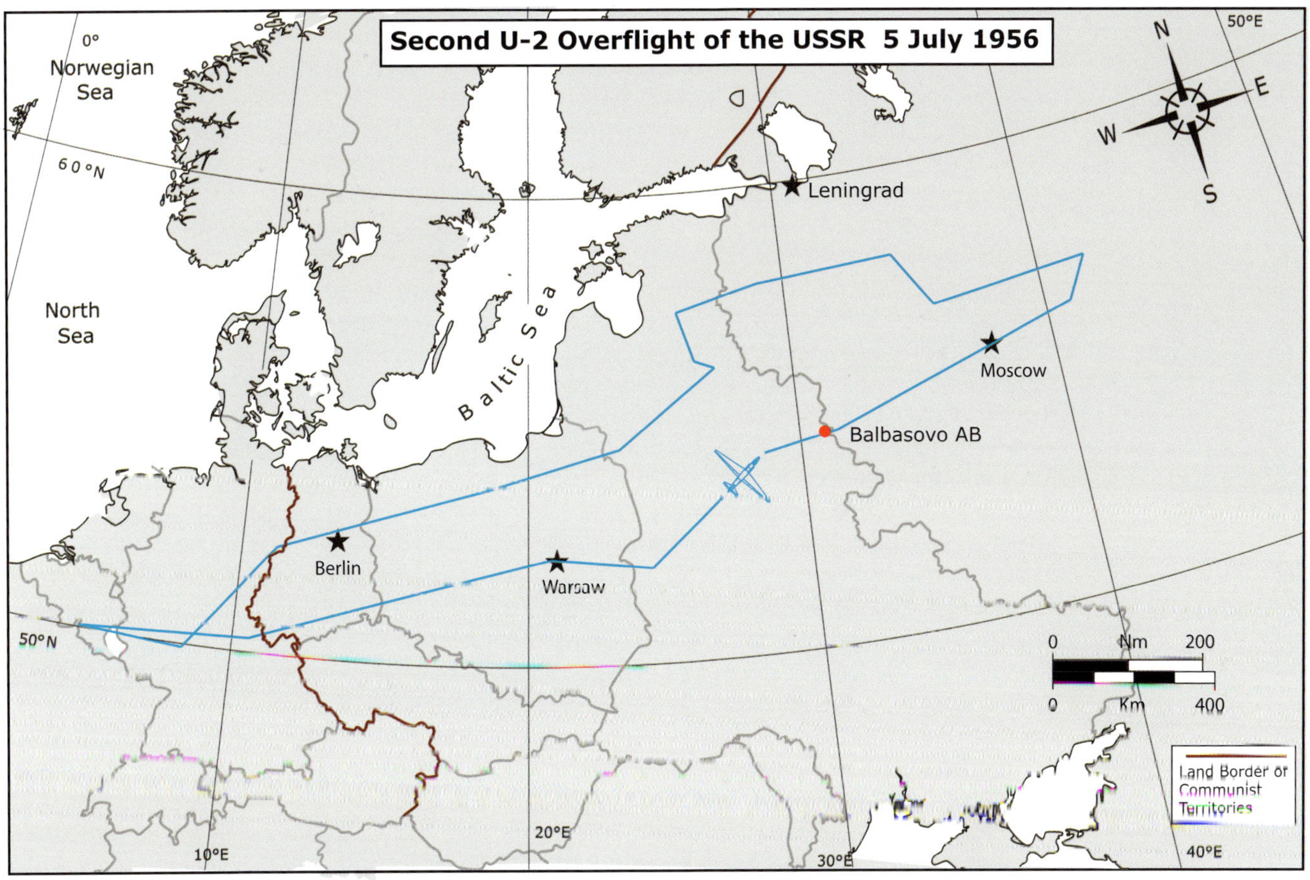

times over Moscow and Leningrad, had been going on since Stalin's time,' but had been kept secret because the 'USSR had no means of preventing them.' As he told his son Sergei in April 1960, any protest was useless: 'the weak complain against the strong; the strong pay no attention and continue their insolent action.'[51] Should the Soviets acknowledge the overflights and admit their inability to react to them or prevent their recurrence, Soviet leaders would reveal to the United States and the world that Russian military forces were not as capable as their propaganda suggested. This perception of Soviet weakness applied equally to allies such as Red China, underscoring Mao's view that the Soviet Union was faltering in its strength as a bastion against Western imperialism.[52] So, too, would non-aligned nations wonder if the Soviets could not defend themselves using their best airplanes and tactics, how could they possibly be a model for the defense of other nations and a seller of equipment that didn't work as promised? By remaining silent about these incursions, Soviet officials kept secret their susceptibility to reconnaissance flights and hence to potential US bomber missions should war erupt.

Although the Soviets were reticent to discuss specific overflights, they were not averse to generalizations and abstractions. During 1955 Khrushchev ordered that Soviet defense forces shoot down without fail any aircraft that overflew the Soviet Union. The following year he conspicuously warned General Twining during the Moscow air show – less than a month after the HOME RUN missions and ten days before the first U-2 overflight – that the Soviets would not tolerate spy flights over the USSR and that such missions would be shot down without mercy.[53] Although US officials understood Soviet vulnerability and continued to exploit it discreetly in subsequent reconnaissance missions, expecting a public or even private Soviet admission of this weakness was unrealistic. As Richard Bissell recalled, 'the two governments, even in their deep hostility, found it convenient to collaborate and keep the flights secret.'[54] If the purpose of overflights was to advance a Project CONTROL-like rollback agenda where the United States sought to leverage the missions to compel changes in Soviet behavior, Bissell's observation clearly suggests otherwise. Neither side was willing to admit that the overflights were taking place. The Russians refused to concede their vulnerability, and America refused to acknowledge responsibility and wanted the missions to continue for the intelligence they produced. Flaunting American overflights to intimidate the Russians would have been an admission of culpability and guilt in violating Soviet airspace and would have compromised any future missions, rendering them meaningless. For both sides it was all about saying nothing, a cardinal rule of the spy game since the beginning of time.

Interestingly the Soviets maintained a strict internal secrecy about overflights as well, hiding details of the missions not just from the Soviet public in the pages of *Pravda* but from operational commanders within the halls of Soviet defense ministries. To protect themselves against charges of incompetence because of their failure to destroy these aerial intruders, Soviet defense officials kept the incidents secret from other defense officials. Colonel General Yu V Votintsev, who in 1959 was the commander of the Turkestan Air Defense Corps which tried to intercept U-2 missions from Peshawar, recalled that after each failed attempt to down a U-2 the unsuccessful pilots and radar controllers were transferred to remote posts. This not only punished the 'criminally negligent' pilot or radar operator, it kept the story of the event secret from other essential military personnel. The 'corporate knowledge' relating to prior efforts to shoot down the U-2s – what worked and what did not, what should be tried next and why – was effectively erased. Each attack on overflying airplanes, especially the U-2s, was effectively an *ab initio* attempt which began by repeating the failures of prior interceptions. This ignorance proved especially embarrassing to Soviet aerospace engineers when in 1960, unaware that U-2 overflights had been going on since 1956, they confidently told senior Soviet military leaders that no airplane in the world could possibly fly at altitudes in excess of 68,000 feet for four to six hours. Excessive Soviet secrecy precluded the engineers from examining the radar tapes made of the 20 or so U-2 overflights, knowledge which would have allowed those engineers to develop suitable defenses more quickly than otherwise occurred. In short, the Russians were systemically denying even to themselves that the overflights were taking place and were crippling their ability to defend against them and, implicitly, against American strategic aerial bombardment.[55]

Although these summaries describe how the Soviets responded to CIA and SAC overflights of the USSR, they do not explain why Soviet leaders acted as they did. What did Stalin, Khrusuchev, and their senior advisors think about Western reconnaissance flights as they transpired? Did they distinguish between peripheral missions and overflights? Did they view any of the flights as harbingers of war or a compelling form of 'control'? Did they believe that the flights brought the USSR and United States to a hidden brink of nuclear war? To what degree did they even matter? Until researchers are accorded greater access to archival materials and interviews with the dwindling number of key participants to better illuminate the views of Soviet policy makers, the understanding of the Soviet reaction to Western aerial reconnaissance missions must be largely inferential. Nonetheless, it is possible to make generalizations about how these flights affected Soviet policy and, ultimately, US-Soviet relations during the Cold War.

Critics – Western critics – of US reconnaissance missions argued that the flights antagonized Soviet leaders and needlessly prolonged the Cold War (although these assertions do not distinguish between peripheral missions and overflights). With the benefit of hindsight, for example, George Kennan cited the May 1960 U-2 affair as 'a grievous error' and 'a good example of the damage these activities can do.' No doubt feeling like Cassandra, he lamented that American political interests were 'sacrificed or placed in jeopardy by the avid and greedy pursuit of military intelligence.' In a September 1952 dispatch from Moscow, Ambassador Kennan warned that paranoid Soviet leaders were likely to overreact to US reconnaissance flights and make irrational decisions that could lead to accidental nuclear war. The lack of restraint by the United States on such activities led, as Kennan claims it did in the U-2 episode, 'to the shattering of the political career of the only Soviet statesman of the post-Stalinist period with whom we might conceivably have worked out a firmer sort of coexistence.' Instead of working with a conciliatory Khrushchev, Kennan argued, America was compelled to deal with a 'coterie of military and police officials far more reactionary and militaristic in temper,' the very essence of Soviet hard-line military paranoia.[56]

Kennan's assessment reflects a prevailing Western worldview of Soviet thinking and behavior that has informed much Cold War scholarship and journalism. It assumes that Soviet leaders were inherently paranoid and often acted rashly out of fear. They were constrained by a rigid ideology that offered little room for negotiation. Their foreign policy options and choices were purely defensive in nature, defined by a long history of invasion.[57]

Distinguished diplomat and former US Ambassador to the Soviet Union George F Kennan considered aerial reconnaissance flights around the USSR to be akin to a 'state of war', lamented that the U-2 Incident destroyed the career of Nikita Khrushchev, and risked provoking paranoid Soviet leaders into actions that would trigger global thermonuclear war. Kennan was wrong on all counts. *Author's Collection*

As such, any actions by the West that were unaccommodating or preyed upon this paranoia, rigidity, or fear of attack needlessly painted Soviet decision makers into an ever-decreasing corner with a commensurate risk of nuclear war. Aerial reconnaissance flights, epitomized by the May 1960 U-2 imbroglio, were a perfect example of American insensitivity to Soviet security. Historian William Taubman, for example, writes that aerial reconnaissance flights in general had a 'devastating' psychological impact on Soviet leaders, adding that Khrushchev was 'obsessed' with the U-2 overflights. If peripheral reconnaissance flights constituted examples that were 'devastating' to the psychology of Soviet leaders, then one is compelled to wonder what effect events ranging from the Marshall Plan to US nuclear testing to the Cuban Missile Crisis had on Kremlin psyches. In the grand history of the Cold War, reconnaissance flights were at best a footnote. To ascribe this level of impact on Soviet decision makers suggests either scholarly hyperbole or an admission that Soviet leaders were overwhelmed by arguably trivial events. Other researchers such as Lashmar and journalists such as Wise and Ross have embraced a similar perspective. In the absence of any substantive archival or evidentiary record of Soviet perceptions of these flights, such conclusions derive largely from the few 'sound bite' quotes that appear scattered in self-serving Kremlin memoirs or from Western assumptions that because the flights induced US-Soviet tensions Russians leaders were provoked and profoundly affected by these missions. Most importantly, this Western perspective also assumes that aerial reconnaissance missions, both peripheral and especially overflights, were consistently an important – if not top – priority for Soviet leaders.

We know very little from contemporary sources about how Soviet leaders actually viewed these flights. In one report uncovered by Lashmar, Soviet officials presumed at one point that they were merely part of 'cloak-and-dagger' operations intended to destabilize the Soviet government. In his Top Secret 1952 report to Lavrentii Beria, Soviet Air Chief Marshall Konstantin Vershinin noted that the primary purpose of the Western aerial missions 'which violated our State borders' was to 'paradrop [spies], saboteurs and supplies' to subversive groups within the Soviet Union. He added that the flights posed little threat to Soviet security.[58] There is no record of Beria's response to Vershinin's report, or if Beria informed Stalin of its contents. Similarly, Molotov's published memoirs mention nothing about these flights during Stalin's tenure.

As yet there is no declassified documentary evidence of Stalin's personal view toward Western reconnaissance flights, peripheral or otherwise. Conclusions about his attitudes must be drawn from inferences based on a narrative of Soviet reactions to the flights. He certainly knew about the flights, especially those which resulted in the loss of the airplane or an international incident. The generally restrained Soviet response prior to 1950 suggests that he was unwilling or unable to take a hard-line position to limit or prevent them. Post-war purges of air force commanders, such as the 'Aviator's Affair,' focused on punishing those responsible for the poor Soviet showing during the war because of inadequately tested airplanes rushed into combat (as alleged by Stalin's own son Vasilii) or defaming Soviet commanders whose accomplishments eclipsed Stalin's and who had acquired a high level of public adoration for their wartime achievements (notably Zhukov and Malenkov). Both Stalin's and Khrushchev's sons were pilots. Vasilii Stalin survived the war and rose in rank despite alcoholism and rash behavior. Leonid N Khrushchev, equally delinquent, became a pilot in lieu of assignment to a *shtraf* penal battalion after accidentally killing a sailor during a drunken William Tell stunt. The younger Khrushchev served with distinction but died in an aerial battle on 11 March 1943.[59] None of Stalin's purges have been linked to peripheral or overflight reconnaissance missions.

Khrushchev's views on aerial reconnaissance are ambiguous. In his memoirs (begun in 1967) he described aerial reconnaissance flights as an 'arrogant and aggressive policy...to demonstrate [American] superiority' over the Soviet Union. The former First Secretary did not specifically distinguish between peripheral missions and overflights, but seemed to imply the latter by saying that the planes flew 'deep into our territory, sometimes as far as Kiev,' a likely reference to the RAF RB-45 JU JITSU flights. He said the U-2 missions were designed to 'pressure us,' 'to weaken our resolve,' 'to play on our nerves,' and to 'bend our knees behind our backs.' Sergei Khrushchev recalled that his father was elated upon learning that Frank Powers had been shot down so that he could finally retaliate for 'all the years of humiliation' he had suffered. In the ensuing days Khrushchev was 'simply enjoying the game' of entrapping the United States.[60] A month later, the Soviets shot down the RB-47H on Khrushchev's orders knowing that the airplane 'was not flying over Soviet territory; it was flying over neutral water.' Khrushchev complimented the PVO, saying 'Well done, boys, keep them from even flying close.'[61]

Despite this vitriol he was not inherently hostile to aerial reconnaissance as a tool to achieve a diplomatic advantage for the USSR or to meet its own intelligence requirements. Khrushchev viewed Eisenhower's 1955 OPEN SKIES proposal at Geneva as legalized espionage, but was not averse to accepting the idea provided the US Congress would allow Soviet planes to overfly American territory. The Soviet Presidium, however, rejected the proposal outright. Similarly, the 1963 Partial Test Ban Treaty, which Khrushchev signed, allowed for peripheral reconnaissance aircraft to monitor Soviet nuclear tests. As part of the US National Nuclear Test Readiness Program (NNTRP), three NC-135A RIVET DIGGER airplanes were configured to verify compliance with the treaty with the full approval of the USSR. These examples show that Khrushchev was not inherently hostile to reconnaissance flights in general.[62]

In fact, Stalin, Khrushchev, and their successors were as appreciative of the value of strategic aerial reconnaissance as were Truman and Eisenhower. The extensive nature of Western strategic aerial reconnaissance flights has created a certain tunnel vision about their use during the Cold War. The sheer number of flights by the United States, Britain, and other nations, the longevity of the reconnaissance programs and increasing institutional commitment, and the public attention of events such as the U-2 Incident and the Cuban Missile Crisis all suggest that Cold War aerial reconnaissance was a one-way street circling the Soviet Union and its Communist allies. Indeed, the Russians were hardly the passive, innocent victims of provocative spyflights and aerial espionage that critics charge.

By 1950 the Soviets had established their own strategic aerial reconnaissance program aimed at Western Europe, Southwest Asia, Japan, and the United States. The missions provided the same sorts of intelligence as American flights: early warning of US and NATO war preparations, target and defense data to develop war plans for attacks on the United States and its allies, and assessment of the national industrial infrastructure to support American war production capability in general and American nuclear weapons manufacturing in particular. Because the Soviets were able to collect much of this information through traditional sources, they did not need to develop the same extensive aerial reconnaissance effort as the West but they embraced the ability nonetheless.

Using converted bombers such as the Tu-4, Tu-16, and Tu-95, as well as modified transports configured with cameras and electronic sensors, Russian and Warsaw Pact aerial assets conducted routine missions along the periphery of countries around the world.[63] In Europe, the planes would typically fly parallel to the Iron Curtain, monitoring electronic emissions to determine the status of NATO forces. Airspace over the Baltic Sea was a virtual traffic jam of reconnaissance flights from both East and West given the importance of the Soviet Baltic Sea Fleet and its potential to break through the Danish archipelago and Skagerrak into the North Sea. Soviet SIGINT flights assessed the readiness of Danish and Swedish defenses, as well as NATO naval forces. Similarly, the Soviet Atlantic Fleet – home ported at Murmansk – had to sail through the so-called 'Greenland-Iceland-United Kingdom Gap' (GIUK) to reach open waters of the Atlantic. Russian reconnaissance flights probed British defenses to determine their ability to prevent the fleet, especially submarines, from passing through to launch attacks on the United States. Similar reconnaissance missions supported war planning for the Black Sea and Mediterranean Fleets, especially in escaping bottlenecks such as the Bosphorus, the Dardenelles, and Gibraltar.

Soviet flights proved just as aggressive in their collection efforts as their Western counterparts. ELINT-configured airplanes probed the borders

The Soviet attack on RB-47H 53-4281 bore a striking resemblance to the downing of the *Little Red Ass* seven years earlier. Even though the RB-47H was unequivocally in international airspace, Khrushchev embraced its intentional destruction as a signal of Soviet power. In the wake of the U-2 Incident, few in the global community faulted the USSR for this blatant violation of international law.

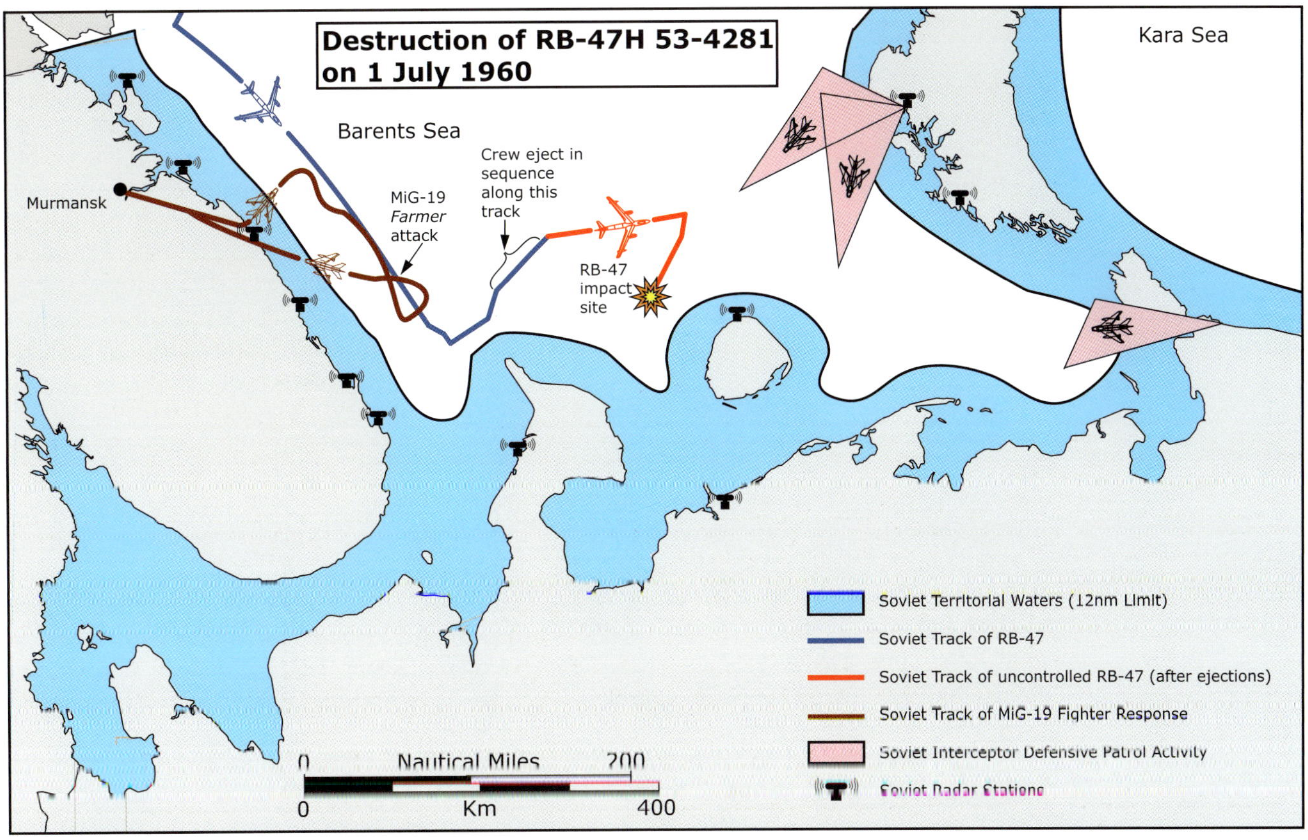

The focus on Western reconnaissance flights and their provocative nature toward the Eastern Bloc fails to account for a similar – but far less known – Soviet reconnaissance effort toward the West. These rare photos show two Li-2 *Cabs* assigned to Group of Soviet Forces Germany converted for ELINT and COMINT duties. Based at Schönfeld, they show fairings and pods beneath wings and fuselage that cover a variety of antennas. Missions included those 'along the fence' between the divided Germanys. *USAF via Geoff Hays*

of Turkey, Iran, and Afghanistan, occasionally making brief incursions into Western airspace.[64] Flights throughout the Sea of Japan provoked regular interceptions and escorts by American fighters stationed in Japan, and eventually those of the Japan Air Self Defense Force (JASDF). Again, short 'inadvertent' forays into Japanese airspace were the norm for these operations.

The first Soviet overflight of American facilities in Greenland took place on 10 December 1952. Soviet aerial reconnaissance around and over North American began in the summer of 1952, with approximately a dozen overflights by the end of the year. Some of these incursions were identified by their contrails and on radar, and they rapidly grew in frequency along the northern coasts. As with Western sorties along Soviet and Chinese borders, Russian peripheral flights were not averse to incursions. One Alaskan Air Command general noted that Soviet reconnaissance planes 'come in at all times and places and some have even penetrated deep into north central Canada.' The mission of these flights was to gather intelligence related to American early warning radars and anti-aircraft defenses, critical to the success of any potential Soviet air strike on the United States. They 'feel out our radar defenses and photograph our coasts, and when our jets go out to meet them they run.'[65] In the aftermath of the Cuban Revolution in 1959, Soviet Tu-95s routinely flew non-stop from the Soviet Union to Havana, following international flight routes parallel to the Eastern Seaboard of the United States. These *Bears* gathered ELINT from American defense installations and from Atlantic Fleet naval vessels based at Norfolk, Virginia. During a 9 August 1960 meeting with Eisenhower, Allen Dulles noted 'the Soviets have run [redacted] missions in the Alaska region but have kept out of range of our fighters.'[66] The Soviets also equipped a number of their commercial airliners with cameras to photograph territory along their flight path and near their destinations.

American, British, NATO, and other interceptor pilots faced the same barriers as did Soviet or Chinese pilots in properly identifying the interloper – limited time, bad weather or lighting, and duress, but no Soviet flights were attacked or shot down. For peripheral encounters adjacent to the United States, for example, American interceptors followed standard international protocols, by flying in close formation between the Russian airplane and US airspace. Soviet flights that actually violated American airspace were escorted back outside US airspace and sent on their way with little diplomatic fanfare, unlike Khrushchev's exploitation of the events of May 1960.

On the surface the U-2 affair was both a priority and a victory for Nikita Khrushchev. At home he was finally able to silence military hawks amid claims that he had recklessly reduced Soviet defense budgets and undertook risky overtures toward greater 'peaceful coexistence' with the West at the very time that US peripheral intelligence-gathering flights increased dramatically in number, when SAC overflights reached their peak, and CIA U-2 missions began their uncontested four-year operation over the Soviet Union. He showed allies – especially Mao – that the USSR was strong militarily and not incapable of standing up to aggressive military adventurism, exemplified by the very same aerial reconnaissance flights that the PLAAF attacked with zeal. His brilliant handling of the timing of announcements regarding the destruction of the aircraft and, most importantly, the capture of a living Frank Powers, made Eisenhower look foolish and appear out of control of the American military and intelligence agencies. His rash behavior at the Paris Summit certainly weakened his ability to take the moral high road in the face of blatant American espionage and complicated his ability to work with French and British leaders, but all in all it appeared that Khrushchev was the political winner in May 1960.

This rosy assessment masks deep underlying faults in Khrushchev's policies and behavior linked to the U-2 problem, a military embarrassment of Khrushchev's own making. Domestic hawks argued that had Khrushchev not emasculated funding for conventional, defensive weapons at the expense of unproven, strategic offensive rocket forces then overflights – which began long before the first U-2 mission in 1956 – would not have happened. Indeed, they argued, it was a 'lucky shot' that accounted for the U-2's destruction, and defense of the Soviet Union in an age of thermonuclear weapons should not rely on luck. Neither was Mao impressed with Russian claims of strength in the face of American aggression and imperialism. Although Khrushchev could point to the apparent effectiveness of Soviet defenses by downing the U-2 in May 1960, this was old news in China. On 7 October 1959 a Red Chinese SA-2 SAM purchased from the USSR shot down RoCAF RB-57D 5643 (53-3978) on an overflight to Beijing. Although the RB-57D operated at a lower altitude than the U-2, the implications were obvious and compelling. If Chinese forces could shoot down aerial violators with an SA-2 (designed and built in the USSR), why couldn't the Soviets do so with their own SA-2s? In the six months following the RB-57D loss there were two successful U-2 flights over the USSR before Frank Powers took off on his ill-fated mission. Again, a 'lucky shot' hardly demonstrated strength.[67] Eisenhower's acceptance of personal responsibility for the U-2 flights (instead of taking Khrushchev's 'out' by blaming rogue military and intelligence officials) enraged Khrushchev. His efforts to establish a constructive relationship with the president now seemed imprudent. Feeling betrayed on a personal level, he demanded the impossible from the president (an apology and promise that the flights would not resume). Khrushchev left for Paris fully prepared to sabotage the summit in an act of 'ham-fisted brinkmanship.' His emotional intransigence at the Paris Summit, according to Presidium Chairman and long-time friend Anastas Mikoyan, delayed 'the onset of détente for fifteen years.'[68]

Khrushchev himself viewed the U-2 affair as his professional watershed. 'From the time Gary Powers was shot down in a U-2 over the Soviet Union,' Khrushchev told a visiting American physician in 1969, 'I was no longer in full con-

Grainy gun camera photo purportedly of RoCAF former HEART THROB RB-57A 52-1431 (5642) taken by the MiG-17 *Fresco* which shot it down on 18 February 1958 near Shandong, PRC. Khrushchev suffered considerable loss of face as Mao's forces shot down several RoCAF overflights, but Soviet forces could do nothing to stop 23 U-2 overflights and 156 RB-47 HOME RUN overflights, plus others over Warsaw Pact territory. *Author's Collection*

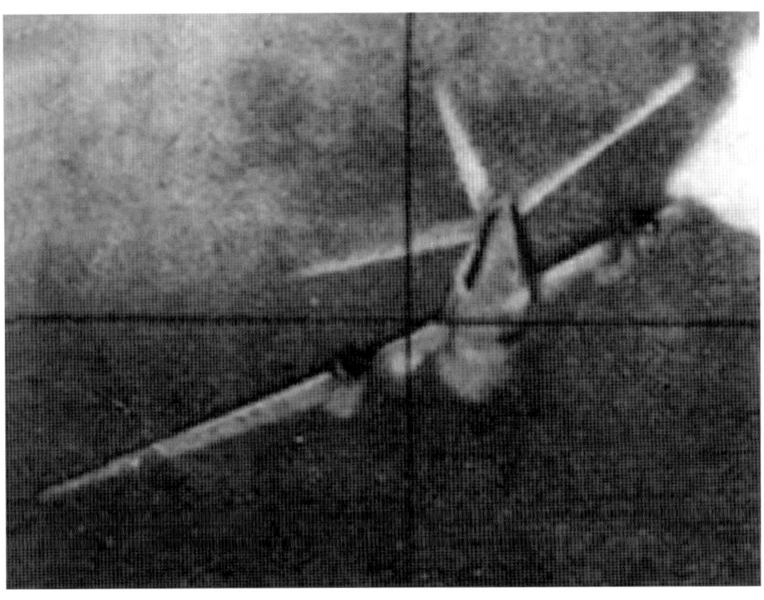

trol.' He added, 'those who felt that America had imperialist intentions and that military strength was the most important thing had the evidence they needed, and when the U-2 Incident occurred, I no longer had the ability to overcome that feeling.'[69]

Was it really the U-2 Incident, as Kennan claims, or perhaps the accumulated history of Western overflights of the Soviet Union – including 156 HOME RUN missions, 23 other U-2 overflights, and literally thousands of peripheral flights – that 'shattered' an otherwise congenial Nikita Khrushchev's career and started his four-year slide from power? Was the U-2 affair simply selective evidence adduced by critics of intelligence flights as proof they had a negative effect on US-Soviet relations? Or was it merely a convenient milestone used as an excuse by a reflective Khrushchev, a leader who had failed on so many fronts?

Kennan's assessment of Khrushchev as 'the only Soviet statesman' with whom the United States could 'do business' is highly contentious. Khrushchev's unyielding stance on Berlin and a separate Soviet-German peace treaty, culminating with his near ultimatum to John Kennedy during their 1961 Vienna meeting, hardly represented a 'conciliatory' international partner. Khrushchev's haphazard instigation of the 1962 Cuban Missile Crisis was an utterly irresponsible act for any leader with a finger on the button. As Taubman notes, in the absence of the 'positive momentum that a Cuban triumph' offered, Khrushchev 'had learned at last that bluff and bluster didn't pay, but they had been his main weapons, and without them, he was lost.'[70]

Soviet Defence Minister Rodion Malinovsky (right) initially accepted Nikita Khrushchev's (left) emphasis on strategic rockets, although he considered them more a deterrent than a useful weapon. As with many Soviet military leaders who endured the Great Patriotic War, Malinovsky still believed that victory required soldiers, tanks, and airplanes, all of which Khrushchev slashed in drastic budget reductions. The effect of these cuts became obvious as U-2s and RB-47s overflew the USSR at will, evading feeble attempts to shoot them down. *Author's Collection*

Following Kennedy's assassination in November 1963 Khrushchev's willingness to accommodate US interests in the spirit of international co-operation vanished given his untested relationship with Lyndon Johnson. Khrushchev equally failed to halt rapidly unraveling Soviet relations with China. This impending split had the unintended benefit of allowing greater US-Soviet comity, but Khrushchev failed to understand this or act appropriately. By the time he was ousted from power in 1964 – four years after Frank Powers was shot down – he was seen by foreign leaders and Soviet colleagues alike as impetuous, reckless, irresponsible, and clownlike. Some even doubted his sanity.[71]

As they confronted him in the Presidium conference room on 13 October 1964, Nikita Khrushchev's former protégés delivered a litany of criticisms to justify removing him from power. Leonid Brezhnev attacked his rudeness, refusal to listen to the Presidium and his unilateral decision making, his crippling failures in industrial and agricultural reform that 'contradicted Lenin's teachings', and his frequent and lengthy absences from the Kremlin on vacations to Crimea and boondoggle trips around the world. Pyotr Shelest spoke next, calling Khrushchev a 'changed person' who had become 'unpredictable, arbitrary, and unrestrained.' His impetuous 1957 decisions on agriculture, made without the advice or consent of his senior advisors, 'turned an embarrassment into a disaster.' Gennadii Voronov decried the new 'cult of Khrushchev', centered around simple peasant tradition masquerading as received truth. Dissent was treated with contempt, insults, profanity, and verbal harangue. Alexasandr Shelepin attacked Khrushchev's Bonapartism and charged him with being 'hasty, erratic, and inclined to intrigues' when making decisions. In foreign affairs, Khrushchev had acted rashly during the 1956 Suez Crisis, nearly leading to war. His policy on Berlin had been consistently mishandled, and he 'juggl[ed] the fate of the world' in Cuba. Leonid Yefromov accused Khrushchev of making foreign policy in an '*ad hoc* fashion'[72]

The laundry list of Khrushchev's domestic and foreign policy failures includes no indication the plotters believed that he put the Soviet Union at risk or weakened its international reputation by failing to stop aerial reconnaissance flights, especially deep SAC overflights and the CIA U-2 missions. Shelepin specifically mentioned Suez, Berlin, and Cuba, all areas where the Soviet Union sought to project its power and influence abroad but failed. He pointedly

Although CIA U-2 operations were undertaken with considerable secrecy, SAC U-2 sorties, especially CROWFLIGHT sampling missions, often took place in the public eye at international bases or even commercial airports. Here crowds gather to watch the pilot exit 56-6700 at RAAF East Sale, Australia. No one cared about these missions until the U-2 Incident, which suddenly revealed to an innocent world that 'spyflights' were an evil impediment to peace. *Kurt Finger*

said nothing about defending the USSR at home; the U-2 Incident would have been a salient example of Khrushchev's national security failures. To be sure, his handling of the U-2 affair was consistent with his impetuous and explosive personal behaviors. His solitary decisions on defense priorities and spending reflected his lack of vision and strategy. Long before the U-2 affair Khrushchev's defense budget emphasized strategic rocket forces at the expense of increasing conventional forces. He opposed raising draft rates and time of obligation for draftees (he even spoke of an all-militia military). He rejected calls to build tactical nuclear weapons to achieve parity with NATO. These and other budgetary reductions had a pronounced effect on air defense forces charged with protecting the *Rodina* from aerial violations, resulting in what one former aviation commander described as 'a difficult time,' and certainly did not engender unassailable good will with the Soviet military.[73] Senior defense officials 'seethed' over Khrushchev's January 1960 troop cuts (he hinted at more), a concern shared by members of the Presidium.[74] By 1964 these questionable defense decisions meant that Brezhnev and his co-conspirators could act to remove Khrushchev without fear of a military countercoup, if not their outright support.

Unpredictable. Arbitrary. Unrestrained. Erratic. Certainly not terms one would want to describe the leader of a nuclear-armed Soviet Union at the height of the Cold War. Was this really Kennan's 'only Soviet statesman' who offered hope for improved US-Soviet relations, cast from office because of a single airplane? Under Brezhnev – Kennan's 'coterie' of 'reactionary and militaristic' officials Soviet policy toward the United States was a measured continuation, if not expansion, of the 'Khrushchev Thaw,' and it ultimately achieved the stability of détente. Brezhnev was hardly as charismatic or volatile as his predecessor, but with this lack of dynamism came a sense of stability that Khrushchev did not offer and Kennan did not seem to appreciate. Given the extensive domestic and foreign policy failures that can be attributed to Khrushchev over the course of his tenure, it is extremely difficult to accept that it was the U-2 Incident four years earlier which ended his political career, and that his departure from power precipitated a worsening of US-Soviet relations.

The issue, though, is not simply Kennan's judgment in assessing the suitability of foreign leaders to engage in productive superpower dialogue or the statesmanship of Nikita Khrushchev. Rather, it is the underlying assertion that American aerial reconnaissance – and the U-2 Incident in particular – severely damaged long-term US-Soviet relations, first under Stalin and then Khrushchev, and therefore these missions were counterproductive to world peace. Even more ominous is the contention that overflights risked a Russian reaction that would trigger nuclear war between the United States and the Soviet Union.

For many years, researchers and observers of US-Soviet relations knew very little about Western aerial reconnaissance missions and their impact on Soviet-American relations. Prior to May 1960, occasional articles in American legal journals and headlines in the *New York Times* addressed Russian attacks on American peripheral reconnaissance flights, but these attracted little scholarly attention. At most there was a brief, transient public outcry and sense of moral indignation. Few argued that the flights were an impediment to improved international harmony; rather, the Soviet Union's reaction to them reflected its inherent hostility toward the West and unwillingness to live in peace. After the May 1960 U-2 loss and the RB-47H loss a month later this attitude began to change. The

Paris summit collapsed, many now argued, because of the U-2, and this premature failure needlessly derailed hopes for greater international peace and stability. Suddenly, strategic aerial reconnaissance achieved a notoriety that had previously gone unnoticed for 15 years.

There is little doubt that the May 1960 U-2 affair is an important event in Soviet-American relations, but did Soviet policy toward the United States change because of the U-2 Incident or because of aerial reconnaissance in general? Did reconnaissance flights, peripheral or otherwise, have a sustained impact on international relations during the early years of the Cold War?

Despite a brief and often highly public imbroglio surrounding an attack or loss of any kind of Western airplane along the periphery of the USSR, relations between the Soviet Union and the West remained unaffected in the long term. Diplomats from either side of the Iron Curtain were not expelled as spies in retaliation for an incursion, real or perceived. Indeed, General Twining was still welcomed at the 1956 Moscow air show only weeks after the HOME RUN overflight missions. Trade and ongoing international diplomatic efforts continued without interruption. Soviet diplomats at the United Nations or ambassadors to the affected countries did not threaten war or the severing of diplomatic relations. American, British, and NATO interceptors did not fire upon Soviet reconnaissance flights in a tit-for-tat response to attacks on Western ferrets. American peripheral flights continued, and in fact increased in quantity and frequency as the Soviet response to them grew less belligerent, reflecting the increasing Soviet acceptance of their legitimacy and unthreatening nature.

Peripheral reconnaissance flights and US-Soviet relations were essentially a 'non issue.' To be sure, there were flashpoints when the Soviets attacked or shot down a single ferret, but these were no different than any other international incident that occupied front-page real estate in the *New York Times* for a week and then was forgotten. For example, on 28 January 1964 USAF North American T-39A 62-4448, a small business jet used for transporting senior officers, inadvertently flew into East German airspace while on a training mission and was shot down by a MiG-19 *Farmer*. In a repeat of events involving early Cold War reconnaissance flights, then-Secretary of State Dean Rusk condemned the attack, and the Soviets claimed they had no choice but to shoot down the airplane after it ignored orders to land. Two days later the bodies of the three crewmen were repatriated, and the affair faded quickly and quietly. The only difference between this unfortunate incident and any of the peripheral reconnaissance flights that were attacked or destroyed between 1945 and 1960 is that the T-39 was not gathering intelligence, but was simply a small transport that had become lost. At no time did anyone in either the American or Russian government (recall that Khrushchev was still in power at this time), in the editorial pages of major newspapers, or in subsequent historical studies of US-Soviet affairs express concern or argue that the T-39 loss adversely affected Russian-American relations. A Soviet attack on a Western airplane had the same repercussions whether it was on a reconnaissance mission or a training flight or was simply a lost airliner: brief diplomatic histrionics followed by a return to the status quo. Aerial violations or the resulting attack were not the issues at hand; it was the *idea* that an airplane was conducting reconnaissance that was considered the impediment to US-Soviet comity. Only the family members of those lost in the incident had reason to keep the memory of the tragedy alive. In the broad sweep of international diplomacy, peripheral reconnaissance missions were irrelevant.

Overflights were little different. Planned overflight missions by American, British, and Swedish crews had been under way over the Soviet Union since at least 1947, totaling perhaps some 200 flights or more through May 1960. None of these has been linked to any change in Soviet policy toward the West. At Camp David in 1959 Khrushchev famously said nothing to Eisenhower about *any* overflights by the CIA or SAC, claiming that he didn't want to show weakness to Eisenhower. Perhaps this was indeed the case, but if overflights (and by extension, hypothetical programs such as Project CONTROL) risked nuclear war – even by accident – then it was totally irresponsible of the Soviet leader not to share with his American counterpart Soviet concerns that aerial reconnaissance flights were a grave danger to world peace. Instead, US-Soviet relations continued unaffected by overflights prior to May 1960. To be sure, there may be as-yet unrevealed policies that were implemented (or those which were not) because of overflights, but the absence of evidence is just that – there is nothing to suggest that overflights prior to May 1960 had a sustained effect, adverse or otherwise, on Soviet-American relations, making the Cold War 'colder'.

Even the U-2 affair passed with minimal undesirable impact on the Cold War. During his 3 June 1960 press conference, Khrushchev 'pledged to seek better relations with the United States after the American election' in November.[75] In the eyes of the Soviet Union it was Dwight Eisenhower – not the United States who was tainted by the U-2 affair. As a lame-duck president with only six months until the election this was hardly significant. His visit to the USSR was cancelled, but with only weeks between the planned trip and the election Eisenhower's presence in the Soviet Union was essentially ceremonial and cosmetic. No matter if Nixon or Kennedy won in November, the new president still had to face Khrushchev's looming threat to sign a unilateral peace treaty with Germany, an issue unrelated to (and arguably uninfluenced by) the U-2 Incident. Indeed, initial Russian post-election reports about Kennedy suggested that he was more sympathetic to better relations with the Soviets and would have apologized for the U-2 Incident. One of Khrushchev's friends told Averill Harriman, former US ambassador to the USSR and now the Democratic Party's elder statesman, that Khrushchev wanted to 'make a fresh start, forgetting the U-2 Incident and the subsequent gyrations' – notably with no conditions attached. Other Soviet leaders asked Kennedy's advisors '[w]hat can we do to help the new administration?' These supplications continued well after the January inaugural.[76] If Khrushchev hoped this 'forgive and forget' approach would attenuate American peripheral reconnaissance efforts he would be sorely disappointed. Just a month after taking office Kennedy approved NSAM 24, authorizing 'the resumption of RB-47 reconnaissance flights on the periphery of the Sino-Soviet bloc' with the caveat that the aircraft remain at least 40nm from Soviet territory. He urged the rapid development and installation of improved navigation equipment for the airplanes as well, and approved an unidentified high-priority mission to be undertaken no later than 5 March 1961.[77] Clearly, peripheral reconnaissance flights around the Soviet Union were a top priority for yet another American president.

If overflights needlessly brought the world perilously close to the brink of nuclear war by provoking the Soviets into an irrational or unintended act, why was Khrushchev suddenly ready to forgive and forget, and actively sought to assist the new administration as a step toward the resumption of congenial Soviet-American relations akin to those under Franklin Roosevelt? This *volte-face* might be yet another example of Khrushchev's impetuous and unpredictable nature were it not for the support it had of other Kremlin leaders. It was certainly in the best interest of both states to back down from Khrushchev's original shrill rhetoric, and with Eisenhower no longer in office the door was open to an amicable return to the status quo. The U-2 affair adversely affected Soviet relations with President Eisenhower, but not with the United States.

Ike and Nikita smile for the press at Camp David on 25 September 1959. There had been 20 U-2 overflights of the USSR, plus the 156 of HOME RUN and dozens of other military incursions at the time the two leaders met. Either the two leaders were grossly irresponsible in allowing the overflights to take place – Eisenhower for approving them and Khrushchev for not protesting them directly to the president – or the missions were simply part and parcel of the routine of international espionage. *US Park Service, Author's Collection*

For the families of reconnaissance crewmembers who were killed or whose fate remains unknown, for the families of interceptor pilots who never returned from their missions or were sent into exile for failing in their mission, for flight crews who limped home with damaged airplanes or who were rescued at sea, and for at least three fliers – Frank Powers, John McCone, and Bruce Olmstead – who were 'non-paying guests' at the notorious Lubyanka Prison in Moscow, Cold War strategic aerial reconnaissance missions were an intensely personal component of Soviet-American relations between 1945 and 1960. It is far more difficult, however, to measure the impact of reconnaissance flights on the relations between nation-states than it is on the lives of fliers over the Barents Sea or their families waiting at home in Kansas.

For nearly 15 years clashes between Western reconnaissance flights and Soviet fighters went largely unnoticed, generally due to the secrecy surrounding the missions. There is no evidence, as yet, that these hidden events affected Soviet-

American relations or otherwise influenced the course of the Cold War. Situations that reached the public eye where Soviet fighters attacked or shot down American reconnaissance airplanes attracted real attention, and were typically considered 'international incidents.' They attracted public attention and led to a flurry of diplomatic discourse between embassies and at the United Nations. They did not, however, escalate into wider disputes or risk greater confrontation between the parties involved. For example, in the immediate aftermath of the North Korean seizure of the USS *Pueblo* intelligence-gathering ship on 23 January 1968, the United States deployed 26 SAC B-52s plus support aircraft to Southeast Asia to prepare for conventional (and nuclear) strikes against the DPRK under Operation PORT BOW. Additional tactical aircraft were deployed to US bases in South Korea.[78] When Israeli aircraft and torpedo boats attacked the USS *Liberty* during the 1967 Six Day War, the US Sixth Fleet prepared to launch protective forces. Similarly, when North Korean MiGs attacked and shot down a US Navy EC-121 in 1969 US carrier- and land-based aircraft were launched. At no time during the early Cold War did American forces increase their alert readiness or deploy overseas as part of preparations to launch possible retaliatory strikes against any nation that attacked or shot down a reconnaissance flight. At no time during the early Cold War did Soviet or Red Chinese military forces mobilize additional troops, aircraft, or naval vessels either at home or abroad in response to Western ferrets along their borders or over their territory. Even the U-2 Incident, an event that is considered standard fare among students of Cold War crises, had limited fallout. Again, there were no larger military mobilizations by either side, no démarche or diktat with threats of war or retaliation, only Khrushchev's bluster and the poor public relations management by the Eisenhower administration.

Whether a muted peripheral incident or a diplomatic tempest associated with an overflight, world opinion remained unchanged. Those leaders (and subsequent researchers and pundits) inclined to view the flights as essential to Western national security remained steadfast in their beliefs that it was the Soviet Union or the People's Republic that acted rashly, resorting to violence when simple diplomatic avenues were available. During the Paris Summit de Gaulle admonished Khrushchev about his spy satellites passing over France and wondered what the difference was between them and the U-2. For many foreign leaders sympathetic to Eisenhower and the reconnaissance missions, the problem with the U-2 Incident was simply that America got caught. Leaders who saw Western flights as aggressive, an impediment to peaceful relations, and even imperialistic remained unchanged in their views; the loss of an RB-50 on a peripheral mission or the U-2 Incident reaffirmed the threatening nature of Western reconnaissance and the inherent hostility of containment. To be fair, there were modest, temporary changes that resulted from the U-2 Incident. Japan, for example, insisted that CIA U-2 operations from Japan end immediately. This was not, however, due to official Japanese criticism of the overflights (USAF overflights of the USSR from Yokota AB began in 1955 and other Japanese bases as early as 1949) but from concerns in 1960 that leftists and radicals in Japan would use the affair to sway public opinion away from the pro-Western Liberal Democratic Party and the controversial Japan-America peace treaty. Given the prompt withdrawal of the U-2s this threat subsided quickly.

So what changed? If, as critics of the flights charge, they made the Cold War a colder and more dangerous place, what was substantially different in the wake of these events? Did any nation break off diplomatic relations? No. Were treaties abrogated or shelved, was international trade or commerce halted? No. Were there threats of escalation or retaliatory military responses either against the United States or against Western interests such as Berlin? No. In the aftermath of the Soviet destruction of Willard Palm's RB-47H in June 1960, what responsible leader in the Soviet Union or the United States would risk general nuclear war over the loss of four American lives? Certainly not Khrushchev, however volatile he might be considered. One might make a case that Mao would use such an incident to precipitate – even welcome – general war. He had several opportunities to do so but did not, likely restrained because an attack by the PRC on the United States would lead to war between America and Russia. Mao could commit Red China, but not the Soviet Union, to global war on behalf of anti-imperialism. The absence of any Red Chinese atomic weapons until 1964 equally limited Mao's calculations. Spy flights and attacks upon them were little different than any other controversial events between nations. Ultimately, strategic reconnaissance flights had far greater effect on historians and journalists in the waning years of the twentieth century than on Soviet-American relations during the early years of the Cold War.

8 Reassessing Eisenhower

The 1962 John Ford film *The Man Who Shot Liberty Valence* tells the fictional story of the death of a notorious gunslinger in the American West. Pacifist attorney Ransom Stoddard – played by the same Jimmy Stewart who previously starred in *Strategic Air Command* – is compelled into a showdown with Liberty Valence, a gunman whose gang has terrorized the growing community. To everyone's surprise, Stoddard miraculously kills Valence, launching Stoddard's successful political career. When Senator Stoddard returns for the funeral of long-time friend Tom Doniphon, portrayed by John Wayne, he agrees to an interview for the local newspaper. In fact, Stoddard recounts, Doniphon was standing in the shadows near the duel, and it was Doniphon who actually shot Liberty Valence yet kept it secret even to his death. Newspaper editor Maxwell Scott then tosses the interview notes into a wood-burning stove and tells a befuddled cub reporter, 'When the legend becomes fact, print the legend.'

The historical understanding of strategic aerial reconnaissance during the early years of the Cold War shares a number of traits with Ford's film. Both took place at a time and in a milieu of ambiguous legal certitude. Dueling, however distasteful and distinct from outright murder, was an illegal but nonetheless acceptable means to resolve personal conflict. Western overflights of the Soviet Union and the People's Republic of China were equally disagreeable and a violation of international norms, but were considered a necessary evil to acquire the intelligence necessary to preserve American, British, and allied security. Stoddard was forced against his will to fight Valence, just as Western leaders felt they had no choice but to use overflights. The key events in both film and real life – Doniphon's hidden killing of Valence and the sheer number of intelligence flights – took place in the periphery and shadows of the local and global communities. After the duel Stoddard's community lived in peace and prospered, free from the threat of terror meted by Valence and his gang. Similarly, reconnaissance flights reduced Western fears of Communist aggression, and allowed for greater domestic economic and social prosperity. Perhaps the most important similarity, however, is that many of the key historical interpretations of Cold War aerial reconnaissance, like the legendary belief that it was Stoddard who killed Valence, have become accepted as fact and entered the canon of Cold War historiography.

In some cases the legends of early Cold War aerial reconnaissance are about events such as the 1953 Operation ROBIN Canberra overflight of Kapustin Yar. Distinguished CIA photoanalyst Dino Brugioni repeatedly asked to see the images gathered on this flight but was told they were unavailable – too blurry to be useful due to hostile action. If the films were reported as unusable then surely the flight must have occurred, yet Chris Pocock has convincingly shown that such a flight never took place. How and why the myth started remains to be determined, but it was sufficiently persuasive to convince even Brugioni of its credibility. The Canberra overflight of Kapustin Yar is first mentioned in a 1964 Columbia University oral history of CIA Deputy Director Robert Amory. Although Kapustin Yar became a major missile test center, by 1953 it was only a modest facility involved in testing Soviet-built V-2 rockets and short-range surface-to-surface missiles. Reports from intelligence sources supposedly piqued British officials, who ordered the flight. This was certainly an important site, but hardly carried the urgency which motivated U-2 overflights in the late 1950s, and certainly would not have justified the political risk of a compromised mission. Why the airplane would have flown over a huge portion of the USSR at great risk by departing from Giebelstadt AB in West Germany, when it could have easily flown a shorter, safer route from RAF Habbaniya in Iraq, further undermines the story. It is likely that Amory has conflated the RAF RB-45C JU JITSU mission over Kiev in 1952 with the peripheral RAF Canberra flights along the Iron Curtain, just as Twining similarly confused USAF overflights.

Similarly, there is an old canard that Kennedy won the 1960 presidential election because neither Eisenhower nor Nixon would betray the secrets of the U-2 overflight intelligence to refute JFK's wild campaign charges that the Eisenhower administration was soft on defense and allowed the Missile Gap to develop in Russia's favor.[1] Kennedy's claim made Nixon appear weak in foreign policy and defense. This in turn undermined Nixon's slight advantage and tipped the election in Kennedy's favor. In fact, the American electorate learned of the U-2 program and its benefits during the opening weeks of May, months before either Kennedy or Nixon was officially nominated as his party's presidential candidate. Eisenhower's reluctance to campaign for Nixon – especially on national defense issues – was more the result of Mamie Eisenhower's insistence that he not risk his health than any effort by Eisenhower and Nixon to keep the U-2 program and its results a national secret.

In other cases aerial reconnaissance legends have arisen as artifacts perpetuated by historians and journalists. Richard Bissell asserted that the greatest benefit of the U-2 program was that it allowed Eisenhower to prevent excessive and wasteful defense spending, and hence supported his vision of a balanced budget and economic prosperity. Despite the absence of any supporting evidence, Bissell's claim was uncritically accepted as Eisenhower revisionists saw it as a salient example of the president's leadership. In fact, defense spending rose after 1956 when U-2 overflights began. Spending on strategic systems supposedly obviated by U-2 intelligence, such as ICBMs, bombers, and ballistic missile submarines, increased substantially – in some cases doubled – at the cost of conventional military preparedness. Aerial intelligence also fueled 'target creep' and hence created pressure for more weapons and delivery systems to attack them, adding to demands for increased defense spending.

Charges by Lashmar and Rhodes that rogue Air Force generals, particularly Curtis LeMay, undertook overflights of the Soviet Union without presidential authorization or knowledge as provocations of war quickly became standard fodder for international television documentaries, books, and blistering exposés in *The New Yorker* and elsewhere. These claims were based on sound bites and selective evidence, but as with many conspiracy theories were plausible and could not be disproven with existing evidence. Critics of Lashmar and Rhodes fared little better, offering only praise for LeMay's professional integrity as proof the flights were authorized; neither side made a compelling case. The debate ultimately devolved into ideological fisticuffs between the Left (guilty as charged) and the Right (innocent and indignant). Regardless of political viewpoint, the myth of LeMay's duplicity became a major distraction in the accountability of aerial reconnaissance in American political history under Truman and Eisenhower.

Understanding the impact of intelligence on policy is a considerable challenge, and efforts to associate aerial reconnaissance flights with distinct policy decisions are even more difficult. Aside from the Cuban Missile Crisis when the U-2 was the premier, critical source of accurate intelligence used by the ExComm, histories and memoirs have been generally lacking in their ability to link individual flights to specific foreign policy choices. The apparent successes of the U-2 in resolving the 1956 Suez Crisis and 1958 Taiwan Straits Crisis have both become classic case studies in the application of timely aerial intelligence to prudent policy decisions by President Eisenhower and his advisors. Researchers have been content to accept these examples as gospel without evaluating their deeper implications. This has perpetuated the myth that the U-2's success in resolving the Suez Crisis, for example, demonstrated the ability of aerial intelligence to detect imminent conflict and to enable an expedient and peaceful resolution in a crisis. In fact the evidence suggests the opposite: two month's worth of incontrovertible U-2 imagery failed to prevent the outbreak of war, and intelligence gathering during the crisis did nothing to bring it to a close. If American security rested on early detection by predominantly aerial means of an impending Soviet attack on the United States and its allies, then that security was a hollow capability. After all, critics could argue, the US intelligence community failed to detect and deter the attack on Pearl Harbor in 1941, the North Korean invasion of South Korea in 1950, the Israeli attack on Egypt in 1956, and preparations for war by Mao's forces in 1958. If Eisenhower could not use U-2 intelligence to persuade America's closest allies and long-time personal friends in Britain and France not to invade Egypt, what hope did he have to dissuade a Soviet or Red Chinese leader convinced of the 'historical inevitability' of a global nuclear clash not to attack the United States?

The intellectual heart of the Cold War aerial reconnaissance narrative is the issue of risk and reward. Reduced to its simplest, the risk was war with the Soviet Union and its Communist allies, particularly Red China. The reward was the knowledge essential to the survival of the United States and the global liberal capitalist world order. The central critique of Cold War strategic aerial reconnaissance is that American flights were sufficiently provocative that they might well induce the Soviet Union to consider them a *casus belli*. As such, the missions could needlessly and unintentionally lead the superpowers into general war, an atomic holocaust with global implications for the 'soul of all mankind'. Whatever incremental information the flights might garner on behalf of the US military and intelligence community paled in comparison to the horrors of atomic war and the ensuing centuries of nuclear winter. This accords with an interpretive framework associated with Revisionist and New Left studies which argues that American actions during the Cold War failed to accommodate legitimate Soviet security concerns and organizing ideology, were senselessly antagonizing to the Soviets, and therefore gratuitously risked nuclear war. However undesirable such a war would be, the belief that it could easily be precipitated by American reconnaissance flights is perhaps the most fundamental myth of all.

The Soviet response to Western aerial reconnaissance flights was hardly the violent knee-jerk portrayed in existing histories of the early Cold War. Russian reaction to flights varied widely from silence to outright attacks, and was applied equally to any airplane – an American spyplane or a British airliner – perceived to be a threat to the USSR. Indeed, for years the Soviets could not distinguish a ferret from any other type of airplane near its borders, so had no policy of hostility specifically toward reconnaissance flights. International conventions and courts at the time all agreed that peripheral flights were legal and were therefore immune to attack. Eventually the Soviets became desensitized to peripheral flights as they grew in number and frequency, and as Soviet defenses grew more capable in their assessment that the peripheral flights were hardly a threat. Overflights proved more complex. Although they violated Soviet territorial sovereignty, their implications as a *casus belli* were far less ominous than critics suggest. Neither Stalin nor Khrushchev was willing to unleash nuclear war over aerial reconnaissance flights. U-2 overflights did not topple Khrushchev from power, nor did they have a sustained, adverse impact on Soviet-American relations.

Critics railed at Eisenhower's willingness to risk war by authorizing U-2 overflights of the USSR. In Paris Khrushchev pointed accusingly and shouted at Eisenhower (left) for his duplicity and dishonesty. Pundits and world leaders alike decried the president's foolhardiness in approving GRAND SLAM so close to the summit. One wonders how their vitriol might have changed had they known – especially Khrushchev – that Prime Minister Harold Macmillan (right) approved British participation in the Chalice missions, including two overflights of the USSR. *Author's Collection*

These examples provide the basis for a more nuanced insight into the relationship of aerial reconnaissance to policy. These conclusions also suggest the need to revise our understanding of Dwight Eisenhower, who inherited a nascent aerial reconnaissance community and embraced its transformation into a worldwide source of ready intelligence. It is tempting to ascribe the failure of aerial intelligence to prevent the Suez Crisis or the inability to use aerial intelligence to constrain defense spending as shortcomings in Eisenhower's leadership abilities, requiring a reassessment of his presidential legacy. These case studies, however, reveal the inherent limits of intelligence to influence policy rather than any personal weaknesses on the president's part. How Eisenhower managed *demands* for intelligence derived from aerial reconnaissance is far more valuable in determining his success or failure as president during the early years of the Cold War.

It was not just ivory tower academics or critics of a particular political ilk who feared that reconnaissance missions might lead to war. Western leaders, including Truman and Eisenhower, were well aware of the potential for conflict that an aerial incident might precipitate. Both Truman and Eisenhower were willing to take that gamble in the interest of American national security. For Harry Truman it was a relatively low-risk proposition; it was part of the cost of understanding a dangerous adversary. Peripheral missions were fundamentally routine. Whereas the Soviets or Chinese might complain about the flights, attack them, or even shoot them down, Truman did not see them as a provocation of greater conflict. In the case of overflights Truman restricted or prohibited specific missions because they put *the crew* at unnecessary risk, not because he feared war with the USSR. In discussions leading to his approval of the 1952 overflight of Siberia, for example, there was no debate of the implications of the flight in terms of instigating Soviet military action against the United States. Although Truman clearly understood that this overflight (and those that followed) could lead to hostilities with the USSR, he considered that such conflict would be limited to a localized incident and would not spiral out of control into general war.

This was hardly true for Dwight Eisenhower. In insisting that U-2 overflights of the Soviet Union be undertaken by civilian pilots, for example, Eisenhower said emphatically '[i]f uniformed personnel of the armed services of the United States fly over Russia, it is an act of war – *legally* – and I don't want any part of that.'[2]

Or was it? In all of the declassified records associated with Eisenhower's decisions about overflights of the Soviet Union, there is no evidence that the president and his advisors specifically discussed the international legal implications of the missions. They certainly debated the justification for such flights, but there is no clear indication they explored the legality of these flights. To be fair, there may still be classified documents or working papers from State Department legal experts that offer opinions and recommendations about overflights. Perhaps the legal issues were considered but subsumed in minutes of the meetings as part of any 'general discussion.' To date, however, scholars and researchers – as did some contemporary observers – have taken as axiomatic Eisenhower's assertion that an overflight of the Soviet Union by a *military* pilot was a legal 'act of war' against the USSR. As a corollary, they have accepted Eisenhower's notion that however provocative it might be to the Soviets, a U-2 mission flown by a *civilian* pilot (in this case a CIA pilot) would not be a legal 'act of war.' An assessment of the international legal history of overflights suggests that neither of these cases is true.

By the mid-1950s international conventions and legal precedents on the matter of overflights were both clear and ambiguous. They were forthright in defining specific rights of commercial airplanes to overfly foreign territory with permission. Commercial overflights that did not have permission were generally considered allowable if they were under duress – such as an in-flight emergency – or had entered the airspace due to navigational error or were blown off course by winds aloft.[3] Beyond these cases, agreements such as the Paris and Chicago Conventions were deliberately vague in defining non-commercial aircraft. Although these clearly included military airplanes, other types such as customs or police airplanes were considered state aircraft as well. Most signatories of the Chicago Convention agreed, however, in a broad definition of military aircraft based on the 'status of the [pilot], the functional purpose for which the aircraft was designed, the functional use to which the aircraft is put, and the status of the owner or operator.'[4] In the case of the U-2, the design purpose and the functional use were clearly the collection of intelligence by the American government, which both owned and operated the airplane. CIA civilian U-2s were identical in design, purpose, and operation to SAC military U-2s, further undermining any claim that CIA U-2s were in fact commercial (hence non-military) airplanes, particularly as the CIA had no functional commercial role. Even the weather-sampling cover story reaffirmed the status of CIA U-2s as state-sponsored airplanes because of NASA's government affiliation (the British cover story for RAF pilots was the same – they were part of the government's Meteorological Office). Moreover, as early as the 1922 Washington Naval Conference an aircraft was considered a military airplane if it was used to collect information.[5] No matter how Eisenhower dissembled or rationalized his decision, civilian CIA U-2 overflights of the Soviet Union were no different in the eyes of international law and precedent than military SAC RB-47 overflights.

But what of Eisenhower's focus on the pilot as the essential difference between a military and civilian airplane? Although some early efforts to codify an airplane's legal status were based on the pilot's military rank and branch of service, these were never adopted.[6] International custom dictated that a pilot (or crew) be considered either as a commercial pilot or as a pilot in the service of the state – a military pilot. Again, it made no difference under international law if the pilot of an overflight was an Air Force captain or a CIA civilian, he was a pilot in the service of the state and therefore equally representative of the United States government and as such a *de facto* and *de jure* military pilot. Indeed, a compelling argument can be made that a military U-2 pilot would be afforded some protection under international law from criminal prosecution if he was captured, whereas a civilian U-2 pilot could justifiably be considered a spy and subject to summary trial and execution. All airplanes are required by international convention to display nationality and registration marks. CIA U-2s carried no national markings, which reinforced the implication that the pilots could be treated as spies. Moreover, CIA U-2 pilots carried a 'blood chit.' This document identified the pilot as an American (or a Briton). In the event the pilot was forced down over Russia, he was to show this to 'friendly civilians.' Written in multiple languages, the blood chit promised that any help accorded the downed pilot would be rewarded by the American (or British) government. There was no doubt a CIA U-2 pilot was an agent of the government.[7]

Eisenhower's legal quibbling over the status of CIA U-2 pilots was largely smoke and mirrors. From his time as supreme commander in Europe when he learned about the JU JITSU overflights using American planes and RAF crews, through his inauguration in 1953 when he learned about the extant SAC overflight program of the USSR, through December 1956 when he shut down all overflights of Communist countries, Eisenhower clearly knew that military crews flew military airplanes over the Soviet Union. He showed little reluctance as president about allowing these flights – including the massive SAC HOME RUN overflights during 1956 – to continue, and expressed no fear that their military crews would lead to open conflict with the USSR. By stipulating in 1955 that CIA U-2 overflight pilots must be civilians to avoid provoking war with the USSR but allowing SAC military overflights to continue for at least a year, Eisenhower contradicted his own policy and eviscerated his argument that military overflights risked war whereas civilian overflights did not.

Irrespective of the military or civilian status of a CIA U-2, Eisenhower believed (or at least claimed) that a U-2 overflight of the Soviet Union was an 'act of war.' Again, there is no evidence to suggest that the president and his advisors deliberated this point or merely held it as axiomatic. Nonetheless, Eisenhower argued that a U-2 overflight would, mirroring his own beliefs, give Khrushchev a *casus belli* to declare war on the United States. In a 1959 meeting the president told Secretary of Defense McElroy, Air Force Secretary Donald Quarles, and General Twining that '[n]othing would make [Eisenhower] request authority to declare war more quickly than violation of our air space by Soviet aircraft.'[8] Eisenhower's misuse of the phrase 'act of war' is equally out of place. By international agreement the idea of an act of war is some event that takes place after a war has been declared, and is not some event on a laundry list of acceptable reasons to declare war. He clearly understood the implications of global war with the Soviet Union, and throughout his tenure as president worked to prevent the miseries of war and its subsequent nuclear winter. That he would unleash the deaths of millions of people because a Soviet reconnaissance aircraft violated American airspace and overflew the atomic laboratory at Los Alamos, New Mexico, is insane, yet he told his advisors that he would and, by implication, that Khrushchev would too. If the president truly believed that an RB-47 or U-2 overflight of the Soviet Union could trigger a global holocaust, then he acted utterly irresponsibly in authorizing *any* overflights.

Assuming that Eisenhower was correct in his concern that Khrushchev would consider U-2 overflights as a *casus belli*, on what grounds would the Soviet premier declare war? Article 2, Section 4 of the United Nations Charter requires members to refrain from the 'threat of or use of force against the territorial integrity or political independence of any state,' but does not define failure to do so as a belligerent act legitimizing a declaration of war. Although U-2 or RB-47 overflights violated the territorial integrity of the Soviet Union, the People's Republic of China, and other nations, they did not represent the 'threat of or use of force' against those countries. Arguably they could have carried bombs and – in the case of the unimplemented Project CONTROL – been a threat of force. Indeed, the president held no compunction about overflying France, Israel, Laos, Syria, Tibet, Indonesia, Egypt, and other nations with U-2s, but at no time was he concerned that such overflights constituted a true *casus belli* with those countries. Granted, the implications of Laos or Egypt declaring war on the United States were generally trivial, but the legal precedent and standing remained the same as with Russia or Red China. An overflight was certainly a violation of territorial sovereignty, but it was not a justifiable reason under the UN Charter and international law to declare war.

Similarly, Eisenhower was inconsistent in his approval of U-2 overflight requests. At a 7 April 1959 meeting, for example, the president revealed that he had discussed a proposed U-2 overflight with Secretary Dulles. Both agreed that the overflight – planned for the 'north and south' of the Soviet Union – should not be undertaken because a compromised mission would not be worth the political costs. Both Eisenhower and Foster Dulles agreed, however, that if the proposed U-2 overflight was planned for the 'east' then neither would object to it. ('North' refers to the northwest region of the USSR, including Leningrad, Moscow, and the nuclear test facility at Novaya Zemlya. 'South' refers to central Soviet Asia, including the ballistic missile test facilities at Kapustin Yar and Tyuratam, and the nuclear weapons facility at Semipalatinsk. 'East' covered the Pacific Far East and Siberia, which were overflown by U-2s operating from Japan.)[9]

Herein lies an essential paradox in Eisenhower's handling of overflight missions. If he rejected an overflight of one region of the USSR because it was politically unacceptable, then he should have rejected as politically unacceptable *any* overflight of the USSR. He did not do this. The 7 April debate illustrated Eisenhower's ambivalence: a compromised U-2 mission over one part of the USSR *was not* politically acceptable, but a U-2 mission compromised elsewhere over the Soviet Union *was* politically acceptable. The 24 April 1958 suspension of all high-altitude overflights, military and civilian, further underscores Eisenhower's inconsistency. On the same day the president approved a low-altitude mission over the USSR (likely an agent insertion flight). Paradoxically, a compromised high-flying mission over the USSR was not politically acceptable, but the compromise of a low-altitude flight was politically acceptable.

During the Second World War the 'special relationship' between the United States and Britain facilitated the exchange of knowledge and resources associated with the development of the atomic bomb. After the war this high degree of collaboration extended beyond merely the sharing of sensitive information and extended into the collection of intelligence, particularly via overflights of Communist territory. Under Truman and Eisenhower programs like JU JITSU used RAF crews to fly American RB-45s over Eastern Europe and the western Soviet Union. Indeed, two British pilots each flew one U-2 overflight of the Soviet Union.

Throughout the early years of the Cold War such joint operations were far more prevalent than these few US-UK missions might suggest. Joint operations between the United States and a foreign military should be distinguished from basing or overflight privileges accorded to American airplanes by a host nation. Norway, Japan, Pakistan, Morocco, Iran, Thailand, Saudi Arabia, Turkey, West Germany, and other countries allowed US reconnaissance flights to orig-

Japan has long been the Pacific cornerstone of US strategic reconnaissance missions, and hosted more types of overflight aircraft than any other location. HEART THROB RB-57As and BLACK KNIGHT RB-57Ds, as well as CIA U-2s, all departed from Japanese bases for overflights of the USSR and PRC. An RB-45C from the 91st SRS joins with HAYMAKER RF-86Fs and SLICK CHICK RF-100As for a unique group photo of the other US overflight aircraft operating from Japan. *Bob Gould via Doug Gordon*

Swedish pilots (Goliath and Brycker seen here next to Spitfire S31) brought considerable personal experience flying in the Baltic to their peripheral and overflight missions of the USSR. Such 'local talent' added to American intelligence by providing regular, reliable missions that could identify small but significant changes in the region. *Axel Carleson via Lennart Andersson*

inate or recover at bases in those countries. At no time did personnel from these countries participate in US aerial reconnaissance missions, either from local bases or on a global operational level. However, these nations were often beneficiaries of intelligence gleaned from American reconnaissance flights or accorded other forms of American largesse. Other nations were far more involved in collaborative aerial intelligence. Using airplanes supplied by Britain and the United States, Swedish pilots undertook a handful of overflight and hundreds of routine peripheral missions on behalf of the United States, including those over the Baltic States, the former Nazi rocket research facility at Peenemünde in East Germany, and even as deep into the Soviet Union as Murmansk. Pilots from Iran flew similar missions along the southwestern borders of the USSR. Throughout Europe, Malaysia, Indonesia, and Tibet, expatriate crews under the CIA OSTIARY, CHERRY, and RED CHERRY programs flew specially converted airplanes near or over their former homelands, not all friendly to the United States. Many of these overflights simultaneously served a dual purpose of dropping agents or supplies as well as gathering SIGINT, COMINT, and PHOTINT. Greek and expatriate Polish pilots were selected for U-2 flights but did not complete the rigorous training. Beginning with the Truman administration and continuing until the end of the Nixon administration, crews from Nationalist China conducted hundreds of overflights of the People's Republic of China using both surplus and modern American airplanes, including the U-2. As with the OSTIARY missions, these routinely collected intelligence while fulfilling other clandestine tasks.

This collaboration with other nations made sense for a variety of reasons. Pilots from Sweden had considerable operational experience in flying around the Baltic Sea and could safely execute the precise missions using traditional techniques such as route following and timing, as well as by recognizing visual landmarks. OSTIARY and Chinese crews had a similar knowledge of the local terrain as well as the added benefit of understanding the local language. This enabled them to listen in on hostile radio communications that might warn of an impending attack on the airplane. Moreover, these crews could 'fit in' should they be shot down over hostile territory given their language skills, knowledge of local customs and behaviors, as well as their physical appearance. A blonde-haired, blue-eyed, six-foot-tall American could never blend in trying to evade capture after being shot down over the People's Republic of China. Most importantly, these crews were motivated to risk life and limb to complete each mission out of a strong sense of national pride. Americans were certainly willing to risk their lives to overfly Communist countries to meet US intelligence needs, but they had less 'dog in the fight' compared with Nationalist Chinese or Czechoslovakian pilots who believed that their participation in overflights would lead to the liberation of their homelands from Communist occupiers and usurpers.

The 2013 declassification of the complete CIA history of the U-2 program has added a new dimension to this use of proxy nations to meet US intelligence requirements. Following Eisenhower's December 1956 moratorium on all American overflights of Communist countries, Richard Bissell proposed the use of foreign pilots in the U-2 program, much like those in OSTIARY and RED CHERRY. In the event of a compromised flight, Bissell argued, the United States could deny any responsibility if the pilot was British or Polish or Greek – as long as he was not an American. Bissell's argument proved persuasive to the CIA, Defense, and State Departments. On 6 May 1957 'Eisenhower [tentatively] approved the concept of British participation in the U-2 project' as 'a natural aspect of their alliance with the United States.'[10] Prime Minister Harold Macmillan gave the joint project his blessing on 27 August 1958. By November 1958 three fully qualified RAF pilots had been assigned to the CIA's Detachment B at Adana, Turkey.

For the British, participation in the U-2 program – renamed Chalice to reflect this new partnership – provided the opportunity for additional overflights of the USSR and the intelligence windfall that would offer. Even more appealing was the potential for British-manned U-2 flights to cover areas of greater interest to British intelligence such as the Middle East. Indeed, RAF pilots undertook 27 U-2 missions over the Middle East from 1958 through 1960. Britain's 'front row seat' in U-2 operations also meant that they would continue to share in the U-2's collection, eliminating the temporary loss of regular access to U-2 photography that took place during the 1956 Suez Crisis.[11]

Given the RAF's considerable experience of high-altitude photo-reconnaissance using Canberras, it was natural that RAF pilots should find their way into the CIA U-2 program. Two flew overflights of the USSR – Squadron Leader Robbie Robinson (seen here) in Mission 8005 on 6 December 1959 and Squadron Leader John McArthur in Mission 8009 on 5 February 1960. If Eisenhower believed that an RAF pilot in a compromised U-2 would deflect Soviet blame he was badly mistaken. RAF pilots also flew more than two dozen overflights of the Middle East after the 1956 debacle. *Photo courtesy of Chris Pocock*

For the CIA, or at least Bissell, the British role meant greater operational latitude. In a move that many could easily expect of Curtis LeMay, Bissell thought that British participation would 'facilitate operations by them at times or under circumstances beyond the scope of authority accorded by US political authorities.'[12] In short, if Eisenhower or his advisors at CIA, State, and Defense would not authorize an American U-2 overflight of the Soviet Union, then perhaps the mission could still be undertaken if authorized by Macmillan. It is not altogether clear if Bissell's intent was total circumvention of the president and his approval authority or if Bissell thought that British approval would then compel a reluctant Eisenhower into giving his assent for the mission.[13]

Eisenhower saw the intimate British connection as a means to 'confuse the Soviets as to the sponsorship of particular overflights.' Equally important was the ability 'to spread the risk in the event of a loss.'[14] Eisenhower pursued this line of reasoning with other nations' participation in aerial reconnaissance, especially with overflights. A downed Nationalist Chinese PB4Y-2 in Manchuria could be dismissed with minimal international opprobrium to the United States by asserting that it was a Taiwanese mission undertaken without the knowledge or approval of US officials. America's fault was not violating sovereign Red Chinese airspace but failing to constrain a client state's actions that might create or exacerbate international tensions.

On the surface Eisenhower's decision to share the risk seems sensible. 'Plausible deniability' has long been an inherent part of intelligence gathering whether in international military affairs or domestic political scandals such as Watergate. If a U-2 flown by a British pilot was lost over the Soviet Union then Khrushchev and Soviet military officials could not blame just the United States. In fact, Eisenhower hoped that the Soviets would be unable to decide exactly who to blame. British complicity also meant Britain's endorsement of the flights, which translated to unity of action against the USSR. The Soviet Union was not only a threat to the United States but to other free-world countries as well, and they were all willing to share the necessary risks to safeguard

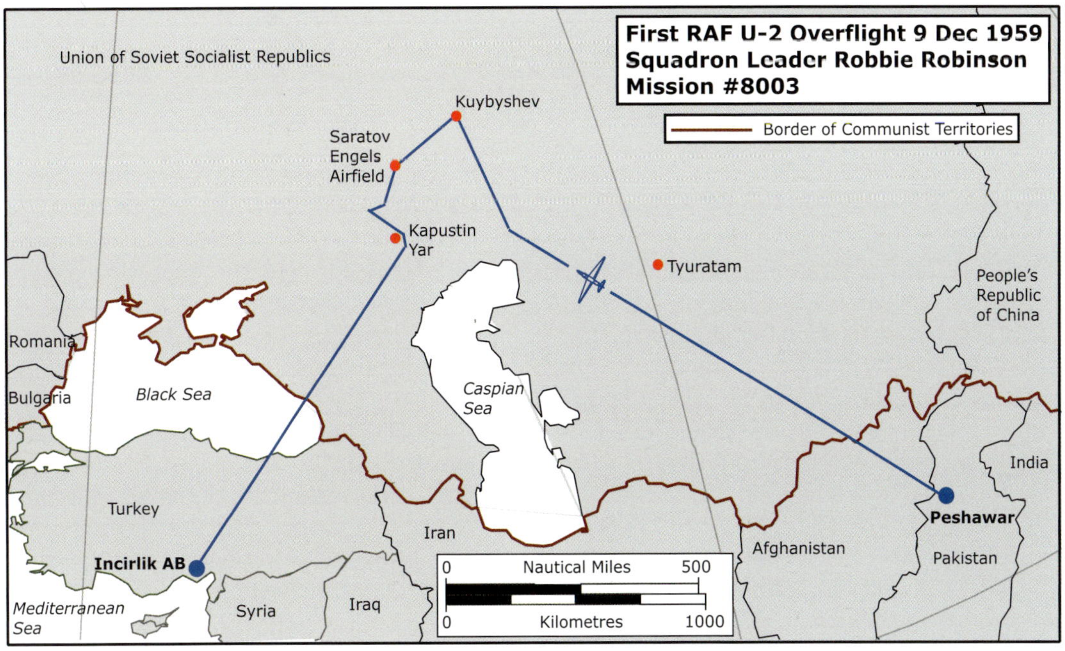

RAF pilots flew two missions over the USSR. Aside from the shared intelligence benefits, Eisenhower saw political advantages. A downed RAF pilot might shift Soviet anger away from the US, and remind the British that any retaliation would be aimed at London as well as Washington. For Bissell, the British connection was a way to circumvent Eisenhower's strict control of overflights.

their security in the face of Soviet hostility. Despite these good intentions Eisenhower's thinking was badly flawed.

The JU JITSU RAF overflight missions, begun under Truman, utilized American-built RB-45s in RAF markings and flown by RAF crews. These were modern airplanes but were hardly beyond the capability of other countries to produce. Indeed, the Canberras and RB-57s used for overflights of the Soviet Union were British designs. Throughout the mid-1950s fully a half-dozen countries ranging from the United States to the Soviet Union to Britain and even Canada had the capacity to design, develop, and manufacture multi-engine jet aircraft suitable for use in aerial reconnaissance. As such the origins of an RB-45 or an RB-57 lost over the Soviet Union could not be unequivocally ascertained by analyzing the remains. The U-2 was an entirely different animal. However simple the airframe was in design – it was little more than a jet-powered high-altitude glider with a camera – it was still at the cutting edge of aerospace production technology. Given the small number built and the secrecy surrounding the program, many parts were hand crafted or required a level of manufacturing sophistication available only to airplane builders with resources analogous to the Manhattan Project.

Eisenhower's hope that British participation would 'confuse the Soviets' was incredibly naive. It assumed that Khrushchev and his advisors would be incapable of determining the source of origin for the U-2. Originally Soviet aerospace designers did not believe that a single-engine airplane such as the U-2 existed, and they argued instead that it was a multi-engine bomber derivative. Once they were able to inspect Frank Powers' airplane it became readily apparent that only America could have built such an aircraft, so ownership – and blame – devolved solely to the United States. In practice, no one was fooled. A crucial unanswered question remains as to how and why the Soviets knew (or believed) that the U-2 overflights were American. Beginning with Stockman's 4 July 1956 overflight the Soviets protested the missions in diplomatic messages to the United States, not, for example, to the Federal Republic of Germany from where Stockman departed and returned. Perhaps the Soviets had a far better understanding of the U-2 program than previously believed.

Indeed, a 21 April 1958 Soviet note protested CIA pilot Tom Crull's overflight, saying on '2 March, 1958, at 4:05 a.m. Moscow time, an American military reconnaissance aircraft of the Lockheed U-2 type, having appeared from the direction of the Sea of Japan, violated the state border of the Soviet Union.'[15] Clearly the Soviets knew the airplane was a U-2 and not some 'twin-engine bomber of the Canberra type'. No matter the nationality of the pilot, the markings (or lack thereof) on the airplane, or the base of origin, the Russians knew that the U-2s were not British or Japanese or Turkish but American and reacted accordingly.[16] Similarly, following the loss of RoCAF U-2s, Mao Zedong railed against the United States, not Taiwan. Even Eisenhower understood that no matter the markings on the airplane or the nationality of the pilot it was a fantasy to hope that a foreign leader would not hold the United States primarily, if not solely, accountable for an incursion. In the aftermath of the Bay of Pigs fiasco, John Kennedy told Eisenhower that JFK's unwillingness to use more overt American force to preserve the invasion was a vain effort 'to keep our hands from showing the affair.' Eisenhower, perhaps now keenly aware of the realities of the U-2 crisis, excoriated Kennedy for failing to appreciate what Eisenhower failed to understand less than a year earlier. 'Mr President,' Ike asked, 'how could you expect the world to believe that we had nothing to do with it? Where did these people get the ships to go from Central America to Cuba? Where did they get the weapons?'[17] Indeed, where would any British pilot get a U-2?

What accounts for this inconsistency in Eisenhower's thinking and actions? Why would the president simultaneously allow U-2 overflights of the USSR yet tell his senior advisors that such an act perpetrated against the United States would lead him to declare war against the Soviet Union? Knowing his public and private commitment to avoid nuclear war, why did he say he was prepared to unleash the destruction that would kills tens, if not hundreds, of millions of people and leave the survivors in a irradiated world all because of a single airplane? Why did he exaggerate the legal status of overflights as an 'act of war' when he understood that they were merely a violation of Soviet national sovereignty, hardly the *casus belli* he made them out to be. A U-2 that crashed or was shot down over one part of the USSR was just as compromising as a U-2 that was lost over a different part of the Soviet Union, but the president was inconsistent in approving equally risky missions. How do we explain the inconsistency in his requirement that U-2 pilots, perhaps totaling one or two dozen, had to be civilians to avoid a military provocation of the Soviet Union when in fact he had for years approved hundreds of military pilots, navigators, and ravens to overfly the USSR? Eisenhower knew that his efforts to 'spread the blame' in the event of a compromised U-2 flight by including British, Polish, Greek, and Taiwanese pilots would fool no one as to the ultimate American culpability for the missions.

Perhaps Eisenhower's critics were right. Perhaps old age, ill health, and a penchant for the golf course instead of the Oval Office predisposed the president to make contradictory or poor decisions. Perhaps Wise and Ross were right when they claimed that the CIA and intelligence community really called the shots on the U-2 missions, and that Eisenhower was just a doddering figurehead whose sole contribution was to give legitimacy to needlessly provocative overflights. Perhaps there was another reason.

Students of Eisenhower's presidential management style, articulated through Greenstein's 'hidden hand' framework, argue that despite his rambling statements and appearance of ineptitude the president's public persona masked a keen manipulator who made decisive and prudent choices to the benefit of the nation and global harmony. Certainly this could explain the inconsistencies in Eisenhower's choices – saying one thing but doing another – about the U-2 flights. But this interpretation only accounts for the president's actions, not his motivation. If we dismiss as reductionist the explanation that Eisenhower was clinically incompetent, affecting his decisions regarding the U-2 overflights, then how are we to explain *why* he felt compelled to act as he did? Why would Eisenhower see the *need* to dissemble over key decisions related to the U-2 missions in particular, and overflights of the USSR and Red China in general?

The memoirs of U-2 pilots like Frank Powers, the accounts by U-2 program participants like photo analyst Dino Brugioni, and the histories of the U-2 and the Cold War by researchers like Michael Beschloss and Chris Pocock paint a consistent picture of a patient, methodical, and ultimately deeply conservative Eisenhower approving each of the two dozen overflights of the Soviet Union and an unknown number over the People's Republic of China. This glacial pace suggests that the entire mechanism – from proposing to approving to conducting each overflight – was a commendable example of prudence and caution on the part of everyone involved. Given the gravity of a compromised mission, U-2 overflights were intentionally difficult to authorize. This onerous and burdensome process to approve a mission, however, did not mean that an overflight was inherently difficult. In fact, overflights were easy. Perhaps too easy.

As the 156 Operation HOME RUN RB-47 missions showed, putting multiple airplanes over the Soviet Union was not a particularly unmanageable problem. Aside from the relatively straightforward logistical issues of basing and fuel, SAC demonstrated the ability to sustain ongoing and extensive overflights of the Soviet Union. With a similar logistics commitment U-2s could achieve a similar mission capability. As Bissell noted in his memoirs, with the appro-

Given the promise of satellite reconnaissance, overflights were never intended to be an indefinite undertaking. Western leaders recognized the risks and worked to mitigate them through high-tech solutions including satellites, improved ground-based interception, and drones. Peripheral sorties continued, but by the end of the Cold War their role shifted markedly to contingency operations. RB-47H 53-4304 awaits the scrapper's torch on 8 May 1976. *Gerald Markgraf via Stephen Miller*

priate political will U-2s could overfly the USSR with ease, not only gathering essential national intelligence but could, if need be, carry atomic weapons in time of war.[18] U-2 reconnaissance overflights, coupled with ongoing SAC overflights, were thus both appealing and accessible. Left unchecked, this appeal could lead to spiraling demands for multiple, regular (even daily) overflights of the USSR and Red China. Any losses would be, to paraphrase LeMay, equal to those from routine training attrition. Eisenhower appreciated that to be effective in detecting preparations for war reconnaissance overflights had to be both continuous and expansive. Given the promise of satellites to provide this capability, overflights were a limited-duration proposition – they were never intended to be an indefinite operation. Eliminating military overflights entirely reflected Eisenhower's commitment to future satellite-based intelligence and his intent to shut down overflights with their attendant opprobrium. More ominously, the accessibility of the flights meant that Sleeper's Project CONTROL was not merely a theoretical exercise but a realistic capability. For extremists who advocated preventive war, the easy accessibility of overflights demonstrated that the United States had the immediate capability to launch the massive and essentially uncontested aerial assault needed to destroy and defeat the Soviet Union.

If the actual execution of overflights of Communist nations was limited only by the logistics necessary to put fuel in a U-2 and bases at either end of the mission, what was Eisenhower to do? How could he limit the demand for overflights in a way that would defy rebuttal by those seeking more flights? He could deny all requests for overflights as dangerous and addictive, but he nonetheless wanted some overflights even with their attendant risks. Advocates of more flights could claim that HOME RUN, JU JITSU, HEART THROB, and other overflight missions demonstrated the minimal risk of such flights and that more U-2 missions could be undertaken with confidence and safety. If the president approved *some* U-2 missions, they could argue, he should approve *any* U-2 missions. Eisenhower's solution was both masterly and shrewd.

It is doubtful if anyone believes that Eisenhower really would have started World War Three because a lone Soviet reconnaissance aircraft overflew Offutt AFB or Yucca Flats, Nevada, the site of nearly 80 per cent of America's nuclear tests. By telling his advisors that he would do so he conveyed an indisputable and absolute unwillingness on his part to authorize excessive overflights. Neither Allen Dulles nor Nate Twining could adduce a persuasive, objective counterargument to Eisenhower's irrational, subjective diktat. Similarly, by grossly inflating the significance of overflights as a provocative 'act of war' he reinforced his subjective claim that the missions were profoundly dangerous and that as president he alone could pass judgment on their need. Eisenhower's opinion, however accurate or reasonable, trumped any argument calling for more flights. Eisenhower's apparent irrationality may have made an impression on his vice president. Nixon used a similar approach as president when he used his 'Madman Theory' to influence Soviet policy during negotiations over Vietnam.[19] Eisenhower's preposterous thinking translated into his approval of some U-2 overflights and rejection of others. He was the ultimate arbiter of the need, risk, and benefit for each mission. Despite equally compelling justification for different flights, he rejected some not from objective concerns but because he could. This does not mean his decisions were random or capricious. Rather, he showed that there were only so many potential trips to the well that Dulles or Twining could make, and that he as president was in absolute control of both the military and civilian intelligence community.

By requiring U-2 pilots to be civilians he took the first step to shut the door on future military overflights, which he ultimately did in December 1956. In doing so Eisenhower eliminated the central mechanism of efforts like Project CONTROL and removed from the military any possibility of armed reconnaissance that might tempt someone in SAC – from a crew of three in a B-47 to Tommy Power – to start global nuclear warfare on their terms. Civilian U-2 pilots were less about provoking the Soviets or Red Chinese than they were about eliminating future US military overflights and denying the tools of preventive war. This is not to suggest that Eisenhower took this action specifically in response to Project CONTROL or that he even knew about it, only that he sought to prevent efforts like it to lead to or precipitate preventive war.

Demanding that allied nation pilots be part of the U-2 program in an effort to 'spread the blame' showed that the missions were not simply about American domination of Russian skies but were part of the West's collaborative commitment to peace. If Britain and the rest of NATO, as well as Taiwan, Japan, and the ASEAN nations wanted to benefit from the American nuclear defense umbrella – informed by U-2 intelligence – they must share in the risks. By claiming that he wanted to shift potential political responsibility from the United States to Britain if a U-2 piloted by an RAF officer was lost over the USSR, the president achieved a higher purpose. He made Britain fully complicit in the overflights. If U-2 overflights were to provoke a Soviet military response, then Eisenhower wanted the British to understand that Russian atom rockets would not only reach New York but London as well. British leaders should not lightly seek to undertake U-2 overflights (especially with Bissell's scheme) with the assumption that they could do so with the United States carrying all the territorial risk of military retaliation. Again, Eisenhower was the ultimate judge as to the need for and approval of U-2 overflights, American or British.

This new interpretation of Eisenhower's efforts to constrain demand for overflights of the Soviet Union comports well with existing assessments of his presidential leadership. He insisted on keeping his options open to allow for overflights of the Soviet Union that he deemed essential and appropriate while simultaneously limiting calls for the potentially unlimited overflights that defense and intelligence officials sought. The president reaffirmed absolute civilian control over the military by eliminating the potential for preventive war based on the accessibility and appeal of overflights. He deftly managed the international component of the U-2 program to limit any British inclination to undertake overflights by circumventing his approval. In another example Eisenhower used 'organizational decisions and policy strictures to impede development of the [1957] Dyna-Soar Program' championed by Air Force planners seeking to militarize space, further reflecting his systematic willingness to constrain military officials through civilian administrative processes and his own ambiguity.[20]

The U-2 itself is a good metaphor for Eisenhower's handling of the U-2 program. It was highly effective but terribly unforgiving of poor oversight. Minor incidents – such as sliding off the runway like U-2A 56-6721 – could be mitigated. A compromised mission, however, proved fatal. Ike understood this, and his seemingly contradictory decisions served to constrain escalating demands for overflights. *USAF photo, Author's Collection*

Critics of the U-2 program, and especially the 1 May 1960 flight, may well argue that despite having these controls in place, Eisenhower failed to use them and allowed Powers' ill-fated mission to take place. At worst this is an *ad hoc* fallacy, which presumes that the president should have prevented the flight because it led to an international crisis. At best it presumes that any risk linked to overflights was unacceptable, and because Eisenhower authorized the flight it demonstrated his poor judgment. This assessment, however, confuses bad judgment with bad luck. There were 23 previos U-2 overflights of the Soviet Union, not to mention the nearly 200 military overflights undertaken during Eisenhower's administration and others under Truman. Whether or not the president acted wisely or imprudently in authorizing these missions they were all the beneficiaries of good fortune. It was chance that allowed the Soviets to shoot down Frank Powers, not bad judgment on Eisenhower's part. The only way to eliminate luck from presidential actions would be to avoid them altogether. As a soldier Eisenhower was unwilling to forego a risky operation he deemed essential – such as Operation OVERLORD – to avoid possible failure. Understanding this tolerance for essential risk enables a better understanding of presidential willingness to embrace strategic aerial reconnaissance during the early years of the Cold War.

We can now more fully appreciate Harry Truman's oversight of strategic reconnaissance flights at their birth after the Second World War. He approved of their purpose, enabled their operational ability by providing the necessary organizational requirements, established the precedent for military overflights of the Soviet Union, and supported the symbiotic relationship between the United States and other nations – initially Great Britain – to conduct joint overflight operations of Communist countries. For Truman the flights had a sense of urgency. The United States knew little about its new Cold War adversary, and American national security hinged directly on how quickly American planners could overcome that gap. The missions focused primarily on military matters: Soviet offensive capabilities and nuclear program, targeting information, and war planning. Although these were an integral part of US national security policy, their primary purpose was to meet actual and projected military intelligence needs essential to the prevention of or, failing that, prosecution of general war with the Soviet Union. A secondary goal of the missions was to gather information that would guide the evolution of American political policies abroad. The changing technical nature of aerial reconnaissance meant that the photographs and electronic intelligence the flights gathered had little immediate value in achieving such foreign policy development. Truman accepted the need for both peripheral missions and overflights. He delegated the authority to conduct those flights to the appropriate agencies within the Department of Defense, the Navy and Air Force, and ultimately the Strategic Air Command. Having done so, he maintained the right to disapprove missions which he felt were not in the national interest or carried unacceptable risk to American servicemen.

Dwight Eisenhower inherited Truman's adolescent aerial reconnaissance capacity and was quick to embrace its value in meeting US security requirements. He increased the organizational support for SAC, USAFE, and Navy missions, and expanded the aerial reconnaissance community by adding the CIA and the U-2, as well as a number of other technical intelligence tools including the nascent satellite program. Ever the commanding general, Eisenhower strengthened Truman's presidential oversight of the missions. He understood the extent of the military overflight effort in the early 1950s, and acted decisively in 1956 in ending SAC incursions of the Soviet Union and Red China, in turn precluding their value to preventive war. He established organizational controls of peripheral reconnaissance. At the same time the value of strategic aerial intelligence began to achieve a balance between military and political needs. Not only did the flights inform military planning, they influenced the conceptual policies related less to fighting a war with the Soviet Union and instead to suggesting ways to coexist with Russia in a peaceful and less dangerous world. For all his efforts, however, Eisenhower was unable to take full advantage of what reconnaissance flights could offer. He could not use the intelligence they gathered to prevent war or international crises. Even though he is credited with using the U-2s to end the Bomber and Missile Gaps, he could not use this knowledge to constrain needless, excessive defense spending. In using intelligence derived from strategic aerial reconnaissance, Eisenhower was prudent but not always effective.

Most importantly the flights contributed to Cold War stability and a less violent world. US military planners learned that their potential Soviet adversary was not as great a threat as they imagined. However insane the belief that a nuclear war was 'winnable,' both presidents used strategic aerial intelligence to know that nuclear war was neither imminent nor necessary. Truman and Eisenhower were committed to US security and embraced strategic aerial reconnaissance to achieve that, but were unwilling to write a blank check that would turn America into a garrison state or cripple the domestic economy. Eisenhower was especially receptive to a broad spectrum of scientific and professional experts who validated his belief in the value of strategic aerial reconnaissance, a belief acquired from his experience as supreme allied commander during the Second World War. He was equally sensitive to domestic political and economic considerations affected by intelligence derived from these flights. Despite guidance from both Truman and Eisenhower on the conduct of strategic aerial reconnaissance, real-world exigencies and human foibles meant that there were variations and exceptions to these directives, as well as unintended and undesired consequences of the flights. Organizational tensions further complicated these processes and outcomes.

Despite charges that Eisenhower had lost control of the military and civilian intelligence communities, the president established a clear chain of command for the approval of military overflights, provided organizational oversight for ongoing peripheral reconnaissance missions – military and civilian – through the JRC, and, most importantly, constrained demand for civilian U-2 overflights. These actions demonstrated not only his robust awareness of aerial reconnaissance operations during his presidency but his commitment to minimizing the risk to world peace that excessive U-2 overflights would create. For Eisenhower, that risk did not derive from a compromised overflight or a Soviet leader fed up with U-2 incursions and who then acted irrationally to start the road to war. Instead, Eisenhower feared that left unchecked overflights of the Soviet Union and the People's Republic of China could easily grow in number and frequency. At some point this unarmed reconnaissance could transition into armed reconnaissance or even the opening salvo of a preventive war. By ending all military overflights and through his seemingly irrational approval process for U-2 overflights, Eisenhower prevented schemes like Sleeper's or Bissell's from becoming a reality, and disarmed advocates of both more overflights as well as those who championed preventive war with the Soviet Union.

***

When Alan Shepherd became the first American in space, when John Glenn became the first American in orbit around the Earth, and when Neil Armstrong became the first American (and human) to set foot on the moon, they were each properly fêted as national heroes. Each phase of his journey was reported in minute-by-minute detail thanks to television commentators like Walter Cronkite and on the front page of newspapers around the world. Afterward he enjoyed a ticker-tape parade, luncheon with the President, and a secure place in history books as an exemplar of courageous exploration under hostile and life-threatening conditions. Each wore a space suit to prevent certain death if he was exposed to the harsh environment. Each was snugly cocooned inside a tiny metal capsule to provide him with a minimal atmosphere and protection from the hazards of space. Each enjoyed great fame for his genuinely heroic accomplishment. Indeed, a generation of boys (and not a few girls) grew up with one purpose – to follow in an astronaut's footsteps on their own journey into space.

At the same time another group of aviators undertook similar risks but under far more secretive circumstances. Each wore a space suit to keep him alive in the event of rapid decompression. Each sat in a seat – crammed into a space smaller than half a phone booth – fitted with an explosive charge to eject him in the event of an emergency into the emptiness on the fringe of the atmosphere. Each knowingly agreed to anonymity for life. There would be no TV interviews, no trip to the Oval Office for tea with Mamie or Jackie, and no exclusive (and lucrative) agreement to have his family featured

Three of the seven Mercury astronauts look on as President Kennedy congratulates Alan Shepherd, the first American in space. They were heroes to more than one generation of youngsters who aspired to their fame. No one, however, wanted to grow up to be a U-2 pilot, in part because of secrecy and in part because few appreciated the risks they took in the name of US national security. *Author's Collection*

weekly in the pages of *Life*. In 1957 no one wanted to grow up to be a U-2 pilot.

When Francis Gary Powers became a household name it was not because of his skills as an intrepid aviator willing to risk his life for something he believed was important to the survival of the United States. Rather, it was because he had somehow humiliated the United States by getting caught in the act of espionage, because he had not committed suicide rather than be taken prisoner and was thus subjected to the national embarrassment of a Soviet show trial, or even, as some believed, because he betrayed his country by intentionally compromising the U-2 program or was attempting to defect to the USSR. Powers epitomized the recklessness of the American intelligence community in its 'avid and greedy pursuit' of information about the Soviet Union. Sadly, Frank Powers was never recognized in his lifetime as an American icon on par with Shepherd, Glenn, or Armstrong. Instead, he became a symbol of an intelligence system gone amok.

There were other unknown fliers besides those associated with the U-2. Pilots, navigators, ravens, radio operators, linguists, flight engineers, gunners, and others from the air forces of the United States, Britain, Taiwan, Sweden, and other allied nations all undertook equally risky and equally secretive missions around and over the Soviet Union and its allies. No matter where they called home, they had all foresworn any publicity about their missions – their purpose, their successes and failures, their experiences. Even some 50 years later, with only a few still living in their twilight years, many still refuse to talk about what they did and where they flew.

They all shared one common trait: a covenant with their government. This was not some agreement that simply promised to rescue them should they be shot down or taken prisoner – a blood chit to provide for their personal safety. They all acknowledged that their mission carried life-threatening risks yet they were all willing to make that flight. Rather, their unspoken agreement with their government was that the information they collected would be used wisely to preserve peace or, if need be, would enable the United States to survive any attack and allow future generations to enjoy the American promise. That covenant reassured them that their sacrifices made a difference, that the losses in men, airplanes, family life, and international political good will was worth it.

It would be easy to say 'no' it was not worth it, and as proof point to the inability of aerial intelligence to prevent war in Suez in 1956, or to the critical belief that overflights were really about conservative 'troglodyte' roll-back generals trying to provoke World War Three, or to the shibboleth that the U-2 Incident poisoned US-Soviet relations for years to come. But the evidence clearly shows that the flights did matter. Truman, Eisenhower, and their advisors all benefitted from the intelligence they collected. In many cases they made better decisions and acted wisely; in other circumstances they were constrained by organizational or practical boundaries that served to limit the effectiveness of aerial intelligence no matter how well intentioned the president's actions. In any case, there was no 'historically inevitable' nuclear war from any cause (including reconnaissance flights) between the United States and the Soviet Union. Both sides benefitted from the stability that strategic reconnaissance provided. The Russians were less threatening than alarmist Americans believed, and although the flights led to increased expenditures for defense on both sides of the Iron Curtain, an arms race was arguably a preferential alternative to preventive or accidental war.

Strategic aerial reconnaissance during the early years of the Cold War, both peripheral missions and overflights, took place in general obscurity until May 1960. For all practical purposes these flights did not exist nor did they have any discernable public impact on the evolution of American Cold War national security or on Soviet-American relations. In the shadowy world of US defense planning, the intelligence derived from these flights had a real effect on understanding the nature of the Soviet threat and how to defeat it should war erupt, and hence on US defense strategy and budgets. Beyond this, intelligence from aerial reconnaissance became simply another source in the ongoing effort to assess threats to US security. When the Russians shot down Frank Powers, however, public and scholarly attention focused not on the intelligence requirements or benefits associated with these missions but on the flights themselves. As Eisenhower said during his 12 May 1960 press conference: *We must not be distracted from the real issues of the day by what is an incident or a symptom of the world situation today. This incident has been given great propaganda exploitation. The emphasis given to a flight of an unarmed, non-military plane can only reflect a fetish of secrecy. The real issues are the ones we will be working on at the Summit – disarmament, search for solutions affecting Germany and Berlin, and the whole range of East-West relations.*[21] Recon-

The personal sacrifice made on behalf of early Cold War strategic aerial reconnaissance went beyond the fliers. Thousands of maintenance personnel kept each aircraft in flying condition, rebuilt their engines, repaired broken hydraulic lines, emptied post-flight toilets, got sunburned and frostbitten, and are too often forgotten. RB-36H 52-1384 undergoes maintenance at Fort Worth. *Lockheed Martin via Dennis Jenkins*

naissance flights suddenly became the problem, not the justifiable need for either side to know about a potential adversary or how to live in peace with that adversary. This abrupt shift gave the flights an inflated historical and public agency disproportionate to their actual influence on Soviet-American relations during the early years of the Cold War. Irrespective of its availability, accuracy, technical objectivity, and timeliness, aerial intelligence was more limited in its effect on Cold War policy in the United States and the Soviet Union than previously believed. In terms of military planning the impact was greater than held but far less desirable as it stimulated and sustained a global arms race. Strategic aerial reconnaissance flights certainly mattered, but not as much as their champions and critics have long argued – the legend of their exaggerated importance had become fact.

Young wrench-turners smile during a break while performing engine maintenance on SLICK CHICK RF-100A 53-1551 at Bitburg AB. *Cecil Rigsby via Doug Gordon*

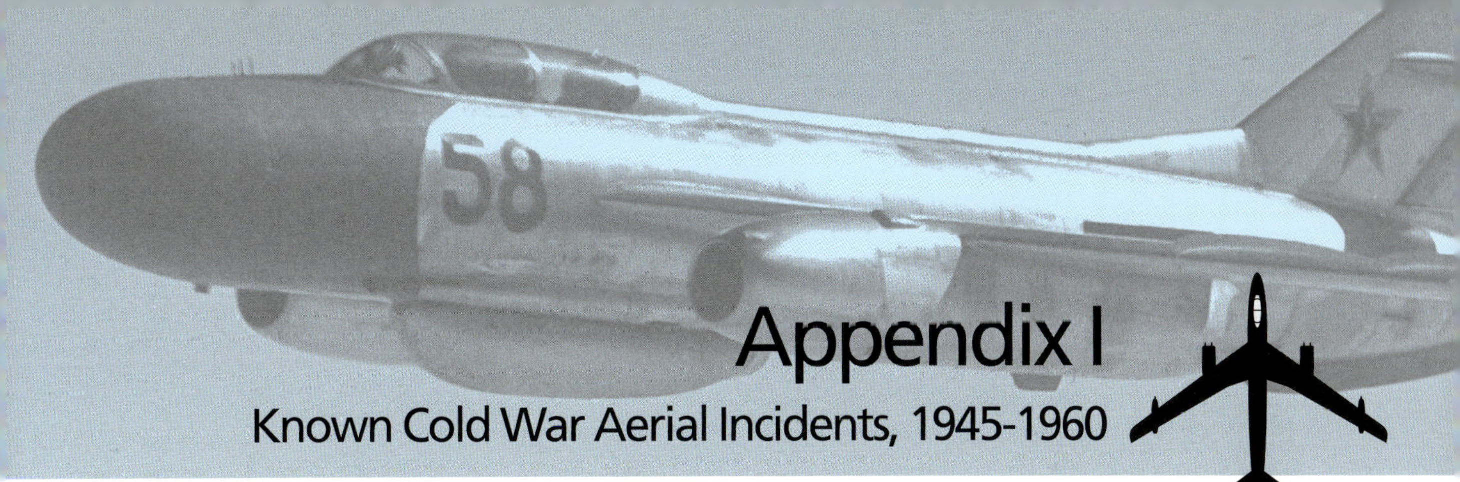

Appendix I

Known Cold War Aerial Incidents, 1945-1960

Date	Aircraft	Service	Reacting Nation	Type of Contact	Outcome	Remarks
29 Aug 45	B-29A	USAAF	USSR	Yak-9	forced down	Near Kanko; also reported as November 1945
15 Oct 45	PBM-5	USN	USSR	fighter	attacked	25 miles from Dairen after overflying Port Arthur
20 Feb 46	PBM-5	USN	USSR	fighter	attacked	After inadvertent overflight of Port Arthur
5 Apr 46			USSR		protest	Near Astara, Azerbaijan; claims of prior flights as well
22 Apr 46	C-47	USAAF	USSR	P-39	attacked	While landing at Tulln Airport near Vienna, Austria
9 Aug 46	C-47A 43-15376	USAAF	Yugoslavia	Yak-3	forced down	Near Yugoslavia/Italian border
7 Aug 46	B17L	Sweden	USSR	fighter	intercepted	During attempted overflight of Peenemunde
19 Aug 46	**C-47A**	**USAAF**	**Yugoslavia**	**Yak-3**	**destroyed**	**Near Bled, Yugoslavia**
5 Sep 46	Spitfire	Greece	Yugoslavia	fighter	forced down	Overflight of Yugoslavia
9 Sep 46		Turkey	USSR		missing	After overflight of eastern border adjacent to USSR
5 Oct 46		RAF	Yugoslavia	fighter	forced down	Overflight of Yugoslavia
1 Dec 46	A-26	USAAF	Bulgaria		landed	Became lost in bad weather and landed
2 Dec 46		Greece	Bulgaria		protest	Claims of 7 overflights in previous 5 weeks
25 Feb 47		US	USSR		protest	Soviets claimed 3 overflight Ratmonov Island, Bering Strait, between 8 March 1946 and 31 January 1947
27 Mar 47		Iran	USSR		landed	Recon flight over Azerbaijan
3 Aug 47		US	USSR		protest	Claimed overflight 35 miles NE Cape Wellen, Chukotskii
28 Oct 47		US	USSR		protest	Claimed 3 airplanes overflew Kuriles
29 Oct 47		US	USSR		protest	Claimed overflight of Kuriles
23 Dec 47		US	USSR		protest	Claimed incursion over Big Diomede Island
25 Dec 47		US	USSR		protest	Claimed incursion over Big Diomede Island
29 Dec 47		USMC	PRC		landed	Unknown incursion, crew repatriated in 1948
9 Feb 48	**2 Spitfires**	**Turkey**	**Bulgaria**	**AAA**	**destroyed**	**One pilot killed, one returned**
5 Apr 48	**Viking G-AIVP**	**Civil**	**USSR**	**Yak-3**	**destroyed**	**British European Airways Vickers VC.1 Viking collides with Soviet Yak-3 near RAF Gatow in Berlin**
19 Oct 48		USN	PRC		crashed	Unknown incursion, crew repatriated in 1950
27 Oct 48	**P-38 MM4175**	**Italy**	**Yugoslavia**		**destroyed**	**Overflight of Yugoslavia**
Nov 48		US	USSR		protest	Overflight by 6 aircraft of Soviet zone in Austria
Feb 49		Finland	USSR		protest	Claims of Finnish overflights of Soviet border area as a proxy for US intelligence-gathering
5 Oct 49		USN	USSR	fighter	intercept	Baltic Sea
22 Oct 49	RB-29A	USAF	USSR	La-7	attacked	Vladivostok, Sea of Japan; OVERSALT mission
6 Mar 50	RB-17	USAF	USSR	Yak-9	intercept	Baltic Sea
14 Mar 50	**RB-25 07**	**RoCAF**	**PRC**	**fighter**	**destroyed**	**Over China; reconnaissance B-25 Mitchell**
22 Mar 50	RB-29	USAF	USSR	fighter	intercept	Near Dairen
1 Apr 50		USAF	PRC		overflight	Inadvertent overflight of Shantung, PRC
7 Apr 50		US	USSR		overflight	Major deviation' 65-mile penetration of USSR
8 Apr 50	**PB4Y-2 59645**	**USN**	**USSR**	**La-11**	**destroyed**	**Baltic Sea 35 miles WSW of Latvia**
11 May 50	PB4Y-2	USN	USSR		destroyed	Claimed but unverified
14 May 50		Iran	USSR		protest	Multiple border incursions under the guise of 'oil exploration flights' employing 'American experts'
May-Jun 1950	multiple	US	USSR		protest	Claimed US planes dropped Colorado beetles over East Germany to destroy German potato crop
May-Jun 1950	multiple	US	Czechoslovakia		protest	Claimed US planes dropped Colorado beetles over Czechoslovakia to destroyfood crops

Jun-Aug 1950	multiple	RAF	PRC		protest	Claimed 100 RAF planes overflew Chinese territory 50 different occasions
10 Jul 50	multiple	US	Czechoslovakia		protest	8 alleged violations of 'illegal overflights'
15 Jul 50	RB-29A	USAF	USSR	fighter	intercept	Near Permskoye AB, USSR
19 Jul 50	B-45	USAF	USSR		protest	Claimed incidiaries dropped on Klietz, East Germany, to destroy food crops
27 Jul 50	B-45	USAF	USSR		protest	Claimed incidiaries dropped on Oranienbaum East Germany, to destroy food crops
22 Aug 50		USAF	PRC	AAA	attacked	Close to Manchurian-Korea border
27 Aug 50		USAF	PRC		protest	Overflight of Manchurian border
30 Aug 50			USSR		detection	European theater
Oct 50 - Jun 51	multiple	USAF	Czechoslovakia		protests	Recon and espionage overflights/incursions – Oct 50: 8; Nov 50: 18; Dec 50: 6; Jan 1-15 51: 26; Jan 15-Jun 51: 116
15 Oct 50	F-51D	USAF	PRC	AAA	claimed	Over Manchuria, but not proven
Nov 50		France	PRC		protest	Claimed hundreds of overflights of PRC since Dec 49
9 Nov 50	**RB-29A 44-61813**	**USAF**	**DPRK/USSR**	**MiG-15**	**destroyed**	**Crash landed at Johnson AB; 1 MiG-15 shot down**
4 Dec 50	**RB-45C 48-015**	**USAF**	**DPRK/USSR**	**MiG-15**	**destroyed**	**Near Antung, China, but crashed in North Korea**
26 Dec 50	RB-29A 44-61855	USAF	DPRK/USSR	MiG-15	attacked	Violating Soviet Far East airspace
late 50	P2V	USN	USSR	MiG-15	attacked	Near Vladivostok; one MiG-15 shot down
7 Feb 51	2 jets	USAF	Czechoslovakia		protest	Overflight to Prague
8 Jun 51	2 F-84E (1 was 49-2273)	USAF	Czechoslovakia		detained	Airplanes landed and were detained. 2 pilots returned in July; 1 to America and a Norwegian USAF exchange pilot to Norway
Jun 51		CIA	USSR		overflight	USSR executed 2 spies (Osmanov and Sarancev) after parachuting into Moldavia
4 Jul 51	RB-45C	USAF	PRC	MiG-15s	attacked	Overflight of Harbin, China
17 Jul 51		Sweden	USSR		protest	Airspace violation by Swedish aircraft near Libau, Baltic
26 Jul 51		Sweden	USSR		protest	Airspace violation by Swedish aircraft near Vindau, Baltic
13 Aug 51	8 jets	Turkey	USSR		protest	Overflight of border region
28 Sep 51		USN	PRC	fighter	intercept	Shantung region
29 Sep 51		USN	PRC	fighter	intercept	Shantung region, repeat of 28 Sep mission
30 Sep 51		USN	PRC	ship-based AAA	attacked	75 miles south of Shantung Peninsula
4 Oct 51		USN	PRC	ship-based AAA	attacked	Vicinity of Shantung Peninsula
13 Oct 51	**P-38 MM4203**	**Turkey**	**Yugoslavia**		**destroyed**	**Overflight of Yugoslavia**
18 Oct 51		CIA	Romania		protest	Parachute drop of 5 spies from base in Athens, Greece
6 Nov 51	**P2V-3W 124283**	**USN**	**USSR**	**MiG-15**	**destroyed**	**Sea of Japan near Siberia. Also reported as two La-11s**
18 Nov 51	C-47	USAF	Hungary	fighter	forced down	Crew of 4 ransomed for $30k each; charged with espionage in Hungary following overflight of Romania
23 Jan 52	P4M-1Q	USN	USSR	fighter	attacked	Baltic Sea; 'rocket attack' by fighters
7 Feb 52	**P4M-1Q 124371**	**USN**	**USSR**	**fuel starvation**	**destroyed**	**Ukraine periphery; evaded attack; ditched north of Cyprus**
29 Feb 52	RB-50G	USAF	USSR			Armed follow up to 23 Jan 52 mission; third cancelled
29 Mar 52	RB-50	USAF	USSR	SAM	attacked	Near Dairen
1 Apr 52		USN	PRC		attacked	Over China Sea
18 Apr 52		USN	USSR	fighter	attacked	Black Sea area, also attacked by SAM
29 Apr 52	DC-4 F-BELI	Civil	USSR	2 MiG-15s	attacked	Air France civil flight from Frankfurt to Berlin, 2 passengers wounded and aircraft reached Berlin
8 May 52	C-49	Civil	USSR		protest	French civil aircraft alleged overflight in Berlin corridor
11 May 52	PBM-5	USN	USSR	2 MiG-15s	attacked	Near Port Arthur 75 miles SSW Takushan AB
15 May 52	DC-4	Civil	USSR		protest	Overflight along Berlin corridor
18 May 52		UK	USSR		protest	Overflight along Berlin corridor
18 May 52		UK	PRC	ship-based AAA	attacked	Vicinity of Hong Kong
22 May 52		Civil	USSR	MiG-15	intercepted	British European Airways cargo aircraft buzzed in Berlin corridor
26 May 52		USAF	USSR		protest	Alleged overflight of East Germany
Jun-Jul 52		USAF	USSR		protest	Alleged corridor violations of over Soviet-occupied Austria
26 Jun 52	'DC-4'	USAF	Czechoslovakia		protest	Alleged overflight to drop Colorado beetles
Jun 52		USAF	East Germany		protest	Alleged overflight to drop Colorado beetles
Jun 52		USAF	East Germany		protest	US acknowledged inadvertent overflight by 'hospital aircraft'

Jun 52		RAF	USSR		protest	Alleged overflight by 'jet fighter'
4 Jun 52		USAF	USSR	2 MiG-15s	forced down	Carrying US High Commissioner Donnelly
5 Jun 52		Italy	Albania		protest	Alleged overflight of Albania
6 Jun 52		France	PRC		protest	Overflights of PRC along Indochina border
7 Jun 52		USAF	USSR		protest	Alleged overflight of East Germany
12 Jun 52		Italy	Albania		protest	Alleged overflight of Albania
13 Jun 15		RAF	USSR		protest	RAF 'jet fighter' overflight of East Germany
13 Jun 52	**RB-29A 44-61810**	**USAF**	**USSR**	**MiG-15**	**destroyed**	**Sea of Japan, north of Hokkaido; mission 6-13-12. Moscow reported one survivor rescued**
13 Jun 52	**DC-3 79001 (42-5694)**	**Sweden**	**USSR**	**MiG-15**	**destroyed**	**Swedish SIGINT in Baltic**
14 Jun 52		Italy	Albania		protest	Alleged overflight of Albania
16 Jun 52	**Catalina 47002**	**Sweden**	**USSR**	**MiG-15**	**destroyed**	**During rescue search for SIGINT DC-3 lost on 13 June**
19 Jun 52	C-54	USAF	USSR		protest	Alleged overflight of East Germany
19 Jun 52		USAF	USSR		protest	Alleged overflight of East Germany by single-engine airplane
24 Jun 52		USAF	Czechoslovakia		protest	Alleged overflight by multiple aircraft
Jul 52	RB-26	USAF	DPRK/USSR	MiG-15s	attacked	Over Korea Bay
Jul 52	P4M-1Q	USN	DPRK/USSR	MiG-15s	attacked	Over Korea Bay
2 Jul 52		Turkey	Bulgaria		protest	Claimed 2 jets overflew Bulgaria to conduct reconnaissance
4 Jul 52	**RB-29A 44-61727**	**USAF**	**DPRK/USSR**	**MiG-15s**	**destroyed**	**Possibly over PRC**
15 Jul 52		USAF	USSR		protest	Alleged overflight of East Germany
15 Jul 52		Civil	USSR		protest	Alleged overflight of East Germany
16 Jul 52	RB-26	USAF	USSR	MiG-15	attacked	45 miles SE Dairen
31 Jul 52	PBM-5 59277	USN	PRC	MiG-15	attacked	60 miles east of Port Arthur; 2 crew killed
Aug 52		US			disappeared	Lost in NW Pacific
4 Aug 52		UK	PRC	ship-based AAA	attacked	Vicinity of Hong Kong
8 Sep 52	DC-4	Civil	USSR		protest	SABENA overflight of East Germany
15 Oct 52	B-47B	USAF	USSR	MiG-15	intercept	MiGs attempted to intercept RB-47 during overflight of Chukostskii region
20 Sep 52	PB4Y-2	USN	PRC	MiG-15	attacked	East China Sea; MiG pilot claimed as B-29 destroyed
7 Oct 52	**RB-29A 44-61815**	**USAF**	**USSR**	**La-11**	**destroyed**	**North of Hokkaido; also struck by AAA, mission 10-7-22**
8 Oct 52	C-47A	USAF	USSR	MiG-15	attacked	Unmarked USAF hospital aircraft in Berlin corridor
4 Nov 52		USAF	Poland		protest	Claimed overflight to paradrop 2 spies
23 Nov 52	PB4Y-2	USN	PRC	MiG-15	attacked	Off the coast of Shanghai
29 Nov 52	**C-47**	**CIA**	**PRC**		**destroyed**	**During attempted exfiltration of agent in Jilin Province**
13 Jan 53	**RB-29A 44-62217**	**USAF**	**USSR/DPRK**	**MiG-15**	**destroyed**	**Leaflet drop over North Korea; mission R-7011**
18 Jan 53	**P2V-5 127744**	**USN**	**PRC**	**AAA**	**destroyed**	**Formosa Strait off Swatow**
10 Mar 53	**2 F-84Es**	**USAF**	**Czechoslovakia**	**MiG-15s**	**destroyed**	**Alleged overflight, one F-84 escaped**
12 Mar 53	Lincoln RF503	RAF	USSR	MiG-15s	intercepted	Buzzed while in Berlin corridor prior to Lincoln RF531 loss
12 Mar 53	**Lincoln RF531**	**RAF**	**USSR**	**MiG-15s**	**destroyed**	**Likely mistaken for SIGINT overflight**
12 Mar 53	Viking	Civil	USSR	MiG-15s	intercepted	In Berlin corridor 6 hours after Lincoln RF531 was shot down
15 Mar 53	RB-50E 47-0128	USAF	USSR	MiG-15	attacked	Kamchatka, 100 miles NE of Petropavlovsk
15 Apr 53	RB-50	USAF	USSR	MiG-15	claimed	Kamchatka near Zhoopanovo; claimed but not proven
23 Apr 53	P4M-1Q 124369	USN	PRC	MiG-15	attacked	Near Shanghai
25 Apr 53		CIA	USSR		protest	Alleged airdrop of spies over Ukraine
15 May 53	WB-29	USAF	USSR	MiG-15	attacked	Kamchatka
19 Jun 53	PBM-5	USN	PRC	AAA	attacked	In Formosa Straits
28 Jun 53	P2V-5	USN	PRC	AAA	attacked	Near Natien
21 Jul 53	PBM-5	USN	PRC	MiG-15s	attacked	Over the Yellow Sea
29 Jul 53	**RB-50G 47-0145**	**USAF**	**USSR**	**MiG-17**	**destroyed**	**Near Cape Povorotny, Sea of Japan; Likely in retaliation for US downing of Soviet IL-12 on 27 July 1953**
17 Aug 53	LT-6G	USAF	USSR/DPRK		claimed	North of DMZ but unverified

Sep 53			USSR/DPRK	MiG-15	attacked	Yellow Sea; F-86 escort to attack MiGs
Oct 53	PBM-5 84713	USN	PRC	MiG-15	attacked	30 miles east of Tsingtao
7 Nov 53	PBM-5 58152	USN	PRC	MiG-15	destroyed	Near Qianlidao in Qingdao; reported lost on 10 Nov 53
18 Nov 53	PBM-5 84747	USN	PRC	MiG-15s	attacked	Inadvertent overflight near Shanghai
4 Jan 54	P2V-5 127752	USN	USSR/DPRK	MiG-15	destroyed	Crashed while attempting to land at K-13, South Korea, after possible attack causing engine failure
27 Jan 54	RB-45C	USAF	USSR/DPRK	MiG-15	attacked	Yellow Sea; 16 F-86 escorts, 8 MiGs attacked, 1 destroyed
12 Mar 54	AD-4	USN	Czechoslovakia	MiG-15	1 damaged	Accidental incursion
9 Apr 54	P2V-5	USN	PRC	MiG-15	attacked	Over the Yellow Sea
29 Apr 54	RB-45C	RAF	USSR	AAA	attacked	During JU JITSU overflight
8 May 54	RB-47E	USAF	USSR	MiG-17	attacked	Austin overflight of Murmansk
12 May 54	F2H	USMC	PRC	MiG-15	intercepted	Overflight of Fukien
3 Jun 54	DC-3 OO-CBY	Civil	Yugoslavia	fighters	attacked	SABENA cargo flight; landed in Austria after attack
23 Jul 54	DC-4 VR-HEU	Civil	PRC	La-7	destroyed	Cathay Pacific Airliner shot down over Hainan
2 Aug 54	RB-29A	USAF	USSR	fighter	attacked	Mission R-2003
4 Sep 54	P2V-5	USN	USSR	MiG-15	destroyed	Sea of Japan near Siberia
12 Sep 54	PB4Y-2 '12'	RoCAF	PRC	AAA	destroyed	FOX CHASE ELINT
7 Nov 54	RB-29A 42-94000	USAF	USSR	MiG-15 1K	destroyed	Sea of Japan near Hokkaido, crash landed in Hokkaido
17 Nov 54	RT-33A '2'	RoCAF	PRC	MiG-15	destroyed	Crashed into mountains near Fujian evading attack
Feb 55	P2V-5	USN	PRC	AAA	attacked	Over Straits of Formosa
5 Feb 55	RB-45C	USAF	USSR/DPRK	MiG-15	attacked	Yellow Sea; 12 F-86 escort, 2 MiG-15s shot down
Apr 55	P4M-1Q 124362	USN	PRC	MiG-15	attacked	Shot down 22 Aug 56
2 Apr 55			PRC		protest	Claimed multiple overflights
17 Apr 55	RB-47B-I 51-2054	USAF	USSR	MiG-15s	destroyed	Near Petropavlovsk
1 May 55		NATO	USSR		claimed	Alleged overflight of multple cities; Kiev, Leningrad
22 Jun 55	P2V-5 131515	USN	USSR	MiG-15	destroyed	Bering Sea; crash landed on St Lawrence Island
27 Jun 55	RT-33A '7'	RoCAF	PRC	MiG-15	destroyed	Off the coast of Fujian
27 Jul 55	L-049 4X-AKC	Civil	Bulgaria	MiG-15	destroyed	El Al Airliner shot own near Petrich, Bulgaria
18 Aug 55	LT-6G	USAF	USSR/DPRK		destroyed	Near North Korea
10 Sep 55	RB-50	USAF			destroyed	Reported shot down over Sea of Japan. Unconfirmed
10 Jan 56		US	PRC		protest	Claimed multiple overflights
23 Jun 56	RB-17	RoCAF	PRC	MiG-17	destroyed	FOX CHASE ELINT over Jiangxi
Jul 56	P2V	USN	USSR	MiG-15	claimed	Sea of Japan; unverified loss
22 Aug 56	P4M-1Q 124362	USN	PRC	fighter	destroyed	PRC coast near Wenchow
10 Sep 56	RB-50G 47-0133	USAF	USSR	MiG-17s	destroyed	Sea of Japan; NOT lost in Typhoon Emma, but shot down by radio silent MiG-17 attack from Vladivostok
Oct 56	RF-84F 52-7366	USAF	USSR	MiG-15s	attacked	During a day reconnaissance mission over Kurile Islands
11 Dec 56	RB-57D	USAF	USSR		protest	SAC RB-57D overflight of Vladivostok
12 Jan 57		USN	PRC	AAA	attacked	Formosa Straits
14 May 57	RF-84F	RoCAF	PRC	MiG-17	attacked	Overflight of Shanghai; one of two planes attacked
14 May 57	RF-84F	RoCAF	PRC	MiG-17	destroyed	Overflight of Shanghai; crashed upon landing in South Korea
27 Jul 57		USAF	Czechoslovakia		protest	Claimed overflight
Dec 57	DC-4	Civil	Albania	MiG-15s	forced down	BOAC commercial flight
23 Dec 57	RT-33A 51-4413	USAF	Albania	MiG-15	force down	Forced to land at Rinas Airport in Albania following overflight
24 Dec 57	RB-57D	USAF	USSR		claimed	Claimed destroyed over Black Sea; unverified
18 Feb 58	RB-57A 52-1431	RoCAF	PRC	MiG-17	destroyed	Overflight of PRC near Shandong; ex-HEART THROB aircraft '5642'
13 Mar 58	RB-17	RoCAF	PRC	MiG-17	attacked	Overflight of PRC

25 Mar 58	RF-84F 52-7237 (H8-N)	Belgium	USSR	MiG-17s	force down	Landed at Parchim, East Germany. Pilot and aircraft returned
21 Apr 58	**RB-17**	**RoCAF**	**PRC**	**MiG-17**	**destroyed**	**Overflight of PRC**
1 May 58	RB-47	USAF	USSR		protest	Alleged overflight of Kiev, vicinity of Moscow
17 Jun 58	**RF-84F 52-8751 '5609'**	**RoCAF**	**PRC**	**fighter**	**destroyed**	**Struck ground while evading attack over PRC**
27 Jun 58	**C-118A 51-3822**	**USAF**	**USSR**	**MiG-17**	**destroyed**	**Near Yerevan**
26 Jul 58	RB-57	USAF	USSR		protest	Alleged overflight
26 Jul 58	RB-47	USAF	USSR	fighter	intercept	Claimed from Iran over Caspian Sea
21 Aug 58	RB-17	RoCAF	PRC	MiG-17	attacked	Multiple attacks over PRC
2 Sep 58	**C-130A-II 56-0528**	**USAF**	**USSR**	**MiG-17**	**destroyed**	**SIGINT flight near Armenia**
10 Sep 58	multiple	US	PRC		protest	Claimed PBM-5 and U-2 overflights of PRC
22 Sep 58		US	PRC		protest	Claimed overflight
30 Sep 58		US	USSR		protest	Claimed 3 overflights of Chuktosk Penninsula and Ratmanov Island
7 Oct 58		US	PRC		protest	Claimed multiple overflights
31 Oct 58	RB-47	USAF	USSR	MiG-17	attacked	Black Sea
7 Nov 58	RB-47	USAF	USSR	MiG-17	attacked	East of Gotland Island in the Baltic
17 Nov 58	RB-47	USAF	USSR	MiG-17	attacked	Sea of Japan
17 Nov 58	RB-47	USAF	USSR	fighter	attacked	Sea of Japan
15 Dec 58	RB-17, RB-69	RoCAF	PRC	fighter	attacked	Overflight near Nanching
29 May 59	**RB-17 '835'**	**RoCAF**	**PRC**	**MiG-17**	**destroyed**	**Overflight of PRC**
16 Jun 59	**P4M-1Q 122209**	**USN**	**DPRK/USSR**	**MiG-17**	**destroyed**	**Sea of Japan; 85 miles east of Wonsan, Korea; landed at Miho AB, Japan, written off**
19 Jul 59		USN	PRC		protest	Claimed overflight near Fukien
7 Oct 59	**RB-57D 53-3978**	**RoCAF**	**PRC**	**SA-2**	**destroyed**	**Overflight of PRC; also claimed by MiG-19 pilot**
15 Jan 60	RB-69	RoCAF	PRC	AAA, MiG-17	intercept	ELINT overflight of PRC
16 Jan 60	**P4M-1Q 124365**	**USN**	**USSR**	**fighter**	**destroyed**	**Near Incirlik, Turkey. Details unknown but some report this crashed in Mediterranean or Black Sea due to fighter attack**
1 Mar 60	RB-69	RoCAF	PRC	MiG-17	intercept	ELINT overflight of PRC
1 May 60	**U-2C 360/56-6693**	**CIA**	**USSR**	**SA-2**	**destroyed**	**Sverdlovsk. Frank Powers taken prisoner**
20 May 60	C-47	USAF	USSR	fighters	forced down	Near Kleutz, East Germany
1 Jul 60	**RB-47H 53-4281**	**USAF**	**USSR**	**MiG-19**	**destroyed**	**Barents Sea. John McCone and Bruce Olmstead taken prisoner**

Note: All CIA U-2 overflights generated reactions ranging from diplomatic protest to attack by fighters and SAMs

The future of US strategic aerial reconnaissance: RC-135B 64-14841 rolls out of the Boeing Factory on 24 September 1964 prior to delivery to Martin for the BIG TEAM conversion to an RC-135C. Scheduled to serve through 2040 – nearly 80 years of flying – the RC-135 has become the primary platform for a wide variety of reconnaissance missions. *Boeing Photo P37266*

Appendix II

Known Intentional Western Overflights 1946-1960

Date	Number of Overflights	Agency	Aircraft	Pilot/Commander or Unit	Departure Base	Recovery Base	Comments
1946	multiple	USAF	RB-29	46th RS	Ladd Field, AK	Ladd Field, AK	
Oct-Dec 1947	multiple	USAF	RB-29	72nd RS	Ladd Field, AK	Ladd Field, AK	Project 23 Siberian PHOTINT mission
Dec 48 - Sep 50	multiple	SAF	Spitfire PR19	F11	Nyköping	Nyköping	Baltic states
5 Aug 48	single	USAF	RB-29	72nd RS	Ladd Field, AK	Yokota AB	Siberia
8 Aug 48	single	USAF	RB-29	72nd RS	Yokota AB	Ladd Field, AK	Siberia
1 Sep 48	single	USAF	RB-29	72nd RS	Ladd Field, AK	Yokota AB	Siberia
6 Sep 48	single	USAF	RB-29	72nd RS	Yokota AB	Ladd Field, AK	Siberia
10 Jul 48	single	SAF	P-51	J26	Linköping	Linköping	Baltic states
10 Nov 48	single	SAF	P-51	J26	Linköping	Linköping	Baltic states
23 Nov 48	single	SAF	P-51	J26	Linköping	Linköping	Baltic states
10 May 49	single	USAF	RF-80	Bryce Poe	Misawa AB	Misawa AB	Kuriles
10 May 49 - 18 Aug 50	multiple	USAF	RF-80	8th TRS	Misawa AB	Misawa AB	Kuriles, Vladivostok, Dairen, Shanghai
10 Mar 50	single	USAF	RF-80	Bryce Poe	Misawa AB	Misawa AB	Vladivostok
29 Sep 49	single	SAF	Spitfire PR19	F11	Luleå	Luleå	South of Murmansk
1950-Feb 55	multiple	USAF	fighter				Eastern Europe and USSR
15 Jan 51-Jun 52	multiple	RAF	Spitfire PR19	Edward Powles	Hong Kong Kai Tak	Hong Kong Kai Tak	Hainan Island and Coastal PRC
13 May 51	single	USAF	RF-80A	Jean Woodyward	Suwon AB	Suwon AB	Mukden PRC (Tu-4 base)
5 Jun 51	single	USAF	RB-45	Stacy D Naftel	Yokota AB	Yokota AB	Central PRC
4 Jul 51	single	USAF	RB-45	Stacy D Naftel	Yokota AB	Yokota AB	Central PRC
8 Aug 51	single	USAF	RB-45	Stacy D Naftel	Yokota AB	Yokota AB	Vladivostok
25 Aug 51	single	USAF	RB-29	91st SRS	Yokota AB	Yokota AB	Shanghai
Oct 51	single	USAF	RB-26	12th TRS	Kimpo AB	Kimpo AB	Vladivostok
9 Oct 51	single	USAF	RB-45	91st SRS	Yokota AB	Yokota AB	Kuriles
1951-1953	multiple	USAF	RF-86 / RF-80	15th TRS			PRC
1952-1953	multiple	USAF	RB-45	91st SRS	Yokota AB	Yokota AB	Vladivostok, Kuriles, PRC
1952	multiple	RoCAF	RB-25		Taoyuan AFB	Taoyuan AFB	RoCAF/CAT PHOTINT
21 Mar 52	3 aircraft	RAF	RB-45	John Crampton	RAF Sculthorpe	RAF Sculthorpe	JU JITSU: East Germany, Berlin
2 Apr - 29 Jun 52	10 missions	USAF/ USN	P2V / RB-50	Richard A Koch	Shemya AFB	Shemya AFB	Kamchatka, Chukotskii
17 Apr 52	3 aircraft	RAF	RB-45	John Crampton	RAF Sculthorpe	RAF Sculthorpe	JU JITSU: 1-Baltic, Ukraine 2-Belorussia, Orel 3-Ukraine, Rostov
Jun 52	3 aircraft	USAF	RF-86A	Cecil Rigsby	Kimpo AB	Kimpo AB	Harbin PRC (IL-28)
17 Sep 52	single	USAF	RB-50	Roy Kaden	Thule AB	Thule AB	Franz Josef Island
15 Oct 52	single	USAF	B-47B	Don Hillman	Eielson AFB, AK	Eielson AFB, AK	Siberia, Chukotskii Peninsula
late 1952	multiple	USAF	RB-36		Yokota AB	Yokota AB	Overflights of Manchuria
17 Dec 52	single	USAF	RB-45	Howard S 'Sam' Meyers	Yokota AB	Yokota AB	Vladivostok, Harbin, Mukden
3 Jan 53	single	USAF	RF-86	Mele Vojvodich, Jr			PRC (later a CIA A-12 pilot)
27 Jul 53	single	USAF	RF-86	LaVerne 'Griff' Griffin	Kimpo AB	Kimpo AB	Harbin
1954	multiple	RoCAF	multiple	SMG	Taoyuan AFB, Hsinchu AFB	Taoyuan AFB, Hsinchu AFB	40 PB4Y-2/RB-24 and 14 B-17 overflights of PRC
22 Mar 54 - 19 Feb 56	multiple	USAF	RF-86F	15th TRS	Osan AB	Misawa AB	Vladivostok, Khabarovsk, PRC
22 Mar 54	2 aircraft	USAF	RF-86F	LaVerne 'Griff' Griffin	Osan AB	Misawa AB	Vladivostok
3 Apr 54	2 aircraft	USAF	RF-86F	LaVerne 'Griff' Griffin	Osan AB	Misawa AB	Vladivostok
21 Apr 54	2 aircraft	USAF	RF-86F	LaVerne 'Griff' Griffin	Osan AB	Misawa AB	Vladivostok
28 Apr 54	3 aircraft	RAF	RB-45	John Crampton	RAF Sculthorpe	RAF Sculthorpe	Kiev, Stalingrad
1 May 54	3 aircraft	USAF	RF-86F	Jerry DePew	Kunsan AB	Misawa AB	Dairen PRC

8 May 54	single	USAF	RB-47E	Harold 'Hal' Austin	RAF Fairford	RAF Brize Norton	Murmansk
11 May - 12 Jun 54	77 sorties	USMC	F2H	VMJ-1	NAS Atsugi	NAS Atsugi	Fukien PRC
11 May 54	2 aircraft	USMC	F2H	Major Turcott	NAS Atsugi	NAS Atsugi	Fukien PRC
12 May 54	4 missions	USMC	F2H	Marion Carl	NAS Atsugi	NAS Atsugi	Fukien PRC
6 Jun 54	1 mission	USMC	F2H	Marion Carl	NAS Atsugi	NAS Atsugi	Fukien PRC
12 Jun 54	1 mission	USMC	F2H	Marion Carl	NAS Atsugi	NAS Atsugi	Fukien PRC
Aug 54	27 missions	USAF	RB-45	91st SRS	Yokota AB	Yokota AB	Vladivostok, Harbin, Mukden
1954-1955	multiple	CIA	RB-69	Expatriate Poles, Czechs, etc	Wiesbaden, FRG	Wiesbaden, FRG	OSTIARY, CHERRY, WILD CHERRY: COMINT Eastern Europe
early to mid 1950s	multiple	USAF	RB-36				PRC, Murmansk
Feb 55-early 56	multiple	USAF	GRB-36 / RF-84K	99th SRW 71st SRW	Fairchild AFB, WA Larson AFB, WA		USSR
19 Feb 55	single	USAF	RF-86F	Robert E Morrisson			Khabarovsk
1 Mar 55	3 aircraft	USAF	RB-45	John Anderson, et al	RAF Sculthorpe	RAF Sculthorpe	Ukraine
mid 55 - mid 56	3 missions	USAF	RF-100A	7407th SS	Bitburg AB	Bitburg AB	SLICK CHICK: Eastern Europe
mid 55 - mid 56	multiple	USAF	RF-100A	6021st RS	Yokota AB	Yokota AB	SLICK CHICK: Eastern USSR
26 Nov 55	single	USAF	RB-57A	Joseph A Guthrie, Jr	Chitose AB	Chitose AB	HEART THROB: Sakhalin
1955-1956	single	USAF	RB-57A	Jim Bryant			HEART THROB: USSR
1955-1956	single	USAF	RB-57A	Robert E Hines, Sr			HEART THROB: USSR
1955-1956	multiple	USAF	RB-47	26th SRW			APQ-56 SLAR border incursions
17 Aug 55 - 24 Apr 56	15 missions	RoCAF	PB4Y-2				FOX HUNT ELINT over PRC
18 Sep 55	single	USAF	RF-100A	Cecil H Rigsby	Bitburg AB	Bitburg AB	SLICK CHICK Czechoslovakia
23 Sep 55	single	USAF	RF-100A	Bert Dowdy	Bitburg AB	Bitburg AB	SLICK CHICK Czechoslovakia
Sep 55-Aug 56	15-19 missions	USAF	RB-57A	7407th SS	Rhein-Main AB	Rhein-Main AB	HEART THROB: Eastern Europe
9 Mar 56	single	USAF	RF-100A	Bert Dowdy	Bitburg AB	Bitburg AB	SLICK CHICK Czechoslovakia
21 Mar - 10 May 56	156 missions	USAF	RB-47	26th SRW, 55th SRW	Thule AB	Thule AB	Siberia
6 May 56	6 aircraft	USAF	RB-47	26th SRW	Thule AB	Eielson AFB, AK	Ambarchik, Siberia, Chukotskii
20 Jun 56	Mission # 2003	CIA	U-2	Carl Overstreet	Wiesbaden, FRG	Wiesbaden, FRG	Czechoslovakia, Poland, East Germany
23 Jun 56	single	RoCAF	RB-17	Ye Zheng Min	Hsinchu AFB	shot down	FOX HUNT over Jiangxi
2 Jul 56	Mission # 2009	CIA	U-2	Jake Kratt	Wiesbaden, FRG	Wiesbaden, FRG	Austria, Hungary, Yugoslavia, Bulgaria
2 Jul 56	Mission # 2010	CIA	U-2	Glen Dunaway	Wiesbaden, FRG	Wiesbaden, FRG	East Germany, Poland, Czechoslovakia, Hungary, Romania
4 Jul 56	Mission # 2013	CIA	U-2	Hervey Stockman	Wiesbaden, FRG	Wiesbaden, FRG	East Germany, Poland, Minsk, Leningrad, Estonia, Latvia, Poland
5 Jul 56	Mission # 2014	CIA	U-2	Carmine Vito	Wiesbaden, FRG	Wiesbaden, FRG	East Germany, Warsaw, Minsk, Moscow, Estonia, Latvia, Lithuania, Poland
9 Jul 56	Mission # 2020	CIA	U-2	Marty Knutson	Wiesbaden, FRG	Wiesbaden, FRG	East Germany, Poland, Minsk, Poland
9 Jul 56	Mission # 2021	CIA	U-2	Carl Overstreet	Wiesbaden, FRG	Wiesbaden, FRG	Czechoslovakia, Vienna, Hungary, L'Vov, Kiev, Minsk, Poland
10 Jul 56	Mission # 2024	CIA	U-2	Glen Dunaway	Wiesbaden, FRG	Wiesbaden, FRG	Poland, Kishinev, Kerch', Sevastapol', Simferopol', Odessa, Romania, Hungary
Sep-Dec 56	multiple	USAF	RB-57D	4080th SRW	Yokota AB	Yokota AB	USSR
6 Sep 56	single	CIA	U-2				Yugoslavia, Albania
Oct 56	single	USAF	RB-57A	Joseph A Guthrie, Jr			HEART THROB: USSR
12 Oct 56	single	CIA	U-2				Yugoslavia, Albania
20 Nov 56	Mission # 4016	CIA	U-2	Frank Powers	Incirlik AB	Incirlik AB	Iran, Yerevan, Baku, Astara, Caucasus
10 Dec 56	single	CIA	U-2	Carmine Vito	Wiesbaden, FRG	Wiesbaden, FRG	Albania, Bulgaria, Yugoslavia
10 Dec 56	single	CIA	U-2		Wiesbaden, FRG	Wiesbaden, FRG	Albania, Bulgaria, Yugoslavia
11 Dec 56	three	USAF	RB-57D	William Shuman Bob Chalmers Keith Simms	Yokota AB	Yokota AB	Vladivostok; 3 aircraft plus 3 spares
1957-1960	multiple	CIA	RB-69	RoC crews			PRC
2 Jan 57	single	RoCAF	RB-17	Zhao Qin	Hsinchu AFB	K-8 (Kunsan AB)	FOX HUNT ELINT over PRC
18 Mar 57	Mission # 4020	CIA	U-2	Jim Cherbonneaux	Incirlik AB	Incirlik AB	Soviet border to Afghanistan, Azerbaijan, Armenia, Georgia (unintentional)
25 Apr 57	single	CIA	U-2		Giebelstadt, FRG	Giebelstadt, FRG	Albania

8 Jun 57	single	CIA	U-2				'Russia'
20 Jun 57	Mission # 6005	CIA	U-2	Al Rand	Eielson AFB, AK	Eielson AFB, AK	Khaylyulya, Ust'-Kamchatsk, Kozrevsk, Karaganskiy-Ostrov, Kura (Klyuchi) Test Range
Jun 57 - Jun 58	multiple daily	RoCAF	RF-84F	6th PRG	Taoyuan AFB	Taoyuan AFB	PRC
4 Aug 57	single	CIA	U-2				China, Mongolia, 'Russia'
5 Aug 57	Mission # 4035	CIA	U-2	Eugene 'Buster' Edens	Lahore	Lahore	Afghanistan, Tashkent, Tyuratam, Kazalinsk, Aral Sea
12 Aug 57	Mission # 4039	CIA	U-2	Bill McMurray	Lahore	Lahore	Alma-Ata, Ust'-Kamenogorsk, Sinkiang
21 Aug 57	Mission # 4045	CIA	U-2	Sammy Snyder	Lahore	Lahore	Novokuznetsk, Tomsk
21 Aug 57	Mission # 4048	CIA	U-2	E K Jones	Lahore	Lahore	Lake Balkhash, Karaganda, Omsk, Alma-Ata
22 Aug 57	Mission # 4049	CIA	U-2	Tom Birkhead	Lahore	Lahore	Merket Bazar, Kuldja, Abakan, Krasnoyarsk, Kansk, Sinkiang
22 Aug 57	Mission # 4050	CIA	U-2	Jim Cherbonneaux	Lahore	Lahore	Lake Balkhash, Semipalatinsk, Bamaul, Prokop'yevsk, Novokuznetsk, Leninogorsk
22 Aug 57	Mission # 4051	CIA	U-2	Bill Hall			Tibet
28 Aug 57	Mission # 4058	CIA	U-2	E K Jones	Lahore	Lahore	Dushanbe, Tashkent, Tyuratam, Kazalinsk, Aral Sea
10 Sep 57	Mission # 4059	CIA	U-2	Bill Hall	Incirlik AB	Incirlik AB	Krasnovodsk, Gur'yev, Astrakhan', Tbilisi
16 Sep 57	Mission # 6008	CIA	U-2	Barry Baker	Eielson AFB, AK	Eielson AFB, AK	Kamchatka Peninsula, Milkovo
13 Oct 57	Mission # 2040	CIA	U-2	Hervey Stockman	Giebelstadt, FRG	Giebelstadt, FRG	Norway, Finland, Murmansk, Kandalaksha
20 Nov 57	single	RoCAF	RB-17	Zhu Zhi He	Hsinchu AFB	K-8 (Kunsan AB)	FOX HUNT: PRC
6 Dec 57	single	RoCAF	RB-57A	Si Lang Lu	Taoyuan AFB	Taoyuan AFB	LARGE CHARGE; Hainan Island
15 Dec 57	single	RoCAF	RB-57A	Yu Pao Chang	Taoyuan AFB	Taoyuan AFB	LARGE CHARGE: PRC
7 Jan 58	single	RoCAF	RB-57A	Tso Shi Lin	Taoyuan AFB	Taoyuan AFB	LARGE CHARGE: PRC
28 Jan 57	single	CIA	U-2				Albania
18 Feb 58	single	RoCAF	RB-57A	Kwan Hua Chao	Taoyuan AFB	shot down	LARGE CHARGE: Shot down over Shandong by MiG-19
1958	multiple	USAF	RB-57D	4080th SRW			Overflights of PRC
1 Mar 58	Mission # 6011	CIA	U-2	Tom Crull	Atsugi NAS	Atsugi NAS	Dal'nerechensk, Khabarovsk, Blagoveschensk, Belagorsk, Komsomolsk, Sovetskaya Gavan'
13 Mar 58	single	RoCAF	RB-17	Wang Guo Shan	Hsinchu AFB		FOX HUNT ELINT
20 Mar 58	single	RoCAF	RB-69	Zhao Qin	Hsinchu AFB	Hsinchu AFB	Operation CHERRY ELINT
21 Apr 58	3 aircraft	RoCAF	RB-17/RB-69				2 FOX HUNT RB-17s (1 shot down); CHERRY RB-69
17 Jun 58	2 aircraft	RoCAF	RF-84F	S H Yang, M C King	Taoyuan AFB	Taoyuan AFB	1 RF-84F destroyed over PRC
19 Jun 58	Mission # 6012	CIA	U-2	Lyle Rudd	Naha AB	Naha AB	Fujian, Jiangxi, Peking, Shanghai
20 Aug 58	Mission # 6017	CIA	U-2	Lyle Rudd	Naha AB	Naha AB	PRC
10 Sep 58	Mission # 6019	CIA	U-2		Naha AB	Naha AB	PRC
22 Oct 58	Mission # 6023	CIA	U-2	E K Jones			PRC
6 Nov 58	Mission # 4093	CIA	U-2	John Shinn	Bodo	Incirlik AB	Peripheral along USSR, overflight of Poland, Romania
6 Dec 58	single	RoCAF	RB-57D		Taoyuan AFB	Taoyuan AFB	1st STAGE SHOW Mission, Jiangxi Province
15 Dec 58	3 aircraft	RoCAF	RB-17/RB-69				2 FOX HUNT RB-17s; CHERRY RB-69
1959	multiple	RoCAF	RB-17/RB-69				FOX HUNT RB-17; CHERRY RB-69
Jan 59-May 60	multiple	USAF	RB-57D	4080th SRW	Rhein-Main AB	Rhein-Main AB	BORDERTOWN SIGINT, possibly over Eastern Europe, Finland. PAPER DOLL and DINAH LEE
6 Jan 59	single	RoCAF	RB-57D	Si Lang Lu	Taoyuan AFB	Taoyuan AFB	STAGE SHOW mission, PRC
7 Jan 59	single	RoCAF	RB-57D	Yu Pao Chang	Taoyuan AFB	Taoyuan AFB	STAGE SHOW, Najiang, Shanghai
14 Jan 59	single	RoCAF	RB-57D	Tso Shi Lin	Taoyuan AFB	Taoyuan AFB	STAGE SHOW
14 Jan 59	single	RoCAF	RB-57D	Yu Pao Chang	Taoyuan AFB	Taoyuan AFB	STAGE SHOW
19 Jan 59	single	RoCAF	RB-57D	Si Lang Lu	Taoyuan AFB	Taoyuan AFB	STAGE SHOW
3 Feb 59	single	RoCAF	RB-57D	Yu Pao Chang	Taoyuan AFB	Taoyuan AFB	STAGE SHOW

3 Mar 59	single	RoCAF	RB-57D	Chien Nan Tien	Taoyuan AFB	Taoyuan AFB	STAGE SHOW
10 Mar 59	single	RoCAF	RB-57D	Ying Chin Wang	Taoyuan AFB	Taoyuan AFB	STAGE SHOW
11 Mar 59	single	RoCAF	RB-57D	Chien Nan Tien	Taoyuan AFB	Taoyuan AFB	STAGE SHOW
26 Mar 59	single	RoCAF	RB-57D	Si Lang Lu	Taoyuan AFB	Taoyuan AFB	STAGE SHOW
26 Mar 59	single	RoCAF	RB-57D	Ying Chin Wang	Taoyuan AFB	Taoyuan AFB	STAGE SHOW
5 Apr 59	Mission # 7350	RoCAF	RB-57D	Si Lang Lu	Taoyuan AFB	Taoyuan AFB	STAGE SHOW
5 Apr 59	Mission # 7351	RoCAF	RB-57D	Ying Chin Wang	Taoyuan AFB	Taoyuan AFB	STAGE SHOW
9 Apr 59	single	RoCAF	RB-57D	Si Lang Lu	Taoyuan AFB	Taoyuan AFB	STAGE SHOW
9 Apr 59	single	RoCAF	RB-57D	Yu Pao Chang	Taoyuan AFB	Taoyuan AFB	STAGE SHOW
30 Apr 59	single	RoCAF	RB-57D	Ying Chin Wang	Taoyuan AFB	Taoyuan AFB	STAGE SHOW
12 May 59	Mission # 6025	CIA	U-2	Tom Crull	NAS Cubi Point	Kermitola AB	MILL TOWN: Tibet, Laos, North Vietnam, PRC
14 May 59	Mission # 6028	CIA	U-2	Lyle Rudd	NAS Cubi Point	Kermitola AB	MILL TOWN: Tibet, China
29 May 59	2 aircraft	RoCAF	RB-17				FOX HUNT ELINT; One shot down
14 Jun 59	single	RoCAF	RB-57D	Si Lang Lu	Taoyuan AFB	Taoyuan AFB	STAGE SHOW mission to Beijing
18 Jun 59	single	RoCAF	RB-57D	Ying Chin Wang	Taoyuan AFB	Taoyuan AFB	STAGE SHOW
22 Jun 59	single	RoCAF	RB-57D	Yu Pao Chang	Taoyuan AFB	Taoyuan AFB	STAGE SHOW
9 Jul 59	Mission # 4125	CIA	U-2	Marty Knutson	Peshawar	Zahedan	Tyuratam
29 Aug 59	single	CIA	U-2		Takhli RTAFB	Takhli RTAFB	SOUTH GATE: North Vietnam, Laos
3 Sep 59	single	CIA	U-2		Takhli RTAFB	Takhli RTAFB	SOUTH GATE: Tibet, PRC
4 Sep 59	single	CIA	U-2		Takhli RTAFB	Takhli RTAFB	SOUTH GATE: Tibet, PRC, Laos
7 Sep 59	single	CIA	U-2		Takhli RTAFB	Takhli RTAFB	SOUTH GATE: Laos, North Vietnam
9 Sep 59	single	CIA	U-2		Takhli RTAFB	Takhli RTAFB	SOUTH GATE: Tibet, PRC
12 Sep 59	single	CIA	U-2		Takhli RTAFB	Takhli RTAFB	SOUTH GATE: Laos, North Vietnam
2 Oct 59	single	RoCAF	RB-57D	Si Lang Lu	Taoyuan AFB	Taoyuan AFB	STAGE SHOW
6 Oct 59	single	RoCAF	RB-57D	Yu Pao Chang	Taoyuan AFB	Taoyuan AFB	STAGE SHOW
7 Oct 59	single	RoCAF	RB-57D	Ying Chin Wang	Taoyuan AFB	shot down	STAGE SHOW mission to Peking; Shot down by SA-2
14 Oct 59	single	RoCAF	RB-57D	Si Lang Lu	Taoyuan AFB	Taoyuan AFB	STAGE SHOW
4 Nov 59	single	CIA	U-2		Takhli RTAFB	Takhli RTAFB	SOUTH GATE/QUICK KICK: Vietnam, Cambodia, Laos, Tibet, Burma
6 Dec 59	Mission # 8005	RAF	U-2	Robbie Robinson	Peshawar	Incirlik AB	Kuibishev, Kapustin Yar, Caucusus
1960	multiple	USAF	RB-66	7544th SG			WET STONE Eastern Europe
1960	multiple	RoCAF	RB-69		Taoyuan AFB	Taoyuan AFB	PRC
8 Jan 60	Mission # 7393	RoCAF	RF-101A	6th PRG	Taoyuan AFB	Taoyuan AFB	SENTRY DOG mission opposite Quemoy Island
13 Jan 60	single	RoCAF	RB-69	Yin Yan Shan	Hsinchu AFB	K-8 (Kunsan AB)	ELINT
14 Jan 60	single	RoCAF	RB-69	Zhao Qin	Hsinchu AFB	Hsinchu AFB	ELINT
15 Jan 60	single	RoCAF	RB-69	Yin Yan Shan	Hsinchu AFB	K-8 (Kunsan AB)	ELINT
5 Feb 60	Mission # 8009	RAF	U-2	John McArthur	Peshawar	Incirlik AB	Tyuratam, Kazan
26 Feb 60	single	RoCAF	RB-17	Li De Feng	Hsinchu AFB	Hsinchu AFB	PRC
1 Mar 60	single	RoCAF	RB-69		Hsinchu AFB	Hsinchu AFB	PRC
30 Mar 60	Mission # 6049	CIA	U-2		Takhli RTAFB	Takhli RTAFB	Operation TOPPER: PRC and Tibet
30 Mar 60	Mission # 6050	CIA	U-2		Takhli RTAFB	Takhli RTAFB	Operation TOPPER: PRC and Tibet
5 Apr 60	Mission # 6054	CIA	U-2	Bill McMurray	Takhli RTAFB	Takhli RTAFB	Operation TOPPER: PRC and Tibet
9 Apr 60	Mission # 4155	CIA	U-2	Bob Erickson	Peshawar	Zahedan	Lake Balkhash, Semipalatinsk, Kyzylespe, Dzhezhkazgan, Tyuratam
1 May 60	Mission # 4154	CIA	U-2	Frank Powers	Peshawar	shot down	Tyuratam, Kyshtym, Sverdlovsk
21 Nov 60	single	RoCAF	RB-57D	Yu Pao Chang	Taoyuan AFB	Taoyuan AFB	STAGE SHOW

Notes: This is not an absolute list all overflights, especially of China; Brief unplanned border incursions are not listed here; The CIA U-2 history includes one such mission on 18 March 1957, among its listing of the 24 U-2 overflights of the USSR; RoCAF flights are included as they were US aircraft operating on behalf of the CIA despite having Chinese pilots and crews under Projects BGMARQUE and STPOLLY; Many of the RoCAF overflights were agent or supply drops with additional PHOTINT or ELINT tasks; CIA U-2 overflights of Eastern Europe without mission numbers are unverified due to discrepancies in official CIA reports.

Appendix III

Primary US Strategic Reconnaissance Aircraft 1945-1960

Compiling a list of specific aircraft used in early Cold War strategic aerial reconnaissance is particularly challenging. In some cases a handful of aircraft – such as RB-17s – were converted from the thousands of airplanes built during the Second World War. Units often kept few accurate records so identifying what equipment was installed on which aircraft is a daunting, if not impossible task. In other cases, aircraft intended primarily for tactical reconnaissance in a combat environment – such as RF-86s and RB-26s – were tasked with strategic reconnaissance missions against the Soviet Union or People's Republic of China. As such, it is a more useful exercise to select those airplane types which flew dedicated peripheral or overflight missions rather than one-off sorties. Even so, a serial number of a given type might have flown multiple overflight missions whereas another serial number never flew any. Without unfettered access to pilot logs, mission reports, or maintenance logs, it is not possible to identify the aircraft used on each overflight. In other cases the programs were so secret that official records do not specify which aircraft were involved, and often list different (or unofficial) Mission-Design-Series (MDS) for the same airplane, for example, RB-57D and RB-57D-0.

Losses or retirements are especially problematic. Variation in dates often results from the different time zones involved, such as the 17 April (US time) or 18 April (Kamchatka time) 1955 loss of the ROMAN I RB-47B-I. Retired aircraft were typically scrapped after a stay at the Military Aircraft Storage and Disposal Center (MASDC), and records of early aircraft dispositions are frequently unreliable or altogether missing. Some aircraft reverted to basic configuration or traditional missions for the type, but when and with what unit is often unclear.

Reconciling Soviet or Chinese claims with actual losses is always a challenge. On 26 December 1950 Soviet pilots Stepan Bakhayev and 'N. Kotov' claimed to have shot down RB-29A 44-61855 (it landed and was repaired). The location of this incident has been reported variously as near 'Cape Seiskora', over the 'Tyumen'-Oola' River, and in the 'Soviet Far East'. There is a Cape Seiskari in the Gulf of Finland where RB-29s are not known to have operated, nor were there Soviet MiG-15s deployed in that region at that time. 'Oola' is the Russian suffix for river. Tyumen is a major city on the Tura River in south-central Siberia, thousands of miles from any Soviet border. Bakhayev says the airplane was shot down after violating airspace in the Soviet Far East, which is most likely as the RB-29 was from the 91st SRS based in Japan. In fact, the location was the Tumen River (Romanized Manchu as Tumen Ula), which flows along the border of Russia, China, and Korea, which accords with Bakhayev's claim. The confusion surrounding this incident reflects the complexity of trying to correlate Soviet claims with actual events, placing specific locations in vast geographic areas, and reconciling multiple conflicting accounts in different languages of the same event.[1]

Even trying to define what constitutes a loss can be an insurmountable task. On 14 December 1965 RB-57F 63-13287 crashed while operating in international airspace over the Black Sea, killing its crew of two, Les Lackey and Bob Yates. Many aviation historians and writers were not shy about including this loss as a successful Soviet attack. Officially, however, this crash has been attributed to mechanical issues leading to pilot incapacitation from hypoxia, and it was not among the military incidents identified by Yeltsin in 1992. NSA historian Michel Peterson argues that the loss was not associated with a hostile Soviet act, and reveals what the NSA heard as the event actually transpired: *There was extensive SIGINT on the incident, both HF Morse air surveillance tracking and VHF tactical air-ground voice communications. The Soviets tracked not only the RB-57 but also a US Navy reconnaissance aircraft and a USAF ACRP aircraft, all generally at the same time and generally in the same area. Two Soviet fighters were detected in defensive patrols, but SIGINT showed that the closest approach of the fighters to the RB-57 was 90 kilometers, with no hostile intent demonstrated. NSA concluded that despite 'analysis of all available SIGINT data,' there was 'no indication of Soviet involvement in the loss of the US Reconnaissance aircraft (RB-57F).'*[2]

General Dynamics personnel who examined the wreckage, however, had no doubt that the airplane was shot down not by a MiG but by a SAM. One such person – who asked to remain anonymous – told me there was a hole in the wing large enough to drive a car through, as well as other damage that could only have occurred *before* the airplane struck the water. Photos of a recovered wing reveal significant pre-impact damage. Even more compelling evidence that this was a 'combat' loss is the posthumous award of the Purple Heart medal to both crewmembers, a decoration given only to US service members wounded or killed by hostile fire. Finally, one person familiar with the program claims that from the moment of the initial 'event' until just prior to surface impact, the crew was in constant communication with an ACRP aircraft, almost certainly a SUN VALLEY C-130.

So which is it? Mechanical failure? Pilot incapacitation? One possibility might be that the RB-57F was shot down *accidentally* by an SA-N-1 (SA-3 GOA) or SA-N-2 (SA-2 GUIDELINE) surface-to-air-missile launched from a Soviet naval vessel operating in the Black Sea, similar to the 3 July 1988 destruction of an Iran Air Airbus A300 by a SAM launched from the USS *Vincennes*. Another possibility is that it was shot down *accidentally* by a land-based SA-2. Both cases would explain the lack of communication heard by the NSA (especially the land-based scenario) and the omission from the official Soviet list of incidents, but they are *purely speculative*. As with so much about Cold War aerial reconnaissance, it remains for future research to determine.

The following tables include dedicated primary US Cold War strategic reconnaissance aircraft, that is, those specifically configured for intelligence collection rather than unmodified airplanes which performed reconnaissance missions on an *ad hoc* basis. The tables include – where known – serial numbers, dates of service, configurations, attrition, and other appropriate comments but do not attempt to provide an exhaustive service record of each aircraft.

US Air Force (USAF)

Boeing B-17 Flying Fortress

The B-17 first flew in 1935 but earned its considerable reputation as a four-engine, long-range daylight bomber over Europe beginning in 1942. Some two dozen Boeing B-17 Flying Fortress bombers were converted during the war into PHOTINT platforms. Converted B-17Fs were designated as F-9s (F for 'foto' reconnaissance), F-9As, or F-9Bs depending on their camera configuration. PHOTINT B-17Gs became F-9Cs but were later redesignated RB-17Gs. A small number of these served with SAC from 1947 until 1950 and USAFE from 1946 through 1951. SAC RB-17Gs included those which had been perviously assigned to Continental Air

RB-17G Serials

7499th SS (USAFE)			
44-83282	44-8891	44-8846	44-8889
44-83378			
Strategic Air Command			
43-38651	44-83515	44-83726	44-83792
43-39271	44-83582	44-83763	44-83867
43-39487	44-83584	44-83765	44-84596
43-39489	44-83586	44-83766	44-85496
43-39498	44-83626	44-83767	44-85514
44-83365	44-83653	44-83778	44-8930
44-83514			

Rare aerial photo of a 338th SRS RB-17G. SAC used the RB-17G briefly for photomapping duties between Alaska and Greenland as part of Operation EARDRUM. The pressurized RB-29 provided a far better platform with greater range, altitude, and airspeed, so the RB-17G was quickly phased out. *George Smith photo, Author's Collection*

Opposite page, top and centre: Contrary to long-standing belief, the dark room in the photo compartment in Bomb Bay 1 of the RB-36 did *not* have the capability to develop film but was used simply to change the film in each camera. The camera operator monitored the number of frames exposed and changed canisters when needed. Water thermos, cup dispenser, and coffee maker were among the minimal crew comforts on 24-hour missions. *USAF via Dennis Jenkins*

Opposite page, bottom: Once attached to the trapeze, the RF-84K would be hoisted back into the modified GRB-36D bomb bay. The film would be replaced, guns rearmed, the aircraft refueled, and the pilot given hot coffee and a sandwich (not to mention a bathroom break). These were luxuries which pilots in TIP TOE and TOM TOM wingtip-mounted fighters would do without. Neither of these bomber defense programs saw service. *USAF photo via Dennis Jenkins*

Force and photomapping units in the Philippines and Bermuda. Although it could carry a variety of camera and electronic gear, as well as a large crew to operate the equipment, its slow cruise speed of 160 KIAS and service ceiling of 35,000 feet made it highly vulnerable in unescorted, single-aircraft reconnaissance operations near hostile territory.

Boeing B-29 Superfortress

During the Second World War the B-29 gained equal measures of fame and notoriety for its use against targets in Japan. Planners expected the four-engine bomber to duplicate what they saw as the high-altitude bombing success by B-17s over Europe. The results, however, were disappointing, and operations changed to low-altitude incendiary raids, notably over Tokyo in April 1945. In August 1945 B-29s dropped the atomic bombs on Hiroshima and Nagasaki. Less well known are the 138 photoreconnaissance B-29s that saw service during and after the war as F-13As. Eventually 84 of these were assigned to SAC and strategic reconnaissance duties as RB-29As in both the PHOTINT and ELINT roles. Communist forces shot down six of these. In addition, one B-29A (44-62290) was converted directly into a COMINT prototype, which led to a fully operational COMINT capability in RB-29s and RB-50s, as well as the C-130A-II.

The B-29 was pressurized which meant that crews were not exposed to the minus 40°C/F temperatures at altitude nor did they have to wear oxygen masks, as did their predecessors in the B-17 or B-24. This made it extremely well suited as a reconnaissance platform in terms of crew comfort and endurance, as well as a suitable operating environment for sensitive electronic listening gear.

High-altitude B-29 operations in the Pacific theater revealed that the jet stream would be a significant factor in any SAC long-range bombing operations, as well as other traditional weather considerations. It made sense to utilize modified B-29s in weather reconnaissance and atmospheric sampling roles. Initially these were standard B-29s with filters installed in place of the lower aft gun turret. These were eventually supplanted by 104 WB-29s which had all armament removed and a full suite of weather monitoring gear (including dropsondes) installed.

Strategic Air Command RB-29s

Year	Assigned	Year	Assigned
1946	12	1951	77
1947	12	1952	70
1948	24	1953	10
1949	84	1954	10
1950	84		

Convair B-36 Peacemaker

Design of the Consolidated-Vultee (later Convair) B-36 arose from the early 1941 requirement for a bomber capable of reaching Nazi Germany from the United States. The airplane first flew on 8 August 1946, however, well after the end of the war. Its intercontinental range and massive payload capacity made it well suited to serve as SAC's primary strategic bomber until the delivery of the first B-52 in 1955. The B-36's reconnaissance potential was immediately apparent, and 143 were configured for PHOTINT and ELINT.

RB-36 evolution is somewhat confusing. The 21 B-36As and the YB-36 were reinserted into the production line and literally remanufactured as RB-36Es concurrent with the production of 24 identical RB-36Ds. These had their four cavernous bomb bays converted for reconnaissance-related functions. The first bomb bay carried anywhere from 14 to 23 cameras and even a small curtained area to reload film canisters while airborne. The second bomb bay held 80 T-86 flash bombs for night photography. A 3,000-gallon fuel tank was located in the third bomb bay, and ECM and ELINT equipment was installed in the fourth.

Generic improvements to the basic B-36 airframe resulted in the B-36F, and Convair delivered 24 additional RB-36Fs, although their reconnaissance capability was identical to the earlier RB-36D. Similarly, SAC ordered 73 RB-36Hs along with procurement of the more advanced B-36H. Again, the RB-36H's reconnaissance suite was essentially the same as the RB-36D. Ultimately many of the RB-36s had the ELINT gear in the fourth bomb bay removed to make room for nuclear weapons, providing an armed reconnaissance capability.

Ten RB-36s were further converted into GRB-36Ds, designed to carry a single 'parasite' GRF-84K single-seat photoreconnaissance jet suspended on an extendable trapeze in the GRB-36D's bomb bay. Some 25 RF-84Ks were converted with a large retracting hook in front of the cockpit, and were otherwise distinguishable by their downward slanting horizontal stabilizers (required to allow the tail to fit inside the bomb bay). Known as FICON (for 'FIghter CONveyer'), the operational premise was that the GRB-36D would carry the parasite fighter to a point near Communist territory. The RF-84K pilot would climb into his jet which would then be lowered into the slipstream for engine start. The parasite would then speed off to take photos of targets in denied territory. Once the photos were taken, the RF-84K would return to the GRB-36D 'mothership,' hook back onto the trapeze, and be hoisted into the bomb bay. The RF-84K would then be refueled and prepared for another sortie. Initial flight testing began in 1952 and continued through the following year, entering service with the 99th SRW in 1955. It is not altogether clear if this was a fully operational capability. The hook-up procedure was complex and difficult enough for a highly experienced pilot during daylight, let alone at night. Still, there are consistent reports from GRB-36D crewmembers that there were at least some flights near or over the USSR or PRC with the RF-84Ks, but these may have been proving flights rather than examples of a mature program. Despite LeMay's personal interest in this project, he ultimately ended it after only 18 months, with the last flight taking place on 27 April 1956. The cancellation was largely due to pilot proficiency limits and the imminent operational debut of the U-2. (A similar cancelled program was the 1950 proposal to use drone RB-29s and JB-2 Doodlebugs – US-built German V-1 rockets – equipped with television cameras, directed or launched from RB-29 motherships.)[3]

GRB-36D Serials

44-92090	49-2687	49-2695	49-2701
44-92092	49-2692	49-2696	49-2702
44-92094	49-2694		

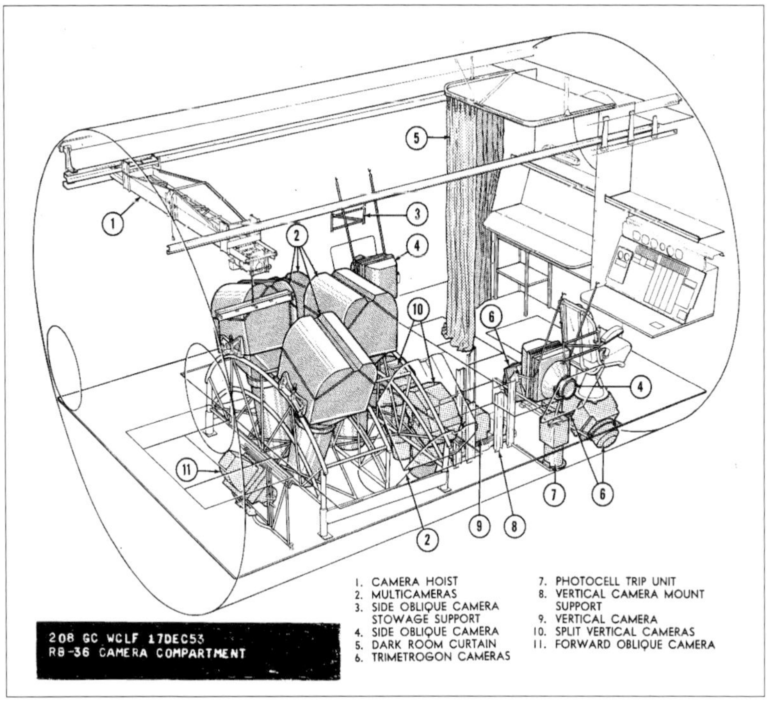

Four RB-45Cs lined up at the 'home 'drome' of the 91st SRW at Lockbourne AFB. One notable RB-45C pilot – Harold 'Hal' Austin – transferred to the RB-47Es at Lockbourne AFB and flew the 8 May 1954 overflight of Murmansk. Despite its small size, the RB-45C had a crew of four: pilot, copilot, navigator, and tail gunner. The vertical fin on the *front* of the drop tank adds to the overall odd appearance of the airplane. *NMUSAF via Geoff Hayes*

North American B-45 Tornado

At first glance the B-45 looks strikingly similar to the Luftwaffe Arado Ar 234C four-engine bomber developed at the end of the Second World War. Indeed, the B-45 was the first American effort to produce a multi-engine jet bomber, and its appearance was reflected in other straight-wing jets such as the Martin B-48. The US Air Force ordered nearly 200 B-45s, although post-war budget cuts reduced this to some 150 of all types, including converted RB-45Cs for reconnaissance. B-45Cs and RB-45Cs were the first jet bombers capable of aerial refueling. This provided the extended range and endurance which made the RB-45C well-suited to deep overflights of the USSR and PRC, most notably in RAF service during the JU JITSU missions. With the outbreak of the Korean War, SAC's RB-45Cs operated from Yokota AB while assigned to the FEAF. One was shot down while on an overflight of North Korea. The RB-45C was plagued by engine trouble and was vulnerable to MiG-15s, limiting its operational value. With the delivery of the YRB-47B and RB-47E, the RB-45C was withdrawn from service by the end of 1957.

Boeing B-47 Stratojet

The B-47 began life as a 1944 proposal for a twin-engine, high-speed piston-powered reconnaissance aircraft. Following its first flight on 17 December 1947, Boeing's medium jet bomber experienced protracted development problems which were not resolved until well after its operational debut with SAC in 1951. The B-47 was extremely fast – around 500 KIAS at 30,000 feet – which made it an ideal replacement for the lumbering RB-50s and RB-36s in SAC's reconnaissance fleet. The B-47 was also air refuelable, allowing for long-distance and long-duration missions, especially from forward operating locations in England and Japan.

The initial effort to use a B-47 in the reconnaissance role met with failure. B-47B 49-2645 had a camera pod installed in the bomb bay for an overflight mission of the Chukotskii Peninsula from Eielson AFB. While undergoing routine maintenance on 20 September 1951 the airplane caught fire on the ramp, destroying both the airplane and the camera pod. Mission 52 AFR-18 was finally flown on 15 October 1952. This time two B-47Bs – 50-0028 and 50-0073 – were assigned, and Lieutenant Colonel

RB-45C Serials

Serial	Comments	Serial	Comments	Serial	Comments
48-011		48-022		48-033	
48-012		48-023		48-034	
48-013		48-024	w/o 28 Apr 51	48-035	
48-014		48-025	w/o 5 Mar 52	48-036	
48-015	shot down 4 Dec 50	48-026	w/o 15 May 51	48-037	
48-016		48-027		48-038	
48-017	to JRB-45C	48-028	w/o 9 Feb 51	48-039	w/o 24 Dec 52
48-018	w/o 7 Jul 51	48-029		48-040	
48-019		48-030	w/o 7 May 51	48-041	
48-020	w/o 26 Mar 52	48-031		48-042	
48-021	w/o 7 Jun 51	48-032	w/o 4 Aug 51	48-043	

EB-47E(TT) 53-2315 sits alert at Incirlik AB. The nose-mounted TELINT fairings changed over the life of the program, ranging from Boeing's BLUE OCEAN slender 'boxes' to the Douglas-Tulsa dipole antenna seen here. New crewmembers often had their first deployment on the TELL TWOS before moving on to other variants. *John Kovacs*

Don Hillman flew the primary mission aircraft (believed to be 50-0073) with 50-0028 an airborne spare.

Pending delivery of the reconnaissance RB-47E, SAC directed that 91 B-47Bs receive the bomb bay camera pod and be redesignated as YRB-47Bs. Two of these (51-2054 and 51-2142) were further modified into RB-47B-I ROMAN Is with the installation of a 100-inch camera on the left side of the fuselage. The YRB-47B was indistinguishable externally from the B-47B other than the camera ports in the bomb bay. Modification delays meant that the YRB-47Bs, intended only as an interim reconnaissance platform, slowly entered service in 1953, almost concurrently with its replacement. The RB-47E became operational in 1954, with some 240 delivered. The following year

B-47 Reconnaissance Variants

MDS	Serial	Attrition	Comments
B-47B	49-2645	20 Sep 51	Burned during ground fuelling for USSR overflight mission
	50-0028	July 1952	306 SW airplane. OCAMA installed the photo pod and tail gun turret in DATE; believed to be the backup overflight aircraft on 15 Oct 52
	50-0073		Believed to be the primary overflight aircraft on 15 Oct 52
RB-47B-I	51-2054	17 Apr 55	Shot down by 2 MiG-15s near Petropavlovsk, USSR
	51-2142		
EB-47E(TT)	53-2315		
	53-2316		
	53-2320	03 Apr 65	Crashed during out-of-limits crosswind landing at Incirlik AB following an operational sortie
RB-47E (PETER PAN)	52-0701		
	52-0702	21 Oct 59	Crashed in Missouri, details unknown
	52-0703		
	52-0704		
	52-0705		
	52-0706		
	52-0708		
	52-0711		
	52-0712		
	52-0714		
	52-0715		
	52-0716		
	52-0721		
	52-0725		
ERB-47H	53-6245		
	53-6246		
	53-6249		

Boeing RB-47H/K Variants

MDS	Serial	Comments	Serial	Comments	Serial	Comments
RB-47H	53-4280		53-4292		53-4304	
	53-4281	Shot down 1 Jul 60	53-4293		53-4305	
	53-4282		53-4294		53-4306	
	53-4283	w/o 10 Feb 56	53-4295		53-4307	
	53-4284		53-4296		53-4308	
	53-4285		53-4297	w/o 12 Dec 62	53-4309	w/o 29 Apr 60
	53-4286		53-4298		53-6245	to ERB-47H
	53-4287		53-4299		53-6246	to ERB-47H
	53-4288		53-4300		53-6247	
	53-4289		53-4301		53-6248	w/o 27 Oct 62
	53-4290	DPRK 10 Apr 65	53-4302		53-6249	to ERB-47H
	53-4291		53-4303			
RB-47K	53-4265		53-4270		52-4275	
	53-4266		53-4271		52-4276	
	53-4267		53-4272		52-4277	
	53-4268		52-4273		52-4278	
	53-4269		52-4274		52-4279	w/o 27 Sep 62

Boeing began deliveries of 35 newly built SIGINT RB-47Hs. Three of these were further modified into ERB-47Hs. Three B-47Es were converted into the TELL TWO EB-47E(TT)s for the IRON WORKS ICBM TELINT collection program. In addition, Boeing built 15 RB-47Ks for SAC's weather missions. On 20 March 1963 Lockheed-Marietta began conversion of 34 B-47Es into WB-47Es as part of the BIG BLUE program to replace the structurally unsound WB-50s with Air Weather Service.[4]

Boeing B-50 Superfortress

Design improvements to the B-29 beginning in late 1944 led to the installation of better engines, the use of different metal alloys yielding stronger and lighter wings, a taller vertical stabilizer, and higher gross operating weights. Originally designated the XB-44, these modifications resulted in the proposed B-29D. The end of the war, however, eliminated the requirement for these airplanes. Boeing cleverly changed the B-29D designation to B-50A to preserve at least a modest order for 'new' airplanes.

Beginning in 1949 reconnaissance-configured RB-50s were produced in three primary variants. Boeing-Wichita initially delivered 28 B-50Bs as RB-50Bs. Of these, 14 were configured for photoreconnaissance and in April 1951 were redesignated RB-50Es, and the other 14 were equipped for photo mapping and were redesignated RB-50Fs, also in April 1951. The basic camera suites were interchangeable between the two variants. The RB-50Fs carried palletized SHORAN (SHOrt RANge) navigation gear for precise mapping and geodetic surveys. Between 1955 and 1956, Texas Engineering

RB-50D 49-307, seen on 3 October 1957 at RAF Bovingdon, was one of the three HALF TRACK airplanes configured for the ATRAN program. The intent was to map terrain over which the Matador missile would fly, using the images to verify its position en route to the target. Although this would become standard technology with cruise missiles in the 1970s and 1980s, the program was fraught with difficulties and technical setbacks and was canceled in short order. *Arthur Pearcy via Geoff Hayes*

Boeing RB-50 Variants

MDS	Serial	Comments	Serial	Comments
RB-50B	47-119	to RB-50E	47-134	to RB-50F
	47-120	to RB-50E	47-135	to RB-50E
	47-121	to RB-50F	47-137	to RB-50F
	47-122	to RB-50E	47-138	to RB-50F
	47-123	to RB-50E	47-139	to RB-50F
	47-124	to RB-50E	47-140	to RB-50F
	47-125	to RB-50E	47-141	to RB-50F
	47-126	to RB-50E	47-142	to RB-50F
	47-127	to RB-50E	47-144	to RB-50F
	47-128	to RB-50E	47-146	to RB-50F
	47-129	to RB-50E	47-158	to RB-50F
	47-130	to RB-50E	47-159	to RB-50F
	47-131	to RB-50E	47-160	to RB-50F
	47-132	to RB-50E	47-162	to RB-50F
RB-50D	48-107	ex B-50D, to KB-50D		
(HALF TRACK)	49-307	ex JB-50D, to TB-50D		
	49-312	ex EB-50D, to JTB-50D		
RB-50E	47-119	to ERB-50E	47-127	to RB-50E ARCP
	47-120	to RB-50E ARCP	47-128	
	47-122	MASDC 29 Apr 66	47-129	to RB-50E ARCP
	47-123	MASDC 25 Jan 65	47-130	
	47-124	to RB-50E ARCP	47-131	
	47-125	MASDC 29 Jul 64	47-132	
	47-126	to RB-50E ARCP	47-135	
RB-50E ARCP	47-120	to RB-50E-II		
(HAYSTACK)	47-124	to RB-50E-II		
(DREAM BOAT)	47-126	to RB-50E-II		
	47-127	to RB-50E-II		
	47-129	to RB-50E-II		
RB-50E-II	47-120	MASDC by Sep 61		
(HAYSTACK)	47-124			
(DREAM BOAT)	47-126	MASDC by Jul 61		
	47-127			
	47-129	MASDC by Jul 61		
RB-50F	47-121	MASDC 20 Jan 66	47-142	MASDC 29 Jan 65
	47-134	MASDC 1 Oct 64	47-144	MASDC 1 Oct 64
	47-137	MASDC 29 Mar 66	47-146	
	47-138	MASDC 12 Apr 66	47-158	
	47-139	MASDC 25 May 66	47-159	MASDC 11 May 66
	47-140	MASDC 19 Jul 64	47-160	MASDC 17 Apr 65
	47-141	MASDC 31 Mar 65	47-162	MASDC 29 Jul 65
RB-50G	47-133	to RB-50G ARCP	47-151	to RB-50G ARCP
	47-136	to RB-50G ARCP	47-152	
	47-143		47-153	
	47-145	shot down 29 Jul 53	47-154	
	47-147		47-156	to TB-50G
	47-148	to TB-50G	47-157	to RB-50G ARCP
	47-149	to RB-50G ARCP	47-161	
	47-150			
RB-50G ARCP	47-133	shot down 10 Sep 56		
(HAYSTACK)	47-136	to RB-50G-II		
(DREAM BOAT)	47-149	to RB-50G-II		
	47-151	to RB-50G-II		
	47-157	to RB-50G-II		
RB-50G-II	47-136			
(HAYSTACK)	47-149			
(DREAM BOAT)	47-151			
	47-157	MASDC by Aug 61		

and Manufacturing Company (TEMCO) modified five of the RB-50Es for 'armed SIGINT' as well as the Airborne COMINT Reconnaissance Program (ACRP) for use by USAFE and the Far Eastern Air Forces (FEAF) under the HAYSTACK program, where they were known operationally as DREAM BOAT ACRP aircraft. TEMCO further modified these in 1958 into RB-50E-IIs for PACAF with improved SIGINT gear and removed the armament. Boeing-Wichita also converted 14 B-50Bs into RB-50Gs for SIGINT collection, carrying five additional Ravens. As with the RB-50Es, beginning in 1955 TEMCO enhanced the SIGINT and COMINT suites on five of the RB-50Gs as part of HAYSTACK, and in 1958 further upgraded four of these (one had been shot down) into unarmed RB-50G-IIs. In addition, Goodyear modified three B-50Ds into RB-50Ds for the Automatic Terrain Recognition and Navigation (ATRAN) terrain mapping program for the Martin TM-61B Matador, an early cruise missile. Beginning in 1953 Lockheed Air Services converted 78 B-50Ds into WB-50D weather reconnaissance platforms to replace older WB-29s. The WB-50Ds had the inflight refueling system removed (additional bomb bay fuel tanks increased the unrefueled range) and had the distinctive E-1 air sampling scoop installed on the upper fuselage, as well as F-50 sampling pods on wing pylons.[5]

Martin B-57 Canberra

The Martin Company built the English Electric Canberra under license for the US Air Force as a light to medium twin-engine jet bomber. The British success in high-altitude Canberra operations prompted a similar effort by the Americans. Thirteen early production B-57As had the bomb bay removed and sealed, the navigator position eliminated, and the engines uprated for improved thrust and high-altitude operation. Known as the 'Featherweight' modification (similar to that applied to RB-36s), this reduced the overall weight of the RB-57A by 5,600 pounds and increased its ceiling by 5,000 feet to 50,000 feet. Ten of these were used for HEART THROB overflight missions. Another two were used in European peripheral sorties under the RB-57A-2 designation. One received a 240-inch focal length camera as part of the SHARP CUT program.

In addition to the HEART THROB RB-57A overflight missions, SAC operated a specialized unit of highly modified RB-57Ds. First developed under the BALD EAGLE program, Martin substantially extended the length and width of the wing, replaced the J65 engines with more powerful J57 engines, and considerably decreased the overall weight of the aircraft. As such, the RB-57D could reach altitudes of 65,000 feet and had an endurance of some seven hours. Known as BLACK KNIGHT RB-57Ds, the first flight took place on 5 November 1955. Eventually 20 were assigned beginning on 30 April 1956 to the 4025th SRS, 4080th SRW at Turner AFB, Georgia. The wing relocated to Laughlin AFB on 1 April 1957, some two months before the wing also acquired SAC's first U-2.[6]

There were three primary variants of the BLACK KNIGHT aircraft. The 'basic' RB-57D (sometimes referred to as RB-57D-0) had a crew of one pilot and was configured for PHOTINT. There were 13 of these, of which seven were capable of inflight refueling. A single RB-57D-1 was equipped with high-resolution radar and had a single pilot. Six RB-57D-2s were configured for ELINT and had a crew of two, a pilot and a systems operator. The first of the D-2s was delivered on 10 February 1957.

As with many new aircraft, especially those manufactured in small numbers with nonstandard design and equipment, the RB-57D expe-

The 7407th SS briefly operated two RB-57A-2s (52-1435 and -1437) from late 1957 through mid 1958, although in what operational capacity is unknown. After their service, these and several of the HEART THROB RB-57As were configured for test roles and electronic warfare evaluation platforms. NRB-57A 52-1435 was assigned to the Rome Air Development Center when photographed on 2 October 1965. *Thomas Cuddy via Stephen Miller*

rienced more than its share of problems. After being forced to land right after takeoff at a heavy gross weight, for example, the wing spar on RB-57D 53-3973 broke, although the airplane was repaired as an NRB-57D with ARDC in December 1959. The System 320 ECM suite on the RB-57D-2 was prone to failure, and occasionally was jammed by navigation equipment on board the airplane. The MM-4 autopilot used in all 20 of the RB-57Ds failed routinely, leading to frequent critical mission aborts. Between tanker mission aborts and unreliable air refueling couplings, the RB-57Ds did not consistently meet training requirements for air refueling proficiency, earning the wrath of the 'bean counters' at SAC Headquarters.

As the number of SAC U-2s assigned to the 4080th SRW increased, the BLACK KNIGHT RB-57Ds were reassigned to the 7407th SS at Rhein-Main AB, Germany, and SAC was not particularly sorry to see them go.[7] On 9 June 1959, five RB-57Ds and one RB-57D-2 left for Europe. A week later, three additional RB-57Ds departed Laughlin AFB for Rhein-Main AB. By 15 July 1959 the remaining four RB-57D-2s and two RB-57Ds were transferred to the 7407th SS.

Two of the BLACK KNIGHT RB-57Ds continued overflight missions while assigned to the Republic of China Air Force (RoCAF). On 3 July 1958 three RoCAF pilots began training with the 4080th SRW and two airplanes (53-3978 and 53-3981) identified for transfer under the DIAMOND LIL program. The program was renamed FAIR TREAT on 20 September 1958, and ten days later the aircraft (now renumbered 5643 and 5644, respectively) reached Taoyuan AB, Taiwan. There were 24 RoCAF overflights of the PRC in the BLACK KNIGHT airplanes. RB-57D 5644 was lost over Red China on 7 October 1959, becoming the first airplane to be shot down by a surface-to-air missile.[8]

RB-57A 52-1492, seen here on 16 October 1970 after preservation, was modified under the BIG SAFARI program with a 240-inch focal length camera for the SHARP CUT program. It served for some five years with the 7407th SS at Rhein-Main AB, which also operated the HEART THROB RB-57As, although it is uncertain if the SHARP CUT airplane conducted any overflights or was used exclusively for peripheral PHOTINT sorties. *Jack Morris via Stephen Miller*

USAFE and PACAF RB-57As

MDS	Serial	Unit	From	To	Comments
RB-57A	52-1427	6021st RS, Yokota AB	04 Sep 55	1957	RoCAF 5641; Converted to RB-57F 53-13300; to WB-57F
	52-1429	7407th SS, Rhein-Main AB	24 Aug 55	10 Aug 59	
	52-1431	6021st RS, Yokota AB	04 Sep 55	1957	RoCAF 5642; shot down by PRC J-5 18 Feb 58
	52-1432	6021st RS, Yokota AB	04 Sep 55	by 1957	Converted to RB-57F 63-13301; to WB-57F
	52-1433	6021st RS, Yokota AB	04 Sep 55	by 1957	Converted to RB-57F 63-13302; to WB-57F
	52-1439	7407th SS, Rhein-Main AB	24 Aug 55	29 Jul 59	
	52-1440	7407th SS, Rhein-Main AB	24 Aug 55	29 Jul 59	
	52-1442	7407th SS, Rhein-Main AB	24 Aug 55	29 Jul 59	
	52-1462	7407th SS, Rhein-Main AB	24 Aug 55	29 Jul 59	
	52-1464	7407th SS, Rhein-Main AB	24 Aug 55	10 Aug 59	
	52-1492	7407th SS, Rhein-Main AB	May 55	30 Nov 60	SHARP CUT
RB-57A-2	52-1435	7407th SS, Rhein-Main AB	Sep 57	Jun 58	
	52-1437	7407th SS, Rhein-Main AB	08 Aug 57	Jun 58	

SAC Black Knight RB-57Ds, 1956-1960

MDS	Serial	SAC Flyaway	IFR	Crew	Mission	Comments
RB-57D	53-3970	26 Aug 56	Yes	1	PHOTINT	To 7407th SS on 9 June 1959; to MASDC 16 Mar 64; converted to RB-57F 63-13502.
	53-3971	14 Jun 56	Yes	1	PHOTINT	To Robins AFB by December 1959, wfu.
	53-3972	01 Jun 56	Yes	1	PHOTINT	To 7407th SS on 9 June 1959; to MASDC 25 Feb 64; converted to RB-57F 63-13500
	53-3973	30 May 56	Yes	1	PHOTINT	To NRB-57D Dec 1959. Wright-Patterson AFB.
	53-3974	15 Jun 56	Yes	1	PHOTINT	To 7407th SS on 9 June 1959; to US 20 May 64; converted to RB-57F 63-13503.
	53-3975	30 Jun 56	Yes	1	PHOTINT	To 7407th SS on 9 June 1959; to US 25 Jan 64; converted to RB-57F 63-13501.
	53-3976	17 Jul 56	Yes	1	PHOTINT	To 7407th SS on 9 June 1959
	53-3977	23 Jun 56	No	1	PHOTINT	To 7407th SS on 16 June 1959. Later converted to WB-57D then EB-57D.
	53-3978	28 Nov 56	No	1	PHOTINT	To RoCAF on 3 July 1958 as 5643. Shot down by SA-2 on 7 October 1959.
	53-3979	28 Sep 56	No	1	PHOTINT	Crashed at Laughlin AFB 2 October 1958.
	53-3980	23 Jun 56	No	1	PHOTINT	To 7407th SS on 16 June 1959. Converted to EB-57D.
	53-3981	09 May 56	No	1	PHOTINT	To RoCAF on 3 July 1958 as 5644.
	53-3982	29 Apr 56	No	1	PHOTINT	To 7407th SS on 16 June 1959. Converted to EB-57D.
RB-57D-1	53-3963	02 Feb 57	Yes	1	Radar	To 7407th SS on 9 June 1959. To MASDC 16 Mar 64.
RB-57D-2	53-3964	16 Jan 57	Yes	2	ELINT	To JRB-57D by December 1959. wfu by June 1960; converted to EB-57D.
	53-3965	05 Apr 57	Yes	2	ELINT	wfu by June 1960; converted to EB-57D.
	53-3966	31 Oct 56	Yes	2	ELINT	To 7407th SS on 15 July 1959. Later converted to EB-57D.
	53-3967	10 Nov 56	Yes	2	ELINT	To 7407th SS on 15 July 1959. Later converted to EB-57D.
	53-3968	27 Nov 56	Yes	2	ELINT	To 7407th SS on 15 July 1959. Later converted to EB-57D.
	53-3969	11 Dec 56	Yes	2	ELINT	To 7407th SS on 15 July 1959. Later converted to EB-57D.

Douglas C-54 Skymaster

The Douglas DC-4 was designed as a long-range, high-capacity replacement for the Douglas DC-3. It could cruise at nearly 170 KIAS at 22,000 feet in pressurized comfort over 4,000nm. It also represented the shift away from converted bombers for strategic aerial reconnaissance. Along with the C-97 and C-135 (derived concurrently with the civilian Boeing 377 and 707, respectively), the C-54 provided an excellent platform for peripheral reconnaissance.

BIG SAFARI converted seven into specialized PHOTINT and ELINT platforms. Of these, three were part of the SARA JANE program. This involved the placement of 14 P2 cameras in the airplane's wings interspersed with the standard fuel tanks. These were sufficiently well hidden 'that even an X-ray of the wing would not have detected' the cameras or the doors.[9] At the

Douglas C-54 Reconnaissance Variants

Variant	MDS	Serial	From	To	Comments
HOT PEPPER	C-54D	42-17248	18 Mar 54	08 Dec 59	s/n changed to 43-17235
PRETTY GIRL	C-54D	42-72465	18 Jun 55	08 Oct 59	#2 aircraft
PRETTY GIRL	C-54D	42-72667	18 Mar 55	27 Aug 60	#1 aircraft; reportedly reserialed 42-72255 in 1955
LULU BELLE	C-54D	42-72684	23 Jun 55	05 May 60	Noted as '17206'
SARA JANE	C-54E	classified	26 May 55	05 Jan 61	#1 aircraft
SARA JANE	C-54E	classified	29 Jun 55	20 Nov 59	#2 aircraft
SARA JANE	C-54D	classified	20 Jul-55	23 Mar 60	#3 aircraft

Identifying the SARA JANE C-54s has been a daunting task. Even the BIG SAFARI records list the actual serial numbers of the C-54D and two C-54Es as classified. By inference and observation three plausible candidates have been identified, including VC-54D 42-72748, seen here in 1961 on final approach to Berlin Tempelhof. *Ralf Manteufel*

same time, the airplane received a VIP interior and external paint scheme. This masked its true covert mission of PHOTINT over sensitive areas while carrying ambassadors and diplomats to meetings. The actual serial numbers of these three airplanes were marked 'classified', even in the original BIG SAFARI records. Tail spotters noted VC-54D 42-72748, C-54E 44-9075, and C-54E 44-9123 operating in VIP configuration throughout Europe, but specific tie-ups or confirmation is purely speculative.

The 7405th SS also operated the HOT PEPPER C-54D 42-17248 primarily in the PHOTINT role. As with the SARA JANE aircraft, the cameras on board HOT PEPPER were obscured by immaculately machined doors that defied visual detection when on the ground. In addition to its Berlin corridor missions, it flew peripheral sorties throughout Europe. Beginning in 1957 it acquired an ELINT capability. The airplane was 'recycled' in 1962, but given a new lease on life as the HILO HATTIE PHOTINT airplane, although with the new serial number 43-17235 for use in Southeast Asia. C-54D 42-72684 LULU BELLE was also configured for PHOTINT missions, including IR night photography. It has been photographed '17206'.

ELINT missions fell to the two PRETTY GIRL C-54Ds assigned to the 7499th SS. Its crew included seven Ravens and an in-flight maintenance technician, as well as the regular crew of two pilots, two navigators, and crew chief. According to one source, these airplanes never flew the Berlin corridor missions, and were instead used exclusively for peripheral sorties.[10] Sometime in 1955 the first PRETTY GIRL C-54D (42-72667) was reportedly given the new serial 42-72255, but the BIG SAFARI records fail to show this, suggesting that it was a temporary assignment, if at all (that serial was assigned to a C-54D that by then was in commercial cargo service).

Boeing C-97 Stratocruiser

The successful testing during 1951 of the 'Big Bertha' 240-inch focal length camera in an RB-36 led to the acquisition of a suitable cargo aircraft to undertake operational evaluation and full-scale PHOTINT missions. Boeing began the PIE FACE modification using one of its YC-97s

PIE FACE C-97A 49-2592 prepares to depart Berlin Tempelhof AP for its return flight to Rhein-Main AB. After the end of the Cold War, a crew member chanced to meet a Soviet MiG pilot who asked him which C-97s he flew, the 'camera or the listening version.' As with so many reconnaissance missions, both sides knew and it was only the public who was kept in the dark. *Ralf Manteufel*

(serial unknown, but possibly 45-59593). Boeing's handling and security proved unsatisfactory so General Dynamics took over the program at its Convair plant in Ft Worth, TX. Following final conversion, the airplane undertook six weeks of operational testing in Europe. The 'Big Bertha' camera proved highly successful, but the YC-97 with its early engines lacked the altitude and flight capability desired. Consequently, General Dynamics removed the camera from the YC-97 and installed it in C-97A 49-2592.

The new combination proved effective and between July and December 1953 the airplane flew 13 missions. The Soviets limited flights through the Berlin Corridors to a maximum altitude of 10,000 feet, so the PIE FACE could not operate at its optimal altitude of 32,000 feet. Missions north of Norway and over Greece, Turkey, and Iran, as well as border missions 'along the fence' separating Germany demonstrated the system's full potential. The 7499th SS operated the airplane (reportedly sporting the bogus serial 49-2612 on occasion) until 1962, when it returned to the US for missions associated with the Cuban Missile Crisis. It was scrapped in 1965 and the camera displayed at the NMUSAF.

Lockheed C-130 Hercules

The ubiquitous C-130's large cargo compartment made it an excellent choice to serve in a COMINT collection role. TEMCO modified 10 C-130As into SUN VALLEY I ACRP platforms to replace the elderly RB-50E-IIs and RB-50G-IIs. Following conversion the airplanes were redesignated as C-130A-IIs. The SUN VALLEY I airplanes (later known as RIVET VICTOR I) were a substantial improvement over the DREAM BOAT ACRP RB-50s in terms of equipment capability, number of linguists, and cabin comfort. One of these – 56-0528 – accidentally entered Soviet airspace over Armenia and was shot down with the loss of all crewmembers. A single SUN VALLEY I airplane (56-0535) served 'to evaluate various system developments under realistic operating conditions,'

Sun Valley I C-130A-II Serials

Serial	Comments
56-0484	to AMARC as CF063
56-0525	
56-0528	Shot down 5 Sep 58
56-0530	to AMARC as CF064
56-0534	to AMARC as CF060
56-0535	STRAWBRIDGE to AMARC as CF059
56-0537	
56-0538	w/o 17 Jun 02
56-0540	w/o 13 Aug 94
56-0541	to AMARC as CF058

Sun Valley II C-130B-II Serials

Serial	Comments
59-1524	to Bolivian AF as TAM66
59-1525	to AMARC as CF099
59-1526	to Argentine AF TC-57
59-1527	to Turkish AF as 91527 then Romanian AF as 5927
59-1528	to Tunisian AF as TS-MTG
59-1529	to AMARC as CF108
59-1530	To Romanian AF as 5930
59-1531	
59-1532	To Bolivian AF as TAM 67 w/o 31 Dec 94
59-1533	To Tunisian AF as TS-MTD
59-1535	To Columbia AF as 1011
59-1537	To AMARC as CF144, to Bangladesh as S3-AGB

A rather incongruous afterlife as 'trash haulers' for the SUN VALLEY-I C-130A-IIs followed their clandestine COMINT missions 'along the fence' in Europe. Most retired to AMARC, where several were withdrawn for fire-fighting duties (with two lost in crashes). West Virginia ANG C-130A 56-0540, seen at Martinsburg AP on 13 August 1972, met a similar fate when it crashed on 13 August 1994. *Stephen Miller*

In a fitting tribute, BIG SAFARI refurbished C-130A 57-0453 to appear exactly like SUN VALLEY-I C-130A-II 56-0528 on its final flight on 2 September 1958. The memorial resides in the National Vigilance Park adjacent to NSA Headquarters in Ft Meade, Maryland, and is open to the public. *Stephen Miller*

and was known as the STRAWBRIDGE aircraft.[11] Further technical enhancements in the reconnaissance suite coupled with airframe improvements associated with the C-130B resulted in the 1960 SUN VALLEY II modification program, with 11 C-130B-IIs converted.

After retirement from the US Air Force, the SUN VALLEY I airplanes were stored in AMARC, where they were purchased (although not all were actually taken up) for service as airborne fire fighters, with two lost in crashes. The C-130B-II SUN VALLEY II airplanes were retrofitted as C-130Bs, and most were transferred to foreign air forces in the cargo role.

Republic F-84F Thunderflash

Efforts by Republic to improve the performance of its straight-wing F-84 Thunderjet to a level comparable to the North American F-86 resulted in the swept-wing F-84F Thunderflash. Some 2,700 were eventually built, with almost half delivered to NATO air forces. The overall improvements were sufficient to merit the production of 715 reconnaissance versions, although to carry cameras the RF-84F had its engine intakes relocated to the wing roots, resulting in a slight loss of thrust. As part of the FICON parasite program, 25 RF-84Fs had a large retractable hook installed in the top of the forward fuselage to attach to the extendable trapeze in the GRB-36D. In order to provide clearance for the tailplane while mated to the GRB-36D, the horizontal stabilizers on the RF-84F were slanted downward with a 23-degree anhedral. These airplanes were redesignated as RF-84Ks, and were assigned to the 91st SRS at Larson AFB, Washington. Cancellation of the FICON program in 1956 resulted in these airplanes returning to service with other RF-84F units.

RF-84K Serials

52-7254	52-7261	52-7268	52-7275
52-7255	52-7262	52-7269	52-7276
52-7256	52-7263	52-7270	52-7277
52-7257	52 7264	52-7271	52-7278
52-7258	52-7265	52-7272	
52-7259	52-7266	52-7273	
52-7260	52-7267	52-7274	

Looking a bit nervous, this test pilot shows the narrow passage between the stowed parasite F-84 (in this case the prototype) and the GRB-36D crew compartment. The hook is visible at extreme right. Despite the hazards of coupling two airplanes in flight, there were no losses of airplanes or pilots during the years the program was in development or saw operational service. *USAF Photo, Author's Collection*

The RF-86F proved to be an effective tactical reconnaissance airplane given its speed and maneuverability against the MiG-15 *Fagot*. It was equally effective in making short overflights of the USSR and PRC, although the deployment of the MiG-17 *Fresco* spelled the end of the Sabre's suitability for overflights. ASHTRAY RF-86F 52-4529, piloted by 1LT Charlie Witmer, is seen here with Mickey Mouse nose art. *Charlie Witmer via Doug Gordon*

RF-86 Overflight Aircraft

MDS	Serial	Configuration	Comments
RF-86A	48-187	HONEYBUCKET / ASHTRAY	w/o 21 Dec 52
	48-195	ASHTRAY	
	48-196	ASHTRAY	
	48-217	HONEYBUCKET / ASHTRAY	w/o 27 Jun 52
	48-246	ASHTRAY	w/o 5 Sep 52
	48-257	ASHTRAY	
RF-86F	52-4330	ASHTRAY	
	52-4357	ASHTRAY	
	52-4377	HAYMAKER	
	52-4379	HAYMAKER	
	52-4492	HAYMAKER	
	52-4510	HAYMAKER	
	52-4518	ASHTRAY	w/o 3 Jun 53
	52-4522	HAYMAKER	
	52-4523	HAYMAKER	
	52-4528	ASHTRAY	
	52-4529	ASHTRAY	
	52-4585	HAYMAKER	
	52-4767	HAYMAKER	
	52-4800	HAYMAKER	
	52-4808	HAYMAKER	
	52-4823	HAYMAKER	
	52-4857	HAYMAKER	
	52-4864	HAYMAKER	

SLICK CHICK RF-100A

Serial	Unit	Comments
53-1545	7407th SS, Det 1, Bitburg AB	
53-1546	6021st RS, Yokota AB	To RoCAF Dec 58
53-1547	6021st RS, Yokota AB	To RoCAF Dec 58
53-1548	6021st RS, Yokota AB	Crashed June 57
53-1551	7407th SS, Det 1, Bitburg AB	Crashed 1 Oct 56
53-1554	7407th SS, Det 1, Bitburg AB	To RoCAF Dec 58

CAROL ANN CT-29A Serials

49-1910	49-1912	49-1917	49-1933

North American F-86 Sabre

The F-86 Sabre became famous for its outstanding kill record against the MiG-15 during the Korean War. The Sabre's speed (520 KIAS at 35,000 feet) also made it an ideal replacement for the Lockheed RF-80 (350 KIAS at 35,000 feet) in the tactical photoreconnaissance role. With a proven track record of eluding MiGs and its high performance, the RF-86 was an excellent choice to use for ongoing combat reconnaissance as well as overflights of the Soviet Union and Red China during and after the war. At least six RF-86As were converted in the field for the HONEYBUCKET and ASHTRAY programs. North American delivered at least 18 RF-86Fs for ASHTRAY and HAYMAKER missions. Following USAF service the airplanes flew with both the Taiwanese and Korean air forces.

North American F-100 Super Sabre

During 1954 the US Air Force asked North American to modify six F-100As into high-altitude, high-speed reconnaissance aircraft for SLICK CHICK overflights of Eastern Europe and the People's Republic of China. This proved a significant technical challenge as the F-100 had a large central air intake, making the placement of cameras particularly problematic. Ultimately five cameras – three trimetrogon and two side-oblique – were installed. Missions were flown at Mach 1 and 50,000 feet, which necessitated external drop tanks, although the use of four drop tanks created yaw and center-of-gravity problems, and was not liked by the pilots. Operations began in 1955, but the success of the CIA U-2 program spelled the end of the SLICK CHICK missions, and the surviving airplanes were transferred to the RoCAF.

Convair T-29

Convair built its CV-240 airliner as a replacement for the ubiquitous Douglas DC-3. The design was well suited for military transport as well. Beginning in 1950 the USAF and USN acquired some 350 T-29s for navigator training. Not surprisingly, the airplane's bland, inconspicuous appearance made it an excellent choice for the peripheral reconnaissance role, especially with the 'Berlin for Lunch Bunch'. Between March 1958 and March 1959, BIG SAFARI modified four airplanes into CT-29As as part of the CAROL ANN program. These were equipped with a secret camera compartment in the aft cabin that could be configured with standard high-resolution cameras, trimetrogon cameras, and infrared cameras. A US Army observer would fly on each mission to identify

Above and right: The two ventral camera fairings are easily seen on the SLICK CHICK RF-100As, but the side fairing containing the flush-mounted camera door blends in to the fuselage making it difficult to see. Posing in front of 53-1445 are pilots (l to r) Maj Cecil Rigsby, Maj Bert A Dowdy, Capt Edgar H Hill and CWO, W-2 Edward Brosche. *Cecil Rigsby via Doug Gordon*

Left and below: Placement of the two K-38 split-vertical cameras in the SLICK CHICK RF-100A proved a difficult engineering assignment due to the engine intake running through the center of the fuselage and the position of the cockpit. Instead of pointing downward the cameras point forward and use a mirror to angle the image into the cameras. With the camera bay closed, the result is a clean opening. *North American Aviation photo via Cecil Rigsby via Doug Gordon*

areas of interest. The navigator had a covert control panel which operated the cameras. Flush doors covered the camera openings rendering them indiscernible to observers when on the ground. The missions added to their 'innocent' role as courier/cargo flights by carrying materiel and passengers who were oblivious to the actual PHOTINT nature of their flight.

The airplanes operated with the 7405th SS at Rhein-Main AB beginning in 1959. The program was renamed OCEAN GEM, and operations continued through 1968. BIG SAFARI further modified the three surviving airplanes (49-1917 crashed on 13 February 1967) as part of RIVET KITE for the SENTINEL STRING COMINT mission and they were reassigned to operations in Korea.

By the time this PB4Y-2 visited Springfield, IL, in 1956, the Privateer had been replaced as the US Navy's primary ELINT platform. Following the first US reconnaissance loss to Soviet interceptors (PB4Y-2 BuNO 59645) on 8 April 1950, President Truman said that arming US platforms 'made good sense.'

The P4M-1Q Mercator was an odd egg. Unlike the P2V or B-36 which had external jet engines added, the Mercator was designed with both props and internal jets. It was well liked by its crews and proved an effective ELINT and COMINT platform. *Author's Collection*

US Navy (USN)

PB4Y-2 Privateer

Convair PB4Y-2s were naval patrol/bomber variants of the famous B-24 Liberator. During the war some of these were converted into early SIGINT platforms, a role which they continued after the Japanese surrender in September 1945. The first US strategic reconnaissance aircraft shot down by the Soviets was PB4Y-2 BuNO 59645 on 8 April 1950.

PBM-5 Mariner

US Navy strategic reconnaissance airplanes during the early Cold War years were all derived from maritime patrol aircraft. The Martin PBM-5 Mariner twin-engine flying boat entered service prior to World War, and saw combat in transport and anti-submarine warfare (ASW) duties. Following the war it continued patrol missions, especially in the Pacific and Sea of Japan.

P2V Neptune

Near the end of World War Two, Lockheed and Martin competed for a US Navy contract to produce a fleet of long-range land-based maritime patrol aircraft. Lockheed's twin-engine P2V Neptune won the competition. Beginning with the P2V-5F, Neptunes were configured with two additional jet engines to increase performance against MiGs. Communist forces claimed five US Navy P2Vs conducting reconnaissance missions, and attacked a handful of others.

P4M-1Q Mercators

MDS	BuNO	Comments
P4M-1Q	121451	
	121452	Crashed on 8 Mar 51 during flight tests; not a P4M-1Q.
	121453	
	121454	
	122207	
	122208	
	122209	Attacked by DPRK MiG-17s on 16 Jun 59; crash landed in Japan.
	124362	Shot down by PRC MiG on 22 Aug 56 near Wenchow, China.
	124363	
	124364	
	124365	Crashed on 16 Jan 60 near Incirlik AB, Turkey, possibly from Soviet fighter activity.
	124366	
	124367	
	124368	
	124369	Attacked near Shanghai, 23 Apr 53.
	124370	
	124371	Ditched on 7 Feb 52 north of Cyprus due to fuel starvation after engine failure, allegedly after evading MiGs over the Black Sea.
	124372	w/o 27 Jul 58
	124373	Crashed on 6 Jan 58 in Virginia.

P4M-1Q

Although Martin lost the patrol contract to Lockheed, the US Navy procured 19 P4M-1 Mercators for high-speed mine laying. As with later P2V variants, all P4M-1s were equipped with two piston- and two jet-powered engines. This speed advantage proved ideal, and the US Navy opted to replace its SIGINT Convair PB4Y-2s with the 18 remaining Mercators. Redesignated as P4M-1Qs, they operated in both the Pacific and European theaters, primarily in the Black Sea. Soviet, Red Chinese, and North Korean forces attacked at least five Mercators. Two are known to have been shot down, and two others were lost in incidents that have been attributed to hostile action.[12]

Central Intelligence Agency (CIA)

Lockheed RB-69A

Lockheed's 'Skunk Works' converted seven P2Vs into RB-69s for CIA covert penetration missions. They were all eventually transferred to the Taiwan. Red Chinese MiGs and AAA shot down three of these, and two crashed or disappeared. The remaining two resumed ASW duties with the US Navy.

RB-69A Serials

MDS	Serial	BuNO	Comments
RB-69A	54-4037	135612	to RoCAF; Shot down by PRC MiG-17 on 11 Jan 64
	54-4038	140438	to RoCAF; Disappeared on 8 Jan 62
	54-4039	140440	to RoCAF; Shot down by PRC AAA on 6 Nov 61
	54-4040	140442	to RoCAF; Crashed on 25 Mar 60
	54-4041	141233	to RoCAF; Shot down by PRC MiG-17 on 19 Jun 63
	54-4042	141241	to RoCAF; Returned to use as SP-2H
	54-4043	141244	to RoCAF; Returned to use as SP-2H

Lockheed U-2

No aircraft is more intimately associated with Cold War strategic reconnaissance than the U-2. The product of famous designer Clarence 'Kelly' Johnson, its rapid development, technological advances, and clandestine operations are the stuff of aviation legend. Bureaucratic infighting between the CIA and SAC over ownership led to parallel programs, with the CIA responsible for overflights and SAC responsible for peripheral missions and aerial sampling.

Lockheed converted seven US Navy P2Vs into USAF RB-69As for covert operations seconded to CIA crews of 'displaced' nationals under the OSTIARY and CHERRY programs in Europe and Taiwan. Surprisingly, this RB-69 was on display – perhaps accidentally – at an airshow as NAS Westminster, PA. *Stephen Miller*

Early in their operational career U-2s were not black, either with the CIA or SAC. In this case, SAC U-2A 56-6700 was overall natural metal. They eventually acquired the overall black color and the mystique that has made the U 2 an icon of Cold War aerial reconnaissance. *Kurt Finger*

Initial CIA/SAC Lockheed U-2 Disposition

MDS	USAF Serial	CIA Article	W/O	Comments
U-2A		341	04 Oct 57	Crashed on Nevada Test Range
U-2A	56-6675	342	25 Feb 66	U-2F prototype; lost during a/r test
U-2A	56-6676	343	27 Oct 62	Shot down over Cuba
U-2A	56-6677	344	01 Mar 62	Lost during a/r training
U-2A	56-6678	345	15 May 56	Crashed at Groom Lake
U-2A	56-6679	346	17 Sep 56	Crashed in West Germany
U-2A	56-6680	347		1st O/F USSR; display at Udvar-Hazy
U-2A	56-6681	348		to NASA; display at Ames
U-2A	56-6682	349		to NASA; display at Robins
U-2A	56-6683	350	20 Nov 63	Crashed Gulf of Mexico
U-2A	56-6684	351	19 Mar 61	Crashed at Taoyuan, Taiwan
U-2A	56-6685	352	22 Oct 65	Crashed on training flight, Taiwan
U-2A	56-6686	353	14 Sep 61	Crashed at Edwards AFB
U-2A	56-6687	354	31 Aug 56	Crashed at Groom Lake
U-2A	56-6688	355	01 Nov 63	Shot down by PLAAF SA-2
U-2A	56-6689	356	22 Mar 64	Crashed in Taiwan Straits
U-2A	56-6690	357	19 Dec 56	Crashed in Arizona; see also Article 390
U-2A	56-6691	358	10 Jan 65	Shot down by PLAAF SA-2
U-2A	56-6692	359		Display at Imperial War Museum, Duxford
U-2A	56-6693	360	01 May 60	Last O/F USSR; shot down by SA-2
U-2A	56-6694	361	26 Sep 57	1st SAC U-2; crashed on maintenance test
U-2A	56-6695	362	07 Jul 64	Shot down by PLAAF SA-2
U-2A	56-6696	363	22 Mar 66	Crashed near Tucson, RoCAF pilot training
U-2A	56-6697	364	06 Aug 58	Crashed at Laughlin AFB
U-2A	56-6698	365	09 Jul 58	Crashed in New Mexico
U-2A	56-6699	366	28 Jun 57	Crashed in New Mexico
U-2A	56-6700	367	29 May 75	Crashed in West Germany
U-2A	56-6701	368		Display at SAC Museum
U-2A	56-6702	369	28 Jun 57	Crashed at Del Rio, TX
U-2A	56-6703	370	18 Sep 64	Crashed at Davis-Monthan AFB
U-2A	56-6704	371	28 Nov 57	Crashed at Laughlin AFB
U-2A-1	56-6705	372	17 Feb 66	Prototype HASP; crashed Taichung, Taiwan
U-2A	56-6706	373	08 Feb 67	Shot down by PLAAF SA-2
U-2A	56-6707	374		Display at Laughlin AFB
U-2A	56-6708	375	01 Jul 67	Crashed near Barksdale AFB
U-2A	56-6709	376	02 Jan 62	Crashed in Mississippi
U-2A	56-6710	377	11 Sep 58	Crashed at Edwards AFB
U-2A	56-6711	378	09 Sep 62	Shot down by PLAAF SA-2
U-2A	56-6712	379	19 Dec 64	Crashed near Tucson, RoCAF pilot training
U-2A	56-6713	380	08 Jul 58	Crashed in Texas; RAF pilot in training
U-2A-1	56-6714	381	31 Jan 80	Crashed at Beale AFB; display at Beale AFB
U-2A-1	56-6715	382	26 Apr 65	Crashed at Edwards AFB
U-2A-1	56-6716	383		Display at Davis-Monthan AFB
U-2A-1	56-6717	384	21 Jun 66	Crashed off Taiwan
U-2A-1	56-6718	385	05 Jan 69	Crashed in Yellow Sea
U-2A	56-6719	386	28 Jul 66	Crashed in Bolivia
U-2A	56-6720	387	14 Jul 60	Crashed in Texas
U-2A	56-6721	388		Display at Palmdale, CA
U-2A	56-6722	389		Display at Air Force Museum,
U-2A	56-6690	390	08 Oct 66	Duplicate serial Article 357; crashed Vietnam
U-2A	56-6951	391	19 Oct 66	Crashed at Davis-Monthan AFB
U-2A	56-6952	392	18 Nov 71	Crashed at Davis-Monthan AFB
U-2A	56-6953	393		Display Cold War Museum, Bodø, Norway
U-2A	56-6954	394	31 May 68	Crashed near Tucson
U-2A	56-6955	395	14 Aug 64	Crashed near Boise, ID; RoCAF pilot training

Appendix IV

Major Strategic Reconnaissance and Related Programs 1945-1960

Aquatone	CIA U-2 program
ASHTRAY	RF-86A/F PHOTINT program
BALD EAGLE	Initial RB-57D conversion program
BIG BLUE	Boeing conversion of B-47Es to WB-47Es
BIG SAFARI	USAF special conversion program
BIOGRAPH	RB-29 reconnaissance of the Baltic
Black Beauty	Alleged CIA RB-47C overflight capability
BLACK KNIGHT	SAC RB-57D program
BLUE NOSE	SAC RB-36 PHOTINT missions
BLUE OCEAN	Initial Boeing TELL TWO modification program
BLUE SKY	RC-47 COMINT missions in Korea
BONUS BABY	Proof of concept for B-47 COMINT capability
BORDER TOWN	USAFE RB-57D peripheral ELINT missions
BOX TOP	RB-47H automated COMINT capability
CAROL ANN	USAFE CT-29A PHOTINT program (later OCEAN GEM)
CASEY JONES	USAFE RB-17G ELINT and PHOTINT missions
CENTERING	LRDP peripheral sampling mission
Chalice	CIA/RAF U-2 cover name
CHERRY	CIA expatriate missions
COBRA BALL	SAC RC-135S TELINT/MASINT aircraft
COMBAT SENT	SAC RC-135U special electronic reconnaissance aircraft
CONGO MAIDEN	SAC U-2 peripheral PHOTINT missions
CONSTANT PHOENIX	USAF aerial sampling program
Corona	First US satellite recon program
COTTONSEED	LRDP peripheral sampling mission
CROWFLIGHT	SAC U-2 HASP peripheral sampling missions
DESERT ROCK	US conventional maneuvers following an atomic blast
DIAMOND LIL	RoCAF RB-57D training (renamed FAIR TREAT)
DINAH LEE	USAFE RB-57D PHOTINT program
DREAM BOAT	RB-50F and RB-50G ACRP program
DUALISM	1948 USAF leadership conference
EARDRUM	SAC RB-17G mapping of Alaska-Canada-Greenland
FAIR TREAT	RoCAF RB-57D training (previously DIAMOND LIL)
Featherweight	USAF weight reduction/high altitude conversion
First Lightning	First Soviet atomic detonation
FLEETWOOD	Early US war plan
FLOODLIGHT	RB-29 Alaska/Siberia PHOTINT (previously Project 5)
FORTUNE FINDER	SAC U-2 peripheral sampling missions
FOX HUNT	RoCAF ELINT peripheral and overflights of PRC
FROLIC	Early US war plan
GENETRIX	USAF balloon reconnaissance
GIANT FISH	SAC B-52H sampling program (previously SEA FISH)
GOPHER	USAF balloon reconnaissance
GRAND SLAM	CIA U-2 overflight by Frank Powers on 1 May 1960
Grandad	SAC B-52B/F SEA FISH sampling tracks
GRANDSON	USAF balloon reconnaissance
GRAYBACK	USAF balloon reconnaissance
HALF TRACK	RB-50D ATRAN mission
HALFMOON	Early US war plan
HARD TACK	High altitude sampling missions for US nuclear test
HAYMAKER	RF-86F PHOTINT missions
HAYSTACK	RB-50 ACRP COMINT modification program
HEART THROB	USAF RB-57A overflight program
HOME RUN	SAC 1956 RB-47 overflights of USSR
HONEYBUCKET	RF-86A PHOTINT missions
HOT PEPPER	USAFE C-54 PHOTINT program
IRON WORKS	CIA-sponsored program to collect ICBM data
JACK POT	US recovery plan for downed SAC bomber crews

JEFFERSON	Beacon Hill Group (later WINCHESTER)
JU JITSU	RAF RB-45C overflight missions
LEOPARD	RB-29 PHOTINT of Chukotskii Peninsula
LIDA ROSE	CIA PHOTINT conversion of Air Force One VC-137B
LINCOLN	USAF/MIT technology development program
LOW CARD	Proposed U-2 ICBM launch detection program
LULU BELLE	USAFE C-54D PHOTINT platform
MILL TOWN	CIA U-2 overflights of Southeast Asia
MONTICELLO	SAC RB-47E reconnaissance program
OCEAN GEM	CT-29A PHOTINT program (previously CAROL ANN)
OFFTACKLE	Early US war plan
Open Skies	Proposed overt US-USSR aerial reconnaissance program
Operation 21	Reported RB-36 overflight mission
Operation BARBAROSSA	Nazi German invasion of the Soviet Union
Operation HAIK	CIA support for Indonesian rebels
Operation KADESH	1956 Israeli invasion of Sinai
Operation MUSKETEER	Franco-British invasion of the Suez Canal
Operation OVERLORD	1944 Allied invasion of Normandy
Operation PORT BOW	SAC response to the seizure of the USS *Pueblo*
Operation ROBIN HOOD	CIA U-2 deployment to photograph Indonesia
Operation VITTLES	Aerial resupply of Berlin during 1948 blockade
OSTIARY	CIA expatriate missions
OVERCALLS	RB-29 operation from Ladd Field
OVERSALT	RB-29 operation from Ladd Field
OXCART	CIA A-12 program
PAPER DOLL	USAFE RB-57D PHOTINT program
PEGASUS	USN F2H-P overflights of Eastern Europe
PETER PAN	RB-47E configured with APQ-56 SLAR
PIE FACE	Boeing C-97A with 240-inch Boston Camera
PINCHER	Early US war plan
PRETTY GIRL	USAFE C-54D ELINT program
Project 5	RB-29 Alaska/Siberia PHOTINT (later FLOODLIGHT)
Project 23	RB-29 ELINT border incursion of Siberia
Project CIRCUS	RoCAF support for Tibetan rebels
Project CONTROL	Proposed SAC armed recon overflights of the USSR
Project No.52 AFR-18	B-47B overflight of Siberia
Project POLARIS	RB-29 PHOTINT search for Arctic islands
Project WRINGER	Interrogation of German and Japanese POWs from USSR
REDSKIN	Debriefing of Western travellers after USSR visits
REDSOX	Deployment of US moles into the USSR
RICKRACK	RB-29 search for Siberian bomber bases
RIVET AMBER	SAC LISA ANN RC-135E side-looking radar aircraft
RIVET DIGGER	US NNTRP NC-135A
ROBIN	Unverified 1953 RAF Canberra overflight of Kapustin Yar by ROBIN peripheral aircraft
ROSE BOWL	RC-47 COMINT missions in Korea
ROUNDOUT	SAC PHOTINT of Western Europe and North Africa
SAND SHARK	SAC RB-57D peripheral ELINT missions from Alaska
SARA JANE	Clandestine USAFE C-54 PHOTINT program
SEA FISH	B-36 and B-52 aerial sampling mission, later GIANT FISH
SEA LION	RB-57D operational deployment to Yokota AB
SEASHORE	SAC RB-47 peripheral PHOTINT mission
SHAKEDOWN	Early US war plan
SHARP CUT	USAFE RB-57A PHOTINT program with 240-inch camera
SILVER KING	RB-47H configuration
SILVERPLATE	B-29 configured to carry an atomic bomb
SKYSCRAPER	JKC-135A ICBM launch and re-entry detection program
SLICK CHICK	RF-100A overflight missions
SNOWBALL	Soviet conventional maneuvers following an atomic blast
SOLARIUM	Analysis of US national policy under Eisenhower
SOUTH GATE	CIA U-2 overflights of Southeast Asia
SQUINT	HOT PEPPER operational mission
STAGE SHOW	RoCAF RB-57D overflights of PRC
STONEWORK	RB-29 operation from Ladd Field
STRAWBRIDGE	SUN VALLEY development aircraft
SUN VALLEY I	USAF COMINT C-130A-IIs
SUN VALLEY II	USAF COMINT C-130B-IIs
TELL TWO	SAC EB-47E(TT) TELINT mission
TOY SOLDIER	SAC U-2 peripheral sampling missions
TREASURE ISLAND	Library of Congress search for information on the USSR
TROJAN	Early US war plan
ULCER GULCH	C-97 COMINT capability
VULTURE	SAC support plan for French at Dien Bien Phu
WET STONE	USAFE RB-66C reconnaissance missions
WHITE WOLF	JCS advisory warning program
WILD CHERRY	CIA RB-69 expatriate missions
WINCHESTER	Beacon Hill Group (previously JEFFERSON)

End Notes

Preface

1 As part of the 1987 US-USSR Intermediate Nuclear Force (INF) treaty, the COBRA BALL was a key part of the verification process for Soviet compliance in destroying their intermediate-range and short-range ballistic missiles. Section III of the elimination protocol allowed missiles to be destroyed by launching them from known test facilities to known impact sites, with unimpeded observation by any national technical means. This process was referred to as 'shoot to destruction.' The COBRA BALL was very active, particularly in monitoring SS-20 *Saber* re-entries. In addition to the usual 'light show', SS-20 launches were accompanied by a unique phenomenon known as the 'dome of light.' Western intelligence sources suggest this may have served to disable incoming ballistic missiles or mask a Soviet first strike launch from US detection satellites. The Russians know but aren't saying. On the elimination protocol, see http://www.state.gov/www/global/arms/treaties/inf4.html accessed 10 July 2015. On shoot to destruction and dome of light, see Thomas C Reed and Danny B Stillman, *The Nuclear Express: A Political History of the Bomb and its Proliferation* (Minneapolis, MN: Zenith Press, 2009), 199-200, and Don Shannon, 'Helms Asks CIA to Check if Soviets Cheated on Accord,' *Los Angeles Times*, 24 January 1988, n.p.

2 See Robert S Hopkins, 'COBRA BALL and COBRA EYE: Alaskan Observers,' *World Air Power Journal* 8 (Spring 1992): 128-39; and idem, *The Boeing KC-135 Stratotanker – More Than Just a Tanker* (Leicester, England: Midland Publishing, 1997), 146-49, 191. The RC-135E RIVET AMBER carried a large radar which tracked incoming ballistic objects. It routinely operated in conjunction with the COBRA BALL.

3 Established in April 1964 DEFSMAC provides for a 'management arrangement to (a) task and technically control DoD missile and space intelligence collection and processing activities directed against foreign missile and space activities and (b) provide current analysis and reporting of foreign missile and space events.' Richard L Bernard, 'The Defense Special Missile and Astronautics Center,' 31, 33, http://www.nsa.gov/public_info/_files/cryptologic_spectrum/desfmac.pdf accessed 10 July 2015; and idem, 'In the Forefront of Foreign Missile and Space Intelligence: History of the Defense Special Missile and Astronautics Center, 1960-2010,' brochure from Center for Cryptological History, National Security Agency, 2012. A robust summary by distinguished intelligence scholar Jeffrey Richelson is available at http://www2.gwu.edu/~nsarchiv/nukevault/ebb489/ accessed 10 July 2015.

4 'Strategic Fireworks,' 6 May 2011, posted on Russian Defense Policy, http://russiandefpolicy.wordpress.com/tag/klyuchi/ accessed 10 July 2015; and http://kiksssr.narod.ru/O_Y_Kamchatka.htm (in Russian only) accessed 10 July 2015.

5 It was an RC-135S COBRA BALL that was airborne near Kamchatka on 31 August 1983 when an errant Korean Air Lines Boeing 747 flew close enough that Soviet tracking radars confused the two airplanes. Within a few hours, the RC-135S was back on the ground at Shemya AFB and the 747 shot down by a Soviet Su-15 *Flagon*. Among the veritable cottage industry of literature on Korean Air Lines flight 007, David E Hoffman provides the most current and accurate summary of this event in *The Dead Hand: The Untold Story of the Cold War Arms Race and its Dangerous Legacy*, (New York: Doubleday, 2009), 72-86.

6 For other photographs of actual intercepts and the close proximity of the airplanes, see Bruce Bailey, *We See All: A Pictorial History of the 55th Strategic Reconnaissance Wing,* (Privately printed, 1982), 246-50.

7 The J-8 pilot, Wang Wei, was close enough to the EP-3E that he could show them a hand-written copy of his e-mail address. Steven Lee Myers and Christopher Drew, 'US Aides Say Chinese Pilot Reveled in Risk,' *New York Times*, 6 April 2001, n.p. For the EP-3E pilot's account, see Shane Osborn with Malcolm McConnell, *Born to Fly* (New York: Broadway Books, 2001). Summaries appear in Larry Tart and Robert Keefe, *The Price of Vigilance: Attacks on American Surveillance Flights*, (New York: Ballantine), xix-liv; and William E Burrows, *By Any Means Necessary: America's Secret Air War in the Cold War*, (New York: Farrar, Straus and Giroux, 2001), 310-18. A photograph of Wang Wei holding up his e-mail address appears in Burrows in the photograph section following page 110.

8 David Cenciotti, 'U.S. Spyplane Aggressively Intercepted by Russian Su-27 Over the Baltic Sea,' 13 April 2015; http://theaviationist.com/2015/04/13/su-27-aggressively-intercept-rc135/; and idem, 'U.S. RC-135U Spyplane and Russian Su-27 in One of the Most Dangerous Aerial Encounters Since the Cold War,' 3 June 2014; http://theaviationist.com/2014/06/03/combat-sent-intercepted-su27/ (both accessed on 10 July 2015).

9 By way of *de rigeur* full disclosure, this manuscript has never been vetted by any government agency and contains nothing which *at the time it was acquired* was classified. Recently the US Air Force has begun reclassifying documents that were previously declassified. Whether this inane process affects any of the material used in this research is beyond my knowledge. Moreover, I have not utilized nor revealed any classified information acquired during the time I held any security clearance, nor have I used that experience to link together unclas-

sified information to derive results or conclusions which are classified.
10 Gregory W Pedlow and Donald E Welzenbach, *The Central Intelligence Agency and Overhead Reconnaissance: The U-2 and OXCART Programs, 1954-1974* (Washington, DC: CIA History Staff, 1992), [Preface, 2].

Chapter One
A Better Understanding

1 On the expectation by planners, officials, and the president that a U-2 pilot would not survive an attack on the airplane, see Michael Beschloss, *Mayday: Eisenhower, Khrushchev, and the U-2 Affair*, (New York: Harper and Row, 1986), 15-16, 36, 64-65.
2 Gregory W Pedlow and Donald E Welzenbach, *The Central Intelligence Agency and Overhead Reconnaissance: The U-2 and OXCART Programs, 1954-1974* (Washington, DC: CIA History Staff, 1992), 174; and Francis Gary Powers and Curt Gentry, *Operation Overflight*, (New York: Holt, Rinehart and Winston, 1970), 13-18, 72. Powers' parents called him Francis, his first wife Barbara called him Gary, his friends called him Frank, but his historical reputation will forever be Francis Gary Powers. E-mail from Gary Powers, Jr, to Chris Pocock, 12 January 2015.
3 *Ibid*., 73-84; and Chris Pocock, *The U-2 Spyplane: Toward the Unknown – A New History of the Early Years*, (Altglen, PA: Schiffer, 2000), 164-65, 184-91.
4 David Wise and Thomas B Ross, *The U-2 Affair*, (New York: Random House, 1962), 259-60, 265.
5 [Unknown], 'An Interview With Former DDCI John N McMahon,' *Studies in Intelligence*, (1999): 3-5; Pocock, *The U-2 Spyplane*, 242-43. MUDLARK was the program to determine what actually happened to Powers on 1 May 1960.
6 George F Kennan, *Nuclear Delusion: Soviet American Relations in the Atomic Age*, Rev. ed. (New York: Pantheon, 1983) 111-12; and idem, *Memoirs: 1950-1963*. (Boston: Little, Brown, 1972), 347-48, 351.
7 Allan R Millett, review of *The Origins of Nuclear Strategy, 1945-1953,* by Samuel R Williamson, Jr, and Steven L Rearden, In *Diplomatic History* 18 (Spring 1994): 283.
8 J Garry Clifford, 'Bureaucratic Politics,' in *Explaining the History of American Foreign Policy,* ed. Michael J Hogan and Thomas G Paterson (New York: Cambridge University Press, 1991), 147.
9 Richard J Aldrich, "Grow Your Own': Cold War Intelligence and History Supermarkets,' *Intelligence and National Security* 17 (March 2002): 135.
10 John Ferris, 'Coming in from the Cold War: The Historiography of American Intelligence, 1945-1990,' *Diplomatic History* 19 (Winter 1995): 92.
11 John Lewis Gaddis, 'Intelligence, Espionage, and Cold War Origins,' *Diplomatic History* 13 (Spring 1989): 210-12.
12 National Archives and Records Agency [hereafter 'NARA'], Record Group [hereafter 'RG'] 59, Department of State, Office of the Legal Advisor, Sam Klaus Files, Aircraft Incidents, 1944-62, Lot 64 D 551, MLR E1588A, Boxes 55, 56, 57, 100, 101, and 102; US Department of Defense, 'Summary of Cold War Losses;' A L George, *Case Studies of Actual and Alleged Overflights, 1930-1953* [hereafter *Case Studies]*, RAND Research Memorandum RM-1349, 15 August 1955, Secret, 303-310; idem, *Case Studies of Actual and Alleged Overflights, 1930-1953-Supplement* [hereafter *Case Studies–Supplement]*, RAND Research Memorandum RM-1349 (S), 15 August 1955, Top Secret; Bruce Bailey, *We See All: A Pictorial History of the 55th Strategic Reconnaissance Wing* (Privately printed, 1982), 47-48; Douglas Stanglin, Susan Headden, and Peter Cary, 'Flight of the Ferrets,' *US News & World Report,* 15 March 1993, 44-45; idem, 'Secrets of the Cold War,' *US News & World Report,* 15 March 1993, 32-33; William E Burrows, 'Beyond the Iron Curtain' *Air & Space,* August/September 1994, 27-35; Paul Lashmar, 'Shootdowns,' *Aeroplane Monthly,* August 1994, 10; and Charles Maechling, 'Intrusions, Overflights, and Shootdowns,' *Air Power History* 36 (Summer 1989): 6-15.
13 Bill Gertz, 'Soviet Lying on US POWs Spanned Nearly Five Decades,' *Washington Times,* 13 June 1992, 4. Jason Gertzen, 'US Hunts For 89 Lost in Cold War,' *Omaha World-Herald,* 8 September 1996, Bl, B3.
14 John M Deutch, speech given at the 'CORONA and the Revolution in Intelligence' Conference, George Washington University, 23 May 1995. As one example of the excessive number of overflights accorded to the U-2, see Peter Grose, *Gentleman Spy: The Life of Allen Dulles* (Boston: Houghton Mifflin, 1994), 470.
15 Letter from Major George Budway, Alaskan Air Command Director of Intelligence, to Major General C P Cabell, USAF Director of Intelligence, 17 November 1948, Top Secret, NARA, RG341, Entry 214, 2-5466; Memorandum for Director of Operations, from Colonel Chas. M Townsend, '(Restricted) Recent Electronic Reconnaissance Flights,' AFOIN-1A3, 1 October 1953, Top Secret-Security Information, NARA, RG 341, Headquarters Air Force; '91st Strategic Reconnaissance Squadron History,' August 1954, Air Force Historical Research Agency [hereafter AFHRA]; AAOID-IO 062, Subject: Photographic Coverage of Northwestern Siberia, 4 November 1949, Top Secret, NARA, RG341, Entry 214, 2-10097.
16 In the absence of information since declassified, David Rosenberg suggested that USAF overflights of the USSR did not begin until 1956, ostensibly because that was the year of the first civilian U-2 overflight. David Alan Rosenberg, 'The Origins of Overkill: Nuclear Weapons and American Strategy.' In *The National Security: Its Theory and Practice, 1945-1960,* ed. Norman A Graebner, 123-95 (New York: Oxford University Press, 1986), 128. In fact, President Eisenhower permanently suspended all military overflights of the USSR on 18 December 1956.
17 Paul Lashmar, 'Stranger Than 'Strangelove': A General's Forays into the Nuclear Zone,' *Washington Post,* 3 July 1994, C9; idem, 'Killer on the Edge: The Warmongering Career of Curtis LeMay,' *New Statesman and Society,* 15 September 1995, 20-22; idem, *Spy Flights of the Cold War* (London: Alan Sutton, Ltd, 1996); 'General Curtis LeMay: The Man Who Wanted World War III,' produced by Paul Lashmar, aired in the United States by Arts & Entertainment Network on 22 February 1997; Richard Rhodes, *Dark Sun: The Making of the Hydrogen Bomb* (New York: Simon and Schuster, 1995), 564-66, 568; and idem, 'The General and World War III,' *The New Yorker,* 19 June 1995, 47-59.
18 Mark J Conversino, 'Back to the Stone Age: The Attack on Curtis E LeMay,' unpublished paper presented 16 May 1996, at the Strategic Air Command Symposium at Offutt AFB, Nebraska; revised as idem, review of *Dark*

Sun: The Making of the Hydrogen Bomb, by Richard Rhodes, In *Strategic Review25* (Spring 1997): 60-68; R Cargill Hall, 'The Truth About Overflights,' *MHQ: The Quarterly Journal of Military History* 9 (Spring 1997): 24-39; and idem, 'Strategic Overflight Reconnaissance in the Cold War,' 21, note 44.

19 Robin Winks, review of *Gentleman Spy: The Life of Allen Dulles,* by Peter Grose, in *Foreign Affairs* 73 (November/December 1994): 148, 149.

Chapter Two
From Post War to Cold War

---

1 Matthew A Evangelista, 'Stalin's Postwar Army Reappraised,' *International Security* 7 (Winter 1982-83): 110-38.

2 John Keegan, *The Battle for History: Re-fighting World War II* (New York: Vintage Books, 1995), 84; quoted in John T Greenwood, 'The Atomic Bomb: Early Air Force Thinking and the Strategic Air Force, August 1945-March 1946,' *Aerospace Historian* (Fall 1987): 159, 161; *The United States Strategic Bombing Survey, Summary Report (European War),* 30 September 1945, reprinted in *US Strategic Bombing Surveys (European War and Pacific War),* October 1987, 39; and General of the Army Henry H Arnold, *Third Report of the Commanding General of the Army Air Forces to the Secretary of War,* USAAF, 12 November 1945, 65.

3 Speech by Lieutenant Colonel Richard S Leghorn, 'Objectives for Research and Development in Military Aerial Reconnaissance,' 13 December 1946, 26-27.

4 J C Hopkins and Sheldon A Goldberg, *The Development of Strategic Air Command, 1946-1986 (The Fortieth Anniversary History)* (Offutt AFB, NE: Office of the Historian, Strategic Air Command, 1986), 2.

5 Sherman Kent, *Strategic Intelligence for American World Policy* (Princeton: Princeton University Press, 1949; reprint, Hamden, CT: Archon Books, 1965), xxi-xxii, 212. Emphasis in original.

6 This language is from the Eisenhower administration but correctly summarizes the demands for strategic intelligence throughout the Cold War. NSC 5501, 'Basic National Security,' 7 January 1955, in *FRUS,* 1955-1957, vol. XIX, 38. See also Richelson, *American Espionage and the Soviet Target,* 38-39.

7 Clark Clifford, 'American Relations with the Soviet Union,' reprinted in Arthur Krock, *Memoirs: Sixty Years on the Firing Line* (New York: Funk & Wagnalls, 1968), 422, 425; and Clark Clifford and Richard Holbrooke, *Counsel to the President: A Memoir* (New York: Random House, 1991), 109-13, 115-16, and 123-29. Clifford's self-serving role in the preparation, importance, and impact of the report should not obscure the fact that it did represent the opinion of a number of senior Truman advisors. John Acacia, *Clark Clifford: The Wise Man of Washington* (Lexington, KY: University Press of Kentucky, 2009), 36-56.

8 Douglas Frantz and David McKean, *Friends in High Places: The Rise and Fall of Clark Clifford* (Boston: Little, Brown, 1995), 56. For a critique of the report, see Melvyn P Leffler, *A Preponderance of Power: National Security, the Truman Administration, and the Cold War* (Stanford, CA: Stanford University Press, 1992), 130-38.

9 John Thomas Farquhar, 'A Cold War in Flames: The Impact of Aerial Reconnaissance on US-Soviet Relations, 1948-1960,' M.A. thesis, Creighton University, 1986, 25.

10 'NSC Directive to CIA,' NSC Meeting #5, 13 January 1948, 1, Harry S Truman Library [hereafter 'HSTL'], President's Secretary's Files [hereafter 'PSF'], National Security Council (A-D), Subject File-Actions, Record of, 1947-1949, Box 191; 'Coordination of Collection Activities Abroad,' NSCID 2, 13 January 1948, Confidential, NARA, RG59, Department of State, Records of the Executive Secretariat, NSC Files: Lot 66 D 148, Dulles-Jackson-Correa Report, Annex 8; and 'Coordination of Intelligence Production,' NSCID 3, 13 January 1948, Secret, ibid., Annex 9. Eisenhower confronted similar turf battles over aerial reconnaissance between the Air Force and the CIA. Dino A Brugioni, *Eyes in the Sky: Eisenhower, the CIA, and the Cold War* (Annapolis, MD: Naval Institute Press, 2010), 97, 115, 161-62.

11 Memorandum for the Secretary of Defense, Subject: Special Electronic Airborne Search Operations (SESP), 5 May 1950, Top Secret; Memorandum to the President, Subject: Special Electronic Search Operations (SESP), 24 May 1950, Top Secret; and Memorandum for the Secretary of Defense, Subject: Special Electronic Airborne Search Operations [SESP], 22 July 1950, Top Secret, HSTL, PSF, General File, Bradley, Omar N [All hereafter 'SESP-date'].

12 Kent, *Strategic Intelligence for American World Policy,* xxiii.

13 H H Martin, 'Are Our Big Bombers Ready to Go?' *Saturday Evening Post,* 30 December 1950, 19.

14 CIA photo analyst Dino Brugioni identifies some 38 sources by 1953. Brugioni, *Eyes in the Sky,* 50-64.

15 Memorandum for General McDonald, Subject: Strategic Reconnaissance, 31 January 1948, Top Secret, 2, NARA, RG341 Entry 214, 2-848; and James A Walsh, 'Strategic Thinking and Air Intelligence,' *Studies in Intelligence* 2 (Winter 1958): 7.

16 *History of SAC Reconnaissance, 1950,* K416.01-5, 1114054, AFHRA, 1-2; and Lieutenant General Curtis E LeMay, Commanding General, SAC, to Lieutenant General Lauris Norstad, USAF Deputy Chief of Staff for Operations, 15 December 1948, Top Secret, 1, NARA, RG341.

17 Memorandum for Lt Pusta, Headquarters USAF/AFOIP-FL, from AFOIR-RC, 10 January 1950, Sub: Organization of Strategic and Tactical Reconnaissance. Copy printed in R Cargill Hall and Clayton D Laurie, eds., *Early Cold War Overflights, 1950-1956: Symposium Proceedings, Vol. II: Appendixes* [hereafter *'Appendixes'*], (Washington DC: Office of the Historian, National Reconnaissance Office, 2003), 427.

18 James T McElhone, 'Determination of the Need for Electronic Reconnaissance,' Air Command and Staff School Research Paper, December 1949, AFHRA, 3, 4, and 9; and John Farquhar, 'A Need to Know: The Role of Air Force Reconnaissance in War Planning, 'Ph.D. diss., Ohio State University, 1991 68-69.

19 John Ponturo, *Analytical Support for the Joint Chiefs of Staff: The WSEG Experience, 1948-1976,* Study S-507 (Arlington, VA: Institute for Defense Analysis, July 1979), 5, 52-53, 74.

20 Memorandum for Record, AFOIN-E/CE, Colonel Thomas/76472, 29 November 1951, Top Secret-Security Information, NARA, RG341, Entry 214, 2-21928; and *Beacon Hill Report: Problems of Air Force Intelligence and Reconnaissance* (MIT, 15 June 1952).

21 Eisenhower made this remark in justifying U-2 overflights of the USSR. 'Memorandum of Discussion at the 445th Meeting of the National Security Council,' 24 May

1960, Top Secret, DDEL, Whitman File, NSC Records; and Dwight D Eisenhower, *The White House Years: Waging Peace, 1956-1961* [hereafter *Waging Peace*] (New York: Doubleday, 1965), 559.

22 'Meeting the Threat of Surprise Attack, ' 14 February 1955, Top Secret, Restricted Data, NARA, RG59, Department of State, S/S-RD Files: Lot 71 D 171. Emphasis in original.

23 'Memorandum of Discussion at the 257th Meeting of the National Security Council, Washington, August 4, 1955,' in *FRUS,* 1955-1957, vol. XIX, 106. NSCID 17 'Electronic Intelligence' was dated 16 May 1955, and NSC 5520 'US Scientific Satellite Program' was dated 20 May 1955. The latter appears in *FRUS,* 1955-1957, vol. XI, 723.

24 Quoted in James R Killian, Jr, *Sputnik, Scientists, and Eisenhower* (Cambridge: MIT Press, 1977), 80.

25 Richard M Bissell, Jr, with Jonathan E Lewis and Frances T Pudlo, *Reflections of a Cold Warrior: From Yalta to the Bay of Pigs* (New Haven: Yale University Press, 1996), 94.

26 Congress, Joint Committee on Defense Production, *Deterrence and Survival in the Nuclear Age: (The 'Gaither Report' of 1957),* 94th Cong., 2d sess., 1976, Joint Committee Print, 21.

27 Paul Nitze, *From Hiroshima to Glasnost: At the Center of Decision, A Memoir,* with Ann M Smith and Steven L Rearden (New York: Grove-Weidenfeld, 1989), 167.

28 U Alexis Johnson and Jef Olivarius McAllister, *The Right Hand of Power: The Memoirs of an American Diplomat* (Englewood Cliffs, NJ: Prentice-Hall, 1984), 352; and Shulsky, *Silent Warfare.* 35-40.

29 Richelson, *American Espionage and the Soviet Target,* 42-43, 275- 85; John Ranelagh, *CIA: A History* (London: BBC Books, 1992), 211; and Ernest Volkman, *Warriors of the Night: Spies, Soldiers, and American Intelligence* (New York: William Morrow and Company, 1985), 16.

30 R Cargill Hall, 'The Eisenhower Administration and the Cold War: Framing American Astronautics to Serve National Security,' *Prologue* 27 (Spring 1995): 61; and, Harry Rositzke *The CIA's Secret Operations* (New York: Reader's Digest Press, 1977), 18-20, 38.

31 Secretary of Defense Memorandum from Robert LeBaron, 'Basis for Estimating Maximum Soviet Capabilities for Atomic Warfare,' 20 February 1950, Top Secret, HSTL, PSF, NSC Atomic, Atomic Energy–Russia, Box 201. Emphasis added.

32 Letter from Brigadier General John B Ackerman, Chief, Collection Division, USAF Directorate of Intelligence, to Colonel James H Walsh, SAC Director of Intelligence, 30 November 1951, Top Secret, 1, NARA RG341, Entry 214, folder 2-21300-2-21399.

33 Leo D Carl, *The International Dictionary of Intelligence,* (McLean, VA: International Defense Consultant Services, 1990), 70-71, 181, 184-85, 193, 384-85.

34 Telegram From the Embassy in Pakistan to the Department of State, 13 December 1955, Top Secret, Priority, NARA, RG59, Department of State, Central Files, 711.56390D/12-1355; Bissell, *Reflections of a Cold Warrior,* 115-16; and Memorandum for the Deputy Secretary of Defense from General G B Erskine, Assistant to the Secretary of Defense (Special Operations), 'Installation of AN/FPS-17 Radar on Shemya Island,' 11 March 1958, Top Secret, NARA, RG 330, OSD Office of Special Operations, OSO Chronological File, 2 January thru 31 March 1958.

35 Bob W Rush, *A History of USAFSS Airborne SIGINT Reconnaissance Program (ASRP), 1950-1977,* 20 September 1977 (TSC), 8; CCH Collection, Series X.J.4.f.; cited in Michel L Peterson, 'Maybe You Had to Be There: The SIGINT on Thirteen Soviet Shootdowns of US Reconnaissance Aircraft,' Cryptologic Quarterly 12 (Summer 1993): 3, n 4.

36 NSCID-17 'Electronic Intelligence (ELINT),' *FRUS: The Intelligence Community, 1950-1955,* 715; and Jeffery Richelson, *The US Intelligence Community* (Cambridge: Ballinger, 1985), 118.

37 *History of SAC Reconnaissance 1950,* K416.01-5, 1114054, AFHRA, 9.

38 William H Nance, 'Quality ELINT,' *Studies in Intelligence* 12 (Spring 1968): 8.

39 Letter from Colonel Willard W Smith, Commander, 97th Bombardment Wing, Medium, to the Commander, 810th Air Division, [9 November] 1955, 'Recommendation for Award of the Air Force Outstanding Unit Award,' Library of Congress [hereafter 'LoC'], Curtis E LeMay Papers, Box B60, Nathan F Twining correspondence.

40 Charles A Kroger, 'ELINT: A Scientific Intelligence System,' *Studies in Intelligence* (Winter 1958): 74, 77.

41 Quoted in Richelson, *US Intelligence Community,* 118.

42 Letter from Richard M Bissell, Jr, Farmington, CT, to the author, 5 February 1992; Robert S Hopkins, III, 'The TELL TWO Stratojets,' *Air Enthusiast Quarterly* 41 (Midsummer, 1990):18-21; and Kroger, 'ELINT,' 77.

43 Memorandum for the Deputy Secretary of Defense from General G B Erskine, Assistant to the Secretary of Defense (Special Operations), 'Army ELINT Installation on Shemya,' 4 June 1958, Top Secret, NARA, RG 330, OSD Office of Special Operations, 080 Chronological File, 1April thru 30 June 1958.

44 M C Wonus, 'The Case of the SS-6,' *Studies in Intelligence* 13 (Winter 1969): 25, 27.

45 Hopkins, 'TELL TWO Stratojets,' 18-21; and 'How US Taps Soviet Missile Secrets,' *Aviation Week,* 21 October 1957, 26-27.

Chapter Three
Aerial Containment

1 William E Burrows, *By Any Means Necessary: America's Secret Air War in the Cold War* (New York: Farrar, Straus and Giroux, 2001), 30-36, and inside front dust jacket. Brugioni considers the unwillingness to repatriate lost crewmembers and the treatment of their families to be a blemish on Eisenhower's record, in particular the State Department. Dino Brugioni, *Eyes in the Sky: Eisenhower, the CIA, and the Cold War* (Annapolis, MD: Naval Institute Press, 2010), 71-72.

2 DIRNSA message to JCS/JRC, subject: White Wolf Advisory Warning Plan, serial P04-184-64, 1 April 1964 (TSC); Cryptologic Archival Holding Area; Accession No.43050, box H03-0504-1, NSA; Correspondence and papers relating to the White Wolf Plan, 1961-1964 (TS-CCO); Cryptologic Archival Holding Area; Accession No.43050, box H03-0504-1, NSA; and Operations Plan, UHF Air/Air Advisory Warning Plan, Serial No.6-61, 31 May 1961 (TS); Cryptologic Archival Holding Area; Accession No.15157, box CBRE67, NSA, cited in Peterson, 'Maybe You Had to Be There,' 37-38, n 108, 109, 112.

3 John F Murphy, Jr, 'The Alaskan Mystery Flights,' *International Journal of Intelligence and Counterintelligence* 9 (Spring 1996): 103-105.
4 'Army Mass Flight to Alaska in July,' *New York Times,* 22 June 1934, 3; 'Army Planes Mapping Alaska,' *New York Times,* 6 August 1934, 17; DeWitt S Copp, *A Few Great Captains* (McLean, VA: EPM Publications, 1980), 244- 46; Goddard, *Overview,* 224-29; and Murphy, 'Alaskan Mystery Flights,' 109.
5 Walter Durany, 'Japan is Warned on War by Russia,' *New York Times,* 4 February 1934, 1; and Harold Denny, 'Peace in Far East Seen by Diplomats; Soviet Skeptical,' *New York Times,* 2 April 1934, 1, 11.
6 Robert Dallek, *Franklin D Roosevelt and American Foreign Policy, 1932-1945,* with a new Afterword (New York: Oxford University Press, 1995), 88-89.
7 Murphy does not make this claim in 'The Alaskan Mystery Flights.' He clearly states this, however, in his response to criticism of his initial article. See *International Journal of Intelligence and Counterintelligence* 9 (Fall 1996): 329-36, especially 334.
8 Copp, *A Few Great Captains,* 240.
9 Bruce Bidwell, *History of the Military Intelligence Department of the Army General Staff, 1775-1941* (Washington, DC: University Publications of America, 1986), 462.
10 On early Navy aerial reconnaissance operations, see Don C East, 'A History of US Navy Fleet Air Reconnaissance. Part 1: The Pacific and VQ-1,' *The Hook* (Spring 1987): 15-33; idem, 'A History of US Navy Fleet Air Reconnaissance. Part 2: The European Theater and VQ-2,' *The Hook* (Summer 1987): 32-47; and Wyman H Packard, *A Century of US Naval Intelligence* (Washington, DC: Naval Historical Center, 1996).
11 Undated Top Secret memorandum, HSTL, PSF, Subject File– Agencies-Military: 'Danger of War-Increase in Air & Naval Forces.'
12 Memorandum for the Record, 15 March 1949, Top Secret, NARA, RG341, Entry 214, 2-6725; AFOIR-RC, Subject: Classification of Photography, 28 October 1949, NARA, RG341, 2-981?? [complete number not visible on original document]; *History of Strategic Air Command, 1948,* vol. 1, *January – December, 1948,* AFHRA 416.01, 248-49; Letter, Colonel J E Mallory, Chief, USAF Directorate of Intelligence Reconnaissance Branch, 'Polaris Projects Photographs,' 2 December 1948, Top Secret, NARA, RG341; and Air Intelligence Information Report, Subject: Severo Airfield, 5 July 1949, Top Secret, NARA, RG341; and Major General C P Cabell to Commanding General, Alaskan Air Command, Subject: ECM Ferret Program-Alaskan Air Command, 26 July 1948, Top Secret, NARA, RG341, entry 214, file 2-3000-2-3099.
13 Memorandum for Record, Major Langbohm/rm/ 4544, 27 July 1947, NARA, RG341; and *History of SAC Reconnaissance, 1950,* 6.
14 Memorandum for Files, Subject: History of the Long-Range Detection Program, 21 July1948, Top Secret-Restricted Data, HSTL, PSF, Box 199; David Holloway, *Stalin and the Bomb: The Soviet Union and Atomic Energy, 1939-1956* (New Haven: Yale University Press, 1994), 216; and Jeffery Richelson, *Spying on the Bomb: American Nuclear Intelligence from Nazi Germany to Iran and North Korea* (New York: Norton, 2006), 88-89.
15 A number of original documents discussing the benefits and restrictions related to these distances are reproduced in Hall and Laurie, *Appendixes,* 413-26.
16 Memorandum for Record, 20 February 1948, Top Secret, NARA, RG341, Entry 214, 2-934a; Letter to Commander-in-Chief, Alaska, [?] February 1948, Top Secret, NARA, RG341, Entry 214; and Letter to Francis B Stevens, Acting Chief, Division of Eastern European Affairs, Department of State, from Brigadier General F J Timberlake, 2 March 1948, Secret, RG341, Entry 214, 2-934.
17 Memorandum for Chief, Air Intelligence Requirements Division, from Maj Carl M Green, Reconnaissance Branch, Air Intelligence Requirements Division, USAF Directorate of Intelligence, 11 December 1947, Sub: Coordination of Photo and Photo Intelligence Activities, reproduced in Hall and Laurie, *Appendixes,* 409.
18 'Memorandum of Discussion at the 444th Meeting of the National Security Council,' 9 May 1960, Top Secret, DDEL, WF, NSC Records; 'Memorandum of Discussion at the 445th Meeting of the National Security Council,' 24 May 1960, Top Secret, DDEL, WF, NSC Records; Congress, Senate, Committee on Foreign Relations, *Events Incident to the Summit Conference: Executive Session Hearing Before the Senate Foreign Relations Committee,* 86th Cong., 2d sess., 2 June 1960, 395, 403; and OH-274, Interview with General Nathan Twining [hereafter 'Twining Oral History'], 17 August 1967, Columbia University Oral History Project, 134. Lashmar is unconvinced that so many airplanes were over the USSR at that one time and agrees that Twining was boasting. Lashmar, 'Stratojets Over the USSR,' 22.
19 White, *World in Peril,* 37, 63-64; and interview with 'Doc' Savage and Rex Knaak, former 46th RS crewmembers, 6 September 1996, at Omaha, Nebraska. Both Savage and Knaak said that in his book White takes personal credit for many of the squadron's accomplishments. Animus combined with amnesia may explain the uncertainty about these overflights.
20 Burrows, 'Beyond the Iron Curtain,' 31; and quoted in Richelson, *Century of Spies,* 221.
21 Michael Dobbs, *One Minute to Midnight: Kennedy, Khrushchev, and Castro on the Brink of Nuclear War* (New York: Knopf, 2008), 270.
22 *History of Strategic Air Command, 1949,* vol. 1, *January–December, 1949,* AFHRA, 416.01, 121, 122, 124-25.
23 Hillman and Hall, 'Overflight,' 33; and R Cargill Hall, 'Cold War Overflights: Military Aerial Missions Over the USSR and China,' 14 November 1996, 15. Hall kindly shared this manuscript with me prior to its publication as idem, 'The Truth About Overflights.' See also Doug Gordon, *Tactical Reconnaissance in the Cold War* (Barnsley, England: Pen and Sword Aviation, 2006), 15-56.
24 Brugioni, *Eyes in the Sky,* 73.
25 A W Jessup, 'MiG-15 Dims USAF's A-Bomb Hopes,' *Aviation Week,* 4 February 1952, 16; and Robert F Futrell, *The United States Air Force in Korea, 1950-1953,* rev. ed. (Washington, DC: Office of Air Force History, 1983), 548.
26 *History of SAC Reconnaissance, 1950,* 17; and speech to the National War College by General Curtis E LeMay, 'The Strategic Air Command,' 28 January 1954, Top Secret, 35-37, NSArch.
27 *Unit History Report, 91st Strategic Reconnaissance Squadron, 1 Nov 50-31 Dec 50,* AFHRA; and 'Intelligence Requirements for B-47's for Special Reconnaissance Missions,' AFOOP, 1 December 1950, Top Secret, NARA,

RG341, Entry 214, Box 54, 2-17352; 'Intelligence Requirements for B-47's for Special Reconnaissance Missions,' AFDRQ-SNR, 4 January 1951, Top Secret, NARA, RG341, Entry 214; Memorandum for Record, AFOIN-C/RC, 5 January 1951, Top Secret, NARA, RG341, Entry 214; and Memorandum for Record, AFOIN-1A2, 78061, 26 August 1954, Top Secret, NARA, RG341, Entry 214, Box 77, 4-2104.

28 *History, 14th Air Division, August 1953*, AFHRA, K-DIV-14-HI, 426052, 28.

29 Quoted in Frederick A Johnsen, *Thundering Peacemaker* (Tacoma, WA: Bomber Books, 1978), 10, 12; Larry Davis, *Planes, Names, and Dames: Korea Nose Art*, vol. II, *1946-1960* (Carrollton, TX: Squadron Signal Publications, 1993), 17; John Prados, *The Soviet Estimate* (New York: Dial Press, 1982), 29; and Larry Davis, *Air War Over Korea* (Carrollton, TX: Squadron Signal Publications, 1982), 55.

30 Interview with a former RF-84K crew chief who requested anonymity; Charles A Ravenstein, *Air Force Combat Wings-Lineage and Honors, 1947-1977* (Washington, DC: Office of Air Force History, 1984), 111, 142; Meyers K Jacobsen and Ray Wagner, *B-36 in Action* (Carrollton, TX: Squadron/Signal Publications, 1980), 45-48; Johnsen, *Thundering Peacemaker*, 24-26; and Meyers K Jacobsen, *Convair B-36: A Comprehensive History of America's 'Big Stick'* (Altglen, PA: Schiffer, 1997), 347-50.

31 Peterson, 'Maybe You Had to Be There,' 3; and Larry Tart and Robert Keefe *The Price of Vigilance: Attacks on American Surveillance Flights* (New York: Ballantine, 2001), 202, 205-14.

32 Richard A Koch, 'Joint Service Overflights in the Soviet Far East,' in R Cargill Hall and Clayton D Laurie, eds. *Early Cold War Overflights, 1950-1956: Symposium Proceedings, Vol. I: Memoirs* [hereafter '*Memoirs*'] (Washington DC: Office of the Historian, National Reconnaissance Office, 2003), 148. Koch was the pilot on the P2V-3W.

33 Kenneth J Conboy and James Morrison, *Feet to the Fire: CIA Covert Operations in Indonesia, 1957-1958* (Annapolis, MD: Naval Institute Press, 1999), 67-74; and Jay Miller, *Lockheed's Skunk Works: The Official History*, rev. ed. (Leicester, England: Midland Publishing, 1995), 57-58.

34 'Development of Evasive Tactics for the RB-45,' HQ/91st SRW(M), Barksdale AFB, 30 July 1951, Secret, AFHRA. Emphasis in original.

35 Letter from RAF Air Marshal Sir John C Slessor to USAF General Hoyt S Vandenberg, 12 September 1952, LoC, Hoyt S Vandenberg Papers; Hall, 'Cold War Overflights,' 6-8; Duncan Campbell, *The Unsinkable Aircraft Carrier: American Military Power in Britain*, Rev. ed., (London: Paladin, 1986), 126, 128-31; Paul Lashmar, 'Skulduggery at Sculthorpe' *Aeroplane Monthly*, October 1994, 10-15;' John W Sheehan, Jr, 'The USAF's Tornado,' *Air International*, November 1988, 248; Roy Braybrook, 'Let's Hear it for the Hairy Apes,' *Air International*, January 1990, 25-26; and Maury Seitz, telephone interview with the author, 28 June 1994.

36 Wolfgang W E Samuel, with a Foreword by Ken Hechler, *I Always Wanted to Fly: America's Cold War Airmen* (Jackson, MI: University Press of Mississippi, 2001), 175, 186; and John Crampton, 'RB-45C Overflight Operations in the Royal Air Force,' in Hall and Laurie, *Memoirs*, 153-63.

37 Gordon, *Tactical Reconnaissance in the Cold War*, 44-73.

38 Hall, 'Cold War Overflights,' 22-23; Lashmar, 'Canberras Over the USSR,' 32-35; and Burrows, *By Any Means Necessary*, 151-52; Brugioni, *Eyes in the Sky*, 86-87.

39 Chris Pocock, 'Operation 'Robin' and the British Overflight of Kapustin Yar: A Historiographical Note,' *Intelligence and National Security* 17 (September 2002): 185-193. Pocock has found a fascinating article in a model airplane magazine which gives a similarly meticulous but totally fabricated operational history of a hypothetical Cold War reconnaissance airplane. This was not malicious but a tongue-in-cheek effort to justify the author's desire to build a unique variant of the 'RAF's Most Secret Spy-plane'. Indeed, the cover of the magazine reads 'Warning: This issue breaches the Official Secrets Act!' 'Meteor PR19,' *Mushroom Monthly*, 9(4) April 1994, n.p.; and idem, 9(5) May 1994, n.p.

40 Samuel, *I Always Wanted to Fly*, 148-49, 185, 188; Crampton, 'RB-45C Overflight Operations in the Royal Air Force,' 160-63; and Hall, 'Cold War Overflights,' 23-24, 26, 28.

41 John C Fredriksen, 'Detachment 2 Goes to War: RB-45C Reconnaissance Activity in Korea, 1950-1953,' *AAHS Journal* 41 (Winter 1996): 282-86; and Robert Burns, 'Mystery of Korean War's Secret Air Force Mission is Unraveled,' *Los Angeles Times*, 18 December 1994, Al; Samuel, *I Always Wanted to Fly*, 163, 169-70, 191; *History of the 91st Strategic Reconnaissance Squadron, Medium, Photo, 1 August 1951-31 August 1951*, 30, Top Secret map supplement, AFHRA; *Historical Report, 91st SRS, Supplement, March 1952, May 1952*, AFHRA; and Hall, 'Cold War Overflights,' 16-18.

42 91st SRS Histories, March, April, June, and August 1954, AFHRA.

43 *Ibid.*; John Prados, *The Sky Would Fall: Operation Vulture: The US Bombing Mission in Indochina, 1954* (New York: Dial Press, 1983); and Frank Logevall, *Embers of War: The Fall of an Empire and the Making of America's Vietnam* (New York: Random House, 2014), 454-80.

44 *History of 14th Air Division, August 1953*, AFHRA, K-DIV-14-HI, 426052, 47.

45 Brugioni, *Eyes in the Sky*, 72.

46 Hillman and Hall, 'Overflight,' 30-31; Operations Plan Serial No.X-52, 6th Sir *[sic]* Division, MacDill Air Force Base, 10 July 1952, LoC, Nathan F Twining Papers, Box 122, Folder Top Secret File 1952-57 (2); Hillman and Hall, 'Overflight,' 35-37; and interview with the aircraft commander, Colonel Donald E Hillman, USAF (retired), 15 May 1996.

47 Austin, 'A Cold War Overflight of the USSR;' Holt, 'Comments from the Back Seat;' Lashmar, 'Stratojets Over the USSR,' and interview with the aircraft commander, Colonel Harold Austin, USAF (retired), 15 and 16 May 1996.

48 Letter from Director of Naval Intelligence to Director of Intelligence, US Air Force, Subject: Photography; request for, 25 May 1954, Top Secret, NARA, RG341, Entry 214, Box 77, 4-1114-4-1290.

49 Pocock, *U-2 Spyplane*, 57.

50 Marion E Carl, with Barret Tillman, *Pushing the Envelope: The Career of Fighter Ace and Test Pilot Marion Carl* (Annapolis, MD: Naval Institute Press, 2005), 81-85.

51 R Cargill Hall to the author, 4 September 1996; idem, remarks on 15 May 1996, at the Strategic Air Command Symposium, Offutt AFB, Nebraska; and idem, 'Cold War Overflights,' 19-21, 27.
52 Pocock, *U-2 Spyplane*, 60; and Jim Tuttle, 'Slick Chick,' *American Aviation Historical Society Journal* 42 (1997): 124-130; *Eyes in the Sky*, 75; Cecil H Rigsby, 'Project Slick Chick Overflights in Europe, 1955-1956, in Hall and Laurie, *Memoirs*, 165-81; and Gordon, *Tactical Reconnaissance in the Cold War*, 67-73
53 Joseph A Guthrie, 'RB-57A Heart Throb Overflight Operations in Asia,' in Hall and Laurie, *Memoirs*, 89-97; Robert E Hines, Sr, 'Project Heart Throb in the Far East,' in idem, 105-13; Louis J Picciano, Jr, 'RB-57A Heart Throb Overflights,' in idem, 127-33; and Gerald E Cooke, 'Heart Throb Pilot: Overflights in the European Theater,' in idem, 183-210.
54 Hall, 'Cold War Overflights,' 29-33; Samuel, *I Always Wanted to Fly*, 149-219; Lloyd F Fields, 'Wrangel Island and Project Home Run Overflights,' in Hall and Laurie, *Memoirs*, 259-72; George A Brown, 'Project Home Run Operations,' in idem, 273-84; Burton S Barrett, 'Project Home Run Electronic Reconnaissance,' in idem, 285-92; Hyko Gayikian, 'Meteorology for Project Home Run and Other Special Operations,' in idem, 293-303; Earl T O'Laughlin, 'A Project Home Run Experience,' in idem, 305-313; and Hall and Laurie, *Memoirs*, 259-72.
55 Austin, 'A Cold War Overflight of the USSR;' Holt, 'Comments from the Back Seat;' Lashmar, 'Stratojets Over the USSR,' and interview with the aircraft commander, Colonel Harold Austin, USAF (retired), 15 and 16 May 1996.
56 Lloyd, *Boeing's B-47 Stratojet*, 181, cf. interview by the author with the pilot Walt Savage, published in Robert S Hopkins, III, 'The TELL TWO Stratojets,' *Air Enthusiast Quarterly* 41 (Midsummer, 1990): 18-21. It may well be that Lloyd mis-transcribed the entry for RB-47H 53-4290, the next chronological B-47 loss following the TELL TWO loss, which was in fact attacked by two DPRK MiG-17s.
57 Tegler, *B-47 Stratojet*, 144; Donald, *Spyplane*, 40; and Peterson, 'Maybe You Had to Be There,' 5.
58 Brugioni, *Eyes in the Sky*, 115, 161-63, 333; and Pedlow and Welzenbach, *The CIA and the U-2 Program*, Foreword, n.p., 321.
59 Pocock, *U-2 Spyplane*, 115-119.
60 *Ibid.*, 119-21, 129-30.
61 *History, 4080th Strategic Reconnaissance Wing, April-May 1959*, AFHRA, K-WG-4080-HI, 460412.
62 *History, 92nd Bombardment Wing, November 1958*, AFHRA, K-WG-92-HI, 452495; *History, 93rd Bombardment Wing, May 1959*, AFHRA, K-WG-93-HI, 452739; and *History, 93rd Bombardment Wing, March 1960*, AFHRA, K-WG-93-HI, 452749.
63 *History, 4080th Strategic Reconnaissance Wing, November 1956*, AFHRA, K-WG-4080-HI, 460386, 21, 25-31.
64 *History, 4080th Strategic Reconnaissance Wing, November 1956*, AFHRA, K-WG-4080-HI, 460386, 21, 25-31; Hall, 'Cold War Overflights,' 34; and US Department of State *Bulletin*, volume 36, 28 January 1957, 135 (the December 1956 history of the 4080th SRW remains classified); Pedlow and Welzenbach, *The CIA and the U-2 Program*, 127; Richard H Kohn and Joseph P Harahan, eds, *Strategic Air Warfare: An Interview with Generals Curtis E LeMay, Leon W Johnson, David A Burchinal, and Jack J Catton* (Washington, DC: Office of Air Force History, 1988), 95-96; and Robert M Kipp and John T Bohn, Oral History of General Curtis E LeMay [hereafter 'LeMay Oral History-1972'], 16 November 1972, USAF Oral History Program, Confidential, [now declassified] AFHRA K239.0512-1774, 24.
65 *History, 4080th Strategic Reconnaissance Wing, July 1959*, AFHRA, K-WG-4080-HI, 460414, Exhibit 3.
66 *History, 4080th Strategic Reconnaissance Wing, June 1959*, AFHRA, K-WG-4080-HI, 460413.
67 Robert C Mikesh, *B-57 Canberra at War, 1964-1972* (New York: Charles Scribner's Sons, 1980), 124, 126.
68 Pocock, *U-2 Spyplane*, 170, 178-79; and Brugioni, *Eyes in the Sky*, 333-34.
69 DDEL, WF, DDE Diaries. 'Memorandum for the Record,' 1 June 1960, Secret, DDEL, Project Clean Up. Richard M Nixon banned all overflight of the PRC, including those of the RoC Black Cat squadron.
70 Doubek, *Strategic Reconnaissance 1956-1976*, 28-29.
71 Mitchell, 'The Air Force and Peripheral Reconnaissance;' Jerry E Knotts and Patrick R O'Malley, *The Big Safari Program Story: ...as Told by the Big Safari People*, n.p.d., [1994], 8-13; and Bill Grimes, *The History of Big Safari* (Bloomington, IN: Archway Publishing, 2014), 10-16, 27-28, 36-42.
72 Nance, 'Quality ELINT,' 9.

Chapter Four
Targets and Tactics

1 Russell E Dougherty, 'The Psychological Climate of Nuclear Command,' in *Managing Nuclear Operations*, ed. Ashton B Carter, John D Steinbruner, and Charles A Zraket (Washington, DC: Brookings Institution, 1987), 407.
2 Bernard Brodie, *The Absolute Weapon: Atomic Power and World Order* (New York: Harcourt, Brace, 1946), 25, 28.
3 Robert A Lovett to General Carl Spaatz, 4 April 1946, LoC, Carl A Spaatz Papers.
4 Harry R Borowski, *A Hollow Threat: Strategic Air Power and Containment Before Korea* (Westport, CT: Greenwood Press, 1982), 168-69; and William S Borgiasz, *The Strategic Air Command: Evolution and Consolidation of Nuclear Forces, 1945-1955* (Westport, CT: Praeger, 1996), 109, 115-17, 121-27.
5 Quoted in Kaplan, *The Wizards of Armageddon*, 246; and 'The Operational Side of Air Offense: Remarks by General Curtis LeMay to USAF Scientific Advisory Board at Patrick AFB,' 21 May 1957, Top Secret, LoC, Manuscript Division, Curtis E LeMay Papers, Box 206, Top Secret File Number 60725. Emphasis in original.
6 'Intelligence Briefing for Reconnaissance Symposium,' Maxwell AFB, 11 April 1955, Top Secret, 4, NSArch.
7 Letter from Harry S Truman to Jno. N Garner, 21 September 1946, HSTL, PSF, Foreign Affairs File (Russia I), 1945-48 (2 of 4), Box 187.
8 'Supplemental Classified Report of the President's Air Policy Commission,' 31 December 1947. HSTL, President's Air Policy Commission, July 1947-January 1948, Box 41; and 'Memorandum for the Secretary of the Air Force,' 3 January 1950, from Jimmy Doolittle, 2. HSTL, Papers of Stuart Symington, 1946-50, D, General-Democratic National Committee [Box 4], Correspondence File

1946-50, Declassified Documents.

9 'Estimate of the World Situation Through 1954,' in 'Current Policies of the Government Relating to National Security,' vol. I, 'Geographic Area Policies,' 1 November 1952, Top Secret, I, HSTL, PSF, NSC Memoranda-Reports 1, Box 194; and Walsh, 'Strategic Thinking and Air Intelligence,' 19.

10 Quoted in Krock, *Memoirs,* 425; 'Study Prepared by the Director of the Policy Planning Staff (Nitze),' 8 February 1950, in *FRUS,* 1950, vol. 1, 145-46; and 'Estimate of the World Situation Through 1954.'

11 Gordon Prange, *At Dawn We Slept: The Untold Story of Pearl Harbor* (New York: McGraw Hill, 1981), 605. For a succinct summary of the controversy and its implications for intelligence analysis, see Harold P Ford, *Estimative Intelligence: The Purposes and Problems of National Intelligence Estimating,* rev. ed. (Lanham, MD: University Press of America, 1993), 3-42.

12 'Brief on the Pattern of War in the Atomic Warfare Age,' 16 December 1948, Secret, in Gaddis and Etzold, *Containment,* 45; and Ross, *American War Plans, 1945-1950.*

13 Carl A Spaatz, 'Spaatz Board Report,' 23 October 1945. LoC, Spaatz Papers, Box 22; 'Warns on Atomic Attack,' *New York Times,* 9 June 1946, 29; and JIC 435/12, 30 November 1948, NARA, RG 218, CCS, 092-USSR (3-27-49), Section 34.

14 *Report of the Joint Chiefs of Staff Evaluation Board for Operation Crossroads,* 30 June 1947, 'The Evaluation of the Atomic Bomb as a Military Weapon,' Enclosure 'A,' 28. HSTL, PSF, Box 202.

15 Memorandum, 'Discussion at the 306th Meeting of the NSC, December 20, 1956,' in *FRUS,* 1955-57, XIX, 380. See also Letter from General Power to General White, 21 October 1957, October 1957 folder, Nuclear History Series, NSArch; and *Gaither Report,* 25. For an analysis of the Gaither Committee's assessment of US intelligence weaknesses and recommended corrective action, see Snead, *The Gaither Committee.*

16 Excerpt from *Pravda,* 8 September 1957, trans. and quoted in Memorandum for the Steering Committee, 7 October 1958, DDEL, WHO, Office of the Special Assistant for Science and Technology, Series 1: Alphabetical Series, Subseries B: non-Top Secret File, Box #6, Department of Defense (1957) (1), 1-2. I am indebted to David Snead for sharing this reference with me.

17 LeMay, 'Strategic Air Command: Question Period,' 28 January 1954, 2.

18 'SAC Targeting Concepts,' History of SAC, Historical Study #73A, Top Secret, 5. This document was declassified at my FOIA request, and a copy provided to the National Security Archives. See also LeMay to Chief of Staff, 'Strategic Air Command Capabilities,' 20 January 1951, LoC, LeMay Papers, Box 197; LeMay to Vandenberg, 'SAC Capability,' 15 January 1951, LoC, LeMay Papers, Box 197; LeMay to Vandenberg, 'SAC Capability,' 23 April 1951, LoC, LeMay Papers, Box 197; USAF Deputy Inspector General to USAF Inspector General, 'Report on Strategic Air Command Capabilities to Initiate and Sustain Combat Operations,' 19 March 1951, LoC, LeMay Papers, Box 197.

19 Memorandum for the Chief of Staff, USAF, 20 June 1956, LoC, Twining Papers, Box #92, 1956 Top Secret Material (2), 1. See also Memorandum for the Chairman, Joint Chiefs of Staff, 18 October 1955, NARA, RG 218, JCS, Radford Records, CJCS 381 (Continental Defense), 1; and Memorandum for the Air Force Council (from Twining), 2 March 1956, *ibid.*, 1956 Top Secret Material (1), 1-2; and 'SAC Targeting Concepts,' 5.

20 James R Fuchs, Oral History Interview with General Robert B Landry, 28 February 1974, Scottsdale, Arizona, HSTL, 77-78.

21 Gerald K Haines, 'A Die Hard Issue: CIA's Role in the Study of UFOs, 1947-90,' 1 *Studies in Intelligence* (1997).

22 Compare Edward Oxford, 'Night of the Martians,' *American History Illustrated,* 23 October 1988, 14-23; Hadley Cantril, *The Invasion from Mars* (Princeton: Princeton University Press, 1940); and Howard Koch, *The Panic Broadcast* (Boston: Little, Brown, 1970) with Brad Schwarz, *Broadcast Hysteria: Orson Welles's War of the Worlds and the Art of Fake News* (New York: Hill and Wang, 2015).

23 Thomas J Patton, 'The Monitoring of War Indicators,' *Studies in Intelligence* 3 (Winter 1959): 55-56, 61.

24 'Spaatz Board Report;' and Rositzke, *CIA's Secret Operations,* 21.

25 Patton, 'The Monitoring of War Indicators,' 56-59; Cynthia M Grabo, 'The Watch Committee and the National Indications Center: The Evolution of U.S. Strategic Warning 1950-1975,' *International Journal of Intelligence and Counterintelligence* 3 (Fall 1989): 363-85; R Cargill Hall, 'Origins of US Space Policy: Eisenhower, Open Skies, and Freedom of Space,' in *Exploring the Unknown: Selected Documents in the History of the US Civil Space Program,* vol. I, *Organizing for Exploration,* ed. John M Logsdon (Washington, DC: NASA History Office, 1995), 220; and Mary McCarthy, 'The National Warning System: Striving for an Elusive Goal,' *Defense Intelligence Journal* 3 (Spring 1994): 6.

26 Grabo, 'The Watch Committee and the National Indications Center,' 369-70; and Hall, 'Origins of US Space Policy,' 220.

27Charles P Cabell, *A Man of Intelligence: Memoirs of War, Peace, and the CIA*, Charles P Cabell, Jr, ed. (Colorado Springs, CO: Impavide, 1997), 249; and Grabo, 'The Watch Committee and the National Indications Center,' 370.

28 Report of the Technological Capabilities Panel of the Science Advisory Committee, 15 February 1955, in *FRUS,* 1955-57, XIX, 41. This topic is discussed in depth in Matthew D Taylor, 'Toward a Nuclear Strategy: Eisenhower and the Challenge of Soviet Power' (Ph.D. diss., Rice University, 1992), 366-416. Hall suggests that Eisenhower was fixated on 'surprise attack and his dedication to forestalling such an event.' Hall, 'Origins of US Space Policy,' 220, note 33; and idem, 'The Eisenhower Administration and the Cold War,' 60-63, 65, 68, 70 note 7.

29 Bissell, *Reflections of a Cold Warrior,* 103; and 'Intelligence Briefing for Reconnaissance Symposium,' 2, NSArch. Emphasis in original.

30 'US Policy on Continental Defense,' NSC 5802/1, 19 February 1958; 'Official Report of the United States Delegation to the Conference of Experts for the Study of Possible Measures Which Might Be Helpful in Preventing Surprise Attack and for the Preparation of a Report Thereon to Governments,' Geneva, Switzerland, November 10-December 18, 1958,' NARA, RG359, Subject Files, 1957-62, Box 47; Jeremi Suri, 'America's Search for a Technological Solution to the Arms Race: The Surprise Attack Conference of 1958 and a Challenge for 'Eisenhower Revisionists',' *Diplomatic History* 21(Summer1997): 417-51; and Gregg Herken, *Counsels of War* (New York: Alfred A Knopf, 1985), 123-25.

31 L Wainstein, et al, *The Evolution of US Strategic Command and Control and Warning, 1945- 1972,* Study S-467 (Arlington, VA: Institute for Defense Analysis, June 1975), 89-112, 195-220; 'Meeting the Threat of Surprise Attack,' in Marc Trachtenberg, ed., *The Development of American Strategic Thought: Basic Documents from the Eisenhower and Kennedy Periods, Including the Basic National Security Policy Papers from 1953 to 1959* (New York: Garland Publishing, 1988), 356-57; 'Memorandum From the Joint Chiefs of Staff to the Secretary of Defense (Wilson),' 19 August 1955, in *FRUS,* 1955-1957, vol. XX, 184; 'United States Outline Plan for the Implementation of President Eisenhower's Aerial Inspection Proposal, Submitted to the Disarmament Subcommittee, August 30, 1955,' in Department of State, *Documents on Disarmament, 1945-1959,* vol. 1, *1945-1956* (Washington, DC: Department of State Historical Office, August 1960), 502; and Diary entry, 11 October 1950, LeMay Diary #2, Box 103, LeMay Papers.

32 'Meeting the Threat of Surprise Attack,' in Trachtenberg, *Development of American Strategic Thought,* 356-57; and 'Brief on the Pattern of War in the Atomic Warfare Age,' 16 December 1948, Secret, in Thomas H Etzold, and John Lewis Gaddis, eds., *Containment: Documents on American Policy and Strategy, 1945-1950* (New York: Columbia University Press, 1978), 45.

33 'Probable Warning of Soviet Attack on the US Through Mid-1957' Special National Intelligence Estimate SNIE-11-8-54, 3, 7, NARA, Military Records Branch, National Intelligence Estimates, Box 2. I am indebted to Gene Matthews for this document; and Curtis E LeMay, 'Interview – We Must Avoid the First Blow,' *US News & World Report,* 9 December 1955, 38, 50. This foreknowledge of an impending attack and the American response raises the thorny issue of intelligence and preemptive or preventive war. See Herken, *Counsels of War,* 94-98; and Kaplan, *Wizards of Armageddon,* 133-34. Examples of the limits of early warning and its potential for error are considered in Scott D Sagan, *The Limits of Safety: Organizations, Accidents, and Nuclear Weapons* (Princeton: Princeton University Press, 1993), 117-55.

34 'Intelligence Briefing for Reconnaissance Symposium,' 6; and Patton, 'The Monitoring of War Indicators,' 66-67.

35 For the original intelligence requirement see 'Request for Reconnaissance on Franz Josef Land,' 3 January 1952, Top Secret, NARA, RG341 Entry 214, Box 62, 2-22137. For a description of the mission by the pilot, see Roy Kaden, 'Overflight of the Franz Josef Land Archipelago,' in Hall and Laurie, Memoirs, 227-244. During a coincidental concurrent press tour of Thule AB, the *New York Times* and *Life Magazine* unwittingly identified Kaden's mission, saying 'The Russians are rumored to have set up a counterpart to Thule somewhere in Franz Josef Land.' Austin Stevens, 'US Creates Huge Air Base in Far North of Greenland,' *New York Times*, 19 September 1952, 1; and 'Birth of a Base: Now US Can be Told of the Huge Effort to Build 'Blue Jay' in Northern Greenland,' *Life,* 22 September 1952, 130-151.

36 'Soviet B-29 Airfields,' SAC Intel Brief 62, 2 August 1948, AFHRA 416.606-62; and 'Soviet Air Facilities in Northeastern Siberia,' SAC Intel Brief 63, 2 August 1948, AFHRA 416.606-63.

37 Diary entry, 22 July 1950, LoC, LeMay Papers LeMay Diary #2, Box 103; 'The Significance of Iceland as a Strategic Air Base,' SAC Intel Brief 30, 16 December 1947, AFHRA 416.606.30; 'The Significance of Spitsbergen (Svalbard) as a Strategic Base,' SAC Intel Brief 32, 26 January 1948, AFHRA 416.606.32; and 'Iceland: Where US May Lose a Base,' *US News & World Report,* 13 April 1956, 43-44, 46.

38 'The Russian B-29,' in Memorandum for Colonel Hugh D Wallace from Colonel Robert Taylor, Collection Branch, Air Intelligence Requirements Division, Directorate of Intelligence, 8 March 1948, 2-8389, NARA, RG341, Entry 214, Box 45, 2-8300-2-8399; Farquhar, 'A Need to Know,' 122; [William Green], 'The Billion Dollar Bomber,' *Air Enthusiast,* September 1971, 215; and R Cargill Hall to the author, 3 February 1997. For evidence of Soviet intentions to develop a 100-division-strong strategic aerial strike force in 1952, see N N Ostroumov, 'Armada, Kotoraia ne vzletela' [The Armada that Never Took Off], *Voenno-Istorisheskii Zhurnal,* October 1992, 39-40 [translated for the author by Michael C O'Brien].

39 Hopkins and Goldberg, *Development of Strategic Air Command, 1946-1986*, 16; Curtis E LeMay, with MacKinlay Kantor, *Mission with LeMay* (Garden City, NY: Doubleday, 1965), 433; and Borowski, *A Hollow Threat,* 139-73.

40 LeMay, 'SAC: Question Period,' 9-10.

41 Owen Lattimore, 'New Road to Asia,' *National Geographic,* December 1944, 641.

42 [Green], 'Billion Dollar Bomber,' 214.

43 Yefim Gordon, *Soviet Strategic Aviation in the Cold War* (Manchester, England: Hikoki, 2009), 75-82.

44 Les Anenson, quoted in Jacobsen, *Convair B-36,* 162-63.

45 'Soviet Capabilities For a Surprise Attack on the Continental United States Before July 1952,' Central Intelligence Agency, SE-10, 15 September 1951, [Top Secret], 2-4, 8, 19, DDRS, 1994, 1851, Fiche 156, CIA

46 Memo from AF Sec Symington to SecDef Johnson 8 Nov 49, HSTL, NSC Atomic, Atomic Energy-Russia, Box 201; 'The Soviet Air Forces: Summary,' CIA IM-203, 25 July 1949, Top Secret, HSTL, PSF, Foreign Affairs File, Russia 1949-1952 (Top Secret) Box 187; [Green], 'Billion Dollar Bomber,' 224; and Piotr Butowski and Jay Miller, *OKB MiG: A History of the Design Bureau and its Aircraft* (Leicester, England: Midland Counties, 1991), 134.

47 Gordon, *Soviet Strategic Aviation in the Cold War*, 27; and Yefim Gordon, Dmitriy Komissarov, and Vladimir Rigmant, *Tupolev Tu-4: The First Soviet Strategic Bomber* (Altglen, PA: Schiffer Military Publishing, 2014), 205-208.

48 Interview with Sergei Khrushchev by William Taubman, quoted in idem, *Khrushchev: The Man and His Era* (New York: Norton, 2003) 243, 347; 'Soviet B-29 Airfields,' SAC Intel Brief 62, 2 August 1948, AFHRA 416.606-62; and 'Soviet Air Facilities in Northeastern Siberia,' SAC Intel Brief 63, 2 August 1948, AFHRA 416.606-63.

49 Amnon Sella, *The Value of Human Life in Soviet Warfare*, (New York: Routledge, 1992); Geoffrey Roberts, *Stalin's Wars: From World War to Cold War, 1939-1953* (New Haven, CT: Yale University Press, 2008); Vasily Grossman, *A Writer at War: A Soviet Journalist with the Red Army, 1941-1945*, trans. and ed. Antony Beevor (New York: Vintage, Reprint edition 2007); and Catherine Merridale, *Ivan's War: Life and Death in the Red Army, 1939-1945* (New York: Picador, 2007).

50 'SAC Targeting Concepts,' 13.
51 Jessup, 'MiG-15 Dims USAF's A-Bomb Hopes,' 16; and Moody, *Building a Strategic Air Force*, 109.
52 SNIE-11-8-54, 9; and Curtis LeMay, speech to the Air War College, Maxwell AFB, AL, 9 January 1952, K239.716252-110, AFHRA, 28.
53 White, *World in Peril*, 31, 45-49, 129-31, 199-200; Memorandum to the Chief of the Air Intelligence Requirements Division, Subject: Coordination of Photo and Electronic Intelligence Activities, 11 December 1947, NARA, RG 341, Entry 214, 2-600 – 2-699; Memorandum for Record, Subject: Photographic Coverage – Chukotskii Peninsula Airfields, n.d., NARA, RG 341, Entry 214, 2-1500 – 2-1599 (May 1948); and Letter, Alaskan Air Command/CC (Armstrong) to USAF/CC (Vandenberg), Subject: Photographic Coverage of Northeastern Siberia, 4 November 1949, NARA, RG 341, Entry 214, 2-10097.
54 'Photographic Coverage of Northeastern Siberia,' [7 November 1949], Top Secret, NARA, RG 341, Entry 214, 2-10097.
55 Memorandum for Record, 'Air Defense Command Reconnaissance Requirements [5 June 1951],' AFOIN-C/CC-2, 23 November 1951, Top Secret, NARA, RG 341 Entry 214; 'Request for Photography,' 26 August 1952, Top Secret-Security Information, NARA, RG 341 Entry 214, Box 67, 2-24800-2-24899; and 'Memorandum for Record,' 13 November 1952, Top Secret-Security Information, NARA, RG 341 Entry 214, Box 67, 2-24800 - 2-24899.
56 Pocock, *U-2 Spyplane*, 136.
57 Hopkins, *The Boeing KC-135*, 89, 102-103. Additional programs included those for mid-course and re-entry identification and targeting. *Ibid.*, 107-108. Nothing came of these tests.
58 'Memorandum for Record,' AFOIN-1A2, 78061, 26 August 1954, Top Secret, NARA, RG341, Entry 214, Box 77, 4-2104.
59 Memorandum for the Deputy Director for Intelligence, The Joint Staff, 'Aerial Photo Reconnaissance,' 1 August 1952, Top Secret-Security Information, NARA, RG341, Entry 214, Box 67, 2-24412.
60 Memorandum for the Records, 15 March 1949, Top Secret, NARA, RG341, 2-6725; and Hall, 'Cold War Overflights,' 14.
61 Memorandum for the Records, 15 March 1949, Top Secret, NARA, RG341, 2-6725.
62 SNIE-11-8-54, 3, 6, 8, 9, 10; and 'Draft Study on Proposed Possible Reconnaissance Routes Over the USSR,' 28 September 1950, NARA, RG341 Entry 214.
63 Operations Plan Serial No.X-52, 6th Sir *[sic]* Division, MacDill Air Force Base, 10 July 1952, LoC, Nathan F Twining Papers, Box 122, Folder Top Secret File 1952-57 (2); Hillman and Hall, 'Overflight,' 35-37; interview with the aircraft commander, Colonel Donald E Hillman, USAF (retired), 15 May 1996; Hall, 'Cold War Overflights,' 9-10; and Koch, 'Joint Service Overflights in the Soviet Far East,' in Hall and Laurie, *Memoirs*, 148.
64 Mitchell, 'The Air Force and Peripheral Reconnaissance, 1946-1990,' 11; and Letter, Alaskan Air Command/CC (Armstrong) to USAF/CC (Vandenberg), Subject: Photographic Coverage of Northeastern Siberia, 4 November 1949, NARA, RG341, Entry 214, 2-10097.
65 SNIE-11-8-54, 3, 4, 6, 8, 9, 10.
66 Eisenhower, *Waging Peace*, 547; and Louis J Halle, *The Cold War as History* (New York: Harper, 1967; Harper Perennial, 1991), 371-72.
67 Memorandum form CIA to Exec Sec NSC, 'Atomic Energy Program of the USSR,' (Top Secret), 20 April 1949, HSTL, PSF, NSC–Atomic Energy-Russia, Box 201.
68 Memorandum from AF Sec Symington to SecDef Johnson, 8 November 1949, (Secret), 1, 6, HSTL, PSF, NSC-Atomic Energy-Russia, Box 201; and Undated Top Secret document, 4, HSTL, PSF, NSC-Atomic, Atomic Energy-Russia, Box 29.
69 Jack H Nunn, *The Soviet First Strike Threat* (New York: Praeger, 1982), 91.
70 Memorandum for the Chairman, Intelligence Advisory Committee, 'Critical National Intelligence Objectives with Respect to the USSR,' 10 July 1950, Top Secret, NARA, RG341, Entry 214, File no. 2-14112.
71 Oleg Bukharin, 'The Cold War Atomic Intelligence Game, 1945-70,' *Studies in Intelligence* 48 ([Fall] 2004): 11.
72 'Indications of Soviet Atomic Energy Facilities in USSR,' 25 November 1947, Top Secret, SAC Intel Brief 26, AFHRA, 416.606-26.
73 Should he be asked during the 1949 announcement about how the US detected the Soviet blast, Truman was to respond, 'You will realize that it would not be compatible with national security to tell you how we know there was an atomic explosion.' Draft of Presidential Remarks re: Soviet A-Bomb, Top Secret, HSTL, PSF, Foreign Affairs File, Russia 1949-1952 (Top Secret), Box 187.
74 Pocock, *Dragon Lady*, 39; and Bissell, *Reflections of a Cold Warrior*, 119.
75 Quoted in Ben Rich and Leo Janos, *Skunk Works: A Personal Memoir of My Years at Lockheed*, (Boston: Little, Brown, 1994), 155. Emphasis in original.
76 *Ibid.*, 156-57; and Chris Pocock, *50 Years of the U-2: The Complete Illustrated History of the 'Dragon Lady'* (Altglen, PA: Schiffer, 2004), 57.
77 Herbert Scoville, 'Policing a Nuclear Test Ban,' *Studies in Intelligence* 3 (Winter 1958): 2, 6.
78 'History of the Long-Range Detection Program,' 21 July 1948, Top Secret-Restricted Data, 2-3, 5. HSTL, PSF, Box 199, NSC Atomic/LRDP. The origins and evolution of the LRDP program are well chronicled in Ziegler and Jacobson, *Spying Without Spies*; and Richelson, *Spying on the Bomb*, 74-94
79 Memorandum for the Acting Director of Central Intelligence, 'Atomic Explosion in the USSR,' 1 October 1951, Top Secret, HSTL, PSF, Box 201, NSC Atomic/Russia; Richelson, *Spying on the Bomb*, 114.
80 Curtis LeMay, speech to the Air War College, Maxwell AFB, AL, 9 January 1952, K239.716252-110, AFHRA.
81 Memorandum for General McDonald, Subject: Strategic Reconnaissance, 31 January 1948, Top Secret, 2, NARA, RG341 Entry 214, 2-848.
82 'Requirements for Expansion of the Air Intelligence Effort to Accelerate and Improve the Air Defense for the United States and Alaska,' 27 Oct 1949, Top Secret, NARA RG 341; Samuel R Williamson, Jr, and Steven L Rearden, *The Origins of US Nuclear Strategy, 1945-1953* (New York: St Martin's Press, 1993), 164; Diary entry, 11 October 1950, LeMay Diary #2, Box 103, LeMay Papers.
83 David Alan Rosenberg, 'The Origins of Overkill: Nuclear Weapons and American Strategy,' in *The National Security: Its Theory and Practice, 1945-1960*, ed. Norman A Graebner, 123-95, (New York: Oxford University Press, 1986), 137; Christopher Simpson, *Operation BLOWBACK: America's Recruitment of Nazis and its*

Effects on the Cold War, (New York: Weidenfeld & Nicolson, 1988), 63, 72; 'Increase in Troop Spaces for the 1134th Special Activities Squadron,' AFOIN-Adm, 19 July 1949, Top Secret, NARA, RG 341, Entry 214, 2- 8041A; and 'Requirements for Expansion of the Air Intelligence Effort to Accelerate and Improve the Air Defense for the United States and Alaska,' 27 Oct 1949, Top Secret, NARA RG 341.

84 'Transmittal of Intelligence Requirements,' from Major General George C McDonald, Director of Intelligence, Office of Deputy Chief of Staff, Operations, 28 January 1948, Top Secret, Appendix I, 2, NARA RG341, 2-823/3.

85 JPS 789/1, Staff Studies of Certain Military Problems Deriving from [JPS 789] 'Concept of Operations for 'PINCHER',' Appendix B, 13 April 1946, 19, in Steven T Ross and David Alan Rosenberg, eds., *America's Plans for War Against the Soviet Union, 1945-1950,* vol. 2, *The Pincher Plans* (New York: Garland, 1989).

86 'Evaluation of Effect on Soviet War Effort Resulting from the Strategic Air Offensive,' [the Harmon Report] 11 May 1949, in Etzold and Gaddis, *Containment,* 360-64; and David Rosenberg, 'American Atomic Strategy and the Hydrogen Bomb Decision,' *Journal of American History 66* (June 1979): 72-73. On Soviet will to resist, see Merridale, *Ivan's War.*

87 Borowski, *A Hollow Threat,* 182-83; Phillip S Meilinger, *Hoyt S Vandenberg: The Life of a General,* (Bloomington, IN: Indiana University Press, 1986), 134; Ponturo, *The WSEG Experience, 1948-1976,* 5, 74; Borgiasz, *Strategic Air Command,* 17, 19; and Farquhar, 'A Need to Know,' 136-38.

88 Paul K Carlton, Major, USAF, diary entry, 23 June 1950, 'Commanding General's Diary,' LeMay Papers, Box 103, LeMay Diary #1 folder, 1 Jan 50 to 30 Jun 50, LoC; Rosenberg, 'Origins of Overkill,' 131, 133; and LeMay, 'SAC,' 5, 32.

89 LeMay, 'SAC,' 31.

90 LeMay Diary, 23 January 1951, LoC.

91 Ross and Rosenberg, *The Pincher Plans;* Ross, *American War Plans,* 25-52; and Farquhar, 'A Need to Know,' 48, 52-55.

92 Farquhar, 'A Need to Know,' 65, 93-99, 109; Rosenberg, 'Origins of Overkill,' 134-41; Ross, *American War Plans, 1945-1950,* 53-78, 103-35.

93 R D Little, *The History of Air Force Participation in the Atomic Energy Program, 1943-1953,* vol. 2, part 1, *Foundations of an Atomic Air Force and Operation Sandstone, 1946-1948* (Washington, DC: Air Force Historical Liaison Office, n.d.), sanitized copy, 249; and Borgiasz, *Strategic Air Command,* 41.

94 LeMay, 'SAC,' 31.

95 Memorandum for General McDonald, Subject: Strategic Reconnaissance, 31 January 1948, Top Secret, 2, NARA, RG341 Entry 214, 2-848; and *SAC Reconnaissance, 1950,* 9.

96 Memorandum for General McDonald, Subject: Strategic Reconnaissance, 31 January 1948, Top Secret, 2, NARA, RG341 Entry 214, 2-848.

97 Natola, *Boeing B-47 Stratojet*, 91-92.

98 Quoted in Rich and Janos, *Skunk Works,* 148.

99 Bissell, *Reflections of a Cold Warrior,* 105; and Ludwell L Montague, 'Priority National Intelligence Objectives,' *Studies in Intelligence* 5 (Spring 1961): 1-8.

100 'Memorandum for the Record,' 12 February 1959, in *FRUS,* 1958-1960, vol. X, 260.

101 Directorate of Targets, USAF, 'Semi-Annual History,' 1 January 1959 thru 30 June 1959, 49-50, Secret, NSArch.

102 Cabell, *A Man of Intelligence*, 323.

103 *SAC Operations in the United Kingdom, 1948-1956,* 7th Air Division Historical Division, 3 January 1956 (Secret-Restricted Data), AFHRA K416.04-11, 25, 27. This document was declassified at my FOIA request, and a copy provided to the National Security Archives. The original report on file at the AFHRA remains classified.

104 Harry Lever, 'Strat Recon + Technical Aids = Pinpoint Bombing,' *Flying,* April 1952, 16.

105 'History of Electronic Countermeasures during the Korean Conflict, June 1950 to July 1953,' 3 May 1954, AFHRA, K720.04C; Leonid Krylov, *Soviet MiG-15 Aces of the Korean War,* (Oxford: Osprey Publishing, 2008); and Jessup, 'MiG-15 Dims USAF's A-Bomb Hopes,' 16.

106 'Transmittal of Intelligence Requirements,' from Major General George C McDonald, Director of Intelligence, Office of Deputy Chief of Staff, Operations, 28 January 1948, Top Secret, Appendix I, 1, NARA RG341, 2-823/3.

107 *Ibid.*

108 'Deficiencies Affecting Combat Capability,' 1 October 1950; F M Sallagar to Brig Gen J B Montgomery, 'Comments on the Initial Atomic Strike Capability of SAC,' 12 September 1950, LoC, LeMay Papers, Box B196; Air Force Director of Intelligence, 'Critique of OFF-TACKLE-DROPSHOT and REAPER-HEADSTONE,' n.d., NARA, RG341, General File July 1945-December 1954, folder 2-17700-2-17799; Wainstein, et al, *Evolution of US Strategic Command and Control,* 21, 150; and Borgiasz, *Strategic Air Command,* 19.

109 'Collection of Foreign Scientific and Technological Data,' Secret, HSTL, PSF, NSC/Directives, Box 192; and 'Draft Study on Proposed Possible Reconnaissance Routes Over the USSR,' 28 September 1950, NARA, RG341. For two examples of how ELINT flights resolved these issues, see Farquhar, 'A Need to Know,' 60-62.

110 Bissell, *Reflections of a Cold Warrior,* 121.

111 'Request for Radar Information and Photography,' 20 December 1951, Top Secret-Security Information, NARA, RG341, Entry 214, 2-2180719.

112 'Intelligence Briefing for Reconnaissance Symposium,' 12.

113 Daniel T Kuehl, 'Refighting the Last War: Electronic Warfare and U.S. Air Force B-29 Operations in the Korean War, 1950-53.' *Journal of Military History* 56 (January 1992): 87, 107, 109.

114 LeMay, 'SAC,' 40.

115 'Intelligence Briefing for Reconnaissance Symposium,' 15.

116 Borgiasz, *Strategic Air Command,* 14.

117 Tegler, *B-47 Stratojet*, 120-21; and Lloyd, *Boeing's B-47 Stratojet*, 111-13.

118 Roy Medvedev, *Khrushchev,* trans. Brian Pearce (Garden City, NY: Anchor Press/Doubleday, 1983), 151.

119 Steven J Zaloga, *Soviet Air Defence Missiles: Design, Development and Tactics* (Surrey, England: Jane's Information Group, 1989), 6-13, 26-48.

120 Farquhar, 'A Need to Know,' 188.

121 Chuck Hansen, *US Nuclear Weapons: The Secret History* (New York: Crown, 1988), 109-171, esp. 143 and 146.

122 David Alan Rosenberg, "A Smoking Radiating Ruin at the End of Two Hours:' Documents on American Plans

for Nuclear War with the Soviet Union, 1954-1955,' *International Security* 6 (Winter 1981/82): 3-38; Desmond Ball and Jeffrey Richelson, eds. *Strategic Nuclear Targeting* (Ithaca, NY: Cornell University Press, 1986); Scott Sagan, 'SIOP-62: The Nuclear Plan Briefing to President Kennedy,' *International Security* 12 (Summer 1987): 22-51; and Peter Pringle and William Arkin. *S.I.O.P.: The Secret US Plan for Nuclear War* (New York: Norton, 1983); John R Glock, 'The Evolution of Air Force Targeting,' *Airpower Journal* 8 (Fall 1994): 14-28; Asher Lee, *Air Power* (New York: Praeger, 1955), 165-84; and Robert F Futrell, *Ideas, Concepts, Doctrine: Basic Thinking in the United States Air Force,* rev. ed. (Maxwell AFB, AL: Air University Press, 1989). On Cold War intelligence and targeting, see Farquhar, 'A Need to Know,' 108-149; Borgiasz, *Strategic Air Command,* 110-41; Rosenberg, 'Origins of Overkill,' 131-38; Peter J Roman, 'Curtis LeMay and the Origins of NATO Atomic Targeting,' *Journal of Strategic Studies* 16 (March 1993): 46-74; and Richard G Hubler, *SAC, the Strategic Air Command* (New York: Duell, Sloan, and Pearce, 1958; reprint, Westport, CT: Greenwood Press, 1977), 243-44.
123 Rosenberg, 'A Smoking Radiating Ruin,' 18.
124 General Bruce K Holloway, interview with the author, 5 September 1996, Offutt AFB, Nebraska.
125 'History of Headquarters Strategic Air Command 1961,' SAC Historical Study 89, Top Secret, 157, 167.
126 Rosenberg, 'A Smoking Radiating Ruin,' 18.
127 Robert F Futrell, 'The Influence of the Air Power Concept on Air Force Planning, 1945-1962,' in Harry R Borowski, ed., *Military Planning in the Twentieth Century: Proceedings of the Eleventh Military History Symposium at the US Air Force Academy* (Washington, DC: Office of Air Force History, 1986), 266.
128 Quoted in Peter J Roman, *Eisenhower and the Missile Gap*, (Ithaca, NY: Cornell University Press, 1995), 90.
129 Sagan, 'SIOP-62,' 42.
130 Quoted in Roman, *Eisenhower and the Missile Gap*, 99.
131 *Ibid.*, 99-102.
132 Sagan, 'SIOP-62,' 44; Rosenberg, 'A Smoking Radiating Ruin,' 16; and Stephen I Schwartz, ed. *Atomic Audit: The Costs and Consequences of US Nuclear Weapons Since 1940* (Washington, DC: Brookings, 1998) 200.
133 David Alan Rosenberg on 'US Planning for a Soviet Nuclear Attack,' at http://www.pbs.org/wgbh/amex/bomb/filmmore/reference/interview/rosenberg02.html; accessed 18 July 2015.
134 'Exposing the US Nuclear War Plan,' at http://www.nrdc.org/nuclear/nwarplan.asp; accessed 18 July 2015.
135 See, for example, Roman, *Eisenhower and the Missile Gap*; Edgar M Bottome, *The Missile Gap: A Study in the Formulation of Military and Political Policy* (Rutherford, NJ: Fairleigh Dickinson University Press, 1971); Prados, *The Soviet Estimate*; and Kaplan, *Wizards of Armageddon*, 155-73.
136 Bissell, *Reflections of a Cold Warrior,* 131; quoted in Schwartz, *Atomic Audit*, 233; Beschloss, *Mayday,* 367; and John Sloan, *Eisenhower and the Management of Prosperity* (Lawrence, KS: University Press of Kansas, 1991), 156.
137 Roman, *Eisenhower and the Missile Gap*, 146. Emphasis added.
138 Neil Sheehan, *A Fiery Peace in the Cold War: Bernard Schriever and the Ultimate Weapon* (New York: Random House: 2009), 269, 299, 301-302; and 'Memorandum of Discussion at the 333d Meeting of the National Security Council, Washington, August 1, 1957,' in *FRUS*, 1955-57, XIX, 571-72.
139 Note the different budget limits of $38 and $39 billion. The actual budget cap was $39 billion, so discussions referred to a $38 billion budget.
140 Roman, *Eisenhower and the Missile Gap*, 119.
141 *Ibid.*, 122, note 42.
142 *Ibid.*, 128, note 59.
143 *Ibid.*, 30-62, and 128-29.
144 Quoted in Roman, *Eisenhower and the Missile Gap*, 134-36.
145 Hopkins, *Boeing KC-135 Stratotanker*, 31, 52.
146 Sheehan says *Sputnik* was a 'blessing out of the blue for [Bernard] Schriever,' the Air Force general leading the ICBM development program. *Sputnik* transformed what Secretary of the Air Force Donald Quarles called the 'Poor Man's' ICBM budget into a top budgetary priority. Sheehan, *A Fiery Peace in a Cold War*, 365.
147 'Despite the president's claims of indifference to a non-negotiable cap, he did nothing to dissuade Wilson and his successor McElroy that he would be flexible in approving the DoD budget.' Roman, *Eisenhower and the Missile Gap*, 234, note 23.

Chapter Five
Who's in Control?

1 General Curtis E LeMay Oral History [hereafter 'LeMay Oral History-1976'], 17 November 1976, AFHRA, K.239.0512-1450, 1-2.
2 Lashmar, 'Stranger Than 'Strangelove',' C9; idem, 'Killer on the Edge,' *New Statesman and Society,* 20-22; idem, *Spy Flights of the Cold War;* 'General Curtis LeMay,' produced by Lashmar; Rhodes, *Dark Sun,* 564-66, 568; and idem, 'The General and World War III,' 47-59.
3 Sheila Kerr, 'KGB Sources on the Cambridge Network of Soviet Agents: True or False?' *Intelligence and National Security* 11 (July 1996): 562.
4 I F Stone, 'Keep 'Em Flying,' review of *Mission With LeMay*, by Curtis LeMay with MacKinlay Cantor. New York Review of Books, 20 January 1966; reprinted in I F Stone, with an Introduction by Peter Onos, *The Best of I.F. Stone* (New York: PublicAffairs, 2006), 326-38.
5 Timothy Naftali and Philip Zelikow, eds., *The Presidential Recordings: John F. Kennedy*, vol. 2 (New York: W W Norton, 2001), 583; and Dobbs, *One Minute to Midnight*, 21.
6 Brugioni, *Eyes in the Sky*, 85, 88, 161. When I first met LeMay in 1975 he spoke in brief, hushed sentences during the entirety of our ten-minute 'conversation,' choosing to nod a lot and constantly relighting his pipe.
7 Warren Kozak, *LeMay: The Life and Wars of General Curtis LeMay* (Washington DC: Regnery, 2009), 280, 388.
8 Rhodes, *Dark Sun*, 21; and Robert S McNamara, *The Fog of War: Eleven Lessons from the Life of Robert S. McNamara*, a film by Errol Morris, 2003.
9 Lashmar, *Spy Flights of the Cold War,* 202, 204, 207.
10 Rhodes, *Dark Sun,* 568.
11 Quoted in Kaplan, *Wizards of Armageddon*, 134.

Kaplan offers no reference for this verbatim conversation, which may be reconstructed from his 23 November 1981 interview with Sprague. *Ibid.*, 392.
12 Lloyd, *Boeing's B-47 Stratojet*, 103; Kozak, *LeMay*, 290-91, 313; Sheehan, *A Fiery Peace in the Cold War*, 448; and Brugioni, *Eyes in the Sky*, 71.
13 'USAF Electronic Reconnaissance Program,' 21 July 1949, Top Secret, NARA, RG 341, Entry 214, 2-8177. Tab E of this document identifies additional directive on the early organization of strategic aerial reconnaissance, but has yet to be made available; USAF Letter, AFOAC 311, subject 'Joint Electronic Countermeasures Policy,' dated 10 February 1948, NARA, RG 341, Entry 214; and USAF Letter, AFOIR 311.5, subject, 'Security of Airborne Electronic Reconnaissance Operations,' dated 3 March 1948, NARA, RG 341, Entry 214. Vandenberg's earlier tenure from June 1946 through May 1947 as Director of Central Intelligence of the Central Intelligence Group and his appreciation of strategic airpower suggest his strong personal commitment to these flights to satisfy US intelligence requirements. See Charles R Christensen, 'An Assessment of General Hoyt S Vandenberg's Accomplishments as Director of Central Intelligence' [hereafter 'Vandenberg as DCI'], *Intelligence and National Security* 11 (October 1996): 754-64.
14 SESP, 22 Jul 1950, 1. No unclassified documents have been identified which show the extent or nature of this liaison.
15 SESP, 5 May 1950, 1.
16 *Ibid.*, 2.
17 See, for example, 'Telegram: Ambassador in Soviet Union to Secretary of State,' in *FRUS,* 1950, vol. IV, 1141-42.
18 SESP, 5 May 1950.
19 Diary entry, 26 June 1950, LeMay Diary #1, Box 103, LeMay Papers, LoC.
20 Farquhar, 'Cold War in Flames,' 24.
21 NSC Action 330, 'Photo Reconnaissance of Certain Portions of the China Coast,' HSTL, PSF, NSC (A-D) Box 191, Subject File NSC Actions, Record of 1950.
22 Oral History Interview with General Robert B Landry, 28 February 1974, Scottsdale, Arizona, 8, James R Fuchs, HSTL.
23 Rosenberg, 'Origins of Overkill,' 127-28. The Navy also performed these missions, although in a significantly smaller proportion.
24 Moody, *Building a Strategic Air Force,* 230-32; and Borgiasz, *Strategic Air Command,* 13. There was also considerable confusion over the issue of delegated authority in the wake of the Defense reorganization act. Anna Kasten Nelson, 'President Truman and the Evolution of the National Security Council,' *Journal of American History* 72 (September 1985): 369-70; Borgiasz, *Strategic Air Command,* 9-11; and Christensen, 'Vandenberg as DCI,' 757-58.
25 'USAF Electronic Reconnaissance Program,' 21 July 1949, Top Secret, NARA, RG 341, Entry 214, 2-8177. For examples of Truman's willingness to delegate planning and operational authority in other intelligence matters, see *FRUS,* 1945-1950, *Emergence of the Intelligence Establishment;* Arthur B Darling, *The Central Intelligence Agency: An Instrument of Government to 1950* (University Park, PA; Penn State University Press, 1990; William M Leary, ed., *The Central Intelligence Agency: History and Documents* (University, AL: University of Alabama Press, 1984); Harry Howe Ransom, *The Intelligence Establishment* (Cambridge: Harvard University Press, 1970); and Thomas F Troy, *Donovan and the CIA: A History of the Establishment of the Central Intelligence Agency* (New York: Alethia Books, 1981).
26 Rosenberg, 'Origins of Overkill,' 129, 130, 140.
27 Mitchell, 'Air Force and Peripheral Reconnaissance,' 18, footnote 22; and 'Memorandum for Record, Problem: Limit on Offshore Distance for Reckon *[sic]* Flights in the Pacific Area,' Undated [May 1948], NARA, RG341, Entry 214, May 1948 Folder, 2-1500-2-1599.
28 SESP, 5 May 1950, 2.
29 Rosenberg, 'Origins of Overkill,' 136; and Farquhar, 'A Need to Know,' 154, note 15. Both Farquhar and Rosenberg drew their conclusions before the declassification of unequivocal proof of US military overflights of the USSR.
30 Alonzo L Hamby, *Man of the People: A Life of Harry S. Truman* (New York: Oxford University Press, 1995), 310.
31 Beschloss, *Mayday*, 249.
32 Twining Oral History, 134
33 *SAC Reconnaissance, 1950,* 19.
34 Diary entry, 12 May 1950, LeMay Diary #1, Box 103, LeMay Papers, LoC.
35 LeMay, 'SAC,' 42.
36 'Transmittal of Intelligence Requirements,' from Major General George C McDonald, Director of Intelligence, Office of Deputy Chief of Staff, Operations, 28 January 1948, Top Secret, Appendix I, 2. NARA RG 341, 2-823/3.
37 Major Raymond B Dunn, 'Penetration Problems of Strategic Reconnaissance,' Air Command and Staff College, April 1949, AFHRA 239.04349A-1 16, 1, 2, 8, and 13
38 'Normal Maximum Distribution of Photo Intelligence Reports and Associated Photography,' 7 October 1952, Top Secret-Security Information-Air Force Eyes Only, NARA, RG341, Box 69, 2-36461.
39 Undated Memorandum 'Photographic Coverage-Chukotskii Peninsula,' NARA, RG 341, Entry 214.
40 'Draft Study on Proposed Possible Reconnaissance Routes Over the USSR,' 28 September 1950, NARA, Entry 214.
41 Letter from Major General C P Cabell, USAF Director of Intelligence, to Colonel William A Adams, SAC/DI, 5 October 1950, NARA, RG341, Entry 214. Emphasis added.
42 *Ibid.*; and Burrows, *By Any Means Necessary*, 122.
43 Memorandum for Record, AFOIN-C/LtCol Bell/pg/71067, 27 November 1951, Top Secret, NARA, RG 341, Entry 214.
44 Memorandum for General Curtis LeMay, USAF, Commanding General, Strategic Air Command, from Major General Robert W Burns, USAF, Acting Deputy Chief of Staff, Operations, 5 July 1952. Sub: Special Aerial Photographic Operations. Reproduced in Hall, *Appendixes*, 449-50.
45 Memorandum for General Omar N Bradley, USA, Chairman, Joint Chiefs of Staff, from Robert A Lovett, Secretary of Defense, 12 August 1952, Sub: Reconnaissance Requirements. Reproduced in Hall, *Appendixes*, 451.
46 Memorandum for Gen Curtis E LeMay, USAF, Commanding General, Strategic Air Command, from Maj Gen Roger M Ramey, Director of Operations, USAF, Office of the Deputy Chief of Staff, Operations, 15

August 1952, Sub: Special Aerial Photographic Operations. Reproduced in Hall, *Appendixes*, 457-58.

47 Hall, 'Cold War Overflights,' 6-8. Most, if not all of the intelligence collected was shared with the United States. For more on the Anglo-American aerial intelligence relationship, see Alex Danchev, 'In the Back Room: Anglo-American Defence Co-operation, 1945-51,' in *British Intelligence, Strategy and the Cold War, 1945-51,* ed. Richard J Aldrich, (London: Routledge, 1992), 215-35. On the British U-2 flights, see Pocock, *Dragon Lady,* 45-46; Bissell, *Reflections of a Cold Warrior,* 116; and Nick Cook, 'How the CIA and RAF Teamed Up to Spy on the Soviet Union,' *Jane's Defence Weekly,* 7 August 1993, 11-15. Despite this close co-operation, one writer's claim that 'one in five' U-2 missions was flown by RAF pilots completely missed the mark. Campbell, *Unsinkable Aircraft Carrier,* 130. There were 24 CIA U-2 overflights of the USSR. Only two were undertaken by RAF pilots.

48 Letter from RAF Air Chief Marshal Sir Ralph A Cochrane to RAF Air Chief Marshal Sir William Elliot, 25 July 1951, Top Secret, Vandenberg Papers, LoC. Elliot was the air liaison at the British Joint Services Mission in Washington, DC; and Letter from RAF Air Chief Marshal Sir William Elliot to USAF General Hoyt S Vandenberg, 16 August 1951, Top Secret, Vandenberg Papers, LoC.

49 Letter from [RAF Air Chief Marshal Sir William Elliot] to RAF Air Chief Marshal Sir Ralph A Cochrane, 15 August 1951, Top Secret, Vandenberg Papers, LoC.

50 Letter from RAF Air Marshal John C Slessor to USAF General Hoyt S Vandenberg, 12 September 1952, Top Secret, Vandenberg Papers, LoC.

51 Lashmar, *Spy Flights of the Cold War,* 105, 202, 208.

52 Quoted in Pocock, *Dragon Lady*, 2.

53 Leghorn Oral History, 7.

54 Leghorn, 'US Can Photograph Russia,' 71. Emphasis in original.

55 Bissell, *Reflections of a Cold Warrior,* 94. Emphasis added.

56 The definitive work on Project CONTROL is Tami Davis Biddle, 'Handling the Soviet Threat: 'Project Control' and the Debate on American Strategy in the Early Cold War Years,' *Journal of Strategic Studies* 12 (September 1989): 273-302. See also David J Dean, 'Project Control: Creative Strategic Thinking at Air University,' *Air University Review* 35 (July-August 1984): 22-32.

57 Biddle, 'Handling the Soviet Threat,' 286, 287.

58 Quoted in Richard Overy, *The Bombing War: Europe 1939-1945* (London: Penguin, 2013), 356, 479.

59 Quoted in Biddle, 'Handling the Soviet Threat,' 288.

60 Lashmar, *Spy Flights of the Cold War,* 100, 103.

61 Curtis E LeMay, with MacKinlay Kantor, *Mission With LeMay* (Garden City, NY: Doubleday & Company, 1965), 481.

62 Bissell, *Reflections of a Cold Warrior,* 140.

63 Bohlen, *Witness to History*, 390.

64 Lashmar, *Spy Flights of the Cold War,* 102, 105.

65 Quoted in Lashmar, *Spy Flights of the Cold War,* 105-106. These remarks do not appear in Austin's own article about the incident. See Austin, 'Cold War Overflight.'

66 Kohn and Harahan, *Strategic Air Warfare,* 95-96; and LeMay Oral History-1972, 24.

67 Kaplan, *Wizards of Armageddon,* 133-34.

68 Austin, 'Cold War Overflight,' 18.

69 LeMay, *Mission With LeMay,* 481-82. Emphasis in original.

70 Quoted in Coffey, *Iron Eagle,* 338. For Eisenhower's approval of this mission see Welzenbach and Pedlow, *CIA and the U-2 Program* (2013), 126.

71 LeMay Oral History-1972, 23-24.

72 Curtis LeMay, speech to the Air War College, Maxwell AFB, AL, 9 January 1952, K239.716252-110, AFHRA, 5.

73 Lashmar, *Spy Flights of the Cold War,* 72-73, 134; and Beschloss, *Mayday,* 78-79.

74 LeMay to Twining, 17 November 1955, [Secret]; and 'Recommendation for Award of Air Force Outstanding Unit Award,' [1955], Secret, LeMay Papers, Box 60, Nathan F Twining Files, LoC.

75 Fredrik Fagertun, 'U-2 Flights in the North-Western Strategy, Intelligence Requirements, and Political Risks,' speech given at the Cold War Forum Conference on the Cold War in Bodø, Norway, 7-8 October 1995. Published in *U-2 Flights and the Cold War in the High North,* ed. Svein Lundestad, Bodø College and Norwegian Aviation Center, Bodø, January 1996, 45, 46.

76 White to LeMay, [10] August 1953, [Top Secret], LeMay Papers, Box 204, Folder B-29239, LoC. See also 'Specialized Reconnaissance Operations,' 6 May 1953, Top Secret-Security Information, Nathan F Twining Papers, Box 103, LoC; and 'Development of FEAF's Intelligence Collection Plan,' FEAF Historical Report, November 1953, 35, 40, AFHRA K-720.02, Box 4.

77 Austin, 'Cold War Overflight,' 16-17; and Forster and Gibson, *Listening In*, 66.

78 Marc Trachtenberg, 'Preventive War and US Foreign Policy,' *Security Studies* 16 (2007): 4-5. Preventive war was equally not unique to a decade-long window in American Cold War national security planning. See John Lewis Gaddis, *Surprise, Security, and the American Experience*, (Cambridge: Harvard University Press, 2004).

79 LeMay Oral History-1972, 8

80 Austin, interview with the author, 15-16 May 1996.

81 Truman quoted in Trachtenberg, 'Preventive War and US Foreign Policy,' 5. See note 7 for further examples and references to Truman's wishful thinking; Eisenhower quoted in *ibid.*, 6, emphasis in original; Eisnehower (Suez) quoted in Nichols, *Eisenhower 1956*, 247; and Vladislav M Zubok and Constantine Pleshakov, *Inside the Kremlin's Cold War: From Stalin to Khrushchev* (Cambridge: Harvard University Press, 1996), 67.

82 Roger K Rhodarmer, 'Recollections of an Overflight 'Legman',' in Hall and Laurie, *Memoirs*, 20-21, 27.

83 *Ibid.*, 30-31.

84 Bissell, *Reflections of a Cold Warrior,* 116-117. According to one source, deGaulle learned of the U-2 program and saw some of its products in 1959, although without apparently knowing their origin, and was fully informed about the program at the Four Power Summit in May 1960. Beschloss, *Mayday,* 276. Another source does not mention the earlier episode but corroborates the May 1960 briefing. Brugioni, *Eyeball to Eyeball,* 47-48.

85 Grimes, *History of Big Safari*, 21-22.

86 J F terHorst, and Ralph Albertazzie *The Flying White House: The Story of Air Force One* (New York: Coward, McCann & Geoghegan, 1979), 195-98.

87 In all fairness, I, too, originally reached similar conclusions about Eisenhower's ignorance of the flights. In a preliminary published conference paper I showed examples of military overflights but no evidence of presidential authorization for them. I believed then that they were undertaken without Eisenhower's explicit approval. Presuming that Eisenhower was inclined to delegate authority as part of his presidential management style, I concluded that Eisenhower delegated authority for overflights to his military commanders, thereby implicitly approving these flights. I used this to argue that Eisenhower's control of the intelligence gathering community was not as centralized as some scholars had asserted. Hopkins, 'An Expanded Understanding of Eisenhower, American Policy, and Overflights,' 334-36.

88 See Robert S Jordan, *An Unsung Hero: The Life of General Andrew J. Goodpaster* (Annapolis, MD: Naval Institute Press, 2013).

89 Quoted in Lashmar, *Spy Flights of the Cold War,* 94; idem, 'Stranger Than 'Strangelove',' C9; and 'General Curtis LeMay: The Man Who Wanted World War III,' produced by Paul Lashmar, aired in the United States by Arts & Entertainment Network on 22 February 1997.

90 Lashmar, *Spy Flights of the Cold War,* 94.

91 'Memorandum of a Conference With the President,' 28 May 1956, in *FRUS,* 1955-1957, vol. XXIV, 105; Telegram from Soviet Embassy to the Department of State, No.15, 14 May 1956; Telegram from the Department of State to the American Embassy in Moscow, 15 May 1956, Official Use Only; and Telegram from the Department of State to the American Embassy in Moscow, 29 May 1956, Confidential, NARA, RG59, Box 3512, 761.5411.

92 Andrew J Goodpaster, 'Cold War Overflights: A View From the White House,' in Hall and Laurie, *Memoirs*, 40.

93 Memorandum of Conference with the President November 15, 1956, 2:30 PM, Others Present: Secretary Hoover, Admiral Radford, Mr Allen Dulles, Mr Bissell, Colonel Goodpaster, by Col Andrew J Goodpaster, CE, USA, 15 November 1956, Sub: [Regarding the Desirability of Certain Reconnaissance Overflights]. Reproduced in Hall and Laurie, *Appendixes*, 572. Emphasis in original.

94 'Memorandum of a Conference With the President,' 28 May 1956, 107.

95 Goodpaster wrote additional memoranda that discussed military overflights of Communist countries. See, for example, Memorandum by Andrew Goodpaster, 8 January 1959, DDEL, WHO, Project Clean Up, Intelligence Matters; 'Memorandum for the Record,' 24 April 1958, in *FRUS,* 1958-1960, vol. X, 163; and 'Memorandum for the Record,' 1 June 1960, *FRUS,* 1958-1960, vol X, 521.

96 In 1961 President John F Kennedy approved LeMay as the Air Force Chief of Staff, and reappointed him in 1963.

97 Quoted in Beschloss, *Mayday*, 151.

98 Quoted in *FRUS,* 1958-1960, vol. X, 180. One can't help but feel for the poor fellow who not only made such a terrible mistake but then earned the visceral wrath of the President of the United States.

99 Gordon, *Tactical Reconnaissance in the Cold War*, 44-73.

100 Letter From the Assistant Secretary of Defense for International Security Affairs (Gray) to the Secretary of State, 24 July 1956, in *FRUS*, 1955-57, vol. III, China, 407-408.

101 Memorandum for Record by Col Andrew J Goodpaster, CE, USA, 18 December 1956, Sub: President Instructs Immediate Stop of US Overflights Over Iron Curtain Countries.' Reproduced in Hall and Laurie, *Appendixes*, 575; and Hall, 'Cold War Overflights,' 35.

102 John S D Eisenhower, Memorandum for Record, 30 October 1958, Top Secret, DDEL, WE DDE Diaries.

103 'Memorandum for the Record,' 24 April 1958, in *FRUS,* 1958-1960, vol. X, 163. Emphasis added. On the same day Eisenhower approved a low-altitude civilian overflight of the Soviet Union or some other Communist country, ostensibly requested by Allen Dulles to deploy an agent on a covert mission.

104 Memorandum by John Eisenhower of a meeting between the President, Secretary of Defense Neil McElroy, and General Twining, 28 November 1958, DDEL, WHO, Project Clean Up, Intelligence Matters.

105 'Memorandum for the Record,' 1 June 1960, *FRUS,* 1958-1960, vol X, 521. This reaffirms that Goodpaster was aware of 'civilian and military' overflights under Eisenhower.

106 Conboy and Morrison, *Feet to the Fire*.

107 Mikesh, *B-57 Canberra at War,* 124, 126. Mikesh did not take part in these or other RB-57 operations such as HEART THROB or BLACK KNIGHT. Cargill Hall, interview with the author, 4 September 1996, Omaha, Nebraska.

108 Yung Pang Tsai, *Through the Eyes of the Night Owl: The Opposite Side of the Taiwan Strait During the Mid 20th Century* (Bloomington, IN: Authorhouse, 2009; Chris Pocock with Clarence Fu, *The Black Bats: CIA Spy Flights Over China from Taiwan, 1951-1969* (Altglen, PA: Schiffer, 2010).

109 Diary Entry, 14 June 1950, LeMay Diary #1, LeMay Papers, Box 103, LoC; and Diary Entry, 12 October 1950, LeMay Diary #2, LeMay Papers, Box 103, LoC.

110 Memorandum for Mr Anderson, from General G B Erskine, 'Clandestine Intelligence Collection by the Armed Services,' 10 June 1955, Top Secret, NARA, RG 330, OSD Office of Special Operations, OSO Chronological File, 1 April thru 30 June 1955.

111 D K R Crosswell, *The Chief of Staff: The Military Career of General Walter Bedell Smith* (Westport, CT: Greenwood, 1991), n.p. On Eisenhower and his management style, see Douglas Kinnard, *President Eisenhower and Strategy Management: Study in Defense Politics* (Lexington, KY: University Press of Kentucky, 1977); Phillip G Henderson, *Managing the Presidency* (Boulder, CO: Westview Press, 1988); and Fred I Greenstein, *The Hidden-hand Presidency: Eisenhower as Leader* (Baltimore: Johns Hopkins University Press, 1982).

112 JCS Message 909321, 302036Z, 30 August 1956, Top Secret B-56404/1, 2, LoC, LeMay Papers, Top Secret Files. Declassified by the author's FOIA request.

113 *FRUS,* 1958-1960, vol. X, 186; Tart and Keefe, *Price of Vigilance.* Memorandum for Major General James H Walsh, AFCIN, from General G B Erskine, Assistant to the Secretary of Defense (Special Operations), 'C-130 Incident,' 9 October 1958, Top Secret, NARA, RG 330, OSD Office of Special Operations, OSO Chronological File, 1 October thru 31 December 1958; and Stanglin, Headden, and Cary, 'Flight of the Ferrets,' 49-50. White replaced Twining as Air Force Chief of Staff on 1 July 1957, when Twining became JCS Chairman.

114 Memorandum by Andrew Goodpaster, 8 January 1959, DDEL, WHO, Project Clean Up, Intelligence Matters.

115 White, *Little Toy Dog*; *FRUS,* 1958-1960, vol. X,

540-55; and Bailey, *We See All,* 93-100, 101-105.

116 Memorandum of Conference with the President, 9 August 1960, Office of the Staff Secretary, Subject Series, Alphabetical Subseries, Box 15, Intelligence Matters (17); NAID #12008941, 3.

117 The President's Foreign Intelligence Advisory Board, founded in 1956, recommended a number of changes to US intelligence-gathering programs and organizations. In a 2 February 1960, meeting, one board member remarked '...that the organization of the intelligence community has improved remarkably in the past four years, due to the directives from the President, the formation of a single integrated [one line of text not declassified] and tighter supervision of covert activity.' Memorandum of Conference with the President, 5 February 1960, DDE Diary Series, 'Staff Notes Feb 1960 (2),' DDEL.

118 'Conversation between Colonel Ernest R Harden (USAF Ret.) and Colonel Thomas G Shepherd, OJCS/JRC, 11August 1977,' Joint Chiefs of Staff Memorandum, 12 August 1977, NSArch, microfilm #00857.

119 Memorandum of Conference with the President, 10 August 1960, Office of the Staff Secretary, Subject Series, Alphabetical Subseries, Box 15, Intelligence Matters (17); NAID #12008941, 4-5.

120 'Establishment of a Joint Reconnaissance Center,' Chairman of the Joint Chiefs of Staff Memorandum 451-60, 20 October 1960, National Security Archives (NSArch), microfilm #00855; and 'Establishment of a Joint Reconnaissance Center,' DoD-OSD Memo from Thomas Gates to the Chairman, Joint Chiefs of Staff, 24 October 1960, NSArch, microfilm #00856.

121 'History of the United States Air Force Security Service, Fiscal Years 1960-61,' Reports Control Symbol AFS-1, Part I, Top Secret (San Antonio, TX: Office of the Historian, Air Force Security Service, 28 November 1961), 15. This was declassified at my FOIA request and a copy provided to the National Security Archives.

122 Brief for Discussion with the President, 23 December 1960, PBCFIA, Seventh Report to the President, NSC, SS, WHO, OSANSA: Records 1952-1961, DDEL; Gordon Gray, Special Assistant to the President, 2 November 1960, PBCFIA, Seventh Report to the President, NSC, SS, WHO, OSANSA: Records 1952-1961, DDEL; and Gordon Gray to the Secretary of Defense and the JCS Chair, 30 December 1960, PBCFIA, Seventh Report to the President, NSC, SS, WHO, OSANSA: Records 1952-1961, DDEL, quoted in Kenneth Absher, Michael Desch, and Roman Papdiuk, *Privileged and Confidential: The Secret History of the President's Intelligence Advisory Board* (Lexington, KY: University Press of Kentucky, 2012), 42.

123 Lashmar, *Spy Flights of the Cold War,* 105.

124 Quoted in Taubman, *Khrushchev*, 456-57; and Beschloss, *Mayday*, 44, 60, 371.

125 *Ibid.*, 49.

126 Quoted in *ibid.*, 248, 257.

Chapter Six
Planes and Policies

1 Donald E Welzenbach, 'How Kissinger Used Intelligence in the SALT Negotiations,' *Studies in Intelligence* 31 (1987): 40.

2 Cline, *The CIA Under Reagan, Bush, and Casey*, 221.

3 'Comment on Recent Soviet Black Sea Fleet Maneuvers,' 3 July 1950, Top Secret, HSTL, PSF, Foreign Affairs File, Russia-2, Russia–Moscow, Box 188.

4 Letter from the Assistant Secretary of Defense for International Security Affairs (Sprague) to the Deputy Under Secretary of State for Political Affairs (Murphy), 14 March 1958, Top Secret, NARA, RG59, Department of State Central Files, 656.56D13/3-1458.

5 Cochran, Arkin, Norris, and Sands, *Nuclear Weapons Databook,* 229-30; and John Prados, *Presidents' Secret Wars: CIA and Pentagon Covert Operations from World War II Through the Persian Gulf,* Rev. ed. (Chicago: Ivan R Dee, 1996), 138.

6 'Memorandum of Discussion at the 358th Meeting of the National Security Council, Washington, 13 March 1958,' Top Secret, DDEL, WF, NSC Records; 'Memorandum of Discussion at the 350th Meeting of the National Security Council, Washington, 6 January 1958,' Top Secret, DDEL, WF, NSC Records; and 'Memorandum of Discussion by Gleason,' 31 January 1958, Top Secret, DDEL, WF, NSC Records.

7 Prados, *President's Secret War*, 130-48; Kenneth J Conboy and James Morrison, *Feet to the Fire: CIA Covert operations in Indonesia, 1957-1958* (Annapolis, MD: Naval Institute Press, 1999); Andrew Roadknight, *United States Policy Towards Indonesia in the Truman and Eisenhower Years* (New York: Palgrave Macmillan, 2002); Brugioni, *Eyes in the Sky*, 280-81; Grose, *Gentleman Spy,* 452; and Hagedorn and Hellstrom, *Foreign Invaders,* 122. CIA-sponsored airplanes from the Republic of China also participated in Operation HAIK, dropping supplies to the rebels. Pocock, *U-2 Spyplane*, 126; and Pocock and Fu, *The Black Bats*, 45-46.

8 Pedlow and Welzenbach, *The CIA and the U-2 Program*, 211; Pocock, *U-2 Spyplane*, 126; Grose, *Gentleman Spy,* 453; and Prados, *President's Secret Wars,* 135.

9 'Memorandum of Substance of Discussion at a State-Joint Chiefs of Staff Meeting,' NARA, RG59, Department of State, State-JCS Meetings, Lot 61 D 417. Gordon, *Soviet Strategic Aviation in the Cold War*, 201; and Robert Bock, *Tu-16 Badger in Action* (Carrollton, TX: Squadron Signal Publications, 1990), 12-13.

10 Prados, *President's Secret Wars,* 142-43.

11 Memorandum from the Joint Chiefs of Staff to Secretary of Defense McElroy, 8 April 1958, Top Secret, NARA, RG218, JCS Records, 092 (6-25-48).

12 'Memorandum of Discussion at the 354th Meeting of the National Security Council, Washington, 6 February 1958,' Top Secret, DDEL, WF, NSC Records; and 'Memorandum of Discussion at the 356th Meeting of the National Security Council, Washington, 27 February 1958,' Top Secret, DDEL, WF, NSC Records.

13 'Memorandum of Discussion at the 359th Meeting of the National Security Council, Washington, 20 March 1958,' Top Secret, DDEL, WF, NSC Records.

14 Brugioni, *Eyeball to Eyeball*, 38-39; and idem, *Eyes in the Sky*, 283-84.

15 Pedlow and Welzenbach, *The CIA and the U-2 Program*, 216-17; and Pocock, *U-2 Spyplane*, 143-44.

16 Brugioni, *Eyes in the Sky*, 274-80.

17 Memorandum for Record, Discussion on Tibet, 4 February 1960, OSANSA, Special Assistant Series, Presidential Subseries, Box 4, 1960 Meetings with the President Volume I (7); Conboy and Morrison, *Feet to the Fire*, 71-72; and Pocock and Fu, *The Black Bats*, 36-37.

18 David A Nichols, *Eisenhower 1956: The President's Year of Crisis – Suez and the Brink of War* (New York: Simon and Schuster, 2012), 245-46.

19 Eisenhower, *Waging Peace,* 295; and 'Memorandum Prepared by Secretary of State Dulles,' 4 September 1958, Top Secret, in *FRUS,* 1958-1960, vol. XIX, 133.
20 William B Pickett, *Dwight David Eisenhower and American Power* (Wheeling, IL: Harlan Davidson, 1995), 47, Ambrose, *Ike's Spies,* 3-152; and Grose, *Gentleman Spy,* 402.
21 NSC 5428, 'United States Objectives and Policies With Respect to the Near East,' 23 July 1954, Top Secret, in *FRUS,* 1952-1954, vol. IX, part 1, 525, 528. Charles A Kupchan, 'American Globalism in the Middle East: The Roots of Regional Security Policy,' *Political Science Quarterly* 103 (Winter 1988-89): 587.
22 Bonnie F Saunders, *The United States and Arab Nationalism: The Syrian Case, 1953-1960* [hereafter *US and Arab Nationalism*] (Westport, CT: Praeger, 1996), vii, 21.
23 Department of State Press Release 401, 19 July 1956, in Department of State *Bulletin,* No.892 (30 July 1956), 188.
24 Richard J Aldrich, 'Intelligence, Anglo–American Relations, and the Suez Crisis, 1956,' *Intelligence and National Security* 9 (July 1994): 544-54.
25 Wayne G Jackson, 'Allen Welsh Dulles as Director of Central Intelligence, 26 February 1953-29 November 1961,' vol. V, 'Intelligence Support of Policy,' Top Secret-Codeword, CIA document DCI-2, July 1973, declassified (with deletions) 29 April 1994, 8. NSArch.
26 Bissell, *Reflections of a Cold Warrior,* 121.
27 Jackson, 'Intelligence Support for Policy,' 15.
28 'Memorandum for the Record,' 15 October 1956, Top Secret, DDEL, WF, Eisenhower Diaries; Eisenhower, *Waging Peace,* 56; and 'Memorandum of Discussion at the 302d Meeting of the National Security Council, Washington, 1 November 1956,' Top Secret, DDEL, WF, NSC Records.
29 'Memorandum of Discussion at the 302d Meeting of the National Security Council, Washington, 1 November 1956,' Top Secret, DDEL, WF, NSC Records; Ambrose, *The President,* 363; and Allen Dulles, *The Craft of Intelligence* (New York: Harper & Row, 1963), 168.
30 Isaac Alteras, *Eisenhower and Israel: US-Israeli Relations, 1953-1960* (Gainesville, FL: University of Florida Press, 1993), 215; and Trevor N Dupuy, *Elusive Victory: The Arab-Israeli Wars, 1947-1974* (New York: Harper & Row, 1978), 129-220.
31 Peter L Hahn, *The United States, Great Britain, and Egypt, 1945-1956: Strategy and Diplomacy in the Early Cold War* (Chapel Hill, NC: University of North Carolina Press, 1991) 227-28. For analyses of the issue of surprise and American policy, see Jackson, 'Intelligence Support for Policy,' 1-38, esp. 36; and Yigal Sheffy, 'Unconcern at Dawn, Surprise at Sunset: Egyptian Intelligence Appreciation Before the Sinai Campaign,' *Intelligence and National Security* 5 (July 1990). 41-42.
32 JCS Message 912389, 290133Z, Top Secret, B-57673. LeMay Papers, Top Secret Files, LoC; and Grabo, 'The Watch Committee and the National Indications Center,' 370.
33 Quoted in Brugioni, *Eyeball to Eyeball*, 34; and Pocock, *U-2 Spyplane*, 56.
34 Charles E Bohlen, *Witness to History, 1929-1969* (New York: W W Norton & Co, 1973), 434.
35 Robert Murphy, *Diplomat Among Warriors* (Garden City, NY: Doubleday, 1964), 392.
36 Memorandum from President Eisenhower to Secretary of State Dulles, 9 April 1953. Box 1, White House Memorandum Series, John Foster Dulles Papers, DDEL.
37 JCS Message 912463, 300238Z, 30 October 1956, Top Secret, B- 576981/1, 3, LoC, LeMay Papers, Top Secret Files. Admiral Arleigh A Burke, the Chief of Naval Operations, told historian Cole Kingseed in an 8 September 1981, interview that on 30 October he cabled the US Sixth Fleet commander, warning him that the 'Situation [was] tense, [and to] prepare for imminent hostilities.' Quoted in Kingseed, *Eisenhower and the Suez Crisis,* 108.
38 Eisenhower, *Waging Peace,* 97. US assessments of Soviet moves in the Middle East were outlined and critiqued in the 3 November 1956, JCS report 'Analysis of Possible Soviet Courses of Action in the Middle East,' Top Secret, JCS 1887/298, JCS Records, CCS 381 EMMEA (11-19-47) Section 47 RB.
39 JCS Message 912773, 022318Z, 2 November 1956, Top Secret, B-57805/1, 3, LoC, LeMay Papers, Top Secret Files; Khrushchev quoted in Taubman, *Khrushchev*, 359; and Zhukov quoted in Heikal, *Cairo Documents,* 112.
40 'Memorandum of a Conference With the President, White House, Washington, November 5, 1956, 10:20 a.m.,' Top Secret, DDEL, WF, Eisenhower Diaries; and 'Memorandum for the Record by the Director of the Executive Secretariat (Howe),' 5 November 1956, Secret, NARA, RG59, Department of State, Secretary's Memoranda of Conversation, Lot 64 D 199.
41 'Letter from Prime Minister Bulganin to President Eisenhower,' 5 November 1956, Secret, NARA, RG59, Department of State, Central Files, 674.84A/1 1-556; and Department of State, *United States Policy in the Middle East, September 1956-June 1957* (Washington, DC: US Government Printing Office, 1957), 180-81.
42 Department of State, *United States Policy in the Middle East, September 1956-June 1957,* 183-88.
43 Bohlen, *Witness to History,* 432-33.
44 'Memorandum of a Conference with the President,' 5 November 1956, 5 p.m., Secret, DDEL, WF, Eisenhower Diaries.
45 Memorandum of a Conversation, 'Soviet Maneuvers on the Middle East Situation; Franco-American Relations,' 5 November 1956, Secret, NARA, RG59, Department of State, Central Files, 974.7301/1 1-556.
46 Eisenhower, *Waging Peace,* 90.
47 Department of State *Bulletin,* 19 November 1956, 795-96.
48 Telegram 1176 to New Delhi, 6 November 1956, NARA, RG59, Department of State, Central Files, 684A.86/11-656; and Nichols, *Eisenhower 1956*, 244-47.
49 JCS Message 912901, 060019Z, 6 November 1956, Top Secret, B- 57865, LoC, LeMay Papers, Top Secret Files.
50 'Memorandum of a Conference With the President, White House, Washington, November 6, 1956, 8:37 a.m.,'' DDEL, WF, Eisenhower Diaries.
51 Telegram from the Embassy in the United Kingdom to the Department of State, 6 November 1956, Secret, Niact [Night Action, requiring immediate reply], NARA, RG59, Department of State, Central Files, 684A.86/ 11-656.
52 'Sino-Soviet Intentions in the Suez Crisis,' SNIE 11-9-56, 6 November 1956, Secret, in *FRUS,* 1955-1957, vol. XVI, 1018-20.
53 'Memorandum of a Conference With the President,

White House, Washington, November 6, 1956,' DDEL, WF, Eisenhower Diaries.
54 Bohlen, *Witness to History,* 434.
55 Alteras, *Eisenhower and Israel,* 243-44, 247.
56 Quoted in Bohlen, *Witness to History,* 435.
57 Ambrose, *President,* 368-69; Neff, *Warriors at Suez,* 412-13; and Brugioni, *Eyeball to Eyeball,* 34.
58 By early December all US forces were returned to normal alert status. JCS Message 912901, 060019Z, 6 November 1956, Top Secret, B- 57865, 2, LoC, LeMay Papers, Top Secret Files; and Headquarters Air Force Message T.S. 5416, 032131Z, 3 December 1956, Top Secret, B- 58427/1, LoC, LeMay Papers, Top Secret Files; and JCS Message XXA914740, 081518Z, 8 December 1956, Top Secret, B-58501/1, LoC, LeMay Papers, Top Secret Files; and Headquarters Air Force Message 5741, 072244Z, 7 December 1956, Top Secret, B-58502/1, LeMay Papers, Top Secret Files.
59 Jon D Glassman, *Arms for the Arabs: The Soviet Union and War in the Middle East* (Baltimore: Johns Hopkins University Press, 1975), 16; and Nichols, *Eisenhower, 1956*, 262, 254.
60 Jackson, 'Intelligence Support for Policy,' 8; Pedlow and Welzenbach, *The CIA and the U-2 Program*, 115.
61 'Memorandum of a Conversation, Secretary Dulles' Room, Walter Reed Hospital, Washington, November 7, 1956,' Top Secret, DDEL, Dulles Papers, Meetings with the President.
62 Pedlow and Welzenbach, *The CIA and the U-2 Program*, 115.
63 Allen S Whiting, 'China's Use of Force, 1950-96, and Taiwan.' *International Security* 26 (Fall 2001): 103-131.
64 Telegram From the Department of State to the Embassy in the Republic of China, 2 August 1958, Secret, in *FRUS,* 1958-1960, vol. XIX, 38.
65 *Ibid.*; 'Memorandum of Discussion at the 375th Meeting of the National Security Council, Washington,' 7 August 1958, Top Secret, DDEL, WF, NSC Records; and Wu Lengxi, 'Inside Story of the Decision Making during the Shelling of Jinmen,' trans. by Li Xiaobing, Chen Jian, and David L Wilson, in 'Mao Zedong's Handling of the Taiwan Straits Crisis of 1958: Chinese Recollections and Documents,' Cold War International History Project *Bulletin* [hereafter CWIHP *Bulletin*] 6-7 (Winter 1995/1996): 209.
66 'Memorandum of Discussion at the 377th Meeting of the National Security Council, Washington,' 21 August 1958, Top Secret, DDEL, WF, NSC Records.
67 Brugioni, *Eyes in the Sky*, 262-67; and Pocock and Fu, *The Black Bats*, 46-47.
68 Memorandum From the Assistant Secretary of State for Far Western Affairs (Robertson) to Secretary of State Dulles, Subject: Emergence of New Situation in Taiwan Straits, 8 August 1958, Secret, in *FRUS,* 1958-1960, vol. XIX, 44.
69 Brugioni, *Eyes in the Sky*, 264.
70 Memorandum of Conversation, MC-5, 26 September 1958, Secret, in *FRUS,* 1958-1960, vol. XIX, 280; and Nancy Bernkopf Tucker, *The China Threat: Memories, Myths, and Realities in the 1950s* (New York: Columbia, 2012), 143.
71 'Probable Developments in the Taiwan Strait Area,' SNIE 100-9-58, 26 August 1958, Secret, in *FRUS,* 1958-1960, vol. XIX, 82; Telegram From the Embassy in the Republic of China to the Department of State, 7 August 1958, Secret, in *ibid.*, 41; Telegram from the Commander, US Taiwan Defense Command (Smoot) to the Chief of Naval Operations (Burke), 14 September 1958, Top Secret, Priority, NARA, RG59, Department of State, Central Files, 793.5/9- 1458; and 'Memorandum of Discussion at the 376th Meeting of the National Security Council, Washington,' 14 August 1958, Top Secret, DDEL, WF, NSC Records.
72 Memorandum of Conversation Between President Eisenhower and Secretary of State Dulles, Washington, 11September 1958, DDEL, Dulles Papers, Meetings with the President.
73 Telegram from the Embassy in the Republic of China to the Department of State, 8 September 1958, Secret, Niact, LimDis, NARA, RG59, Department of State, Central Files, 611.93/9-858.
74 See, in particular, Pocock and Fu, *The Black Bats*; and Yung, *Through the Eyes of the Night Owl.*
75 Memorandum for the Assistant Secretary of Defense (International Security Affairs), 'Additional Reconnaissance Aircraft for the Chinese Nationalist Government,' 6 March 1956, Top Secret, NARA, RG330, Office of the Secretary of Defense, Office of Special Operations, OSO Chronological File, 1 January thru 31 March 1956.
76 Pocock and Fu, *The Black Bats*; and Letter From the Under Secretary of State (Herter) to President Chiang, 11 February 1958, Secret, in *FRUS,* 1958-1960, vol. XIX, 5; Telegram From the Embassy in the Republic of China to the Department of State, 10 May 1958, Secret, LimDis, in *ibid.*, 22-23; and Hagedorn and Hellstrom, *Foreign Invaders*, 169-71.
77 Telegram from the Commander in Chief, Pacific (Felt) to the Chief of Naval Operations (Burke), 24 November 1958, Top Secret, NARA, RG59, Department of State, FE Files: Lot 65 D 497, FE 3500-3699.
78 Marks, *Power and Peace,* 85-86. Memorandum of Conversation, Washington, 2 September 1958, Subject: Taiwan Straits Situation, Top Secret, NARA, RG 59, Department of State, Central Files, 793.00/9-258.
79 Tucker, *The China Threat*, 3.
80 Directorate of Targets, USAF, 'Semi-Annual History,' 1 July 1958 thru 31 December 1958, Secret, 65, NSArch.
81 Memorandum of Conversation, 22 September 1958, Washington, Top Secret, Personal and Private, DDEL, Dulles Papers, General Memoranda of Conversations.
82 Memorandum of Conversation, Washington, 2 September 1958, Subject: Taiwan Straits Situation, Top Secret, NARA, RG59, Department of State, Central Files, 793.00/9-258; Memorandum of Meeting, Washington, 8 August 1958, Subject: Taiwan Straits, Secret, *ibid.*, 793.00/8-1158; and Memorandum From Acting Secretary of State Herter to Secretary of State Dulles, Washington, 15 August 1958, Subject: Recommended Warning to Peiping Against Attacking the Offshore Islands, Top Secret, Ibid., 793.00/8-1558.
83 Letter From Secretary of State Dulles to Prime Minister Macmillan, Washington, 4 September 1958, Top Secret, NARA, RG59, Department of State, Presidential Correspondence: Lot 66 D 204.
84 Memorandum From the Assistant Secretary of State for Policy Planning (Smith) to Secretary of State Dulles, Washington, 3 September 1958, Top Secret, NARA, RG59, Department of State, SIP Files: Lot 67 D 548; Memorandum From the Assistant Secretary of State for

Policy Planning (Smith) to Secretary of State Dulles, 15 August 1958, Top Secret, in *FRUS, ibid.*, 58; and SNIE 100-7-58, 'Sino-Soviet and Free World Reactions to US Use of Nuclear Weapons in Limited Wars in the Far East,' Washington, 22 July 1958, Top Secret, in *ibid.*, 32.

85 Telegram From the Embassy in the Soviet Union to the Department of State, 7 September 1958, Official Use Only, Niact, in *ibid.*, 151; Vladislav M Zubok, 'Khrushchev's Nuclear Promise To Beijing During the 1958 Crisis,' CWIHP *Bulletin*, 6-7 (Winter 1995/1996), 219, 226-27; and Zubok and Pleshakov, *Inside the Kremlin's Cold War*, 220-29.

86 Taubman, *Khrushchev*, 392.

87 Tucker, *The China Threat*, 147-49.

88 *Ibid.*, 81.

89 Eisenhower, *Waging Peace*, 295; and John Lewis Gaddis, *Strategies of Containment* (New York: Oxford University Press, 1982) 170-73.

90 Gordon H Chang, 'To the Nuclear Brink: Eisenhower, Dulles, and the Quemoy-Matsu Crisis,' *International Security* 12 (Spring 1988): 96-123.

91 Ambrose, *President*, 245.

92 Chang, 'To the Nuclear Brink,' 98, 100, 106-108, 111-12.

93 Nancy Bernkopf Tucker, 'John Foster Dulles and the Taiwan Roots of the 'Two China' Policy,' in *JFD and Diplomacy*, 237, 241; and Memorandum of Conversation Between President Eisenhower and Secretary of State Dulles, Washington, 11 September 1958, DDEL, Dulles Papers, Meetings with the President.

94 Lengxi, 'Inside Story of the Decision Making during the Shelling of Jinmen,' 210; and Li Zhisui, *The Private Life of Chairman Mao*, trans. Tai Hung-chao, with a Foreword by Andrew J Nathan (New York: Random House, 1994), 270-71.

95 Ambrose, *President*, 483; Eisenhower, *Waging Peace*, 298; and Peter Lyon, *Eisenhower: Portrait of the Hero* (Boston: Little, Brown, 1974), 854.

96 Marks, *Power and Peace*, 87.

97 Memorandum of Conversation, Washington, 11 September 1958. DDEL, WF, DDE Diaries.

98 Leonard H D Gordon, 'United States Opposition to Use of Force in the Taiwan Straits, 1954-1962,' *Journal of American History* 72 (December 1985): 651; and Telegram From the Embassy in the Republic of China to the Department of State, 13 October 1958, Taipei, Secret, Priority, LimDis, NARA, RG59, Department of State, Central Files, 611.93/10-1358.

99 Major John S D Eisenhower, Memorandum for Record, 30 October 1958, Washington, Top Secret, DDEL, WF, DDE Diaries.

100 Pocock, *Dragon Lady*, 90-106; and Rich and Janos, *Skunk Works*, 142, 180. Of these, the RoCAF lost a total of eight to Communist Chinese SAMs. Telegram From the Commander in Chief, Pacific (Felt) to the Chief of Naval Operations (Burke), 24 November 1958, Honolulu, Top Secret, NARA, RG59, Department of State, FE Files: Lot 65 D 497, FE 3500-3699.

101 Ambrose, *President*, 482-85; and Brugioni, *Eyeball to Eyeball*, 38.

102 Telegram From the Department of State to the Embassy in the Republic of China, 29 October 1958, Confidential, NARA, RG59, Department of State, Central Files, 611.93/10-2958.

103 Tucker, *The China Threat*, 1-3.

104 Brugioni cites historians Stephen Ambrose and Robert Divine in their adoration of Eisenhower for his handling of the Taiwan Straits Crisis, calling it 'a *tour de force*, one of the greatest triumphs of his long career.' Quoted in Brugioni, *Eyes in the Sky*, 265.

105 Brugioni, *Eyes in the Sky*, 177-80.

106 Quoted in Nichols, *Eisenhower, 1956*, 159.

107 Brugioni, *Eyes in the Sky*, 175.

108 Nichols, *Eisenhower, 1956*, 181.

109 *Ibid.*, 236-37. Nichols shows that Eisenhower's health was problematic and far worse than the administration claimed. It was also a terrible strain on the president who was recovering from a heart attack in 1955 and abdominal surgery just months before. Nichols concludes, however, that although Eisenhower's ailments took a great personal toll on the president, they did not adversely affect his decision making during the Suez Crisis. Similarly, Secretary of State Dulles was in chronic ill health and underwent emergency cancer surgery at the height of the crisis. A similar claim about the health of leaders at crucial times has long been made about Franklin Roosevelt at Yalta, as well as his advisor Harry Hopkins.

110 Shu Guang Zhang, *Deterrence and Strategic Culture: Chinese-American Confrontations, 1949-1958* (Ithaca, New York: Cornell University Press, 1992, 326.

111 Farquhar, 'A Cold War in Flames,' 26-53; Futrell, *United States Air Force in Korea*, 545, 548, 551; Aid, 'US HUMINT and COMINT in the Korean War;' and idem, 'American COMINT in the Korean War (Part II).'

112 Aviation historian Walt Boyne argues that the success of aerial intelligence in the Cuban Missile Crisis carried 'the seeds of a future disaster.' Precisely – though not always accurately – informed of ongoing details of this perilous confrontation, Kennedy's ExComm confused strategy with crisis management. Confident in their 'techniques used to *respond* to the behavior of the [Soviets],' these same advisors reached 'ill-founded conclusions' about the situation in Vietnam. With an 'inflated sense of their own value in managing the [Cuban] crisis' they made 'a series of mistaken efforts [disguised as strategy] to 'send signals' to an enemy whom they did not even begin to understand' [emphasis added]. Walter J Boyne, *The Influence of Air Power Upon History* (Barnsley, England: Pen and Sword Aviation, 2005), 313-14.

113 Former arms control specialist and intelligence analyst Mark Lowenthal addresses the issue of how strategic intelligence contributes to the formulation of national security policy. Lowenthal offers a disheartening answer, claiming that strategic intelligence makes little difference to policy makers. For example, he argues there was little the United States could do to compel Iraq not to invade Kuwait in August 1990 even had the US intelligence collection and analysis system been working perfectly. 'Whatever the shortcomings of US intelligence in the period before the invasion of Kuwait, it remains uncertain that [better intelligence] necessarily would have led to a policy that would have deterred Saddam Hussein.' Mark M Lowenthal, *US Intelligence: Evolution and Anatomy*, 2d ed. (Washington, DC: Center for Strategic and International Studies, 1992), 4, 92-93.

Chapter Seven
Rhetoric and Stability

1 Burrows, *By Any Means Necessary*, 3-40; idem,

'Beyond the Iron Curtain,' 27-35; NARA, RG 59, Department of State, Office of the Legal Advisor, Sam Klaus Files, Aircraft Incidents, 1944-62, Lot 64 D 551, MLR E1588A, Boxes 55, 56, 57, 100, 101, and 102; US Department of Defense, 'Summary of Cold War Losses;' George, *Case Studies*, 303-310; Bailey, *We See All*, 47-48; Stanglin, Headden, and Cary, 'Flight of the Ferrets,' 44-45; and Lashmar, 'Shootdowns,' 10. Burrows lists Woods as the tail gunner but a 1974 Air Force summary of the mission lists him as left gunner. To be sure there have been survivors of other attacks, so Roche's good fortune should not be seen as unique.

2 John E Roche, interview with the author, 15 May 1996, Omaha, NE. Burrows, *By Any Means Necessary*, 30. Jeffrey Richelson, *A Century of Spies: Intelligence in the Twentieth Century* (New York: Oxford University Press, 1995), 262.

3 Yefim Gordon and Dmitriy Komissarov, *Soviet Air Defence Aviation, 1945-1991* (Manchester, England: Hikoki, 2012) 37-39; Burrows, *By Any Means Necessary*, 21-23; and Tart and Keefe, *Price of Vigilance*, 42-49.

4 Wise and Ross, *U-2 Affair*, 262-65; George F Kennan, *Nuclear Delusions: Soviet American Relations in the Atomic Age*, rev. ed. (New York: Pantheon, 1983), 111; Stephen F Cohen, *Rethinking the Soviet Experience: Politics and History Since 1917* (New York: Oxford University Press, 1985), 156-57; Alexander Yanov, *The Drama of the Soviet 1960's: A Lost Reform* (Berkeley: Institute of International Studies, University of California, 1984), 97-98, 103-106; and Michael Beschloss, *The Crisis Years: Kennedy and Khrushchev, 1960-1963* (New York: Harper Collins, 1991), 349-53. Lashmar is the first to consider the effect of all reconnaissance flights on Soviet-American relations, and reaches the same conclusions. Lashmar, *Spy Flights of the Cold War*, 202, 204, 207.

5 Farquhar, 'A Cold War in Flames,' 54-55.

6 Lashmar has undertaken considerable research in Russia on the Soviet reaction to Western reconnaissance flights, but has focused primarily on the military response to specific incursions rather than on a general assessment of Soviet policy toward the flights. He does say that the flights led to a 'colder Cold War,' but offers no specific evidence of why Soviet leaders would have agreed with this assessment. Lashmar, *Spy Flights of the Cold War*, 207.

7 'Paris Convention on the Regulation of Air Navigation, 1919,' [hereafter 'Paris Convention'] at http://library.arcticportal.org/1580/1/1919_Paris_con-evention.pdf [*sic*], accessed on 20 July 2015; and 'Chicago Convention on International Civil Aviation, 1944,' [hereafter 'Chicago Convention'] at http://www.icao.int/publications/pages/doc7300.aspx, accessed on 20 July 2015.

8 Oliver J Lissitzyn, 'Some Legal Implications of the U-2 and RB-47 Incidents,' *American Journal of International Law* 56 (January 1962): 140-41.

9 *New York Times,* 2 March 1946, 1; and George, *Case Studies,* 27-30.

10 George, *Soviet Reactions,* 2, 7.

11 *Ibid.,* ix.

12 Zubok and Pleshakov, *Inside the Kremlin's Cold War,* 27, 89-90; and quoted in Taubman, *Khrushchev*, 332.

13 Edvard Radzinsky, *Stalin: The First In-Depth Biography Based on Explosive New Documents from Russia's Secret Archives,* trans. H T Willetts (New York: Doubleday, 1996), 561-62, 568-69; and R C Raack, 'Stalin's Role in the Coming of World War II,' *World Affairs* 158 (Spring 1996): 198-211.

14 See, for example, Montifiore, *Court of the Red Tsar*, 626-632 and esp. 633. Quoted in Taubman, *Khrushchev*, 272.

15 Burrows, *By Any Means Necessary*, 30.

16 George, *Soviet Reactions,* xii-xiii, 20-23; George, *Case Studies,* 27-36, 81-83, 97-100; and Telegram from the Embassy of the USSR, 5 January 1948, NARA, RG341, Entry 214

17 Steven J Zaloga, *Soviet Air Defence Missiles: Design, Development and Tactics* (Surrey, England: Jane's Information Group, 1989), n.p.; David C Isby, *Weapons and Tactics of the Soviet Army*, (London: Jane's, 1981), 220-72; and *Soviet War Machine: An Encyclopedia of Russian Military Equipment and Strategy*, (London: Salamander, 1976), 51-58.

18 Peterson, 'Maybe You Had to Be There,' 14.

19 'Report from K A Vershinin to L P Beriya, N A Bulganin, and A M Vasilevskij [hereafter 'Beria Report'],' Top Secret, 19 December 1952, 3. I am indebted to Paul Lashmar for providing English and Russian copies of this report to me.

20 George, *Case Studies-Supplement,* 1-2.

21 Tart and Keefe, *Price of Vigilance*, 190.

22 Vojtech Mastny, *The Cold War and Soviet Insecurity: The Stalin Years* (New York: Oxford University Press, 1996), 60, 74, 113, 127; Evangelista, 'Stalin's Post War Army Reappraised,' 132-33; and MccGwire, *Perestroika and Soviet National Security,* 19.

23 Zaloga, *Soviet Air Defence Missiles,* 6-13, 26-48.

24 Interview with General [?] Abramov, 28 September 1993, transcript courtesy Paul Lashmar.

25 William T Lee, *The Estimation of Soviet Defense Expenditures, 1955-75: An Unconventional Approach* (New York: Praeger, 1977), 141, 143, and Table 5.1, n.p.

26 Taubman, *Khrushchev*, 448-49, 451; and Vladislav M Zubok, *A Failed Empire: The Soviet Union in the Cold War from Stalin to Gorbachev* (Chapel Hill, NC: University of North Carolina Press, 2007), 129-36.

27 Forster and Gibson, *Listening In*, 32-43.

28 Carroll, 'The Silent War,' 77; George, *Case Studies,* 26-312; and idem, *Case Studies-Supplement,* 1-94. These figures do not include efforts to attack each of the 24 U-2 overflights of the Soviet Union other than the loss of Frank Powers' U-2.

29 See, for example, Oliver J Lissitzyn, 'The Treatment of Aerial Intruders in Recent Practice and International Law,' *American Journal of International Law* 47 (1953): 559-63; and the Sam Klaus files from the State Department.

30 Quoted in George, *Case Studies*, 141.

31 George, *Soviet Reactions,* ix.

32 Peterson, 'Maybe You Had to Be There,' 18-19.

33 Alexander L George, *Intelligence Value of Soviet Notes on Air Incidents, 1950-1953,* RAND Research Memorandum RM-1348, 15 October 1954, Confidential, 2.

34 Grimes, *History of Big Safari*, 113.

35 Prados, 'High-flying Spies,' 12; Carroll, 'Silent War,' 81; and Paul M Cole, *POW/MIA Issues,* vol. 2, *World War II and the Early Cold War* (Washington, DC: National Defense Research Institute, 1994), n.p.

36 Examples of active Soviet *dezinformatsia* regarding the shoot-down include M Kalanasundaram, *Flight 007* (Delhi: New Literature, 1983); Akio Takahashi, *Presi-*

dent's Crime: Who Ordered the Espionage Flight of KAL 007? (Tokyo: Ninegasha, 1984); and the infamous 'P. Q. Mann' essay appearing in issue no. 3 (1984) of *Defence Attache,* exposed by James E Oberg in 'Sakhalin: Sense and Nonsense,' *Defence Attache,* no. 1 (1985), 37-47; and Oberg's 'The Sky's No Limit on Disinformation,' *Air Force Magazine*, March, 1986, 52-56. On Soviet revelations, see 'Black Box Mystery,' *US News & World Report,* 24 December 1990, 22; Keith Crowden, 'The Korean Airliner Shootdown–New Evidence,' *Aviation News,* 19 July-1August 1991, 209; Michael Dobbs, 'Soviet Journalists Attack KAL Story,' *Washington Post,* 26 May 1991, 1, 42-43; 'Glasnost Gets the Story,' *US News & World Report,* 14 January 1991, 19; and James Oberg, 'Soviets Report: Moscow Lied About KAL 007,' *Wall Street Journal,* 23 April 1991, n.p; and Gordon *Soviet Air Defence Aviation*, 191-202. There remain a number of discrepancies regarding the official conclusions about why flight 007 overflew the Soviet Union. See, for example, the unpersuasive but nonetheless highly provocative James Gollin, 'Stirring Up the Past: KAL Flight 007,' *International Journal of Intelligence and Counterintelligence* 7 (Winter 1994): 445-62; and James Gollin and Robert Allardyce, *Desired Track: The Tragic Flight of KAL Flight 007* (Findlay, OH: American Vision Publishing, 1994); not to mention the ridiculous, Michel Brun, *Incident at Sakhalin: The True Mission of KAL Flight 007* (New York: Four Walls Eight Windows, 1995). I am also indebted to the late Dick Witkin of the *New York Times* for his thoughts on KAL 007.

37 *Bortom Horisonten*, 155-74, 222-23; *Attack upon Two Swedish Aircraft over the Baltic in June 1952: Documents Published by the Royal Ministry for Foreign Affairs,* New Series II: 2, Stockholm, 1952; George, *Case Studies,* 171-99; and idem, *Soviet Reaction,* 21-22.

38 Walter Sullivan, 'Soviets Regret R.A.F. Loss, Shuns Blame but Asks Talks,' *New York Times,* 20 March 1953, 1.

39 George, *Soviet Reaction*, 7-11.

40 Telegram from the Ambassador in the Soviet Union (Kirk) to the Secretary of State, Top Secret, Priority, 15 April 1950, in *FRUS,* 1950, vol. IV, 1145.

41 Mastny, *The Cold War and Soviet Insecurity,* 115.

42 George, *Diplomatic Aspects,* 10-11.

43 Stalin feared that the West's concern about an inevitable Soviet attack might lead the West to preempt such an attack. Mastny, *The Cold War and Soviet Insecurity,* 60, 113; and Christopher Andrew and Oleg Gordievsky, *KGB: The Inside Story of Its Foreign Operations from Lenin to Gorbachev* (London: Hodder & Stoughton, 1990), 326. I have yet to uncover any specific evidence linking the American political analysis of Western reconnaissance losses to the associated vulnerability of American nuclear strike forces. LeMay's 1954 remarks to the Air War College suggest that the reconnaissance loss rate, when applied to the bomber force, was still acceptable in the prosecution of any pre-emptive war. For senior civilian policy makers, US reconnaissance losses could well have further discouraged them from giving serious credence to a preventive strike, but there is no evidence to support or deny such an assertion.

44 Michael McCGwire, *Perestroika and Soviet National Security* (Washington, DC: Brookings Institution, 1991), 20; Zubok, *Failed Empire*, 86; Zubok and Pleshakov, *Inside the Kremlin's Cold War,* 138-39; and R Craig Nation, *Black Earth, Red Star: A History of Soviet Security Policy, 1917-1991* (Ithaca, NY: Cornell University Press, 1992), 202-204.

45 Bohlen, *Witness to History,* 464. Bohlen incorrectly attributes this remark to R A Rudenko – Roman Andreyevich Rudenko – the Soviet lawyer who served, *inter alia*, as Chief Soviet Prosecutor at the Nuremburg Trials.

46 Interview with Vasilii A Polyakov, transcript courtesy of Paul Lashmar. This contrasts sharply with the Western portrayal of Polyakov, with one caption of his photo reading 'The killer is not smiling.' William L White, *The Little Toy Dog* (New York: Dutton, 1962), ff 54.

47 Taubman, *Khrushchev*, 443.

48 'Paris Convention'; 'Chicago Convention'; Lissitzyn, 'Some Legal Implications of the U-2 and RB-47 Incidents,' 135-42; idem, 'The Treatment of Aerial Intruders in Recent Practice and International Law,' 559-89; Quincy Wright, 'Legal Aspects of the U-2 Incident,' *American Journal of International Law* 54 (October 1960): 836-54; Spencer M Beresford, 'Surveillance Aircraft and Satellites: A Problem of International Law,' *Journal of Air Law and Commerce* 27 (Spring 1960): 107-118; Frank Fedele, 'Overflight by Military Aircraft in Time of Peace,' *USAF Judge Advocate General Law Review* 8 (1967): 8-25, 56.

49 Taubman, *Khrushchev*, 444.

50 Telegram from the Soviet Embassy to the Department of State, No.15, 14 May 1956, NARA, RG59, Box 3512, 761.5411.

51 Medvedev, *Khrushchev,* 151; and quoted in Taubman, *Khrushchev*, 444.

52 Zubok, *Failed Empire*, 136-38.

53 Zubok and Pleshakov, *Inside the Kremlin's Cold War,* 189.

54 Bissell, *Reflections of a Cold Warrior,* 113.

55 Colonel General Yu V Votintsev, 'Unknown Troops of the Vanished Superpower,' *Voyenno-Istoricheski Zhurnal* 9 (1993): 26-38; Taubman, *Khrushchev*, 445; and Pocock, *U-2 Story*, 51.

56 Kennan, *Memoirs: 1950-1963,* 475; George F Kennan, 'The Soviet Union and the Atlantic Pact,' 8 September 1952, reprinted in idem, *Memoirs: 1950-1963*, 141, 347-48, 351.

57 One should not take the argument of Russian sensitivity to invasion too seriously. Since the reign of Catherine the Great during the latter half of the 18th century, Russia was invaded by Napoleon's *Grande Armée* in 1812, Western troops during the 1917 Revolution (at the behest of White forces), and by the Nazis in 1941. During the same period Russia absorbed vast portions of Poland through multiple partitions, repeatedly attacked the Ottoman Empire to gain access to the Black Sea, acquired Finland from Sweden, provoked both the Crimean and Russo-Japanese Wars through blatant territorial expansionism, attacked Germany and the Austro-Hungarian Empire at the start of the Great War, invaded Poland in 1919 starting the Polish-Soviet War and again in 1939 as part of the Molotov-Ribbentrop Pact, and in 1939 invaded Finland in the Winter War.

58 Beria Report, 2.

59 Michael Parrish, *The Lesser Terror: Soviet State Security, 1939-1953* (Westport, CT: Praeger, 1996), 177-90.

60 Quoted in Taubman, *Khrushchev*, 244, 446; 455, 456.

61 Oleg Penkovsky, *The Penkovsky Papers* (New York: Doubleday, 1965), 369.

62 Taubman, *Khrushchev*, 350; and Anatoly Dobrynin,

In Confidence: Moscow's Ambassador to America's Six Cold War Presidents (NY: TimesBooks, 1995), 37-38. Additional airplanes were added under the BURNING LIGHT program to assess French nuclear tests in the Pacific, and were used to monitor Soviet subterranean tests as well. Hopkins, *Boeing KC-135*, 98-99, 101-103, 139-43.
63 Gordon, *Soviet Strategic Aviation in the Cold War*, 17; and Yefim Gordon, *Soviet Spyplanes of the Cold War* (Barnsley, England: Pen and Sword Aviation, 2013).
64 *Ibid.*
65 'Infrequent Soviet Flights Over Alaska Are Reported,' New York Times, 17 March 1953, 8; and William A Ulman, 'Russian Planes Are Raiding Canadian Skies,' Collier's 16 October 1953, 33-34, 36, 39, 42, 43.
66 Memorandum of Conference with the President, 9 August 1960, Office of the Staff Secretary, Subject Series, Alphabetical Subseries, Box 15, Intelligence Matters (17); NAID #12008941, 2.
67 Pocock, *U-2 Spyplane*, 168-69.
68 Quoted in Taubman, *Khrushchev*, 468.
69 A McGehee Harvey, 'A 1969 Conversation with Khrushchev: The Beginning of His Fall from Power,' *Life* (18 December 1970), 48B.
70 Taubman, *Khrushchev*, 581.
71 *Ibid.*, 467; and Zubok, *Failed Empire*, 153.
72 Taubman, *Khrushchev*, 11-13.
73 Matthew Evangelista, "Why Keep Such an Army?': Khrushchev's Troop Reductions,' Working Paper 19, Cold War International History Project, December 1997, 10.
74 Taubman, *Khrushchev*, 454.
75 *Ibid.*, 469.
76 Quoted in *ibid.*, 485-87.
77 Papers of John F Kennedy. Presidential Papers. National Security Files. Meetings and Memoranda. National Security Action Memoranda [NSAM]: NSAM 24, RB-47 Reconnaissance Flights. JFKNSF-328-025. John F Kennedy Presidential Library and Museum.
78 See, for example, Hopkins, *Boeing KC-135 Stratotanker*, 58; Mitchell B Lerner, *The Pueblo Incident: A Spy Ship and the Failure of American Foreign Policy* (Lawrence, KS: University Press of Kansas, 2002); and Jack Cheevers, *Act of War: Lyndon Johnson, North Korea, and the Capture of the Spy Ship Pueblo* (New York: New American Library (Penguin), 2013).

Chapter Eight
Reassessing Eisenhower

1 See, for example, Schwartz, *Atomic Audit*, 16.
2 Quoted in Beschloss, *Mayday*, 106. Emphasis in original.
3 Frank Fedele, 'Overflight by Military Aircraft in Time of Peace,' *USAF Judge Advocate General Law Review* 8 (1967): 9-13.
4 *Ibid.*, 13.
5 'Draft Convention on Rights and Duties of Neutral States in Naval and Aerial War, with Comments,' Research in International Law of the Harvard Law School, *American Journal of International Law Supplement* 33 (1939): 223-24.
6 Fedele, 'Overflight by Military Aircraft in Time of Peace,' 12.
7 Beschloss, *Mayday*, 15.
8 Memorandum for the Record, 12 February 1959, in *FRUS*, 1958-1960, vol. X, 261.
9 Memorandum for the Record, 24 April 1958, *FRUS*, 1958-1960, vol. X, 264.
10 Welzenbach and Pedlow, *The CIA and the U-2 Program, 1954-1974* (Washington, DC: CIA Center for the Study of Intelligence, 1998 [declassified 2013 version]), 154, 156.
11 *Ibid.*, 155-56.
12 *Ibid.*, 155.
13 Bissell, *Reflections of a Cold Warrior*, 116-17.
14 Welzenbach and Pedlow, *CIA and the U-2 Program* [2013], 155.
15 Copy of Soviet Note on Overflights, 21 April 1958, Office of the Staff Secretary, Subject Series, Alphabetical Subseries, Box 14, Intelligence Matters (5); NAID #12008422, 2.
16 Beschloss, *Mayday*, 125.
17 Quoted in Larry J Sabato, *The Kennedy Half-Century: The Presidency, Assassination, and Lasting Legacy of John F. Kennedy* (New York: Bloomsbury, 2013), 83-84.
18 Bissell, *Reflections of a Cold Warrior*, 140.
19 See, for example, William Burr and Jeffrey Kimball, 'Nixon's Secret Nuclear Alert: Vietnam War Diplomacy and the Joint Chiefs of Staff Readiness Test, October 1969,' *Cold War History* 3 (2, 2003): 113-56; and explored more fully in Jeffrey Kimball and William Burr, *Nixon's Nuclear Specter: The Secret Alert of 1969, Madman Diplomacy, and the Vietnam War* (Lawrence: KS: University Press of Kansas, 2015).
20 Nicholas Michael Sambaluk, 'US Policymakers Confront Aerospace Doctrine, 1957-1959,' *Cold War History* 14 (1, 2012), 91.
21 Quoted in Beschloss, *Mayday* 265.

Appendix III

1 Compare, for example, Gordon and Komissarov, *Soviet Air Defence Aviation*, 25 and Thomas Polak, *Stalin's Falcons: The Aces of the Red Star* (London: Grub Street, 1999), 80.
2 NSA report, title: 'Summary of SIGINT Reflections of the Loss of a U.S. Reconnaissance Aircraft in the Black Sea, 14 December 1965,' serial: 2/0IRUK/R54-65, 20 December 1965 (SC); Cryptologic Archival Holding Area; box 31729, temporary location AOI-0 104-2, NSA, cited in Peterson, 'Maybe You Had to Be There,' 44, n. 114.
3 *History, Strategic Air Command, January-June 1950*, AFHRA, K416.01 v. 1.
4 Peacock, *Boeing B-47 Stratojet*, 157-69; Tegler, *B-47 Stratojet*, 61-62, 122-24, 132-33, 135-151; and Lloyd, *Boeing's B-47 Stratojet*, 172-80.
5 Geoffrey Hays, *Boeing B-50* (Simi Valley, CA: Steve Ginter Books, 2013), 224-26.
6 Doubek, *Strategic Reconnaissance 1956-1976*, 24-27. See also Memorandum for the Chief of Staff, USAF, Subject: (Unclassified) Special Reconnaissance Systems, 22 December 1954, Top Secret, LoC, Nathan F Twining Papers, Box 72, Folder 1954 Top Secret Material.
7 Doubek, *Strategic Reconnaissance 1956-1976*, 32-37.
8 *History, 4080th Strategic Reconnaissance Wing, April-May 1959*, AFHRA, K-WG-4080-HI, 460412, 1-5.
9 Grimes, *Big Safari*, 21-22.
10 *Ibid.*, 19.
11 *Ibid.*, 117, 126-27.
12 Steve Ginter, *Martin P4M-1/-1Q Mercator* (Simi Valley, CA: Steve Ginter Books, 1996).

Index

MEDIA

OPERATIONS

ORGANIZATIONS

POLICY AND FOREIGN AFFAIRS

SHIPS AND SPACECRAFT

STRATEGIC WARFARE

UNITS

WEAPONS